The Comprehensive Guide For Every Angler

FISHING
DIGEST

Edited By Dennis Thornton

Published by

 krause publications
An F&W Publications Company

700 East State Street • Iola, WI 54990-0001
715-445-2214 • 888-457-2873
www.krause.com

Please, call or write us for our free catalog of publications.
Our toll-free number to place an order or obtain a free catalog is 800-258-0929
or please us our regular business telephone 715-445-2214.

ISBN: 0-87349-454-7
Library of Congress Number: 2002107612
Printed in the United States of America

Edited by: Dennis Thornton
Designed by: Brian Brogaard

TABLE OF CONTENTS

ACKNOWLEDGMENTS

Anglers and the makers of fishing gear are a friendly and helpful lot. Just ask and they'll come to your assistance.

We put out the call for articles for Fishing Digest and soon assembled a great group of professional writers and photographers, many of whom have written their own books on their fishing specialties.

Likewise, a mailing to manufacturers, resort owners, guides, and retailers in the fishing industry netted a wealth of material that anglers will find beneficial in the "digest" portion of Fishing Digest.

We'd like to thank everyone who contributed to this book. Besides the all-star list of writers, we had lots of other assistance. Jim Brown, Doug Blodgett, and Glenda Kelley provided information about the world records kept by the International Game Fish Association. Ted Dzialo, director of the National Fresh Water Fishing Hall of Fame provided the list of North American record fish kept by that group.

Jim Dicken loaned us his impressive list of fishing guides and charters that he keeps online at the Fishing Guides Home Page.

Tourism and conservation department officials were helpful in providing details about fishing license fees and where to fish.

And hundreds of companies were willing to share information and photos of their products.

We'd also like to acknowledge help and guidance from the following:
Debbie Bradley
Bill Hahn
Cheryl Hayburn
Bill Krause
Rick Lodholz
Steve Massie
Gena Pamperin
Brian Brogaard
Gordon Ullom
Kevin Ulrich

—Dennis Thornton, editor

INTRODUCTION

A kid walks toward the riverbank, carrying a can of worms and a primitive pole, hoping a perch or bullhead will pull down the red-and-white bobber. A man sets out in a 22-foot bass boat powered by a 200-horsepower motor, equipped with the latest in fish finders and GPS units, hoping a record bass will chase a state-of-the-art lure so he can catch, photograph, and release it.

As different as this pair of images might appear, the two anglers have much in common. They're about to participate in one of the world's most popular sports.

More than 34 million Americans fish, according to a recent report released by the U.S. Fish & Wildlife Service. That's one in every six persons. Anglers spent about $36 billion on equipment, transportation and lodging, and other expenses for their sport.

Fishing Digest set out to provide a complete package of information useful to those anglers, whether they fish for panfish or swordfish. This book contains articles on the latest in fishing equipment and fishing boats, as well as hundreds of listings for products ranging from bait to underwater cameras.

Experts who were tapped to contribute articles in their specialties have more than a dozen fishing books and dozens of magazine articles to their credit. They include Mark Romanack, who prowls the Great Lakes in search of walleye; saltwater expert Milt Rosko; fly fisherman and veteran fly-tier C. Boyd Pfeiffer; Tom Gruenwald, whose idea of a good time is sitting on a frozen lake and pulling up northern pike; and Dan Donarski, who takes time off from his outdoors writing in Upper Michigan to catch bonefish in the Caribbean, stalk rainbows in the Rockies, and go on fly-ins to Canada. Also, Edie Franson shares some of her fish recipes, especially for a shore lunch; Ross Bielema reports on the latest fishing equipment and boats; and outdoors writer Craig Cooper interviews B.A.S.S. founder and industry legend Ray Scott, pokes into the smelly confines of catfish bait, and tries to determine when were the "good old days" of fishing.

Also available is a wealth of valuable information, including fishing license fees for every state, a list of more than 1,400 fishing guides and charters, world and North American records for fish, books and magazines about fishing, and state tourism offices that can be helpful in planning a trip.

So, whether your preference is fly fishing, bass fishing, saltwater fishing, or just dunking a worm to pass the time and catch panfish, you can use Fishing Digest to make your sport even more enjoyable.

— Dennis Thornton, editor

Chapter One: Gearing Up
New Horizons Benefit Saltwater Fishing
Breakthroughs in tackle technology include super lines, rods, and reels
By Milt Rosko

Today's recreational saltwater anglers are experiencing a revolution in fishing tackle technology that many never dreamed possible just a few years ago. Looking back more than half a century, the introduction of spinning reels to America was a big event. So were monofilament line and fiberglass fishing rods. The next giant step forward was the graphite rod. Then, for a period of many years there was a modicum of progress.

Suddenly, however, fishing tackle technology might well be termed on a rampage, and the beneficiary is the saltwater angler. For hardly a day goes by that there isn't something new that often makes existing gear obsolete.

Anglers who enjoy fishing with spinning tackle and like to target their favorite species while using live bait were always handicapped. Their spinning reels lacked the capability of free spool–as was capable with a multiplying reel–and this inhibited their ability to present live baits to striped bass, tarpon, yellowtail, and other game fish.

Photos by Milt Rosko

Circle hooks have become increasingly popular among anglers who use live bait. As a fish takes the bait into its mouth, the Circle hook lodges in the corner of the jaw which enables it to be removed with ease, especially important when catch-and-release fishing.

Pete Karura just netted this big striped bass for Glenn Sapir, who hooked it while drifting a live eel from the charter boat "Tophook" off Montauk, Long Island. Each year sees more anglers employing light tackle to catch a wide variety of game fish.

Jeff Melito hooked this big bluefish while deep-jigging with light line, while fishing aboard the party boat "Gambler" sailing from Point Pleasant Beach, N.J. Today's Dyneema and Spectra braided lines have a diameter only 20 percent of that of monofilament of comparable strength.

Milt Rosko holds aloft a school striper he hooked while casting from coastal rockpiles. He's wearing newly designed Korkers footwear that ensures secure footing on slippery rocks. His line is designed for abrasion resistance for those occasions when it comes in contact with sharp rocks and mussels.

New, state-of-the-art live-liner-type spinning reels enable an angler to live-bait fish with a firm, pre-set drag, and with a flip of a lever engage completely free spool, or a very light amount of pressure. This permits the baitfish to swim about freely, and once a game fish has taken the bait, the angler simply flips a lever, which engages the spool and the firmly set drag, and the hook is set.

There's a line for every purpose

In its heyday, monofilament line didn't vary much between manufacturers. Today's lines are designed for specific uses, with some companies producing as many as eight variations, including casting, trolling, jigging, ultra-fine diameter, and abrasion resistance for fishing from jetties.

The introduction of Spectra filament braided lines has been a giant step forward, as the line has an extremely fine diameter. The fine diameter, coupled with practically no stretch, enables anglers who fish deep water for grouper, snapper, sea bass, codfish, and rockfish, to do so with lighter tackle. They're also able to employ lighter sinker weights, maximizing the sporting qualities of catching these species.

The introduction of fluorocarbon was heralded as a major breakthrough because it was a leader material that was invisible in the water. Suddenly anglers had a leader material that resulted in strikes from finicky albacore and tuna that would ignore hook baits on monofilament leaders drifted back in a chum line. The cost of fluorocarbon was prohibitive at first, which resulted in its being used primarily as leader material.

However, as anglers came to appreciate its sterling qualities, fluorocarbon came into vogue as the line of choice. With the passage of time there have been four generations of fluorocarbon technology, resulting in an advanced fluorocarbon resin process that gives it a soft inner core and tough outer shell. It resists abrasion, has outstanding strength and flexibility, and has become the line of choice of many saltwater anglers.

There are also fluorocarbon/monofilament blends that bring the best qualities of both to a single line. Indeed, the days of just buying an ordinary line are a thing of the past.

Graphite rods aid fly fishermen

Rod technology has also made tremendous strides. Fiberglass has almost become a thing of the past. Graphite is the material of choice for its strength, responsiveness, and importantly, its weight is extraordinarily light. When

High density fly lines enables casters to present their offering to bottom-feeding species like the summer flounder being unhooked by the author. Today's saltwater fly fishing equipment enables anglers to execute long casts with ease.

Captain Jim Carey holds aloft a big bluefin tuna hooked by Milt Rosko 45 miles southeast of Montauk Point, N.Y. Tuna are often finicky when attracted to a chum line, and often ignore hook baits. It's remarkable how the success rate improves with the use of fluorocarbon leader material, which is virtually invisible in the water.

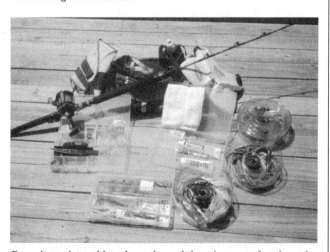

Every item pictured here has enhanced the enjoyment of anglers who fish from long range party boats on the Atlantic, Pacific, and Gulf coasts. The rod, reel, line, fighting belt, shoulder harness, lurebox, and wide assortment of high-speed trolling lures enable anglers to subdue pelagic species such as tuna and marlin.

casting from the surf for hours, the feather-light weight of the rod, and corresponding reduction in the weight of new reels, result in far less fatigue, and more enjoyment than with the tackle of an earlier era.

By far the greatest advances in rod design have been for the saltwater fly fisherman. Fly fishermen who fish the briny generally employ rods rated from No. 8 through No. 15, on which they challenge everything from bonefish to blue marlin. Today's superb rods, most made of graphite, have been painstakingly designed to enable the caster to deliver a streamer fly–often little more than a tuft of feathers and a hook–to a moving target that may be 75 feet or more distant.

Fly lines and the reels on which they are stored have been part of this revolution too. It's safe to say that if your fly line is more than two years old, it's obsolete. There are literally dozens of different weights and tapers of fly lines, from fast tapered floating lines to make a delicate presentation to a permit on the flats, to high-density, quick sinking lines that probe the depths for bluefish and white sea bass. Some manufacturers provide anglers with a

For deep trolling, fine diameter stainless steel cable has replaced the bulky single strand trolling wire of years ago. Keith Kaufman probed the depths at the entrance to the Chesapeake Bay to score with this pretty-hued weakfish.

There are no tackle shops at sea, and anglers who fish on long-range party boats require dependable tackle. Any equipment in your tackle locker that's over 5 years old may well need to be retired, for you'll enhance your fishing enjoyment with the newest gear.

This selection of stand-up tackle and high-speed trolling lures just didn't exist years ago. With the great improvement in tackle of this type, anglers are able to subdue tuna and marlin of several hundred pounds while fishing from the decks of party boats on all three coasts.

selection of four fly line sections, ranging from floating to fast sink rate, that may be slipped onto the fly line with a simple loop, negating the necessity of carrying several reels or extra spools.

Needle sharp hooks penetrate better

When I was a youngster, I vividly recall being taught to use a fine file to hone a sharp point on a brand new hook before using it. Under magnification, many brand new hooks were really dull. The test was to sharpen it until when scraped across your fingernail it would begin to penetrate. Hooks manufactured with that technology are still on the shelves of many tackle shops, although they quite properly should be discarded.

Today when you place a hook under the magnifying glass the point is needle sharp, and hard, so it penetrates with ease. The hooks are laser sharpened, and chemically treated, resulting in an excellent quality hook that holds its point and strength, and resists rust in the hostile salt water environment. You actually dull today's hooks if you attempt to sharpen them with a file!

In addition, there are many new hook designs,

Surf anglers subject their tackle to the worst elements saltwater fishing has to offer. The new reels are impervious to salt water's corrosive action when properly cared for. Each season sees a host of lures enter the market, offering usability and reliability to the serious surf fisherman.

Andy Newman just landed this black drum about to be unhooked by Richard Stanczyk. It was landed on extremely light tackle and fluorocarbon line, while fishing the thin water adjacent to a mangrove island in Florida Bay, while they sailed from Islamorada in the Florida Keys.

Jack Noll is about to unhook a big dolphin hooked by Al Ristori while fishing from the Sea Lion II. Dolphin of this size jump repeatedly, and test an angler and his tackle to the limit. High speed trolling lures account for many dolphin, wahoo, tuna and billfish, especially when worked around weed lines.

especially the ringed hook systems offered by some manufacturers. The free-swinging ring is ideal for live bait fishing, for it offers the baitfish more freedom to move about.

The Circle style hook, while dating back centuries, found little application in the sport fishing community until recently. By virtue of its design, the Circle hook is seldom swallowed by a fish, but instead lodges in the corner of the fish's jaw, where it may easily be removed. This is extremely important when seeking species that are regulated by states where there are size limits, or where an angler wishes to practice catch and release.

Circle hooks are even being used with excellent results while seeking billfish and tunas on the offshore grounds. While with the "J" style hook the angler customarily hooks the fish by striking back with his rod, with Circle hooks the best success rates are achieved by hesitating and not reeling until the fish has turned and moved off with the bait.

For years anglers have used a small barrel swivel to join their leader to their line. While small, they were still bulky, and you couldn't go to too small a swivel because they just didn't have sufficient breaking strength. Suddenly, the Spro power barrel swivel came to market, and it's only a third the size of a conventional barrel swivel of the same test. This results in a connection between line and leader that is barely noticeable.

The same is true with the variety of snaps and hardware used to attach lures, all of which are now available in small sizes with greatly improved strength and resistance to the onslaughts of a saltwater environment.

Plethora of lures tempt lunkers

When it comes to lures in the arsenal of the saltwater angler, today's selection is beyond comprehension. As I look back over more than three score years of fishing the briny, I can't imagine how successful I might have been had I today's lures at my disposal.

Today's plugs are designed for every application, from swimming enticingly on the surface, to probing the depths. They're made of plastic for the most part, nearly indestructible, and their colors replicate in detail the baitfish they're meant to imitate. Some have metal rattles

Climbing around coastal rockpiles requires dependable equipment that can take a lot of abuse. Today's anglers have the opportunity of using lightweight tackle of the finest quality, and they have a huge selection of excellent lures at their disposal.

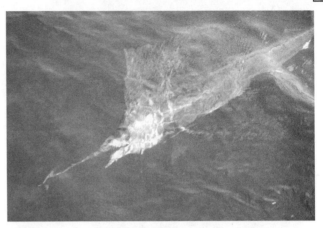

Years ago anglers fought sailfish while strapped into a harness in a fighting chair. Today's quality light tackle enables anglers to catch the magnificent game fish while using stand-up tackle, and 15- to 20-pound test fine diameter lines balanced to equally light tackle, maximizing the enjoyment.

built into their body, which aid in casting, but also emits fish-attracting sound. Most important of all, the split rings and through-wire hook hangers are made of stainless steel that is virtually impervious to corrosion. The same improvements observed earlier for "J" style and Circle hooks have also occurred with treble hooks. The hooking qualities of the triple grip style treble is awesome. One style still lacking is a quality treble without a barb, so as to facilitate quick release. On a triple grip style hook this would be a godsend, so go to it manufacturers, as every catch and release angler will replace barbed trebles with your offering!

The anglers who troll blue water for pelagic species, including the tunas, billfish, wahoo, and dolphin, now enjoy a selection of high-speed trolling lures that are virtually guaranteed to bring results. Much the same is true for anglers who probe estuaries with light tackle and use lead head jigs. Years ago there were but a handful of jigs available, and today the lead heads are airbrushed to resemble every baitfish imaginable, with finite detail right down to their eyes. The skirts were once but bucktail or feathers. Today they're soft plastic, in every color imaginable, with such minute detail that if you hold a live sand launce in the palm of your hand and a soft plastic replica, it's virtually impossible to tell the difference.

While the tackle and lures have changed, there is one technique that I'd like to share with all saltwater anglers, on all three coasts. Throughout the season, while having upgraded to the equipment just described, make yourself a promise to try a teaser ahead of your primary lure.

Begin with a 4-foot long piece of fluorocarbon leader material. Tie a tiny Spro power swivel within a dropper loop, with one end measuring 12 inches and the other 36 inches. Tie a tiny duo-lock snap to the short leader end to accommodate the teaser, and a somewhat larger duo-lock snap to the terminal end of the leader for your primary lure. Use a small saltwater fly like the Clouser minnow as a teaser, although most any saltwater fly will do. By

June Rosko regularly employs fluorocarbon leader material while drifting for summer flounder in the shallow reaches of coastal bays and rivers. The fluorocarbon is virtually invisible in the water, and enhances her score as a result.

Today's anglers enjoy maximum sport by engaging great gamefish with very little tackle. The author employed a popping outfit and lead head jig to entice a strike from this bluefish, while fishing adjacent to the Statue of Liberty in New York Harbor.

Light spinning tackle enables saltwater anglers to tangle with great gamefish, like this fine wahoo being brought to boatside while drifting across Challenger Banks off Bermuda.

season's end you may find yourself catching more fish on the teaser than on the primary lure. Importantly, you'll receive strikes from species that normally would not strike the large primary lure. I never like to use the word "never" with respect to fishing, but I "almost never" use any lure without a teaser ahead of it, whether I'm casting from beach or boat. By the way, my new book, *The Complete Book of Saltwater Fishing*, is full of techniques such as these. Contact me at miltrosko@worldnet.att.net to obtain an autographed copy.

One thing I can say without equivocation. If you haven't kept pace with the fishing tackle revolution, it would serve you well to do so. Take an evening or two, collect your rods and reels together, and rummage through the tackle box. I daresay you'll agree that many of the items might well be retired, mementos of days past. Step up and join those of us who now enjoy the most contemplative of all pastimes, of seeking saltwater adversaries from both beach and boat on our picturesque Atlantic, Pacific and Gulf coasts.

Rosko has written several books on fishing, including *The Complete Book of Saltwater Fishing.*

Milt Rosko uses light tackle as he tangles with an acrobatic sailfish while fishing with Andy Heild off Walker's Cay, northernmost of the Bahamas archipelago.

Tarpon are great acrobats, jumping repeatedly as they tear line from the reel with a smooth as silk drag being used by the author as he fished out of Islamorada in the Florida Keys. Light tackle provides anglers the opportunity of maximizing their enjoyment of the sport, and today's reliable, state of the art tackle makes it all possible.

Chapter One: Gearing Up
Anglers Hooked On High Tech
Electronics, space age materials dominate today's hot fishing gear
By Ross Bielema

In slower times, fishing was nothing more than a cane pole, a stout line, a hook, a bobber, and a coffee can of worms.

While this gear worked fine for Huck Finn, today's anglers have largely abandoned such romantic, inefficient equipment gear in favor of the Star Trek approach.

Bank fishermen and boaters alike have embraced Global Positioning System units that use orbiting satellites to mark favorite fishing holes, LCD-readout sonar to find fish in their rocky, brushy habitat and even devices that let anglers look into the water.

Cane and bamboo have been replaced with graphite and fiberglass materials to create fishing rods that allow anglers to feel the lightest tap on the lure.

Fishing line made of natural materials or Dacron has been largely abandoned in favor of monofilament or the new breed of Kevlar-stranded wire-type lines that sometimes require special tools and glue just to attach a lure.

Hooks are laser-honed, bobbers now come in hundreds of sizes and shapes, and the worms have been replaced with artificial baits that mimic the shape, scent, and wiggle of the real thing.

If Huck Finn were here today, he'd probably use this stuff, too. Why? Simply because the new gear catches more fish, and that means more fun.

Some of this gear is fun to play with even when the fish aren't biting!

Here's a glimpse at a few of the items available at larger sporting goods stores and mail-order outlets:

Rods

Only a few decades ago, fishermen had limited choices when it came to fishing rods. Fiberglass rods dominated the sport.

Today, graphite rods – known for their unbeatable combination of strength and sensitivity – are the first choice for most serious anglers. But fiberglass is still a good choice for the casual angler on a budget.

As with most equipment, price is a good guideline of quality. Buy the best you can afford, if you want to increase your odds of success, particularly on shy-biting finesse fish, such as walleyes or panfish.

As more companies use high-quality rod blanks, the price of a decent graphite rod continues to tumble. Casual fishermen can land a decent rod for $25 to $40, while the angler who takes the sport more seriously

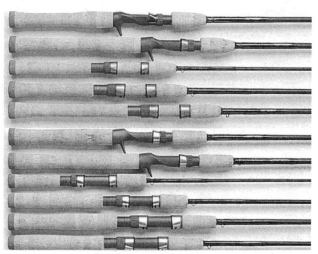

St. Croix, which has been making fishing rods for more than 50 years, offers the Legend Elite, Premier, and Avid series of rods.

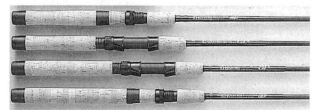

G. Loomis is known for its high quality and sensitive graphite rods, which it advertises as 25 percent lighter than rods of similar strength.

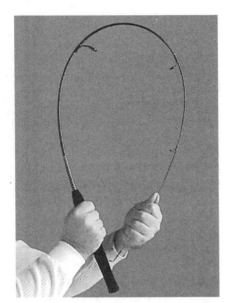

Shakespeare's Ugly Stik rods are tough, with Howald Process Double-Built construction and a 70-day/7-year limited warranty.

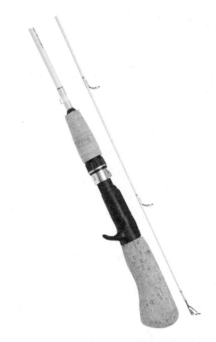

Eagle Claw's FLT105 casting rod is just 4 feet, 10 inches in two sections, featuring ultra light action with lures from 1/16 to 3/8 ounces.

won't mind paying $50 to $300 or even more – especially if that sensitive rod helps him win a walleye or bass tournament.

Virtually all high-quality rods still feature natural cork handles and aluminum oxide or ceramic guides to prevent nicks in the line.

Here are just a few rod companies worth a look:

G. Loomis (gloomis.com)

G. Loomis rods are known worldwide as some of the best. This company offers graphite rods in four quality levels: entry-level GL2, high-modulus GL3, super-high-modulus IMX and top-of-the-line GLX, which are 25 percent lighter than rods of comparable strength.

G. Loomis rods are offered in four actions (extra-fast, fast, moderate, and slow), as well as power ratings of 00 to 6. Plan to spend $95 to $400 on a G. Loomis rod.

The company's newest offerings include a line of 12 muskie rods and the Pelagic Series of eight rods for tackling the largest ocean fish in the sea.

St. Croix (stcroixrods.com)

St. Croix rods have been built in Park Falls, Wis., by a family-owned business for the past 50 years – a rarity in the days of imported products owned by conglomerates. Serious anglers speak in hushed tones about the performance of these rods. The Avid and Legend Elite series are hand-built and carry lifetime warranties, while the more economical Premier series carry two-year warranties.

In 2000, St. Croix developed Integrated Poly Curve (IPC) tooling technology, which allows the graphite to be rolled and compacted in an even taper from the rod tip to the butt. This method eliminates the weak spots associated with the uneven tapers of most other rods. St. Croix offers a full line of spinning, casting, fly-fishing, and ocean-fishing rods, as well as fiberglass Classic Cat rods for handling big flathead and channel catfish.

Expect to pay $75 to $100 for a Premier rod, $100 to $160 for an Avid rod, and $240 to $300 for a Legend Elite rod. You get what you pay for.

Others

Not everyone needs to own the best. Many other companies offer quality rods that will do the job for most casual anglers.

Rapala (rapala.com), the world's largest fishing lure company, this year introduces its new line of Signature and Long Cast rods. The graphite rods with cork handles are priced at $35 to $120.

Fenwick (fenwickfishing.com), which offers a huge line of fishing rods, has something for every budget. Fenglass fiberglass rods cast delicate baits with pinpoint accuracy. Their graphite rods are offered in several lines (Eagle GT, GoldenWing, HMX and HMG) from $50 to $125.

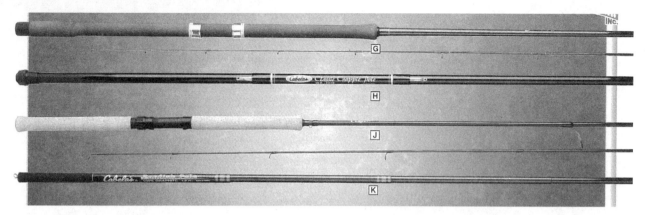

Cabela's Crappie system features four different poles, including a telescopic model.

Shakespeare (Shakespeare-fishing.com) may be the best known of all economy-line rods. Their Ugly Stik models are great values. Their graphite blanks are made in the United States, too. You'll have plenty left for fishing tackle, as Ugly Stiks sell for $25 to $60. Don't overlook rods made by **Eagle Claw (eagleclaw.com)**, *Cabela's* **(cabelas.com)**, **Berkley (Berkley-fishing.com)**, **Daiwa (daiwa.com)** and **Quantum (quantumfishing.com)**, either. Most are economically priced.

Reels

Now that you have selected a sturdy, sensitive rod for your fishing needs, it's time to look at the angler's "engine," or line-moving, fish-winching, hook-setting device. Call it a reel for short. It is the mechanism that can make or break your day on the water. While there are some bargain reels that can do the job, it is best to pay a little more for a reel that will last.

Most of the best feature ball-bearing drives (more bearings means smoother casting), aluminum spools (even machined aluminum on some models), oversized handles for cranking in the big ones and an easy-to-set drag system for tiring a fish without snapping the line. Select a gear ratio that will allow you to retrieve a lure at the speed you desire.

Abu Garcia (abu-garcia.com)

Legendary reel maker Abu Garcia, known for such lines as the Ambassadeur and Cardinal, isn't content to rest on its laurels. The new Ambassadeur C5 Mag-X is a baitcasting beast that is built to bearing tolerances of .0002 (2/10,000ths of an inch!) for ultra-smooth casting and cranking. The five-bearing reel retails for $100. Abu Garcia offers a full range of baitcasting and spinning reels, as well as its bargain-priced spincasting

Quantum's Bill Dance Signature Series rods come in 17 actions and feature a three-year limited waranty.

The Quantum Catalyst PTI spinning reel features eight bearings and a TiMAG II bail system with a lifetime warranty.

The old favorite among Zebco reels, the Zebco 33, has received a new dual-cam all-metal drag system.

Abumatic Pro Guide rod-reel combos for $25 to $60.

Shimano (shimano.com)

The same company that probably built the gears of your bicycle also makes other things that spin smoothly – namely fishing reels. The new Calcutta TE (Total Efficiency) combines the Super Free System with High Efficiency Gearing to create an ultra-smooth baitcasting reel. Aluminum-bodied Stella spinning reels use titanium-coated ball bearings for smoothness. Expect to pay more than $300 for a Calcutta TE, and $450 to $660 for a Stella. Of course, Shimano makes many lesser grades, too. A Sidestab spinning reel with a trigger bail (your finger never touches the line) retails for $30. A nearly backlash-free Curado baitcasting reel with a Variable Brake System sells for $120 to $150. Shimano offers a full range of spinning and baitcasting reels in your price range.

Quantum (quantumfishing.com)

Quantum reels are known for performance and value. This is the high-end line of the famed Zebco company. Quantum has a bounty of new reels this season. Snapshot SX, SS, XR, and Vector spinning reels have been redesigned with new body styles for enhanced performance, better balance, and more comfortable use. All have aluminum Long Stroke spools, Twist-Reducer line rollers, and selective anti-reverse. Prices start at $15 for the Vector, up to $30 for XR and some other Snapshot models.

New PT (Performance Tuned) baitcast and spinning reels include Energy E600PT and Accurist AC500PT baitcasters, and the new Catalyst PTi and Kinetic PTi spinning reels. All models feature special high-speed bearings, super-tough gears, high-tech ceramic components, and special Quantum Hot Sauce lubrication, a unique formulation that bonds molecularly with the base metal. The PT baitcasters have high-speed 6.2:1 gear ratios and ACS II externally adjustable centrifugal cast control braking system, as well as Continuous Anti-Reverse. The spinning reels use a multi-pole magnetic system instead of a spring for bail functions. Retail prices are $160 for the Energy E600PT, $100 for the Accurist, $90 for the Catalyst PTi and $70 for the Kinetic PTi.

Others

Zebco (zebcofishing.com) and its Rhino line are both excellent choices for kids and adult anglers on a budget. Who didn't cut their fishing teeth on a Zebco 202 or 404 spincast reel? These unbeatable values are still offered, along with a full line of spincast reels with stainless steel covers, like the 33, 33 Classic, improved 733 The Hawg, and Gold series. New Rhino models include four spinning reels: the RSP2 and RSP3, which hold 110 yards of 6-pound-test line and 160 yards of 8-pound-test line, respectively; and the RSPXL6 and RSPXL8, big boys that hold 220 yards of 16-pound-test line and 240 yards of 20-pound-test line, respectively. They range from $25 to $45, and unlike baitcasting models selling for up to 10 times as much, they will never backlash.

Daiwa (daiwa.com) offers an extensive line of spinning and baitcasting reels at various price points. The very definition of smooth is a Team Daiwa-Z spinning reel, featuring a magnesium rotor, machined-aluminum body, stainless steel Air Bail, Tournament Drag and 13 ball bearings. Prepare to plunk down nearly $500 for this model. At the other end, Daiwa has

The Team Daiwa-Z line of reels feature ultra-precision magnesium and titanium components and start at just 6.2 ounces.

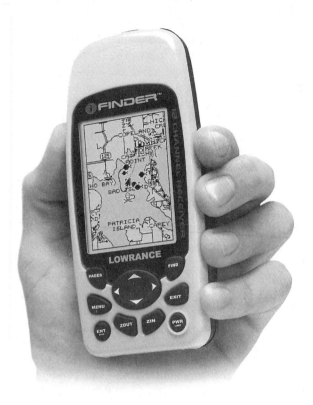

Lowrance's new line of iFinder GPS units are palm-sized but loaded with mapping information.

SS Tournament spinning reels with three-bearing drives for about $30. New offerings include Team Daiwa S and X baitcasting reels. The S series has five bearings and a seven-disc drag system for $150. The X series has six ball bearings and one roller-bearing drive with a titanium nitride line guide that won't nick line for $200.

The Meridian Marine GPS unit from Magellan features a 16 MB database of waterways and navigational aids.

Global Positioning System (GPS) units

Although some Global Position System units can be permanently mounted in a boat (see boats story for more boat-mounted electronics), many of them are battery-powered and small enough to stow in a coat pocket. It is safe to say that a GPS unit is the hottest toy for hikers, hunters, and certainly anglers, too.

GPS units are far more than a practical form of Game Boy, however. They can help you find the fishing hole where you tied into a seven-pound largemouth bass last week (of course he shook loose), and find your way through the rocky shallows of Dead Man's Slough. Some have mapping capabilities that allow for downloading of lake maps or almost any land area, too. They even link to a home computer so you can download your data and print your own maps.

Today's GPS units are more accurate than a few years ago (when the government intentionally maintained a 100-yard margin of error in its military-based satellites which bounce the signals that make GPS work). More channels means the unit can lock onto more satellites for greater accuracy (most good ones are 12-channel).

Garmin (garmin.com)

Garmin, one of the biggest names in GPS, has added three new models to its popular e trex series: Vista, Legend, and Venture. The Vista stores detailed maps and features an electronic compass and barometric altimeter, plus a PC interface cable ($350). The Legend includes a base map of North, Central and South America (with cities, highways, lakes, and rivers), and a rocker switch that allows fast viewing of the maps ($250). The Venture has a smaller memory (1 MB, vs. 8

Aqua-Vu's underwater cameras locate fish as well as underwater obstacles, cover, and bottom features to help anglers.

MB and 24 MB respectively for the Legend and Vista), but the same rocker switch ($170). Garmin's most feature-packed new model is the GPS V. It has an auto-routing function that selects the fastest route, gives turn-by-turn directions, and estimated time of arrival. It includes a CD-ROM of city maps that can be downloaded. Automatic Track Log lets you retrace your last steps. There's an odometer, too *($500)*.

Lowrance (lowrance.com)

Four models of iFinder GPS (iFinder, iFinder Plus, iFinder Atlantis, and iFinder Express) offer plenty of pocket-sized options. All include mapping abilities and WAAS (Wide Area Augmentation System) navigation for improved accuracy. The iFinder Plus offers create-your-own maps with PC software. Atlantis and Express models come with thumbnail-sized memory cards that provide thousands of navigation aids on U.S. coastal and Great Lakes waters, plus a database to find airports, hotels and restaurants (the latter to be used only if the fish aren't biting). The Atlantis model retails for $280; others are less.

Magellan (magellangps.com)

Magellan's new Meridian line includes the Meridian Marine model. It has a 16 MB database of major waterways, navigation aids, highways, airports and more. Memory can be increased for downloading maps, simply by plugging in memory cards. It's also waterproof and it floats! It retails for $300.

Portable fish finders

Aqua-Vu (www.aqua-vu.com)

In 1998, *In-Fisherman* magazine co-founder Jeff Zernov released a new product that lets anglers see the underwater world of fish.

Aqua-Vu consists of a waterproof camera (sealed in military-grade epoxy resin) linked to a monitor with Kevlar-stranded cable also waterproofed in epoxy. The system includes a battery and charger.

Zernov's Nature Vision Inc. is a spin-off of one of his other companies, Zercom Marine, a maker of sonar and other fishing electronics.

The camera allows anglers to see walleyes, bass and

other game fish as they swim in their natural world. Even if they aren't biting, it is enjoyable to watch this ultimate "reality TV show."

The camera unit has a stabilizer fin so it will point forward. It even can be attached to a downrigger, allowing an angler to watch his lure as it trolls through the water. And a video camera can be attached to the monitor, allowing the recording of your favorite aquatic scenes. In fact, many TV fishing shows use Aqua-Vu to film their underwater scenes.

Nature Vision Inc. offers a variety of Aqua-Vu models, starting at $300.

Bottom Line

One last whiz-bang item that the BMW-driving angler would not be caught without is a Bottom Line Fishin' Buddy fishfinder. It looks a bit like a trolling motor with a screen. Powered by 3 C-size batteries, a Fishin' Buddy can be clamped to a small boat, a dock or even used through the ice. They don't offer great screen detail, but can be helpful at finding schools of fish, both straight down and to the side of the built-in transducer. They are priced from $170 to $280.

The Tournament Master HR fish finder from Bottom Line offers a high resolution screen, digital water temperature, and digital boat speeds. It can be connected to a GPS unit for precision fishing.

Hot new products honored at ICAST trade show

Shimano American Corp.'s update to its "Stella" reels series and newly designed hard lure cases were among fishing gear that won honors at the ICAST 2002 New Products Showcase. ICAST is the sportfishing industry's largest annual trade show. "Best of Show honors went to Johnson Outdoors for its Minn Kota Co-Pilot, an accessory that allows a trolling motor to be steered remotely with a small cordless sending unit.

The American Sportfishing Association, which puts on the ICAST show, is the recreational fishing trade association, with 450 members representing the fishing and boating industry, state and federal natural resource agencies, angler advocacy groups, and outdoor journalists.

Suspending Charlie from Pace Products won in the lure category at ICAST's New Products Showcase.

ICAST NEW PRODUCT SHOWCASE WINNERS

Overall Best of Show: Johnson Outdoors' Minn Kota Co-Pilot

CATEGORY	COMPANY	PRODUCT
Rod	Sirrus Rods	Co-Matrix
Reel	Shimano American Corp.	Stella FA
Rod/Reel Combo	American Rod & Gun	Tourney Series
Terminal Tackle	Gamakatsu U.S.A., Inc.	G-Stinger
Lure	Pace Products, Inc.	Suspending Charlie
Tackle Management	Shimano American Corp.	Hard lure case
Boating Accessory and Electronics	Wonder Winder, Inc.	Fishhunter II
Fishing Accessory	Xplores, Inc.	Pliers
Clothing and Giftware	Luhr-Jensen & Sons, Inc.	Legendary Blade
Line	Pure Fishing, Inc.	Iron Silk

The Xplores floating pliers, which comes in 6.5-inch and 9-inch sizes, was ICAST's top fishing accessory in the New Products Showcase.

Chapter One: Gearing Up
A Boat For Every Pocketbook

*Huge variety in fishing boats and motors provides
plenty of choices to lure anglers*

By Ross Bielema

When sportsmen first become drawn into angling (usually just after potty training), they quickly learn that proper gear can mean the difference between sitting on a river or lake shore for hours in solemn boredom, or going home with a stringer of fish. But the pocketbook dictates many equipment decisions. Backwater, blue-collar anglers learn that you don't have to end up in bankruptcy court to find a decent, sturdy, and reliable boat and motor.

Eventually, perhaps as income improves or fishing becomes more important than say, groceries, a fisherman realizes he needs a better boat or bigger motor.

There is plenty of variety afloat today, with something to fit the pocketbook of the bayou river rat, the corporate attorney, and everyone in between. Whether aluminum or fiberglass, deep-V or flatboat, inboard console or outboard steering, pedestal seats or cushions on planks, boat choices are dictated by price, quality and the seriousness of the angler.

Here are just a few of the many choices offered today in fishing boats, motors and gear.

Bass Cat (www.basscat.com)

Building all-fiberglass fishing boats is a way of life for the Pierce family of Mountain Home, Ark. Bass Cat boats have offered such innovations as recessed trolling-motor wells, lighted interior compartments, in-dash fish flashers, and other ideas now used by other companies.

In 1999, Bass Cat was the first to use a true vinyl ester (VE) resin throughout the structure. This greatly reduces the chances of stress cracks and blistering of the hulls (for details, go to www.ResinNavigator.org). Vacuum compression methods have produced stronger hulls. Bass Cat is the only company to use all-fiberglass hulls, stringers, floors, and transoms.

Amazingly, the boats, trailers, seating, wiring harnesses and even the seat embroidery are all made from raw materials at the Bass Cat factory, elsewhere.

Bass Cat's Jaguar model has a 20-foot, 3-inch fiberglass hull and can handle a 175 hp to 285 hp motor.

Smokercraft's Escape and Infinity series of pontoon boats can provide a fishing platform or a cruising craft. Smokercraft also makes several models of deck boats and runabouts.

Lowe's Sea Nymph V Series fishing boats are 15 feet long and the standard package includes a 25 hp motor and trailer.

Bass Cat offers a 20-foot Jaguar, 20-foot Cougar, 19-foot Pantera III, 19-foot Pantera Classic, and 18-foot Sabre.

These top-of-the-line boats offer a myriad of standard and optional features, including fuel tanks up to 52 gallons, dual aerated livewells with timers, sound systems, flush-mount controls, handrails, footrests, rod organizers, security systems, dual steering, lighted storage boxes, and even a sophisticated digital dashboard system that resembles a jet cockpit. Perhaps the Bass Cat's best feature is its transferable lifetime warranty on the hull, transom, floor, and stringers.

Champion (www.championboats.com)

Champion has been building premium fiberglass fishing boats since 1975, and currently offers 14 models.

The Elite Series offers four hull sizes, from 18 feet, 8 inches (the 188 Elite) to the 22-foot, 3-inch 223 Elite. Tournament-ready CX models come in three sizes: the 203 CX, 193 CX, and 187 CX (which again refer to the hull length).

Saltwater anglers typically need a bigger boat to face larger waves and provide a more comfortable day on the water. The Saltwater Series offers the 24 Bay Champ, 21 Bay Champ, and 22 Tunnel Champ. Those who like to fish and water ski can select one of three Fish-N-Ski models: the 21 SX, 190 SX, and 181 SX.

Champion even makes a good all-around fishing boat, the Multi-Species Fishhunter. This 19-foot, 4-inch boat has a deep V-hull and extra-wide 97-inch beam for plenty of room to stretch as well as creating a comfy fishing platform. Dual 26-gallon fuel tanks, dual

Lowrance transducers, dual livewells with hydro-aeration, dual bucket seats…two anglers go in comfort on this rig! It will handle 1,600 pounds of cargo and fishermen.

If you spend more time on the water than at home, know most pro bass anglers' current standings, and don't mind a second mortgage on your house to finance a boat, the 223 Elite is Champion's champion model. Can you say 300 horsepower? You'll never be late for a weigh-in again. The livewell holds 27 gallons, so invite the neighbors along.

Smoker Craft (www.smokercraft.com)

Fishing boats can take many forms. Some favor the run-and-gun style of a fiberglass boat that can move tournament anglers quickly from rocks to weed beds to flooded trees to the weigh-in docks. Others prefer a big, lazy pontoon boat big enough for the wife, kids, Aunt Edith, and the family dog.

At Smoker Craft®, you can take your pick of these designs.

The Alante series of fiberglass runabouts offers five models from 19 to 21 feet. Standard features include 37-gallon fuel tank, ski ring, boarding ladder, navigational lights, built-in coolers, and plenty of in-floor and bow storage space. A CD player is optional.

The Commander series of deck boats offers the spunk of a runabout with a deck fishing platform. Features include 31- to 60-gallon fuel tanks, portable toilets, built-in aerated livewells, bass seats, built-in coolers, wrap-around couches, and pop-up cleats.

If your idea of fishing is a nice nap possibly interrupted by an occasional tug on a bobber, then you might prefer one of Smoker Craft's 20 models of pontoon boats.

This family-owned, Indiana-based company still makes 'em the old-fashioned way, from high-tech materials, like full-length, 1/2-inch aluminum keels,

The Fishfinder Series from Lowe features 16-foot aluminum boats with room for a family to fish.

welded aluminum tube chambers (to stay afloat even with a puncture) and pressure-treated plywood decks with lifetime warranties.

The Paradise series of pontoon boats is for big families or party animals. With room for up to 18 people and motors to 135-horsepower, you may never come home. Sure, you can get options like a galley with stove, pull-out lounges, and a baby-changing station. All feature bimini tops, padded seating, sundecks, and many other comfort items. Fishing doesn't have to be a chore with a boat like this, and if the fish aren't biting, relax and enjoy the ride.

The Serenity, Classic, and Infinity Fish series are aimed at anglers who want to cruise in style. They offer up to 24 feet of space, built-in livewells, lockable rod boxes, four bass seats and 18- to 24-gallon fuel tanks. Bimini tops, carpet, and sound systems are standard. The Infinity Cruise series is intended for multi-use boaters who may fish one week and have a floating cookout the next. These pontoon boats are offered in

18- to 24-foot models, and can be fitted with 50- to 115-horsepower motors as the boat size increases. Two models feature L-group seating with lounge arms, two front couches, convert-a-tables, sundecks, and other creature comforts.

Lowe (www.lowe.com)

In the heart of the Ozarks, hunting and fishing are legendary. In Lebanon, Mo., Lowe makes high-quality aluminum boats that are known for durability and value.

Lowe offers a variety of jon boats, with riveted or welded hulls; a Stinger series, with welded deep-vee hulls to smooth big-water chop; a Classic Bass series, with a riveted 6-degree modified vee hull for a smoother ride and a stable fishing platform; extra-affordable Fishfinder series with a riveted 6-degree modified vee hull; Fishing Machine series in 16- to 19-foot Sea Nymph designs with a choice of backtroller tiller, side console or twin console and V-Tech hull; and

The 223 Elite is Champion's flagship model at 22 feet, 3 inches, and comes with a livewell, rod storage, front and rear fishing decks, and a motor from 225 hp to 300 hp.

The Pro Angler 16 from Lund is a nice choice in smaller fishing boats, with livewells, rod compartments, and dual pedestal seats.

the Angler series of Sea Nymphs, offering affordable models with plenty of options.

Features on some Lowe boat models include dry storage lockers, computer-designed hulls, aluminum casting decks, tinted windshields, 16-ounce marine carpet, lockable rod storage, full instrumentation, aerated baitwells and a variety of motor, trolling motor and fish finder options.

Lund (www.lundboats.com)

If you frequent any lakes or rivers very often, you'll notice lots of Lund boats. Lund makes a strong case for traditional aluminum boats. The company uses aluminum I-beams placed longitudinally deep in the hull, then tied to transverse stringers in the bow, for exceptional strength. They use rivets, because it's the best system (just look at airplanes and 18-wheelers as proof, the company argues). Twin plates are used only

at midship, where the boat takes the most pounding. Two layers across the entire hull would hurt boat performance, Lund argues. They've been making boats for more than 50 years, so they likely have a good case. Lund also is a major sponsor of numerous walleye and other tournaments across the nation.

Lund added a line of 20 jon boats to its offerings in 2002. These are welded hulls, ranging from a little 10-foot NVJR1031 that takes a 3-horsepower motor to a big 20-foot NVJWMV2070SFC model that can take a 115-hp motor. NVJRMV models have modified-V hulls. Hull seams carry a limited lifetime warranty. Lund has 14 other new models. They include the 2150 Baron Magnum, 1950 Tyee and 1850 Tyee in the Sport & Fish Series, the 2025, 1900, 1800 and 1775 Pro-V models in the Tournament Series, the 1700 Angler and Pro Angler 16 in the Sportsman Series, the 1650 Laker in the Legend Series and the 1675 Pro in the Adventure Series.

If you need a big-lake boat, the 2150 Baron Magnum is a monster, with nearly a 22-foot hull, 80-gallon fuel tank, three pedestal seats, lighted livewells, wraparound walk-though windshield, and an outboard up to 225 horsepower.

A nice choice in a smaller fishing boat with a wide profile is the Pro Angler 16. Like most new Lunds, it has the IPS™ (Integrated Power Strake) hull for better maneuverability, in a 16 ½ -foot length. Lighted, aerated livewells, seven lockable rod and storage compartments, dual pedestal seats, and many other features make this a comfy fishing boat.

Lund offers a total of 32 V-hull designs, including its popular Mr. Pike models with 16- and 17-foot hulls.

New from Ranger Boats is the 185 VS, an 18-foot, 5-inch hull set for a 175-hp motor and 1,365 pounds.

Lund has added a line of 20 aluminum, welded jon boats, ranging from 10 feet to 20 feet, to its extensive fishing fleet.

The Tracker Pro Team 185 aluminum bass boat comes with a 50-hp motor and trailer.

Ranger (www.rangerboats.com)

If you've ever seen a bass tournament or talked to serious bass anglers for more than 15 minutes, you've heard about Ranger® boats. Forrest L. Wood is undoubtedly the Henry Ford of fishing boats, particularly fiberglass-hull bass boats, and his Flippin, Ark., company is still making them with meticulous attention to detail, just as they were 35 years ago when Wood founded the company. They are named for the legendary lawmen, the Texas Rangers.

But here's something you probably didn't know:

Ranger also makes aluminum jon boats! There are 12 models in the Cherokee jon boat series, including some that can be outfitted with duck blinds. They range from the JW1448, a 14-footer, to the MV2070DLX, a massive 20-footer that can handle up to eight people or more than 1,000 pounds total. Ranger puts a 20-year warranty on its main hull weld and a 10-year warranty on its support beams, ribs and braces.

For value, it is hard to beat the Fisherman series. There are seven models in this fiberglass-hull series, from the 617DVS, a 17 1/2-foot model that can use up

A fishing boat heads into the sunset sporting a trio of 250-horsepower V-6 Evinrude motors.

to a 150-horsepower motor and float 1,350 pounds of gear and anglers, to the 620T, a big, deep 20-footer that can use up to a 125-hp motor and haul 1,820 pounds of rods, reels, dogs and guys.

The Comanche series of fiberglass-hull fishing boats provides serious anglers with a top-grade boat, but ready for your choice of motors and electronics. They range from the 518DVX, a 19-foot model that can handle up to a 200-horsepower motor and hold 1,400 pounds of cargo and anglers, to the 522SVX, a 22-foot beast that can handle up to a 250-hp motor and 1,600 pounds of gear and crew. All have built-in rod storage, coolers, livewells/baitwells and either single or twin windshields with console steering.

Ardent tournament anglers or well-to-do weekend anglers can choose from nine models in the VS/R series, including four new models. All come outfitted with motors, trolling motors and electronics. They range in size from the R61, a 16-footer that can handle a 90-hp motor and 1,110 pounds of anglers and gear, to the 210 Reata, a family-sized boat at 21 feet that can scoot in front of a 225-hp motor, and handle 1,840 pounds of people and gear. Most in this series are available in single- or double-windshield models. The Reata has an 8-foot center rod holder, while the others have port and starboard rod holders.

The new models include the 175VS, a 17-foot, 5-inch hull that accommodates a 130-hp motor and handles 1,145 pounds; the 185VS, an 18-foot, 5-inch hull set for a 175-hp motor and 1,365 pounds; the 195 Intracoastal, with a 19-foot, 5-inch hull ready for a 200-hp motor and 1,430 pounds; and the 195VS, a 19-foot, 5-inch craft that matches the Intracoastal's other specs, with minor styling differences.

Tracker (www.trackerboats.com)

There's a very good reason why Tracker® boats are pegged as the top-selling line of bass-style fishing boats. They are priced right. But these aluminum watercraft are performers, too, especially some of the newer models designed to perform like fiberglass boats, including the Avalanche. Tracker® is part of the Tracker Marine line that includes Sun Tracker® pontoon boats, Nitro® bass and bay boats and Tahoe family sport boats. Tracker has a line of distributors, including the mighty Bass Pro Shops.

The Bass series of Tracker® boats has 10 models, from the new Avalanche to the Panfish 16. They range from $19,000 for the Avalanche to a mere $6,500 for the Panfish. Those prices include a motor and trailer! The Avalanche is made with a formed aluminum process (similar to that used for aircraft construction) and .125-gauge aluminum to create a sculpted, strong hull. It comes with a 115-horsepower Mercury motor, Motorguide® trolling motor, Humminbird®-designed Tracker® LCR and a color-coordinated trailer.

Motors

Now that you've found a boat in your price range that matches your interests, you need some power. The trick is getting enough power for efficient operation without overdoing it and getting you in way over your head – literally.

Not so many years ago, outboards were smoky, two-stroke affairs that required at least one mechanic on board at all times and still only worked about half the time.

Today's motors are extremely reliable and efficient. Many are four-stroke designs, meaning that you don't need to mix oil in the gasoline. Most of the remaining two-stroke engines, usually low-powered models, use oil injection: again, no mixing.

Here is a basic peek at the most popular engines on the water. Most anglers will tell you that it is hard to

Yamaha's four-stroke outboard motors get up to 67 miles per gallon of gas, setting a world record.

A fisherman is armed with a pair of Johnson motors on his boat, including a new 9.9 horsepower four-stroke model.

The OptiMax line of outboards by Mercury ranges from 135 to 225 horsepower.

buy a bad outboard motor today.

Outboard Marine Corp., which produced about 30 percent of the 349,000 outboards sold in 2000, filed for Chapter 11 protection from creditors around Christmas 2001. At press time, it appeared that OMC has accepted a joint bid from Bombardier and Genmar to purchase the troubled company for $95 million. Bombardier would get the outboard motor business while Genmar (parent company of Ranger and many other boat brands) would get the boat business.

Evinrude (www.evinrudeoutboards.com)

Evinrude, owned by Bombardier, boasts that its Direct Injection system provides more horsepower and less emissions with a lighter overall weight than typical four-stroke outboards. Its series of 200-, 225- and 250-horsepower V-6 motors get up to 35 percent better fuel economy than other brands, according to the company. Their V-4, two-stroke engines boast a 25 percent increase in fuel economy over similar two-stroke motors, while using 50 percent less oil. These mid-range motors are offered in 75-, 90- and 115-horsepower versions. This same Ficht® Ram Injection system is offered on the mid-sized V-6 engines, too, including the 135-, 150- and 175-horsepower models.

Johnson (www.johnson.com)

Johnson, also owned by Bombardier, still offers a full line of traditional two-stroke motors. They range from 25 to 175 horsepower. Even some of the smaller ones offer electric starters. Some feature Power Trim and Tilt and Digital Sequential Multi-Port fuel injection. This isn't your grandpa's Johnson! Of course,

there are some mid-sized and small four-stroke models, too, from a cute little 6-hp model for the duck boat to a 70-hp model with all the bells and whistles. There's also a new line of four-stroke motors ranging from 6 horsepower up to 70 horsepower.

Mercury (www.mercurymarine.com)

Mercury offers a wide array of watercraft engines, from a handy 75-cc, 2.5 horsepower motor to the Pro XB 250 250-horsepower V-6 with enough thrust to make you want to take up bowling instead of fishing. Another Mercury motor line worth considering is its series of jet motors. Jet as in jet-propelled, meaning no propellers to hit stumps or rocks. Jet motors are a consideration if you fish in shallow, stumpy, and rocky backwaters a lot. Come to think of it, that's where the fish are, too. Mercury offers jet motors in 20-, 40-, 65- and 80 horsepower models.

Yamaha (www.yamaha-motor.com)

Sure, you've heard of their motorcycles. But did you know they made outboard motors?

If you are a serious angler, you have. Proving once again that the Japanese build high-quality motors, Yamaha has created several outboard innovations, including the Labyrinth Exhaust system, which quiets the motor even at full throttle. After all, fishing is supposed to be peaceful. Yamaha makes both two- and four-stroke models, as well as jet drives, from 225-horsepower V-6 rocket launchers to the sweet little F4 4-hp model that holds a record for gas mileage (67.27 miles per gallon, according to the *Guinness Book of World Records*).

Chapter One: Gearing Up
Doing It Yourself Pays Off
Tying flies at home saves money, enhances angling experience
By C. Boyd Pfeiffer

You see a snaggy patch of water and realize that you might not get your fly back, but you throw to the spot anyway. Minutes later, you land a nice fish that took the fly from a spot where others would fear to tread.

That's just one of the advantages of tying your own flies. That fly might not have taken more than a few cents of materials and a few minutes to tie so you had little to risk if you lost your offering. Store-shopping anglers, buying flies for a buck or more apiece (often more) might hesitate about casting a fly that might not come back.

Other than saving money, advantages of tying your own flies are that you can always tie in advance the flies that you need for a given trip, that you can custom tie anything that you like, and that you begin to explore the relationship of natural fish foods to the offerings that you tie and fish.

Proper tools, materials important
To do this, of course, you do need to make an initial investment in tools and materials and to learn the basics. Regardless of the type of tying that you will do (trout, bass, panfish, salt water, other) the basics are all pretty much the same. In turn, you will need:

• Vise – Special fly-tying vises hold the hook through cam or lever operated jaws. They come in two basic styles – one with a pedestal base to sit on a table and one with a C-clamp to clamp onto a table. The C-clamp type is more secure, but should not be used on expensive tables. Some vises have rotary cranks to turn the jaws for adding materials and viewing the fly from all sides, but these are not necessary for starting out.

• Hackle pliers – Hackle pliers are just what they say – spring-loaded pliers to grip hackle (a feather) so that you can wind it around the hook. Some now have a universal joint on a handle to make it easier to wrap a hackle without twisting it.

• Scissors – Special fly-tying scissors have large finger holes (necessary for most tyers) and fine pointed blades. For best results, get two – one with coarse blades for heavy cutting of fur and coarse materials, and one with short fine blades for delicate work such

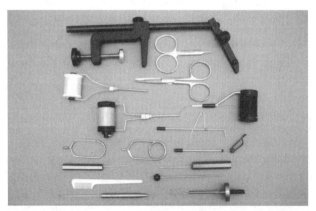

Tools for fly tying. These include, left to right: top row – simple fly tying vise. Second row, fine and coarse scissors. Third row, standard bobbin, Griffin adjustable tension bobbin and Merco adjustable tension bobbin. Fourth row, two types of standard hackle pliers, Griffin rotating hackle pliers and whip finisher. Fifth row, two bodkins. Sixth row, comb and bobbin cleaner. Seventh row, bobbin threader and dubbing loop tool.

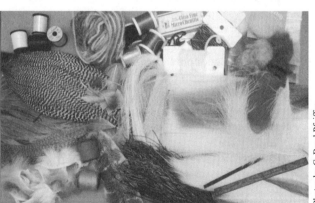

Some of the many materials used in tying trout flies. Left to right, top to bottom, top row: spools of thread, bundle of yarn, spools of floss, packages of chenille and packages of dubbing. Second row, hackle necks, teal and mallard feathers, stranded flash materials, synthetic streamer wing material, and marabou feathers. Third row, feathers, rabbit (Zonker) strips, spools of mohair, turkey feather, peacock herl, bucktail and foam strips.

Photos by C. Boyd Pfeiffer

1. Beginning step in tying a woolly bugger. Tie the thread down to the hook just in front of the bend of the hook. Do this by wrapping the thread around the hook shank a few times, then crossing over the existing wraps.

as trimming thread and hackle.

- Bobbin – A bobbin is a spool holder with a tubular shaft through which the thread runs. They make it easy to apply the thread in a precise location and to control thread tension. The best have ceramic tubes or a ceramic ring at the end (like a guide ring) to prevent thread fraying. If making a variety of flies, get one with a long tube that will be easier to use on large flies.

- Bodkin - A bodkin is nothing more than a needle point on a short handle. You can buy them or make your own by inserting a needle, eye first, into a wood dowel or short handle. They are useful for adding sealer and head cement, pulling out hackle strands and other tasks.

- Light - A good light is a must, and special fly-tying lights are available. A small halogen light for hobby work or reading is ideal.

Materials for fly tying can be found in any fly shop or mail order fly-tying catalog. Basics include hackle or a neck (which has the hackle feathers), various tinsels, chenilles, yarn, nylon tying thread, peacock herl, bucktail and other furs, floss, synthetic materials, body fur, vinyl body materials, rubber legs, Mylar, and plastic foam. With these, in the many colors and sizes available, almost any style or type of fly can be tied.

While a fly can be tied on almost any hook, special fly-tying hooks are available from all the hook companies. These include hooks of regular length, some with longer than normal shanks for tying baitfish patterns, and those with bent shanks for tying scud and swimming nymph trout flies. Hump shank hooks are made for gluing into cork or balsa bass bug bodies.

Tying techniques apply to all flies

The basics of tying flies are to tie materials, in sequence, onto the hook using special fly tying thread. Once the fly is complete, the thread is tied off with a special whip finish. Fortunately, the fundamentals for doing this apply to virtually all flies of all types for all

2. Next, clip a bundle of dark marabou and tie it down using the soft loop wrap as described in the text.

3. Following the tail attachment, tie in a length of body material. Here a length of olive chenille is being used. Other colors are possible.

4. Following the body material attachment, tie down a hackle feather by the tip end as shown here with the purple hackle. Other colors are also possible.

5. At this point, wrap the thread to the front end of the fly, tying down the tag end of the body material and the tip end of the hackle as shown here.

6. Wrap the body by winding the chenille around the hook shank as shown and then tie off with the thread at the front end of the fly.

species of fish.

Learn the basics of tying on, adding materials and tying off, and you can tie any fly for any fish. These basics are:

Placing the hook in the vise – Place the hook in the vise by opening the jaws (loosening the thumb screw or lever) and positioning the bend of the hook in the jaws. Close the vise jaws and make sure that the hook is not too loose.

• Tying on – Thread is "tied" onto a hook by a simple wrapping method. For this, hold the tag end of the thread, wind the thread around the hook shank for a few turns and then wrap at an angle to cover the previous wraps. It is this tension that holds the thread in place on the hook. Clip the excess thread and continue to tie the fly.

• Tying the soft loop to add materials – This is a standard method by which any material of any type can be exactly positioned on the hook. To do this, hold the material in place on the hook shank. Then bring the thread straight up and then loosely straight down on the far side of the hook. This technique keeps the material straight on the hook, without twisting, turning or cocking to one side. The easy way to do this is to grip the material with your left index finger and thumb (assuming a right-handed tyer), then bring the thread up, grip it between the thumb and finger, and then bring it down on the far side before pulling tight.

• Tying tails – Most flies, including wet flies, dry flies, some nymphs and streamers, have tails. These can be fur, feathers or synthetics. Use the soft loop method described above to add the tail to the fly at the junction of the shank and the hook bend. Clip any excess fur.

• Tying bodies – Bodies can consist of chenille, yarn, fur dubbing that is added to ("spun") the tying thread, or tinsel. These are tied in one end of the hook shank,

7. Continue this body by palmering (spiral wrapping) the purple hackle feather around the chenille body, as shown here.

8. Once reaching the head of the fly with the hackle, tie it off with the thread as shown here.

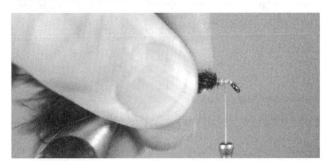

9. Clip the excess hackle, then pull the hackle fibers back and out of the way to complete the head of the fly.

10. Complete the fly by making a whip finish around the head, by wrapping loops of thread over and around the hook shank and the standing end of thread as shown here. Complete the fly, then seal with head cement or nail polish. (Note, in these photos, white thread was used for photo clarity and to differentiate from the other fly materials. Normally, dark thread to complement the dark fly colors would be used.)

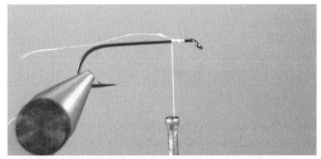

1. To tie a simple streamer, begin by tying down the thread at the front of the hook shank by wrapping around the hook shank and then wrapping over it to secure the thread.

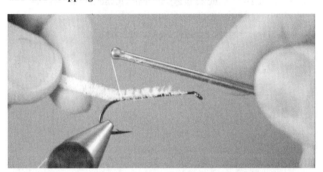

2. Clip the excess thread, then tie in a length of yellow chenille. Then with the bobbin, wrap around the hook shank and the chenille until reaching the bend of the hook. Return the thread by spiral wrapping it to just in back of the hook eye.

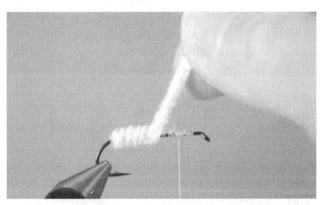

3. With the thread just in back of the hook eye, wrap the chenille forward by winding it around the hook shank as shown here.

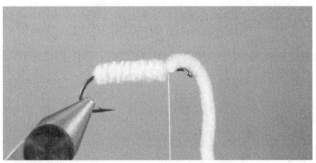

4. Continue to wrap until just in back of the hook eye, then tie off with the thread as shown. Clip the excess chenille.

5. Cut and comb a length of bucktail, then hold it over the fly as shown to position it for the correct length. Generally, the accepted length for a streamer is about 1 1/2 to 2 times the length of the hook.

the thread wrapped to the other end and then the body wrapped until it is tied off by wraps of thread. Excess body material is clipped off.

• Tying ribbing – Ribbing can be thread, tinsel, ribbon or other material that is tied in with the body and then spiral wrapped over it to make for flash or a segmented insect body.

• Tying wings – Wings on wet flies and dry flies are tied differently. Wet fly wings are tied from quills or feathers, with the tips facing to the rear and the wing tied at an angle. Dry fly wings are tied with the tips facing forward, and then brought to a vertical position by wraps of thread in front of the wing. Wings can be upright, divided (two wings, angled to the side) or spent (180 degrees, as with a dead insect).

• Tying hackle – Hackle is the fine feather barbules that are tied to surround the hook shank to make a fly stand up on dry flies, or angled to the rear to make for buggy legs on a wet fly or nymph. Tie hackle in by using thread to wrap in the butt of the feather, then use hackle pliers to wind the hackle around the hook shank. Tie off with the thread and clip any excess hackle. Throat hackle is tied differently, by adding a small bunch of fibers or fur beneath the head of the fly by tying using the soft loop method. Palmered hackle is hackle that is spiral wrapped up the hook shank over the body, as in spiral wrapping tinsel. A woolly bugger is a typical fly tied using this technique.

• Tying streamer wings – Steamer wings are tied on long shank hooks, after the body, ribbing and any tail material have been tied down. Wings are positioned immediately in back of the head. For this, use the soft loop method to secure the wing material straight on top of the hook. Some wings are multilayered with

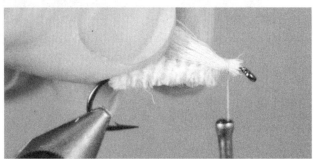

6. Hold the wing by the end with the butts in position over the front end of the fly and tie down, making soft loop wraps with the thread. Secure with several wraps and clip any forward excess bucktail or fur.

7. Use the same method to tie in a length of short red calf tail as a throat, directly under the wing of the fly. This small spot of color can simulate gills of a minnow, and help to provoke strikes.

different materials or colors of the same material.

- Making cork/balsa bug bodies – Cork and foam pre-shaped bodies are available for making floating bugs for bass and panfish. For these, use a regular long shank hook that is glued in place in a foam bug through a hole made in the bug belly. For cork, cut a slot in the belly and glue a hump-shank hook in place. Finish cork bodies with several coats of paint and then tie on a tail and hackle collar. Cork, balsa and foam can also be bought in cylinders and shaped with tools as you desire.

Learn to tie flies by practicing first the basic steps of tying, then tying simple flies such as streamers and woolly buggers on large size hooks. As your skills develop, try tying other flies, more complex patterns and start tying on successively smaller hooks. Consider also some of the many classes given by fly shops and fly fishing clubs, or get some personal instruction from a fly fishing friend who is an experienced tyer.

Developing this fishing hobby of fly tying will provide you with a great off-season activity, help you become a better fisherman by allowing you to throw your flies where others won't and by helping you learn about the habits of fish, their foods and how flies work in the water.

C. Boyd Pfeiffer has written several books on fly fishing and tying, including Tying Trout Flies.

8. Finish by wrapping the rest of the area with thread to make a head of the fly, and then make a whip finish. Begin to make the whip finish by holding the thread in the left hand and using two fingers of the right hand to grasp the thread and fold it over the hook shank and standing part of the thread.

9. Here the first loop has been formed by folding the thread with the two fingers over the hook shank and the standing part of the thread. If having difficulty with this, special easy to use whip finishers are available to make this task easier.

10. Finish the whip finish after several turns of thread by holding the thread loop and pulling the standing end of the thread to pull the loop tight and secure the whipped "knot."

11. Here, the completed simple streamer is being completed by adding head cement or nail polish to the wrapped and secured thread head.

Chapter Two: Heading Out

Hooking Up With Canada's Big Three

Anglers head north for big walleye, northerns, and smallmouth bass
By Mark Romanack

Canada is famous for a lot of things. Hockey, premium whiskey, and beers that are served at room temperature quickly come to mind! No one can measure the amount of pleasure these goods and services provide visitors to Canada, but it's a safe bet that another Canadian resource provides even more anticipation and hair-raising excitement.

The remote, pure, and placid waters of Canada are home to three of the most sought-after gamefish in North America. Staggering numbers of walleye, northern pike, and smallmouth bass await those who journey north. Anglers are frequently treated to the pleasures of fast action and trophy caliber fish that are rarely found elsewhere.

Walleye to 10 pounds, northerns to 20 pounds, and smallmouth topping five pounds aren't fish stories. The fact is, no other region in North America can boast the fishing resources found in Ontario, Manitoba, Quebec, and Saskatchewan: the four provinces where the big three of Canadian sport fish are the most abundant.

There are lots of ways to get in on this outstanding fishing action. Booking a guided trip through a reputable outfitter is the fast track to fishing fun. Outfitters offer prime waters, comfortable accommodations, skilled guides, and other fishing essentials. Many of these trips require a float plane to reach remote destinations. Others can be reached by car or a wilderness train ride.

Cabela's Outdoor Adventures is the nation's leading booking agent for Canadian fishing adventures. Representing dozens of outfitters specializing in

Canada enjoys some of the finest sportfishing opportunities in North America. A wealth of fish live in these waters, but the most popular species are walleye, smallmouth bass, and northern pike.

Photos by Mark Romanack

Smallmouth like this are common in the southern areas of Canada. Big fish and lots of them are a possibility in many waters.

Smallmouth are found in shallow water most of the year throughout Canada. Topwater is always a good technique to try.

Canadian fishing adventures, Cabela's only books for the most trustworthy, dependable, and consistently successful outfitters. Call toll-free at (800) 346-8747 for more information.

Many of the best Canadian fishing waters are also located near or connected to a host of provincial parks found throughout the region. Provincial parks vary a little in the services they offer, but all are great places to camp while exploring new fishing spots. The Web site www.canadaonline.about.com contains a wealth of information about Canada's many provincial and national parks that provide both camping and fishing opportunities.

Walleye, Canada's favorite fish

Throughout Canada, the walleye is more commonly referred to as the pickerel. Walleye are actually members of the perch family. Aside from the fact that both walleye and pickerel sport plenty of sharp teeth, the two species have little in common.

Walleye grow to 15 or more pounds in Canadian waters. Any fish approaching 10 pounds is considered a trophy and most of the specimens taken by sport anglers average 1-3 pounds. Usually modest in size, the walleye makes up for this shortcoming by being amazingly abundant, widespread, and unmatched as table fare.

Where abundant, walleyes aren't difficult to catch. In fact, at certain times of year and in certain waters, catching a walleye on every cast isn't uncommon.

Walleyes are most abundant in the southern half of Saskatchewan, Manitoba, Ontario, and Quebec. The further north an angler travels, the more walleye numbers are replaced by northern pike and lake trout.

Voracious predators, walleye can be caught using a wide variety of terminal tackle and fishing presentations. Medium weight spinning tackle equipped with six- to eight-pound test line is ideal for most walleye fishing situations.

Northern pike, water wolves

Northern pike are the fish that put teeth into the excitement of traveling to Canada. Large, powerful and not afraid to strike at a wide variety of lures and presentations, pike are among the most commonly caught fish in all of Canada.

Distributed widely across every province, the biggest pike tend to come from remote regions. Pike inhabit

Sunset arrives on a Canadian lake.

Small boats are required in many Canadian lakes because launch facilities are often crude.

both lakes and large rivers, and the trophy class specimens tend to come from waters that are rarely fished and accessible only by plane or train.

Because pike are relatively easy to locate and catch, areas that receive heavy to moderate fishing pressure do not consistently produce quality pike fishing. To find the best pike action, you have to get off the beaten path and seek out those overlooked or remote destinations.

Also, certain waters seem to produce big pike more consistently than others. Big lakes with an ample forage base of ciscoes, whitefish, suckers or lake trout grow the most and biggest pike. These soft rayed and protein-rich fishes are the fuel it takes to grow big pike in cold Canadian waters.

Lakes that do not contain this important forage base make poor pike waters. Pike and walleye often inhabit the same lakes, but each species prefers a slightly different niche.

Because pike are often large and powerful, these fish are best handled with heavy action spinning or medium to heavy action baitcasting tackle, 10-20 pound test line and steel leaders to prevent their sharp teeth from cutting the line.

Smallmouth bass, bronzeback fury

Pound for pound, no fish in Canada fights harder or longer than the smallmouth bass. Originally found only in Quebec and Eastern Ontario, stocking efforts have established smallmouth all across the southern rim of Canada as far west as Saskatchewan. The clean and rock-filled waters this area is noted for are the perfect habitat for smallmouth bass. Unfortunately, this outstanding species is slow growing and doesn't do well

A Canadian lake is the setting for a beautiful sunset.

Some of the best fishing in Canada is accessible only from a float plane.

in far north waters. Found primarily in lakes and larger rivers, smallmouth get far less attention from anglers than the more common walleye and northern pike.

Many anglers simply don't realize how good the smallmouth fishing can be in many areas of Canada. Fish to four and five pounds are common, and many lakes yield the potential for 20-30 fish per day catches!

Because of the cool waters, smallmouth throughout Canada are most often found in shallow to moderate water depths all season long. Rarely will an angler have to look deeper than 10-15 feet to find action. Up until late summer, most smallmouth will be concentrated in water less than 10 feet deep, making them accessible to a wide variety of lures and angling presentations.

Gear similar to that used in walleye fishing is ideal for smallmouth. Medium weight spinning or baitcasting tackle equipped with six- to 10-pound test line will handle most any angling situation that comes up.

Tackling the Big Three

The most popular and productive lure groups for catching walleye, pike, and bass include jigs, live bait rigs, and crankbaits. A modest assortment of each of these lure types ensures anglers will experience good fishing results regardless of the conditions encountered.

An ample supply of leadhead jigs is a good place to start. The most popular sizes include 1/8, 1/4, 3/8, and 1/2 ounce.

Often considered "walleye" lures, the fact is jigs are equally effective on pike and bass as well. A jig tipped with a 2- to 3-inch live minnow is legendary for its allure in Canada. There's no way of telling what will bite when this simple yet effective lure and live bait combination is used.

Unfortunately, jig fishing is a rather slow and tedious angling method when it comes to searching for fish. Best employed once a concentration of fish has been located, jigs can be either casted, drifted or fished vertical beneath the boat with great success. The key in

Big pike like this are found most often in remote waters.

most instances is to select a jig that's heavy enough to easily maintain contact with the bottom.

A minnow ranks as the first choice in live baits when jig fishing, but leeches, nightcrawlers, and even salted minnows are also productive. In remote areas where it's difficult or impossible to keep minnows alive, these other alternatives do a fine job. All three bait options work well on Canada's big three.

Soft plastic grub bodies are another essential part of jig fishing. Twister tails, shad bodies, tubes, and a host

Spinnerbaits fished in or near weed beds are always a top technique for northern pike.

Pike in Canada grow big. Fish to 20 pounds are possible in many waters and fish over 10 pounds are common.

of other grub styles serve an important purpose when threaded onto the shank of a leadhead jig. The grub body adds bulk that makes the lure more visible from a greater distance, the soft plastic also adds action to the lure and the opportunity to explore different colors.

In many cases, a jig dressed with a grub body is all it takes to trigger strikes. When the fish are actively feeding, this simple combination works great. As fish become more lethargic, however, it often helps to switch to live bait or to use plastic and live bait in combination.

Good places to use jigs include river mouths, rocky shorelines, the tips of points, saddles between islands, weed edges, and along steeply sloping breaklines that join shallow and deep water.

Jigs are one of the most commonly used lures in Canada, but live bait rigs do a better job of covering water when searching for fish. The biggest chore in catching any type of fish boils down to finding them.

A simple, yet effective live bait rig makes the chore of finding active fish much easier. The rig consists of a weight known as a bottom bouncer. This ungainly

looking device is simply a 12- to 14-inch length of wire that is bent in such a way that it resembles an upside down "L." On the short arm a snap swivel is located that accepts a nightcrawler harness or other live bait snell. On the longer arm a weight is molded midway on the wire. The main line is tied on at the elbow formed when the wire is bent.

Bottom bouncers range in size from 1/2 to three ounces and can be used to fish both shallow and deep waters. The name bottom bouncer suggests that this weight system remains in constant contact with the bottom. Actually, a bottom bouncer armed with a crawler harness or other snell works best when the weight simply ticks the bottom occasionally. Keeping the rig close to bottom, without constantly dragging allows the bait to be presented in the most natural manner and reduces the chances of snagging.

Used while drifting or slow trolling, it's important to

let out only enough line to maintain this "tick and go" balance. The rule of thumb is to fish a bottom bouncer at approximately a 45-degree angle behind the boat and to use enough weight to maintain occasional bottom contact.

A two-hook crawler harness 40 to 60 inches in length and featuring a No. 2 or 3 size blade is the most popular live bait rig used with a bottom bouncer. Deadly on both walleye and smallmouth, Colorado and Indiana style blades seem to produce best. Crawlers are the preferred bait, but minnows can also be fished in combination with single-hook harnesses. Adding a minnow to this bait rig greatly increases the chances of catching big northern pike.

A bottom bouncer rig is a deadly way to explore large flats, deep water in the basin of the lake, outcroppings of submerged gravel or rock, sunken islands, and the saddles between islands.

Crankbaits are the third lure group to explore when fishing for Canada's big three. Trolled or cast, crankbaits are the fastest way to cover water while searching for active fish. Equally effective on walleye, pike, and bass, crankbaits seem to produce best during the warm days of summer when fish are most active.

Crankbaits that float at rest and dive when retrieved are the most versatile. An assortment of shallow, medium and deep diving models enables anglers to fish a wide variety of water depths and fishing situations.

Like other lures, crankbaits produce best when fished in close quarters with bottom structure or another type of cover such as weed growth, submerged timber, boulders, etc.

When targeting shallow waters, stickbaits or what are sometimes referred to as jerkbaits are essential. Most lures in this category feature slender minnow-shaped bodies with a small diving lip. Examples of good jerkbaits include the Rapala Husky Jerk, Storm ThunderStick, Yo-Zuri Crystal Minnow, Reef Runner Ripstick, and Bomber Long A.

When using jerkbaits, cast well past your intended target and work the bait by snapping the rod tip with short and quick motions. When the bait approaches the target area, slow down the retrieve, twitching the bait while moving it as little as possible. This strategy is more than most fish can stand. Sudden and powerful strikes are often the reward.

Jerkbaits work best in water less than 10 feet. For deeper waters, a slightly deeper diving crankbait comes into play.

This 20-pound-plus pike hit on a crankbait trolled over open water.

Walleyes are the jewels of most Canadian lakes. Most lakes have good populations of walleyes in the 2-4 pound range.

Jigs, live bait rigs, and crankbaits are the top lures to take along on a Canadian fishing trip.

Dawn and dusk are always the most productive times to fish for walleye. Early in the year, however, it's common to catch walleyes all day long.

A host of crankbaits will dive from 10 to 17 feet when trolled. Some of the most popular models include the Rapala Shad Raps, Reef Runner Deep Little Ripper, Storm Hot n' Tot and Deep Jr. ThunderStick, Bomber A series, and the Yo-Zuri Diving Minnow.

Crankbaits that reach these moderate depths are excellent tools for trolling. For walleye or bass it's usually best to adjust the lead length so the crankbait dives to within a couple feet of bottom. The angler's guide Precision Trolling (www.precisionangling.com) provides the depth diving ranges of more than 180 popular crankbaits. For northern pike that frequently suspend in the water column, it's not as critical to fish close to bottom.

When trolling crankbaits, in-line style planer boards are a great way to help spread out trolling lines. A couple of these boards makes it easy to cover twice the water in half the time.

For those who long to catch and eat fish in one of the most beautiful settings in North America, Canada is the destination. Fishing licenses are moderately priced and available over-the-counter at most tackle and outdoor shops in Canada and also at all border crossings.

Mark Romanack's books on fishing include *Bassin' With The Pros* and *Catch More Walleyes*.

Chapter Two: Heading Out
Pack Up For That Canadian Adventure

Weight restrictions, weather, and targeted species all play a part in what you'll need to make the most of your dream fishing trip

By Dan Donarski

You've saved your money. You went to all the sports shows to check out the wide variety of destinations and species available. You're ready for that Canadian dream fishing adventure. Right?

Maybe not. Here's a look at three separate areas of Canada and what you can expect once you get there and what you can't. Even more importantly, we'll talk to well-respected lodge/outfitter operators and staff just to make sure you have all that you'll need as well as cut down on the gear you don't.

It should go without saying that where you go, and what fish you are going to target or are available, play a big part in what you decide to bring along on this adventure. Canada is a huge country. Across its length and breadth you'll find snow and sleet a real possibility during July in some locations and in others you'll be in sweltering heat. Making matters even more confusing is that you can find both of these extremes in the same location and often only a day apart.

One article can't begin to cover all the bases in Canada's field. We're going to cover three distinct geographic areas that are varied in species and weather, among other conditions. The chosen three do happen to be the most popular areas, and at the end of each section you'll find phone numbers and Web sites for

more information. We'll also talk a little about areas that aren't covered specifically, but are similar to the ones mentioned.

Northern Saskatchewan

It is next to impossible to talk about a Canadian fishing adventure without Wollaston Lake Lodge, located in northeastern Saskatchewan, popping up in the conversation, accompanied by wide smiles and that far away look in the speaker's eyes. This is arguably one

Photos by Dan Donarski

Central Canada means walleyes and a lot more. Walleye-sized tackle will handle most of your needs for the other species found in this great northern land so don't leave home without it. Canada enjoys some of the finest sportfishing opportunities in North America. A wealth of fish live in these waters, but the most popular species are walleye, smallmouth bass, and northern pike.

The sunsets are late this far north. Be prepared to fish early and late in the day by dressing in layers. A dry bag is a necessity to keep your extra clothes dry whether the sun is shining or not. It will also help protect your camera so you take home those Kodak moments.

of the finest full service operations in the country.

Dave Csanda, the senior editor of In-Fisherman magazine, says simply, "This is the crown jewel of Canadian fly-in fishing destinations." Larry Dahlberg says this about Wollaston: "I would have to place Wollaston Lake Lodge in the top three destinations I've ever visited, and at the very top of my Canadian list." That's high praise indeed from two incredibly well-traveled anglers. It's well deserved, too.

Wollaston boasts some of the finest trophy northern pike fishing found on the planet. In 2001, just under 1,000 pike above 40 inches were caught. More than 400 were over 43 inches with the biggest coming in at 51 inches. Better still, unless old age caught up to these behemoths, they are all still waiting for you as Wollaston has a strict catch and release policy.

The lake, as well as surrounding waters, also contain walleye. Due to the extreme northern location, these do not get into the huge category. They do make up for it in numbers and aggressiveness. You'll also have opportunities at lake trout that can get impressive as well as grayling on some area rivers. Some of these do require an additional fly-out from the lodge.

Like much of Canada, Wollaston has some special regulations. Barbless hooks are mandatory (pinching the barbs down with pliers is fine). You are allowed to use leeches and nightcrawlers but all other types of live bait are illegal. The entire lake, for every species, is

Shore lunches are a fine art up here. Be sure to sign up for one early in your stay so you'll be able to prepare your own later on during your stay. Whether it be walleyes, trout, char or northern pike, these lunches fit the bill.

Early mornings are a bustle of activity at fishing camps. In order to help the outfitter out and get you on the water as quickly as possible make sure your gear is ready before you turn in for the night. Now is not the time to be changing line or sorting out a tackle box.

catch and release.

Unless you own your own long distance plane, you'll first need to get to Winnipeg, Manitoba. In Winnipeg, you'll hook up with a Wollaston representative who will get you on Wollaston's own 50-passenger Convair 580. From Winnipeg, the airfare is on the lodge.

At the lodge, expect fine dining and seriously comfortable rooms. You'll find a superb sauna and daily maid service. There is a guide provided for every two anglers. Mike Lembke and his staff have this lodge

Guides up here are a good investment in success. By hiring a guide on your first couple of days you'll learn enough about the water to be more successful when you choose to go it alone. Their job is to get you into fish and they do their job well.

running impeccably.

"I can't emphasize rain gear enough," says Lembke. "It would be nice if it wouldn't rain the entire season but it does, and once you are uncomfortable, misery isn't far behind. Get a good set of pants, or better yet bibs and a jacket."

As far as tackle goes, leave the saltwater stuff behind–no matter how big you've heard the pike and lake trout get. Don't laugh. Lembke has had more than a handful of anglers bring tackle better suited for small sharks. "Most of your fishing will be handled well by a medium-heavy action rod matched with a good quality baitcasting or spinning reel. Spool the reel with new 15- to 20-pound test and you'll be set."

For the northern, bring along some large Mepp's spinners, a selection of big surface baits, and a few heavy duty spinner baits. Lake trout have a real affinity for the old Five of Diamonds spoon and the walleyes go after simple jig heads with curly tails or Shad Raps. Walleye anglers will also want to bring along some bottom bouncers, according to Lembke. Grayling are handled by smaller spin tackle and grab No. 0 and No. 1 spinners with gusto, according to Lembke.

"The lodge does have a well-equipped tackle shop on site, as well as offering loaner equipment. If you do bring tackle that just isn't working, we will be able to help you out," Lembke says.

Wollaston also highly recommends its guests bring a waterproof, as opposed to water resistant, boat bag. The canoe-style duffels, the type that fold over themselves for added protection, are the best made.

As far as clothing goes, the tried and true method of dressing in layers, and packing so you can dress in layers, is a must. And remember this before you leave, the weight limit per angler is 50 pounds per angler, although there are times that you may be able to bring a few pounds more. The staff will try to accommodate you and your gear, but be well advised that you may be told and should be prepared to leave the excess weight in Winnipeg.

For more information contact Wollaston Lake Lodge at (800) 328-0628 or on the web at www.wollastonlakelodge.com.

Other areas in Canada that will be served by Lembke's suggestions include the Northwest Territories, northern Alberta, Manitoba, and interior British Columbia.

Northern Quebec

How far north? North of the tree line, that's how far. At least it is at Diana Lake Lodge, which is above the 60th Parallel and well above the tree line. Its sister

Chances are you'll be going by air into the camp. Packing light and right is mandatory. Soft sided luggage like a duffle bag is easy to get on board, a suitcase is not. Also, be sure to pack your rods in a protective case so they do not get broken in transit.

lodge is Lake Ternay Lodge, which sits just below the tree line. Both are operated by Joe Stefanski of High Arctic Adventures.

"What clothes you pack really plays a part in your success. If you are miserable, your success goes way down or simply shuts down completely," Stefanski says. "The other show-stopper is what kind of condition you are in before you get here. This is tough country both weather-wise and in the terrain you'll be covering. If you are not in a modicum of good shape, you will have a few troubles here."

Both lodges are comfortable and the meals are hearty but this is definitely not a super-pampered operation. The location itself prevents this due to logistics. What these lodges offer, however, is an adventure in wilderness fly fishing for world-class fish.

Both lodges boast excellent populations of brook trout. You can expect to have fish well over four pounds at the end of your line virtually every day. The largest taken by a guest stretched the scales to 11.11 pounds and numerous fish to eight pounds are taken regularly. Both also have strong populations of lake trout that will top out over 20 pounds. Lake Ternay also has a sizeable population of both northern pike above 15 pounds and quananiche, or land-locked salmon, above 10 pounds.

Diana Lake's claim to real fly fishing passion, besides the huge brookies, are the arctic char that often go well above 10 pounds.

"What our guests bring with them in the way of tackle, snacks and special beverages and, of course, clothing, is what they will have. There is no corner store up here," says Stefanski. "And, for God's sake, do not forget the insect repellent."

Insects here are as numerous as the purified atoms of oxygen you'll be breathing. Without a head net, you may be breathing some of those insects, too. That should not deter you from this area, but it is always best to be forewarned.

As mentioned, this is primarily a fly fishing destination but spin anglers are certainly welcomed. "If a guest brings up a 6- and an 8-weight rod they should do just fine. The eights really come in handy when throwing large flies and when the wind blows, which it will," Stefanski says.

Stefanski also recommends that due to weight restrictions (60 to 70 pounds is allowed), the neoprene waders stay at home. "Bring a set of those lightweight breathable waders and wear long underwear underneath."

Dry flies that need to be included include Wulff's, deer hair mice, humpies, and dark Hendrickson's. Woolly buggers, muddlers, smelt patterns, and large streamers round out the general fly selection. If you're headed to Ternay, bring along some large popping-style surface flies for the northern pike.

At both lodges, you will be required to bring your own sleeping bag. Bags rated to minus 10 degrees should service you well here. Yes, the cabins are definitely heated. And, yes, sometimes things happen. Be prepared; bring the warm bag.

Ed Sutton, a regular at both lodges, so much so that Stefanski has even used him as a guide a time or two, recommends highly that anglers bring along a backpack. "You'll be doing a fair amount of walking up here," says Sutton.

"You will also be away from the cabins during the day so if the weather turns you'll want to get into something warm and/or dry. If you don't have it you will not be happy. At the same time, it could start out windy and with a cold rain and then the sun breaks free and it gets very warm. You'll want something to put those unnecessary clothes in rather than just carrying them."

The lodges also offer photo safaris for such animals as musk ox, polar bear, foxes, golden eagles, and various falcons. In season, they also have caribou and ptarmigan hunts available. For more information,

Jigs catch every species of fish that swim so be sure to bring a good selection along. Whether you'll be fishing lakes or rivers, a selection of 1/8- to 3/4-ounce jigs should be sufficient. A few buck-tail spinners, a small box of cranks and stickbaits, and a few spoons round out the tackle requirements.

contact them at (800) 662-6404 or on the Web at www.higharcticadv.com.

The same tips on insects and gear will serve you well in the Maritimes, and extreme northern Ontario and Manitoba.

North-Central Ontario

OK, we've been to lodges that are going to cook your meals and guide you to the fish. That's not a bad way to go but you will be running on their schedule for meals and fishing. Sometimes that just doesn't cut the mustard. Sometimes you have to go it on your own.

Ernie Leuenberger, along with is brother, Malcolm, operate Leuenberger's Fly-In Lodge and Wilderness Outposts based out of Nakina, Ontario. At the lodge you'll find all the comforts of home including your meals prepared and your bed made. At the outposts those chores will be yours, and so will every other job.

Outpost cabins do offer you the ability to run, or walk for that matter, on your own schedule. Feel like fishing after supper? Go right ahead. How 'bout breakfast at 5 a.m. to get a jump on the day? No problem–as long as you get up and do it yourself.

The cabins also offer one very important intangible. In almost all cases you'll be in the only cabin on the lake where they drop you off. There are a few lakes where they have two, but these are so spread apart that it is unlikely you'll see another soul. In other

words, you are in the bush, the outback, the hinterlands. It is purely wild, and purifying.

"These may be wilderness cabins but we do have a stove and refrigerator which work off propane that we fly in. Cookware and utensils are also at the cabin. The boats are all motorized and we supply the gas, too. Basically, you bring the bedding in the form of a sleeping bag, your food, clothes, and tackle. It's the food that throws some people," says Leuenberger.

In a word, go light. That doesn't mean go without.

"Leave the potatoes at home except for maybe a meal or two. Instead, bring along those rice and pasta dishes where you only add water or powdered milk. Take them out of the box and put them in a zip-lock with the directions and you'll save a lot of weight and space. For breakfast, learn to love oatmeal or something like that. Pancake mix is a good idea to break up the oatmeal monotony.

"Frozen vegetables are a better choice than canned or fresh. Canned is simple, and a few cans of baked beans aren't a bad idea, but you do need to remember weight."

Leuenberger's have a 60-pound weight limit on their float planes. Like the others, a bit over, and I do mean a bit, can normally be accommodated but you can't count on it. They are more than willing to make an extra flight if you insist on bringing along that cooler full of steaks and eggs but you had better be more than willing to cough up the cost of an extra flight.

The area that the brothers operate in is walleye and northern pike heaven. A medium light and a medium heavy spinning or baitcasting outfit is all that is needed. Bring jigs and curly tails, a selection of stickbaits and large spinners, and you should be all set. I'd also recommend a few crawler harnesses and a few dozen crawlers, too. It is possible to trap your own minnows off the dock at your cabin as well.

Mark Martin, one of the top walleye sticks on the Professional Walleye Trail over the past 10 years, also highly recommends a portable fish graph. "Why fish blind? The folks who own the cabins will give you a map that is a good start, but a graph takes the guesswork out. Since you will be self-guided, and on the lake probably for the first time, you need to learn what the bottom looks like. Find the structure and you'll always find the fish. Put up with the weight of the graph and the extra batteries. Certainly there are a lot of fish to be caught, and you'll catch some without a graph but you will catch many more with one along."

For more information on Leuenberger's Fly-In

Lodge and Wilderness Outposts, call (888) 246-6533 or on the Web at www.leuenberger.ca.

Similar areas include all of temperate Canada including central and southern Quebec, Manitoba, and Saskatchewan.

Dan Donarski is an outdoors writer from Upper Michigan.

Solitude and wilderness make the Canadian experience so special. By packing smart and doing your homework it is a sure bet that your initial trip will have that call of the wild bringing you back time and time again.

Chapter Two: Heading Out

Mobile Troller Can Hit Hot Spots

Great Lakes specialists advise anglers to follow the fish

By Mark Romanack

Every fishing lake has its day. It's an accepted fact that specific lakes or even parts of lakes produce their best fishing action at certain times of year. Given these facts it's a logical conclusion to suggest that the best times to fish specific waters are during these peaks of activity.

Ironically, on the Great Lakes it seems many anglers ignore this not so subtle advice and select instead one primary port at which to keep their boat docked all year long. The primary reason Great Lakes trollers saddle themselves with one port for most of the fishing season boils down to boats and docking facilities.

The typical trolling boats used on the Great Lakes range from 25 to 35 feet in length and are more than a little inconvenient to launch and load daily. The hassle in getting in and out of the water stimulates most of these boat owners to pick a favorite port, purchase docking space, and stay put for the entire fishing season.

Such a decision may make for less stress at boat landings, but it also makes for some needlessly tough weeks of fishing. A new breed of angler on the Great Lakes is emerging, however. Anglers content to select smaller boats that can be trailered to hot ports at hot times of year are reaping the benefits of being in the right places at the right times.

Smaller boats ranging from 18 to 23 feet can be trailered and launched easily, yet these fishing machines are large enough to handle the open waters of the Great Lakes on most days. Obviously there are days when smaller boats are no match for the waves and wind so common on these waters. Anglers venturing off shore in small boats must also use extra caution to monitor wave and weather reports.

So long as anglers equipped with smaller boats pay heed to weather reports and storm warnings, they can fish in relative comfort using the same techniques practiced by big boat trollers. Common sense is the key ingredient to a safe and successful fishing trip.

Lake Michigan

Few would argue that Lake Michigan is the richest trout and salmon fishery in the Great Lakes chain. The second largest of the Great Lakes hosts countless lake

Large 25- to 30-foot boats are typical of those used on the Great Lakes. Unfortunately, large boats are a hassle to launch and load. Not surprisingly, most anglers pick a single port, purchase a dock, and stay put all season long.

Smaller boats, like this 22-footer, are big enough to handle the waters of the Great Lakes, yet small enough to be trailered from port to port as the fishing conditions change.

Photos by Mark Romanack

Walleye-sized boats (18-20 feet) can also be versatile Great Lakes fishing boats so long as anglers pay close attention to weather reports and head for shore at the first hint of bad weather.

trout, browns, steelhead, king and coho salmon.

Collectively the four states (Michigan, Illinois, Indiana, and Wisconsin) that border Lake Michigan boast the richest sport fishing harvest in the Great Lakes. King and, to a lesser degree, coho salmon are the fish that made Lake Michigan famous. The annual migrations of these fish are both fascinating and well documented.

The fishing action begins in the spring as soon as ice leaves the harbors and boats can be launched. The bottom or south end of the lake is the first to awaken from the winter deep freeze and in some years the action is beginning by late February. Mixed catches of kings, cohos, brown trout, and steelhead are taken throughout southern Wisconsin, Illinois, Indiana, and southern Michigan waters. Some of the hottest fishing waters are found along the Indiana/Michigan border near the ports of Michigan City, New Buffalo, and Bridgman.

These regions of the lake produce their best fishing during March and April. By early May a clockwise movement of fish occurs that sends kings and cohos on a migration that lasts hundreds of miles. The fish first show up in Illinois waters, then southern Wisconsin, and eventually end up as far north as the Door County region of Wisconsin by early summer.

Some of these same fish then cross Lake Michigan heading east where they turn up in Northern Michigan waters near the ports of Leland, Platte Bay, Frankfort, Arcadia, and Onekama during August and September.

Not all the salmon of Lake Michigan migrate in this clockwise pattern. Kings and cohos that winter in Lake Michigan's southernmost Michigan waters undertake a

Planer boards are frequently used to troll for trout and salmon early in the season and walleyes all year long on the Great Lakes.

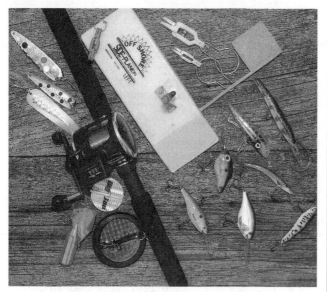

An assortment of tackle typical of the Great Lakes includes crankbaits, spoons, diving planers, and planer boards.

An angler fights a fish.

different journey. Fish that concentrate near the ports of Bridgman, St. Joseph/Benton Harbor, South Haven, and Saugatuck follow the Michigan shoreline north on a gradual migration that will eventually lead these fish to the streams where their parents spawned three to four years earlier. Most of the preferred spawning streams for both salmon and trout are located along the Michigan shoreline. This accounts for the strong migration in Michigan waters.

A natal urge to return to the streams where they were hatched drives the migration, but along the way food resources have a significant impact on the whereabouts of these fish. Early in the season important forage fish such as smelt, alewives, and chubs keep the salmon and trout population near shore. These baitfish are most often found in the warmest available water.

Warm water discharge sites and river mouths tend to be the spots where both fish and anglers concentrate. At Bridgman, the Cook Nuclear Power Plant warm water discharge site is a popular fishing hole. A mix of kings, coho, browns and steelhead are taken from this area during March, April, and early May. Small boats can access this area from a launch located at the end of Livingston Road, but larger boats must launch at St. Joseph or New Buffalo and make the run.

Moving north up the lakeshore, river mouths are some of the hottest fishing sites at St. Joseph, South Haven, and Saugatuck. At Port Sheldon, the Consumers Power Plant has a warm water discharge site known as the "bubblers" that holds significant numbers of early season fish.

North of Port Sheldon, most of the early season action is aimed at brown trout and the occasional steelhead. Browns can be found at Holland, Grand Haven, Muskegon, Pentwater, Whitehall, Ludington, Manistee, Onekama, Arcadia, Frankfort, and Platte Bay.

Spoons and body baits trolled behind planer boards account for most of the early season trout and salmon. Once the near shore waters begin to warm above 50 degrees, most of Lake Michigan's fishing action moves off shore and fishing tactics change as well. It's during this period that trout and salmon can turn up almost anywhere. Often the fish suspend where they find water temperatures and forage fish to their liking. Commonly you'll find kings, cohos, steelhead and lake trout in mixed schools suspended 40 to 100 feet down over 100 to 200 feet of water.

When trout and salmon go deep, spoons fished behind downriggers and Dipsy Divers dominate the fishing scene. Popular spoons include the Wolverine Silver Streak, Michigan Stinger, Northern Kings, Dreamweavers, and Pro Kings.

A fisherman holds a two-year-old salmon.

Big kings like this are what make the Great Lakes trolling fishing famous. Each year countless fish in the 20-35 pound range are taken.

As summer progresses, gradually anglers turn to various forms of attractors, the most common being the dodger/fly or dodger/squid combinations.

During August and September, the popular Luhr Jensen J-Plug is the bait to be pulling. The erratic action of the J-Plug triggers strikes when few other lures produce results.

By early October, most of the salmon have entered the spawning streams and the Great Lakes trolling action focuses on steelhead for the remainder of the fall.

Lake Huron

Lake Huron experiences a seasonal migration of trout and salmon similar to that found on Lake Michigan. Kings, cohos, steelhead, and browns that winter in southern Lake Huron are concentrated in early spring near the cities of Port Huron and Lexington. A significant number of fish are also caught in the St. Clair River that connects Lake Huron to Lake St. Clair.

By early May, most of the salmon are making their way north along the Huron shore to destinations including Port Sanilac, Harbor Beach, Port Hope, Grindstone City, and Port Austin. The primary salmon spawning streams emptying into Lake Huron are located a little further north at Au Gres, Tawas, Oscoda, and Alpena. These ports are where most of the summertime salmon action takes place.

Localized stockings of steelhead and brown trout help to hold fish in many of these ports well into summer. Also resident populations of lake trout are an important part of the catch especially around Harbor Beach, Port Hope, Grindstone City, and Port Austin.

The same angling methods that produce trout and salmon on Lake Michigan are used on Lake Huron. Early in the season most of the action comes on spoons and body baits fished behind planer boards. As the

Dodger and squid combinations are popular with king and coho anglers during the summer trolling season.

surface water warms, trout and salmon seek out deeper waters. Spoons, dodger/fly combinations and J-Plugs fished behind downriggers and Dipsy Divers dominate the trolling scene.

In addition to excellent salmon and trout fishing, Lake Huron is also home to some spectacular walleye fishing. The famed Saginaw Bay is a 20-mile-long appendage of Lake Huron that has become one of the hottest walleye fisheries in the nation.

The native walleye population of this region was destroyed by commercial fishing in the early 1940s. State sponsored stocking efforts aimed at reclaiming the fishery began in the late 1970s. Currently the Saginaw Bay region is planted with more than one million walleye fingerlings annually.

Football-shaped browns are taken mostly during the spring on the Great Lakes.

The results of these extensive stocking efforts are most apparent during the summer when countless boats troll for walleyes throughout Saginaw Bay. Both the east and west shores of Saginaw Bay are productive summer trolling grounds. Some of the most popular ports on the east side include Essexville, Sebewaing, Caseville, and Port Austin.

On the west side of Saginaw Bay anglers find good success near Bay City, Linwood, Pinconning, and AuGres. The region is divided into roughly two halves known as the inner and outer bays. The inner bay is made up of mostly shallow water and produces good catches of walleye May through September. The outer bay is deeper in depth and normally starts producing best around the Fourth of July and remains good all summer.

Trollers on Saginaw Bay depend on two primary techniques. Crankbaits trolled behind planer boards account for the majority of the fish. The Storm Hot n' Tot is the hands-down favorite crankbait on Saginaw

Steelhead are a bonus catch in most Great Lakes waters. Often these fish are found mixed in schools of salmon or walleye.

The best fishing for big kings occurs during the summer and early fall.

Monster browns like this are taken every year on Lake Michigan. This 34-pound plus fish was the state record when caught, but has since been topped twice.

Bay, but a wealth of other lures also produce. Other good baits to try include the Storm Deep Jr. ThunderStick, Reef Runner Deep Little Ripper, Rapala Deep Husky Jerk, and the Daiwa TD Minnow.

Slow trolling with crawler harnesses is also gaining in popularity on Saginaw Bay. Snap weights placed on the line are the most common method used to deploy harnesses at the necessary depths. By varying the weight used (usually 1/2 to three ounces of weight is required), these simple trolling aids can be used to fish shallow or deep. Snap weights can also be easily used in combination with planer boards, further making them the trolling weight of choice on Saginaw Bay.

Some anglers attempt to mix crankbaits and spinners in the same trolling pattern, but the practice doesn't always work as well as you might expect. Crankbaits excel when fished at faster (1.5 to 3.5 mph) speeds while spinners are better when fished slower (.75 to 1.5 mph) than is normally considered good crankbait speed.

Spoons such as these are the bread and butter lures of the Great Lakes trout and salmon fishery.

Lake trout are the native predator fish of the Great Lakes. While kings and cohos get most of the ink, lakers are abundant and fun to catch.

The Great Lakes are the ideal place to share a fishing trip with young people. Limits are generous and the action is often fast paced.

The best advice is to troll crankbaits for awhile to see if they produce, then slow down and experiment with spinners if the fish don't seem to be interested in these hard baits.

Lake Erie

The explosion of walleye on Lake Erie has to be one of the most remarkable fishing success stories ever told. From a polluted and dying sea in the 1960s to the richest walleye fishery in the world in the '90s and new millennium, Lake Erie is the only body of water in the Great Lakes chain that could pull off such a rapid turnaround. The shallow nature of Lake Erie and the fact that it's located near the end of the Great Lakes chain enabled this body of water to literally flush itself clean. Strict water pollution standards enacted in the late '60s and the '70s were also instrumental in the cleanup of Lake Erie.

Today, Lake Erie is the crown jewel of the Great Lakes. Not only does this magnificent lake produce the world's best walleye fishing, Lake Erie is also home to a host of other important game fish including yellow perch, smallmouth bass, steelhead, and king salmon.

The lake is broken down into three divisions known as the Western, Central, and Eastern basins. The Western Basin is shallow by comparison to the other basins and contains most of the critical walleye spawning habitat. Countless walleyes spawn each March on reefs and in tributary rivers throughout this basin. Many of the Western Basin's top spawning reefs are located near the Bass Islands region of Ohio. The town of Port Clinton is the center of this sportfishing activity. The Maumee River near Toledo and the Detroit

The single best month of the year to fish for kings is August.

Coho are almost as common as king salmon in most Great Lakes ports.

River that drains into Lake Erie from the north shore are also important spawning tributaries that attract thousands of fish.

Once the spawning ritual is completed, many of the larger mature walleye begin an eastward migration toward deeper water. Smaller immature fish tend to stay in the shallow waters of the Western Basin.

The trolling fishery in the Western Basin gets started in late April as soon as the spawn wraps up. May and June are the peak trolling months. Top ports include Bolles Harbor, Luna Pier, Toledo, and Port Clinton.

Crankbaits and crawler harnesses trolled behind planer boards are the most popular lures. In recent years spoons trolled behind Dipsy Divers have contributed significantly to the walleye harvest. The most popular crankbaits include the Storm Wiggle Wart and Hot n' Tot series, Rapala Deep Husky Jerk, and Reef Runner Deep Little Ripper. Productive spoons include the Michigan Stinger Scorpion and the Wolverine Silverstreak.

The Central Basin is the transitional waters of Lake Erie. A mix of both shallow and deep water, the Central Basin produces the best walleye fishing in May, June, and July. A good share of this fishing occurs as much as 10-25 miles off shore.

Deep diving crankbaits are among the most

productive lures, but spoons fished on Dipsy Divers and behind downriggers are also important to the overall catch. Good walleye crankbaits include the Reef Runner Deep Diver, Luhr Jensen Power Dive Minnow, Bomber 25A, and Storm Deep Thunderstick.

Trolling spoons will catch both walleye and a surprising number of steelhead during the summer in the Central Basin. One of Lake Erie's greatest secrets is the spectacular summer steelhead action that takes

Diving planers like these are important trolling tools on the Great Lakes.

place off shore near the ports of Cleveland and Lorain.

Mixed catches of walleye and steelhead are very common. Spoons that consistently produce both walleye and steelhead include the Wolverine Silverstreak, Michigan Stinger, and Pro Spoon.

The Eastern Basin of Lake Erie is deep enough to support a surprising trout and salmon fishery. Walleyes are also taken in the Eastern Basin during the summer months. Often these fish are suspended in deep water at or near the thermocline level. Downriggers, Dipsy Divers, and wire line are the methods used to reach these deep water fish.

Walleye anglers use both crankbaits and spoons in the Eastern Basin, while those anglers who are targeting trout and salmon prefer spoons. Dunkirk, N.Y., is one of the most popular fishing ports in the Eastern Basin.

The many ports of the Great Lakes collectively account for some of the best sport fishing waters in America. From tasty walleyes to tackle busting king salmon, the trolling fishery offered in Lakes Michigan, Huron and Erie is without equal. For the mobile Great Lakes troller, the fishing opportunities are almost without limit. From ice out in the spring to ice up in the fall, there's always a good trolling bite going on somewhere in the Great Lakes.

Mark Romanack's books on fishing include *Catch More Walleyes* and *Bassin' With the Pros*.

Here's a close-up of a laker caught on a crankbait.

Chapter Two: Heading Out

Not For Human Consumption

Stinky stuff whipped up by a real comic attracts big cats

By Craig Cooper

The formulas for catfish baits, passed down through generations if they haven't resulted in any untimely deaths or serious injuries, must be similar to chili recipes.

Nearly everyone who cooks believes he or she has the absolute best chili recipe. Everyone who fishes for catfish knows for a fact that he has the recipe that never fails to attract the whiskered demons.
All of the catfish concoctions seem to go something like this:

You catch some field mice. Smash the field mice, mix them up with smashed bananas, smashed garlic, smashed nightcrawlers that have fermented for days in the sun, add a little pancake syrup and cornmeal and oatmeal to hold it all together, and put the stuff in the blender while your wife is out shopping. The most important step may be the last one. You clean the blender before your wife comes home.

There are mass producers like Bowker's, Old Whiskers, Uncle Josh's, Junnies, and Sonny's. They mix up the stuff for you so you don't have to pay for a new blender or pay for a divorce attorney.

Regardless of which of the bait companies prepared the catfish bait or what ingredients have been used, you'll find this standard line on the package: Not For Human Consumption. Duhhhhh.

But if you were so inclined, how would you prepare Bowker's Original Dip Bait for the table?
Do you pan fry the stuff? How do you know when it's done? Does blood bait turn black when cooked properly? Is it served as an entrée or appetizer? Can you grill it and maybe sprinkle a little olive oil on it for seasoning? Does it taste like chicken? How many does one bucket serve?

Catfish Have a Nose for Food

What you find out very early in the catfishing experience is that the fish are not finicky. If the bait has a scent, the catfish and carp will be interested. Catfish

and carp may not be related, but they hang out together and typically enjoy the same menu.

Chicken livers and turkey livers are old standards.

Willie P. Richardson holds a carton of his special bait, Catfish Magic Cheese Dough Bait.

Richardson would put together these elaborate, but basically harmless pranks. Like the time he called the hospital and said somehow he and his wife (he explained they were black) had brought home the wrong baby. Assured that that was impossible, Richardson's punch line was … drum roll, please … "Well, all I know is that I'm not sure I can teach this Mexican child English." And the victims of the prank would explode in laughter. It's funnier the way Richardson does it.

In his mid-40s, Richardson turned his unique "talent" into a career in entertainment. Willie and his wife, Lucretia, have put their best telephone gags on recordings that have made his financial condition better than ever before. They will call up radio stations with the tape recorder running and try out their new stuff. Willie has also turned the gags into a standup act that kept him on the road for several years before he landed

Willie P. Richardson has made a career out of comic phone calls. When he's not creating catfish bait, he's playing a theater in Branson, Mo.

A big gob of worms – nightcrawlers, green or red worms are favored – will catch fish. Corn niblets have been known to work for channel cats.

The more serious a catfish chaser becomes, the more likely it is that the angler will branch out into the formulas. This can be a secretive business. The little companies that make the stuff for you protect their formulas, although a sniff or two can usually identify some of the ingredients.

Anise is a staple. You might recognize the unmistakable scent of garlic. You might recognize the essence of soft dog food. Just about anything could be in the jar or tub of catfish bait you are sniffing.

Entertainer combines comedy, catfish

Willie P. Richardson, who is living "The American Dream," according to his Web site, knows something about prepared catfish baits. Richardson is a colorful Texan who had a number of careers–raising cattle, fishing, delivering furniture, fishing, mowing yards, fishing–until he stumbled upon his real calling. Richardson's calling, by the way, is making prank phone calls.

A caricature of Willie P. Richardson decorates his logo, below, and cartons of Cheese Dough Bait.

AVAILABLE HERE!
WILLIE P. RICHARDSON'S
CATFISH MAGIC!™
CHEESE DOUGH BAIT

Another powerful, and smelly, catfish bait is Top Secret's Catfish Super Strong Ad Hoc Dip that sticks to natural bait and produces a "strong scent cloud."

Gary Van Pelt holds a big catfish caught on an Ultra Point catfish hook by Mustad.

a regular theater show in Branson, Mo.

He makes his living as an entertainer, but what Willie really likes to do is stalk catfish. When he was a kid in the "piney woods" of East Texas, Richardson came up with his own catfish formula that was successful with the cats in the giant reservoir Sam Rayburn Lake.

"The lake filled in 1965 when I was a senior in high school. Over the years we had put some things together like rotten cheese and some grains and we were catching fish. Other fishermen wanted to buy the stuff," Richardson explained.

Richardson went into the catfish bait business in 1999 with an uncle he calls "Rassie." Rassie is a character in his own right. He appears in Richardson's catfishing video.

"Rassie was this old guy around here with no teeth so you couldn't understand him when he talked. It

annoys the heck out of my uncle when I call him Rassie. Rassie's got this James Brown haircut like he is lost in the '60s or something," Richardson said. "He's always been my fishing buddy.

"My daddy didn't have time to fish. He was too busy making a buck so he could support us. Rassie and I would fish all the time. We'd skip from work. We'd tell whoever we were working for we had to make a delivery. We'd show up again two days later."

Flathead Catfish

U.S. Fish & Wildlife Services

One of the baits from the Cat Tracker company is Junnie's Cat Tracker bait.

"Rassie" and one of Richardson's sons now run the bait business out of a warehouse in Nacogdoches, Texas.

The secret's in the spices

Like all good catfish baits, Richardson's "Catfish Magic" has secret ingredients.

"It's like the Colonel's chicken. We have 11 herbs and spices," Richardson joked. "Some of the stuff is pretty raunchy. When I first put it out my label said, 'Not for Human Consumption, Unless You Are Crazy.' We got some complaints from crazy people I guess and had to take that off.

"A real catfisherman will take the top off a bait and put his nose right down in it trying to figure out what's in it. One of the complaints is that dough baits will come off the hook when you try to cast them. We think

Wicked Sticky, from Cat Tracker, is a catfish bait designed for fishing in fast water.

we've got this stuff that keeps it all together so you can cast it."

Stinking cheese is a key ingredient. Richardson said that his supplier brings the stuff to Texas in 55-

Channel Catfish

U.S. Fish & Wildlife Services

gallon drums. Those drums aren't filled with the processed stuff that ends up on grocery store shelves. There are scraps of all sorts of different cheeses and you can't spread the stuff because there are chunks and all sorts of discarded dairy products.

"You take the top off and you just about pass out," Richardson said.

Richardson, who took nearly 50 years to become an overnight success, isn't going to be fanatical about his career move to Branson, where he will do 180 shows in a theater he'll share with the legendary doo-wop group, The Platters. Richardson said his shows may not be politically correct but they are clean. Richardson will be in the morning slot at the theater. By 1 p.m. he says he'll be on Table Rock Lake throwing dough at the catfish.

Dough baits are just one entree on the catfish bait buffet. There are also blood baits and cut baits. Cut bait is what it says. A catfisherman will go after smaller fish, bluegills for example, to use as bait. The smaller fish are chopped up and used as bait for the catfish. Make sure the state law where you are fishing allows this practice. Bluegills are considered to be game fish in some states and cannot be legally used as bait.

Blood baits are also self-explanatory. The base of the concoction is blood from poultry or farm animals. The stuff is not as revolting as it sounds. The fisherman balls up the goo and puts it straight onto the hook or puts it in a scent holder that attracts the fish to the hook.

Dough baits are not something you mix with chocolate chips, walnuts and pop in a hot oven for 12 minutes. They are mixtures that can have any number of ingredients and scents. Dough baits are the interesting stuff with all the different ingredients.

Recipes available on the Internet

There is an entire catfish bait industry in cyberspace. Some sites like www.catfisherman.net have links where catfish bait recipes are exchanged like some sort of twisted social club. They go by names like "Rats for Cats," the feature of which is to smash rats into a goo, and "Joe's Special," which has one can of cola and one cup of honey among its ingredients. You'll need four slices of old bologna and three cups of potato salad to create "The Nasty Smell."

Apparently, if a summer picnic goes bad on a 100-degree day, you can always turn the leftovers into bait. Juice mixes, smelly cheese, and JELL-O are common base ingredients.

On www.texastown.com you can purchase the recipes for "Tried and True Texas Catfish Bait Recipes." For $4.95 plus shipping, you can get the recipes for "The Easy One," "Liver and Cheese Umm," "Liver and JELL-O Variety," and "Chicken Express." A bit of abuse to several of the five human senses can result in a very active fishing trip.

Catfish are prolific, they aren't sensitive to hot weather, they are strong fighters, and they eat well. In the heat of summer, when other fish may have turned off, the catfish will still be active. All you need is some nasty smelling stuff for your hook.

Craig Cooper is an outdoors writer from Iowa.

Blue Catfish

U.S. Fish & Wildlife Services

Chapter Two: Heading Out

Wranglers, Rednecks, and Cutthroats

Wyoming issues a siren song tempting fly fishermen
By Dan Donarski

Wyoming may not have the reputation as a trout Mecca like Montana, its neighbor to the north. That's just fine, keep it that way–and we'll keep Wyoming's secrets to ourselves.

Wyoming, to those who know it well, is the promised land of trout fishing. Some may choose the Jackson area, just south of Teton National Park as the best of the best. Maybe. But, for my hard-earned coin, send me to Cody or Powell, located east of Yellowstone Park, and I'll show you more public water than you can shake a stick at. Not to mention some of the hungriest trout, and sizeable trout, this side of heaven.

If this sounds like it will be a story of a love affair you'd be dead on the money. If you want to truly get away from it all and experience what life on the trail was like, along with some fabulous fishing, this is the place. Or, if you want your fishing experience more refined and the highway a stone's throw away and fine dining awaits you at nightfall, where the fish grow huge

and the crowds are remarkable absent, this is the place too.

Getting remote

Ron and Teresa Lineberger operate Double R Ranch and Butte Creek Outfitters just east of Cody. Each summer they take trips of various lengths into the high country with guests, or dudes as they are called, to give these tenderfeet a taste of true wilderness. One of their premier offerings is a weeklong adventure into the Thorofare River, a trip they call Cowboys and Cutthroats.

It's a day-long unforgettable ride into camp.

Immediately you start to climb above the South Fork of the Shoshone River's valley. Before you know it you'll be in the Washakie Wilderness and after countless switchbacks, if you look down to the left you'll be staring into a thousand foot fall into Deer Creek. If you look right you'll come eye-to-eye with a

The Cowboy State offers hundreds of miles of high quality public trout water. The Cody and Powell areas are smack dab in the center of the action. Twenty-inch fish are not at all rare in the large waters of the Shoshone's North Fork. Cutthroat, cut-bows and rainbows provide plenty of action here.

Cut-bows, a cross between cutthroats and rainbows, are common in the area.

Photos by Dan Donarski

A small net with a cotton basket helps to land the fish quickly and without undue harm.

On cool days and early in the morning bead-head nymphs are a great fly to prospect with. As the day warms the fish will start keying on flies like humpies, Wulffs and stimulators. Green drakes and hoppers, along with a good stone fly imitation will get you through most conditions.

solid rock wall after your hat brim brushes the wall first. What you do is stare straight ahead, and trust the horse.

Once away from the wall on the right and the fall on the left you open up into high alpine meadows where wildflowers paint themselves against the backdrop of lush, Kelly-green grass, still higher snow fields and an azure sky. Now you're just below Deer Creek Pass and you break for lunch.

After crossing a rather intimidating snow field you pop up over the pass and start down the other side and enter the Teton Wilderness. Bighorn sheep frequent the pass, elk favor the meadows. And, lest we forget, you have an excellent chance of crossing paths with a grizzly. Following Butte Creek, the trail cuts through more alpine meadows on its way down before winding through forests of spruce and aspen. The farther down you go the bigger Butte Creek becomes.

The last hour or two seem to last forever. Your butt will be sore, your legs a bit cramped. If you are allergic to horses like I am, those pills you took in the morning will have worn off. It is time to "Cowboy up."

There is no sniveling allowed. You are doing this for a reason – cutthroat trout that don't come any wilder. Trout in a land that has been declared "the most remote section in the lower 48" by the U.S. Geological Society. Somehow the gods have smiled on you–you'll be here for a week before the ride out. This is what you can expect.

Early start isn't necessary

It will be hard not to rush to the Thorofare at first light if you wake up then. You'll have fallen asleep to the river's song and awoken to its hushed alarm. You'll

Canyon fishing the lower stretches of the North Fork brings anglers into the realm of fast water and slippery bottoms. Felt-soled wading shoes are the way to go here.

The North Fork runs from the east gate of Yellowstone National Park to the Buffalo Bill Reservoir near Cody. This is a wide river characterized by a rocky bottom. Most of the river is held publicly. The lower five miles is generally in private ownership but does offer numerous public access areas.

be ready for them, but they won't be quite ready for you.

Up here, in the high country, chances are good there will be frost on the meadow grasses where you made camp last night. There's even a chance of skim ice on the water bucket. The river will be cold, so will the fish.

Rather than rush in this section of trout heaven linger over a second cup of cowboy coffee, warm your hands by the fire, stretch out the kinks left over from yesterday's ride. Wait for the sun to climb above the mountains and begin to warm the water. Mid morning is certainly not too late to wait.

You'll be well served to start out with nymphs as those adults that hatched yesterday will still be fighting off the cold and those that will hatch today are just now starting to think about it. A good mix of stone fly nymphs, some caddis pupae, green drake nymphs and assorted other mayfly nymph patterns will serve you well in the morning.

You'll start to see the adults lifting off the water by noon most days and this hatching and flight activity will continue until dusk. Stones and green drakes should dominate the activity accompanied nicely by elk hair caddis and yellow sallys. If, by chance, you hear some buzzing along the riverbank and in the grasses don't be alarmed, it is only grasshoppers making their presence known. Pack along a few of these patterns, too.

When absolutely nothing seems to be going on at all, you'll have to experiment a bit. If you enjoy nymphing, try bitch creeks or any big bushy subsurface pattern that gives off a good impression of something good to eat. Surface searching should include patterns like red humpies and royal wulffs.

You'll want to bring two rods with you. A four weight is perfect for the size of the fish and the flies you'll be using. However, a six weight will come in mighty handy when the wind begins to blow, which it undoubtably will. There is no reason at all to bring any other line than a matching weight forward floating line here. True some holes may be six feet deep but a weighted fly and a small piece of splitshot will get that fly down just fine.

Thirty minutes from Powell, the Clark's Fork public waters begin. You'll find a lot of cutthroats in this section along with a growing population of grayling.

The South Fork adds bruiser browns to the trout equation. This river runs cold and fast. Fish the pockets and eddies along with the tail-outs to get in on this technical trout fishing river.

Waders and a vest are completely up to you. I brought waders on my first trip here almost 10 years ago and only wore them once. Now I don't even bother and wade wet. I would recommend a pair of felt-soled wading shoes as the rocks are a bit slick in the river. If you have studded felts so much the better.

As for fly vests, they can come in handy but aren't necessary. Instead think about carrying your flies, fly float goop, tippet, forceps and other assorted gadgets in a "possibles bag." The folks at Duluth Pack make a dandy over-the-shoulder bag that carries everything I need with plenty of room to spare.

Now, before you get sucked up into the mindset that cutthroat are easy, let me set the record straight. They aren't. Sometimes they seem to be the definition of obstinate. But, by and large, cutthroat trout are certainly gluttons, they love to eat, and for fly anglers what is even better is that they love to eat on the surface.

A good angler should expect to touch 18 to 20 fish a day on the average on the Thorofare assuming a normal winter and summer. My best day over five trips has been 52 fish, the worst day, a still-impressive 13.

(You can get more info on this trip as well as many others offered by the Double R by calling (307) 587-6016. You will be surprised how affordable this trip really is.)

Closer To Civilization

Cody, and its smaller sister 22 miles to the north, Powell, have more public and easily accessible water to offer trout anglers than can be fished in a multiple of seasons.

Thousands, millions actually, travel through here every year in the warm weather months. Statistics say that one in 10 are going to do some type of trout fishing. If you've ever been through Yellowstone you'll already know where they are headed. Straight for the park, and straight to the cast of thousands that ply these waters. And, in getting to these overused waters, these same anglers drive right on past seemingly untouched, and definitely uncrowded rivers.

North Fork of the Shoshone

"This has to be listed as one of the top freestone rivers in the country," says Scott Aune referring to the North Fork. Aune should know, too, as his family has been fishing the area for decades. Aune also owns Aune's Absaroka Anglers (307/587-5105), a full-service fly and guide shop. "The trout population is fantastic and when it comes to big fish, as in that 20-inch-plus magic range, the river's loaded with 'em."

The river is completely public once you get eight or so short miles above the Buffalo Bill Reservoir. But, in those lower stretches of mostly private water, there are a number of public access sites that offer quality fishing.

One thing to keep in mind when fishing anywhere in Wyoming is their access laws. Property owners do

Hiring a guide to float the rivers brings you into water otherwise inaccessible. The investment in hiring a guide for a day or two is a small price to pay for the beauty of the landscape and the fishing to be found.

own the river bottom on their land. You are more than welcome to float through but you do need to keep your feet off the bottom.

The North Fork is full of cutthroat, rainbow, cut-bows and a smattering of brook trout. The river is characterized a mainly rock and gravel bottom. Numerous areas of undercut banks and downed timber along with huge boulders provide plenty of cover for the trout. Insects abound with caddis and stones dominating the activity.

The 40 miles or more of public water runs directly through the Shoshone National Forest, alongside US-14/16/20, the highway leading to Yellowstone's east gate. This is a busy road but very few anglers ever pull over and feel the pull of the water against their legs. In fact, in the 20 years or so that I have made pilgrimages to this area there have been only three times when I have ever fished within sight of another angler not in my group.

You're probably saying to yourself, "Sheesh, I don't want to be fishing near any ol' highway." If that's the case drive on and fish the park along with hundreds of your best friends. If not, pick a place to park and start fishing in the Wapiti Valley (some marketing guru named it the East Yellowstone Valley, too), an area that Teddy Roosevelt called, "the most scenic 50 miles in America."

There are two major tributaries which should not be neglected, Elk Fork and Eagle Creek. Both flow into the river from the south and there are campsites for each at the junction of the tributaries and the main

river. Both offer some extremely satisfying meadows fishing.

South Fork of the Shoshone

The South Fork empties into the south arm of the Buffalo Bill Reservoir. It runs cold, tingling cold, and may be the only river in the area where waders are a good idea.

The lower 40 miles of this fork is mainly private and the areas that do have public access are not well marked. Do yourself a favor, drive the South Fork Highway until you can't go any farther. From here the water going up stream is all public.

Unlike the North Fork the South Fork is heavily braided and generally quicker in velocity. Studded felts are a wise move here.

Also unlike the North Fork, the South Fork has a heavy population of brown trout which call the place home, joining the cutts, brookies and cut-bows. One other thing, it is definitely a more technical river to fish. You will need to cast well, choose your flies well, and know how to read a river.

Johnny Stafford, a short and soft-spoken guide working out of Aune's shop has a deep passion for the South Fork.

"Yes sir, the North Fork is truly a fine river. Particularly for big fish and fish that aren't tough to catch," he says. "But the South Fork," his handlebar moustache arched high and wide in a grin, "that's the place to fish, really fly fish. Plenty of fish, some dandies, too. And the ones you get here you earn. There

Land owners along rivers in Wyoming own the river bottom, too. Using rafts gets you to these waters and some great fishing. This is particularly true on the middle section of the Clark's Fork and the lower reaches of the North Fork of the Shoshone.

are no gimmees."

My brother Tom joined Stafford and me last summer for a day on the South Fork. Browns were fussy, and we certainly did earn every one we caught. One particular brown kept me occupied for close to an hour, refusing every fly passed his way, and all the while slurping with abandon under an outstretched cottonwood branch. Next time I'll get him.

Clark's Fork

North and west of Powell, Clark's Fork has a number of public access sites but the public water above and below the sites is limited. The exception to this is the access site and parking area located at the national forest boundary.

From the boundary of the Shoshone National Forest found at the end of Wyoming 292, all you have to do is head into the mountains to the west and there's all the public water you'd want. Most of the fish in this section will be cutthroats but there is something else, something very special found here as well- honest to God grayling. Both species tend to run smaller here than in the downstream stretches.

The downstream stretches are best floated. Bill Fisher, a rancher, beet and barley grower from Powell, Aune, and I floated the Clarks from the boundary to Edelweiss along Wyo-120.

One of the first fish caught was a gorgeous 16-inch blued-steel grayling sporting crimson spots on its sail. Cutts and rainbows followed regularly. Typical of the

region we played hide and seek with hot sun and small showers, along with golden eagles, mule deer and a curious herd of antelope.

That's just a sample of what is available in the Cody/Powell area. There's Sunlight and Little Sunlight, in the same area as Clarks along with Crandall. Then there are the Bighorns just an hour to the east with the Tongue River and Paint Rock Creek to name just two. Add a number of lakes, like the free East and West Newton located just out of Cody, and Monster Lake, a pay to play water. Fish grow big and sassy in these still waters.

Playing cowboy gets you to unbelievably great waters. The Thorofare is one of the finest but it'll take a full day of riding to get into the river valley. Double R Ranch and Butte Creek Outfitters bring guests in for a full week of camping and incredible fishing.

Catch and release fishing is encouraged as it ensures that this fishery will continue to be among the country's finest freestone trout areas.

When You Go

Cody is definitely a western tourist town complete with western shops and staged gunfights in the afternoon outside the Irma Hotel. This place has a lot going for it if you like excitement during your non-fishing times. Every night of the summer there's the Cody Rodeo. You need to take time off the rivers for the Buffalo Bill Historical Museum. The museum is a gorgeous gathering of western history including The Plains Indian Museum, the Whitney Gallery of Western Art and the Cody Firearms Museum, the largest collection of American arms.

Powell, on the other hand, is not touristy at all. It's a quiet ranch and farm community that has all the charm of small country towns. The pace here is relaxed and the people go out of their way to welcome you. Restaurants aren't as varied as in Cody but serve hearty portions. You'll find it a little less expensive, too. (Powell and Cody, The Park County Travel Council: 307/587-2297)

Plan on spending at least a couple of nights at a

guest ranch up the Wapiti/East Yellowstone Valley. There are a number of these historic ranches to hang your hat. Absaroka Mountain Lodge (307/587-3963) treated my family and I very well indeed on our last trip. The lodge serves excellent meals, offers package rates that include horseback riding which can bring you to water otherwise out of reach.

Better still, this lodge sits on Gunbarrel Creek, just before it empties into the North Fork. And, from where it empties into the larger river let's just say you are pretty darn close to what many consider the river's Nirvana section.

Chapter Two: Heading Out

Caribbean Dreams

*Bonefish and warm sunshine draw winter-weary anglers
to saltwater getaways*
By Dan Donarski

It's cold and snowy. It's time to get out of Dodge. Time to head for Belize and Roatan and the warm shallow flats where the bonefish and permit play.

A tail glints in the early morning sun. The only part of the fish you see. Over a shallow flat, the bonefish digs into the turtle grass searching for shrimp or small crabs. Your guide positions the boat about 60 feet off the fish and tells you to cast.

Your bait lands a mere 12 inches in front of the feeding bone and you see a fast push of water making its way to where the bait fell. Slowly you come to a tight line and feel resistance. You hit the fish fast and the fish streaks across the still, dark water like a lightning bolt ripping open the sky as your reel whines in pleasant misery.

"Bonefish!" the guide shouts. "Keep your rod high–your line tight." You just have a smile on your face and determination in your soul. Before the struggle is over, three unbelievably fast runs across the flats, through mangrove shoots and around coral heads, and finally the fish is brought alongside the boat. Its silver sides reflect the water and the sky. The darker stripes running vertically down its back provide a fine contrast now, camouflage before. The "ghost of the flats" is yours for a moment and then quickly released. Your smile is still broad as it fins slowly away.

As this is being written, the last of the snowplow's work has finally melted from the curb in front of my house in Michigan's Upper Peninsula. Springtime seems to finally be here, a good month after its official start. Snow is in the forecast for the day after tomorrow. Hopefully it won't last.

Photos by Dan Donarski

Bonefish are the most sought after species on the flats. Traveling in schools as well as in singles and pairs, this "ghost fish" has the speed of a rocket and the heart of a lion. Knuckle-busting runs are to be expected once the fish is hooked.

The poling platform of a flats boat gives the guides far better visibility than anglers on the casting deck when fishing skinny water. Pay attention to them and when they tell you to cast you had better be ready.

Wading the skinny waters found on the flats is better at times than fishing from the flats boat. Grassy or sand bottoms muffle your footsteps and your lower profile allows an easier stalk.

As much as I love winter in the north country, I also feel the need to head south for a week or two each winter just to make sure there really is a sun somewhere shining on crystal clear warm water. Over the past 10

Hop-scotching from flat to flat is easy with the sea worthiness and shallow draft of a flats boat. When fishing Belize or Roatan you'll be fishing a half dozen or more flats every day.

years or so, my rods and reels and I have traveled to Florida and parts beyond.

Five years ago, two destinations captured my imagination and each year hence I have found myself in Belize and Roatan.

Belize is located just south of Mexico and is wrapped on its west and south by Guatemala. Specifically, where I love to get sunburned in Belize is the small southern village of Placencia. Roatan is a bit farther, and don't be embarrassed if you never heard of it. My travel agent had me going to the South Pacific until I saw her error. Roatan is part of the Bay Islands, a group of three major islands belonging to Honduras and located about 40 miles off her eastern shore.

The fish species found on both are similar, though some species stand out in one place over the other. Each offers tremendous bonefish, snapper, barracuda, and mackerel. Belize has shown me she also shines in the tarpon category along with having a good population of permit. Roatan, on the other hand, shines in the permit category and also has some tarpon. Both also offer snook.

What you'll Need

Before we go any farther, there are few particulars that need to be covered. Tackle is the biggest concern as neither of these places will be able to get you geared up at the local tackle shop–there aren't any. If you don't bring it, you won't have it.

For the sake of making things a bit easier, let's assume that bonefish and permit are your main targets, as they should be. Let's also assume that you and a buddy are going together, which makes things even easier in the gear department as well as in expenses.

Spin fishing

Spin fishermen will find that a seven-foot medium action rod is just about perfect for bonefish. For permit you'll want to go to a medium-heavy stick in the same size. Upscale your normal reel on each. In other words, put a heavy, high line capacity reel on the medium-heavy stick. On the medium rod's reel, make sure it is a high line capacity, medium-heavy reel. Why?

Because you will want to be able to cast a healthy distance and have plenty of line. If that smaller reel doesn't handle at least 200 yards of 10- to 12-pound test mono it is simply too small. The larger reel better have a good 300 yards plus of 15- to 17-pound test. One other thing about the reels: make sure the drag system is flawless.

Rods will break. Count on it. Besides the fish and the bouncing around in a boat, how can we forget about our friends in the baggage handling department of the airports you'll be traveling through? Each of you should bring three rods. One angler brings two mediums and one medium-heavy, the other takes along two medium-

Expect bonefish to make three to five runs of a hundred yards or more. These runs are lightning quick so your drag needs to be reliable and your reel filled with at least 200 yards of line.

heavies and one medium. This leaves a spare in each and keeps everyone fishing when a rod shatters.

For my money it is hard to beat the reels in the Shimano arsenal. Buy the best you can afford, take care of them, and they will last decades. My rods come from St. Croix and Bass Pro. Similar rods by other makers are twice the money and offer no better performance or durability. When it comes to dollars and cents, and fishing sense, it is a wise adage to splurge on the reel and save on the rod.

For fly anglers an 8-weight system will handle most conditions for bonefish and permit. In high winds, which can be common on the flats, a 9- or 10-weight will help cut through the wind.

In the bait category, real shrimp and crabs work well on both bones and permit. But finding these in good quantity is a problem. D.O.A. Shrimp, an already rigged and incredibly lifelike soft plastic imitation, is a favorite. Cajun Crabs are another and both can be found in saltwater specialty shops as well as in major catalogs. A very cheap, yet effective alternative is to use walleye-style curly tails in shrimp colors matched to a 3/8-ounce leadhead jig. All of these are also marvelous baits for snapper and other reef species.

Bring along a box filled with larger stickbaits, Spooks, and Rat-L-Traps. When the tides go slack and the bones and permit are off the flats use the heavier rods to troll the edges of deep water for species like barracuda. Throw a handful of steel leaders in the box as well.

Fly fishing

Fly anglers should count on bringing two different rod weights as well. For the bonefish an 8-weight is just fine. While you can do well with permit on an eight, I'd recommend a 10-weight as the extra beef can come in handy. If tarpon are a possibility, you'll be very glad to have that 10-weight.

Like the spinning outfits, I oversize my reels. Winds on the flats are always a problem. If you get a calm day, count your lucky stars. My 8-weight is matched with a 9/10-weight reel that is loaded to the brim with backing and 9-weight, weight-forward line. The larger rod is matched with an 11/12-weight reel, also loaded to the brim with backing and an 11-weight, weight-forward line.

Why the larger line size? They make it easier to defeat the wind, or at least cheat it a little. Why the larger reel? Because if my fly reels can't handle 350 yards of backing along with the line, they aren't big

Spin anglers will be well served by a medium action, 7-foot rod. Couple that with a high quality reel that can handle at least 200 yards of 10-pound test and you're all set for action.

enough. You only have to be spooled once to learn it is awfully disappointing.

Two other things about reels. The relatively new large arbor reels are the way to go as they allow you to pick line back up quicker. Don't be fooled, however. A lot of reels are marketed as large arbors but are such in name only–they don't provide faster pick-up. And, just like the spinning reels, make sure the drag is flawless. Here again, splurge on the reel.

My outfits include rods by Thomas and Thomas and the Orvis Trident. Both are fast action and fit my casting style well. My reels come from Ross, the Saltwater III and IV, along with the Orvis Vortex in the appropriate weights.

Your fly box should include a variety of patterns that imitate shrimp or crabs. Charlies, Mangrove Critters, Bonefish Bitters, Snapping Shrimp, Bonefish Sliders, and McCrabs all work well. Leaders generally need be no longer than 10 feet. Rio's bonefish and permit leaders are the best in the business, but that's just my opinion. Scientific Anglers makes fine leaders, too, and are a bit cheaper. Bring tippets in 6- to 15-pound test and you'll be all set.

Gear for everyone

Flats booties are an absolute necessity. Tennis shoes just don't cut the mustard. Orvis's Christmas Island Flats Bootie is my favorite as they have lasted longer than any other model I have worn. Good quality polarized sunglasses cannot be forgotten. Amber lenses will work the best for most anglers under a variety of conditions. Bring two pair in case one breaks.

Bonefish like the mangroves due to the food they can find there. It makes fishing a bit more interesting as you'll need to cast precisely in order to not get hung up.

Zip-off pants, those convertible long/short pants, come in handy as do Supplex or cotton blend long-sleeved shirts. At first glance, and with the first heat of the day, Supplex will seem to be best but under an unrelenting hot sun the nylon material can start to feel sort of gummy. A hat is also an absolute must. Get one that has a dark color under its brim to help deflect the reflection coming off the water. A light colored outer fabric will help keep your brains from being mush under the heat.

Early mornings are often cool, at least compared to midday. A light wind shirt is a nice thing to have along to fight off the chill, particularly as you make that first run to the flats at daybreak. A lightweight raincoat is also a good idea. Sure, the showers are generally brief but sometimes last a full day. The air may be warm and you may be able to tough it out with a raincoat but why be miserable?

Belize, what you'll find

Placencia is quaint little fishing/tourist village. Countless small cayes are found offshore. Here, the flats mainly consist of finely ground coral, some mud flats, along with smaller sand flats. Most of the flats fishing will be done from pangas as most are rather soft. Expect to wade about 25 percent of the time, and cast from the boat the rest.

It is also a perfect place for that second, or first,

honeymoon. Of all my travels, I don't know of a more romantic getaway that includes world-class fishing. The area also hosts a number of non-angling opportunities. Options include exploring Mayan ruins, snorkeling the second largest barrier reef in the world, scuba diving, swimming in jungle caves, exploring the jungle rivers or even taking a trip to the Jaguar Reserve. Of course, two unaccompanied anglers will enjoy the place as well and can fish every day.

The Inn At Roberts Grove (011/06-23565 or on the Web at www.robertsgrove.com) is by far the fanciest

Brilliant white sand flats mark the outer flats of southern Belize. These are perfect for wading, providing a very firm bottom.

resort in Placencia, and for my money the single place to take that significant other. There are other resorts and smaller lodging facilities that can be downright cheap and quite comfortable for the budget minded. Roberts Grove also has its own fishing guides and there are plenty of other high quality guides in Placencia. *(Contact the Placencia Tourism Center at 011/06-24045, or on the Web at www.placencia.com for more information.)*

As mentioned earlier, the bonefish here truly shine. They may not be the biggest on the planet, the average is probably around two to three pounds, but they make up for that in pure numbers. Off one of the outer cayes last spring, I took seven fish in seven casts. It should have been eight but I screwed the pooch by not checking a knot. My wife was along that day and even she, a fine lady who has only held a fly rod once before in her life, took three fish.

Look for the permit to be traveling alone or in groups of two or three. Most of these will be in the 5- to 10-pound range and, like permit everywhere, are frustrating. The tarpon will be found in the small bays generally on the lee side of the outer cayes. The cuda, snapper and the like will be in the deeper waters just off the reef or off the flats.

You'll find Belize is very U.S. friendly. Its dollar is tied to ours by law. Two Belizean dollars will always equal one U.S. dollar. English is the official language so communicating is easy.

One other very neat thing about Placencia is that the guides are not tied to a set schedule like other destinations in Belize. If you want to leave the docks at 5 a.m. or even earlier, the guides are willing. Just be sure you know that you'll be on the water until sunset, too, as long as the tides are right and your spirit is willing.

If you have never caught a bonefish this is a perfect place to cut your teeth.

Roatan is great for anglers

This is a gonzo angler's haven. While it has been known as one of the top five dive sights in the world, it hasn't received much attention from serious anglers. That should change shortly.

Opened just two seasons ago, Gibson Point Lodge (888 360-1595 or on the Web at www.gibsonpoint.com) is the only fishing lodge on the 30-plus mile long island. Managed by Tom Johnson, a former member of the U.S. Fly Fishing Team, this place has serious fishing written all over it.

The lodge only handles six anglers each week so crowding is never a problem. Meals here are superb,

Many of Roatan's flats are composed of old, dead coral. These are quite noisy for the wading angler– fishing from a panga or flats boat is the best approach to get close to the fish.

Barracuda also call the flats home. Bright flashy flies, stickbaits and spoons will bring the cudas rushing in.

prepared by Johnson's wife, Chrissy, a French-trained certified chef. A very nice detail here is that one of the best flats on the entire island is located a scant 20 yards out the front door.

Why a gonzo angler's haven? Because you'll get to fish the entire island and chances are you won't see more than one or two other anglers all week. When you leave the lodge and head to the east end, it will entail getting up well before dawn is even thinking about cracking. The goal is to be on the coral-bottomed flats as the sun comes up and catch the permit at their most vulnerable. It is a little more civilized when you fish the flats closer to the lodge, but count on sunup to sundown.

Permit, more than I have ever encountered anywhere before, will be seen every day. Better than that, in the 45 days or so I've fished Roatan, there has

only been one day when I haven't had an honest shot at these haunting fish. On an average day you can expect three to five honest shots, and the average size will be above 10 pounds. There's a good chance you'll see permit topping 50, but leave these big guys alone unless you truly want to be humiliated.

One particular afternoon had me hooked up four different times to permit in the 10- to 20-pound range. Two of these were leadered, that means officially caught according to the IGFA, but I never did touch them or feel them give me that dark stare when they come to hand.

Bonefish as well have a habit of swarming the flats. Most will be in the 3- to 5-pound range, but the largest bonefish of my life came from a place called Horseshoe Flat. On a very gray and drizzle-filled day, a 29-inch bone attacked my Bonefish Bitter and after nearly spooling me four times, and heading for the open once, finally came to hand. Expect to see bones in the 7- to 10-pound class nearly every day.

The tarpon and snook are found in the mangrove-filled bays and cuts that dominate the shoreline. These are low light condition fish so you do have to play the watch game. When the tides are slack it isn't a bad idea to head for the barrier reef, a short half-mile away, and cast big streamers for cuda and snappers.

Because the reef is so close and deep water is right at hand you can also find black and yellow-finned tuna, dorado, wahoo, and even billfish within striking distance of small boats. Gibson Point Lodge does have an agreement with a local offshore guide if you want to take a break from the flats for a day.

At slack tide the flats fishing is nothing to brag about. When you are in a slack tide situation head for the reefs and troll or cast lures and flies. Snapper are always willing and in saltwater you never know what you might catch.

Guides on Roatan are everywhere, just ask. But, let the buyer beware. For my money the Boden family, Cedrin, the father, and sons Kevin and Brian, are the way to go. The Bodens have an exclusive agreement with Gibson Point during the winter and spring. If you find yourself on Roatan at other times, give the lodge a call as they will book them for you. Non-fishing choices include trips to the butterfly gardens, the wild bird sanctuary, and the iguana farm. Don't forget about the world-class diving either.

Roatan is a mainly Spanish-speaking island so communicating can be troublesome at times. English is spoken, with varying degrees of skill, by a fair percentage of the residents. Their currency is the Limpera, which fluctuates between 12 and 17 to the dollar. U.S. dollars are accepted by most merchants.

If you are a permit hunter, or one who simply wishes to fish away from the crowds, this is certainly the place.

Chapter Two: Heading Out

Spinners Are Winners For Walleye

Flash and dash of blades turn on angler's favorite targets

By Mark Romanack

In case you haven't noticed, spinner rigs are the hottest things going on the walleye tournament trail. Even if tournaments are the furthest thing from your mind, the facts speak clearly. Some traditional spinner fishing techniques and a number of new turns (no pun intended) in the world of blade fishing are accounting for some uncanny catches of walleye. The beauty of these old and new fishing techniques is they are easy to learn and they work wherever walleye are found.

The allure of the walleye spinner is tough not to notice. A spinner rig has it all! Flash, vibration, color, sound and, of course, that fat and juicy nightcrawler. Right up front, however, it's important to note that not all "crawler harnesses" are suited for catching walleyes. Because spinner rigs are powerful fish catching machines, variations of these lures are built for everything from bluegills to muskie. Those suitable for walleyes have some very specific features.

Harness length

A spinner suitable for walleye fishing starts with a 10- to 17-pound test monofilament leader that's 40-60 inches long. Shorter harnesses are primarily designed for casting, not the slow trolling and drifting techniques

The components of spinner rigs include blades, hooks, clevices, floats, and beads.

Spinners are among the most productive walleye lures on most waters. Just about anywhere walleye live, spinners are an important fishing tool.

Photos by Mark Romanack

The bottom bouncer and spinner combination is perhaps the best method for fishing spinners near the bottom.

used by walleye anglers.

Hook sizes and types

A good walleye harness is equipped with a pair of No. 4 or No. 2 beak style hooks. The No. 6 hook size commonly appears on walleye harnesses, but these small hooks are notorious for losing their grip at the worst possible moment. Walleyes have tough bony mouths that are difficult to penetrate with a hook. Larger hooks simply grab more real estate inside the walleye's mouth and hold on better than smaller hooks.

Harnesses fished near bottom are best equipped with two single hooks to reduce the chances of snags. Harnesses designed to be fished in open water are better equipped with a single hook in the front and a No. 6 or No. 4 treble hook as the trailing hook. Treble hooks do a better job of sticking walleyes.

Hook spacing

A third feature to look for on harnesses is the hook spacing. Many are situated with the two hooks approximately 1-2 inches apart. Hook spacing this close allows more than half of the nightcrawler to trail along without a hook in it, increasing the chances of short strikes and missed fish. The best harnesses feature a hook spacing of between 5-6 inches.

Spinner clevices

The clevice is another essential part of a walleye

When most anglers think of spinner fishing, they think of traditional bottom bumping methods. This angler used snap weights to troll in open water for suspended walleye.

spinner. Used to hold the blade on the monofilament leader material, most harnesses are tied using fixed clevices. To change blades the angler must cut the leader, thread off the blade and clevice, replace the blade and retie the harness. Quick-change style clevices make it easy to change blades without cutting the harness. Two styles are readily available including plastic ones that thread onto the line and metal styles that clip over the line.

Blade sizes and types

Blade types and sizes are yet another feature of walleye spinners to consider. When fishing spinners near the bottom smaller blade sizes tend to produce best. Colorado and Indiana style blades in sizes 1, 2, and 3 are the best choices. These blade shapes and sizes spin best at the slow speeds incorporated while fishing

An angler nets a walleye on a bottom bouncer/spinner rig.

Note the treble hooks on this open water spinner harness. Many anglers use treble hooks when trolling for big walleye in open water.

near bottom.

Larger blade sizes have a place in walleye fishing as well. Bigger blades produce more flash and vibration that in turn helps attract fish from greater distances. These attributes are especially important when fishing for walleyes that are suspended in the water column. Larger blades including 4, 5, and 6 sizes are often the most productive when fishing suspended fish.

Colorado and Indiana style blades are the most popular with open water anglers, but willow leaf blades and some other special shapes such as choppers (pear shaped) and hatchet styles are also good choices for suspended fish.

Bead and snell floats

Beads and floats are the final component of a spinner harness to examine. Small beads are normally selected when fishing near bottom. Smaller beads add less weight to the harness. However, in open water situations where anglers are primarily concerned with using spinners that are easy to see, bigger beads are the

norm.

Snell floats are common on walleye harnesses and they help in two areas. Because of their buoyancy, snell floats help to prevent a harness from quickly sinking to the bottom in turns or other times when the forward momentum of the boat is interrupted. Also, snell floats are large and colorful, making them great attention getters.

Once an angler understands these basic components of a spinner harness, it's time to explore options on how best to fish these lures for walleye.

Drift or troll?

Both methods of boat control work, but drifting limits anglers to moving in only one direction.

It's hard to beat spinners for walleye. Slow trolling is a good method for covering water quickly.

Hatchet-shaped blades like this are sometimes more productive than traditional blade shapes. Anglers need to experiment with different sizes, shapes, and colors of blades.

Unfortunately, the wind doesn't always blow in the right direction. Slow trolling using an electric motor or a small gasoline kicker motor is a more practical means of fishing spinners.

Spinner fishing is a game best played at slow speeds. Typical trolling speeds range from .75 to 1.5 MPH. A good rule of thumb is to troll only as fast as required to make the blades on your harnesses rotate smoothly. Round blades like the Colorado style spin at the slowest speeds, while Indiana and willow styles require progressively faster speeds to achieve adequate blade rotation.

Spinner-deploying devices

Spinners are great fish catchers, but they need a little help when it comes to presenting these lures at the many depths walleye anglers fish. At some point, a spinner rig is going to be married to a weight or other device designed to deploy them to the desired depth. The most common weight systems for use with

spinners include bottom bouncers, snap weights and rubber-core sinkers. Diving planers are another effective way to get spinners in the strike zone. The smaller sized diving disks and planers are especially handy for walleye anglers. Excellent products in this category include the Luhr Jensen Jet Diver, the Mini-Dipsy, and the Big Jons Diving Disk which is offered in two sizes.

All of these spinner deployments can also be incorporated with in-line planer boards to achieve more lure coverage. The most popular board in this category is the Off Shore Tackle Side-Planer available at www.offshoretackle.com.

Bottom bouncers

The bottom bouncer is the most common sinker style used to deploy walleye spinners. Designed to tick along the bottom while the trailing harness is presented a few inches off bottom, this presentation is tough to beat when walleyes are found on flats or other snag-free

Big walleye like this are found most often in remote waters.

The author holds a nice Great Lakes walleye.

bottoms.

Easy to fish and effective in a variety of situations, the most important rule when fishing bottom bouncers is not to fish them too far behind the boat. To keep the bottom bouncer ticking along bottom in an upright fashion, it's critical that only enough line is played out to allow the weight to touch bottom. It's accepted that a bottom bouncer rig fishes best when set at approximately a 45-degree angle behind the boat.

To achieve this balance, use a bottom bouncer that's heavy enough to get the job done. A one-ounce bouncer is suitable for water 10 feet deep or less, a two-ounce weight works well in up to 20 feet of water, and a three-ounce bouncer will be required in deeper water.

Snap weights

The advent of the snap weight has dramatically changed the way anglers approach spinner fishing. A snap weight is a pinch pad style line clip with a weight attached to a split ring. A strong spring tension insures that once the line has been placed between the rubber pads, the weight will remain on the line until the angler removes it.

Snap weights can be placed anywhere on the line from a few feet in front of the lure to 50 feet or more up the line. The trailing lure enjoys more freedom of movement than with other weight systems.

When a fish is hooked on a spinner rig that incorporates a snap weight, the angler reels in the fish and the weight at the same time. Once the snap weight reaches the rod tip, it is quickly removed. Slick!

Obviously the more weight that's used the deeper the

spinner harness will run below the surface. Most commonly used for fishing suspended fish, a depth guide for the snap weight system is available in the book Precision Trolling available at major sporting goods outlets or online at www.precisionangling.com.

Rubber core sinkers

Rubber core sinkers and keel weights are designed to be fished as in-line weights 36-60 inches in front of a spinner harness. One of the more unique variations of these in-line fixed weights involves the use of a trolling spoon as an attractor with a trailing crawler harness.

This rig consists of a in-line weight positioned 6-12 inches in front of a trolling spoon. The treble hook on the spoon is removed and in its place a 40-60 inch crawler harness is added. The resulting rig has extra flash that seems to produce best when fished in open water for suspended fish.

Weight forward spinners

A final chapter in spinner fishing ranks among the most unique. The classic weight-forward spinner type made popular on Lake Erie has seen a rebirth in a unique lure known as the Pa's Spinner. This particular spinner style features a diving lip that allows the Pa's to achieve differing depths by simply adjusting the lead length, much the same as a crankbait.
Most anglers modify the Pa's spinner by removing the single hook that comes standard and replacing it with a 12- to 18-inch long crawler harness. Because of the Pa's unique design, this spinner can be trolled somewhat faster than other spinner types without fear of line twist.

The Pa's is a difficult lure to locate in some regions. For more information on this particular spinner, try the Internet at www.walleyecental.com or e-mail the owner directly at www.paslures@aol.com.

Summing it up

These days walleye spinners are a lot more involved than the traditional bottom bouncer rig. Anglers are reeling in bigger catches than ever by incorporating both traditional methods and gear with a host of new products and techniques. The spinner has always been a powerful fishing tool. Now it's more effective than ever.

An angler lands a walleye on a spinner.

Chapter Two: Heading Out

Thrills And Chills

Ice anglers conquer winter, enjoying a hot sport

By Tom Gruenwald

3:45 a.m.

Accompanying the pre-dawn darkness is a brutal, penetrating cold that draws warmth from my fingertips and exposed portions of my face. Untamed icy winds gust across open expanses of frozen water with such merciless, sustained force, breathing becomes difficult when facing each icy blast. Hard-hitting flecks of snow rattle against my clothing and sting my cheeks, adding to the frigidity.

Yet I continue reeling. My rod tip bends with increasing resistance, guided only by my shaking arm. The fish suddenly runs. Ice begins forming within the rod tip; the drag zips. I'm hoping a friend might notice my struggle, but none can see me in the inky blackness, and there's little chance anyone will hear my voice over the wind.

I coach myself: Keep the line tight. Adjust the drag. Good.

No, not slack line! Is he gone? Quick. Reel. Raise the rod tip!

I'm relieved to feel resistance, then weight. Heavy weight.

Progress.

Soon, I'm rewarded with the splash of a fat fish wallowing in the hole. Within the gentle, eerie light of my sonar, I guide the monstrous head of a gleaming walleye thrashing side to side before me. With numb, nerve-shaken fingers I grasp the fish and heft 30 inches of yellow-green flanks into the wind.

Sport offers a challenge

For some, ice fishing conjures up images of red-cheeked, backwoods souls venturing upon treacherous fields of ice, taking grave chances to catch fish. While those who participate recognize its dangers, they also understand its potential.

Sport may be defined in different ways, but frozen down to the basics, it involves an ingrained human desire to accomplish something, then acting upon that desire through competition, quest and risk–all with the steadfast belief overcoming the struggle will result in satisfaction.

Ice fishing meets these criteria.

The challenge? Battling seemingly unconquerable

Ice fishing is fast becoming one of winter's most popular activities.

Photos by Tom Gruenwald

Trophy walleyes are a favorite game fish species of anglers through the ice-fishing belt.

Yellow perch are one of the most widely distributed, cooperative, and popular winter panfish.

cold while attempting to catch finicky, cold-blooded fish sealed beneath floating layers of ice. Accomplishment comes later, sharing stacks of fresh, steaming fillets and seasoned potatoes with family and friends, reveling in stories of the day's venture.

Safety comes first

Yet such success must begin with safety. Ice floats, and hence supports the weight of anglers and their equipment. However, ice doesn't always freeze uniformly, and is influenced by numerous variables. Lake size, shape and depth, bottom content, water level fluctuations, presence of snow, strength of wind or currents and the activity of animals all affect ice formation. Even thick ice may cause concerns, because

as ice freezes it expands, occasionally forming dangerous pressure cracks.

Use common sense. Ice must be at least 2-3 inches thick to support an average person. Be certain the area you're traversing meets this requirement. Check with local natural resource agencies, law enforcement officials, business owners and residents prior to fishing. If word is good, proceed with caution, avoiding areas of current, heaves and cracks. Use an ice chisel to test the ice as you progress. Consider wearing a personal flotation device, and always carry a set of commercial "ice picks" or screwdrivers. Either can be used to pull yourself from the water should you fall through.

Staying warm is also critical, and isn't difficult given today's technologically advanced clothing. Start with modern synthetic underwear. It's not only warm, but offers a "wicking" action that draws perspiration away from the skin, keeping you dry. Ideal.

Add layers of lightweight, insulative clothing over the top as necessary, depending on temperature and your expected level of activity. Traditional wool or cotton garments function because they insulate well, and being absorbing, enhance movement of moisture

Sonar units are invaluable ice fishing tools, as they reveal depth, bottom content, structure, cover, and fish. They even allow you to watch fish react to your presentations. (Photo courtesy of Vexilar Electronics)

Global Positioning Systems (GPS) allow anglers to electronically locate or "save" specific locations such as launch sites, fishing hot spots, or areas of bad ice, so anglers can return to desired spots or avoid unsafe regions with the press of a button or two. (Photo courtesy Lowrance Electronics)

away from your skin. Top this with a wind and water resistant set of bibs and coat, well-insulated hat, face mask, pair of pac boots and mitts, and you're ready to battle the elements.

Planning helps find fish

Next, establish what species (and size) you prefer to catch. Ask local biologists, bait shop owners, guides and other anglers which waters support such populations–and ask what seasonal and daily times produce the best success. Separate solid advice from sandwich meat, and you're ready to form a plan.

First, obtain a quality lake map for your chosen waters. Locate productive structure such as sunken islands, reefs, points, deep holes and their surrounding breaks. Features offering fish attracting combinations of weeds, downed timber, submerged stumps, rocks or man-made cover like fish cribs are all possibilities. In fact, provided food and oxygen are available, such areas

Another nice walleye emerges from the hole.

Modern ice augers make cutting holes through the ice a simple task. Note the skimmer in the foreground, used for clearing ice chips from holes after they're cut.

have strong potential for drawing fish.

Yes, this may mean a lot of water to cover, but thankfully, today's better maps often include Global Positioning System (GPS) coordinates, so once you've identified productive looking areas, note these coordinates and enter them into a hand-held GPS–your "electronic compass." Plan to seek your designated coordinates in an organized sequence, starting with the area you consider best for the time you'll be fishing, and allow technology to lead.

Once there, use sonar to confirm your depth, decipher bottom content, determine the best available cover and confirm the presence of fish. No need to drill holes. Provided the ice is solid, dumping a little water atop the ice and placing your transducer level within the puddle will produce readings.

Now to cut holes. Quality hand augers are lightweight and generally work well, but when ice is thick, you'll appreciate power augers. Larger diameter, 8-10 inch diameters are best if you're seeking trophy

Today's portable ice shelters make ice fishing truly comfortable. (Photos courtesy HT Enterprises Inc.)

walleyes, pike or trout; for panfish, 6-8 inches is sufficient. Once cut, a skimmer is used to remove excess ice chips from each hole.

Depending on the weather and how long you plan to spend on the ice, a shelter should be a strong consideration. Today's portable units are economical and lightweight, plus they set up and break down quickly. Position the shelter over your holes, pack a little slush or snow around the base to seal out the wind, and accompanied inside with a small propane heater, you'll fish in comfort.

Jigging will prompt strikes

Inside your shelter, try jigging. For panfish, traditional jig sticks or light action, 24-inch ice rods and ultralight spinning reels spooled with thin, low memory 1 to 4 pound monofilament lines rigged with small grub-tipped jigs work wonders. For larger game fish, use heavier action, 24-30 inch combos spooled with slightly heavier, 4 to 12 pound lines and larger jigs, spoons, bladebaits or jigging lures tipped with a minnow or minnow head.

Lower the bait and set your sonar with the transducer pointing straight down. You'll see the lake

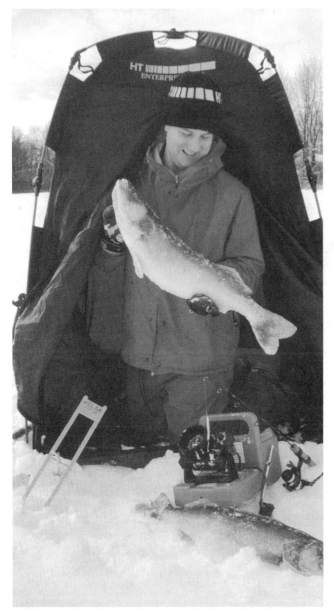

Sheltered from the wind, an angler admires his catch.
(Photos courtesy HT Enterprises Inc.)

For panfish, light-action ice rods combined with smaller, ultralight spinning reels are standard fare. Larger game fish require somewhat heavier-action rods and larger line capacity reels. (Photo courtesy Pure Fishing Inc.)

Tip-ups are a popular, fun way to help increase your winter catches while you're jigging, and are commonly used for a variety of winter-active species, including pike, pickerel, walleyes, trout, crappies, and perch.

bottom, your depth, lure, and if present, cover and fish. Many modern ice anglers are also using underwater cameras. These units consist of a camera lens lowered beneath the ice with images output to a small monitor revealing what's below. Either way, you can watch fish respond to your baits.

Simply position your lure close to marked fish. Usually working the same depth fish are holding or a little higher works best. At times, long lifts or "rips" with the lure will draw surprisingly hard strikes; other times, gentle, periodic lift-drops, simple shaking motions or completely still presentations turn tricks.

Experiment. Try various depths, lure styles, sizes, colors, live baits, hooking methods and jigging motions, carefully watching how fish respond to your presentations and always adjusting your tactics to maximize success.

Modern equipment makes ice fishing comfortable, productive, and fun.

If you're allowed multiple lines in your area, you might also want to try setting tip-ups. Tip-ups are essentially elaborate set lines featuring a spool of line mounted on a frame. Bites are signaled by a release mechanism that trips a brightly colored flag when the spool turns. A variety of designs are available. Some feature underwater spools to prevent line freeze-up, built-in hole covers to keep holes from freezing ... even adjustable rocker arms that allow the wind to jig your bait!

In any case, since fish caught on tip-ups are "hand-lined" to the surface, 15 to 40 pound braided dacron line is typically used on the spool. Dacron is easier to see and handle, and less likely to freeze than monofilament. For smaller or spooky fish, a barrel swivel is often used to attach less visible, light wire or monofilament leaders, although larger fish such as trophy pike may require stronger wire. Leaders are usually tipped with a No. 10-1/0 treble hook adorned with a lively minnow and a split shot to help lower and hold the bait at the desired depth.

In dark or stained water, dressing up your tip-up presentation will help fish find your bait. Try painting your hook bright chartreuse, green or orange. Add colorful strips of yarn to the hook, or beads to your leader. Splice a colorful spinner blade or flashy willow spoon into the rig. Anything to provide additional attraction.

And whether fishing tip-ups or jigging, keep monitoring signs of fish activity on your sonar or underwater camera. If you're not seeing fish or they won't cooperate, move. After all, you can always return. From here, be responsible. Know your local fishing regulations, keep only what you intend to eat, and carefully release the remainder of your catch. Take photos if you wish, but handle fish gently and shoot quickly to minimize potential damage to sensitive tissues, especially the eyes and gills.

Yes, you're likely to pack up tired, cold and hungry at day's end. But the reward of sharing fresh, warmed rye bread, hot, golden-brown fillets, steaming potatoes and vegetables with family and friends within the warmth of home awaits.

And even then, it's not unlike true ice anglers to be occasionally peeking out a window, dreaming about another day of challenging the howling elements outside.

Wisconsin writer and fisherman Tom Gruenwald is the author of *Hooked on Ice Fishing, Hooked on Ice Fishing II: Panfish* **and** *Hooked on Ice Fishing III: GameFish.*

Chapter Three: Changing Times

B.A.S.S. Spells TV Tournament Fishing

Scott's fledgling organization has become big-time, popular competition
By Craig Cooper

Weathered off a Mississippi lake in 1967, Ray Scott was sitting in a Ramada Inn motel room. Cold, wet, mildly annoyed that his fishing day had been ruined, Scott turned on the television to find basketball.

He was an athlete himself so he understood the attraction of competition. He had competed on football fields and in track and field. He certainly was competing in business as a successful insurance salesman.

What he didn't understand was why his favorite sport hadn't grown beyond the weekend fishing shows. Except for fishing derbies and other low-profile competitions, there was nothing in fishing that compared with what he could watch on television from other sports each weekend.

That day in Jackson, Miss., was the day Ray Scott started creating an entire industry, changed the very foundation of fishing, and started becoming a legendary fishing and environmental figure who would be mentioned in a 1995 issue of Field & Stream in the same company with Rachel Carson (author of Silent Spring), Ole Evinrude (outboard motors), and Theodore Roosevelt (expansion of national parks and wilderness areas).

Tournaments add 'sparkle' to fishing

Ray Scott didn't do it all in one afternoon. It did, however, happen pretty much that quickly in his head.

Tournament bass fishing, the best anglers in the country paying $100 each to win each other's money, sponsors who would want to host the fishermen ... the ideas came in neurological flashes.

"I was like a guy who had gotten religion," Scott recalled recently. "I'd always been an idea guy. I thought I had these brilliant ideas to elevate the passive retreat of fishing.

"At the time bass fishermen were loners who left before the sun rose and came home weary and tired.

Bass fishing was something you did when you didn't have work.

"There should be some sparkle to fishing. If was like an inflammation of the whole concept. It was developing in microseconds."

Not even Scott and his fertile imagination could have understood what he had stumbled upon. The ideas that consumed Scott that day became the Bass Anglers Sportsman's Society (B.A.S.S.), a remarkably successful fishing organization and media company.

Within B.A.S.S. is a tournament circuit that has produced Bill Dance, Roland Martin, Rick Clunn, Jimmy Houston, and Denny Brauer. Top fishermen in B.A.S.S. events have become wealthy, probably beyond their imaginations, with national television exposure, big-dollar corporate sponsors, and their own television shows.

B.A.S.S. more than tournaments

Scott's creation of B.A.S.S. did not exactly create the huge fishing industry because it already existed but the fishing industry has prospered with the help of B.A.S.S. Through its successful marketing efforts, B.A.S.S. now has 600,000 members who buy licenses, boats, motors, tackle, and spend money on fishing trips.

B.A.S.S. hasn't only been a financial success. B.A.S.S. fishing has also been an important organization in fisheries management, angler ethics, boating safety, and conservation.

Every time an angler on a Tennessee bass lake boats a wary 5-pounder that has obviously been caught before, Ray Scott and his organization deserve some of the credit.

The live well in your boat can be traced indirectly back to the early years of B.A.S.S., when Scott began to require that all fish caught in the organization's tournaments be weighed in live and released live.

The B.A.S.S. organization has been a watchdog for

clean-water issues since the early '70s. It has a full-time environmental director as well as members who monitor waters and push for sound natural resources policies.

B.A.S.S. was one of the groups instrumental in the development of the Wallop-Breaux Act that funded the expansion of fish hatcheries.

B.A.S.S. competitors were required to wear floatation devices when they were moving from one spot to another. No drinking was allowed, even if it meant turning away big breweries that wanted to sponsor a tournament.

Scott's B.A.S.S. tournaments set the rules for tournament fishing and opened the door for other tournament organizations.

One of the remarkable chapters of the Ray Scott story is that he put those early ideas into action. He didn't just go back to his regular routine and let the ideas die on that day in Mississippi.

Scott's pitch is convincing

Scott had read about Arkansas bass lakes in an outdoors magazine. That was where he would hold his first All-American Bass Tournament. The concept was that Scott, who was a very successful insurance agent who knew how to sell, would sell 100 of the top bass fishermen in the country on competing against each other in Arkansas.

"The very next month I walked into the tourist department of the State of Arkansas and said, 'our organization is going to put on a substantial bass fishing tournament in your fine state,'" Scott laughs of those early beginning. "We didn't have an organization. We had me and my ideas and a lot of folks thought my ideas were crazy.

"I was told to look at Rogers and Springdale in Arkansas. The Chamber of Commerce guy in Rogers wasn't interested at all. He was about to leave the job. The guy in Springdale, Lee Zachery, was pretty new to the job and he was trying to find a way to put Springdale on the map. He tells me, 'I've heard of your fine organization.'"

The board of the Chamber of Commerce was not as excited about the event as Zachery was. The board members weren't sure they trusted the burly Scott, who certainly had a way about him, but was definitely an outsider. The board members went to the trouble of making some calls to Alabama to check on Scott. What they found out was that the insurance agents in Montgomery liked Scott and thought he was honest, but they sure would be happy if he got the heck out of town. Scott could make sales. He had been selling

products since he was a kid.

Zachery couldn't get approval for the fishing tournament but Dr. Stanley Applegate was a chamber member who had not attended the meeting where the vote was taken. Scott made his pitch again specifically for Dr. Applegate, who pulled out his checkbook and wrote a check for $2,500.

"The only strings were that if the event didn't work and I couldn't pay him back, that I would never tell his wife he had written the check," Scott said.

Out of the back room of the chamber's office, with a secretary named Darlene Phillips who agreed to defer her salary until there was some cash flow, Scott began to make his pitch to fishermen. It was textbook salesmanship. He would hear about one possible bass

Ray Scott put tournament fishing into the national sports spotlight when he founded B.A.S.S. in 1968.

Ray Scott, founder of Bass Anglers Sportsman Society, is still comfortable with a microphone years after he put tournament bass fishing on television.

Scott counts among his close friends George Bush. Here former *B.A.S.S. Times* editor Colin Moore, now *Outdoor Life* Executive Editor, interviews him during his presidential run in 1988.

Photos by Larry Teague

Ray Scott and son greet former President George H.W. Bush at the Montgomery, Ala, airport.

fisherman and find out everything he could about the guy. Then he would make his sales pitch, throwing in personal information about the angler, who would be impressed that Scott heard about the prospect's fishing ability. Of course the flattered angler wanted to be part of this.

Just as he used to do in the insurance business, Scott would get one potential competitor to give him a few more names of friends who might be interested. It's called networking these days.

Bill Dance of Tennessee was a name that Scott kept hearing when he asked about the best fishermen. Dance would be one of the first entries.

"I had so much adrenaline. You had to believe in yourself and I sure did," Scott said.
Scott was such a believer that he quit the insurance business. He had no idea how he was going to support his wife, three kids and keep up the mortgage payments but he had sold himself on his own idea and took the gamble.

The first All-American Bass Tournament did

eventually attract 106 competitors, although Scott's prospecting had gone slowly. Stan Sloan was the winner. Scott recalls that Dance was right near the top.

By early in 1968 Scott's fledgling organization had a new name. A friend came up with a perfect acronym for the word bass. Scott started signing up members of B.A.S.S., who would get a patch, a letter from Scott, and a new publication.

Scott didn't have a clue how to write, edit, and design a magazine, but that didn't stop him from trying.

Catch-and-release catches on

Catch-and-release requirements for B.A.S.S. events came in the early '70s. As Scott explains it, he was invited to speak to the Federation of Fly Fishermen in Aspen, Colo. He went fishing with federation members and was amazed how excited the fly fishermen would get when they would catch and release a little trout.

"I thought about these guys releasing these little, biddy fish and how excited they got about that. No

telling how our guys would react to releasing a five-pounder," Scott said. "We started releasing fish in our tournaments in the fall of 1972.

"It was the best thing we ever did. Before that we'd been killing them all. There was no minimum length at the time so we were killing a lot of small fish.

"The problem was that there was no such thing as a live well. By golly our guys bought into it and they would do everything they could to keep those fish alive on coolers, stringers, and buckets.

"We did it because we thought it was right. We were making a statement. A good fish is too precious to be caught only one time.

"Here is the magic ... if a person releases a fish, that individual now has an investment in that water. It is his water."

For many years B.A.S.S. competitors who have a fish die have been penalized.
Catch-and-release is now accepted by not only bass anglers, but anglers who go after other species of fish. Catch-and-release is part of Scott's footprint on fishing.

Scott said it was never his intention to make B.A.S.S. a corporate entity with major sponsors. It happened gradually as companies inside and outside the fishing business could see the benefits of being partnered with B.A.S.S.

The tournaments were gaining media exposure and fans were showing up for weigh-ins.

Scott was the master of ceremonies, cheerleader and ringmaster at B.A.S.S. events. The official weigh-ins Scott orchestrated were entertaining events. Wearing his trademark white Stetson hat, Scott would work the crowd to create excitement about the conclusion of the tournaments that might be decided by an ounce or two.

"The corporate thing came slowly. We didn't have big sponsors for a long time," Scott said. "We were kind of winging it and it was fun.

"In those early days we were happy if we could get the Stren line company to give us six big spools for the guys to use."

Equipment innovations developed because of B.A.S.S. Lines are better, reels and rods are better, and electronics like Global Positioning Systems (GPS) became accepted not only by tournament fishermen, but by recreational anglers. The logic of the recreational anglers seemed to be that if the big guys had all the new gadgets, why shouldn't they. It was no wonder big companies with any sort of tie to fishing – boat manufacturers, equipment companies, gas companies – noticed B.A.S.S. The organization, like its founder, could move products.

Television coverage opened up more doors for the

Top Bass Busters

Denny Brauer
Started as a full-time, professional bass fisherman in 1980 . Had been a mason Twelve-time winner on the B.A.S.S. tournament circuit and B.A.S.S. Angler of the Year in 1987. First pro bass fisherman to earn more than $1 million in his career Has won MegaBucks, Superstars and BASS Masters Classic. First angler to be featured on a Wheaties box has produced two videos and has his own television show Son, Chad, is also a professional bass fisherman Lives in Camdenton, Mo.

Larry Nixon
Two-time B.A.S.S. Angler of the Year (1980 and 1982) Won 1983 BASS Masters Classic and has competed in 22 Classics Has won 14 B.A.S.S. tournaments Member of the Freshwater Fishing Hall of Fame and the Pro Bass Fishing Hall of Fame Lives in Bee Branch, Ark.

Rick Clunn
One of the most successful anglers in B.A.S.S. history. A consistent qualifier for the BASS Master Classic (28 times) who won the premier event in 1976, 1977, 1984, and 1990 Won the 2001 Megabucks event. Second all-time in B.A.S.S. earnings with more than $1.5 million earned Has won 13 B.A.S.S. events in his career 55 years old Lives in Ava, Mo.

Roland Martin
Holds B.A.S.S. record with 19 career victories Named B.A.S.S. Angler of the Year nine times Has fished in the BASS Masters Classic 23 times Hosts "Fishing With Roland Martin" television show.

Bill Dance

Three-time B.A.S.S. Angler of the Year (1969, 1974, 1977) Has written seven fishing books and numerous articles for outdoor publications Eight-time BASS Masters Classic qualifier 23 national bass fishing titles 62 years old Lives in Collierville, Tenn. "Bill Dance Outdoors" is seen on The National Network.

organization.

"We became the preeminent organization for fishing," Scott said.

B.A.S.S. hasn't totally escaped critics. The tournaments are highly competitive with anglers taking no time to enjoy the experience of having a fish on the line. Bass are horsed into the boat, placed in the live well, and the next cast is made within seconds.
The technology that has been spawned by tournament fishing has expanded equipment sales, but observers

Photo by Larry Teague

George Bush helped Scott raise funds for a small church in Pintlala, Ala., by participating in the Eagles of Angling Fishing Tournament held on Scott's 55- acre lake.

have asked if the average guy really needs a 150-horsepower bass boat, GPS system, and all of the expensive gear.

"If you don't want to fish that way you shouldn't. It's an individual choice. Most people, though, are somewhat competitive," Scott said.

B.A.S.S. sold to ESPN

Scott sold B.A.S.S. to company employees and investors in 1986 for $15 million. He stayed on another 12 years as president and "Bass Boss," which is the title of his 1999 biography. In 2001, the Disney conglomerate that includes the cable sports giant ESPN bought B.A.S.S. for $30 million.

Scott is still selling. He is a celebrity endorser for numerous fishing products. He has his own set of instructional videos on how to build a world-class bass pond on a few acres. He makes appearances

THE BEST BASS FISHERMAN IN THE WORLD?

"That's a question I've gotten a lot," said Ray Scott, the founder of the Bass Anglers Sportsman Society. "There are so many good ones but if you had a gun to my head with the hammer cocked, I'd say Roland Martin is the best bass fisherman in the world. He's very open-minded, which is an important thing. You have to be willing to keep learning."

at fishing tournaments and he fishes on his own 55-acre lake in Pintlala, Ala.

Invitations to fish Scott's fantasy lake on his property are treasured, even by bass anglers who have fished the best bass waters in the world. Among Scott's friends are the Bush family of Texas, Washington, D.C., and Kennebunkport, Me. They have a standing invitation. So does Chuck Yeager, the first man to crack the sound barrier in a jet.

Now 68, Scott isn't really retired. He still has ideas. His latest project is a fishing tournament or series of tournaments using only 4-pound test line.

A few years from now there will probably be an entire series of televised events of guys going after 15-pound fish with 4-pound test line and Scott will be there promoting them and cheering them on.

Chapter Three: Changing Times
Are These The Good Ol' Days?

Longing for the past is natural, but many favor today's high-tech sport
By Craig Cooper

The black and white photos on the wall of the lodge of a Northern Minnesota resort tell the story of a different era of fishing. It was an era when the anglers were all men, all wore long pants, all wore jaunty hats, and all had enough fish to provide the main course for the Friday night special at the VFW.

If there were truly "good ol' days" of fishing, the lucky guys in the photos lived them. The anglers could catch so many walleyes or northern pike that at the end of the week they could leave some for the resort owners or give them away to resort guests that hadn't even fished. If there were creel limits, they were "guidelines," not hard and fast rules.

There was no reason to worry about taking too many fish because there were so many available.

It was a simpler time in fishing before 150-horsepower outboards, trolling motors, and fish locators that let the angler actually see the fish and follow them around.

Dan Gapen, who turned 70 years old in April, experienced those days. A professional angler, guide, manufacturer, and outdoors reporter and author, Gapen has never really left those days himself.

"I'm old school. I don't use GPS (global positioning system), rarely use a trolling motor and don't own a motor larger than a 25-horsepower," said

In the simpler days of the 1950s, a fisherman and his son didn't need a fish finder or a big boat and motor. A small aluminum boat, tiny outboard motor, and a rod and reel brought in a lunker. (Photo by Milt Rosko)

Gapen, who has fished all over North America for decades and broke the world record for a northern pike taken by fly rod in 2001. "I don't think there is any question that walleye fishing and pike fishing are not what they once were. "Walleye fishing was so good that it was something you did for the table. You could always catch enough to eat."

But then Gapen throws a curveball into the conversation, saying, "on the other side, catfishing is probably better than it was 30 or 40 years ago and so is bass fishing and muskie fishing and pan fishing is just as good."

Today vs. yesteryear

What Gapen is saying is what many in the fishing business are saying. In many ways, those "good ol' days" of fishing in the photos on the resort wall may not have been any better than today.

Either case can be made.
• There were "good ol' days" when there was less fishing pressure.
  • There were "good ol' days" because Americans were less mobile. The best fisheries were out of range of many anglers.

The pipe and the wooden boat say 1950s in this vintage fishing photo. (Photo by Milt Rosko)

• There were "good ol' days" because the environment was cleaner. There was less chemical use, less pollution, no acid rains.
• There were "good ol' days" because the fishing equipment was much simpler. The fish were everywhere so you didn't need to be able to go 15 miles down the lake.

Or:

• These are the "good ol' days" because of technology. It is easier to get to the best fisheries, and easier and more comfortable to move around once you get on the water because of big outboards and highly maneuverable trolling motors. Rods, reels and line are better and there is always a hot new lure from the television "infomercial" shown at 1 a.m. on channel 114.
• These are the "good ol' days" because of the advancements made in the fisheries biology field. Stocking programs are better.
• These are the "good ol' days" because we recognized we were abusing the environment and we did something about it. The Mississippi River, once a dead sea around populated areas, is a thriving fishery again. The same reversal was made with Lake Erie, which is now generally regarded one of the top walleye fisheries in North America.
• These are the "good ol' days" because of the acceptance of catch-and-release. Those guys in the photos would be ridiculed, or worse, for taking so many fish. Even trophy fish are

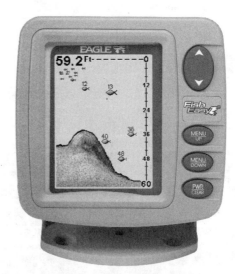

The FishEasy 2 by Eagle is just one of many tools the modern fisherman can employ. The fish finder marks fish by size and depth as well as showing the depth of the water and features of the bottom on a screen.

A father and son proudly display their day's catch next to the wooden fishing boat. Those were the days of low technology but abundant catches. (Photo by Milt Rosko)

In the days before catch and release was ever considered, a nice mess of fish was often easy to bring home. (Photo by Milt Rosko)

routinely being returned to the water.
• It may simply be human nature to long for the past.

"The funny thing is that if you look at the DNR (Department of Natural Resources) publications from the '30s, they were talking about the same things back then," said Scott Pengelly, an information officer for the Minnesota DNR.

Lakes have good, bad times

A number of factors can affect how a fishery is perceived by anglers. Fisheries go through cycles like nearly everything else in our lives. There are good times and bad times for lakes because of factors like fishing pressure and the environment around the lake.

Kevin Storey, a fisheries biologist for the state of Texas, has seen that situation with Lake Fork, a 27,680-acre reservoir in the East Central part of the state. In 1999, Lake Fork was hit with the Largemouth Bass Virus that has hit bass populations in many southern states. Only 4,500 bass were killed by the virus, but the damage had already been done to how the lake was perceived.

"People thought that we weren't giving them the whole story about the number of fish that were killed," Storey said. "The fact is that the lake has never been easy to fish. It's a challenging lake to fish.

"I think the fishing was so good in the early '90s at its peak on the lake the people come to Lake Fork and expect to catch huge numbers of really dumb fish.

"People say that when the lake was at its peak you had a hard time parking at the public ramps because they were full. They say you could almost walk from boat to boat in the best fishing areas on the lake. We don't see that type of intensity."

But at the same time that bass fishermen believe that fishing has declined, the crappie fishing has been outstanding and catfishing is close behind.

And the bass fishing may not have slipped as much as the anglers think. On one day early in 2002, three brood fish weighing 13 to 16 pounds were turned over to state fisheries people to use in their hatchery efforts.

Storey said bass catch rates on Lake Fork remain within range, statistically, of those of a decade ago.

Mississippi River recovers

One of the success stories of the past 30 years has been the recovery of the Mississippi River as a fishery, particularly in urban and highly industrialized areas. Federal requirements that cities and industries clean up their act have worked, according to Ron Benjamin, a river fisheries expert for the Wisconsin Department of Natural Resources.

"There wasn't a fishery on the Mississippi River in the Twin Cities area 25 years ago. You were more likely to find human waste than fish," Benjamin said. "When data was collected in that period in Pools 1, 2 and 3 (pools are numbered based on the closest lock and dam), the crews were happy if they found one or two carp.

Fishing boats have progressed and clothing is much different today, but anglers still enjoy trying to catch big fish. (Photo courtesy of South Dakota Tourism)

Lowrance's GlobalMap 2400 is one of the Global Positioning System units that bring a new dimension to fishing and boating with precise maps. Anglers can tell their exact location at any time.

"There was nothing. The river fishery around the big cities today is no comparison because the water is cleaner. At the same time, that has brought more fishermen. The fishing pressure is much more intense than it was when the river was polluted."

Benjamin said Mississippi River data shows some of the same results that Gapen and many anglers have discovered from their own boats. Muskies, one of the beasts of freshwater fishing, and smallmouth bass, the dancing battlers that probably provide better entertainment than table fare, have exploded in numbers.

"It used to be that a muskie fisherman would be happy with one 31- or 32-inch fish. Now they are all looking for the 40-inch or larger fish," Benjamin said. "Catch-and-release has become so strongly ingrained that there are more fish and larger fish."

Is pressure too intense?

One of Gapen's concerns is that fishing pressure will continue to stress some species. The fishing public is bombarded by a huge industry that thrives by marketing the latest technology to anglers and by reminding them they should be fishing. More people are fishing and they are fishing more, according to statistics of the American Sportfishing Association.

Anglers' purchases are approaching $40 billion a year, compared to just less than $30 billion in 1991. The overall economic impact of sport fishing was $108.4 billion in 1996.

Those numbers mean more anglers with bigger, faster boats and the latest electronics.

"I think some of our fisheries have been over-fished and modern technology also has impacted the fishing," Gapen said. "Walleye fishing, in particular, has become a 12-month-a-year sport. Ice fishing has become so popular that walleyes are being taken almost the entire year."

Gapen's second concern is that some of the fun has been taken out of the sport because of a bigger fish and more fish mentality espoused by tournament fishing. He also sees anglers spending thousands of dollars on equipment they don't need.

"I think we've taken some of the fun out of fishing. It has become a competition like people see on television. You compare your catch to that of whomever is in the boat or your friends in another boat," Gapen said. "And if a fishing buddy has the latest equipment, you have to have it.

"I think we've turned a lot of potential young anglers in the 8 to 18 age group off because we've made it a competition.

"One of the rules in my boat is a 'no compete' rule. It should be fun."

But back to original premise:

Maybe fishing was better in some of those old photos hanging on resort walls. But for some species, these are the "good ol' days" and if catch-and-release continues to be an accepted practice, and water quality continues to improve, the "good ol' days" may last for years into the future.

Chapter Three: Changing Times
Great Eatin' Awaits On Shore

A fresh catch and a campfire mean a mouthwatering meal
By Edie Franson

"When the wind's from the West, the fish bite the best. When the wind's from the East, the fish bite the least" goes part of an old saying among weatherwise anglers. It's always a rush having a fish on your rig, reeling it in, catching the first sight of it, and finally landing it in the boat. There is also the anticipation and pleasure of eating a freshly caught fish.

What better way to enjoy those fresh caught beauties than to have a shore lunch! The words shore lunch summons an image of relaxed, satisfied fishermen sitting around a campfire, enjoying the view of a pristine lake. Overhead is a cloudless blue sky, waves lap against the shoreline, the call of a loon can be heard, and an eagle soars gracefully aloft.

The delicious aroma wafting from the campfire and camp stove is enough to set a person's hunger pangs on high. A skillet is brimming with frying fish fillets and browned potatoes, and a pot of coffee is merrily perking away. Whether it's opening day of fishing season or late season fishing, a shore lunch is a tradition and part of the fishing experience. Good memories are made from simple pleasures such as this.

Caring for your catch

However, before that tasty lunch is a reality, proper care of that freshly caught fish is a must. Freshwater and saltwater fish are at their eating best if properly cared for immediately after they are caught. As soon as you catch a fish, keep it alive in the boat's livewell or place it on ice in a cooler, until you're ready to clean it. If ice is unavailable, keep your catch in the shade. After landing that fish, try not to have it flop around on the bottom of the boat. This flopping around will bruise the fish's delicate flesh and speed up degeneration. Fish deteriorate rapidly when out of water, un-iced, and ungutted. When this happens, bacteria will begin tainting the flesh. This is what produces that "fish" odor. Fresh fish simply do not smell!

For cleaning fresh fish, a preferred method is filleting. When a fish is filleted properly, the bones are removed. If the fish is to be left whole, make sure all

the blood spots are removed and that none of the entrails are attached to the cavity. Wash the fish thoroughly under running water. Pat fillets or whole fish dry with paper toweling. Fish are at their best when cleaned and cooked the day they are taken from the water. However, if the fish is not to be prepared right away, place fish in plastic wrap or a large enough plastic zip-top bag, and refrigerate immediately. Three days is the longest cooking can be safely delayed.

If not preparing your fish within that timeframe, it may be kept much longer by freezing. Using this method, fish can be almost as tasty as the day they were

Photos by Don Donarski

A delicious shore lunch must include freshly caught pan-fried fish fillets. Extras in this case are a salad and roll, but the possibilities are endless.

caught. Freeze your catch immediately after cleaning. Place cleaned fillets in an appropriately sized plastic freezer zip-top bag, then fill with cold water until the level just covers fillets. Carefully press out as much air from the bag as possible, seal, and lay flat in the freezer. Another method is to place fillets in a cleaned milk carton or plastic container, fill with cold water covering fillets, then freeze. If fish is left whole, douse the fish in water first; wrap it tightly in plastic wrap while still wet, then double wrap it in freezer wrap. The wetter the fish while freezing, the longer it lasts. Remember to label and date your packages of fish. This eliminates the guessing game of "what kind and how old is this?"

Some freshwater fish, such as the northern pike and muskie, have a slimy film. If these types of fish are not filleted, scale them and cut the meat into steaks or leave whole for baking. To help eliminate the film, soak fish pieces or whole fish in a saltwater solution made up of 4 cups cold water and ? cup salt. Soak in this mixture for at least one-half hour. Remove, rinse off under cold running water, and wipe off with paper toweling. Refrigerate for use, same as above, or freeze for use later.

When thawing frozen fish, never thaw at room temperature. Place it in the refrigerator to thaw overnight. If time is short, place it still wrapped in a bowl under gently running cold water.

Shore lunch basics

A few basic items are necessary for shore lunch cookery. One is a cast-iron skillet, an all-time favorite for frying fish. Heat is distributed evenly and the high sides prevent the oil from bubbling over as fillets are added.

Fresh, unused shortenings or oils should be used for frying. Peanut oil is a good choice. It has a high smoking point, no unpleasant flavor, and no cholesterol. The oil should be hot – about 365°F, but not smoking, while fish are frying. To test temperature, drop a small cube of bread into hot oil. The cube should brown in about 60 seconds. If possible, adjust frying temperature. Turn up heat higher when adding new fish to the pan, turning it down as the fish heat up.

Fish fillets can be cooked breaded or unbreaded. Breading can be as basic as all-purpose flour. However combinations of biscuit mix, corn meal, corn flake crumbs, cracker crumbs, and, yes, even crushed potato chips make good breading. Any breading requires an agent to hold it to the fillet. An egg wash of beaten

Fishermen prepare a shore lunch over an open campfire.

Photos by Don Donarski

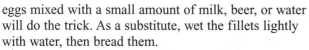

eggs mixed with a small amount of milk, beer, or water will do the trick. As a substitute, wet the fillets lightly with water, then bread them.

Most recipes, fresh and saltwater, will accommodate a substitute, especially if the fish is of similar color and texture as the one called for in the recipe. To gauge when your fish is properly cooked, the meat should have an opaque appearance, but still be moist, and it should flake easily with a fork.

Checklist

It's helpful to prepare a checklist of items to eliminate leaving behind something critical, such as matches, which, I admit, this writer has done on a couple of occasions. Here are some suggestions for your checklist:

Matches or lighter
Paper plates and toweling
Plastic eating utensils
Can opener
2 cast-iron skillets
Spatula(s)
Fillet knife(s)
Aluminum foil or bags
Plastic zip-lock bags (large)
Campstove or grill
Garbage bag
Cooler(s)
Ice

Food Goods

Potatoes
Eggs
Onions
Cooking oil
Butter or margarine
Canned baked beans
Tartar sauce
Lemon(s)
Rye bread and/or sandwich rolls
Package of coleslaw and sauce

Here are some fish tips to help speed up preparation.

* Select enough potatoes for the shore lunch. Wash, clean and leave skins on. Precook potatoes in the microwave until they are ready to soften, but still slightly hard. Cool completely, place in a container for the next day's shore lunch, and refrigerate.

* Crack eggs into a container, cover, and refrigerate. Remember to take along, but keep on ice.
* Larger fillets can be cut into fingers about 3 inches long and 1 inch wide so they fry quickly and evenly.
* When cooking on a campfire grill, wrap aluminum foil around bottom of skillets and pans prior to cooking. This helps eliminate blackening and soot on the bottom, and makes cleanup easier.
* To fry fish, cooking oil should be about 1/4-inch deep.

All that's needed for a quick and easy shore lunch is a campfire with good hot coals. A simple, tasty shore lunch can consist of the basics of fried fish and potatoes, served with tartar sauce or lemon wedges along with thick slices of crusty rye bread. Or, it can be as extravagant as to include baked beans, coleslaw, and delicious steamed apples for dessert. Here are a couple ways to make your shore lunch a special experience, each guaranteed to add to your fishing pleasure.

Photos by Edie Franson

Sizzling Lake Superior Salmon *(fresh or salt water)*

Salmon fillets, cut in serving-size pieces
1 cup finely crushed potato chips
1 cup Bisquick biscuit mix
1 teaspoon seasoned salt
1/4 to 1/2 teaspoon cracked black pepper
2 whole eggs
1/2 cup milk
Dash hot sauce (optional)
Oil

1. Heat oil in cast-iron skillet. To make an egg wash, beat eggs, milk, and a dash of hot sauce together in a bowl.
2. In a plastic zip-top bag or container, combine mix, crushed chips, and seasonings. Dip each fillet in egg

wash, allowing excess to drain off. Dredge fillets in the chip mixture completely coating fillets.

3. Fry breaded fillets in the hot oil, until nicely browned and meat flakes when tested with a fork. Cooking time is about 3 to 5 minutes, depending on thickness of fillets. Drain on paper towels and serve with homemade tartar sauce.

Cleanup is a breeze with foil bags. No pots and pans involved. Just toss the foil bag in with the garbage and you're off, back on the water to catch more fish.

Photos by Edie Franson

No Fuss Fish & Potato Packets

Walleye fillets, or any other firm fish
Potatoes, cleaned and chopped with skin on, cut into bite-size pieces
1 to 2 onions, chopped (optional)
1/2 bell pepper, chopped (optional)
Salt and pepper
Dash garlic powder
1/2 cup shredded cheese (optional)
1/2 to 1 stick butter or margarine
1 Reynolds® foil bag or aluminum foil

1. Have campfire coals hot with no flames, or use a charcoal grill heated to medium-high.
2. Arrange potatoes in an even layer then sprinkle onions and pepper over top. Lay as many fillets over

potatoes as desired. Add salt, pepper, and garlic powder according to taste. Sprinkle cheese over fillets. Place dabs of butter over cheese. Seal bag by tightly double folding open end.

3. If using aluminum foil, use one sheet as the bottom and follow same layering procedure as for the bag. Cover with another same size sheet of foil. Tightly seal all edges. Wrap packet in a second layer of foil, again sealing all edges.
4. Carefully place bag onto grill and bake for 30 to 40 minutes. To check if meal is done, carefully cut a small slit in top of bag. Test potatoes with a fork to see if they're tender. When done, remove from grill and fold back top for steam to escape. Serve and enjoy.

Tartar Sauce

Mix together……..
1/2 cup mayonnaise
1/2 cup finely minced green onions or white onions
3 tablespoons finely minced dill pickles
1 to 2 tablespoons pickle juice
1/8 teaspoon pepper

The perfect end to a shore lunch is yummy dessert served with a hot, steaming cup of coffee.

Cinnamon Apple Delight

Large foil bag or aluminum foil
Apples, cored and cut into wedges
Butter or margarine, 3 to 4 tablespoons per bag
Sugar and cinnamon, to taste
Raisins (optional)
Chopped nuts (optional)

1. Layer apples and remaining ingredients in foil bag. Tightly seal. Over a campfire, place the foil bag at the edge of the coals, or place on the grate. After approximately 20 minutes, cut a small slit in top of bag and test apples for tenderness. When tender, remove and serve.

A shore lunch can be versatile and offers many variations. Hopefully, the suggestions given here will aid in setting your own shore lunch traditions.

Edie Franson is the author of 365 Wild Game Recipes.

Chapter Three: Changing Times
Old Lures Are Alluring To Fishing Tackle Collectors
Millions join the hunt for vintage angling equipment

Collecting old fishing tackle is one of the most interesting and natural extensions to the sport of fishing. Until recent years it has been one of the most unexploited areas of collecting old Americana.
If you are interested in joining in the collecting of old tackle get cracking, because the ranks are growing rapidly. Luckily there have been millions upon millions of pieces of tackle hand-crafted and manufactured since the early days, so there should still be plenty of nice examples to go around. Hundreds of examples, along with a price guide, are pictured in Old Fishing Lures, 6th Edition, as well as the pocket-sized Fishing Lure Field Guide.

Some collectors are mistaken in their claim that the sources are dying up. Don't you believe it. Every day new and fabulous finds are being made. In fact, the newsletter of the National Fishing Lure Collectors Club has a section in every issue entitled It's Still Out There where great new finds are chronicled.

While most of the old lures that collectors find or buy are worth from a few dollars to a few hundred dollars, there are some rare prizes that fetch major money. A seller on eBay, who apparently didn't know what he had, put a vintage Heddon lure up for sale at the modest price of $9. It was advertised as "In good condition. Has some wear/rust. Glass eyes. 5" long." After a couple of days of small incremental raises, the bidding suddenly soared to $2,000, then $4,000, then $8,000. The winning bid was an amazing $31,857.50.

To find vintage lures, try the oldest general stores, drugstores (which once carried bass plugs), bait shops and hardware stores in your area, especially their storerooms and basements. Many treasures have been found by feeling around a dusty top shelf in a storage room. Anywhere tackle has been sold over a period of 40 years or more, there could be some oldies. Some of these places may have sold tackle one time or another. Even if they don't now, they may have some old unsold stock stuck away somewhere.

The garage sales and flea markets of today are good places to try, but so far they haven't been very good hunting grounds. Few of these folks think of old tackle as being very marketable. This source is growing.

Millsite Minnows Bassor Bait: $5-$10

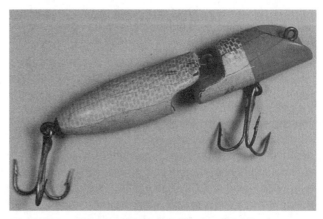
Wooden Merry Widow by Makinen Tackle Co.: $10-$20

The National Fishing Lure Collectors Club (NFLCC) holds many regional shows each year. Join the NFLCC to get an annual schedule of these and other organization events. Chances are you will find one within a reasonable distance from your home. These events are fabulous sources for everything connected to collecting old fishing tackle. The least of this is meeting other folks with a common interest. This is a great way to build your list of contacts for trading and purchasing items for your collection.

A source for contact with collectors who want to buy, sell, trade or just talk about old tackle is the Internet. There are hundreds of sites on the Web. Some are absolutely dazzling sources that are incredibly rich with information.

WHAT DO YOU PAY?

Now this is mighty sticky wicket, this business of pricing old tackle. It is an area probably as full of unseen hazards as there are standing hairs on a mad cat's back.

It would be safe to say that many tackle collectors, particularly among lure collectors, would much prefer swapping and buying. For the most part collectors are "swappers and/or buyers," but generally not sellers. The swap is by far the best way to expand your collection when other sources dry up. The problem is there are precious few instances when one can pin down a value in swapping terms. You just can't say that a "Doctor Catchum's Surefire Killer Diller Spinner" is worth two "Magic Molly Gogglers" and half a "Big Bass Basher." Each swap is an individual negotiation between two collectors, which ends in satisfying both. Most of the time, the only way to avoid the unsatisfactory alternative is to know your business. That takes study.

When hunting for old tackle, most of the time you find it already marked with a price at shows, in stores, garage sales, etc., and that's generally what you pay unless you're that enviable type, the "silver-tongued devil." In the above instances the price is usually more than a fair one, sometimes being a downright steal. The other sources discussed, Grampa's tackle box, etc., usually end up in no monetary outlay at all or if so, an insignificant one. I went prospecting a few years ago and came up with a beat up old metal tackle box with 22 old lures and a reel in it for 20 bucks. That comes to less than $1 per plug. There were only two good collectible plugs in the box, but worth a good bit more than what I paid and the others, while beaters, were still good for parts and a couple went right into my tackle box. The reel was too far gone to count.

I keep hearing collectors talk of their sources

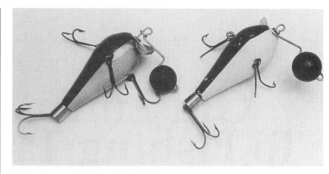

Lake George Floater: $500-$700

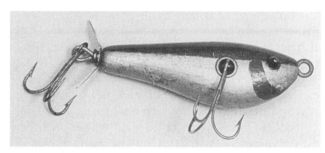

Creek Chub Injured Minnow: $5,000-$10,000

Cisco Kid Topper: $15-$25

Lucky Louie by Minser Tackle Co.: $15-$35

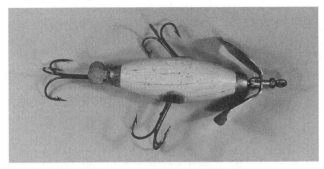

Heddon Dowagiac Underwater (1903): $1,500-$2,500

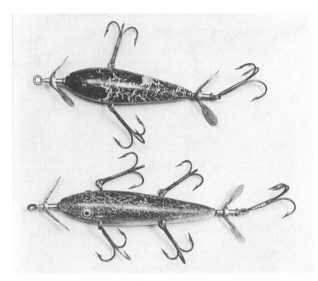

South Bend Worden Wooden Minnow: $200-$400

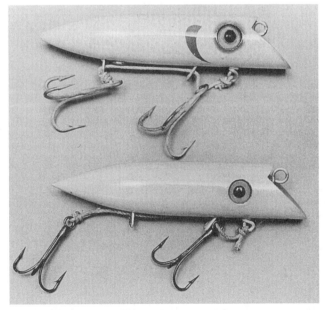

Martin Fish Lure Co.: $20-$35

drying up; that there isn't much left to find. Since it had been several years since that last foray, I decided to try again. I put a couple of ads in local give-away shoppers and waited for the calls. Two weeks later I spent one day on the road visiting the folks who had called. This time the monetary outlay was higher, $255, but some of the lures I came up with were a Heddon blue nose No. 200 Surface, a glass-eyed Lucky-13 and a glass-eyed Creek Chub Plunker and Dingbat, all in great condition. Also included were a couple of dozen lesser baits in varying condition and a sack of Heddon plastics, a metal tackle box in good shape, a nice Bronson Commander reel in the box and a battery-operated toy Mercury outboard motor. You add it up. It wasn't a bad haul especially when you consider how far Alabama is from the mother load of the Midwest. All that for this: Don't tell me it's not out there!

Generally speaking, the older the item the more it's worth, simply because the older it is the less there are available in most cases. The simple law of supply and demand comes into important play in this case. Some old lures, reels, and especially old split cane fly rods can and sometimes do soar into the hundreds, even thousands of dollars. "Older-worth-more" is not necessarily set in concrete. Some lures of the 1920s and 1930s were made for a short period of time and are quite rare and valuable. Some others made in the 1940s through the 1970s are also valuable

Another important consideration is just how bad you want it. It matters not a flit what someone or some book says it's worth if you're in an "I gotta have it" frame of mind.

All that for this: Take the value guide presented in a book as exactly that æ a guide. It is, after all, only one man's opinion. The collector is the final authority. Don't forget it.

SOME HINTS FOR SUCCESSFUL BUYING, SELLING, TRADING

1. Arm yourself with knowledge. Get and study every piece of printed information you can get your paws on.
2. Mutual cooperation builds better collections, good friends, and sources. Ask for help from knowledgeable collectors and give an edge to those who helped you in the beginning, after you get smart.
3. If you find you have a treasure, don't be greedy. Be fair. If you don't deal fairly you may find many of your sources drying up.
4. If you find you have made a bad deal, don't worry over it æ learn from it. Turn lemons into lemonade by knowing better next time.

Top Vintage Lures

Six companies, many of which have gone out of business, are considered top sources of vintage lures.

They are:

Chub Creek
Heddon
Paw Paw
Pflueger
Shakespeare
South Bend

5. Always make an offer. Nothing ventured, nothing gained. Remember one man's trash is another man's treasure.

6. Honest mistakes are made. If you have built up a good rapport with and a good reputation among your collector friends, most mistakes can be rectified. Keep in mind, however, that it is not possible to make all your deals mutually fair, only mutually acceptable. Don't squawk if you find later the deal wasn't so good. You can't win them all.

NEVER MISS A CHANCE

How many times have you been out on the water only to lose that special plug? I mean the only one that works. Or worse, you and your fishing buddy are having a bad day and he starts hauling 'em in like he was bailing out a sinking boat. He found today's secret weapon and he's only got one copy and you're zeroed out in that type. Whatever the reason, we all have modified plugs in our tackle boxes in a sometimes vain attempt to land a lunker. Therein lies a problem the plug collector will invariably encounter. I have replaced spinners, hooks, lips, hook hardware, swivels, and yes, even repainted favorite plugs. Think of the strange concoctions you might run across in an old timer's tackle box! Some may even defy the most expert collector but, most can be identified and eventually the proper hardware may be obtained and the plug restored to its original configuration. Moral: Never discard old, beat up, mistreated plugs you find. Throw them in a box for cannibalization. The same applies to rods and reels.

SOME MISCELLANEOUS CONSIDERATIONS

Insurance - If you find yourself with a collection of old tackle that you cherish and/or is valuable, then please consider some insurance. In the unfortunate event of a house fire, those old wooden plugs and bamboo rods will be great kindling. Many reels have hard rubber and plastic parts, and fires can reach temperatures high enough to melt some metals.

Daredevlets and Daredevle by Lou Eppinger: $50-$100

Al Foss Lures including The Skeik, Shinny Spoon, and Shimmy Wiggler: $10-$25

Magnetic Weedless by General Tool Co.: $40-$60

Gere Featherbait Bass Lure: $80-$100

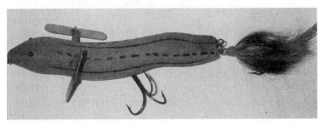

Gopher Bait: $40-$60

Harkauf Minnow: $250-400

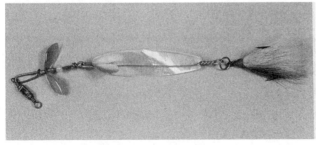

Haynes Pearl Casting Minnow (1907): $50-$100

Check your homeowner's insurance policy or personal effects rider. Most contain a clause that limits or excludes collectibles. It is important to discuss your particular collecting situation with a trusted agent. Alternatively, the National Fishing Lure Collectors Club (NFLCC) has made reasonable insurance available to its members. You might want to look into that possible opportunity.

Protection - There are numerous ways to protect and safeguard your collection, which you can accomplish with ease if you will just take the time to do so. In the unfortunate circumstance of theft or destruction, the law enforcement authorities and/or insurance companies will be able to handle recovery, replacement, or reimbursement much more efficiently if you have done your homework before the fact. This "homework" can be rewarding in itself by increasing your knowledge of the very things you collect.

Write it down - Inventory your collection. Put it on your "Things To Do Today" list. Get yourself some index cards and a file box, a looseleaf notebook, a computer program, or whatever may be easiest for you to use to catalog your collection. Some of the important things to record in your inventory are when, where, and how you obtained each piece. Record the price you paid or what you traded for it. Describe each with name, company name, catalog number, material, measurements, all signatures, and other marks. It would be good even to assign each item a number in your collection and describe the location on the premises. The number may be your own or in the event there is a universal number such as from a company catalog, you may prefer to use it.

Photograph it - Photographs are evidence of original condition, should a piece be damaged. They are a positive means of identification by which items may be traced if stolen and assurance for insurance purposes. They can serve as a valuable tool in either case.

Many collectors find it convenient to use the back of each photo to record the description, etc., for their inventory. It is advisable to maintain duplicates of each, one set in a safe place at home so that you may use them when you wish, and the other set somewhere off the premises, such as in a safe deposit box at a bank.

Identification marks - An additional safeguard is to mark each item individually. If a piece is lost or stolen, the ability to point out a distinctive mark identifying it as your property is quite helpful.
If you are a purist, reluctant to permanently mark an object because it alters the original state, then there are other slightly more difficult ways.

You may want to use descriptions of unique properties of each item such as repairs, imperfections or areas of wear.

Should you choose to mark, do so in an unobtrusive location. However you mark, make sure it is permanent and very small. You could also use an ink that is visible only under ultraviolet or black light.

Reproductions or copies - The forgery is a copy or reproduction of an item specifically for the purpose of deceiving the purchaser. There are a lot of talented folks in this world and some of them are capable of doing an incredible job of copying. That in itself is fine, but where that talent belongs to a dishonest individual his product, the reproduction, becomes a forgery. The purpose of this section is not to help that nefarious forger, but to help the collector protect himself against the varmint, and have a little fun to boot.

There is no substitute for intimate familiarity with the nature and characteristics of what you collect, but the author has found another way to at least add a little to the understanding. Try to make a lure yourself. Reels are just about out of the question. Although not altogether impossible, it would not be economically feasible for anyone to try to forge an old reel. Do watch out for altered markings, however. The same applies to rods.

Old lures are a completely different proposition for obvious reasons. By attempting to reproduce an old plug yourself you will gain some insight into the problems a potential forger may encounter and that might help you to identify counterfeits.

A more enjoyable and satisfying experience however, is the making of lures that catch fish. Some of those old plugs actually were "performing fools." If fish do, as some insist, learn and remember lures that are constantly jerked by their noses then you will present them with a new, unfamiliar delicacy that they might just select for their breakfast. Many of those old successful plugs are not made anymore simply because the making of them costs the manufacturer too much to sell at a profit.

If you like the idea and are fairly handy with your hands, try it. There can't be any greater satisfaction in fishing than landing a lunker with a lure made with your own hands.

DEFINING YOUR COLLECTION

Sooner or later, you will have to decide what kind of collection you are building. The collector may approach his hobby in one of several different ways. You may want to specialize in wooden lures only, lures or reels or rods made by just one manufacturer or even

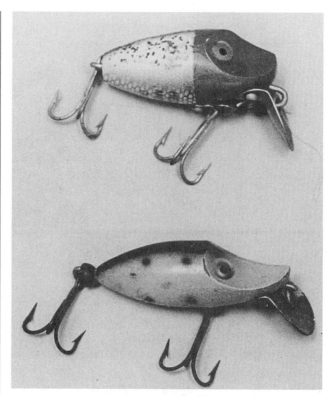
Heddon Midget Digit and Tiny River Runt: $20-$30

Bass Master by L&S Bait Co.: $10-$25

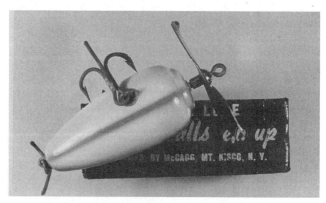
McCagg's Spinning Barney: $20-$35

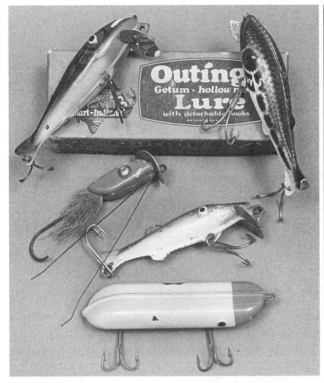

Outing Manufacturing Co.'s Bassy Getum, Pikey Getum without diving lip, Bucky Getum, Pikey Getum with diving lip, and Floatem Getum: $50-$200.

Paw Paw Baits original lure boxes: Original boxes add collector value to lures.

specialize in only one type. Some collectors "color collect." They attempt to find every color and finish option ever offered on a particular lure. Another direction is attempting to collect only lures in one pattern, such as those with a white body and red head. Almost all the companies offered that color. The choices are many. A collector I know, who began over 30 years ago, started out trying to obtain one example of every single lure from one company. His collecting expanded to the same goal for products of several other companies. The collection eventually surpassed 10,000 lures!

An interesting and very attractive collection would be one made up of only those lures, rods, or reels in good to mint condition or collect only those lures that can be found in the original box. This would be difficult but challenging. Some collectors collect only the boxes. To add some variety to your collection and display, even the specialist collector should have a few pieces from other areas of collectible tackle. There are hundreds of accessories to be found illustrated in old catalogs, some quite curious, others interesting but unsuccessful attempts at making the fisherman more comfortable under adverse conditions. The old catalogs themselves are fascinating, incredibly entertaining to read, and some are works of art in themselves.

An old Marshall Field and Company catalog (c. 1915) advertises a FISHING BELL ALARM at five cents, saying, "It is called the sleepy fisherman's friend." A 1919 catalog shows that for $1.35, the unlucky fisherman may obtain a LINE RELEASER complete with leather case. The advertisement states, in part: "Ever have your fly in a tree? Got mad of course." It goes on to claim that the device will not only save your temper but will save your line, leader, lure, and possibly the tip of your rod to boot. It is placed on the tip of the rod, cuts the twig, and "down comes twig and your belongings." I've seen many a day when I could have used one of those. Sometimes I think I should be casting for our feathered friends instead of the fishy variety.

NOW THAT YOU HAVE IT HOW DO YOU DISPLAY IT?

There can be no end to methods of display if you use your imagination. To name but a few: the professionally made, glassed and sealed shadow box; open frames with burlap or other decorative, appropriate substances; custom-made shadow box types with removable glass or Plexiglas; an arrangement on a wall; display shelves and cabinets; hung from ceilings or beams; in antique or modern display fixtures used by

tackle shops or, in the case of some collectors, whole rooms or more, entirely devoted to display and enjoyment. The list is limited only by your imagination and individual requirements. All have advantages, but one will suit your needs.

For the serious or would-be serious collector, I would recommend a method that both protects and allows ease of access and removal. If you don't, you'll regret it later.

One very effective method for lure display is the use of tray-like cases with fabric covered foam rubber backing and a sliding or hinged Plexiglas cover. It is quite easy to remove, add, and rearrange plugs on the using upholsterers' "T pins." The Plexiglas protects from dust and the box itself can be hung on the wall or transported. If you're handy with your hands you can build them yourself. For reels, almost any cabinet with glass fronts and or sides would be very handy. Lights in the interior can add a very dramatic and decorative element to the room as the various metals and surfaces of the reels reflect it.

Rods could be shown to great advantage hung on your walls (removable of course) or perhaps a gun cabinet would be attractive. I have seen some beautiful old wooden rod racks that came out of tackle shops of bygone days. These are ideal for display and ease of removal. Do remember that rods should always be displayed or stored vertically.

You might add interest and contrast to your collection by displaying some of the very old with the very new, modern versions of the same thing.

If you are into rods, reels or lures alone, the inclusion of some example of the others will add enjoyment and interest to your display. An old rod looks a lot nicer with a vintage reel mounted on it.

Add trophy mounts to your collection. Old tackle boxes, patches, and gadgets and accessories add even more interest.

Old catalogs or reproductions of them serve two purposes. One is that they make fascinating reading and more importantly, they are the single most important source of information from which to learn about your hobby. Many of these old catalogs are rare and eminently collectible in themselves. A word about using the catalogs as reference material: The manufacturers were not always entirely accurate when listing. This is especially true with regard to sizes. Frequently the size is rounded to the nearest half or quarter-inch. Some companies used the same illustration for years even

Paw Paw Chub-Caster: $50-$200

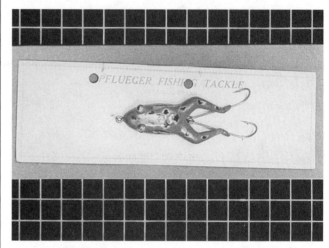

Pflueger Conrad Frog: $80-$100

though there may have been significant changes in hardware or design. Use them as a guide only.

Whatever method or scope of collection and display you arrive at, you will always find it necessary to change, add or delete. That's part of the fun.

From **Old Fishing Lures & Tackle, 6th Edition**
by Carl F. Lucky and Clyde A. Harbin Sr.

HISTORY OF AMERICAN FISHING TACKLE

While there has never been a revolutionary event in the history of fishing to compare with what the invention of gunpowder did for hunting, there have been significant technical advances in lure and tackle manufacture over the years. These can sometimes be identified on an approximate date.

PRE-COLONIAL TIMES

1. The Indians used their hands, traps, spears, and lights at night. The latter, as we know and use them today, obviously attracted some fish. Light could be said to be one of the first artificial "lures."
2. Primitive American Indians as well as primitive peoples of other parts of the world used a "gorge," the crude forerunner of today's modern barbed hook. The gorge, still used in some areas of the world, is a straight bar made of bone, shell, stone or wood, sometimes with a groove around it near the center for tying a line. It was inserted lengthwise in the bait. When the fish swallows the bait, the line is tugged and the gorge becomes lodged lengthwise in the fish.
3. Eskimos and Indians used artificial lures made of ivory or bone. They were customarily used as decoys while ice fishing and/or spear fishing.
4. Eskimos and Indians used gill nets and seines.

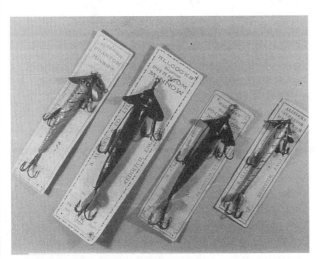

The Phantom Minnow

EARLY COLONIAL TIMES

The first colonists had little interest in sport fishing, as their immediate need was survival. History proves that there was much commercial fishing from the very earliest days of settlement in America.

18th CENTURY

First appearance of fishing for sport in America. Sport fishing probably pre-dates this era, but it was likely to be European aristocrats who brought their fly fishing gear with them.

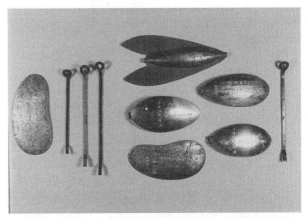

Various parts of Buel spoons and spinners. They may be found with with either J.T. or H.W. Buel (Julio's half brother) and patent date, 1852 or 1854 markings. The metal strips and spoons in the photo are the 1854 patent. The spinner body/blade is from the 1852 patent. Only that was provided. The angler had to attach his own hook and wire armature.

Riley Haskell Minnow. This metal minnow lure measures 4 9/16" in body and 5 5/8" overall (including the hook and line tie).

1800-1810

1. First appearance of the Phantom Minnow in America.
2. George Snyder made the first "Kentucky Reels."

1835-1840

The first commercial manufacture of the "Kentucky Reels" by the Meeks Brothers.

1844-1925
The development of the "Henshall Rod."

1848
Julio T. Buel began commercial manufacture of the spoon lure. He is credited with its invention. Buel was actually fishing with his invention as early as 1821 and made many for friends and neighbors over the years. The 1848 date is subject to speculation as there is a 1904 ad stating "Over 60 Years in Use."

1852
Julio T. Buel - First U.S. patent on spinner bait.

1859
First known patent for a lure that mentions wood as possible material for the lure body, by Riley Haskell, Painesville, Ohio.

1874
First granted patent for an artificial lure specifying the use of wood for the lure body. Patented May 26, 1874, by David Huard and Charles M. Dunbar of Ashland, Wis.

1876
Early manufactured artificial lure incorporating wood as a component. Listed in U.S. patent records as patented by H. C. Brush, Aug. 22, 1876. The 1876 H. C. Brush patent has been thought to be the first wooden plug. However study of patent records reveal the Huard and Dunbar patent precedes Brush by two years. It is not known if it was ever produced.

1880
First known granted patent for an artificial lure specifying glass for the lure body by J. Irgens, Sept. 7, 1880.

1883

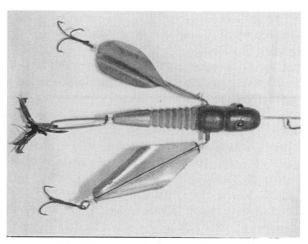

A Flying Hellgrammite. This particular example has red eyes.

Patent for "artificial bait" called The Flying Hellgrammite by Harry Comstock, Fulton, N. Y., January 30,1883.

1883
Patent granted to Earnest F. Pflueger for artificial lures coated with luminous paint for fishing at night.

1885
The development of the "Chicago Rod."

1890
The beginning of widespread bait casting in the United States. Although the bait casting reel was invented about 75 years previously, it wasn't until the 1890s that casting plugs were born in the U.S.

1869-1898
James Heddon is generally credited with the first artificial lure we know as the "plug" today.

1900-1905
The beginnings of major plug manufacturers in the United States.

1907
The first appearance of jointed wooden plugs—the "K and K Animated Minnows."

1910-1920
The first widespread use of luminous paint on plugs began sometime during this period. Pflueger was given the first patent on a luminous lure on Feb. 3,

The Brush Trolling Spoon and papers.

1883.
1912
The first water sonic plugs appeared. Probably the 1912 "Diamond Wiggler."
1914
The first appearance of fluted plugs, probably the Lockhart "Wobbler Wizard." It was later followed by the Wilson "Fluted Wobbler" around 1917.
1914
The Detroit Glass Minnow Tube was introduced; the first of the few and rare glass fishing lures.
1915
First appearance of a self-illuminated plug to utilize a battery-operated bulb. It was called "Dr. Wasweyler's Marvelous Electric Glow Casting Minnow."
1917
Earliest known advertisement of a lure made of celluloid. The first advertisement found was in a May 1917 issue of National Sportsman magazine. It was for an Al Foss "Oriental Wiggler"æa pork rind minnow. Soon after his ads began to say Pyralin instead of celluloid. These may be the first plastic lures.
1922
The Vesco Bait Company of New York City advertised baits and spoons made of Dupont Pyralin, one of the first plastic plugs.
1932
Heddon introduced its "Fish Flesh" plastic lure. The first lures were produced in the No. 9100 and No. 9500 (Vamp) series. Soon thereafter came plastic "Spooks."
1940
Appearance of the first American-built spinning reels.

A 1908 advertisement for the K & K Animated Minnow.

Grading Factors for Wooden Fishing Lures
By Michael Echols

As the dollar value of antique lures rise at a head-spinning rate, the accuracy of grading becomes more and more critical. When it was just a bunch of good old boys trading lures they loved, the fine points of grading didn't matter too much. Today we are talking about $1,500 or $5,000 lures instead of $5 lures, so grading is extremely important.

With higher prices, our collections are going to be smaller. Each addition to a collection can be a major financial decision where you can't afford to make a mistake. Fortunately, the advent of the Internet and the ability to send photos across the country in a matter of seconds has helped solve many grading problems because, as they say, a picture is worth a thousand words.

If you want to get into a fired-up argument, put three lure collectors in a circle, throw a lure in the middle and ask for a grade. More than likely you will get three different opinions. We'll dispense with the usual photos or list showing NFLCC grades and limit the discussion to factors that affect grading rather than making statements about absolutes.

Visual Values:

One of the hottest controversies in any type of collecting, be it coins, guns, or lures, is communicating grading values. The collectors who have seen everything will grade totally different than the novice. Perhaps the most dangerous person is the one who has only seen lures at the flea market and tries to communicate the condition of a lure when all he or she has ever seen is a lure in very good condition at best. What you know about grading is relative to what you have seen. Grading is visual.

How are you going to get through to "an average condition collector" what a pristine condition lure should look like, much less discuss the fine points of plus and minus grades? The representations on eBay.com by non-collectors, and not a few NFLCC members, are typical of this problem. Hopefully we can cover a few topics here to help us better communicate.

When we start getting picky about lure condition,

a 10X handheld glass magnifying lens is handy for examining the paint surface, hardware, and searching for crazing. I frequently look at lures under a 30X binocular dissecting microscope just to get an idea of how the surfaces look at high magnification. If you are looking for fakes, it is an excellent way to detect "workmanship."

Lure Terms and Definitions:

The following are commonly used terms and illustrations of defects that alter the grade of a lure. They are the types of defects that can change a grade by a plus or minus, and understandably the price. No one defect will set the grade, but these are the types of problems that can be used to differentiate between Excellent and Excellent-minus, or between Excellent-minus and Very Good.

Plus and minus are in the eye of the beholder, but they are the variations which can cause large swings in price. Most knowledgeable collectors will pay a lot more for an Excellent-plus lure than for an Excellent-minus. So, let's look at the factors that determine plus or minus and often can change a whole grade level:

- **Pointers:** Marks made by the hook points as they swing around and contact the paint or varnish at a single point. Basically, they are a tiny puncture hole in the paint or varnish. One or two are no big deal, but when the surface looks like the face of the moon it's a whole different matter. When describing pointers, it is best to refer to the exact number, depth, and size. If the hook penetrated into the wood and created a crater, then that is a worse situation than one that just marks the varnish and doesn't touch the paint.
- **Flakes:** Usually in reference to varnish (not people), flakes are the result of the varnish sticking to something and being pulled off the paint, or an actual varnish chip down to, but not including, the paint color. Varnish flakes are highly subjective, but in a heavily varnished lure like a Heddon, large areas of varnish flakes can and do seriously detract. If you are talking about paint flakes, then the matter is serious since value decreases drastically with any paint loss. Heddon Series 00 lures are notorious for flaked varnish due to all the sharp edges that stuck to the box or anything else. Flaking can usually be expressed in terms such as minor, heavy, light, or minimal along with the location. Examination of the surface with a 10X lens should show sharp edges of the flakes as opposed to a smooth, rounded edge caused by buffing or chemical treatment of the

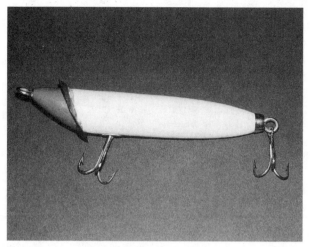

The price of a Heddon EXPERT like this can vary by hundreds of dollars, depending on its condition.

surface.
- **Crazing:** Also known as "checking," crazing refers to minor separation fractures of the paint or varnish. Usually there is a fine quilted pattern to the cracks, which look like brickwork under a 10X magnifying lens. This is not to be confused with deep splits of the paint, or "cracks." In a heavily varnished lure like those produced by Heddon, Pflueger, or South Bend, I personally find it comforting to see crazing because it is indicative of age and quality. It is also extremely difficult to fake subsurface crazing.
- **Hook drag:** A semi-circular scratch made by a hook into the paint or varnish. If it is into the paint, then it's serious and greatly detracts from the value. If it's only into the varnish and very, very light, then it's a personal call, but a hook drag takes any lure out of the "Excellent" range. If you see a semi-circular mark on the surface, then you are talking hook drag and it needs to be described.
- **Cracks:** Separation of the paint or varnish down to the wood and not normal. Cracks allow water to get into the wood, resulting in swelling which causes the paint to flake or pop off in large sections. In some cases, cracks in the paint are like crazing—they are a feature of rare, early lures and are esthetically disturbing, but can verify the origins of the paint on an otherwise excellent lure. Repaints typically would not have cracks. Cracked eyes are something that should be noted and will have influence on condition in the plus and minus department.
- **Chip:** Paint loss in varying sizes, but usually down to the wood. If you are thinking you have to express the amount of paint loss as a percentage, then forget anything above "Very Good" for condition. If there

is enough paint loss to worry about expressing it as a percentage, then you have something in the "fished" or "used" department. Paint chips greatly affect the grade of any lure, be it ancient or just old. One may accept a paint chip, but be sure to carefully note its existence when describing a lure with paint.

- **Shiny:** (a.k.a. lipstick shiny, slick, wet) A term used to describe the slick, smooth, non-dull, quality of well-preserved paint that has not been subjected to chemicals or intense light. The opposite of the shiny surface would be dull, dirty, and lifeless paint as a result of exposure to chemicals, light, dirt, or use. Degree in either direction determines plus or minus grade.

- **Beater:** A lure that is in less-than-average condition. Not collectible, but useful for parts. Many people who do repaints buy beaters to strip and repaint. Some of there are passed as new lures.

- **Rub or scrape:** A rub is a smooth, shallow paint or varnish loss via rubbing. It is not a chip or flake, and more than likely due to rubbing against a hard object like a box top or being deeply cleaned. Depending on the extent, it is a negative factor, but not a big deal if it is very light and small. Scrapes are typically deeper, represent greater damage, and often involve cutting the paint.

- **Otherwise Excellent:** A term used to describe a lure with one small defect that may or may not affect the asking price. Typically a lure with a single minor pointer, flake, chip, or paint off the belly weight.

- **Touch-up:** Typically adding new varnish, gill marks, or an attempt to match the existing antique paint with new paint to hide a defect. This is a no-no and automatically removes the lure from being a true collectible. Touch-ups are easily detectable with a blacklight, which will show the difference in paint age and type.

- **About Very Good:** A term used to avoid listing all the problems on a lure or box.

- **Repaint:** A lure body that has been repainted by an arts and crafts person. Not something that should be in the tackle-collecting scene. If properly marked,

this is a curiosity fit for shadow box displays used by interior decorators and walls in sports bars.

- **Hangs well:** The ultimate euphemism for "It's only good on one side." Otherwise see "Beater."

- **Whizzed:** A term used by coin dealers to describe extensive polishing of a surface. Some people delight in rubbing a lure with cleaner until it is without gill marks or varnish in an attempt to upgrade the value. What they accomplish is destruction of the lure and its value. Cleaning is one thing, polishing to remove the varnish is another. If you remove the varnish on a lure, you have greatly decreased the value and there is no way it can be considered more than Average in grade.

- **Worm burn:** The result of a plastic worm being left against lure paint for an extended time. Typically the paint melts and leaves a messy goo where the worm was in contact. Causes a burn-like mark similar to what a cigarette does to Formica or a laminated furniture surface. Typically earns the lure a "hangs well" grade, but eliminates it from anything above used, or beater condition.

- **Stupid:** What some of us get when we start rationalizing how valuable a ratty old lure is because of its age.

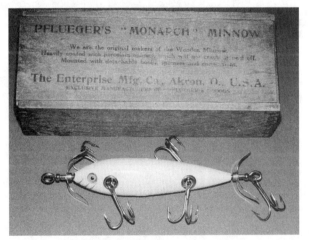

Five-treble MONARCH MINNOWS from Pflueger in this type of condtion are difficult to find..

Chapter Four: The Digest

FISHING DIGEST

- Fishing Tackle
- Fishing Baits
- Fishing Rods & Reels
- Fishing Boats
- Fishing Boat Accessories
- Fishing Apparel
- Fishing Accessories
- Fishing Guides & Charters
- Fishing Resorts
- Other

Tackle

A.H. Rice Corp.
55 Spring St.
Pittsfield, MA 01201
(413) 443-6477
(800) 765-7423
Fax: (413) 442-4650
Founded in 1878, A.H. Rice makes a complete line of rod-wrapping threads in bright and opaque nylon, polyester, acrylic, and metallics.
- **Products:** • Rod-wrapping threads

American Fishing Wire
205 Carter Drive
Westchester, PA 19382
(610) 692-7551
800824-WIRE
Fax: (610) 692-2190
sales@americanfishingwire.com
www.americanfishingwire.com
American Fishing Wire manufactures a complete line of stainless steel, mono, and titanium leader wire, trolling wire, and downrigging wire for sportfishing. Other tackle products include sleeves, snaps, split rings, swivels, thimbles, and tools.
- **Brand Name(s):** Titanium Tooth Proof, Surlon-Micro Supreme, Surfstrand.
- **Products:** • Wire fishing line • Tackle

American Import Co. and Taico Trading Corp.
1453 Mission St.
San Francisco, CA 94103
(415) 863-1506
Fax: (415) 863-0939
tacklestop@aol.com
American Import sells to distributors and Taico Trading is an exporter representing numerous U.S. tackle manufacturers. They handle complete lines of all types of fishing tackle for distributors and components for manufacturers.
- **Brand Name(s):** L.M. Dickson, Bestmade and Premier brands as well as private branding for manufacturers.
- **Products:** • Fishing tackle

Angler's Warehouse
805 Main St.
P.O. Box 1
Montauk, NY 11954
(877) 220-0353
www.anglerswarehouse.com
Angler's Warehouse provides online shopping for a wide variety of fishing equipment, including rods and reels, line, lures, tackle, motors, clothing, electronics, and accessories. Products are searchable in an online catalog.
- **Brand Name(s):** Many leading brands.
- ✔ Online shop.
- **Products:** • Rods and reels • Line • Clothing • Electronics • Motors

Backlash Tackle LLC
P.O. Box 5453
2582 Sand Creek Road
Grants Pass, OR 97527
(541) 955-0312
Fax: (541) 476-2726
info@backlashtackle.com
www.backlashtackle.com
Backlash Tackle offers online and catalog shopping for premium bass tackle, including rods and reels, hooks, baits, and weights from leading manufacturers.
- **Brand Name(s):** Leading brands.
- ✔ Brochure. ✔ Online shop. ✔ Retail shop.
- **Products:** • Rods and reels • Baits • Hooks

Bagley International
5719-1 Corporation Circle
Ft. Myers, FL 33905
(941) 693-7070
(800) 869-9941
Fax: (941) 693-2282
www.baghome.com
Bagley International is a distribution company for fishing tackle, including the Bagley, Key Largo, Wazp, and Capt. Jax's brands. Products include lures, baits, spoons, jigs, and floats.
- **Brand Name(s):** Bagley, Key Largo, Wazp, Capt. Jax's.
- ✔ Brochure.
- **Products:** • Baits • Lures • Floats

Bear Paw Tackle Co.

4904 Aero Park Drive
Bellaire, MI 49615
(231) 533-8604
Fax: (231) 533-9974
info@bearpawtackle.com
www.bearpawtackle.com
Bear Paw Tackle, in business for more than 55 years,
  makes a variety of terminal fishing tackle and
  accessories, including snelled hooks, crawler
  harnesses, electric fish scalers, fish grips, and fillet
  knives.
- ■ **Brand Name(s):** Bear Paw Tackle.
- ■ **Products:** • Terminal tackle • Electric scalers •
  Fillet knives

Top: **Berkley is known for its variety of power baits, including this
selection of Tournament Strength Dropshot Bass Minnows.** *Bottom:*
**Berkley Series One rods are for serious fishermen, with lightweight
graphite and titanium guides, which are 20 times tougher than
ceramic but 55 percent lighter.**

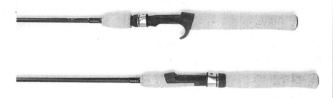

Berkley

1900 18th St.
Spirit Lake, IA 53160
(800) 237-5539
berkley@purefishing.com
www.berkley-fishing.com
Berkley is a leading fishing tackle company, making
  fishing rods, Trilene fishing line, Frenzy Hardbaits,
  and PowerBait, as well as terminal tackle, clothing,
  and accessories.
- ■ **Brand Name(s):** Berkley, Trilene, PowerBait,
  Frenzy Hardbaits.
- ✔ Brochure.
- ■ **Products:** • Fishing tackle • Line • Rods and reels •
  Baits • Lures

Betts Tackle Ltd.

1701 W. Academy St.
Fuquay-Varina, NC 27526
(919) 552-2226
(800) 334-9114
Fax: (919) 552-3423
bettstackle@mindspring.com
Betts Tackle makes a variety of tackle and lures,
  including Betts Spins, cork body poppers, sponge
  bugs and flies for panfishing, and floats, tube tails
  and jigs.
- ■ **Brand Name(s):** Betts.
- ■ **Products:** • Spinners • Floats • Jigs

Big Ten Tackle

412 Thompson St.
Latrobe, PA 15650
(800) 480-4216
bigtentackle@bigtentackle.com
www.bigtentackle.com
Big Ten Tackle manufactures the "bobber with a brain,"
  plus a new line of ceramic sinkers. Orders are taken
  online and the products are available in stores.
- ■ **Brand Name(s):** Bobber With A Brain.
- ✔ Online shop.
- ■ **Products:** • Bobbers • Sinkers

Bimini Bay Outfitters Ltd.

43 McKee Drive
Mahwah, NJ 07430
(201) 529-3550
(800) 688-3481
Fax: (201) 529-0258
Bimini Bay manufactures and markets fishing rods and
  reels, lures, accessories, giftware, and clothing for
  freshwater and saltwater anglers. It's the exclusive
  source for Ande rods, Jarvis Walker-Outback Tough
  Fishing products and Tsunami Lures.
- ■ **Products:** • Rods and reels • Lures • Clothing •
  Accessories

Bullet Weights Inc.

P.O. Box 187
Alda, NE 68810
(308) 382-7436
Fax: (308) 382-2906
www.bulletweights.com
Bullet Weights produces many variety of fishing
  sinkers and rigs. It has added environment friendly
  Ultra Steel sinkers to its line of lead sinkers.
- ■ **Brand Name(s):** Bullet Weights, Ultra Steel.
- ■ **Products:** • Sinkers

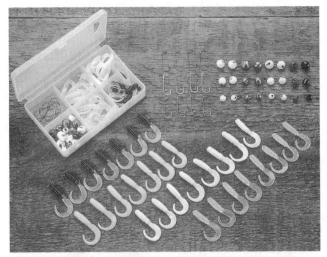

Top: The Ultra Steel Jig Kit from Bullet Weights has weights that are slotted so that they can be added or removed from the hooks without retying the line. *Bottom:* The Drop Weight system by Bullet Weights comes in lead or Ultra Steel and includes torpedo, teardrop, and egg-shaped weights.

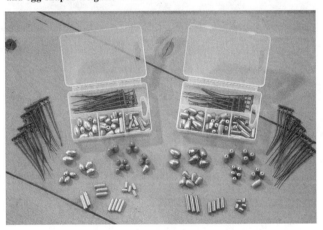

Cajun Line Co.

P.O. Box 9015
Houma, LA 70364
(877) 722-5863
www.cajunline.com
Cajun Line Co. produces specialty low visibility fishing lines, including Cajun Lightnin, Cajun Cast, and Cajun Camo.
- **Brand Name(s):** Cajun Line.
- **Products:** • Fishing line

Carlson Tackle Co. Inc.

1752 N. Market St.
Monticello, IL 61856
(217) 762-7746
Fax: (217) 762-7747
www.carlsontackle.com
Carlson Tackle makes several fishing products, including Mr. Wiggly lures, Wing-it Bobbers, Fishin' Glue, Injector Series Hollow-Floating worms, Wing-Lite Bobbers, and Fisherman's Hand Cream.
- **Brand Name(s):** Wing-it, Fishin' Glue, Mr. Wiggly.
- **Products:** • Tackle • Lures • Bobbers

Church Tackle Co.

7075 Hillandale Road
Sodus, MI 49126
(616) 934-8528
Fax: (616) 934-7229
www.churchtackle.com
Church Tackle manufactures planer boards, trolling weights, downrigger clips, and portable outriggers. Orders are taken online and products are available in stores.
✔ Online shop.
- **Products:** • Planer boards • Trolling weights • Outriggers

Covema Filaments Ltd.

14-B Cochin Special Economic Zone
Kerala, IN 682 030
mail@covema.com
www.covema.com
Covema Filaments, based in India, produces sport and commercial fishing lines under the brands Arctic Strong and Flying Fisher. Orders are taken online.
- **Brand Name(s):** Arctic Strong, Flying Fisher.
- **Products:** • Fishing line

Daiichi

P.O. Box 1177
Wetumpka, AL 36092
(334) 567-2078
info@tticompanies.com
www.daiichihooks.com
Daiichi manufactures the "world's sharpest hooks" in many sizes and styles for different types of fishing and Sabiki Rigs. It has added the Daiichi Bleeding Bait Circle Chunk hook with a red bait holder barb. Internet shopping is available.
- **Brand Name(s):** Daiichi, Bleeding Bait, Gill Flash, Circle Wide, Circle Chunk.
✔ Online shop.

Daiwa Corp.

P.O. Box 6031
Artesia, CA 90702
(562) 802-9589
Fax: (562) 404-6212
www.daiwa.com

Daiwa is a worldwide manufacturer of a wide variety of fishing tackle, including rods and reels, line and lures, combos, and accessories for freshwater and saltwater.

- ■ **Brand Name(s):** Daiwa.
- ■ **Products:** • Rods and reels • Line • Lures • Accessories

Danielson Company Inc.

4510 B Street NW
Auburn, WA 98001
(253) 854-1717
Fax: (253) 852-2794

Danielson provides a wide variety of fishing equipment, including terminal tackle, rods, knives,sinkers, line, hooks, lures, nets, leaders, and tools.

- ■ **Products:** • Fishing equipment

Do-It Corp.

501 N. State St.
Denver, IA 50622
(319) 984-6055
Fax: (319) 984-6403
www.do-itmolds.com

Do-It manufactures lure and sinker molds and other tackle-making products for fishermen. Available are molds for jigs, spinners, and sinkers, as well as hooks, wire, tools, and finishes to make homemade fishing tackle. Sales are by catalog and online

- ✔ Brochure. ✔ Online shop.
- ■ **Products:** • Lure and sinker molds • Tools

Don Iovino Products

3220 W. Wyoming Ave.
Burbank, CA 91505
(818) 848-6180
www.iovino.com

Don Iovino, a charter member of the International Fishing Hall of Fame, has produced a line of products designed for finesse bass fishing, including topwater baits, worm kits, custom jigs, fishing videos, and Ambassadeur Reels. Sales are on the Inter

- ■ **Brand Name(s):** Don Iovino.
- ✔ Brochure. ✔ Online shop.
- ■ **Products:** • Baits • Reels • Lures

The Circle Chunk´® with Stop Gap® Baitholder!

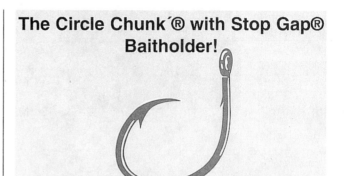

The Daiichi Circle Chunk hook featuring the Stop Gap Baitholder is one of the Bleeding Bait Hooks series.

Top: Necessary equipment for making lures including lead, melting equipment and Do-It molds. *Bottom:* The finished products from Do-It molds are homemade jigs and lures.

Eagle Claw Fishing Tackle

4245 E. 46th Ave.
P.O. Box 16011
Denver, CO 80216
(303) 321-1481
www.eagleclaw.com

Eagle Claw makes many varieties of fish hooks, as well as rods and reels, floats, leaders, rigs, and spinners. It also has a line of clothing.

- ■ **Brand Name(s):** Eagle Claw.
- ■ **Products:** • Hooks • Rods and reels • Leaders and rigs

eders.com

85 Forest Ave.
P.O. Box 774
Locust Valley, NY 11560
(877) 656-0808
feedback@eders.com
www.eders.com
Eders sells a wide variety of marine, boating, and
   fishing products by catalog and on the Internet. It also
   operates Web pages with news, information, and
   discussion about freshwater and saltwater fishing.
■ **Brand Name(s):** eders.
✔ Brochure. ✔ Online shop.
■ **Products:** • Fishing gear • Boating gear

Gamakatsu USA Inc.

P.O. Box 1797
Tacoma, WA 98401
(253) 922-8373
Fax: (253) 922-8447
mailbox@gamakatsu.com
www.gamakatsu.com
Gamakatsu, a division of the Japanese company,
   manufactures fishing hooks, jig heads, and fishing
   line.
■ **Brand Name(s):** Gamakatsu, G-Power.
■ **Products:** • Fishing hooks • Line • Jig heads

Gibbs/Nortac Industries Ltd.

7455 Conway Ave.
Burnaby, BC V5E 2P7
(604) 439-1394
(800) 661-1984
Fax: (604) 439-9996
syd@gibbsfishing.com
www.gibbsfishing.com
Gibbs/Nortac has been producing Quality Gibbs
   Fishing Tackle since 1908. Products include lures,
   nets, sinkers and accessories for saltwater and
   freshwater fishing, with more than 7,000 products.
■ **Brand Name(s):** Quality Gibbs Fishing Tackle.
■ **Products:** • Lures • Nets • Sinkers

Griffin Enterprises

465 A Ash Road
Kalispell, MT 59901
(406) 257-7027
Fax: (406) 257-7061
griff@montana.com
www.griffinenterprisesinc.com
Griffin Enterprises makes a variety of fly-tying
   equipment, including bobbins, vises, scissors, and
   accessories. Products are available in stores.
■ **Brand Name(s):** Griffin.
■ **Products:** • Vises • Bobbins • Fly-tying accessories

Gudebrod

274 Shoemaker Road
Pottstown, PA 19464
(610) 327-4050
Fax: (610) 327-4588
sales@gudebrod.com
www.gudebrod.com
Gudebrod manufactures fly tying and fly fishing
   equipment and tackle as well as Dacron fishing line.
   Line and tackle are sold under the Super G,
   Champion, Monarch, NCP, HT, Trimar and EZ-Dub
   brand names.
■ **Brand Name(s):** Super G, Champion, Monarch,
   NCP, HT, Trimar, EZ-Dub.
■ **Products:** • Fishing line • Fly tying materials

Kumho Hook Mfg.

4915 W. Rosecrans Ave.
Hawthorne, CA 90250
(310) 679-8777
Fax: (310) 679-6777
Kumho makes a variety of sizes and styles of fish
   hooks.
■ **Products:** • Fish hooks

Land O' Lakes Tackle Co.

P.O. Box 145
Land O' Lakes, WI 54540
(715) 547-1111
www.landolakestackle.com
Land O' Lakes Tackle makes the Big Kahuna Bucktail
   that is prescented, live bait rigs, jigs, and fish
   attractants as well as clothing. Its Web site includes
   fishing tips, chat, a newsletter, and other fishing
   information. Online shopping is available.
■ **Brand Name(s):** Land O' Lakes, Big Kahuna
   Bucktail.
✔ Online shop.
■ **Products:** • Bait rigs • Jigs • Lures

Lee's Tackle

8227 NW 54th St.
Miami, FL 33166
(305) 599-9324
Fax: (305) 599-0830
www.leetackle.com
Lee's Tackle, in business since 1920, produces big-game fishing reels, rod holders, outriggers, and fighting chairs for saltwater fishing, as as miscellaneous fishing gear. Sales are by catalog or at the Miami store.
■ **Brand Name(s):** Lee's Tackle.
✔ Brochure.
■ **Products:** • Outriggers • Fighting chairs • Reels • Rod holders

Lindy Legendary Fishing Tackle

P.O. Box 973
Brainerd, MN 56401
(218) 829-1714
Fax: (218) 829-5426
patty@lindylittlejoe.com
www.lindylittlejoe.com
Lindy makes and sells Lindy Little Joe products, including lures, spinners, crankbaits, floats, stringers, sinkers, rigs, and marker buoys. Online shopping is available and products are in stores.
■ **Brand Name(s):** Lindy, Little Joe.
✔ Brochure. ✔ Online shop.
■ **Products:** • Lures • Sinkers • Floats • Rigs • Buoy markers

Marudaka USA Inc.

3899 Nobel Drive, Apt. 1127
San Diego, CA 92122
(858) 558-6294
Fax: (858) 558-6331
Marudaka USA is a sales office of Taicana Marudaka Leisure Goods Co., which offers hooks, lures, swivels, floats, reels, sinkers, leaders, and other terminal tackle.
■ **Products:** • Hooks • Floats • Reels • Terminal tackle

Mason Tackle Co.

P.O. Box 56
Otisville, MI 48463
(810) 631-4571
Fax: (810) 631-8695
Mason Tackle Co. manufactures a variety of fishing lines, tackle, and fly tying gear under many brand names, including Bass-On, Big Muskie, Falcon, Fish Tamer, Legend, Mill Ends, and Tiger Braid.
■ **Brand Name(s):** 49 Strand, Bass-On, Big Muskie, Falcon, Fish Tamer, Legend, Tiger Braid.
■ **Products:** • Fishing line • Tackle

The nearly invisible Maxima Perfexion monofilament line helped persuade this bass to leap at the bait.

Maxima America

3211 S. Shannon St.
Santa Ana, CA 92704
(714) 850-5966
Fax: (714) 850-5963
maximaline@aol.com
www.maxima-lines.com
Maxima manufactures monofilament fishing lines in various colors and strengths.
■ **Brand Name(s):** Maxima.
✔ Brochure.
■ **Products:** • Fishing line

Melton International Tackle

2600 E. Katella Ave., Suite B
Anaheim, CA 92806
(714) 978-9192
(800) 372-3474
Fax: (714) 978-9299
info@meltontackle.com
www.meltontackle.com

Melton International Tackle provides online and catalog
shopping, as well as a retail store in Anaheim, for
deep sea fishing. Products include lures, rods and
reels, boat accessories, clothing, fighting chairs, line,
terminal tackle, and outriggers.

✔ Brochure. ✔ Online shop.
■ **Products:** • Rods and reels • Saltwater fishing gear
• Clothing • Terminal tackle

Mud Hole Custom Tackle Inc.

1714 N. Goldenrod Road, Unit A3
Orlando, FL 32807
(407) 447-7637
(800) 420-6049
sales@mudhole.com
www.mudhole.com

Mud Hole sells a wide variety of fishing tackle and
rod- building components on its Internet store,
including freshwater and saltwater gear, fly fishing
equipment, gifts, fishing magazines, apparel,
footwear, and fishing charts.

■ **Brand Name(s):** Many brands are available.
✔ Brochure. ✔ Online shop.
■ **Products:** • Fishing tackle • Rod-building gear •
Fishing information

N.A.S. Bait & Tackle

8682 E. Bayshore Road
Marblehead, OH 43440
(800) 955-8795
Fax: (419) 798-9556
dewworms@aol.com
www.bestbait.com

N.A.S. Bait & Tackle sells a variety of bait and fishing
equipment, both by retail and wholesale, including
sales by Internet and catalog. Included are live and
preserved baits, lures, bobbers, hooks, nets, stringers,
rods and reels.

✔ Brochure. ✔ Online shop.
■ **Products:** • Baits • Fishing gear

Top: Among a wide variety of rod blanks available from Mud Hole
Custom Tackle are the IGFA Trolling Blanks from Seeker. *Bottom:*
Cork Handle Kits of various sorts are among the build-it-yourself
features at Mud Hole Custom Tackle.

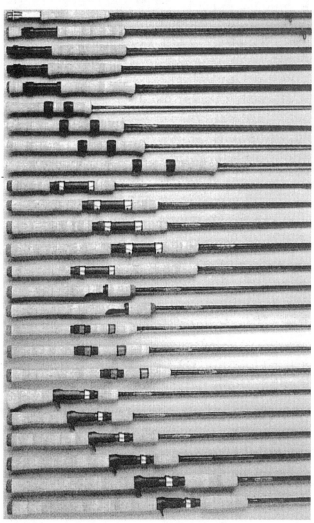

Normark Corp./Rapala

10395 Yellow Circle Drive
Minnetonka, MN 55343
(612) 933-0046
www.normark.com
Normark manufactures the well-known Rapala lures, as
well as several types of fishing rods, Long Cast and
Saltwater fishing lines, Rapala/VMC Premium
Hooks, and fishing accessories including fillet knives,
pliers, scales, and aerators.
- ■ Brand Name(s): Rapala, Long Cast, Rapala/VMC,
  Premium.
- ✔ Brochure.
- ■ Products: • Rods • Line • Lures • Knives • Hooks

O. Mustad & Sons (USA) Inc.

P.O. Box 838
Auburn, NY 13021
(315) 253-2793
Fax: (315) 253-0157
custserv@mustad-usa.com
www.mustad.no
- ■ **Brand Name(s):** Mustad, Ultra Point, Signature
  Series, Partridge.
- ✔ Online shop.
- ■ **Products:** • Hooks • Tackle

Owner American Corp.

3199-B Airport Loop Drive
Costa Mesa, CA 92626
(714) 668-9011
Fax: (714) 668-9133
www.ownerhooks.com
Owner American makes Owner Cutting Point Hooks,
with triple edges, for freshwater and saltwater fishing,
as well as Cultiva Lures featuring Living Eyes,
internal rattles and foil finishes.
- ■ **Brand Name(s):** Owner Cutting Point Hooks,
  Cultiva.
- ■ **Products:** • Fish hooks • Lures

Pokee Fishing Tackle Co. Ltd.

No. 16 Shinping Road
Tainan, Taiwan
www.pokeefishing.com
Pokee Fishing Tackle, based in Taiwan, is a leading
manufacturer and exporter of fishing rods, line,
Dyneema braided lines, and chemical lights.
- ■ **Products:** • Rods • Line

Pro-Troll Products

5700A Imhoff Drive
Concord, CA 94520
(925) 825-8560
Fax: (925) 825-8591
mail@protroll.com
www.protroll.com
Pro-Troll, originally known as Scotty Downriggers,
makes several products for trolling, including lures,
bait holders, weights, planers, and how-to books.
- ✔ Brochure.
- ■ **Products:** • Trolling gear • Lures

Pure Fishing

1900 18th St.
Spirit Lake, IA 51360
(800) 228-4272
www.purefishing.com
Pure Fishing is the world's largest fishing tackle
company, featuring Abu Garcia, Berkley, Fenwick,
Johnson, Mitchell, Red Wolf, and Spider Gear brands.
Products include rods and reels, lures, and line.
- ■ **Brand Name(s):** Abu Garcia, Berkley, Fenwick,
  Johnson, Mitchell, SpiderCast, SpiderLine, Red
  Wolf, Trilene.
- ✔ Brochure.
- ■ **Products:** • Rods • Reels • Line

Redfish-Bluefish Tackle Co.

P.O. Box 12630
Research Triangle Park, NC 27709
(919) 949-4003
Fax: (928) 438-9537
redfish.bluefish@att.net
www.redfishbluefishtackle.com
Redfish-Bluefish Tackle offers online shopping for
fishing tackle, primarily for saltwater fishing. Orders
are also taken by phone, fax or mail.
- ■ **Brand Name(s):** Leading brands of fishing
  equipment.
- ✔ Online shop. ✔ Retail shop.
- ■ **Products:** • Fishing tackle

S&C Brinkman Corp.

4805 N. St. Mary's #1
Beeville, TX 78102
(361) 354-5700
(888) 943-7592
Fax: (361) 358-9327
www.slidingweight.com
Brinkman makes Sliding Weight Hooks & Baits for
crawfish, worms, and shrimp. Tips and tactics are also
available on the Web site.
- ■ **Brand Name(s):** Sliding Weight Hooks & Baits.
- ✔ Online shop.
- ■ **Products:** • Hooks and baits

Sampo Inc.

119 Remsen Road
P.O. Box 328
Barneveld, NY 13304
(315) 896-2606
Fax: (315) 896-6575
info@sampoinc.com
www.sampoinc.com
Sampo specializes in terminal tackle, including swivels,
  beads, leaders, and snaps.
■ **Brand Name(s):** Sampo.
■ **Products:** • Terminal tackle

Shakespeare Fishing Tackle

3801 Westmore Drive
Columbia, SC 29223
(800) 347-3759
Fax: (803) 754-0707
help@shakespeare-fishing.com
www.shakespeare-fishing.com
Shakespeare has been making fishing tackle since
  1897, and is well known for many brands of rods and
  reels including Ugly Stik, Synergy, XTerra, EZ Cast,
  and Wondereel. It also makes Sigma and Alpha
  monofilament line, combos, and fishing kits.
■ **Brand Name(s):** Shakespeare, Sigma, Ugly Stik,
  Synergy, XTerra, Alpha, Wonder Pole, Wondereel.
■ **Products:** • Rods • Reels • Line • Furniture

South Bend Sporting Goods

1910 Techny Road
Northbrook, IL 60065
(847) 715-1400
www.south-bend.com
South Bend has been making fishing tackle for nearly a
century, including registering the trademark Spincast.
Products include rods and reels in many designs,
terminal tackle, and accessories. Sales are by Internet
or catalog as well as in stores.
■ **Brand Name(s):** South Bend.
✔ Brochure. ✔ Online shop.
■ **Products:** • Rods • Reels • Tackle

Spiderline

1900 18th St.
Spirit Lake, IA 51360
(877) 502-6482
spiderline@purefishing.com
www.fishspiderwire.com
Spiderline makes SpiderWire line in a variety of types
  and sizes for freshwater and saltwater fishing.
■ **Brand Name(s):** Spiderline, SpiderWire.
✔ Brochure.
■ **Products:** • Fishing line

SPRO Corp.

3900 Kennesaw 75 Parkway, Suite 140
Kennesaw, GA 30144
(770) 919-1722
Fax: (770) 919-8141
sales@spro.com
www.spro.com
SPRO manufactures a number of fishing products,
  including baitcasting and spinning rods, lures ranging
  from crankbaits to jigs and soft baits, and terminal
  tackle including rigs, snells, and swivels.
■ **Products:** • Rods • Lures • Terminal tackle

Stren Fishing Lines

870 Remington Drive
P.O. Box 700
Madison, NC 27025
(800) 243-9700
Fax: (336) 548-7801
info@remington.com
www.stren.com
Stren, a division of Remington Arms Co., is a major
  manufacturer of fishing line in many varieties and
  ratings. It also makes Classic Soft Plastic Lures and
  fishing accessories, including fillet knives, clips,
  scales, and terminal tackle.
■ **Brand Name(s):** Stren, Pal.
■ **Products:** • Fishing line • Plastic lures •
  Accessories

Easy Cast, in a variety of strengths, is one of many types of line
available from Stren.

Strike King Lure Co.

466 Washington St.
Collierville, TN 38017
(901) 853-1455
Fax: (901) 853-7606
info@strikeking.com
www.strikeking.com

Strike King makes a wide variety of lures, including spinnerbaits, buzzbaits, and jigs, as well as catfish baits and pork lures. It also sells sunglasses, clothing, and caps. Its All Star Pro Team includes top anglers.

■ **Brand Name(s):** Strike King.
✔ Brochure.
■ **Products:** • Lures • Baits • Clothing

Sufix USA

2000 Nuggett Road
High Point, NC 27263
(800) 554-1423
Fax: (336) 434-5870
sufixusa@nr.infi.net
www.sufixfishing.com

Sufix is one of the largest monofilament line manufacturers in the world, with offices in Taiwan and China, largely to private label customers. It makes enough line every year to stretch around the world 15 times, in many sizes and types.

■ Brand Name(s): Sufix.
■ Products: • Fishing line

TICA USA Inc.

1450-Q West Pointe Drive
West Pointe Business Park
Charlotte, NC 28214
(704) 398-2850
(800) 390-5268
www.ticaglobal.com

TICA, based in Thailand and China, is one of the major fishing tackle makers in the world. Products include rods and reels for fly fishing, bass fishing, trolling, bait casting, and spinning in fresh and salt water.

■ **Brand Name(s):** TICA.
■ **Products:** • Rods • Reels

Top: TICA's TP-B Series of reels features an aluminum alloy frame, brass gear, and 13 ball bearings. *Bottom:* The TC3 Fly Rods from TICA are ultra light and sensitive, with TC3 graphite construction and stainless steel snake eyes.

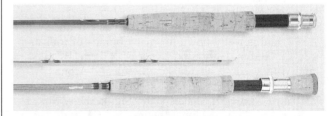

A lineup of Precision Brass Weights is part of the collection of brass sinkers made by Top Brass Tackle.

Top Brass Tackle

P.O. Box 209
Starkville, MS 39760
(662) 323-1559
Fax: (662) 323-7466
info@topbrasstackle.com
www.topbrasstackle.com

Top Brass makes a line of brass sinkers and glass beads that add a noise-making aspect to attract fish to a worm or bait. Products can be found in tackle shops.

■ **Brand Name(s):** Top Brass Tackle.
✔ Brochure.
■ **Products:** • Brass fishing tackle

The Blood Red worm Hook is one of many styles of Tru-Turn hooks.

Tru-Turn Hook More Fish

P.O. Box 1177
Wetumpka, AL 36092
(334) 567-2011
info@tticompanies.com
www.truturnhooks.com
Tru-Turn Hooks are the original cam action hooks and now include the Blood Red line of bait hooks. Sales are available on the Internet as well as in stores.
■ **Brand Name(s):** Tru-Turn, Blood Red, HitchHikers, Brute, E-Z Link.
✔ Online shop.
■ **Products:** • Fishing hooks

TyGer Leader

P.O. Box 26
Bonners Ferry, ID 83805
(208) 267-6292
Fax: (208) 267-8822
info@tygerleader.com
www.tygerleader.com
TyGer Leader is a stainless steel knottable leader designed to handle toothy fish, nylon-coated to resist rock and coral. It is sold in 2 pound to 120 pound strengths. Online shopping is available.
■ **Brand Name(s):** TyGer Leader.
✔ Online shop.
■ **Products:** • Stainless steel leaders

VMC Inc.

1901 Oakcrest Ave.
St. Paul, MN 55113
(651) 636-9649
Fax: (651) 636-7053
jkiklas@vmchooks.com
www.vmchooks.com
VMC makes what it advertises as the "world's finest fish hooks" in a variety of styles and sizes, including bass, walleye, muskie, fly, and saltwater hooks.
■ **Brand Name(s):** VMC.
■ **Products:** • Fish hooks

Water Gremlin Co.

1610 Whitaker Ave.
White Bear Lake, MN 55110
(651) 429-7761
www.watergremlin.com
Water Gremlin makes many fishing sinkers in a variety of shapes, styles, and sizes, including Snap-Loc, Split Shot, Rubbercor, Pinch-Grip, Needle Nose Worm Weights, Bull Shot, and Egg Sinkers.
■ **Brand Name(s):** Water Gremlin.
■ **Products:** • Sinkers

Wolf Wire Forms Inc.

3640 Investment Lane #18
West Palm Beach, FL 33404
(561) 845-6225
Fax: (561) 845-0207
www.wolfwire.com
Wolf Wire Forms produces stainless steel Duo Lock Snaps and Split Rings.
■ **Brand Name(s):** Duo Lock.
■ **Products:** • Snaps • Split rings

XPoint

100 Red Eagle Road
Wetumpka, AL 36092
(334) 567-2011
www.xpointhooks.com
XPoint, a division of TTI Companies, is "the world's fastest hook," made of 110-Carbon Steel. Sales are available online as well as in stores.
■ **Brand Name(s):** XPoint, XGap.
✔ Online shop.
■ **Products:** • Fishing hooks

Bait

AA Worms
P.O. Box 176
Temecula, CA 92593
(909) 676-6384
Fax: (909) 695-6746
www.aaworms.com
AA Worms manufactures custom hand-poured plastic lures, worms, grubs, and swimbaits. Brands are AA's, AAT, and Optimum Baits.
■ **Brand Name(s):** AA's, AAT, Optimum Baits.
■ **Products:** • Plastic worms • Baits

Acme Tackle Co.
P.O. Box 72771
Providence, RI 02907
(401) 331-6437
Fax: (401) 272-7821
www.acmetackle.com
Founded in 1950, Acme Tackle makes a number of metal fishing lures, including Little Cleo, Dixie Flash, Kastmaster, and K.O. Wobbler. Online shopping is available, and products are in stores.
■ **Brand Name(s):** Little Cleo, Kastmaster.
■ **Products:** • Metal lures

Atlas-Mike's Bait Inc.
P.O. Box 608
Fort Atkinson, WI 53538
(920) 563-2046
Fax: (920) 563-7207
Atlas-Mike's has been making quality baits for more than 65 years, including salmon eggs, marshmallows, floating trout bait, steelhead accessories, egg cures, and fish attractor scents.

■ **Brand Name(s):** Mike's.
✔ Brochure.
■ **Products:** • Baits

Bagley International
5719-1 Corporation Circle
Ft. Myers, FL 33905
(941) 693-7070
(800) 869-2282
www.baghome.com
Bagley International is a distribution company for fishing tackle, including the Bagley, Key Largo, Wazp, and Capt. Jax's brands.
■ **Brand Name(s):** Bagley • Key Largo • Wazp • Capt. Jax's
✔ Brochure
■ **Products:** Baits • Lures • Floats

Above Right: The Small Fry is just one of many sizes and styles of bagley baits. *Above:* A bass lunges at a Bagley Small Fry, ready to inhale the bait.

Two of Atlas-Mike's trout baits are Floating Glo Bait and Floating Glo Pellets.

Some of Atlas-Mike's marshmallow baits include Micro Mallows, Super Scented Marshmallows in several colors and scents, and Glitter Mallows.

Besides its line of fishing lures, Bandit Lures offers its raccoon logo on caps and shirts.

Bandit Lures

444 Cold Springs Road
Sardis, MS 38666
(662) 563-8450
www.banditlures.com
Bandit Lures makes fishing lures in a variety of sizes and color patterns, as well as a line of shirts and caps. Online shopping is available.
- **Brand Name(s):** Bandit Lures
- ✔ Brochure. ✔ Online shop.
- **Products:** • Lures

Bass Assassin Lures Inc.

Route 2, Box 20
Mayo, FL 32066
(386) 294-1049
Fax: (386) 294-3495
sales@bassassassin.com
www.bassassassin.com

Left: The Fire Tiger is one of more than two dozen crawdads offered by Bass Assassin. *Right:* A pair of Louisiana Softshell lizards, that come in 5 1/2 inch, 7 inch and 9 inch sizes, are among Bass Assassin baits.

Bass Assassin manufactures and sells, online and through retailers, a full line of freshwater and saltwater lures and jigs. Its Web site also offers articles and news about fishing, free classified ads, and links to guide services and fishing gear.
- **Brand Name(s):** Bass Assassin.
- ✔ Brochure. ✔ Online shop.
- **Products:** • Lures • Jigs

Bay de Noc Lure Co.

P.O. Box 71, Dept. INT
Gladstone, MI 49837
(906) 428-1133
Fax: (906) 428-1414
sales@baydenoclure.com
www.baydenoclure.com
Bay de Noc Lure Co. makes a variety of fishing lures and baits, including the Swedish Pimple, Do-Jigger, Flure Spoon, and Laker Taker.
- **Brand Name(s):** Swedish Pimple, Do-Jigger.
- **Products:** • Lures

Bill Lewis Lures

P.O. Box 7959
Alexandria, LA 71306
(318) 487-0352
(800) 633-4861
Fax: (318) 445-8301
www.rat-l-trap.com
Bill Lewis Lures makes the Rat-L-Trap line of fishing lures for saltwater and freshwater fishing, using the Liv-N-Sound attraction system.
- **Brand Name(s):** Rat-L-Trap.
- ✔ Brochure.
- **Products:** • Lures

Sits
Upright

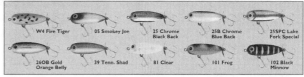

W4 Fire Tiger | 05 Smokey Joe | 25 Chrome Black Back | 25B Chrome Blue Back | 25SPC Lake Fork Special
26OB Gold Orange Belly | 39 Tenn. Shad | 81 Clear | 101 Frog | 102 Black Minnow

Right: The improved Rat-L-Trap from Bill Lewis is 10 percent bigger than the old model and features sonic weld technology for additional strength. *Left:* The Slap-Stik from Bill Lewis Lures sits upright at water level because of its shifted tail weight. Sound chambers contain "rattlers" just like the Rat-L-Trap.

Blakemore Lure Co.

P.O. Box 1149
North Highway 65
Branson, MO 65615
(417) 334-5340
Fax: (417) 334-5220
www.blakemore-lure.com
Blakemore makes the Road Runner lure in a variety of
  sizes and styles, Jaker weedless jigs, as well as
  Electro-Carv fillet knives, and fishing accessories.
- **Brand Name(s):** Road Runner.
- **Products:** • Lures • Jigs • Fillet knives • Accessories

Boone Bait Co.

P.O. Box 2966
Winter Park, FL 32790
(407) 975-8775
Fax: (407) 975-8776
boonebait@earthlink.net
Boone Bait Co. has been selling saltwater lures since
  1951, including skirts, plugs, floats, rigs, jigs,
  terminal tackle, lure bags, and spinning baits.
- **Products:** • Lures

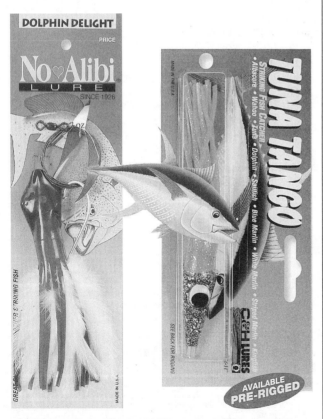

Left: **The Dolphin Delight, by C&H Lures, is a combination feather
lure with rubber skirt and leaded head.** *Right:* **The Tuna Tango lure
with weighted head, by C&H Lures, comes in a wide variety of
colors and styles.**

Bowker's

841 W. 11th St.
Crete, NE 68333
(402) 826-2516
info@bowkersbait.com
www.bowkersbait.com
Bowker's has created the "Original Dip Bait" for catfish
  for more than 40 years. A new product is Catfish Bits
  in a 6-ounce zip lock bag. Online shopping is
  available.
- Brand Name(s): Bowker's Original Dip Bait.
- ✔ Brochure. ✔ Online shop.
- **Products:** • Catfish bait

C&H Lures

13051 Beach Blvd.
Jacksonville, FL 32246
(904) 992-9600
Fax: (904) 992-7367
www.candhlure.com
C&H Lures makes a variety of fishing lures, including
  the Lil' Stubby, Tuna Tango, Tuna Witch, Seawitch,
  No-Alibi, and Alien.
- **Products:** • Lures

Calcutta Baits

300 Dunbar Ave., Suite 100
Oldsmar, FL 34677
(813) 855-3450
(800) 362-7675
Fax: (813) 854-3184
www.calcuttabaits.com
Calcutta sells saltwater baits, rigs, teasers, soft plastic
  artificial baits, and a line of clothing. An online
  catalog is available for ordering.
- **Brand Name(s):** Calcutta Baits.
- ✔ Brochure. , Online shop.
- **Products:** • Baits • Clothing

Cat Tracker Bait Co.

2095 Kerper Blvd.
Dubuque, IA 52001
(319) 557-5174
(888) 248-9183
www.cattracker.com
Cat Tracker Bait Co. was founded by Junnie Mihalakis
  and sells Junnie's CatTracker Original Dip as well as
  catfish baits such as Junnie's Sewer Bait, Wicked
  Sticky, and Jo Jo's Pole Snatcher. It also sells worms
  and rigs as well as apparel.
- **Brand Name(s):** Cat Tracker, Junnie's.
- ✔ Brochure. ✔ Online shop.
- **Products:** • Catfish bait

STC316 PEARL PEPPER STC222 NATURAL/BLUE GLITTER STC17 GREEN PUMPKIN/BLACK FLAKE

STC368 GLASS MINNOW STC819 WATERMELON/RED FLAKE (Also available but not shown) STC19 BLACK/RED FLAKE

Top: New from Charlie Brewer's Slider Co. is the Slider 4-inch Tube Crawfish in several color schemes. *Bottom:* Spider Web Jigs rigged weedless and featuring silicone skins, are among Charlie Brewer's Slider Co.'s featured items.

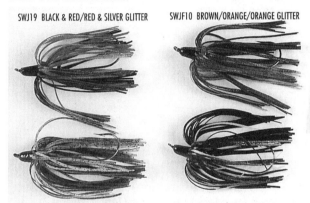

SWJ19 BLACK & RED/RED & SILVER GLITTER SWJF10 BROWN/ORANGE/ORANGE GLITTER

SWJ2516 PURPLE/CLEAR/CHARTREUSE/ BLACK & PURPLE GLITTER SWJF51 BLACK/CHARTREUSE/GOLD GLITTER

Charlie Brewer's Slider Co.

P.O. Box 130
511 E. Gaines St.
Lawrenceburg, TN 38464
(931) 762-4700
(800) 762-4701
Fax: (931) 762-0435
slider@sliderfishing.com
www.fishingworld.com/slider/
Charlie Brewer's Slider technique of fishing imitates nature with artificial worms, frogs, and grubs. Online shopping is available for those products as well as hooks, jigs, rods, and clothing.
- **Brand Name(s):** Charlie Brewer's Slider Co.
✔ Online shop.
- **Products:** • Artificial baits • Fishing gear • Clothing

Competitive Edge

1345 Vista Way
Red Bluff, CA 96080
(530) 529-4080
customerservice@cefishing.com
www.cefishing.com
Competitive Edge is dedicated to bass fishing, offering a variety of baits, jigs, Magic Worms, and Wacko Tackle to anglers. Sales are online, by catalog, and in stores.
- **Brand Name(s):** Magic Worms, Wacko Tackle.
✔ Brochure. ✔ Online shop.
- **Products:** • Bait • Tackle

Crafty's TackleWorks

480 Pat Ave.
P.O. Box 613
Overton, NV 89040
(702) 397-2662
(888) 286-8061
www.ScentHead.com
Products: The ScentHead is a spinner bait that adds a trail of scent to attract fish.
- **Brand Name(s):** ScentHead
✔ Brochure. ✔ Online shop.

Above: The ScentHead Spinner Bait by Crafty's TackleWorks features a head with refillable scent holder.

Crave Fishing Research

13479 Baker Road
Red Bluff, CA 96080
(530) 528-9254
Fax: (530) 528-9258
sales@cravebait.com
www.cravebait.com

Crave makes several types of baits with SEXattract, the company's trademark for the reproductive, biological stimulant. They include Ultra Violet, Premium, Glow Bright, and Action Gel.

- **Brand Name(s):** Crave.
- **Products:** • Bait

Creme Lure Co.

P.O. Box 6162
Tyler, TX 75711
(903) 561-0522
Fax: (903) 561-0555
www.cremelure.com

The originator of the plastic worm, Creme Lure provides a wide variety of soft plastic lures, including worms, lizards, bugs, frogs, crawlers, minnows, lure kits, and trailers. It also offers snelled hooks, walleye rigs, and a large fishing umbrella.

- **Brand Name(s):** Creme Lure.
- **Products:** • Lures

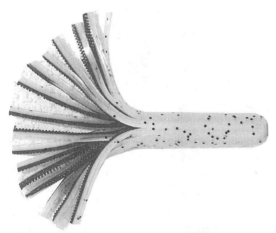

Top: Creme Lure offers its Super Tube Heavy lure in a variety of patterns and colors. *Bottom:* Scoundrel Worm Rigs from Creme Lure are 6-inch worms with a wire leader and propeller.

D.O.A. Lures

3461-b Palm City School Ave.
Palm City, FL 34990
(561) 287-5001
877-DOALURE
Fax: (561) 287-3843
doalures@adelphia.net
www.doalures.com

D.O.A. fishing lures are made of soft plastic and impregnated with farm-grown shrimp to resemble real shrimp, crabs, and bait fish. Orders are taken online, by mail or by fax.

✔ Online shop.
- **Products:** • Lures

Erie Dearie Lures Inc.

2252 Greenville Road
Cortland, OH 44410
(330) 638-6675
(888) 433-2743
Fax: (330) 638-2575
erielure@aol.com
www.eriedearie.com

Erie Dearie makes a variety of fishing lures, including the Erie Dearie, Weapon, Top Doc, and Ambassadear. The company has acquired Hog Hunter and is expanding its line of lures.

- **Brand Name(s):** Erie Dearie.
- **Products:** • Lures

Falcon Lures

112 Plainview Drive
Lafayette, LA 70508
(800) 488-9679
www.falconlures.com

Falcon Lures makes lures, jigs, and hooks that were designed for tournament fishing by Wayne Falcon. Included are the Bait-Jerker Hook, "K" Wacky Hooks, and Flipping Tube Jigheads. It offers online shopping.

- **Brand Name(s):** Falcon Lures.
- ✔ Online shop.
- **Products:** • Jigs • Hooks

Gene Larew Tackle

8121 N. 116th E. Ave.
Owasso, OK 74055
(918) 272-7337
(800) 937-7258
Fax: (918) 272-7317
genelarewtackle@aol.com
www.genelarew.com

Gene Larew introduced the salt-impregnated process in
soft plastic baits in its Salt Craw and patented the
process. The company has a full line of bass, crappie,
walleye, and other soft plastic baits, including Salt
Eggs for trout. It also makes the

■ **Brand Name(s):** Gene Larew.

✔ Online shop.

■ **Products:** • Plastic baits • Jigheads

H&H Lures Co.

10874 N. Dual St.
Baton Rouge, LA 70814
(225) 275-1471
Fax: (225) 275-9953
hhlure@catel.net

H&H Lures produces a variety of fishing lures,
including spinners, hard and soft plastic, rubber
skirts, jigs, spoon, as well as terminal tackle, floats,
and accessories.

■ **Products:** • Lures

Top: The Rattlin' Stick by H&H Lures has been a fishermen's
favorite for many years. *Bottom:* The Original Monster Mullet,
made of white cedar in several varieties, is among the lures produced
by H&H Lures

Hawaii Lure

45-343 Namoku St.
Kaneohe, HI 96744
(808) 247-6796
Fax: (808) 247-2077
fish@hawaiilure.com
www.hawaiilure.com

Hawaii Lure has a variety of lures and fishing tackle for
offshore, shorecasting, and inland fishing, including
Pacific Lure Poppers, Aloha Lures, Island lead
sinkers, Lanikai Lures, Jaslures, TubeBait Flies and
Vibra Lures.

■ **Products:** • Lures

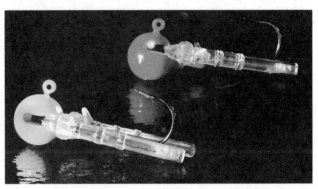

**Headlights use natural light-gathering fiber optics for fish-eye
realism.**

Headlights

34370 E. Frontage Road
Bozeman, MT 59715
(406) 586-0747
Fax: (406) 486-0853
www.headlightlures.com

Headlights use fiber optic materials to gather available
light and concentrate it in the eyes of the fishing jigs.
It uses no chemicals or batteries to light lures on
cloudy days or at twilight. Orders are taken online.

✔ Brochure. ✔ Online shop.

■ **Products:** • Fiber-optic fishing lures

High Tide Tackle Inc.

P.O. Box 41355
Long Beach, CA 90853
(562) 439-6901
Fax: (562) 856-8941
sptfishing@aol.com

High Tide Tackle offers a variety of lures and baits,
including a line of Magic Metals, a Magic Probe, and
Dan's Magic Squid Strips.

■ **Products:** • Lures • Baits

The Magic Probe from High Tide Tackle comes in five sizes to catch saltwater and freshwater fish.

HighRoller Fishing Lure Co. LLC

P.O. Box 357147
Gainesville, FL 32635
(877) 205-1764
Fax: (352) 378-1060
info@hroller.com
www.hroller.com
HighRoller produces a variety of hand-painted fishing lures, including the HighRoller, ChugRoller, RipRoller, and WiggleRoller. Orders are taken online and products are available in stores.
- **Brand Name(s):** HighRoller.
- ✔ Online shop.
- **Products:** • Lures

Hildebrandt Co. LLC

P.O. Box 50
Logansport, IN 46947
(574) 722-4455
Fax: (574) 722-3712
hildyco@hildebrandt.net
www.hildebrandt.net
Hildebrandt, which has been fooling fish since 1899, produces several lines of lures, including original spinners, Premium Blades, No-Lead Series, MicroLite, and Premium Skirts. Catalog orders are taken and products are in stores.
- **Brand Name(s):** Hildebrandt.
- ✔ Brochure.
- **Products:** • Lures

Left: A fisherman who used a Hildebrandt Sareena Spinner shows off a double-header catch. *Right:* A large Indiana steelhead fell for a Colorado Spinner from Hildebrandt.

Hopkins Fishing Lures

3300 Chesapeake Blvd.
Norfolk, VA 23513
(757) 622-0977
Fax: (757) 624-1120
info@hopkinslures.com
www.hopkinslures.com
Hopkins manufactures a line of stainless steel lures, including the Shorty, No=EQL, Smoothie, and Prism. It also offers apparel and accessories. Online shopping is available.
- **Brand Name(s):** Hopkins, Shorty, No=EQL, Smoothie.
- ✔ Online shop.
- **Products:** • Lures • Apparel

Hot Spot Fishing Lures Ltd.

#3-745 Vanalman
Victoria, BC V8Z 3B6
(250) 727-9956
888-744APEX
Fax: (250) 727-9935
www.hotspotlures.com
Hot Spot, based in Canada, manufactures Hot Spot Flasher lures and Apex Trolling Lures as well as Lake Ontario Series Flashers.
- **Brand Name(s):** Hot Spot Flasher, Apex Trolling Lures.
- **Products:** • Lures

Hover-Lure

4530 N. Dixie Highway
Fort Lauderdale, FL 33301
(954) 351-2222
Fax: (954) 351-0500
www.hover-lure.com
Hover-Lure makes lures and lure kits that resemble dragonflies. Orders are taken online.
- **Brand Name(s):** Hover-Lure.
- ✔ Online shop.
- **Products:** • Lures

Illusion Lures Inc.

2401 Tee Circle, Suite 201
Norman, OK 73070
(405) 364-4600
Fax: (405) 364-4604
info@illusionlures.com
www.illusionlures.com
Illusion Lures makes a variety of crankbaits, soft plastics, and soft plastic kits. An online store is available.
- ✔ Online shop.
- **Products:** • Baits

Top: The Bass Buster Kit from Illusion Lures contains a variety of plastic baits. *Bottom:* The Rainbow Trout bait from Illusion Lures is six inches long.

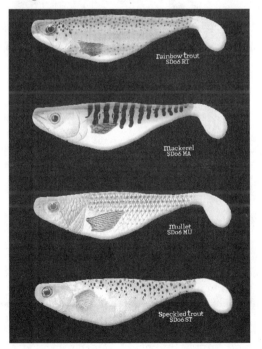

Jack's Juice Bait Spray comes in four flavors: lizard, crawfish, garlic oil, and salty shad.

Jack's Juice

P.O. Box 310
Orchard Hill, GA 30266
800-835FISH
info@jacksjuice.com
www.jacksjuice.com
Jack's Juice makes a variety of bait spray fish attractants, including saltwater sprays, freshwater sprays, as well as accessories such as caps and patches. Products can be ordered online as well as in stores.
- **Brand Name(s):** Jack's Juice.
- ✔ Online shop.
- **Products:** • Bait spray attractants

L&S Bait Co.

1415 E. Bay Drive
Largo, FL 33771
(727) 584-7691
Fax: (727) 487-0784
info@mirrolure.com
www.mirrolure.com
L&S Bait Co. makes L&S original freshwater lures, MirrOlure saltwater lures, and Tournament Tackle Ilander Lures.
- **Brand Name(s):** MirrOlure, L&S Lures, Ilander Lures.
- ✔ Brochure.
- **Products:** • Lures

Lil' Hustler Tackle Co.

639 Fourth Range Road
Pembroke, NH 03275
(603) 224-8856
Fax: (603) 228-4364
www.lilhustler.com
Lil' Hustler Tackle is the manufacturer of premium
  spinner baits, buzz baits, jigs, tubes, and jigheads.
- **Brand Name(s):** Lil' Hustler.
- **Products:** • Lures

Luck E Strike

#1 Industrial Drive
Cassville, MO 65625
(417) 847-3158
Fax: (417) 847-3010
www.luckestrike.com
Luck E Strike has an assortment of soft plastics,
  spinner baits, crankbaits, jigheads, crappie and
  panfish baits.
- **Brand Name(s):** Luck E Strike.
- **Products:** • Baits

Lucky Craft

3001 Red Hill Ave., Building 2-109
Costa Mesa, CA 92626
(714) 241-8484
(800) 270-3117
Fax: (714) 241-8480
info@luckycraft.com
www.luckycraft.com
Lucky Craft makes an assortment of baits and lures,
  including the Pro-Tune Series of crankbaits, spinners,
  jerk baits, big game and saltwater lures, and
  accessories. Online shopping is available and products
  are in stores.
- **Brand Name(s):** Lucky Craft.
- ✔ Brochure. ✔ Online shop.
- **Products:** • Baits

Lucky Strike Bait Works Ltd.

Route 3
2287 Whittington Drive
Peterborough, ON K9J 6X4
(705) 743-3849
Fax: (705) 743-4043
info@luckystrikebaitworks.com
www.luckystrikebaitworks.com
For more than 70 years, Canada-based Lucky Strike has
  been making an assortment of baits as well as fishing
  accessories, including spoons, wobblers, plugs,
  spinners, terminal tackle, and nets.
- **Brand Name(s):** Lucky Strike.
- ✔ Brochure.
- **Products:** • Lures • Terminal tackle • Nets

Luhr Jensen & Sons

P.O. Box 297
400 Portway Ave.
Hood River, OR 97031
(800) 535-1711
info@luhrjensen.com
www.luhr-jensen.com
Luhr Jensen, in business since 1932, manufactures
  fishing tackle, including lures and accessories. It also
  makes Big Chief and Little Chief food smokers.
  Online and catalog sales are available and products
  are in stores.
- **Brand Name(s):** Luhr Jensen.
- ✔ Brochure. ✔ Online shop.
- **Products:** • Fishing tackle • Smokers

Among the arsenal of Lunker Lures is the Triple Rattleback
Monster Grass Jig.

Lunker Lure

P.O. Box 100
Union, SC 29379
(800) 842-0582
Fax: (864) 427-3883
www.lunkerlure.com
Lunker Lure and Hawg Caller merged in 2000 but have
  kept both brand names and complete lines of lure and
  baits, including jigs, spinnerbaits, buzzbaits, plastics,
  and accessories. The www.hawgcaller.com site is also
  active.
- **Brand Name(s):** Lunker Lure, Hawg Caller.
- ✔ Brochure.
- **Products:** • Lures

Mad Man Lures

4217 Canyon Drive
Amarillo, TX 79109
(806) 331-0030
(866) 623-6261
Fax: (806) 463-2051
www.madmanlures.com
Mad Man Lures specializes in crawfish tubes and
   crawfish worms in various colors and sizes. Online
   shopping is available, as well as a catalog.
■ **Brand Name(s):** Mad Man Lures.
✔ Brochure. ✔ Online shop.
■ **Products:** • Lures

Top: **Buss Bed-ding by Magic Products keeps nightcrawlers and
worms clean, fresh, and lively.** *Bottom:* **Rainbow Marshmallow Bait
from Magic Products comes in garlic, cheese, shrimp, and anise
flavors.**

 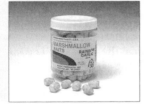

Magic Products Inc.

3931 Second St.
Amherst, WI 54407
(715) 824-3100
Fax: (715) 824-5225
sales@magicproducts.com
www.magicproducts.com
■ **Brand Name(s):** Aerobait, Buss, Brown Bear,
   Magic, Tournament Series

✔ Brochure.
■ **Products:** • Bait containers • Marshmallow bai •
   Preserved baits • Simulated salmo • Plastic lures •
   Trout bait

Mann's Bait Co.

1111 State Docks Road
Eufaula, AL 36027
(334) 687-5716
mannsbait@us.inter.net
www.mannsbait.com
Mann's Bait is a diversified lure maker with
   manufacturing capabilities in crankbaits, soft plastics,
   spinnerbaits, lead lures, and hollow body baits. The
   company's products are used by fishermen in more
   than 50 countries. An online store is available.
✔ Brochure. ✔ Online shop.
■ **Products:** • Lures

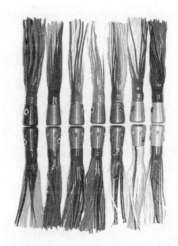

**MP Lures' line of aluminum head lures comes in a variety of colors
for the heads and skirts.**

Marine Products Group LLC

2482 Clark St.
Apopka, FL 32703
(407) 523-1350
866-MPLURES
Fax: (407) 523-2033
www.mplures.com
Marine Products Group makes MP Lures, most with
   machined aluminum, stainless steel, or chrome-plated
   heads and skirts, in a variety of colors and sizes. The
   company also makes line guides, rod tips, and rod
   holders. Online shopping is available.
■ **Brand Name(s):** MP Lures.
✔ Brochure. ✔ Online shop.
■ **Products:** • Lures

Matzuo America Inc.

4770 C Forest St.
Denver, CO 80216
(720) 941-9400
customerservice@matzuo.com
www.matzuo.com

Matzuo America offers an assortment of baits, including soft baits, bass plastics, jigs, the Depth Charge, Jitter Rat, Warthog, and Lizards. Online shopping is available.

✔ Online shop.
■ **Products:** • Lures

Meier's Fish Bait

P.O. Box 833
Draper, UT 84020
866-FISHBAIT
sales@predatorfishbait.com
www.predatorfishbait.com

Meier's Fish Bait makes Predator Baits from ground meat in several colors and garlic, cheese, fish, corn, anise, and caramel flavors.

■ **Brand Name(s):** Predator Baits.
✔ Brochure. ✔ Online shop.
■ **Products:** • Baits

Millennium Lures Inc.

P.O. Box 885
306 S. Hayes
Wagoner, OK 74477
(918) 485-9311
(866) 485-0072
Fax: (918) 485-1664
mlures@aol.com
www.millennium-lures.com

Millennium Lures is a manufacturer of hard plastics and soft plastics, including the Lookalike series, Illusion series of holographic lures, and Bass Candy soft plastics.

■ **Brand Name(s):** Millennium Lures.
✔ Brochure.
■ **Products:** • Soft and hard plastic baits

Mizmo Bait Co.

3221 Shelby Drive
Jonesboro, AR 72404
(870) 932-2490
Fax: (870) 932-0146
pam@mizmo.com
www.mizmo.com

Mizmo is a premier tube manufacturer, making soft plastic lures including lizards, grubs, and many sizes and styles of tubes. Its Web site also includes fishing tips, a Bragging Board, and information on their pro fishing team.

■ **Brand Name(s):** Mizmo.
■ **Products:** • Lures

NGC Sports

60 Church St.
Yalesville, CT 06492
(800) 873-4415
www.ngcsports.com

NGC Sports markets the Kicktail and Walking Worm baits.

■ **Brand Name(s):** Kicktail, Walking Worm.
■ **Products:** • Baits

The **Illusion Series** from **Millennium Lures** features holographic high-loss reflective, double-gel coated lures.

The new Nils Master Big Mouth has an open mouth to allow water to flow through to lure and give it a swimming motion.

Nils Master USA Inc.

P.O. Box 160
Jericho, VT 05465
(802) 899-1209
(800) 650-7472
Fax: (802) 899-5535
www.nilsmaster.com
Nils Master USA offers a full line of freshwater and saltwater lures, including ice fishing jigs. Its latest product is the Big Mouth lure with an open mouth that allows water to flow through.
■ **Brand Name(s):** Nils Master.
✔ Brochure.
■ **Products:** • Lures

Old Bayside Tackle Co.

P.O. Box 35543
Tulsa, OK 74153
(918) 477-7543
oldbayside@aol.com
www.oldbayside.com
Old Bayside makes a variety of baits, including freshwater soft plastic, jigheads, saltwater soft plastic, and OldBayside Kits.
■ **Brand Name(s):** Old Bayside.
■ **Products:** • Baits

Old Whiskers Catfish Bait

P.O. Box 145
O'Fallon, IL 62269
(618) 632-5561
Fax: (618) 632-5773
whiskers@icss.net
www.oldwhiskersbait.com
Old Whiskers, founded in 1952, produces dough bait, dip bait, and accessories to catch catfish. Online shopping is available.

■ **Brand Name(s):** Old Whiskers Catfish Bait.
✔ Online shop.
■ **Products:** • Catfish bait

Pace Products Inc.

1050-A S. Cypress St.
La Habra, CA 90631
(714) 773-4132
Fax: (714) 773-0562
www.pacemarine.com
Pace Products is the manufacturer of MegaBait Lures, including jigs, jerk baits, crankbaits, plastic worms, and trolling lures for saltwater and freshwater, as well as leaders, fish pens, and gift items.
■ **Brand Name(s):** MegaBait.
■ **Products:** • Lures

Panther Martin/Harrison Hoge Industries

19 N. Columbia St.
Port Jefferson, NY 11777
(631) 473-7308
(800) 852-0925
Fax: (631) 473-7398
www.panther-martin.com
Panther Martin lures include a wide variety of spinners, the Superior Frog line, and lure kits. The Web site has a discussion board, trophy fish photos, and online shopping.
■ **Brand Name(s):** Panther Martin.
✔ Online shop.
■ **Products:** • Lures

Paragon Plastics Inc.

P.O. Box 100
Union, SC 29379
(800) 842-0582
Fax: (864) 427-3883
sales@lunkerlure.com
www.lunkerlure.com
Lunker Lure and Hawg Caller, two regional bass lure companies, joined in 2000 and now bring a variety of spinnerbaits, buzzbaits, jigs, and soft plastics. Online shopping is available and products are in stores.
■ **Brand Name(s):** Lunker Lure, Hawg Caller.
✔ Online shop.
■ **Products:** • Bass lures

Persuader American Angling

P.O. Box 3207
Danville, CA 94526
(925) 820-5543
Fax: (925) 831-3502
www.persuaderamerican.com

Persuader American makes Persuader Bass Baits and Assassinator Bass Baits. Online shopping is available and products are in stores.
- **Brand Name(s):** Persuader, Assassinator.
- ✔ Online shop.
- **Products:** • Baits

Pradco Outdoor Brands

P.O. Box 1587
Fort Smith, AR 72902
(479) 782-8971
Fax: (479) 783-0234
www.lurenet.com

Pradco features fishing brands, primarily lures, line and fish attractants, including Rebel, Excalibur, Bomber, and Cotton Cordell. Lurenet.com is an online sales outlet and also offers fishing information.
- **Brand Name(s):** Bomber, Cotton Cordell, Excalibur, Lazy Ike, Quik Bite, Rebel, Silver Thread.
- ✔ Online shop.
- **Products:** • Lures • Line • Attractants

Preston Lures

1640 Evans Ave.
San Francisco, CA 94124
(415) 641-0492
info@prestonlures.com
www.prestonlures.com

Preston Lures has introduced its new Flyin' Fish Lure, with a patented Afterburner system that provides a magnetic heartbeat. The rotating internal magnetic pulse system activates soft plastic wings.
- **Brand Name(s):** Preston, Flyin' Fish Lure.
- **Products:** • Lures

Producers/LMN Enterprises

327 W. Kalamazoo Ave., Suite 105
Kalamazoo, MI 49007
(616) 345-8172
(888) 830-9211
Fax: (616) 345-3077

The Producers carry a full range of hard baits, spinners, spoons, and soft plastics for freshwater and saltwater.
- **Brand Name(s):** The Producers.
- **Products:** • Lures

Realures LLC

9010 River Road, Building 91
Chalmetto, LA 70123
(504) 279-0683
(800) 455-9395
realures@aol.com
www.realures.com

Realures manufactures lures that are true replicas of living creatures.
- **Brand Name(s):** Realures.
- **Products:** • Lures

The Afterburner system powers the soft plastic wings on Preston Lures' new Flyin' Fish.

"Topwater chuggers" of Duff's Beer and Imitation Gruel from "The Simpsons" are among the collectable lures marketed by Relic Lures.

Relic Lures
31387 Pacific Coast Highway
Malibu, CA 90265
(760) 736-0057
info@reliclures.com
www.reliclures.com
Relic Lures has developed several collectible lures based on licensed TV or movie characters, including The Simpsons, Reservoir Dogs, and Guardians of Atlantis.
■ **Brand Name(s):** Relic Lures.
✔ Brochure.
■ **Products:** • Collectible lures

RT Tackle Inc.
5719-1 Corporation Circle
Ft. Myers, FL 33905
(239) 693-7070
(800) 869-9941
Fax: (239) 693-2282
RT Tackle makes Key Largo Tackle branded lures and Wazp Quality Fishing Tackle. It is also affiliated with the Bagley line of lures.
■ **Brand Name(s):** Wazp, Key Largo.

✔ Brochure.
■ **Products:** • Lures • Floats

Silver Buddy Lures
Route 1, Box 80
Greenup, KY 41144
(606) 473-6331
(888) 862-8339
information@zoomnet.net
www.silverbuddy.com
After 20 years of making Silver Buddy blade baits for freshwater, Silver Buddy has added Big Gamefish Series stainless steel saltwater baits in three sizes.
■ **Brand Name(s):** Silver Buddy Lures.
■ **Products:** • Lures

Sliding Weight Hooks & Baits
4805 N. Saint Mary's, Suite 1
Beeville, TX 78102
(361) 354-5700
Fax: (361) 358-9327
www.slidingweighthooksandbaits.com
Sliding Weight makes a variety of hooks and weights for soft plastic baits, using a sliding weight system on the hook.
■ **Brand Name(s):** Sliding Weight Hooks & Baits.
✔ Brochure.
■ **Products:** • Weighted hooks

Smirk Tackle Co.
8282 Atlanta Ave. #10
Huntington Beach, CA 92646
(800) 475-5954
www.smirktackle.com
Scott Mueller of Smirk Tackle makes "S" Series Plugs, which are designed, turned, drilled, painted and filled by hand, one at a time.
■ **Products:** • Lures

Smith Bait Manufacturing Co.
P.O. Box 462
Minocqua, WI 54548
(715) 356-5565
Fax: (715) 356-5381
Smith Bait makes the Smity Muskie Baits in sizes from four to 10 inches, plus leaders, hook sharpeners, and sucker rigs.
■ **Brand Name(s):** Smity Muskie Bait.
■ **Products:** • Lures

A big bass grabs a taste of a Snag Proof frog bait.

Southern Lure Company

P.O. Box 2244
201 North Browder
Columbus, Mississippi 39704
662/327-4548
FAX 662/327-4557

The Scum Frog line by Southern Lures is soft plastic in many color choices.

Snag Proof Mfg. Inc./Sea Bay Lures

11387 Deerfield Road
Cincinnati, OH 45242
(513) 489-6483
800-SNAGPRF
Fax: (513) 489-0387
www.snagproof.com
Snag Proof produces 23 different styles of weedless lures, including frogs, mice, lizards, worms, crankbaits, buzzbaits, and poppers. It has added the Sea Bay line of saltwater lures. The Web site features an online store.
■ **Brand Name(s):** Snag Proof, Sea Bay.
✔ Online shop.
■ **Products:** • Lures

Southern Lure Co.

P.O. Box 2244
201 N. Browder
Columbus, MS 39704
(662) 327-4548
Fax: (662) 327-4557
Southern Lure makes Scum Frog and Bassrat weedless, soft body lures, poppers, Thundertoad buzzbaits, and TinyToads.
■ **Brand Name(s):** Scum Frog, Bassrat.
■ **Products:** • Lures

The Powerbuss Bait is one of many lures produced by Strike On as part of its Hammerin' Hare Series.

Strike On Lures

P.O. Box 1935
Edwards, CO 81632
(877) 634-8170
info@strikeon.com
www.strikeon.com
Strike On makes a variety of baits and lures, including rabbit hair jigs, spinnerbaits, and power buzz bait, as well as the Kickin' Bass Scent. Online shopping is available.
- **Brand Name(s):** Strike On Lures.
✔ Online shop.
- **Products:** • Lures

Thompson-Pallister Bait Co. Inc.

5860 Len Thompson Drive
Lacombe, AL T4L 1E7
(403) 782-3528
Fax: (403) 782-3533
www.lenthompson.com
Len Thompson Lures have been manufactured since 1929. They are available in 12 sizes and a wide array of color patterns. Online shopping is available.
- **Brand Name(s):** Len Thompson Lures.
✔ Online shop.
- **Products:** • Lures

Thornwood Lures Inc.

P.O. Box 186
Thornwood, NY 10594
(914) 773-0523
Fax: (914) 769-5136
www.thornwoodlures.com
Thornwood Lures are hand-carved from white cedar and basswood, then hand-tuned. Lures include poppers, prop baits, and bird lures.
- **Brand Name(s):** Thornwood Lures.
✔ Brochure.
- **Products:** • Hand-carved lures

Timberline Fisheries

201 E. Timberline Road
Marion, IL 62959
(800) 423-2248
Fax: (618) 997-4692
www.timberlinefisheries.com
Timberline Fisheries is a leading live bait producer of crickets, worms, nightcrawlers, as well as containers.
✔ Brochure.
- **Products:** • Live bait

Uncle Josh Bait Co.

P.O. Box 130
Fort Atkinson, WI 53538
(920) 563-2491
Fax: (920) 563-8622
www.unclejosh.com
Uncle Josh, in business since 1920, makes an assortment of baits from pork rinds and other products for bass, trout, panfish, catfish, and walleyes. It also sells preserved natural baits, inclluding worms, leeches, minnows, and crawfish. Products are
- **Brand Name(s):** Uncle Josh.
✔ Brochure.
- **Products:** • Pork baits • Preserved baits

WiggleFin Inc.

2109 Madison Ave.
Boise, ID 83702
(208) 388-8539
Fax: (208) 338-5227
info@wigglefin.com
www.wigglefin.com

WiggleFin makes Action Discs to attach to bait that is cast or trolled and adds a swimming action.

Top: The new Muskie Tail Spinner from Worden's Lures comes in 12 colors and is constructed of heavy duty wire. *Bottom:* The popular Worden's Rooster Tail is now available in four new colors featuring glitter blades.

FlashDance decals can be added to the discs for color, and Drunken Stripper trolling rigs or WiggleRigs are also available for online or catalog shoppers.

■ **Brand Name(s):** WiggleFin, Action Discs.
✔ Brochure. ✔ Online shop.
■ **Products:** • Swimming bait discs • Trolling rigs

Wigston's Lures

28 Gepp Parade, Derwent Park
Tasmania, AU 7010
enquiries@wigstonslures.com.au
www.wigstonslures.com.au

Wigston's Lures, located in Tasmania, Australia, offers many variations of its Tasmanian Devil Lures for trolling, casting or jigging.

■ **Brand Name(s):** Tasmanian Devil.
■ **Products:** • Lures

Yakima Bait Co.

P.O. Box 310
Granger, WA 98932
(509) 854-1311
(800) 527-2711
Fax: (509) 854-2263
www.yakimabait.com

Since 1932, Worden's Lures have been produced, including the Rooster Tail spinner, Lil' Corky and Spin-N-Glo drift bobbers, FlatFish, and new Timber Tiger crankbaits.

■ **Brand Name(s):** Worden's Lures.
■ **Products:** • Lures • Drift bobbers

Yamashita USA

P.O. Box 1197
Honolulu, HI 96807
(808) 591-6500
Fax: (808) 596-9468

Yamashita makes baits and lures, including octopus and squid skirts, hard lures, bass lures, and bait rigs.

■ **Products:** • Lures

Rods and Reels

Ambassadeur Reels from Abu Garcia are well known among anglers for their performance.

Abu Garcia

1900 18th St.
Spirit Lake, IA 51360
(800) FISH838
www.abu-garcia.com
Abu Garcia has been making rods and reels for more than 60 years, including Ambassadeur reels. A division of Pure Fishing, it also has a line of clothing and merchandise.
- **Brand Name(s):** Abu Garcia, Ambassadeur.
- **Products:** • Rods and reels • Clothing

All Star Graphite Rods Inc.

9817 Whithorn
Houston, TX 77095
(281) 855-9603
www.allstarrods.com
All Star uses seven different advanced graphite materials in its 12 lines of hand crafted fishing rods.
- **Brand Name(s):** All Star Graphic Rods.
- **Products:** • Fishing rods

American Fishing Tackle Co. (AFTCO Mfg.)

17351 Murphy Ave.
Irvine, CA 92614
(949) 660-8757
(800) 452-3726
Fax: (949) 660-7067
www.aftco.com
For 40 years, AFTCO has been making saltwater fishing tackle. It has added pliers, downriggers, gaffs, bait nets, and clothing to its product line.
- **Products:** • Downriggers • Gaffs

American Premier Corp.

13771 Roswell Ave. #6
Chino, CA 91710
(909) 590-8680
Fax: (909) 590-1686
American Premier makes fishing rods and reels, blanks, combos, fishing line, wooden floats, leaders, and terminal tackle.
- **Brand Name(s):** Premier.
- **Products:** • Rod and Reels • Terminal Tack

Anglers Resource LLC

400 E. Section Ave.
Foley, AL 36535
(251) 943-4491
Fax: (215) 943-4493
Anglers Resource is the agent/distributor for quality rod components of Fuji, Hopkins & Holloway, and Fish Hawk, marketing rod guides, tops, reel seats, handles, glue, grip material, and rod-wrapping threads.
- **Products:** • Rod components

Avet Reels

9687 Topanga Canyon Place
Chatsworth, CA 91311
(818) 576-9895
(877) 487-4476
Fax: (818) 576-9896
reels@avetreels.com
www.avetreels.com
Avet Reels makes fishing reels in a variety of models, including the JX Series, LX Series, and new single-speed model, as well as parts and accessories.
- **Brand Name(s):** Avet Reels.
- **Products:** • Fishing reels

Biscayne Rod Manufacturing Inc.

425 E. 9th St.
Hialeah, FL 33010
(305) 884-0808
Fax: (305) 884-3017
bisrod@aol.com
www.biscaynerod.com
Biscayne Rod has been manufacturing fine fishing rods since 1948 in every pound and weight class, including trolling, casting, spinning, and fly rods.
- **Brand Name(s):** Biscayne, Billy Baroo.
- **Products:** • Fishing rods

BnM Pole Co.

P.O. Box 231
West Point, MS 39773
(662) 494-5092
(800) 647-6363
Fax: (662) 494-7211
buck@bnmpoles.com
www.bnmpoles.com
Since 1940, BnM Pole Co. has provided fishing poles for the panfishing market. Products include Buck's Series graphite poles and rods, Sam Heaton Signature Series, Sunny's Bamboo Poles, fiberglass telescopic poles, the Tuff-Lite Series.
- **Brand Name(s):** BnM Poles.
- **Products:** • Fishing poles

Cape Fear Rod Co.

302-A Raleigh St.
Wilmington, NC 28412
(910) 350-0494
Fax: (910) 350-2878
hextek@capefearrod.com
www.capefearrodcompany.com
Cape Fear Fishing Rods feature Hextek Technology in its graphite rods, including the Blue Water Series, Live Bait Series, Big Game Fly Rods, Advance Tech Series, and EXT Series. It also makes Fin-Nor Fishing Reels.
- **Brand Name(s):** Cape Fear Fishing Rods, Fin-Nor Reels.
- **Products:** • Fishing rods

CastAway Graphite Rods

118 Cape Conroe Drive
Montgomery, TX 77356
(936) 582-1677
Fax: (936) 582-1679
castaway@flex.net
www.castawayrods.com
Castaway makes graphite fishing rods, including bass rods, saltwater rods, high modulus graphite, and a new line of titanium rods. They carry a five-year limited replacement warranty. It also sells a line of outdoor clothing.
- **Brand Name(s):** CastAway.
- ✔ Brochure.
- **Products:** • Fishing rods

Falcon Graphite Rods

1823 W. Reno
Broken Arrow, OK 74012
(918) 251-0020
Fax: (938) 250-0021
www.falconrods.com
Falcon Rods pioneered making different rods for specific types of fishing and offers a wide range of products, including the Silver, LowRider XG, Cara, and Expert Series of freshwater rods, and the Coastal, Kingfish Special, and Deep Blue Series.
- **Brand Name(s):** Falcon Graphite Rods.
- ✔ Online shop.
- **Products:** • Fishing rods

Fenwick Fishing

1900 18th St.
Spirit Lake, IA 51360
877-FENRODS
www.fenwickfishing.com
Fenwick Fishing manufactures graphite fishing rods, including fly rods, freshwater and saltwater rods, salmon/steelhead rods, as well as fly reels and fly line, and clothing.
- **Brand Name(s):** Fenwick, Fenglass, Eagle GT, Saltstik, HMG AV, Pacificstik Supreme.
- ✔ Brochure.
- **Products:** • Rods • Fly reels • Fly line • Clothing

G. Loomis Inc.

1359 Down River Drive
Woodland, WA 98674
(360) 225-6516
800-GLoomis
Fax: (360) 225-7169
loomis@gloomis.com
www.gloomis.com
G. Loomis manufactures several lines of spinning, casting, and fly fishing rods, including rods for bass, muskies, walleye, salmon, trout, and panfish, as well as travel rods and push poles for boats.
- **Brand Name(s):** G. Loomis.
- **Products:** • Fishing rods

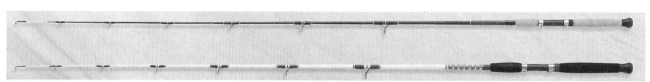

Biscayne rods offers several models of spinning rods in the graphite Billy Baroo Series and the Shakespeare Ugly Stick Spin Series.

Hookhider Fishing Rods

P.O. Box 811
22C Court Square
Gainesville, MO 65655
(417) 679-2622
(877) 999-4665
Fax: (417) 679-3515
www.hookhider.com
Hookhider Rods feature a patented grip design with a slotted tubular section that stores the lure when not in use. The grip can be used on other rods and Hookhider manufactures its own lightweight graphite rods with gold stainless steel line guides a
■ **Brand Name(s):** Hookhider.
✔ Brochure.
■ **Products:** • Fishing rods • Rod grips

Johnson

1900 18th St.
Spirit Lake, IA 51360
(877) 508-3474
johnson@purefishing.com
www.fishjohnson.com
Johnson Reels have been made for more than 50 years, and the company also makes Johnson Lures, including the Silver Minnow, BassBuster Beetle Spin, Sprite, and others.
✔ Brochure.
■ **Products:** • Reels • Lures

Lamiglas Inc.

1400 Atlantic Ave.
P.O. Box 1000
Woodland, WA 98674
(360) 225-9436
Fax: (360) 225-5050
fishon@lamiglas.com
www.lamiglas.com
Lamiglas manufactures quality graphite and fiberglass fishing rods and blanks for fly fishing, bass, salmon and steelhead, and freshwater and saltwater specialty uses. Online shopping is available and products are in stores.
■ **Brand Name(s):** Lamiglas.
✔ Brochure. ✔ Online shop.
■ **Products:** • Fishing rods

Lew's

6505 Tower Lane
Claremore, OK 74017
(800) 588-9030
www.lews.com
Lew's has been making rods and reels since the 1940s. Included are baitcast reels, spinning reels, and Dave

Lew's Laser Baitcast reel features a three-bearing system, continuous anti-reverse, and thumb bar spool release.

Fritt's Signature Series Rods.
■ **Brand Name(s):** Lew's.
✔ Brochure.
■ **Products:** • Rods and reels

Marado Rods & Reels

19247 80th Ave. South
Kent, WA 98032
(253) 395-3355
(800) 748-7153
Fax: (253) 395-9594
maradoz@msn.com
www.marado.com
Marado manufactures quality rods and reels.
■ **Brand Name(s):** Marado
■ **Products:** • Rods and reels

Martin Classic Fly Tackle

P.O. Box 270
Tulsa, OK 74101
(918) 836-5581
Fax: (918) 836-0154
www.martinfishing.com
Martin produces a variety of fly fishing equipment, including rods, reels, and combos.
■ **Brand Name(s):** Martin.
✔ Brochure.
■ **Products:** • Rods and reels

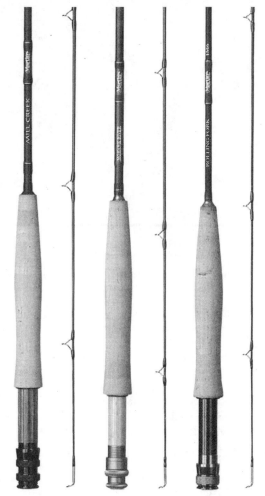

Martin Classic Fly Tackle has added three new rods to its arsenal, including the Mill Creek, Mohawk River, and Rolling Fork.

Master Fishing Tackle Corp.

1009 E. Bedmar St.
Carson, CA 90746
(310) 631-5188
Fax: (310) 631-6054
Master Fishing Tackle offers a complete line of freshwater and saltwater rods and reels.
- ■ **Products:** • Rods and reels

Mitchell

1900 18th St.
Spirit Lake, IA 51360
(877) 502-6482
mitchell@purefishing.com
www.fishmitchell.com
Mitchell manufactures spinning reels, and combos, as well as clothing.
- ■ **Brand Name(s):** Mitchell.
- ✔ Brochure.
- ■ **Products:** • Spinning reels • Clothing

Oceaner Products USA

1345 S. Parkside Place
Ontario, CA 91761
(909) 673-1819
(866) 275-9577
Fax: (909) 673-0648
Oceaner Products offers a full line of quality freshwater and saltwater King Hawk rods and reels as well as combos.
- ■ **Products:** • Rods and reels

Penn Fishing Tackle Mfg. Co.

3028 W. Hunting Park Ave.
Philadelphia, PA 19132
(215) 229-9415
Fax: (215) 223-3017
www.pennreels.com
Penn, which has been making fishing tackle since 1933, makes an extensive line of reels, rods, and downriggers, with 280 products in all. Included are bait casting, spinning and fly reels, Tuna Stick, Power Stick, Spinfisher, Sabre and Power Graph rods.
- ■ **Brand Name(s):** Penn.
- ■ **Products:** • Rods and reels • Downriggers

Pflueger

3801 Westmore Drive
Columbia, SC 29223
(803) 754-7000
www.pfluegerfishing.com
Pflueger, which has been making fishing equipment since 1881, is now part of the Shakespeare company. Pflueger makes fly fishing rods and reels, as well as vests, plus the Trion line of spinning and baitcasting rods and reels.
- ■ **Brand Name(s):** Pflueger, Trion.
- ✔ Brochure.
- ■ **Products:** • Rods and reels

Quantum

6505 Tower Lane
Claremore, OK 74017
(800) 588-9030
www.quantumfishing.com
Quantum makes a variety of rods, reels, combos, and fishing gear under the brand names Quantum, Zebco, Lew's, Browning, and Martin.
- ■ **Brand Name(s):** Quantum, Zebco, Lew's, Browning, Martin.
- ✔ Brochure.
- ■ **Products:** • Rods and reels

Quarrow

2325 Vancouver St.
Broken Arrow, OK 74012
(888) 568-5026
www.quarrow.com
Quarrow makes fishing rods for every kind of water
and every kind of fish, including lines of freshwater,
saltwater, and fly fishing rods.
- ■ Brand Name(s): Quarrow.
- ■ Products: • Fishing rods

Rods by Sirrus

4820 Intrepid Drive
Las Vegas, NV 89130
(702) 395-2173
Fax: (702) 395-5429
ken@sirrusrods.com
www.sirrusrods.com
Rods by Sirrus has introduced a new line of titanium
Ultimate Ti rods to its existing Co-Matrix Filament
Wound line. It makes rods for casting, spinning,
cranking, muskies, and fly rods.
- ■ **Brand Name(s):** Sirrus.
- ■ **Products:** • Fishing rods

Shikari Inc.

P.O. Box 549
Kellyville, OK 74039
(918) 247-3090
Fax: (918) 247-3269
www.shikariblanks.com
Shikari makes fishing rod blanks in graphite and
fiberglass for a variety of fishing, both freshwater and
saltwater. A line of clothing is also available. Products
are sold online as well as in stores.
- ■ **Brand Name(s):** Shikari.
- ✔ Brochure. ✔ Online shop.
- ■ **Products:** • Fishing rod blanks

Shimano American Corp.

One Holland Drive
Irvine, CA 92618
(949) 951-5003
(877) 577-0600
www.fish.shimano.com
Shimano produces baitcasting reels, spinning reels,
conventional reels, freshwater rods, saltwater rods,
combos, and accessories.
- ■ **Brand Name(s):** Shimano.
- ■ **Products:** • Rods • Reels • Accessories

The **Shimano** spinning reel family is available to fishermen though a variety of sources, including White's Outdoor catalog.

Silstar/Pinnacle Corp. of America Inc.

P.O. Box 6505
1141 Silstar Road
West Columbia, SC 29170
(803) 794-8521
Fax: (803) 794-8544
www.silstar.com
Silstar manufactures rods and reels under the brand
names Silstar, Pinnacle, Pinnacle Limited Edition, and
FishBonz.
- ■ **Brand Name(s):** Silstar, Pinnacle, Pinnacle Limited
Edition, FishBonz
- ■ **Products:** • Rods • Reels

Spidercast

1900 18th St.
Spirit Lake, IA 53160
(877) 502-7743
spidercast@purefishing.com
www.fishspidercast.com
Spidercast Reels are designed for spinning and
baitcasting. The division of Pure Fishing also makes a
line of clothing.
- ■ **Brand Name(s):** Spidercast.
- ✔ Brochure.
- ■ **Products:** • Fishing reels

St. Croix Rods

856 4th Ave. North
P.O. Box 279
Park Falls, WI 54552
(715) 762-3226
(800) 826-7042
Fax: (715) 762-3293
www.stcroixrods.com
St. Croix Rods, more than 50 years old, makes a wide
assortment of fishing rods, including fly rods,
spinning and casting rods, and saltwater rods. It also
sells clothing and accessories.
- ■ **Brand Name(s):** St. Croix.
- ■ **Products:** • Fishing rods • Clothing

Supreme Products Inc.
Route 1, Box 8A
Superior, NB 68978
(402) 879-4755
(888) 298-7918
Fax: (402) 879-4755
Supreme Products makes Catfish Getters, new
  lightweight fiberglass bankline poles complete with
  line, sinker, swivel, and hook.
- **Brand Name(s):** Catfish Getters.
- ✔ Online shop.
- **Products:** • Fishing poles

The namesake Teton line of reels is available in more than a dozen
models from Teton Fly Reels.

Teton Fly Reels Inc.
924 Church Hill Road
San Andreas, CA 95249
(209) 754-4709
Fax: (209) 754-4716
info@tetonflyreels.com
www.tetonflyreels.com
Teton makes several models of fly fishing reels,
  machined from premium aluminum and sealed for
  saltwater durability.
- **Brand Name(s):** Teton Fly Reels.
- ✔ Brochure.
- **Products:** • Fly fishing reels

Thomas & Thomas Rodmakers Inc.
627 Barton Road
Greenfield, MA 01301
(413) 774-5436
Fax: (413) 774-5437
info@thomasandthomas.com
www.thomasandthomas.com
Thomas & Thomas makes several series of fly-fishing
  rods, including double-handed rods, split cane rods,
  and briefcase rods. It also makes reels and accessories
  such as clothing, leather goods, fly boxes, and nets.
  Sales are by catalog and through de
- **Brand Name(s):** Thomas & Thomas.
- ✔ Brochure.
- **Products**: • Fly rods • Reels • Clothing

An angler holds a rainbow trout caught fly fishing using a Thomas
and Thomas Double-Handed Series fly rod.

Titan Rods
2805 Silverglade Drive
Oklahoma City, OK 73120
405-74TITAN
sales@titanrods.com
www.titanrods.com
Titan Rods have a dual grip that is ergonomic for
  comfort and sensitivity. Orders are taken online as
  well as through dealers.
- **Brand Name(s):** Titan Rods.
- **Products:** • Fishing rods

Ultracom International
3760 Prospect Ave.
Yorba Linda, CA 92886
(714) 792-0838
800-GOUKUMA
Fax: (714) 792-0983
www.okumafishing.com
Ultracom International makes the Okuma line of rods
  and reels, including a full line of trolling reels,
  spinning reels, a variety of rods, combos, and fly
  fishing rods and reels, as well as accessories.
- **Brand Name(s):** Okuma.
- ✔ Brochure. ✔ Online shop.
- **Products:** • Rods and reels

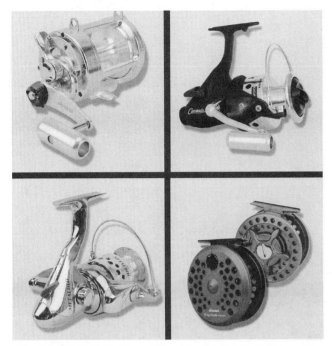

A variety of reels, including trolling, spinning, and fly fishing, awaits the angler from Okuma.

A selection of YAD America's fishing rods are displayed.

Van Staal

3-B Landing Lane
Hopedale, MA 01747
(800) 718-7335
Fax: (631) 734-2251
www.vanstaal.com
Van Staal makes VS Series spinning reels, C-Vex Series fly reels, and titanium fishing pliers.
- **Brand Name(s):** Van Staal.
- **Products:** • Reels • Pliers

WristSaver Rods Inc.

P.O. Box 223
Prior Lake, MN 55372
Near Minneapolis
(952) 440-1152
(877) 721-0020
info@wristsaverrods.com
www.wristsaverrods.com
Rod/reel combinations range from $39.99 to $155. WristSaver specialized in ergonomic spinning rods and reels; ergonomic ice-fishing rods and reels.
- **Brand Name(s):** WristSaver Rods
- **Products:** • Spinning rods • Reels

YAD America

99 Grand St. #17
Moonachie, NJ 07074
(201) 672-0216
Fax: (201) 672-0217
YAD America is a rod company that produces all categories of fishing rods, including freshwater rods, saltwater rods, fly rods, and poles.
Products: • Rods

Zebco

6505 Tower Lane
Claremore, OK 74017
(80) 058-9030
www.zebco.com
Zebco has been making fishing rods and reels for more than 50 years, since R.D. Hull invented the spincast reel in 1945. It is now a division of Quantum.
- **Brand Name(s):** Zebco.
- ✔ Brochure.
- **Products:** • Rods and reels

Zebco's Omega reel features a six-bearing system with oscillating spool and aircraft aluminum covers.

Boats

Action Craft Inc.

2603 Andalusia Blvd.
Cape Coral, FL 33909
(941) 574-7008
Fax: (941) 574-1152
www.actioncraft.com

Action Craft makes several models of coastal and inshore fishing boats of fiberglass, with deep-V design, a wide beam, and a Pocket Drive for navigating in eight inches of water. Models include the Action Craft line of flats and fly fishing boats.
- ■ **Brand Name(s):** Action Craft, Coastline.
- ✔ Brochure.
- ■ **Products:** • Fishing boats

Aquasport

1651 Whitfield Ave.
Sarasota, FL 34243
(941) 753-7811
Fax: (941) 751-7822
www.aquasport.com

Aquasport, in operation since 1964 and a part of Genmar, manufactures 14 models of fiberglass and urethane boats from 16 feet to 27 feet, designed for offshore and big inland water use. Its fishing boats have had a number of industry firsts.
- ■ **Brand Name(s):** Aquasport.
- ✔ Brochure.
- ■ **Products:** • Fishing boats

Aries Boats/Fiberglass Works Inc.

2111 Highway 47 East
Dickson, TN 37055
(615) 446-8513
(888) 296-2821
ariesbts@bellsouth.net
www.ariesboats.com

Fiberglass Works has been manufacturing custom-built Aries Boats since 1981 in sizes from 16 feet to 21 1/2 feet. The fiberglass boats are hand-laid and feature a limited lifetime transom warranty.
- ■ **Brand Name(s):** Aries Boats.
- ✔ Brochure.
- ■ **Products:** • Fishing boats

An Aquasport 275EXP loaded with fishing gear trolls for fish as a trio of fishermen await a bite.

The Aries 2100 Series features rod lockers, ice chests, a 50-gallon fuel storage tank, and an outboard up to 300 horsepower.

Bass Baby

1000 Flag Road
Adair, IA 50002
(877) 742-3071
info@connectadock.com
www.connectadock.com

Connect-A-Dock Inc. makes a portable, eight-foot, two-person boat that fits in a pickup truck bed and weighs 143 pounds, with space to attach a motor.
- ■ **Brand Name(s):** Bass Baby.
- ■ **Products:** • Portable fishing boats

Bass Cat

P.O. Drawer 1688
Mountain Home, AR 72654
(870) 481-5135
www.basscat.com

Bass Cat has been making fishing boats since 1971 and its current line runs from the 17-foot Phelix to the 20-foot Jaguar. All have fiberglass construction with a transferrable lifetime warranty. Bass Cat also makes boat trailers.
■ **Brand Name(s):** Bass Cat
✔ Brochure.
■ **Products:** • Bass boats

Bass Hunter

2066 Highway 72 East
Colbert, GA 30628
(800) 345-4689
Fax: (706) 783-5027
www.basshunter.com

Bass Hunter manufactures thermoformed fishing and hunting boats in one- and two-person models.
■ **Brand Name(s):** Bass Hunter.
■ **Products:** • Boats

Bassmaster Boats

P.O. Box 803
Danville, KY 40423
(859) 792-4339
Fax: (859) 792-6054
info@bassmasterboats.com
www.bassmasterboats.com

Bassmaster Boats manufactures several models of bass fishing boats from 16 feet to 20 feet, as well as an 18-foot Bass Skier and the Crappie Master and Crappie King models.
■ **Brand Name(s):** Bassmaster.
✔ Brochure.
■ **Products:** • Fishing boats

The two-person **Bass Baby** boat weighs just 143 pounds and comes with wheels for unloading and moving to the water.

The Bass Hunter Duck Boat comes with a blind, Mossy Oak camo hull, and two bucket seats.

A fisherman heads to his favorite spot, piloting the Cougar model Bass Cat 20-foot, 3-inch fishing boat.

Bayliner

1 N. Field Court
Lake Forest, IL 60045
(847) 735-4765
www.baylinerboats.com
Bayliner has been building boats since 1955 and is now part of the Brunswick Corp. Models include Capri runabouts, Ciera Cruisers, Rendezvous deckboats and motoryachts.
■ **Brand Name(s):** Bayliner.
✔ Brochure.
■ **Products:** • Boats

Blazer Boats Inc.

3300 Bill Metzger Lane
Pensacola, FL 32514
(850) 478-2290
Fax: (850) 478-8701
www.blazerboats.com
Blazer Boats, founded in 1978, manufactures high performance bass boats. Included are a line of bass fishing boats from 18 feet to 21 feet and a line of bay sportfishing boats from 18 feet to 24 feet, with Yamaha or Mercury motors.
■ **Brand Name(s):** Blazer Boats.
✔ Brochure.
■ **Products:** • Fishing boats

Boston Whaler

100 Whaler Way
Edgewater, FL 32141
(904) 428-0057
Fax: (904) 409-8559
www.whaler.com
Boston Whaler boats, featuring the unsinkable Unibond foamcore, run from 12 feet to 35 feet.
■ **Brand Name(s):** Boston Whaler.
■ **Products:** • Fishing boats

Brunswick Corp.

1 N. Field Court
Lake Forest, IL 60045
(847) 735-4700
Fax: (847) 735-4765
www.brunswick.com
Brunswick is the parent company to several boat- and motor-manufacturing companies, including Mercury Marine, Sea Ray Boats, Baja Marine, Boston Whaler, U.S. Marine, Bayliner, Trophy, and Maxum. Fishing boat and motor lines are listed separately.
■ **Brand Name(s):** Mercury Marine, Trophy, Bayliner, Maxum, Boston Whaler.
■ **Products:** • Boats • Motors

Bullet Boats Inc.

P.O. Box 2202
Knoxville, TN 37901
(865) 577-7055
info@bulletboats.com
www.bulletboats.com
Bullet Boats, established in 1980, builds eight models of fiberglass fishing boats in 20-foot and 21-plus foot sizes. It also sells accessories and apparel.
■ **Brand Name(s):** Bullet Boats.
✔ Brochure.
■ **Products:** • Fishing boats

Power is the hallmark of Blazer boats and the 190 Pro-V and 180 Pro-V show off some of their speed.

Bumble Bee Boats

210 Industrial Blvd.
P.O. Box 128
Tullahoma, TN 37388
(931) 455-9728
Fax: (931) 455-1481
www.bumblebeeboats.com
A veteran of 30 years of boat building, Bumble Bee
  manufactures fiberglass fishing boats ranging from
  the 16-foot Back Bay model to 2100 Pro Sport model.
  It also features Bumble Bee Trailers by MFI and a
  line of apparel.
■ **Brand Name(s):** Bumble Bee Boats.
✔ Brochure.
■ **Products:** • Fishing boats • Trailers

Champion Boats

880 Butler Road
Murfreesboro, TN 37127
(615) 494-2090
info@championboats.com
www.championboats.com
Champion Boats manufactures five lines of fishing
  boats with several models of each, including Elite,
  CX, Saltwater, Fish-n-Ski, and Multi-Species. The
  fiberglass boats feature an exclusive V-Wing hull.
  Also available is a line of apparel.
■ **Brand Name(s):** Champion Boats.
✔ Brochure.
■ **Products:** • Fishing boats

Charger Boats Inc.

Box 709
Richland, MO 65556
(573) 765-3265
Fax: (573) 765-5881
charger2@dam.net
www.chargerboats.com
With more than 30 years of experience, Charger Boats
  manufactures 10 models of fiberglass fishing boats
  from 16 feet, 9 inches to a 21 foot, 9 inches. They
  include a Triple-Step Hull design and a patented Pro-
  Air Livewell System.
■ **Brand Name(s):** Charger Boats.
✔ Brochure.
■ **Products:** • Fishing boats

Top: **The 24 Bay Champ is the top of the line in Champion Boats'
Saltwater Series, carrying a 200- to 300-hp motor and a 90 gallons of
fuel.** *Bottom:* **Charger Boats have developed a more streamlined look
to its lineup of bass boats, and still offer livewells, easy access to the
engine compartments, and rod lockers.**

A family sets out on a fish excursion aboard a FishHawk 16 fishing boat by Crestliner.

Crestliner
609 13th Ave. NE
Little Falls, MN 56345
(320) 632-6686
Fax: (320) 632-2127
jantolik@crestliner.com
www.crestliner.com
Crestliner, founded in 1946, manufactures 55 models of aluminum boats, including several fishing models, and 28 models of pontoons from 10 feet to 24 feet. It features a 20-year warranty plan. The company is a Genmar subsidiary.
■ **Brand Name(s):** Crestline.
✔ Brochure.
■ **Products:** • Boats

Dabbie Products
P.O. Box 34171
Northdene
Durban, SA 4064
info@dabbie.za.net
www.dabbie.net
Dabbie, based in South Africa, produces a line of Personal Flotation Craft -- one- or two-person pontoon boats for fishing. It also produces accessories, including oars, anchors, rod holders, and storage pouches.
■ **Brand Name(s):** Dabbie.
■ **Products:** • Pontoon boats

Davis Boats
2601 Germaine Way
Paso Robles, CA 93446
(805) 227-1170
(888) 600-2628
Fax: (805) 227-1173
davisboats@thegrid.net
www.davisboats.com
Davis Boats makes fishing boats for sport or commercial use, ranging from 22 feet to 26 feet. Boats are custom built to its owners' needs.
✔ Brochure.
■ **Products:** • Fishing boats

Dorado Marine Inc.
270 Hedden Court
P.O. Box 427
Ozona, FL 34660
(727) 786-3800
Fax: (727) 786-4842
sales@doradoboats.com
www.doradoboats.com
Dorado manufacturing a line of handmade custom fishing boats that are light, strong, and fuel-efficient, in sizes from 23 feet to 40 feet, primarily for saltwater fishing.
■ **Brand Name(s):** Dorado.
■ **Products:** • Fishing boats

Duckworth Boat Works Inc.
P.O. Box 580
1061 16th Ave.
Clarkston, WA 99403
(509) 758-9831
(800) 261-7617
Fax: (509) 758-8809
duckworth@clarkston.com
www.duckworthboats.com
Duckworth, for 30 years, has been building heavy-duty welded aluminum jet boats designed to survive whitewater rapids and shallow runs of the Snake River Hell's Canyon. Some models are also designed for outboard motors or sterndrives.
■ **Brand Name(s):** Duckworth.
✔ Brochure.
■ **Products:** • Boats

Falcon Boats
300 E. Sycamore St.
Sherman, TX 75090
(903) 868-1265
Fax: (903) 893-5054
Falcon makes several types of fishing boats, including Striper King, Striper Pro, Grande Pro, and Tiger Pro.
■ **Products:** • Boats

G3 Boats

901 Cowan Drive
Lebanon, MO 65536
(877) 877-4348
www.g3boats.com

G3 Boats makes several lines of aluminum fishing
boats, including the HP Series, MV Pro Series,
Panfish Series, Deep V Series, Gator Series, and Jon
Boats. It also makes Sun Catcher pontoon boats,
many equipped for fishing. Yamaha motors are
standard.

■ **Brand Name(s):** G3 Boats, Sun Catcher.
✔ Brochure.
■ **Products:** • Fishing boats • Pontoon boats

Glastron

P.O. Box 460
Little Falls, MN 56345
(320) 632-8395
Fax: (320) 632-1438
glastron@brainerd.net
www.glastron.com

Founded in 1956, Glastron is well known for its family
runabout and sports boats, as well as fishing boats.
The patented Super Stable Vee hull and light weight
allow for agile handling and good fuel economy. Boats
are of trailerable size.

■ **Brand Name(s):** Glastron.
✔ Brochure.
■ **Products:** • Boats

A couple fishes from a Glastron SX170, a fiberglass fishing boat that
can double as a family runabout.

Top: The line of Jon Boats from G3 Boats are "gator tough" welded
aluminum work horses. *Bottom:* The Panfish Series from G3 Boats
includes this Model 175, with trailer, trolling motor and fish finder
included.

Godfrey Marine

4500 Middlebury St.
P.O. Box 1158
Elkhart, IN 46515
(574) 522-8381
Fax: (574) 522-5120
info@godfreymarine.com
www.godfreymarine.com
Godfrey Marine manufactures several lines of boats,
including the Polar Kraft and Polar fishing boats, and
pontoon models including Sweetwater, Sanpan, Aqua
Patio, Parti Kraft, and Hurricane lines.
- **Brand Name(s):** Polar Kraft, Polar, Sweetwater,
Aqua Patio, Parti Kraft, Hurricane.
- ✔ Brochure.
- **Products:** • Fishing boats • Pontoon boats

Greg Tatman Wooden Boats Inc.

36250 Enterprise Road
Creswell, OR 97426
(541) 746-5287
Fax: (541) 744-2190
woodn@gregboats.com
www.gregboats.com
Greg Tatman builds wooden driftboats, primarily in kits
that can be assembled, from 12 feet to 17 feet.
Accessories include trailers, oars or motors, and
anchors.
- **Brand Name(s):** Greg Tatman Wooden Boats.
- ✔ Retail shop.
- **Products:** • Wooden driftboats

Hawk Boats

1 Capitol Drive
McAlester, OK 74501
(918) 429-1200
Fax: (918) 429-1300
info@hawkboats.com
www.hawkboats.com
Hawk Boats manufactures fiberglass fishing boats in 11
models, ranging from 19 feet to 22 feet. A Mercury
motor is standard.
- **Brand Name(s):** Hawk Boats.
- ✔ Brochure.
- **Products:** • Fishing Boats

A fisherman holds his catch while navigating in the Hobie Float Cat.

Hobie Cat Co.

4925 Oceanside Blvd.
Oceanside, CA 92056
(760) 758-9100
Fax: (760) 758-1841
hobieboats@aol.com
www.hobiekayaks.com
Hobie Cat makes fishing boats and kayaks as well as
sailboats. Fishing boats include the single-seat pedal-
powered Hobie Mirage Outback and the Hobie Float
Cat with polyethylene hulls that can be disassembled
in minutes.
- **Brand Name(s):** Hobie Cat.
- ✔ Brochure.
- **Products:** • Portable fishing boats

Hydra-Sports

1651 Whitfield Ave.
Sarasota, FL 34243
(941) 753-7811
Fax: (941) 751-7822
www.hydrasports.com
Hydra-Sports, in business since 1973, produces 14
models of fiberglass fishing boats, from 18 feet to 28
feet, designed to withstand a saltwater environment. It
is part of the Genmar boat family.
- **Brand Name(s):** Hydra-Sports.
- ✔ Brochure.
- **Products:** • Saltwater fishing boats

Hydra-Sports Boats

1651 Whitfield Ave.
Sarasota, FL 34243
(941) 751-7831
www.hydrasports.com

Hydra-Sports has been manufacturing fiberglass fishing boats since 1973. It was acquired by Genmar in 2001. The Hydra-Sports series ranges from 18 feet to 24 feet and the Vector series ranges from 24 feet to 28 feet, designed for saltwater fishing.

- ■ **Brand Name(s):** Hydra-Sports, Vector.
- ✔ Brochure.
- ■ **Products:** • Saltwater fishing boats

Javelin Boats

800 Butler Road
Murfreesboro, TN 37130
(615) 895-5190
Fax: (615) 494-2061
www.javelinboats.com

Javelin Boats, founded in 1987 and a part of Genmar, offers 12 models of fiberglass bass and fish-and-ski boats ranging from 17 feet to 21 feet.

- ■ **Brand Name(s):** Javelin Boats.
- ✔ Brochure.
- ■ **Products:** • Fishing boats

Johnson Outdoors Inc.

555 Main St.
Racine, WI 53403
www.johnsonoutdoors.com

Johnson Outdoors produces a wide variety of watercraft, motors, and outdoors equipment, including Old Town canoes, Ocean Kayak, Leisure Life Limited boats, Necky Kayaks, Dimension kayaks, Escape sailboats, extrasport life jackets, Minn Kota electric motors.

- ■ **Brand Name(s):** Minn Kota, Airguide, Old Town, Dimension, Ocean Kayak, Leisure Life Limited, extrasport.
- ■ **Products:** • Boats • Canoes • Motors • Marine products

KL Industries Inc.

1790 Sun Dolphin Drive
Muskegon, MI 49444
(231) 733-2725
Fax: (231) 739-4502
www.klindustries.com

KL Industries makes several lines of small fishing boats, sport boats, canoes, kayaks, and paddle boats. It also produces ice fishing shelters. Online shopping is available.

- ✔ Brochure. ✔ Online shop.
- ■ **Products:** • Fishing boats • Ice fishing shelters

Larson Boats

Paul Larson Memorial Drive
Little Falls, MN 56345
(320) 632-1427
Fax: (320) 632-1423
www.larsonboats.com

Larson Boats dates back to 1913 when Paul Larson built his first fishing boat. Now a part of the Genmar boat family, Larson uses VEC technology to craft 19 models of fiberglass boats ranging from 18 feet to 33 feet, including several fishing models.

- ■ **Brand Name(s):** Larson Boats.
- ✔ Brochure.
- ■ **Products:** • Boats

Legend Boats

Regional Road 55
Whitefish, ON POM 3E0
(705) 866-2821
Fax: (705) 866-2616
www.legendboats.com

Legend Boats, based in Canada, produces Legend GenX Series and Legend Pro Classic Series models, including side console, full windshield, tiller model, and pontoon boats, made of aluminum and powered by Mercury motors.

- ■ **Brand Name(s):** Legend.
- ✔ Brochure.
- ■ **Products:** • Boats

Leisure Life Limited

4855 Broadmoor SE
Grand Rapids, MI 49512
(616) 698-3000
(800) 552-6287
www.llboats.com

Leisure Life Limited, a division of Johnson Outdoors, makes several lines of small boats, including Basstender fishing boats, ElDeBo electric deck boat, WaterTender dinghy, WaterQuest canoes, as well as kayaks and pedal boats.

- ■ **Brand Name(s):** Basstender, ElDeBo, WaterTender.
- ✔ Brochure.
- ■ **Products:** • Fishing boats • Canoes • Kayaks

Lowe

2900 Industrial Drive
Lebanon, MO 65536
(417) 532-8923
Fax: (417) 532-8988
www.lowe.com

Lowe builds 191 models of aluminum fishing and recreational boats, ranging from utility boats to pontoons and deck boats from 10 feet to 25 feet. Fishing boats include Roughneck jon boats, Angler, Fishing Machine, Stinger, and Bass Striker models.

■ **Brand Name(s):** Lowe, Bass Striker, Roughneck, Stinger.
✔ Brochure.

Lund

West Centennial Drive
New York Mills, MN 56567
(218) 385-2235
Fax: (218) 385-2278
www.lundboats.com

Founded in 1948, Lund manufactures 75 models of aluminum fishing boats, ranging from 12 feet to 21 feet. Lund uses the Integrated Power Strake hull to enhance performance and installs the new ProControl console for handling.

■ **Brand Name(s):** Lund.
✔ Brochure.
■ **Products:** • Fishing boats

A family enjoys a day on the water in one of the Lund Sport & Fish Series boats, Model 1950 OB. Lund makes about 75 models of boats.

A pair of fishermen haul in a catch aboard Lowe's Stinger, part of the All-Welded Bass Series of Lowe fishing boats.

Maverick Boat Co. Inc.

3207 Industrial 29th St.
Ft. Pierce, FL 34946
888-SHALLOW
Fax: (772) 489-2168
sales@maverickboats.com
www.maverickboats.com
Maverick Boat Co. manufactures skiff, bay, and
offshore boats ranging in size from 17 to 24 feet.
Besides the Maverick line, it builds Hewes Light
Tackle Boats and Pathfinder bay boats and skiffs.
■ **Brand Name(s):** Maverick, Hewes, Pathfinder.
✔ Brochure.
■ **Products:** • Fishing boats

National Marine Manufacturers Association

200 E. Randolph Drive, Suite 5100
Chicago, IL 60601
(312) 946-6200
www.nmma.org
The National Marine Manufacturers Association is a
trade group that works to improve the boating
experience through safety, certification, and product
quality. It operates a Discover Boating program for
consumers.
■ **Products:** • Boating information

Norris Craft Boat Co. Inc.

P.O. Box 209
Memorial Drive
LaFollette, TN 37766
(423) 562-7629
info@norriscraftboats.com
www.norriscraftboats.com
Norris Craft has been making bass boats for 45 years.

Its newest addition is the 2000 FXLD Vee, a
fiberglass boat with a 20-foot, 5-inch length and
maximum 300 horsepower, with a five-year warranty.
■ **Brand Name(s):** Norris Craft.
■ **Products:** • Bass boats

Outcast Sporting Goods

P.O. Box 44499
Boise, ID 83711
(208) 343-3281
info@outcastboats.com
www.outcastboats.com
Outcast makes float tubes and one- and two-person
pontoon fishing boats from 7-feet to 16-feet,
including the Fat Cat, Backpacker Lite, and PAC
series, as well as accessories.
■ **Brand Name(s):** Outcast Boats.
✔ Brochure.
■ **Products:** • Pontoon boats • Float tubes

Pelican International Inc.

1000 Paul-Kane
Laval, QC H7C 2T2
(450) 664-1222
(800) 463-6960
Fax: (450) 664-4522
sales@pelicanintl.com
www.pelican-intl.com
Pelican International is a leading manufacturer of
thermoformed canoes, kayaks, pedal boats, mini-bass
boats and jon boats. It manufactures and markets the
Coleman line of thermoformed boats.
■ **Brand Name(s):** Pelican, Coleman.
■ **Products:** • Fishing boats • Canoes • Kayaks

The Pathfinder 1806-V by Maverick Boats offers angler-and family-friendly features in a quality bay boat with open cockpit and forward casting deck.

Penn Yan Boat Co.

P.O. Box 228
Cheriton, VA 23316
(757) 331-1818
pennyan@worldnet.att.net
www.pennyanboats.com
Penn Yan has been building boats for more than 80
  years. They range from 17-foot Surfrider with an
  outboard motor to the 33-foot Commander cruiser,
  powered by twin inboards. Most are designed for
  saltwater fishing.
- ■ **Brand Name(s):** Penn Yan.
- ✔ Brochure.
- ■ **Products:** • Fishing boats

Playbuoy Pontoon Manufacturing Inc.

903 Michigan Ave.
P.O. Box 698
Alma, MI 48801
(989) 463-2112
Fax: (989) 463-8226
www.playbuoy.com
Playbuoy manufactures Playbuoy and Tahoe lines of
  pontoon boats, which can be outfitted for fishing or
  pleasure uses.
- ■ **Brand Name(s):** Playbuoy, Tahoe.
- ✔ Brochure.
- ■ **Products:** • Pontoon boats

Porta-Bote International

1074 Independence Ave.
Mountain View, CA 94043
(800) 227-8882
info@porta-bote.com
www.porta-bote.com
Porta-Bote makes folding, portable botes in 8-foot, 10-
  foot, and 12-foot models that can be folded for storage
  or transport.
- ■ **Brand Name(s):** Porta-Bote.
- ■ **Products:** • Portable boats.

Princecraft

P.O. Box 220160
St. Louis, MO 63122
(800) 395-8858
princecraft@princecraft.com
www.princecraft.com
Princecraft makes a variety of boats, including fishing
  boats, deck boats, jon boats, and pontoons. They range
  from a 10-foot jon boat to a 26-foot pontoon.
- ■ **Brand Name(s):** Princecraft.
- ✔ Brochure.
- ■ **Products:** • Boats

Ranger Boats

P.O. Box 179
Flippin, AR 72634
(870) 453-2222
info@rangerboats.com
www.rangerboats.com
Ranger makes 40 models of premium fiberglass and
  aluminum fishing boats, including the VS/R Series,
  Fisherman Series, Commanche Series, Saltwater
  Scrics, and Cherokee Series. Many Ranger boats are
  used in fishing tournaments.
- ■ **Brand Name(s):** Ranger Boats.
- ✔ Brochure.
- ■ **Products:** • Fishing boats

A pair of fishermen head out for a day of fishing aboard Ranger's Cherokee Model 216S, one of about 40 models of elite fishing boats.

River Ridge Custom Canoes

5865 River Ridge Court NE
Rochester, MN 55906
(507) 288-2750
Fax: (507) 280-0029
plantan@aol.com
www.riverridgecustomcanoes.com
River Ridge makes custom canoes for fishing and
 navigating in small bodies of water.
■ **Brand Name(s):** River Ridge Custom Canoes.
■ **Products:** • Canoes

San Augustine Fiberglass Products Inc.

P.O. Drawer 596
San Augustine, TX 75972
(936) 275-3456
Fax: (936) 275-5755
info@raycraftboats.com
www.raycraftboats.com
San Augustine Fiberglass makes Ray-Craft Boats,
 which have been manufactured since 1968. Fishing
 boat styles range from the V-156 Pro 15-footer to the
 19-foot V-190 Pro with custom trailer, two built-in
 fuel tanks, rod box, livewell, and raised casting
 platforms.
■ **Brand Name(s):** Ray-Craft.
■ **Products:** • Fishing boats

Sea Ray International

2600 Sea Ray Blvd.
Knoxville, TN 37914
(865) 522-4181
Fax: (865) 525-5977
www.searay.com
Sea Ray makes more than 40 models of boats, from 17
 feet to 68 feet. Many are designed for or can be used
 for fishing.
■ **Brand Name(s):** Sea Ray.
✔ Brochure.
■ **Products:** • Boats

Sea Ray International makes more than 40 models of boats, from 17-footers to yachts.

Seaswirl Boats

P.O. Box 167
Culver, OR 97734
(541) 546-5011
Fax: (541) 546-7244
www.seaswirl.com
Seaswirl Boats, founded in 1955, makes 19 models of
 fiberglass offshore fishing boats ranging from 17 feet
 to 25 feet. It is part of the Genmar boat company.
■ **Brand Name(s):** Seaswirl.
✔ Brochure.

Splash Marine Inc.

135 N.E. 38th Terrace
Oklahoma City, OK 73105
(800) 786-6552
www.busterboats.com
Splash Marine makes the Buster Boats line of small,
 portable fishing boats, from 8 feet to 10 feet. Models
 include Buster Boats, Pond Hopper, Bass Brat, Bass
 Wagon, and Trophy Series, as well as trailers and
 accessories.
■ **Brand Name(s):** Buster Boats
✔ Brochure.
■ **Products:** • Small fishing boats

Armed with saltwater trolling gear, a couple heads out to fish aboard a Seaswirl 2101 Center Console boat.

Storm Boats

377 S.W. 14th Ave.
Pompano Beach, FL 33069
(800) 336-0520
www.stormboats.com
Founded in 1976, Storm Boats hand-builds about 25
  bass fishing boats a year and is now in Florida for its
  quality.
- **Brand Name(s):** Storm Boats.
- **Products:** • Bass boats

Stratos Boats

880 Butlers Road
Murfreesboro, TN 37127
(615) 494-2008
Fax: (615) 494-2062
www.stratosboats.com
Stratos has become one of the most popular freshwater
  fishing boats, with 12 models ranging from 17 feet to
  21 feet. The boats feature composite construction with
  foam floatation. Included are XL bass boats and 290
  Ski and Fish models.
- **Brand Name(s):** Stratos.
- ✔ Brochure.
- **Products:** • Fishing boats

Stroker Boats

3944 Old Niles Ferry
Maryville, TN 37801
(865) 983-2482
www.strokerboats.com
Stroker makes fishing boats that it calls the "world's
No. 1 wide body performance bass boat," a 21-foot
boat of composite construction.
- **Brand Name(s):** Stroker Boats
- **Products:** • Boats

Tracker Marine

2500 E. Kearney
Springfield, MO 65803
(417) 873-5900
www.trackermarine.com
Tracker Marine manufactures Tracker Fishing Boats,
  Nitro Bass and Bay Boats, and Sun Tracker pontoons.
  New models include the aluminum Avalanche and
  Tundra.
- **Brand Name(s):** Tracker, Nitro, Sun Tracker.
- **Products:** • Boats

Triton Boats

15 Bluegrass Drive
Ashland City, TN 37015
(888) 887-4866
Fax: (615) 792-9053
fun@tritonboats.com
www.tritonboats.com
Triton makes a wide variety of fishing boats, including
  aluminum boats from 15-feet to 18-feet, Summit
  Pontoon fishing boats, Tournament bass boats, Fish
  and Ski boats, saltwater Bayflight and Seaflight
  models, and multi-species boats.
- **Brand Name(s):** Triton Boats
- ✔ Brochure.
- **Products:** • Fishing boats • Apparel

Triumph Boats

100 Golden Drive
Durham, NC 27705
(919) 382-3149
Fax: (919) 382-6395
www.triumphboats.com
Triumph produces freshwater and saltwater boats using
  the Roplene roto-molded polyethylene construction
  system to build dual-hull boats in one seamless piece.
  It features 13 models from 12 feet to 21 feet for
  fishing, skiing and cruising.
- **Brand Name(s):** Triumph Boats.
- ✔ Brochure.
- **Products:** • Boats

Two fishermen cast along a weedy shoreline aboard the Triumph 170 bass boat.

Trophy Sportfishing Boats

1 N. Field Court
Lake Forest, IL 60045
(847) 735-4765
www.trophyfishing.com
Trophy Sportfishing Boats are built for saltwater
  fishing, including 17-foot to 21-foot center console
  models and 18-foot to 25-foot walkarounds. Trophy is
  a division of Brunswick Corp.
- **Brand Name(s):** Trophy.
✔ Brochure.
- **Products:** • Fishing boats

Viper Boats Inc.

1055 Cardinal Drive
Mountain Home, AR 72653
(870) 424-4244
www.viperboatsinc.com
Viper Boats makes a variety of bass and walleye
  fishing boats in the Viper Cobra line as well as the
  Viper Coral fish and ski boat line and Aztec ski boats.
- **Brand Name(s):** Viper, Cobra, Coral, Aztec.
✔ Brochure.
- **Products:** • Boats

Vivian Industries

P.O. Box 232
680 S. Pardue
Vivian, LA 71082
www.vipboats.com
Vivian Industries, which began making boats in 1968,
  now manufactures several lines, including VIP
  Runabouts and Fish-N-Ski models, BayStealth fishing
  boats, Vindicator, and Deckliner. See
  www.baystealth.com for more information on the
  BayStealth line.
- **Brand Name(s):** VIP, BayStealth, VIP Blue Water,
  Vindicatork, Deckliner.
✔ Brochure.
- **Products:** • Boats

Warrior Boats

400 Highway 55
Industrial Park, Box 367
Maple Lake, MN 55358
(320) 963-5005
Fax: (320) 963-3215
warrior@lakedalelink.net
www.warrior-boats.com
Warrior Boats manufactures the Eagle, Falcon, and

Hawk lines of fishing boats, featuring deep vee
reverse flare bow, Smart Trolling Keel and Pro Tiller
Hydraulic Steering. The company features a 21-year
hull and three-year top-side warranty.
- **Brand Name(s):** Warrior Boats
✔ Brochure.
- **Products:** • Fishing boats

Wellcraft Marine

1651 Whitfield Ave.
Sarasota, FL 34243
(941) 753-7811
Fax: (941) 751-7822
www.wellcraft.com
Wellcraft Marine manufactures 39 models of fiberglass
  boats, including fishing boats, sport cruisers, and
  Scarab performance boats. The fishing boats are
  designed for offshore use, with secure handling and
  seaworthiness stressed.
- **Brand Name(s):** Wellcraft.
✔ Brochure.
- **Products:** • Boats

Xpress Boats

199 Extrusion Place
Hot Springs, AR 71901
(501) 262-5300
Fax: (501) 262-5053
info@xpressboats.com
www.xpressboats.com
Xpress Boats manufactures all-welded aluminum
  fishing and hunting boats, including jon, bass, and
  bay models
- **Brand Name(s):** Xpress Boats.
✔ Brochure.
- **Products:** • Boats

Zephyr Boats

6837 #2 Highway 126 North
Midway, AR 72651
(870) 481-4014
Fax: (870) 481-4015
www.zephyrboats.com
Zephyr Boats manufactures the ZS/ZD-720 lineup of
  20-foot fishing boats with 50-gallon fuel tanks and
  choice of V-6 Mercury or Yamaha engines, with EZ
  Loader trailers.
- **Brand Name(s):** Zephyr Boats.
- **Products:** • Boats

Boat Products

ACDelco
6200 Grand Pointe Drive
P.O. Box 6020
Grand Blanc, MI 48439
800-ACDELCO
Fax: (810) 606-2920
www.acdelco.com
ACDelco makes the Voyager Battery for boats. The batteries are rechargeable and carry 12-month free replacement warranty and 36-month limited warranty.
- **Brand Name(s):** ACDelco.
- **Products:** • Boat batteries

Action Products Inc.
P.O. Box 100
One Action Ave.
Odessa, MO 64076
(816) 633-5514
www.actionp.com
Action Products makes seats for fishing boats as well as accessories, including anchors, battery cases, oars, and rod holders.
- **Brand Name(s):** Action Products.
- **Products:** • Boat seats • Anchors • Oars

Airguide
1326 Willow Road
Sturtevant, WI 53177
(800) 227-6433
motors@johnsonoutdoors.com
www.airguideinstruments.com
Airguide makes precision marine compasses and navigation instruments, including speedometers, gauges, weather temp sensors and digital hygrometers.
- **Brand Name(s):** Airguide.
- ✔ Brochure.
- **Products:** • Compasses • Marine instruments

American Suzuki Motor Corp.
P.O. Box 1100
Brea, CA 92822
(800) 247-4704
www.suzukimarine.com
Suzuki manufactures four-stroke and two-stroke outboard motors ranging from five horsepower to 225 horsepower. It also offers accessories, including propellers, chemicals, control boxes, and instruments.

- **Brand Name(s):** Suzuki.
- ✔ Brochure.
- **Products:** • Outboard motors

Top: Twin DF115 Fuel-Injected 4-Strokes from American Suzuki power this fishing boat. **Bottom:** A couple enjoys the water on their boat powered by American Suzuki's DF9-.9 4-Stroke motor.

Attwood Corp.

1016 N. Monroe St.
Lowell, MI 49331
(616) 897-9241
Fax: (616) 897-2247
www.attwoodmarine.com
Attwood makes several boating accessories, including
seats, pumps, ventilation and lighting equipment,
fishing accessories such as downriggers, trailer parts,
and boat covers.
- **Brand Name(s):** Attwood.
- **Products:** • Boat equipment • Fishing accessories

Boat Master Trailers

12301 Metro Parkway
Ft. Myers, FL 33912
(239) 768-2292
Fax: (239) 768-6389
www.boat-trailers.com
Since 1980, Boat Master has been building fully
submersible all-aluminum boat trailers for many
models and sizes of boats. The company also makes
custom trailers for air boats, personal watercraft, and
other vehicles. Online shopping is now available.
- **Brand Name(s):** Boat Master Trailers.
- ✔ Brochure. ✔ Online shop.
- **Products:** • Boat trailers

Carlisle Paddles Inc.

4562 North Down River Road
P.O. Box 488
Grayling, MI 49738
(989) 348-9886
(800) 258-0290
Fax: (989) 348-8242
reply@carlislepaddles.com
www.carlislepaddles.com
Carlisle, a division of Johnson Outdoors, makes paddles
and oars for canoes, boats, and kayaks.
- **Brand Name(s):** Carlisle
- ✔ Brochure. ✔ Online shop.
- **Products:** • Oars • Paddles

Champion Trailer Parts Supply

56705 I-10 Service Road
Slidell, LA 70458
(800) 229-6690
Fax: (800) 359-8169
freecatalog@championtrailers.com
www.championtrailers.com
Champion Trailer sells a wide variety of aluminum and
galvanized boat trailers and parts for trailers,
including wheels, brakes, axles, bolts, rollers, and
winches.

✔ Brochure.
- **Products:** • Boat trailers • Trailer parts

CMC

P.O. Box 1737
2930 S. 13th
Duncan, OK 73534
(800) 654-3697
Fax: (580) 252-2970
www.cook-mfg.com
CMC, a division of Marine Accessories Corp., makes
transom jacks, tilt and trim gear, and accessories for
boats.
- **Brand Name(s):** CMC.
- **Products:** • Transom jacks • Tilt and trim

Co-Star VII

Thousand Oaks Corporate Park
51A Thousand Oaks Blvd.
Morgantown, PA 19543
(888) 853-4484
Fax: (610) 286-7246
www.co-starvii.com
Co-Star VII has been making Detwiler outboard motor
jack plates for several years, and has added a Pack-A-
Pole line of high quality fishing rod cases.
- **Brand Name(s):** Co-Star VII, Detwiler
- **Products:** • Jack plates • Rod cases

Coleman Company Inc.

P.O. Box 2931
Wichita, KS 67201
(800) 835-3278
consumerservice@coleman.com
www.coleman.com
Coleman makes a wide variety of fishing and camping
products, including flashlights, inflatable boats,
fishing boats, raingear, and coolers. Products are
available in retail stores as well as Camp Coleman
Stores across the country.
- **Brand Name(s):** Coleman
- ✔ Brochure. ✔ Online shop. ✔ Retail shop.
- **Products:** • Coolers • Boats • Raingear •
  Flashlights

Coleman offers many outdoors products, including coolers and flashlights.

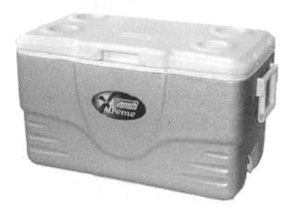

DeLorme Mapping Co.

2 DeLorme Drive
P.O. Box 298
Yarmouth, ME 04096
(800) 511-2459
Fax: (800) 575-2244
sales@delorme.com
www.delorme.com
DeLorme Mapping offers a variety of maps, both paper and software, as well as GPS receivers and cables.
- **Brand Name(s):** Earthmate GPS Receiver, Street Atlas USA.
- ✔ Online shop.
- **Products:** • Maps • GPS

Evercel

5 Pond Park Road
Hingham, MA 02043
(781) 741-8800
Fax: (781) 740-8919
general@evercel.com
www.evercel.com
Evercel makes nickel-zinc batteries for many applications, including boats. They are lighter than lead acid batteries and contain less than 2 percent lead.
- **Brand Name(s):** Evercel.
- **Products:** • Boat batteries

Exide Technologies

210 Carnegie Center, Suite 500
Princeton, NJ 08540
(609) 627-7200
800-STARTIT
www.exideworld.com
Exide manufactures and markets a number of marine batteries, including the Orbital Marine Starting, Orbital Deep Cycle, Stowaway Tournament, Stowaway Marine Deep Cycle, and Stowaway Marine Starting Batteries. It also makes Champion products.
- **Brand Name(s):** Exide, Orbital, Stowaway, Champion.
- **Products:** • Batteries.

EZ Loader Boat Trailers

P.O. Box 3263
Spokane, WA 99220
(509) 489-0181
www.ezloader.com
Since its beginning in 1953, EZ Loader has expanded its boat trailer production to more than 60,000 trailers a year in many sizes and types. The company invented the all-roller trailer.
- **Brand Name(s):** EZ Loader.
- ✔ Brochure.
- **Products:** • Boat trailers

Fentress Marine

577 Isham St., #2-B
New York, NY 10034
(212) 304-9660
Fax: (212) 304-9759
www.fentressmarine.com
Fentress Marine provides boating, fishing, marine, and diving accessories, including fishing rod holders, tool and drink holders, rigging and fillet tables, roof racks, and rod and reel racks.
- **Brand Name(s):** Fentress Marine.
- ✔ Brochure.
- **Products:** • Boat accessories

Fulton/Wesbar Corp.

50 Indianhead Drive
Mosinee, WI 54455
(715) 693-1700
Fax: (715) 693-1799
www.wesbar.com
Fulton/Wesbar makes boat trailer and marine
accessories, including taillights, hub bearing kits, tire
carriers, ramps, and ladders.
- **Brand Name(s):** Wesbar.
- **Products:** • Trailer accessories

Grady-White Boat Co.

P.O. Box 1527
Greenville, NC 27835
(252) 752-2111
Fax: (252) 752-4217
www.gradywhite.com
Grady-White builds 18 models of sportfishing boats,
from 18 feet to 33 feet, including cabin, center
console and dual console models. It also offers an
online catalog for shopping for apparel and boating
accessories.
- **Brand Name(s):** Grady-White.
- ✔ Brochure. ✔ Online shop.
- **Products:** • Fishing boats

Hillman Marine

Route 3, Box 411
Dickinson, TX 77539
(281) 339-1546
(800) 452-1795
Fax: (281) 339-1581
rhillman@wt.net
www.hillmanmarine.com
Hillman Marine offers an online catalog of marine
fishing and boating products, including fishing gear,
hardware such as anchors and cables, and hull
maintenance supplies.
- ✔ Online shop.
- **Products:** • Fishing gear • Hull maintenance •
Hardware

Honda Marine Group

4900 Marconi Drive
Alpharetta, GA 30005
(800) 426-7701
Fax: (678) 339-2670
www.honda-marine.com
Honda Marine manufactures four-stroke outboard
motors in horsepower ranges from two horsepower to
225 horsepower, as well as parts and accessories.
- **Brand Name(s):** Honda.
- **Products:** • Outboard motors

International Concepts Inc.

P.O. Box 677
St. Joseph, MI 49085
(616) 556-0608
Fax: (616) 556-0609
intercinc@hotmail.com
www.motowasher.com
International Concepts makes the MotoWasher tool for
cleaning boats, RVs or autos, and the AnglersBest
fillet knives.
- **Brand Name(s):** MotoWasher, AnglersBest.
- **Products:** • Boat cleaner • Fillet knives

Top: **The new Model 7MX Charter Master LCD GPS unit offers the improved speed and perfomance of an internal GPS receiver coupled with a small external antenna.** *Bottom:* **The Sea Scout sonar unit from Interphase scans horizonally and from side to side at forward ranges up to 1,2000 feet.**

Interphase Technologies Inc.

2880 Research Park Drive, Suite 140
Soquel, CA 95073
(831) 477-4944
888-77SONAR
Fax: (831) 462-7444
comments@interphase-tech.com
www.interphase-tech.com
Interphase Technologies offers a forward scanning
sonar that offers the fisherman, sailor, or boater a
virtual image of the underwater area ahead of the boat.
It also offers Chart Master chart plotters complete with
built-in GPS receiver/antenna.
- **Brand Name(s):** Interphase.
✔ Brochure.
- **Products:** • Sonars • Chart plotters

Interstate Batteries

1700 Dixon St.
Des Moines, IA 50316
(866) 842-5368
www.interstatebatteries.com
Interstate Batteries makes a line of marine batteries as
well as battery chargers and many other types of
batteries.
- **Brand Name(s):** Interstate Batteries.
- **Products:** • Batteries • Battery chargers

Magic Tilt Trailers

2161 Lions Club Road
Clearwater, FL 33764
sales@magictilt.com
www.magictilt.com
Magic Tilt has been making boat trailers since 1953 and
produces a full line of aluminum and galvanized steel
trailers, from personal watercraft to 40-foot deep vee
fishing boats. Sales are through dealers only.
- **Brand Name(s):** Magic Tilt Trailers.
- **Products:** • Boat trailers

Magnum Trailers

10806 Highway 620
Austin, TX 78726
(512) 258-4101
(800) 662-4686
Fax: (512) 258-2701
www.magnumtrailers.com
Magnum Trailers, in business since 1973, builds custom
boat trailers, with each trailer handcrafted one at a
time, for boats from 16 feet to 51 feet weighing up to
60,000 pounds.
- **Brand Name(s):** Magnum Trailers.
- **Products:** • Boat trailers

Maptech Inc.

10 Industrial Way
Amesbury, MA 01913
(978) 792-1000
(888) 839-5551
www.maptech.com
Maptech makes maps, GPS gear and marine maps for
fishing or navigation. Many are available by
downloading from the Web site.
- **Brand Name(s):** Maptech
✔ Brochure. ✔ Online shop.
- **Products:** • Maps

The EFI (electronic fuel-injected) outboard is one of many Mercury
Marine motors available to power fishing boats.

Mercury Marine

W6250 W. Pioneer Road
P.O. Box 1939
Fond du Lac, WI 54936
(920) 929-5000
Fax: (920) 929-5060
www.mercurymarine.com
Mercury Marine manufactures Mercury Outboards,
Mariner Outboards, Mercruiser Sterndrives and
Inboards, Smartcraft engine monitoring systems,
propellers, jet drives, as well as Mercury Inflatable
Boats.
- **Brand Name(s):** Mercury, Mercruiser, Mariner.
✔ Brochure.
- **Products:** • Outboard motors • Inboard motors •
Inflatable boats

Midwest Industries Inc.

401 East Highway 59 and 175
Ida Grove, IA 51445
(800) 859-3028
Fax: (712) 364-3361
www.shorelandr.com
Midwest Industries makes the Shoreland'r brand of boat
trailers, available to haul everything from small
fishing boats to 15,000 pound cruisers. Trailers in
standard sizes as well as aluminum, pontoon, and
inboard trailers are available.
- **Brand Name(s):** Shoreland'r.
- **Products:** • Boat trailers

Minn Kota

1326 Willow Road
Sturtevant, WI 53177
(800) 299-2592
www.minnkotamotors.com
Minn Kota is the world's leading manufacturer of bow-
and transom-mount trolling motors, including
Genesis, Vantage, Maxxum, All Terrain, AutoPilot,
PowerDrive, Endura, Riptide, and Turbo models, as
well as accessories including batteries and chargers.
- ■ **Brand Name(s):** Minn Kota.
- ✔ Brochure.
- ■ **Products:** • Trolling motors

Nikon USA

1300 Walt Whitman Rd.
Melville, NY 11747
800NIKONUS
www.nikonusa.com
Nikon produces a line of binoculars and scopes as well
as cameras.
- ■ **Brand Name(s):** Nikon, StabilEyes.
- ✔ Brochure. ✔ Online shop.
- ■ **Products:** • Binoculars

Nissan Marine & Power Products

1624 W. Crosby Road, Suite 101
Carrollton, TX 75006
(972) 323-6003
Fax: (972) 323-5277
www.nissanmarine.com
Nissan Marine manufactures two-stroke and four-stroke
outboard motors in 17 horsepower levels, from 2.5
horsepower to 140 horsepower. It also sells
accessories, including motor oil, fuel tanks, gauges,
and water pumps.
- ■ **Brand Name(s):** Nissan Marine.
- ✔ Brochure.
- ■ **Products:** • Outboard motors

Orion Safety Products

12 Windswept Road
Holmdel, NJ 07733
(410) 822-0318
(800) 637-7807
Fax: (410) 822-7759
www.orionsignals.com
Orion Safety Products is the nation's largest producer of
marine and outdoor signals. Products include marine
signal kits, flares, lightsticks, and first aid kits.
- ■ **Brand Name(s):** Orion.
- ✔ Brochure.
- ■ **Products:** • Signal kits • Flares • First aid kits

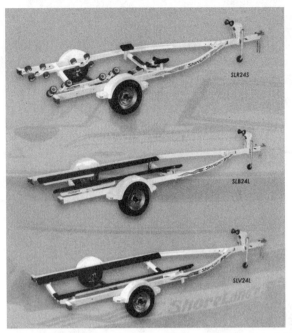

Three versions of Shoreland'r boat trailers are for boats in the 2,000
to 2,400-pound class.

Besides its line of electric trolling motors for fishing boats, Minn
Kota has introduced Universal Sonar transducer technology that
works with fish finders.

Top: Boat covers in many sizes and fabrics are among the popular boating accessories available from Overton's. *Bottom:* The Tempo Gas Walker, available from Overton's, transports 29 gallons of fuel to the dock to make refueling easy.

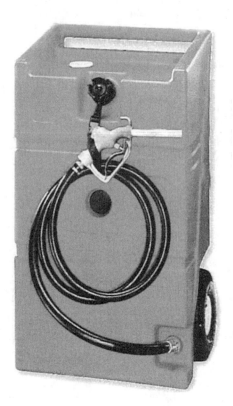

Overton's

111 Red Banks Road
P.O. Box 8228
Greenville, NC 27835
(800) 334-6541
www.overtons.com
Overton's is a catalog and online source of hundreds of boating products, including trailers, propellers, electronics, covers, lights, accessories, and safety gear.
- ■ **Brand Name(s):** Dozens of leading brands.
- ✔ Brochure. ✔ Online shop.
- ■ **Products:** • Boating accessories • Trailers • Electronics

Panther Marine Products

3276 Fanum Road
St. Paul, MN 55110
(651) 486-2010
Fax: (651) 486-6989
www.panthermarineproducts.com
Panther makes boating products and outboard motor accessories, including jack plates, motor lifts, remote auxiliary steering, trim and tilt, and accessories.
- ■ **Brand Name(s):** Panther.
- ■ **Products:** • Outboard accessories

Para-Tech Engineering Co.

2117 Horseshoe Trail
Silt, CO 81652
(970) 876-0558
(800) 594-0011
Fax: (970) 876-5668
paratech@rof.net
www.seaanchor.com
Para-Tech Engineering makes a number of boating accessories, including Sea Anchors, Boat Brakes, and accessories.
- ■ **Products:** • Sea anchors

Raymarine Inc.

22 Cotton Road Unit H
Nashua, NH 03063
(603) 881-5200
Fax: (603) 864-4756
www.raymarine.com
Raymarine, which was founded in 2001 following a management buy-out of Raytheon Marine, provides a complete marine electronics package, including instrumentation, autopilots, radar, chartplotters, fish finders, communications, and PC charting software.
- ■ **Brand Name(s):** Raymarine.
- ✔ Brochure.
- ■ **Products:** • Marine electronics • Fish finders

SI-TEX Marine Electronics Inc.

11001 Roosevelt Blvd., Suite 800
St. Petersburg, FL 33716
(727) 576-5734
Fax: (727) 570-8646
www.si-tex.com

SI-TEX makes several marine electronics products,
including charting systems, marine radars, autopilots,
depth sounders, GPS units, radios, and transducers
and accessories. It is a subsidiary of Koden
Electronics Co. of Japan.
■ **Brand Name(s):** SI-TEX.
✔ Brochure.
■ **Products:** • Marine electronics

SMR Marine Electronics

7205 NW 68th St., Suite 10
Miami, FL 33166
(305) 884-3399
Fax: (305) 884-4466

SMR Marine Electronics handles VHF handhelds, VHF
base stations, and accessories.
■ **Products:** • Marine radios

The Worth Co.

P.O. Box 88
Stevens Point, WI 54481
(715) 344-6081
(800) 374-3021
Fax: (715) 344-3021
sales@worthco.com
www.worthco.com

The Worth Co. makes several marine products,
including the Anchormate anchor system, Moormate,
and fishing lure components.
■ **Brand Name(s):** Anchormate.
■ **Products:** • Anchor systems • Lure components

Trojan Battery Co.

12380 Clark St.
Santa Fe Springs, CA 90670
(562) 946-8381
(800) 423-6569
Fax: (562) 906-4033
custcare@trojanbattery.com
www.trojanbattery.com

Trojan Battery makes several deep cycle battery
products, including some for boats. It also makes the
MasterCharge Battery Charger.
■ **Brand Name(s):** Trojan Battery.
■ **Products:** • Marine batteries

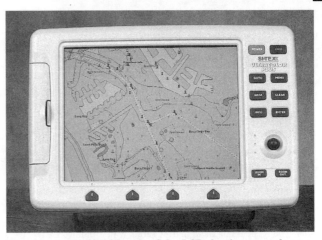

Top: **The new SI-TEX Ultraplus Color LCD charting system has a built-in GPS receiver and self-contained navigation, display on a vivid LCD screen. Bottom: The T-721 is part of the line of True-Color Radars from SI-TEX that displays radar echoes in different colors depending on signal strength.**

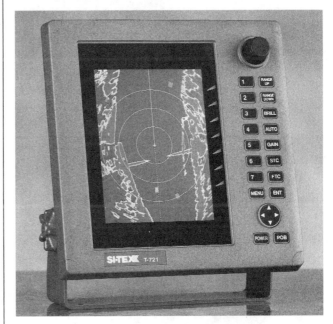

Top: The Icom Single Band marine radio, with expanded LCD display, is among electronics available from West Marine. *Bottom Left:* Expensive outboard motors are protected by Soft Touch fabric covers, available from West Marine. *Bottom Right:* Compact Bait/Fillet Mate cutting tables from West Marine are easy to clean and virtually indestructable.

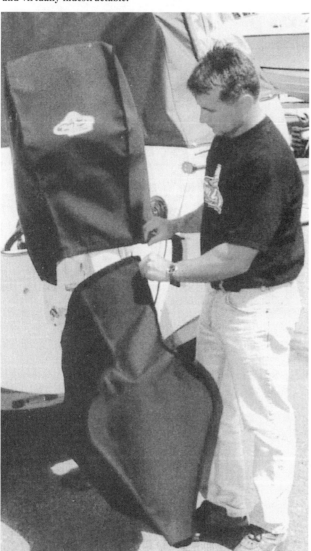

West Marine

P.O. Box 50070
Watsonville, CA 95077
800-BOATING
Fax: (831) 761-4421
webmaster@westmarine.com
www.westmarine.com

West Marine offers online shopping for many boating-related products, including anchors, engines, seats, trailers, electronics, as well as fishing products including rods and reels, tackle, and accessories. West Marine also has more than 220 U.S. sto
✔ Online shop. ✔ Retail shop.
■ **Products:** • Boating products • Fishing gear

Yamaha Motor Corp. USA

1270 Chastain Road NW
Kennesaw, GA 30144
(800) 962-7926
www.yamaha-motor.com

Yamaha manufactures several models of outboard motors, including two-stroke and four-stroke, from a two horsepower portable to a 225 horsepower four-stroke V-6. Honda also makes several models of sports boats.
■ **Brand Name(s):** Yamaha.
✔ Brochure.
■ **Products:** • Outboard motors • Boats

Apparel

Academy Broadway Corp.

1224 Fern Ridge Parkway
St. Louis, MO 63141
(314) 576-8044
(800) 338-7000
Fax: (314) 576-8010
Academy Broadway produces a variety of outdoor equipment, including hip and chest waders, and rainwear.
■ **Brand Name(s):** Academy Broadway.
✔ Brochure.
■ **Products:** • Waders

Action Optics

280 Northwood Way
P.O. Box 2999
Ketchum, ID 83340
(208) 726-4477
(800) 654-6428
Fax: (208) 727-9584
www.actionoptics.com
Action Optics produces polarized sunglasses for fishing, shooting, and other uses, including photochromatic glass lenses, polycarbonate lenses, and prescription lenses including bifocals.
■ **Brand Name(s):** Action Optics.
■ **Products:** • Polarized glasses

Top: **Stocking Foot Waders are among several types of waders available from Academy Broadway.** *Bottom:* **Academy Broadway's lineup of Two Piece Rainsuits are made of heavy gauge viynl with two storm pockets and a drawstring hood.**

Action Optics has added a ready-to-wear bifocal series to its line of polarized sunglasses.

American Needle

1275 Busch Parkway
Buffalo Grove, IL 60089
(847) 215-0011
Fax: (847) 215-0013
American Needle is the manufacturer of high quality
    fashion headwear, both in licensed and non-licensed
    categories.
■ **Products:** • Headwear

Bug-Out Outdoorwear Inc.

P.O. Box 185
901 E. Stewart
Centerville, IA 52544
(641) 437-1936
(877) 928-4688
Fax: (641) 437-4805
bugout@hotmail.com
www.bug-out-outdoorwear.com
Bug-Out produces clothings that includes micro fibers
    that screen out insects including mosquitoes, ticks,
    and black flies. Included are jackets, pants, mitts,
    head covers, and bed covers. The products are
    available online, by catalog, and in retail stores.
■ **Brand Name(s):** Bug-Out.
✔ Brochure. ✔ Online shop.
■ **Products:** • Insect-proof clothing

C.C. Filson Co.

P.O. Box 34020
Seattle, WA 98124
(800) 624-0201
Fax: (206) 624-4539
www.filson.com
C.C. Filson has been making outdoors clothing since
    1897 and has heavy-duty fishing gear, including
    coats, pants, sweaters, and caps. It also has fishing
    shorts, bibs, fishing vests and tackle packs.
■ **Brand Name(s):** Filson.
✔ Brochure. ✔ Online shop.
■ **Products:** • Outdoors clothing • Fishing vests •
    Tackle packs

Top: **The Shelter Cloth Dry Finish Fly Fishing Strap Vest is one of Filson's specialty fishing vests.** *Bottom:* **Feather cloth, weighing three ounces, is the secret of Filson's new Fly Fishing Shirt.**

The Abrams Creek Lightweight Stocking Foot Waders offer Chota's premium features in a lightweight design.

Chota Outdoor Gear

P.O. Box 31137
Knoxville, TN 37930
(865) 690-1814
Fax: (865) 690-5605
info@chotaoutdoorgear.com
www.chotaoutdoorgear.com
Chota makes clothing and equipment for fly fishing and canoeing, including waders, boots, booties, knee-highs, sandals, and other gear. Sales are through dealers.
- **Brand Name(s):** Chota.
- **Products:** • Fly fishing gear • Footwear • Waders

Cordura/DuPont

P.O. Box 80711
Wilmington, DE 19880
cordura-na@usa.dupont.com
www.dupont.com/cordura
DuPont's Cordura is used in a variety of fishing and hunting equipment and apparel.
- **Brand Name(s):** Cordura

- **Products:** • Apparel

Costa Del Mar

123 N. Orchard St. #6
Ormond Beach, FL 32174
(386) 677-3700
(800) 447-3700
Fax: (386) 677-3737
www.costadelmar.com
Costa Del Mar Sunglasses are a leading brand of polarized, performance eyewear for watersports enthusiasts. It has introduced a revolutionary new lens, the Wave 580, that improves visibility on colored objects.
- **Brand Name(s):** Costa Del Mar.
- **Products:** • Sunglasses

The eight-inch River Gripper by Danner has extra-thick felt soles to offer traction on slick rocks and streambeds.

Danner Inc.

18550 NE Riverside Parkway
Portland, OR 97230
(503) 251-1100
(800) 345-0430
Fax: (503) 251-1119
www.danner.com
Danner makes a variety of rugged shoes and boots, including the River Gripper and Studded River Gripper specifically for fishing.
- **Brand Name(s):** Danner.
- ✔ Brochure.
- **Products:** • Boots

Fishboy

9 Aerial St.
Arlington, MA 02474
866-FLATALE
Fax: (781) 646-6474
fishboy@getfishy.com
www.fishboy.com

Fishboy offers a variety of novelty T-shirts, shirts, caps, coffee mugs, and bumper stickers with fish slogans, such as "Camp Ketabigwun," "French Flies," and "Crankenstein Lures." Sales are online and by catalog.

- ■ **Brand Name(s):** Fishboy.
- ✔ Brochure. ✔ Online shop.
- ■ **Products:** • Shirts • Coffee mugs

Fisherman Eyewear

1700 Shelton Drive
P.O. Box 261
Hollister, CA 95024
(510) 848-4700
(800) 393-9273
Fax: (831) 637-8343
mail@fishermaneyewear.com
www.fishermaneyewear.com

Fisherman Eyewear, founded in 1974, produces polarized glasses designed for fishing.

- ■ **Brand Name(s):** Fisherman Eyewear.
- ■ **Products:** • Polarized sunglasses

Fitovers Eyewear USA

2600 McHale Court, Suite 175
Austin, TX 78758
(512) 832-6131
(888) 834-8872
Fax: (800) 416-4887
ussales@fitover.com
www.fitovers.com

Fitovers produces sunglasses that slip over 98 percent of all prescription eyewear. With a virtually indestructible nylon frame, the Sport model provides complete wraparound protection with glare-blocking polarized lenses and side shields.

- ■ **Brand Name(s):** Fitovers.
- ✔ Online shop.
- ■ **Products:** • Sunglasses

Top: The Big Dead Stinky Fish T-shirt is one of the Fishboy products. *Bottom Right:* A T-shirt from Fishboy advertises "Crankenstein Reels."

Sport Fitovers are lightwieght, polarized sunglasses with impact-resistant lenses that fit over regular glasses.

Top: The Calcutta model of Action Angler Series polarized sunglasses from Flying Fisherman offers wraparound protection with a nylon frame. Bottom: The Blue Marlin is one of four new designs of Native Anglers Caps from Flying Fisherman.

Flying Fisherman

P.O. Box 545
Islamorada, FL 33036
(305) 852-8989
800-3FLYFISH
Fax: (305) 853-0100
info@flyingfisherman.com
www.flyingfisherman.com

Flying Fisherman markets polarized sunglasses as well as apparel, including head gear and sportswear. It also operates Flying Fisherman Television Productions.
- **Brand Name(s):** Flying Fisherman.
✔ Brochure.
- **Products:** • Sunglasses • Clothing

Frogg toggs

517 Gunter Ave.
P.O. Box 428
Guntersville, AL 35976
(256) 505-0075
(800) 349-1835
Fax: (256) 505-0307
froggtoggs@localaccess.net
www.froggtoggs.com

Frogg toggs makes guaranteed waterproof, breathable, lightweight, affordable rainwear, including the Pro Angler rain suit. Sales are on the Internet and in stores.
- **Brand Name(s):** Frogg toggs.
✔ Brochure. ✔ Online shop.
- **Products:** • Rainwear

Korkers

9333 SE Alansa Drive, #200
Clackamas, OR 97015
(503) 723-7100
(800) 524-8899
www.korkers.com

Korkers has been known for its traction footwear for more than 50 years. Its new wading boot allows an angler to change boot soles quickly to adapt to conditions. It also makes sandals and felt products.
- **Brand Name(s):** Korkers.
✔ Brochure. ✔ Online shop.
- **Products:** • Wading boots

A close-up shows the interchangeable soles of the Korker's Wading Boots, which can swap a trail sole, felt or carbide cleated traction sole or carbide rubber sole.

Frogg Toggsmakes a variety of rainwear.

L.L. Bean

15 Casco St.
Freeport, ME 04033
(800) 441-5713
Fax: (207) 552-3080
www.llbean.com

Besides its line of outdoor clothing, L.L. Bean offers an extensive line of fishing equipment, including fly rods and reels, waders, fly lines and leaders, and accessories. It also sponsors Outdoor Discovery Schools about fly-fishing.

■ **Brand Name(s):** L.L. Bean, Outdoor Discovery School.
✔ Brochure. ✔ Online shop.
■ **Products:** • Fly rods • Fly reel • Waders • Accessories

LaCrosse Footwear Inc.

18550 NE Riverside Parkway
Portland, OR 97230
(503) 766-1010
800-323BOOT
Fax: (503) 766-1015
customerservice@lacrossefootwear.net
www.lacrosse-outdoors.com

LaCrosse makes a variety of boots as well as rubber footwear, waders, and apparel.

■ **Brand Name(s):** LaCrosse.
■ **Products:** • Boots • Waders

Lure-Eyes

602 SW 14th St.
Bentonville, AR 72712
(501) 464-2800
(866) 587-3393
www.lureeyes.com

Lure-Eyes makes the "ultimate marine sungear." Its sunglasses offer lightweight titanium frames, polarized shatterproof lenses, and 100 percent UV protection in many styles.

■ **Brand Name(s):** Lure-Eyes.
✔ Brochure.
■ **Products:** • Sunglasses

The Buckmasters PFT by LaCrosse Footwear feature Thinsulate insulation and Trac-Lite soles for traction.

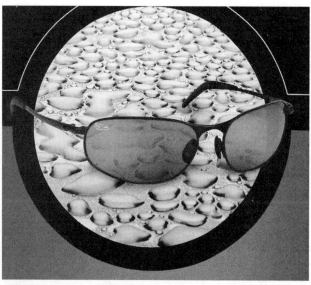

Lure-Eyes offers a complete line of the "ultimate marine sungear."

Adirondack waders from LaCrosse Footwear is a waterproof boot with Thinsulate insulation.

The Storm Jacket from Navarro is 100 percent polyester D.W.R. shell with waterproof, breathable polyurethane laminate.

Navarro Weather Gear

3017338 Canada Inc.
201-975 Vernon Drive
Vancouver, BC V6A 3P2
(604) 251-1756
(800) 663-7740
Fax: (604) 251-9862
info@navarro.ca
www.navarro.ca
Navarro makes heavy duty outdoors clothing, much of it specifically for water sports, including jackets, pants, and rainwear.
- **Brand Name(s):** Navarro.
- **Products:** • All-weather clothing

Nikwax

P.O. Box 1572
Everett, WA 98206
(425) 303-1410
Fax: (425) 303-1242
nixwax@watershedusa.com
www.nikwax-usa.com
Nikwax makes waterproofing products for a variety of uses, including outerwear, footwear, and equipment.
- **Brand Name(s):** Nikwax.
- ✔ Brochure.
- **Products:** • Waterproofing products

Ocean Waves Sunglasses Inc.

76 Levy Road
Atlantic Beach, FL 32233
(904) 247-7871
(800) 247-7871
Fax: (904) 249-1126
brad@oceanwaves.com
www.oceanwaves.com
Ocean Wave Sunglasses have polarized, distortion-free and spring-loaded frames made of acetate, nylon and metal. Online shopping is available.
- **Brand Name(s):** Ocean Waves Sunglasses.
- ✔ Online shop.
- **Products:** • Sunglasses

PolarEyes

51 Zaca Lane
San Luis Obispo, CA 93401
(800) 549-0063
www.polaroptics.com
PolarEyes offers premium sunglasses with polycarbonate UV-400 lenses with lightweight frames.
- **Brand Name(s):** PolarEyes.l
- **Products:** • Sunglasses

Rain Shield Inc.

5110A Cedar Lake Road South
Minneapolis, MN 55416
(888) 543-1894
Fax: (952) 543-1896
www.rainshield.com
Rain Shield creates O2 branded rainwear from 3M's Propore Fabric, which is waterproof and breathable.
- **Brand Name(s):** Rain Shield, O2.
- **Products:** • Rainwear

Red Wing Shoe Co.

314 Main St.
Red Wing, MN 55066
(651) 388-8211
888-SETTER0
customer.service@irishsetterboots.com
www.irishsetterboots.com
For more than 50 years, Red Wing has been making shoes and boots, including the Irish Setters lline of outdoor footwear developed for freshwater and saltwater fishermen.
- **Brand Name(s):** Irish Setters.
- **Products:** • Footwear

Schott International Inc.

2850 Gilchrist Road
Akron, OH 44305
(866) 853-4563
Fax: (330) 773-7856
www.schottint.com
Schott International makes waterproof fabrics, finishes, and tarps for the fishing and hunting industries.
- ■ **Products:** • Fabrics

Sportif USA

1415 Greg St., Suite 101
Sparks, NV 89431
(775) 359-6400
800-SPORTIF
Fax: (775) 353-3400
www.sportif.com
Sportif USA makes outdoor clothing "for the everyday extremist," including a line of fishing attire, including pants, shirts, and shorts, some with UV sun protection. Sales are made online, by phone, by catalog, and through stores.
- ■ **Brand Name(s):** Sportif USA.
- ✔ Brochure. ✔ Online shop.
- ■ **Products:** • Clothing

Tarponwear International

P.O. Box 1170
Jackson Hole, WY 83001
(800) 291-9402
Fax: (307) 739-9817
tarponwear@tarponwear.com
www.tarponwear.com
Tarponwear manufactures hot weather clothing that offers maximum sun protection, including shirts, pants, shorts, jackets, and hats. Product lines are UV-

Top: Tarponwear's UV-Pro Flats Long Sleeve Shirt has 30+ UV sun Protection, an extended collar for neck protection, and front pocket to hold extra gear. *Bottom:* The Women's UV-Pro Original Flats Pants from Tarponwear is 100 percent Supplex nylon with 30+UV sun protection and two front cargo pockets. *Bottom Left:* Tarponwear's Flats Cap is 100 percent Micro Polyester offers extreme sun protection, including a stowable back flap.

Pro and UV Max-Pro.
- **Brand Name(s):** UV-Pro, UV Max-Pro, Tarponwear.
- ✔ Brochure.
- **Products:** • Clothing

Top Line Manufacturing Co.

901 Murray Road
East Hanover, NJ 07936
(973) 560-9696
Fax: (973) 560-0661
www.toplineus.com
Top Line produces quality footwear for sportsmen, including a variety of Pro Line waders, boots, and accessories.
- **Brand Name(s):** Pro Line.
- ✔ Brochure.
- **Products:** • Waders

W.L. Gore & Associates

551 Paper Mill Road
Newark, DE 19711
(888) 914-4673
info@wlgore.com
www.gore.com
W.L. Gore makes Gore-Tex and Windstopper fabrics for outdoors wear, as well as Gore-Tex Immersion Technology for fishing waders and waterproof products, and Gore-Tex Ocean Technology outerwear.
- **Brand Name(s):** Gore-Tex, Windstopper.
- ✔ Online shop.

Wickers America

20 Wickers Drive
Wolfboro, NH 03894
(800) 648-7024
www.wickers.com
Wickers specializes in high-performance underwear for active people.
- **Brand Name(s):** Wickers
- ✔ Brochure. ✔ Online shop.
- **Products:** • Apparel

Chest waders that are waterproof and breathable, with rubber boot feet are part of the Pro Line arsenal made by Top Line Manufacturing.

VASQUE

The Vasque Gore-Tex is a light fabric/leather boot with material from W.L Gore & Associates.

Fishing Accessories

3rd Grip Products

P.O. Box 217
San Marcos, CA 92079
866407-GRIP
www.3rdgrip.com

3rd Grip makes the "ultimate pole and tool holster," a carrier for a fishing pole, knife, and pliers that straps to an angler's lower leg or waist. That allows the angler to hold the pole while baiting, removing a hook, changing lures, or removing tackle.

■ **Brand Name(s):** 3rd Grip Pole Holster.
✔ Brochure.
■ **Products:** • Fishing pole holder

5K Enterprises

999 Route 910
Allison Park, PA 15101
(888) 757-2800
Fax: (724) 443-1344

5K Enterprises manufactures and distributes the Wonder Bar and Wash-A-Way odor cleansing metal bars for fishing, hunting, camping, and hiking.

■ **Brand Name(s):** Wonder Bar, Wash-A-Way.
■ **Products:** • Odor cleaners

Aerated Bait Container Co. Inc.

Route 1, Box 68R
Brook Park, MN 55007
(320) 629-5065
abccoinc@ecenet.com
www.ecenet.com/abccoinc

Aerated Bait manufactures insulated aerated bait containers that operated on batteries for up to 48 hours to keep bait fresh.

■ **Brand Name(s):** Aerated Bait Container.
■ **Products:** • Bait containers

Albackore

23705 Van Owen St. #288
West Hills, CA 91307
(818) 704-5731
Fax: (818) 702-6824
troutman@westval.com
www.albackore

The Ultimate Pole & Tool Holster, from 3rd Grip, allows an angler to hold a fishing pole, pliers, and knife while having hands free to do other tasks.

Albackore makes a freshwater/saltwater fishing tackle bag that features soft-sided/rigid frame construction, removable lunchbox, and adjustable shelves and dividers.

■ **Brand Name(s):** Albackore.
■ **Products:** • Fishing tackle bags

Altrec.com
135 Lake St. South #1000
Kirkland, WA 98033
(425) 827-5159
(800) 369-3949
www.altrec.com
Altrec.com offers information and sells a wide variety
of outdoors products online, including fly fishing
equipment such as fly line, float tubes, clothing, rods
and reels, tools, and waders. The Web site contains
articles on fishing.
✔ Online shop.
■ **Products:** • Fly fishing gear • Information

American Angler
P.O. Box 29
Walnut Ridge, AR 72476
(870) 886-6774
Fax: (870) 886-9162
bwilcoxson@douglasquikut.com
www.quikut.com
American Angler makes electric fillet knives that can
plug into electrical outlets or a cigarette lighter or
clamps onto a battery. It also makes manual fillet
knives and aerators.
■ **Brand Name(s):** American Angler, Quikut.
■ **Products:** • Fillet knives

American Fly Fishing Co.
3523 Fair Oaks Blvd.
Sacramento, CA 95864
(916) 483-1222
(800) 410-1222
www.americanfly.com
American Fly Fishing has online shopping for a wide
variety of fishing equipment, including fly rods and
reels, lines and leaders, nets, waders, clothing, flies,
tubes, and books. It also arranges fishing trips with
guide service, and classes.
■ **Brand Name(s):** Leading brands.
✔ Online shop. , Retail shop.
■ **Products:** • Fly fishing gear • Guide service • Trips
• Fishing information

Angler Sports
6312 E. Santa Ana Canyon Road, #200
Anaheim Hills, CA 92807
(714) 685-9664
www.anglersports.com
Angler Sports makes the ultimate tackle containment
systems, backpack tackle boxes designed to carry

The BFP 5000 model backpack tackle box from Angler Sports can
carry up to eight boxes of equipment and has five wet/dry pouches.

fishing equipment with ergonomically designed
padded backs. Also available are jig packs and line
keepers.
■ **Brand Name(s):** Angler Sports.
✔ Brochure.
■ **Products:** • Backpack tackle boxes

Angler's Aluminum Products
920 Harbor Road
Wanchese Industrial Seafood Park
Wanchese, NC 27981
(252) 473-2905
888-RODRACK
Fax: (252) 475-1421
info@rodrack.com
www.rodrack.com
Angler's Aluminum Products makes fishing rod racks
for vehicles in several models, as well as an
installation kit and accessories.
■ **Products**: • Rod racks

A boy's unhappiness with a tangled fishing line could be prevented by The Tangle Tamer, a new product from Apex Outfitters that isolates the line with flexible tubing.

Anglers Attic

P.O. Box 460489
Escondido, CA 92025
(760) 736-0057
Fax: (760) 736-4967
www.anglersattic.com

Anglers Attic provides online shopping for a wide variety of fishing tackle, specializing in bass. Products available include lures, baits, tackle boxes, sinkers, and more.

■ **Brand Name(s):** Leading brands.
✔ Online shop.
■ **Products:** • Fishing tackle • Lures

Anglers Mart

P.O. Box 73
Woodland, MI 48897
sales@anglersmart.com
www.anglersmart.com

Anglers Mart is an online store for discount fishing tackle and equipment, including lures, baits, floats, ice fishing equipment and jigs.

✔ Online shop.
■ **Products:** • Tackle • Lures • Baits • Ice fishing gear

Apex Outfitters Inc.

P.O. Box 9071
Fort Wayne, IN 46899
(260) 615-0431
Fax: (260) 459-2851
dan@thetangletamer.com
www.thetangletamer.com

Apex Outfitters makes The Tangle Tamer, a kit that installs onto most fishing poles and works by isolating the fishing line with flexible tubing, virtually eliminating tangles.

■ **Brand Name(s):** The Tangle Tamer.
■ **Products:** • Fishing line guide

Aqua Gem

P.O. Box 250
Branford, CT 06405
(203) 483-8293
Fax: (203) 483-8293
mail@aquagemtackle.com
www.aquagemtackle.com

Aqua Gem makes the Snap Float, an environmentally safe float in four sizes to suspend bait at a given depth, for saltwater and freshwater fishing, including fishing for shark.

■ **Brand Name(s):** Snap Float.
✔ Online shop.
■ **Products:** • Fishing floats

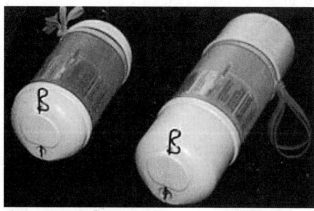

The Snap Float is operational in five seconds and is easy to attach.

Atlantic & Gulf Fishing Supply Corp.

7000 N.W. 74th Ave.
Miami, FL 33166
(305) 888-9646
(800) 327-6167
Fax: (305) 888-6027
www.atagulf.com

Atlantic & Gulf sells a wide variety of fishing equipment through its catalog and online. Products include anchors, aerators, clothing, hooks, tackle, tools, and accessories.
- **Brand Name(s):** Many leading brands.
- ✔ Brochure. ✔ Online shop.
- **Products:** • Tackle • Hooks • Tools • Clothing • Fishing gear

Axial Technologies Inc.

8111 28th Ave. N
New Hope, MN 55427
(763) 582-0438
(888) 805-6339
Fax: (763) 557-1062
www.axialtech.com

Axial makes the CatchCam underwater viewing system, which combines a camera and monitor and accessories.
- **Brand Name(s):** CatchCam.
- **Products:** • Underwater camera

B&L Sport Products

2115 Center Road
Clinton, OH 44216
(330) 882-6800
(866) 411-3269
Fax: (330) 882-5362

B&L manufactures Hard Plastic Rod Cases and has added a Rod Tote Carrier.
- **Products:** • Rod cases

B3 Sports Manufacturing Inc.

147 Old Milford Road
Brookline, NH 03033
(802) 893-2203
Fax: (719) 623-3162
info@b3sports.com
www.b3sports.com

B3 Sports specializes in Professional Catch Tools for anglers, allowing fishermen to land, weigh and release a catch, featuring in-haldle scales. Products include Accurra, Sure-Handle, and Twist-Lip Gaff.
- **Products:** • Weighing tools

Top: The Helmsman Compass series is among many fishing products available in the Atlantic & Gulf Fishing supply catalog.
Bottom: A variety of plastic handled knives combine stainless steel with vanadium and carbon for hardness at Atlantic & Gulf Fishing Supply.

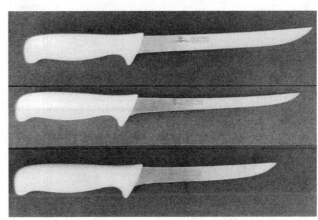

Backbone Fishing Products

P.O. Box 12126
Costa Mesa, CA 92627
(949) 646-2741
www.backbonefishing.com

Backbone Fishing Products produces reel clamps that offer strength, light weight, durability, and a place to secure a rigged hook, jig or lure. They are designed to fit with a number of reels.
- **Brand Name(s):** Backbone.
- ✔ Brochure.
- **Products:** • Reel clamps

Top: A Deluxe Rod Rack stores an angler's complete arsenal in this offering from the Bass Pro Shops catalog. *Middle:* The Extreme Boat Bag from Bass Pro Shops is made to be kicked, thrown, stepped on, or drenched. *Bottom:* New from Bass Pro Shops is the Tourney Special Round Baitcast Reel with four bearings for increased casting distance.

Bag-em Products LLC

2341 Morton St.
Flint, MI 48507
(810) 694-0189
(888) 665-0189
Fax: (810) 579-0754
bag-em@voyager.net
www.bag-em-com

Bag-em Products specializes in bags to carry fish from the boat to the weigh-in scales or cull fish, as well as bass tags, measuring devices, and hats, patches, and decals. Orders are taken online, by phone or by catalog.
- **Brand Name(s):** Bag-em.
- ✔ Brochure. ✔ Online shop.
- **Products:** • Fish bags • Measuring devices

Bass Pro Shops

2500 E. Kearney
Springfield, MO 65898
800-BASSPRO
Fax: (800) 566-4600
www.basspro-shops.com

Bass Pro Shops offers online and catalog shopping for a wide variety of fishing equipment and products, including rods and reels, baits, terminal tackle, videos and books, waders, clothing, marine products, electronics, and saltwater fishing tackle.
- **Brand Name(s):** Bass Pro Shops, Outdoor World.
- ✔ Brochure. ✔ Online shop.
- **Products:** • Rods and reels • Apparel • Tackle • Books, videos • Marine products • Electronics

Basstackle.com

P.O. Box 7025
Lee's Summit, MO 64064
(816) 350-8252
877-4TACKLE
Fax: (816) 478-1323
service1@basstackle.com
www.basstackle.com

Basstackle.com offers online shopping for a wide variety of fishing products, including lures, rods and reels, line, tackle boxes, rainsuits, and books.
- **Brand Name(s):** Leading brands.
- ✔ Online shop.
- **Products:** • Rods and reels • Lures • Clothing • Line

Bert's Custom Tackle
1250 Ladd Road
Walled Lake, MI 48390
(248) 624-8200
(800) 367-3726
Fax: (248) 624-4421
www.teclausa.com
Bert's Tackle makes a versatile rod-holder system,
  mounted on a track that is adjustable to most
  fishermen's needs. The rod holder can be removed
  from the track and replaced by accessories including a
  step pad, cup holder, tool holder, or fillet board.
- **Products:** • Rod holders

Bigfishtackle.com Inc.
P.O. Box 2287
Los Alamitos, CA 90720
(714) 799-1510
(877) 282-2553
Fax: (714) 799-1720
bigfish@bigfishtackle.com
www.bigfishtackle.com
Bigfishtackle.com offers online shopping for a wide
  variety of fishing gear in its Superstore. The Web site
  also has fishing reports, message boards, classified
  ads, resources, articles, and photos.
- **Brand Name(s):** Many name brands.
- ✔ Online shop.
- **Products:** • Fishing equipment • Fishing
  information

Bill's Sport Shop
1566 Highway One
Lewes, DE 19958
(302) 645-7654
www.billssportshop.com
Bill's Sport Shop has two retail fishing equipment
  stores in Lewes and Rehoboth Beach, Del., and also
  offers online sales of fishing gear. It also operates a
  fishing charter boat, the Slicker III.
- ✔ Online shop. ✔ Retail shop.
- **Products:** • Fishing equipment • Charter

BobWards.com
1600 North Ave. W #5
Missoula, MT 59801
(800) 800-5083
www.bobwards.com
BobWards.com started as Bob Ward & Sons, a
  Montana sporting goods retailer. It stocks fly rods and
  reels as well as men's and women's outerwear,
  activewear and footwear, including waders.
- **Brand Name(s):** Columbia, Cortland, G. Loomis,
  Montana Classic, Scientific Angler, St. Croix, and

other brands are featured.
- ✔ Online shop.
- **Products:** • Fly rods and reels • Apparel

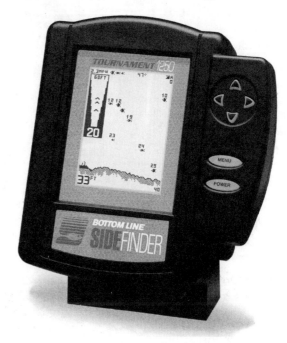

The SideFinder is one of Bottomline's fish finders.

Bottomline Electronics/Cannon
499 E. Corporate Drive
Meridian, ID 83642
(208) 887-1000
Fax: (208) 887-2000
customerservice@computrol.com
www.bottomlinefishfinders.com
Bottom Line Electronics produces several models of
  fish finders as well as a GPS module. It also produces
  Cannon downriggers. Online shopping is available
  and products are available in stores.
- **Brand Name(s):** Bottomline, Cannon.
- ✔ Online shop.

Bradley Technologies
2118-21320 Westminster Highway
Richmond, BC V6V 2X5
(604) 270-3646
(800) 655-4188
Fax: (604) 279-0553
info@bradleysmoker.com
www.bradleysmoker.com
Bradley Smokers offer wood barbecuing of seafood as
  well as beef, pork and ribs. The Web site includes
  recipes.
- **Brand Name(s):** Bradley Smoker.
- **Products:** • Smokers

THE DIGEST

The Ulti-Mate Ocean fillet knife is the largest in Buck Knives' arsenal, with an 8 ¼ -inch stainless steel blade.

Braid Products Inc.

538 E. Rancho Vista Blvd.
Palmdale, CA 93550
(661) 266-9791
(800) 716-4558
Fax: (661) 266-9849
info@braidproducts.com
www.braidproducts.com

Braid Products has a line of more 200 products for offshore fishing, including lures, fishing belts, hook sharpeners, pliers, rigs, and leaders. Sales are made online and through dealers. The Web page also includes fishing trips, tips, techniques.

- ■ **Brand Name(s):** Braid.
- ✔ Brochure. ✔ Online shop.
- ■ **Products:** • Saltwater fishing gear • Lures • Belts • Tools

Buck Knives

P.O. Box 1267
El Cajon, CA 92022
(800) 326-2825
www.buckknives.com

Buck Knives makes three types of fish fillet knives, plus a folding knife called the Fishlocker. Online shopping is available.

- ■ **Brand Name(s):** Buck Knives.
- ✔ Brochure. ✔ Online shop.
- ■ **Products:** • Fillet knives

Bushnell Performance Optics

9200 Cody
Overland Park, KS 66214
(800) 423-3537
Fax: (913) 752-3550
www.bushnell.com

Bushnell makes the H2Optix Marine Vision System for serious water sports enthusiasts. The polarized sunglasses are durable, fit comfortably, and include a floating sport strap and clip-on neoprene case.

- ■ **Brand Name(s):** Bushnell.
- ■ **Products:** • Sunglasses

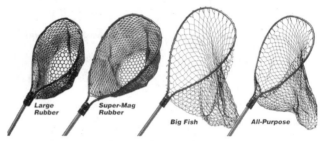

Top: Cabela's markets fish nets in several sizes. *Bottom:* An angler can carry all his rods at once with a Cabela's carrier.

Cabela's

812 13th Ave.
Sidney, NE 69160
(800) 237-4444
Fax: (800) 496-6329
www.cabelas.com

Cabela's offers a large catalog of fishing equipment, including rods, reels, lures, tackle, line, tools, GPS gear, and waders, for freshwater or saltwater fishing. It takes orders by phone, online, or in its Midwestern retail stores.

- ■ **Brand Name(s):** Cabela's as well as leading brands of fishing equipment.
- ✔ Brochure. ✔ Online shop. ✔ Retail shop.
- ■ **Products:** • Rods and reels • Lures • Line • Tackle • Waders • Tools

Caddis Manufacturing Inc.

4201 Riverside Drive
McMinnville, OR 97128
(503) 472-3111
(800) 824-4671
Fax: (503) 434-5038
www.caddis.com
Caddis Manufacturing designs, manufactures, and sells
float tubes and accessories for the fishing industry.
Included are round float tubes, u-shaped float tubes,
pontoon boats, and float tube accessories.
- **Brand Name(s):** Caddis.
- **Products:** • Float tubes • Pontoons

Capt. Harry's Fishing Supply

100 NE 11th St.
Miami, FL 33132
(305) 374-4661
(800) 327-4088
Fax: (305) 374-3713
www.captharry.com
Capt. Harry's provides online and catalog shopping for
a wide variety of fishing equipment, including rods
and reels, lures, tackle, line, tools, clothing, books,
and other gear. Its Web site also includes a newsletter,
fishing resources, and a photo album
- **Brand Name(s):** Many leading brands.
- ✔ Brochure. ✔ Online shop. ✔ Retail shop.
- **Products:** • Rods and reels • Tackle • Line • Tools •
Clothing • Accessories

Catalina Technologies Inc.

4740 E. Sunrise Drive, #393
Tucson, AZ 85718
(520) 529-2601
(800) 999-7745
Fax: (520) 529-0402
service@technocat.com
www.technocat.com
Catalina manufactures the ClineFinder, a digital
temperature and depth sounder, the Sportfisher digital
floating surface thermometer, and SportStrap, a rod
and reel wrap. Sales are by Internet and catalog.
- **Brand Name(s):** Technocat.
- ✔ Brochure. ✔ Online shop.
- **Products:** • Thermometers • Rod and reel wraps

Challenge Plastic Products Inc.

P.O. Box 278
Edinburgh, IN 46124
customerservice@fishingbuckets.com
www.fishingbuckets.com
Challenge makes plastic products for fishing, including
tackle boxes, fishing buckets, cricket cages, and
fishing accessories.
- **Products:** • Fishing buckets • Tackle boxes •
Cricket cages

Columbia River makes several knives for fishermen.

Columbia River Knife & Tool

9720 S.W. Hillman Court, Suite 805
Wilsonville, OR 97070
(503) 685-5015
(800) 891-3100
Fax: (503) 682-9680
info@crkt.com
www.crkt.com
Columbia River makes makes a variety of hunting and
outdoor knives, including fish fillet knives.
- **Brand Name(s):** Columbia River.
- ✔ Brochure.
- **Products:** • Fillet knives

Compleat Angler/Camas Designs

555 W. 25th St.
Idaho Falls, ID 83402
(208) 522-1794
Fax: (208) 523-3148
Since 1973, Compleat Angler has manufactured fishing
and outdoor accessories, including felt soles,
suspenders, Duraflex patch kits, rod bags, and gear
packs.
- **Products:** • Fishing accessories

Component Systems Inc.

5004 Sherman St.
Wausau, WI 54401
(715) 845-3009
Fax: (715) 845-3907
www.csipaint.com
Component Systems is a paint manufacturer for the
fishing tackle industry, as well as consumers, for
fishing lures and jigs. Products include ProTec
Powder Paint and Pro-Flake Metallic Glitter.
- **Products:** • Paint for lures

Pro-Tec Powder Paint from Component Systems produces a durable, high-gloss fluorescent finish for lures and dries in seconds.

Coverlay Manufacturing Inc.

4017 Highway 67 N
San Angelo, TX 76905
(800) 633-7090
Fax: (915) 658-8885
coverlay@coverlaymfg.com
www.coverlaymfg.com
Coverlay manufactures a number of fishing accessories, including Ken Cook's Fishing Tool Kit, rod organizers and reel racks, Peter T's Rigmaster, and utility box caddies. Online shopping is available.
- **Brand Name(s):** Coverlay.
- ✔ Online shop.
- **Products:** • Tool kits • Rod and reel organizers

Dan Bailey's Fly Shop

209 W. Park St.
P.O. Box 1019
Livingston, MT 59047
(406) 222-1673
(800) 356-4052
Fax: (406) 222-8450
info@dan-bailey.com
www.dan-bailey.com
Based in Montana, Dan Bailey's Fly Shop has been outfitting flyfishers since 1938. Dan Bailey sells through an online catalog, as well as traditional catalog sales, including flies, rods and reels, waders, lines, clothing, and accessories.
- **Brand Name(s):** Leading brands of fly equipment.
- ✔ Brochure. ✔ Online shop. ✔ Retail shop.
- **Products:** • Online fly fishing gear sales • Guide service • Fishing information

Duluth Pack

1610 W. Superior St.
Duluth, MN 55806
(800) 777-4439
orders@duluthpack.com
www.duluthpack.com
Besides its trademark Duluth Packs, the company makes camping gear, totes, and luggage. It stocks fly fishing equipment. There is a retail store in Duluth.
- **Brand Name(s):** Duluth Pack.
- ✔ Online shop. ✔ Retail shop.

Eagle Electronics' new Tri-Finder 2 produces three-beam-wide underwater sonar coverage to give anglers a view of left, right, and center fish and objects.

Eagle Electronics

P.O. Box 669
Catoosa, OK 74015
(918) 437-6881
(800) 324-1354
www.eaglesonar.com
Eagle Electronics makes sonar fish fishers and Global Positioning Systems for mapping and navigation. Sonar units include the FishEasy, FishMark, and TriFinder2. Also available is mapping softwear.
- **Brand Name(s):** Eagle Sonar, FishEasy, FishMark.
- ✔ Brochure. ✔ Online shop.
- **Products:** • Fish finders • GPS units

eAngler Inc.

8401-A Benjamin Road, Suite A
Tampa, FL 33634
(813) 639-9636
877-979FISH
Fax: (813) 639-9736
www.eangler.com
eAngler operates the eAngler.com Web site, which has
  online sales of fishing equipment, including clothing,
  electronics, engines, fly fishing gear, tackle, lures,
  rods and reels, tools, and accessories. The Web site
  also provides fishing information,.
- **Brand Name(s):** Leading brands.
✔ Online shop.
- **Products:** • Fishing equipment • Clothing •
  Reference information • Newsletter

Ed Cumings Inc.

2305 Branch Road
Flint, MI 48506
(810) 736-0130
Fax: (810) 736-7701
www.cumingsnets.com
Since 1927, Ed Cumings has supplied top quality fish
  landing nets and accessories.
- **Brand Name(s):** Ed Cumings.
- **Products:** • Nets

Evergreen Fly Fishing Co.

768 Locust Ave.
Clarksburg, WV 26301
(304) 623-3564
www.evergreenflyfishing.com
Evergreen Fly Fishing combines online fly fishing
  tackle sales with a guide service and fly fishing
  instruction. It operates a retail store in West Virginia
  with more than 10,000 flies in stock as well as 100
  books, fly tying materials.
- **Brand Name(s):** Leading brands.
✔ Online shop. ✔ Retail shop.
- **Products:** • Fly fishing tackle • Guide service •
  Instruction

F.J. Neil Co. Inc.

1064 Route 109
P.O. Box 617
Lindenhurst, NY 11757
(631) 957-1073
(800) 969-6345
Fax: (631) 957-1005
canefish@aol.com
F.J. Neil sells a wide variety of fishing products,
  including rods and reels, bamboo poles, line, terminal
  tackle, floats, sinkers, nets, tools, lures, and jigs.

- **Products:** • Fishing equipment

Fish Hawk Electronics Corp.

P.O. Box 340
Crystal Lake, IL 60039
(815) 363-0929
Fax: (815) 363-0966
www.fishhawkelectronics.com
Fish Hawk Electronics makes sport fishing instruments
  to monitor temperature, light/lure color, trolling speed,
  and lure speed to 200 feet deep.
- **Brand Name(s):** Fish Hawk Electronics.
- **Products:** • Depth, temperature measuring devices

Fish-N-More Inc.

1135 Springfield Road
Union, NJ 07083
(908) 355-1613
info@fishnmore.com
www.fishnmore.com
Fish-N-More offers a line of bobbers, including the
  Master Beacon lighted bobbers, the Master Sensor
  bite sensor, lures, and food spirals for carp.
✔ Online shop.
- **Products:** • Bobbers • Lures

Fisherman's Line

P.O. Box 236
Assonett, MA 02702
(508) 644-5812
Fax: (508) 946-3456
www.fishermansline.com
Fisherman's Line sells a variety of fishing products,
  including Yankee lures, rigs, tubing, tools, and books.
  Sales are by catalog and online.
- **Brand Name(s):** Several brand names.
✔ Brochure. ✔ Online shop.
- **Products:** • Rigs • Tools • Lures • Books

Fishin' Musician

P.O. Box 50102
Richmond, VA 23250
fishinmusicians@hotmail.com
www.thefishinmusician.com
The Fishin' Musician operates a Web site that offers
  online shopping for fishing tackle, fishing reports and
  current conditions on the Virginia area, a guide
  service, picture gallery, and an online magazine with
  articles on fishing.
✔ Online shop.
- **Products:** • Online shopping • Fishing information

Fishing Buddy System

2510 Robinson St.
Colorado Springs, CO 80904
(800) 615-6461
www.fishingbs.netmegs.com
Fishing Buddy System makes the Shore Fishing Buddy, a fishing rod holder, and the Ice Fishing Buddy. Orders are taken by phone or the Internet.
- **Brand Name(s):** Fishing Buddy System.
- **Products:** • Fishing rod holders

Fishypete's Fly Co.

P.O. Box 16084
Savannah, GA 31416
(912) 356-3474
Fax: (912) 356-3483
www.fishypete.net
Fishypete's offers online fly fishing shopping. It also enrolls members on its Web site, offering them special Fly Club flies and members' privileges such as discussion groups and fishing news.
- **Brand Name(s):** Fishypete.
- ✔ Online shop.
- **Products:** • Fly fishing gear

Flambeau Products Corp.

15981 Valplast Road
Middlefield, OH 44062
(440) 632-1631
(800) 457-5252
Fax: (440) 632-1581
www.flambeau.com
Flambeau Outdoors manufactures plastic products for sportsmen, including tackle boxes, bait buckets, rod tubes, and utility boxes.
- **Brand Name(s):** Kwikdraw, Tackle Station, Bazooka Rod Tubes.
- **Products:** • Tackle boxes • Bait buckets • Rod tubes

Flow-Rite

3412 Lousma Drive SE
Grand Rapids, MI 49548
(616) 243-2750
Fax: (616) 243-5151
www.flow-rite.com
Flow-Rite has developed a number of Livewell and Baitwell Systems to keep fish and bait alive.
- **Brand Name(s):** Flow-Rite.
- **Products:** • Livewells

Top: **Fly Logic offers a RTG** *(ready to Go)* **family of fishing rods for freshwater, saltwater, and travel.** *Bottom:* **Optimum and Premium lines of fly lines of fly fishing reels are available at Fly Logic.**

Fly Logic Inc.

P.O. Box 270
Melba, ID 83641
888-FLYLOGIC
Fax: (208) 495-2064
fli@flylogic.com
www.flylogic.com
Fly Logic offers online catalog shopping for its rods, reels and kits, which include the new ready-to-go Travel Logic Kit. It also has started the TryLogic program that offers a 14-day trial period to test equipment before buying.
- **Brand Name(s):** Fly Logic.
- ✔ Brochure. ✔ Online shop.
- **Products:** • Rods • Reels • Fly fishing kits

Fly Shop International

11060 Alpharetta Highway, Suite 112
Roswell, GA 30076
(770) 649-9866
atlflyfishing@mindspring.com
www.flyshopinternational.com
Fly Shop International is an Internet shopping site for fly fishing equipment, including rods and reels, line, fly tying, clothing, and accessories. Its sister site, Atlanta Fly Fishing Outfitters, offers fly fishing instruction, fishing reports.
- **Brand Name(s):** Leading fly fishing brands.
- ✔ Online shop.
- **Products:** • Fly fishing gear • Fly fishing instruction

Top: The FPI Fishing Vest features the Pocket Pak Fishing system with convenient cases for lures or hooks. *Bottom:* Lure Holster from Form Plus Industries keep lures tuned and untangled.

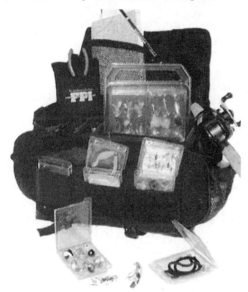

Force Fin
715 Kimball
Santa Barbara, CA 93103
800-FINSWIM
Fax: (805) 564-8240
info@forcefin.com
www.forcefin.com
Force Fin makes swimming and paddling fins, including some that can be used with float tube fishing to propel and maneuver the tube.
■ **Brand Name(s):** Force Fin.
■ **Products:** • Float fishing fins

Form Plus Industries
700 Colorado St., Suite A
Kelso, WA 98626
(360) 575-9203
www.formplusindustries.com
Form Plus Industries manufactures PocketPak fishing

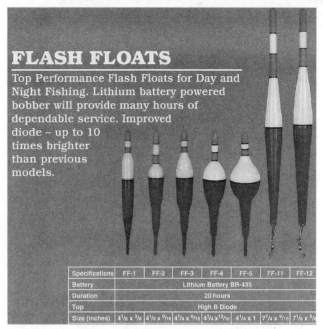

FLASH FLOATS

Top Performance Flash Floats for Day and Night Fishing. Lithium battery powered bobber will provide many hours of dependable service. Improved diode – up to 10 times brighter than previous models.

Specifications	FF-1	FF-2	FF-3	FF-4	FF-5	FF-11	FF-12
Battery	Lithium Battery BR-435						
Duration	20 hours						
Top	High B Diode						
Size (inches)	$4^{1}/_{8}$ x $^{3}/_{8}$	$4^{1}/_{8}$ x $^{9}/_{16}$	$4^{1}/_{4}$ x $^{9}/_{16}$	$4^{1}/_{4}$ x $^{13}/_{16}$	$4^{1}/_{4}$ x 1	$7^{1}/_{4}$ x $^{9}/_{16}$	$7^{1}/_{8}$ x $^{5}/_{8}$

Lighted Flash Floats from Fuji-Toki are powered by lithium batteries for day or night fishing.

and hunting systems, including fly boxes and tackle boxes, vests, spinners, and fishing tools.
■ **Brand Name(s):** PocketPak.
✔ Brochure. , Online shop.
■ **Products:** • Tackle boxes • Fishing tools • Spinners

Frabill
P.O. Box 49
Jackson, WI 53037
service@frabill.com
www.frabill.com
Frabill manufactures bait containers, landing nets, worm bedding boxes, portable ice shelters, tip-ups, and jig rods.
■ **Brand Name(s):** Frabill.
■ **Products:** • Bait containers • Nets • Ice shelters • Tip-ups

Fuji-Toki California Inc.
P.O. Box 7032
1673 Donlan St. # 208
Ventura, CA 93003
(805) 674-8190
(800) 336-0669
Fax: (805) 644-0431
Fuji-Toki makes several types of lighted botters, including Flash Floats, Lighted Slip Bobbers, Jumbo Flash Floats, as well bobber stops and headlamps.
■ **Brand Name(s):** Fuji-Toki.
■ **Products:** • Lighted bobbers

Furuno USA Inc.
4400 N.W. Pacific Rim Blvd.
Camas, WA 98607
(360) 834-9300
Fax: (360) 834-9400
www.furunousa.com
Furuno USA manufactures a variety of marine
electronics, including radar, sonar, GPS, fish finders,
autopilots, NavNet, Weather fax, and VHF and Single
Side Band radios.
■ **Brand Name(s):** Furuno.
✔ Brochure.
■ **Products:** • Fish finders • Radars • Radios •
NavNet

G. Pucci and Sons
P.O. Box 140
43 Park Lane
Brisbane, CA 94030
(415) 468-0457
(800) 537-2394
Fax: (514) 468-5147
www.p-line.com
G. Pucci and Sons makes P-Line fishing lines with
copolymer-based and fluorocarbon technology.
Products include Floroice, CXX X-tra Strong, and
CX Premium lines, as well as pliers and crimpers.
■ **Brand Name(s):** P-Line.
■ **Products:** • Fishing line

Gander Mountain
4567 W. 80th St.
Minneapolis, MN 55437
8889GANDER
Gander Mountain operates more than 50 stores in seven
midwestern states, specializing in fishing, camping,
and hunting equipment. Fishing equipment includes
rods and reels, lures, electronics, marine products,
and ice fishing equipment.
■ **Brand Name(s):** A variety of brands of fishing
equipment.
✔ Retail shop.
■ **Products:** • Rods • Reel • Elec • Lure • Boat

Garmin International Inc.
1200 E. 151st St.
Olathe, KS 66062
(913) 397-8200
Fax: (913) 397-8282
www.garmin.com
Garmin International manufactures several types of
Global Positioning Systems for mapping and
navigation, and a line of fishfinders.
■ **Brand Name(s):** Garmin.

■ **Products:** • GPS gear • Fishfinders

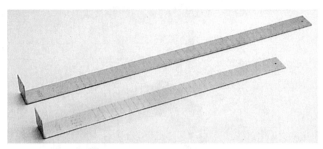
**Bluewater Measuring Boards from Gator Grip are made of
aluminum and handle fish up to 38 inches and 48 inches.**

Gator Grip
1441 Miller Ave.
Shelbyville, IN 46176
(317) 398-6281
Fax: (317) 392-4267
www.gatorgrip.com
Gator Grip produces fishing accessories, including
Golden Rule fish measuring boards, hook sharpeners,
reel handles, and hex nuts. Online shopping is
available.
■ **Brand Name(s):** Gator Grip.
✔ Brochure. ✔ Online shop.
■ **Products:** • Fish measurement tools • Reel handles

Gearout Outdoor GearStore
100 E. Corsicana St., Suite 200
Athens, TX 75751
(866) 443-2768
Fax: (903) 675-8179
info@Gearout.com
www.gearout.com
Gearout offers online shopping for a wide variety of
fishing, marine, and electronics products. Included
are rods and reels, bait, clothing, line, lures, boating
accessories, radios, depth finders, and fish finders.
■ **Brand Name(s):** Leading brand names.
✔ Online shop.
■ **Products:** • Rods and reels • Boating access • Fish
finders • Clothing • Bait • Tackle

Gonefishinshop.com
5069 Johnston Road
Port Alberni, BC V9Y 5L6
(250) 723-1172
Fax: (250) 723-1173
info@gonefishinshop.com
www.gonefishinshop.com
Gonefishinshop.com is a Canadian Web site that offers
online shopping for fishing, hunting, and outdoor
clothing products. A wide selection of freshwater and

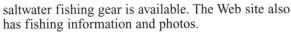

saltwater fishing gear is available. The Web site also has fishing information and photos.
✔ Online shop.
■ **Products:** • Fishing gear

Gorge Fly Shop

201 Oak St.
Hood River, OR 97031
(541) 386-6977
gorgeflyshop@gorgeflyshop.com
www.gorgeflyshop.com
Gorge Fly Shop operates a store in Hood River and offers online shopping for a variety of fly fishing equipment, including rods and reels, waders, float tubes, pontoon boats, and rain jackets from major manufacturers. It also offers guide service.
■ **Brand Name(s):** Major brands.
✔Brochure. ✔ Online shop. ✔ Retail shop.
■ **Products:** • Rods and reels • Float tubes • Rainwear • Guide service

Hagen's

3150 W. Havens
Mitchell, SD 57301
(605) 996-1891
(800) 541-4586
Fax: (605) 996-8946
www.hagensfish.com
Hagen's produces fishing tackle components, hand-crafted rods, live bait coolers, and fish rules.
■ **Brand Name(s):** Hagen's.
✔ Brochure.
■ **Products:** • Fishing rods • Bait coolers

Hanggee-Koehler Corp.

20332 Clark St.
Woodland Hills, CA 91367
(818) 340-6253
Fax: (818) 340-6262
www.reelegood.com
Hanggee-Koehler makes the Reel E Good Winder for reloading spin and bait cast reels and storing fly line on spools. It also makes protectant pads for cleaning and treating fly line, and a fly reel reloader. Online shopping is available.
■ **Brand Name(s):** Reel E Good.
✔ Online shop.
■ **Products:** • Line reloaders

Hi-Liner Fishing Gear & Tackle Inc.

P.O. Box 5225
Lighthouse Point, FL 33074
(954) 783-1320
800-525GEAR
Fax: (954) 941-9323
hiliner@hiliner.com
www.hiliner.com
Hi-Liner provides saltwater fishing equipment to both the recreational and commercial markets, including line, lures, fighting belts, tools, tuna gear, and shark gear. Offices are in Florida and Nova Scotia, and a catalog is available.
✔ Brochure. ✔ Retail shop.
■ **Products:** • Line • Lures • Saltwater gear

High Country Flies

185 N. Center St.
P.O. Box 3432
Jackson, WY 83001
(307) 733-7210
(877) 732-7210
Fax: (307) 733-5382
info@highcountryflies.com
www.highcountryflies.com
High Country Flies provides online shopping as well as its Jackson store for a complete line of fly fishing equipment, including more than 1,700 Umpqua flies and 1,000 other products. Its Web site also offers fly fishing and tourism information.
✔ Online shop. ✔ Retail shop.
■ **Products:** • Fly fishing gear • Fishing information

HoldZit Products Inc.

15355 S. Bradley Road
Oregon City, OR 97045
(503) 655-9576
pat@holdzit.com
www.holdzit.com
HoldZit offers rust-stopping holsters and sheathes for fishing equipment, including vest packs, Tool Saver Holsters, Comfort Grips for rods, and Squeeze Sheathes gear storage. Online shopping is available.
■ **Brand Name(s):** HoldZit.
✔ Online shop.
■ **Products:** • Storage sheathes

Housatonic River Outfitters

24 Kent Road
Cornwall Bridge, CT 06754
(860) 672-1010
Fax: (860) 672-1010
hflyshop@aol.com
www.dryflies.com

Housatonic River Outfitters has two retail stores selling fly fishing equipment, including 50,000 flies. It also offers online shopping, as well as buying and selling used and antique fishing equipment. It also offers guide service and lodging.

✔ Online shop. ✔ Retail shop.
■ **Products:** • Fly fishing gear • Guide service • Lodging

Inside Sportfishing

5814 Van Allen Way, Suite 165
Carlsbad, CA 92008
(760) 930-4094
Fax: (760) 930-4054
info@insidesportfishing.com
www.insidesportfishing.com

Inside Sportfishing offers online shopping for more than 20,000 fishing items from 300 manufacturers. The Web site also provides information on travel, boats, tackle, conservation, fishing reports and sea temperature charts. It also produces TV shows

✔ Online shop.
■ **Products:** • Fishing equipment • Fishing information

Intruder Inc.

P.O. Box 136
Rice Lake, WI 54868
(800) 553-5129
Fax: (715) 234-9462
sales@intruderinc.com
www.intruderinc.com

Intruder offers fishing accessories and fish cleaning items, including fillet knives, boards, and gloves, knife sharpeners, live bait oxygen tabs, and crawler cribs. Online shopping is available and products are in stores.

■ **Brand Name(s):** Intruder.
✔ Online shop.
■ **Products:** • Fillet knives • Knife sharpeners

James Acord's Leather

2612 Armstrong Drive
Wooster, OH 44691
(330) 345-5778
turtles@bright.net
www.turtlemoon.com/acord/

James Acord makes custom fly fishing cases and other handmade leather products. Each piece is hand signed, dated, and numbered.

✔ Retail shop.
■ **Products:** • Fly fishing cases

KeepAlive Inc.

P.O. Box 1952
Tarpon Springs, FL 34688
(727) 841-0407
Fax: (727) 815-8049
keepalive@keepalive.net
www.keepalive.net

KeepAlive makes oxygen infusers designed to keep fish and bait alive. Included are portable oxygen infusers, livewell recirculating kits, and "thru hull" models. Sales are online and in bait shops.

■ **Brand Name(s):** KeepAlive.
✔ Online shop.
■ **Products:** • Oxygen infusers

Top: "Bite" Super Scents, from Lake Hawk, come in seven scents including garlic and crawfish. *Bottom:* The Catch & Release Tournament Bag by Lake Hawk allows fishermen to keep their trophy fish alive and well for weigh-in at tournaments.

Lake Hawk Inc.

512 Campbell Road S.E.
Calhoun, GA 30701
(706) 625-4620
Fax: (706) 625-8592
www.lakehawk.com
Lake Hawk makes a variety of fishing accessories,
including Color-Rite dipping dyes for baits, blades
and plugs, Worm Dye, "Bite" Super Scents for baits,
catch and release tournament bags, and deodorizing
soap. Online shopping is available.
- **Brand Name(s):** Lake Hawk, Color-Rite, "Bite."
- ✔ Brochure. ✔ Online shop.
- **Products:** • Bait dyes • Bait scents • Fish bags

Lake Products Co.

P.O. Box 189
Capac, MI 48014
(810) 395-9100
Fax: (810) 395-8840
info@knottying.com
www.knottying.com
Lake Products makes the Fisherman's Knot Tying Tool,
which comes with a booklet and video. It also makes
the Charger line of fishing lures. Orders are taken by
phone, online, mail or fax.
- **Brand Name(s):** Fisherman's Knot Tying Tool,
Charger.
- **Products:** • Knot-tying tool • Lures

Lansky Sharpeners

P.O. Box 800
Buffalo, NY 14231
(716) 877-7511
(800) 825-2675
www.lansky.com
Lansky makes a line of sharpeners for sportsmen's
equipment.
- **Brand Name(s):** Lansky Sharpeners.
- ✔ Brochure.
- **Products:** • Knife sharpeners

Lee Fisher International Inc.

3922 W. Osbourne Ave.
P.O. Box 15695
Tampa, FL 33684
(800) 356-5464
Fax: (813) 874-8807
leefisher@justfornets.com
www.cherrybombmarkerbuoy.com
Lee Fisher makes a line of high quality fish nets as well
as the Cherry Bomb Marker Buoy. Other Web sites
the company uses include www.justfornets.com and
www.justcastnets.com.

- **Brand Name(s):** Cherry Bomb Marker Buoy.
- **Products:** • Nets • Marker buoys

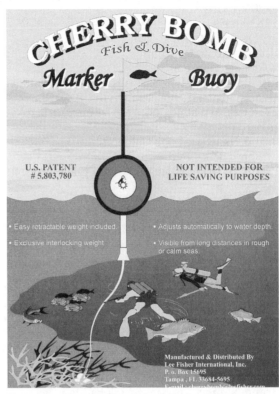

An illustration shows the Cherry Bomb Marker Buoy from Lee
Fisher International.

Loki Nets

3304 Rifle Range Road
P.O. Box 5320
Knoxville, TN 37928
(865) 687-7341
Fax: (865) 687-7343
midlakescorp@aol.com
Loki Nets makes landing nets, livewell nets, and bait
dip nets of all sizes.
- **Brand Name(s):** Loki Nets.
- ✔ Brochure.
- **Products:** • Fishing nets

The Big Fish Nets from Loki are sized for big, heavy fish including
muskie and salmon.

Loon Outdoors

7737 W. Mossy Cup
Boise, ID 83709
(28) 362-4437
Fax: (208) 362-4497
service@loonoutdoors.com
www.loonoutdoors.com
Loon Outdoors develops and sells fly fishing products,
including floatants, sinkets, fly tying materials,
accessories, and attire. Sales are by Internet and
catalog.
- **Brand Name(s):** Loon Outdoors.
✔ Brochure. ✔ Online shop.
- **Products:** • Fly fishing gear • Fly tying materials •
Accessories

Lowrance Electronics Inc.

12000 E. Skelly Drive
Tulsa, OK 74128
(800) 324-4781
Fax: (918) 234-1703
www.lowrance.com
Lowrance Electronics designs and manufactures sonar,
global position systems, and mapping products,
including GPS receivers for marine navigation and
fish finders. Included are a combination GPS and
sonar unit, color and black and white fish finders.
- **Brand Name(s):** Lowrance, GlobalMap.
✔ Brochure.
- **Products:** • Fish finders • GPS units

M and N Distributing

P.O. Box 164
54 Bridge St.
Midvale, ID 83645
(800) 352-5301
info@mandndistributing.com
www.mandndistributing.com
M and N sells several fishing products, including the
Rock-It Fish Scaler, Rocky Mountain T-Pik, U-Serve
String and Separator, Snake River Fish Scents, and
Rock-It Pole Holder. Sales are by Internet and
through dealers.
- **Brand Name(s):** Rock-It, U-Serve.
✔ Online shop.
- **Products:** • Fish scalers • Fish scents • Rod holders

Top: the SporTrak Map from Magellan is a handheld GPS unit that features full mapping capabilities, with 6MB of built-in maps and memory. *Bottom:* Magellan's Meridian Platinum GPS receiver is built for serious navigators, featuring a 16MB built-in map, three-axis electronic compass, and barometer.

Magellan

471 El Camino Real
Santa Clara, CA 95050
(408) 615-5100
Fax: (408) 615-5200
www.magellangps.com
Magellan, part of worldwide Thales Companies, makes
a line of Global Positioning (GPS) units that can be
used for fishing, boating, and other outdoor
recreation.
- **Brand Name(s):** Magellan.
✔ Brochure.
- **Products:** • GPS units

Marine Metal Products Inc.

1908 Calumet St.
Clearwater, FL 33765
(727) 461-5575
Fax: (727) 446-2026
www.marinemetal.com

Marine Metal Products makes livewell aeration systems to preserve live bait, including the Bubble Bag Bait Saver, Bubbles air pumps, Airhead livewell aerator, and Bait Saver Aerators. Products are available in stores, or by mail order.
- ■ **Brand Name(s):** Bubbles, Airhead.
- ■ **Products:** • Live bait aerators

UV Tech is one of the McNett's handy chemical products for fisherman.

McNett Corp.

1411 Meador Ave.
Bellingham, WA 98226
(360) 671-2227
Fax: (360) 671-4521
sales@mcnett.com
www.mcnett.com

McNett offers several products for anglers, including Aquaseal Wader Repair Kit, Tenacious Sealing & Repair Tape, Gore-Tex Fabric Repair Kit, Seal Cement for Neoprene repairs, MiraZyme Odor Eliminator, a line of outdoor knives.
- ■ **Brand Name(s):** MiraZyme, Aquaseal, Tenacious, Seal Cement.
- ✔ Brochure.
- ■ **Products:** • Sealants • Odor fighters • Knives

Mengo Industries Inc.

4611 Green Bay Road
Kenosha, WI 53144
(262) 652-3070
(800) 279-4611
Fax: (262) 652-9910
dotline@mengo-ind.com
www.mengo-ind.com

Mengo Industries manufactures marine and tackle products, including nets, rod holders, gaff hooks, paddles, and boat ladders.
- ■ **Brand Name(s):** Dotline.
- ✔ Brochure.
- ■ **Products:** • Nets • Rod holders • Ladders

Meyerco USA

4481 Exchange Service Drive
Dallas, TX 75236
(214) 467-8949
Fax: (214) 467-9241
meyerco@bnfusa.com
www.meyercousa.com

Meyerco makes several lines of knives, including fillet knives, as well as Camp USA camping tools.
- ■ **Brand Name(s):** Meyerco USA, Camp USA.
- ✔ Brochure.
- ■ **Products:** • Knives • Camping tools

Mid-Lakes Corp.

P.O. Box 5320
Knoxville, TN 37928
(865) 687-7341
Fax: (865) 687-7343
midlakescorp@aol.com

Mid-Lakes manufactures hand-held fishing nets and seines, including bait nets, cast nets and other products.
- ■ **Products:** • Nets

Mil-Comm Products

2 Carlson Ave.
East Rutherford, NJ 07073
(201) 935-8561
(888) 947-3273
www.reelsaver.com

Mil-Comm Products manufactures fishing and boating lubricants, including Reel Saver reel lubricant and Reel Saver Cleaner, Line Saver fishing line coating, Trailer Saver packing grease, and Boat Saver protective spray.
- ■ **Brand Name(s):** Reel Saver, Trailer Saver, Boat Saver.
- ■ **Products:** • Lubricants

THE DIGEST

Morning Dew Anglers

1900 Orange St.
Berwick, PA 18603
(570) 759-3030
mdangler@ptdprolog.net
www.morningdewanglers.com
Besides operating a retail shop in Pennsylvania,
 Morning Dew Anglers offers a guide service for trout
 and smallmouth bass, and a fly fishing school.
■ **Brand Name(s):** Many leading brands.
✔ Retail shop.
■ **Products:** • Guide service • Fly fishing gear

Nature Vision Inc.

213 NW 4th St.
Brainerd, MN 56401
(218) 825-0733
Fax: (218) 825-0721
aquavu@naturevisioninc.com
www.naturevisioninc.com
Nature Vision makes the Aqua-Vu underwater viewing
 system, including the camera, cables, monitor, and
 accessories, allowing anglers to see fish underwater.
■ **Brand Name(s):** Aqua-Vu.
✔ Brochure.
■ **Products:** • Underwater camera

Northern Sport Fishing Products Ltd.

139 Morris St., Unit 2
Guelph, ON N1E 5M6
(519) 824-4023
Fax: (519) 824-1439
sales@flyline.net
www.flyline.net
Northern Sport Fishing makes Aquanova fly lines, Ultra
 monofilament lines, and Ultra braided lines as well as
 lubricants for line and reels.
■ **Brand Name(s):** Aquanova, Ultra.
■ **Products:** • Fishing line

Ocean Anglers Unlimited LLC

1976 Circle Park Lane
Encinitas, CA 92024
(866) 733-5146
Fax: (760) 943-8804
marlin@theanglers.net
www.theanglers.net
Ocean Anglers Unlimited operates an online tackle
 store that stocks a huge inventory of rods and reels,
 line, terminal tackle, lures, accessories and apparel.
 The Web site also offers "hot bite" information,
 weather conditions, and links.
✔ Online shop.

■ **Products:** • Fishing tackle • Apparel • Fishing
 information

Ole Florida Fly Shop

6353 N. Federal Highway
Boca Raton, FL 33487
(561) 995-1929
(877) 653-3567
oleflorida@aol.com
www.oleflorida.com
Ole Florida Fly Shop operates a retail store in Boca
 Raton and also offers classes and schools for fly
 fishing, guide services, and trip packages. Fishing
 gear can be ordered by e-mail or phone.
■ **Brand Name(s):** Leading fly fishing brands.
✔ Retail shop.
■ **Products:** • Fly fishing gear • Guide service •
 Schools • Books • Apparel

**Lunker Lights from OmniGlow are three-inch lightsticks that
increase bait visibility.**

OmniGlow

96 Windsor St.
West Springfield, MA 01089
(800) 762-7548
www.omniglow.com
OmniGlow produces Outdoor Glow Lightsticks,
 survival lights, emergency boat lights, as well as
 Lunker Lights, Hammerhead Bobber Lights, and Rod
 Tip Clip-on Lights for fishing.
■ **Brand Name(s):** OmniGlow, Outdoor Glow.
■ **Products:** • Outdoor lights

PowerPro solves line problems with super slick, non-abrasive Spectra Fiber composition.

The Illuma-Light PR-200 from Optronics is a 2 million candlepower rechargeable spotlight with 100-watt quartz halogen bulb and internal 12-volt battery.

Optronics Inc.

401 S. 41st St. East
Muskogee, OK 74403
(800) 364-5483
www.optronicsinc.com

Optronics manufactures several types of fishing lights, including BlackEye Beam, Submersible Fish-N-Lites, and Floating Fish-N-Lites. It also makes docking lights for boats, spotlights, and head lamps.

■ **Brand Name(s):** Optronics, Illuma-Light, NightBlaster, BlackEye Beam.
✔ Brochure.
■ **Products:** • Fishing lights

Osprey Products

30665 N. Yosemite
Castaic, CA 91384
(888) 965-7225
Fax: (661) 294-9875

ospreyprods@earthlink.net
www.ospreyproducts.com

Osprey Products makes a variety of fishing and boating accessories, including rod racks, tackle box organizers, rod and boat tie-down buckles, battery trays, and the Jens-su Trolling Motor Weed Cutter. Online shopping is available.

■ **Brand Name(s):** Osprey.
✔ Brochure. , Online shop.
■ **Products:** • Rod racks • Tie-downs • Battery trays

Patagonia Inc.

8550 White Fir St.
P.O. Box 32050
Reno, NV 89523
(800) 638-6464
Fax: (800) 543-5522
www.patagonia.com

Patagonia has a variety of outdoors and fishing equipment, including fishing jackets, wading shoes, waders, and other clothing. Purchases can be made online, by catalog, or in stores.

■ **Brand Name(s):** Patagonia.
✔ Brochure. ✔ Online shop.
■ **Products:** • Clothing • Waders

Patagonia offeres a wide variety of Fleeces, shirts and sweatshirts.

Plano Molding Co.

431 E. South St.
Plano, IL 60545
(630) 552-3111
(800) 226-9868
Fax: (630) 552-9737
customercare@planomolding.com
www.planomolding.com
With more than 50 years in business, Plano makes several outdoors products for hunting and fishing, including a line of tackle boxes and gear bags.
■ **Brand Name(s):** Plano.
■ **Products:** • Tackle boxes

PowerPro

2105 I-70 Business Loop
Grand Junction, CO 81501
(970) 242-3002
(800) 650-8003
Fax: (970) 242-3030
www.powerpro.com
PowerPro makes fishing line with Enhanced Body Technology that provides strength, near zero stretch, and abrasion resistance. Sales are made on the Internet or in stores.
■ **Brand Name(s):** PowerPro.
✔ Online shop.
■ **Products:** • Fishing line

Pro Image Distribution Co.

6425 Isles Road
P.O. Box 459
Brown City, MI 48416
(810) 346-3660
(877) 788-3660
Fax: (810) 346-4072
info@ezfishing.com
www.ezfishing.com
Pro Image makes and distributes the Pro Trigger Release Hook Remover as well as Lightning Lure spinner baits. Orders are taken online and by catalog.
■ **Brand Name(s):** Pro Trigger Fish Hook Remover, Lightning Lures.
✔ Online shop.
■ **Products:** • Hook removers • Spinner baits

Rainbow Plastics

P.O. Box 1861
Ft. Collins, CO 80522
(970) 493-4189
Fax: (970) 221-0252
www.rainbowplastics.com
Rainbow Plastics is a manufacturer of floats, fishing accessories, and lures.
■ **Products:** • Floats • Accessories • Lures

Recreational Equipment Inc. (REI)

6750 S. 228th St.
Kent, WA 98032
(800) 426-4840
Fax: (253) 891-2523
www.rei.com
REI is a consumer cooperative that sells a variety of fishing and outdoors equipment online and in its more than 60 stores across the U.S. Fishing gear includes rods and reels, flies, sunglasses, waders, and clothing.
■ **Brand Name(s):** Most major brands are available.
✔ Online shop. ✔ Retail shop.
■ **Products:** • Rods and reels • Waders • Clothing • Flies

Reliance Products

1093 Sherwin Road
Winnipeg, MB R3H 1A4
(204) 633-4403
(800) 665-0258
Fax: (204) 694-5132
www.relianceproducts.com
Reliance Products, based in Canada, makes Woodstream Tackle, including utility boxes, Lid Lockers, rod cases, tackle bags, Pier-Mates, and trunk boxes.
■ **Brand Name(s):** Reliance, Woodstream Tackle.
✔ Brochure.
■ **Products:** • Tackle boxes • Rod cases

Renzetti Inc.

8800 Grissom Parkway
Titusville, FL 32780
(321) 267-7705
Fax: (321) 264-5929
www.renzetti.com
Renzetti makes tools for fly tying and fly fishing, including vises, bobbins, hair stackers, rod lathes, and accessories. Orders are taken online and sales are also made through dealers.
■ **Brand Name(s):** Renzetti.
■ **Products:** • Fly tying gear • Vises • Lathes

Rio Products International Inc.

5050 S. Yellowstone Highway
Idaho Falls, ID 83402
(208) 524-7760
Fax: (208) 524-7763
general@rioproducts.com
www.rioproducts.com

Rio Products manufactures fly lines for steelhead, salmon, bass, saltwater fish, and trout, as well as tapered leaders, tippet materials, and accessories. It also publishes the Rio Magazine online.

■ **Brand Name(s):** Rio.
✔ Brochure.
■ **Products:** • Fly lines • Leaders • Tippet materials • Online magazine

Top: A series of Fish Tail Handle Coffee Mugs are among angling gifts available from River's Edge Products. Bottom: Fish Flags available from River's Edge include this jumping sailfish.

River's Edge Products Inc.

#10 Lofting Industrial Drive
St. Clair, MO 63077
(636) 629-7300
(888) 326-6200
Fax: (636) 629-7557
www.riversedgeproducts.com

River's Edge makes a variety of outdoors accessories, including nautical gift items, can coolers, trailer ball covers, giant display lures, and fish wall hangings.

■ **Products:** • Nautical gifts • Can coolers • Wall hangings

RodMounts

P.O. Box 8105
Bend, OR 97708
(888) 925-4487
Fax: (541) 330-9661
www.rodmounts.com

RodMounts makes fishing rod carriers that can be mounted on boats, cars, pickup trucks, and SUVs.

■ **Brand Name(s):** RodMounts.
✔ Brochure. ╷ Online shop.
■ **Products:** • Fishing rod holders

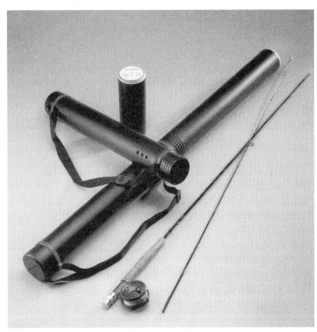

Top: VarioPack tubes by Rose Plastic protects fishing rods from shipping and storage. Bottom: A variety of plastic protectors are made by Rose Plastic to house fishing lures.

Rodtek Sports USA

11626 E. Christy St.
Cerritos, CA 90703
(562) 924-1264
Fax: (562) 927-5984
Rodtek Sports manufactures fishing backpacks, soft
tackle bags, bait, lures, jigs, and other terminal tackle.
■ **Products:** • Tackle bags • Baits • Terminal tackle

rose plastic USA LP

P.O. Box 698
California, PA 15419
(724) 938-8530
Fax: (724) 938-8532
www.rose-plastic.com
Rose plastic makes a variety of creative, protective
plastic packaging for fishing equipment, including
Variopack tubes for rods and lures.
■ **Brand Name(s):** Variopack.
■ **Products:** • Packaging

Scotty Fishing and Outdoor Products

2065 Henry Ave. West
Sidney, BC V8L 5Z6
(250) 656-8102
(800) 214-0141
Fax: (250) 656-8126
scotty@scotty.com
www.scotty.com
Scotty makes an assortment of electric and manual
downriggers and accessories, releases, rod holders;
outdoors products including knife sharpeners, oar
locks, and first aid kits; and boating lifebuoys and
safey items.
■ **Brand Name(s):** Scotty.
■ **Products:** • Downriggers • Rod holders • Boat
safety items

Shark River Mail Order

P.O. Box 115
Avon, NJ 07717
(800) 223-6481
Fax: (732) 774-5462
srmo@srmo.com
www.srmo.com
Shark River Mail Order is an online store that sells rods
and reels, line, lures, rigs, jigs, and a variety of fishing
equipment. Sales are also available through a catalog.
■ **Brand Name(s):** Several leading brands.
✔ Brochure. ✔ Online shop.
■ **Products:** • Rods and reels • Tackle • Rigging

Top: The Tie-Fast Knot Tyer is a one-piece stainless steel tool that
makes tying knots easier. *Bottom:* The Tie-Fast Line Clipper is made
of stainless steel and features a loop spring design and a protected,
enclosed eye pin used for cleaning hook eyes.

Sierra Stream

P.O. Box 7693
Chico, CA 95927
(530) 345-4261
(800) 343-1333
Fax: (530) 899-1038
tiefast1@aol.com
www.tie-fast.com
Sierra Stream manufactures fisherman's vest tools
under the brand name Tie-Fast Tools. Included are
knot-tying kits, line clippers, hook sharpeners,
scissors, and pliers. Sales are by catalog, online, and
in stores.
■ **Brand Name(s):** Tie-Fast Tools.
■ **Products:** • Fishing tools

SKB Corp.

434 W. Levers Place
Orange, CA 92867
(714) 637-1252
(800) 654-5992
Fax: (714) 283-0425
www.skbcases.com
SKB manufactures transport systems for fishermen,
including tackle boxes, rod transport cases, reel
lockers, and fishing bags.
■ **Products:** • Tackle boxes • Rod cases

Speedtech Instruments

P.O. Box 1178
Great Falls, VA 22088
(800) 760-0004
Fax: (703) 759-0509
info@speedtech.com
www.speedtech.com

Speedtech handles a variety of electronics and
instruments for fishing and boating, including depth
meters, compasses, weather radios, weather watches, a
fish feeding forecaster, and wind meters. Online
shopping is available and products are in stores.
- **Brand Name(s):** Speedtech.
- ✔ Online shop.
- **Products:** • Compasses • Depth meters • Weather
radios • Wind meters

Stearns is known for its flotation devices, including this Sportsman's
Vest in plain or camouflage.

Stearns Inc.

1100 Stearns Drive
Sauk Rapids, MN 56379
(320) 252-1642
(800) 333-1179
Fax: (320) 252-4425
stearns@stearnsnet.com
www.stearnsinc.com

Stearns makes several fishing and boating products,
including life vests, Fly Tech waders, float tubes, and
shoes, rainwear and outerwear, and marine products.
Sales are by catalog and online as well as in stores.
- **Brand Name(s):** Stearns, Fly Tech.
- ✔ Brochure. ✔ Online shop.
- **Products:** • Waders • Rainwear • Float tubes • Life
vests

Stillwater Fishing

9860 W. 59th Place
Arvada, CO 80004
(800) 950-0197
Fax: (801) 262-6897
sales@stillwaterfishing.com
www.stillwaterfishing.com

Stillwater specializes in float tubes and accessories for
fishing, as well as single-person pontoon and kick
boats.
- **Products:** • Float tubes • Pontoons and kick boats

The customer service staff of Strikemaster displays the company's
line of power ice fishing augers.

StrikeMaster Ice Augers

P.O. Box 567
17217 U.S. Highway 10 East
Big Lake, MN 55309
(763) 263-8999
Fax: (763) 263-8986
www.strikemaster.com

StrikeMaster manufactures ice fishing augers, including
power augers that use the new LazerMag Ultra blade,
as well as hand ice augers, electronics including the
PolarVision handheld digital sonar, and fishing house
heaters.
- **Brand Name(s):** StrikeMaster, Lazer.
- ✔ Brochure.
- **Products:** • Ice fishing augers • Electronics •
Heaters

Suncoast of America LLC

158 Little Nine Drive
Morehead City, NC 28557
(252) 727-1848
(888) 654-7520
Fax: (252) 727-4851

Suncoast manufactures and imports more than 230
  products, including fishing tools and accessories, fly-
  tying tools, and hunting tools.
- **Products:** • Tools • Accessories

T&L Products

7856 Reinbold Road
Reese, MI 48757
(989) 868-4428
Fax: (989) 868-1550
tandlproducts@aol.com
www.tandlproducts.com

T&L Products makes several fishing-related products,
  including a downrigger deck, Trol-a-Matic trolling
  motor controller, mounts for depth finders, and
  downrigger controls.
- **Products:** • Downrigger aids • Depth finder mounts

Tackle Factory

81 S. Genesee St.
P.O. Box 195
Fillmore, NY 14735
(585) 567-4176
(800) 991-2822
Fax: (585) 567-2366
info@cubaspecialty.com
www.tackle-factory.com

Tackle Factory manufactures fishing products,
  including Gee's Minnow Trap, crab and crawfish
  traps, rod cases, nets, and accessories.
- **Brand Name(s):** Tackle Factory, Cuba Specialty.
- **Products:** • Minnow traps • Rod cases • Nets

TackleDirect

926 Palen Ave.
Ocean City, NJ 08226
(609) 398-2900
888-354REEL
Fax: (609) 398-9962
sales@tackledirect.com
www.tackledirect.com

TackleDirect sells a variety of fishing equipment by
  catalog and online, including saltwater rods and reels,
  lures and tackle; freshwater rods and reels, lures and
  tackle; fly fishing rods and reels; fishing accessories,
  and sportswear.
- **Brand Name(s):** Many leading brands.

✔ Brochure. ✔ Online shop.
- **Products:** • Rods and reels • Tackle • Line •
  Sportswear • Tools

Taylor Cutlery's Smith & Wesson Knives for filleting include the
CHDDS with Kryton handle and 420 C Diamond Dust Coated Steel,
and the CHFF of Surgical Steel with 6.5 inch blade.

Taylor Creek Fly Shop

P.O. Box 799
Basalt, CO 81621
(970) 927-4374
tcreek@sopris.net
www.taylorcreek.com

Taylor Creek Fly Shop, near Aspen, provides fly
  fishing equipment, clothing, and service in its store. It
  also provides guide service in Colorado and arranges
  international trips. It has fishing reports on its Web
  site.
✔ Retail shop.
- **Products:** • Fly fishing gear • Guide service

Taylor Cutlery

P.O. Box 1638
Kingsport, TN 37662
(423) 247-2406
(800) 251-0254
Fax: (423) 247-5371
taylor@preferred.com
www.taylorcutlery.com

Taylor Cutlery handles the Smith & Wesson brand of
  knives, including fish fillet knives. Online shopping is
  available.
- **Brand Name(s):** Smith & Wesson Knives.
✔ Brochure. ✔ Online shop.
- **Products:** • Fillet knives

Team Nu-Mark

2908 Ciffet St.
Victoria, TX 77963
(361) 573-4199
(800) 843-3033
Fax: (361) 573-4712
www.teamnumark.com
Team Nu-Mark manufactures premium fishing equipment and accessories, including fishing tools, wading belts, fighting belts, and bait cages.
- **Products:** • Fishing tools • Fishing belts • Bait cages

Techsonic Industries Inc.

108 Maple Lane
Eufaula, AL 36027
(334) 687-6613
www.humminbird.com
Techsonic manufactures the Humminbird line of fish finders, including Humminbird, Piranha and Legend sonars, as well as Fisheye underwater cameras. It also makes the Teleflex line of marine products, including hydraulics and electrical units.
- **Brand Name(s):** Humminbird, Teleflex, Sierra Marine.
- ✔ Brochure.
- **Products:** • Fish finders • Cameras • Marine products

Tempress Products/Fish-On!

2015 McKenzie Drive, Suite 100
Carrollton, TX 75006
(972) 241-6500
877-2FISHON
www.fish-on.com
Tempress Products makes tackle boxes, seats and cushions, boot-savers, rod mounts, and fishing accessories as well as Fish-On clothing. It also operates the Fish-On! Web site that has fishing information, recipes, and links.
- **Brand Name(s):** Fish-On!, Tempress.
- **Products:** • Tackle boxes • Seats • Rod mounts • Fishing information

The Complete Sportsman

P.O. Box 826
Westborough, MA 01581
(508) 898-2990
Fax: (508) 898-3379
tcs@world.std.com
www.rareandunusual.com/tcs
The Complete Sportsman is dedicated to classic, contemporary, futuristic, and radical fly tying. It sells books about fly fishing and publishes the Art of Angling Journal, and its Web site includes galleries and a reference library on flies.
- **Brand Name(s):** The Complete Sportsman.
- ✔ Online shop.
- **Products:** • Fly-fishing books • Art of Angling Journal

The Fisherman's Store

P.O. Box 202132
Anchorage, AK 99520
(907) 338-6136
Fax: (907) 338-6118
admin@thefishermansstore.com
www.thefishermansstore.com
The Fisherman's Store offers online and catalog shopping for a wide variety of fishing equipment, including rods and reels, lures, hooks, fly-tying equipment, flies, line, apparel, and accessories.
- **Brand Name(s):** Leading brands.
- ✔ Brochure. ✔ Online shop.
- **Products:** • Rods and reels • Hooks • Fly-tying gear • Clothing

The Fly Factory

200 Ingham
P.O. Box 709
Grayling, MI 49738
(888) 768-8286
flyfactory@troutbums.com
www.troutbums.com
The Fly Factory offers fly fishing guide service on the AuSable and Manistee Rivers, as well as a retail store and canoe rentals. It plans to launch online shopping, and offers fishing information on the Troutbums Web site.
- ✔ Retail shop.
- **Products:** • Guide service • Fly fishing gear

The Fly Rod Shop

954 S. Main St.
Stowe, VT 05672
(802) 253-7346
(800) 535-9763
angler@flyrodshop.com
www.flyfishvt.com
The Fly Rod Shop sells fly rods, reels, and apparel in its retail shop and online. It also offers a guide service, classes, and clinics.
- ✔ Online shop. ✔ Retail shop.
- **Products:** • Fly rods • Reels • Guide service • Classes

Tight Lines Fishing Services

P.O. Box 236
Elkins Business Loop
Elkins, NH 03233
(603) 526-9299
(800) 526-6550
Fax: (603) 526-9473
info@nhfishguide.com
www.nhfishguide.com
Tight Lines operates a fly and tackle shop and a guide service in New Hampshire, fly fishing for salmon, trout, and bass.
- **Brand Name(s):** Several leading brands.
✔ Retail shop.
- **Products:** • Fly and tackle gear • Guide service

Tigress Outriggers & Gear

2516 SW 4th Ave.
Ft. Lauderdale, FL 33315
(954) 462-0917
Fax: (954) 524-0441
Tigress Outriggers has a complete line of telescoping and fixed aluminum outriggers, rigging kits, accessories, and outrigger fishing rod holders.
- **Products:** • Outriggers • Rod holders

Tite-Lok

P.O. Box 219
Topeka, IN 46571
(219) 593-2277
(800) 848-3565
weborders@titelok.com
www.titelok.com
Tite-Lok makes fishing rod holders, transducer holders and brackets, mounting systems, net holders, storage systems, and accessories. Products can be purchased online as well as in stores.
- **Brand Name(s):** Tite-Lok.
✔ Online shop.
- **Products:** • Rod holders • Storage systems

Tooltron Industries

103 Parkway
Boerne, TX 78006
(830) 249-8277
Fax: (830) 755-8134
easykut@gvtc.com
www.tooltron.com
Tooltron makes a variety of fly fishing and sport fishing tools, including retracto reels, scissors, threaders, nippers, clamps, and vises.
- **Brand Name(s):** Fly Tyme Products.
- **Products:** • Fishing tools

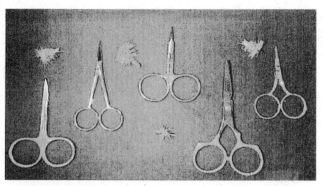

A variety of fishing scissors are among the fly fishing and sport fishing tools made by Tooltron Industries.

Trondak Inc.

11710 Airport Road, #300
Everett, WA 98204
(425) 290-7530
Fax: (425) 355-9101
www.aquaseal.com
Trondak makes Aquaseal brand waterproofing products, including map and fabric sealers, and footwear conditioner.
- **Brand Name(s):** Aquaseal.
- **Products:** • Waterproofing products

Ultimate Angler Inc.

P.O. Box 318037
San Francisco, CA 94131
(415) 695-8885
Fax: (415) 695-8886
www.ultimateangler.com
Ultimate Angler features online shopping for tackle storage, fishing accessories, fly fishing systems, and apparel.
- **Brand Name(s):** Ultimate Angler.
✔ Online shop.
- **Products:** • Tackle storage • Accessories • Clothing

Ultimate NiTi Technologies

200 Central St.
Bristol, CT 06010
(800) 999-6484
Fax: (860) 585-6666
info@ultimateniti.com
www.ultimateniti.com
Ultimate NiTi makes a variety of products from nickel titanium, including Recoil fishing rod guides, spinnerbaits, and the Ultimate LureSaver, a device that couples the hook to the lure.
- **Brand Name(s):** Ultimate LureSaver, Recoil guides.
- **Products:** • Rod guides • Lure savers

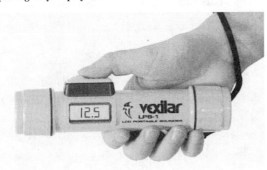

Top: Vexilar's FL-18 is the next generation of color LED flasher technology, with a built-in shallow water mode, Auto Zoom mode fro winter anglers, and a Bottom Lock feature for summer. *Bottom:* The LPS-1 Hand-held Depthfinder from Vexilar is easy to use. A fisherman puts it in the water, points, and pushes the "on" button to get the depth digitally displayed.

Vexilar Inc.

200 W. 88th St.
Minneapolis, MN 55420
(952) 884-5291
Fax: (952) 884-5292
www.vexilar.com

Vexilar is a manufacturer of marine electronics and accessories for freshwater fishing, including color flashers, LCD display depth sounders, and accessories including the Deptherm thermometer, mounts, and battery chargers. Online shopping is available.

■ **Brand Name(s):** Vexilar.
✔ Brochure. ✔ Online shop.
■ **Products:** • Depth finders • Color flashers • Battery chargers

W.R. Case & Sons Cutlery Co.

P.O. Box 4000
Owens Way
Bradford, PA 16701
(800) 523-6350
Fax: (814) 368-1736
casesales.com

W.R. Case makes a variety of pocket and sporting knives, including fish fillet knives.

■ **Brand Name(s):** W.R. Case
✔ Brochure.
■ **Products:** • Knives

West Coast Nets Inc.

930 S.E. 9th Lane
Cape Coral, FL 33990
(941) 573-1175
866-249NETS
Fax: (941) 573-1108
sales@westcoastnets.com
www.westcoastnets.com

West Coast Nets makes a variety of cast nets, primarily for catching bait including sardines, bait fish, minnows, and shrimp.

■ **Brand Name(s):** West Coast Nets.
■ **Products:** • Bait nets

Whistle Creek

P.O. Box 580
Monument, CO 80132
(719) 488-1999
Fax: (719) 488-1950
george@whistlecreek.com
www.whistlecreek.com

Whistle Creek is the largest maker of rustic walking and hiking sticks in the U.S., including a flyfishing wading staff and Field and Stream Walking Sticks. It offers online shopping, a catalog, and distribution through retail stores.

■ **Brand Name(s):** Whistle Creek.
✔ Brochure. ✔ Online shop.
■ **Products:** • Walking sticks • Flyfishing waders

Guides or Charter

A Bass Guide
2808 Dorsey Place
Melbourne, FL 32901
Melbourne is 30 minutes from Vero Beach and an hour from Daytona Beach.
(321) 722-3134
bnscoach@gate.net
www.hughcrumpler.com
Reservations: (352) 406-6925
Hugh Crumpler is A Bass Guide, catching "monster bass" in Florida's Stick Marsh and Farm 13.
■ **Products:** • Guide

Alaska Top Dog Charters
P.O. Box 20424
Juneau, AK 99802
(907) 586-4656
topdogch@alaska.net
www.alaskaboatcharter.com
Alaska Top Dog Charters has fishing trips from one to six days in southeast Alaska. Service includes pickup or dropoff at the airport, sleeping on the boat and "fishing until you drop" as well as whale watching.
✔ Brochure.
■ **Products:** • Guide

Anglers Adventures & Outfitters
P.O. Box 991
Devils Lake, ND 58301
On Devils Lake
(701) 662-8683
(701) 351-2621
itbeme@stellarnet.com
www.anglers-adventures.com
Charter boat and guide services are offered in summer and winter. Rentals of fish houses and spearing houses are available for ice fishing. Fly fishing and instruction classes are offered.
■ **Brand Name(s):** Anglers Adventures & Outfitters
✔ Brochure.

Byrd's Guide Service
12068 Highway 99 East
Red Bluff, CA 96080
150 miles north of Sacramento
(800) 527-3332
dougbyrd@cwnet.com
www.wecatchum.com

Doug Byrd has been a professional fishing guide for 25 years, specializing in the Sacramento and Feather Rivers in California.
■ **Products:** • Guide service

C-Devil II Sportfishing and Lil' Devil Guide Service
331 Burdickville Road
Charlestown, RI 02813
(401) 364-9774
cdevilii@aol.com
www.cdevilsportfishing.com
C-Devil II and Lil' Devil feature a 32-foot Topaz Sportfisherman and an 18-foot Scout Center Console for inshore and offshore fly and light tackle fishing. The boats sail from Point Judith Marina, Snug Harbor, R.I.
■ **Products:** • Fishing guide

Top: A yellowfin tuna was the catch of the day by C-Devil II Sportfishing in Rhode Island. *Bottom:* A striped bass was caught on a fly fishing expedition aboard the Lil' Devil guide service in Rhode Island.

Charles Ireland Guide Service

3389 N. Myrtle Road
Myrtle Creek, OR 97457
90 miles south of Eugene.
(541) 863-6082
charles@cirelandguide.com
www.cirelandguide.com
Reservations: (541) 863-1221
Charles Ireland provides guided salmon and steelhead
 fishing trips on Southern Oregon rivers and bays.
■ **Products:** • Guide service

Classic Alaska Charters

P.O. Box 6117
Ketchikan, AK 99901
(907) 225-0608
www.classicalaskacharters.com
Classic Alaska Charters offers overnight charter service
 for five-day trips aboard a 40-foot yacht with full
 service, including a chef.
■ **Products:** • Charter fishing

**Anglers hold a six-pack of big salmon caught on Lake Michigan
aboard Dumper Dan's Sportfishing Charters.**

Dumper Dan's Lake Michigan Sportfishing Charters

4022 N. 51st St.
Sheboygan, WI 53083
(920) 457-2940
dmprdan@bytehead.com
www.fishdumperdancharters.com
Dumper Dan's provides charter fishing services on
 three full-time boats in Lake Michigan, specializing
 in trout and salmon fishing. Lodging packages are
 available.
✔ Brochure.
■ **Products:** • Charter fishing

Fatman's Flyfishing Guides

209 Kendall St.
Burlington, WI 53105
Between Chicago and Milwaukee
(847) 322-0881
fat@fishinfatman.com
www.fishinfatman.com
Fatman's offers guide services and fly fishing
 instruction, including destination trips to Illinois,
 Wisconsin, Iowa and Canada fly fishing for salmon,
 steelheads, inland trout, and muskies.
■ **Products:** • Fishing guide

Fisherman's Landing

2838 Garrison St.
San Diego, CA 92106
(619) 221-8500
Fax: (619) 222-0799
www.fishermanslanding.com
Fisherman's Landing, which holds several fishing
 world's records, offers trips of one to 23 days off Baja
 California, Mexico, or San Diego for tuna, albacore,
 and wahoo. It also operates the Fisherman's Landing
 Tackle Shop, with online sales.
✔ Online shop. ✔ Retail shop.
■ **Products:** • Guide service • Fishing tackle

Glacier's Edge Sportfishing Charters Inc.

P.O. Box 772442
Eagle River, AK 99577
(907) 227-3151
Fax: (907) 694-5074
young@ptialaska.com
www.glaciersedge.net
Glacier's Edge is a saltwater fishing guide service
 operating out of Seward, Alaska, with a 34-foot boat
 and five-star Coast Guard safety rating. It also
 operates Box Canyon Cabins, with four log cabins
 (www.boxcanyoncabin.com) with kitchens.
■ **Products:** • Fishing guide • Cabins

Great Rocky Mountain Outfitters

P.O. Box 1677
216 E. Walnut
Saratoga, WY 82331
(307) 326-8750
Fax: (30) 732-6390
www.grmo.com
Great Rocky Mountain Outfitters combines a full
  service Orvis fly shop, which sells tackle and gear,
  with a guide service. It also offers fishing trips and
  cottages.
✔ Brochure. ✔ Retail shop.
■ **Products:** • Fly fishing gear • Guide service •
  Lodging

HillBilly Charters

1201 S.E. 8th Ave.
Okeechobee, FL 34974
(800) 472-2036
Captskid@strato.net
www.CaptsKid.com
Wheelchair accessible.
Fishing charters fish for striped bass in Maine and for
  crappies in Florida.

Idaho Angling Services LLC

208 David St., Picabo
Bellevue, ID 83313
(208) 788-9709
info@anglingservices.com
www.anglingservices.com
Idaho Angling Services offers fly fishing guide service
  in Idaho as well as planning for fishing trips. Guide
  David Glasscock spends winters as a fishing guide in
  New Zealand and arranges fishing trips to that nation.
✔ Brochure.
■ **Products:** • Guide services

Lake Texoma Striper Guide Service

1620 Mill Creek Road
Pottsboro, TX 75076
75 miles from Dallas
(903) 786-8400
bannist9@aol.com
www.texoma-fishing.com
Charters specialize in fishing for striped bass on Lake
Texoma.
✔ Brochure.

Mark Kovach Fishing Services

406 Pershing Drive
Silver Spring, MD 20910
(301) 588-8742
www.mkfs.com
Mark Kovach operates fly fishing schools in Maryland
  and leads float trips for fly and spinning rod anglers
  on the Potomac Rivers and other areas in Maryland
  and Pennsylvania.
■ **Products:** • Guide service • Fly fishing school

Montana Flywater Fishing Co.

1426 Knight St.
Helena, MT 59601
(406) 495-0487
pat@montanaflywater.com
www.montanaflywater.com
Patrick and Terri Straub offer fly fishing guide services
  as well as fishing reports, weather, photos, streamflow,
  and other information on their Web site.
✔ Online shop.
■ **Products:** • Guide services

Mountain Angler

Main Street Mall
P.O. Box 467
Breckenridge, CO 80424
970-453HOOK
(800) 453-4669
Fax: (970) 453-4226
info@mountainangler.com
www.mountainangler.com
Mountain Angler provides fly fishing guide service in
  Summit County. It also has an online store and a fly
  fishing equipment store in Breckenridge. It also
  provides lessons and fishing trips.
✔ Online shop. , Retail shop.
■ **Products:** • Guide service • Fly fishing equipment •
  Lessons

Musky Tom Wehler's Guide Service

876 Howard St. North
St. Paul, MN 55119
225 miles from Twin Cities.
(651) 470-9774
muskitom@aol.com
www.muskytomsguideservice.com
Reservations: (612) 617-1983
Musky Tom offers one-to-one professional musky hunts
  for full or half days on Lake Vermillion.
■ **Products:** • Fishing guide

National Bass Guide Service

8619 Camden St.
Alexandria, VA 22308
10 miles south of Washington, D.C.
(703) 360-3472
info@nationalbass.com
www.nationalbass.com
The National Bass Guide Service is a largemouth bass
  guide on the Potomac River.
■ **Products:** • Fishing guide

New Hampshire Lakes Area Bass Guide

P.O. Box 457
Merrimack, NH 03054
75 miles from Boston.
(603) 424-4946
jimfnh@aol.com
http://members.aol.com/jimfnh/ newhampshirebassguid
The New Hampshire Lakes Area Bass Guide provides
  bass guiding service in New Hampshire.
■ **Products:** • Guide service.

North Platte Anglers

P.O. Box 31
Alvoca, WY 82620
(866) 472-9190
flyfishpdk@earthllink.net
www.northplatteanglers.com
North Platte Anglers is a guide service for rainbow
  trout on the North Platte River in Wyoming. It also
  provides fish camps for fly fishermen.
■ **Products:** • Guide service

Northwest Angler

P.O. Box 2925
18804 Front St.
Poulsbo, WA 98370
(360) 697-7100
888-4FISH97
info@nwangler.com
www.nwangler.com
Northwest Angler operates a fly shop in Washington as
  well as a Web store. It offers guide services as well as
  fly fishing schools.
✔ Online shop. ✔ Retail shop.
■ Products: • Guide service • Fly shop

Bass Fishing on the Potomac River

The historic and scenic Potomac River boasts some of the finest largemouth bass fishing in the country, hosting the BASSMASTERS for the past 12 years. With river grasses, sunken wrecks, and creeks, there are fishing opportunities for all skill levels. In addition to the fishing, the sights of Washington DC, George Washington's Mount Vernon home, the Pentagon, and Reagan National Airport offer a different perspective when viewed from the water.

U.S. Coast Guard Licensed

National Bass Guide Service can accommodate beginning and advanced Bass fishing.

Trips are for one or two people. A full day is 8 hours, a half day is 4 hours. You can bring your own tackle, or we will provide.

Supply your own food and beverages.

Call for details and to schedule a trip. A great way to get away during the week with a client! Gift certificates available.

National Bass Guide Service
Phone: 703-360-3472/703-626-0972
Website: www.nationalbass.com
E-mail: info@nationalbass.com

Largemouth bass are held by fishermen who used the National Bass
guide Service to fish the Potomac River.

A fisherman holds the huge largemouth bass he caught using the Renegade Guide Service in Florida.

A happy fisherman holds up a trophy salmon from Lake Michigan on a Renegade Sportfishing Charter trip.

Renegade Guide Service

148 Chobee St.
Okeechobee, FL 34974
(863) 634-1321
(877) 525-7380
renegade@ictransnet.com
www.fishfla.com/renegade.html
Capt. Harry Simmons shares 40 years of experience with customers of his Renegade Guide Service, fishing for bass, crappies, shell crackers, and Mayan Cichlid on Lakes Okeechobee and Istokpoga, and Stick Marsh and the Everglades in Florida.
■ **Products:** • Guide

Renegade Sportfishing Charters LLC

P.O. Box 436
Port Washington, WI 53074
25 miles north of Milwaukee.
(262) 377-4560
(800) 343-0089
rengad@aol.com
www.renegadecharterfishing.com
Renegade Sportfishing Charters operates on Lake Michigan, catching brown trout, coho and chinook salmon, lake trout, and rainbow trout.
■ **Products:** • Charter fishing

Salmon Depot Charter Fishing

P.O. Box 141
Baileys Harbor, WI 54202
(920) 839-2272
(800) 345-6701
Fax: (920) 884-8877
salmondepot@hotmail.com
www.salmondepot.com
Salmon Depot is a charter fishing operation in Wisconsin's Door County resort area, fishing Lake Michigan. All fishing tackle is furnished.
■ **Products:** • Fishing guide

Sea Dog Sportfishing Charters

P.O. Box 912
Sheboygan, WI 53082
(920) 918-2628
(800) 582-9694
schled@nconnect.net
www.fishsheboygan.com
Sea Dog, located on Sheboygan's riverfront, offers Lake Michigan charter fishing on the area's newest 34-foot fishing boat. It also offers current online charter fishing reports.
✔ Brochure.
■ **Products:** • Charter

Happy fishermen hold up a large Lake Michigan salmon taken on a Sea Dog Sportfishing Charters boat.

Sierra Drifters Guide Service

HCR 79, Box 165-A
Mammoth Lakes, CA 93546
325 miles from Los Angeles, 400 miles from San Diego.
(760) 935-4250
driftfish@qnet.com
www.sierradrifters.com
Sierra Drifters provides a fly fishing guide service in California.
■ **Products:** • Guide service

Southern Fishing Schools Inc.

106 Hickory Ridge
Cumming, GA 30040
(770) 889-2654
Fax: (770) 886-5010
www.southernfishing.com
Southern Fishing Schools is a Georgia fishing school and guide service, teaching anglers how to catch largemouth and smallmouth bass, spotted bass, striped bass, and trout. It puts on fishing clinics at Bass Pro Shops Outdoor World as well as teachi

■ **Products:** • Fishing education

The Hook-Up!

P.O. Box 2193
85 Lowell Square
Orleans, MA 02653
70 miles from Boston.
(508) 240-0778
Fax: (508) 240-0963
thehookup@c4.net
www.thehookupcapecod.com
The Hook-Up! operates a charter service with three boats and a tackle store in Massachusetts. Charter boats include the Tammy Rose out of Rock Harbor in Orleans, Hampton Caught II out of Pleasant Bay, and The Hook-Up out of Hyannis.
✔ Retail shop.
■ **Products**: • Charter boats • Tackle store

Tite Line Fishing

540 Moonlite Drive
Idaho Falls, ID 83402
(877) 582-3474
Fax: (208) 542-0652
john@titeline.com
www.titeline.com
Tite Line Fishing offers fly fishing guide service, wading and float trips, and fly fishing schools on the Missouri River. It also sells several fly fishing products online, by catalog, and through dealers.
✔ Brochure. ✔ Online shop.
■ **Products:** • Guide service • Fly fishing accessories

Trophy Specialists Fishing Charters

15555 Cassidy Road
Chelsea, MI 48118
Monroe, Manistee, Au Gres, Mich.
(734) 475-9146
(800) 305-6988
veinemr@aol.com
www.trophyspecialists.com
Charters fish for walleyes, salmon, steelhead and brown trout.
✔ Brochure.

Trout & About

3488 N. Emerson St.
Arlington, VA 22207
Near Washington, D.C.
(703) 536-7494
Fax: (703) 536-0017
trotabot@mindspring.com
www.troutandabout.com
Trout & About, with guide Phil Gay, focuses on catch
and release streams of the tri-state area around
Washington, D.C., and also conducts fly fishing
schools.
■ **Products:** • Fishing guide

Westport Outfitters

570 Riverside Ave.
Westport, CT 06880
45 miles north of Manhattan on I-95.
(203) 226-1915
Fax: (203) 454-0857
godzilla41@aol.com
www.saltwater-flyfishing.com
Westport Outfitters combines charter, guide, and
marina services for saltwater fly fishing and light
tackle spinning. It also offers boat and motor sales
for Maverick, Pathfinder, Yamaha motors, Orvis,
Loomis, Powell rods and reels.
✔ Retail shop.
■ Products: • Charter service • Marina

Wetland Outfitters

119 Yukon Court
Murfreesboro, TN 37129
(615) 904-2556
Fax: (615) 217-7588
www.wetlandoutfitters.com
Wetland Outfitters offers a variety of outdoor products
and service, including online and catalog shopping
for fishing equipment, guide services in Tennessee,
fishing and hunting news and tips, lake reports,
articles
✔ Brochure. Online shop.
■ **Products:** • Guide services • Fishing gear • Fishing
news

Trout & About Guide and Instructor, Phil Gay, in his office.

Guiding Services and Instruction

Guide and instructor Phil Gay holds a trout in his "office" at Trout
& About in Virginia.

Resorts

Top: **Whopper salmon, rainbow trout, artic grayling, and northern pike are caught at Bentalit Lodge in Alaska.** *Bottom:* **A trio of anglers displays their trophy catches at Bentalit Lodge in Alaska.**

Bentalit Lodge
P.O. Box 52
Mile 50, Yentna River
Skwentna, AK 99667
(907) 733-2716
Fax: (907) 733-2716
bentalit@ptialaska.net
www.bentalitlodge.com
Hotel: 11 rooms
Bentalit Lodge is a remote deluxe fishing lodge that also features winter recreation. It includes a dining area, game room, racquetball court, and living area. All fishing gear is supplied, with licensed guides.
✔ Brochure.
■ **Products:** • Resort

Boyette's Resort
Route 1, Box 1230
Highway 21
Tiptonville, TN 38079
(888) 465-6523
Fax: (731) 253-6645
judyatreelfoot@aol.com
www.boyettesresort.com
Hotel: 17 rooms
Boyette's Resort, on Reelfoot Lake, has four family-size houses and 13 cottages. Fishing guides and fishing packages are available, including cottage, boat, gas, bait, and fishing license.
✔ Brochure.
■ **Products:** • Resort

Eagle Lake Lodge
Box 38
Eagle River, ON P0V 1S0
(888) 755-3245
Fax: (807) 755-2422
www.eaglelakelodge.com
Hotel: 10 rooms
Eagle Lake Resort has 10 cabins and a lodge on the American Plan and housekeeping. The resort has a sand beach, offers bait, tackle, and gas, and has fishing for walleyes, northerns, and muskies.
■ **Products:** • Resort

Katahdin Lake Wilderness Camps
Box 398
Millinocket, ME 04462
(207) 723-4050
(207) 723-9867
info@katahdinlakecamps.com
www.katahdinlakecamps.com
Katahdin Lake Wilderness Camps was built in 1885 and includes a main cabin and 10 guest cabins. There are no phones, electricity, or stores. The camp includes 700 acres of spring-fed lake with native brook trout.
■ **Products:** • Wilderness camp

La Reserve Beauchene
C.P. 910
Temiscaming, QU J0Z 3R0
In western Quebec, near North Bay, Ontario.
(819) 627-3865
(888) 627-3865
Fax: (819) 627-3043
beauchene@thot.net
www.beauchene.com
La Reserve Beauchene is a fishing lodge with exclusive rights for fishing, hunting, and trapping on 50,000 acres. A lodge, cabins, deluxe chalet, outpost cabins, and Bear Bay Campground are available for visitors. Guide service and boats are available.
■ **Products:** • Resort

Loon Haunt Outposts

Box 1344F
Red Lake, ON P0V 2M0
(807) 735-2400
fishing@loonhaunt.com
www.loonhaunt.com

Loon Haunt Outposts provides a variety of cabins and locations in Ontario, including some fly-in lakes. Rates include cabins with hot and cold water, showers, cookware, and electricity, and boats, motors, and unlimited gasoline. Several package plans
✔ Brochure.
■ **Products:** • Fishing resort

Red Lodge Resort

Route 1
Sheguiandah, ON P0P 1W0
(705) 368-3843
(877) 553-5585
www.manitoulin.com/redlodge

Red Lodge Resort has 10 one- to four-bedroom bungalows with shower, refrigerator, electric heat, and five rooms in the lodge on Lake Manitou in Ontario. Manitoulin Island is the largest freshwater island in the world at 100 miles long with 108 lakes
✔ Brochure.
■ **Products:** • Resort

Roaring Stony Lodge

Birch Lake
7299 Hill Road
Ely, MN 55792
(218) 741-0174
www.fishingresorts.com
Reservations: (218) 365-2115

Roaring Stony Lodge is a full-service fishing resort that's 100 miles from Duluth, Minn., featuring the American Plan. Remote fly-ins are available.
■ **Products:** • Resort

Tomahawk Resort

P.O. Box 29
Sioux Narrows, ON P0X 1N0
90 miles north of U.S. border.
(807) 226-5622
(800) 465-1091
Fax: (807) 226-5563
www.tomahawkresort.com
Hotel: 11 rooms

Tomahawk Resort is a fishing resort with 11 deluxe cottages, houseboat rentals, and an RV park. Guided fishing trips are available.
✔ Brochure.
■ **Products:** • Resort

Top: A float plane delivers guests to a cabin on Whitelaw Lake in Ontario, one of several locations operated by Loon Haunt Outpost. *Bottom:* A happy fisherman holds a giant northern pike, which was returned to the water in catch-and-release fishing at Loon Haunt Outposts in Canada.

Uchi Lake Lodge

P.O. Box 104
Sioux Lookout, ON P8T 1A1
(800) 946-8244
Fax: (807) 737-0054
judy@uchilake.com
www.uchilake.com

Uchi Lake Lodge is a fly-in remote fishing resort in Ontario, Canada, that features trophy walleye and northern fishing. Three-day and seven-day packages are available, with a full American plan and housekeeping packages. A restaurant is available.
✔ Brochure.
■ **Products:** • Fishing resort

Other

Action Performance Co.

4707 E. Baseline Road
Phoenix, AZ 85042
(602) 337-3700
Fax: (702) 337-3740
www.action-performance.com
Action Performance's newest division, Castaway
Collectibles, combines official motorsports licenses
with licenses for professional anglers, including Hank
Parker, to make scale model die-cast bass boats. The
replicas include scale trailers and motors.
- **Brand Name(s):** Action Performance.
- **Products:** • Die-cast bass boat replicas

Alaska Travel Industry Association

2600 Cordova St., Suite 201
Anchorage, AK 99503
(907) 929-2200
www.sportfishinginalaska.com
The Alaska Travel Industry Association provides
information on fishing in Alaska.

AllFishermen.com

P.O. Box 990
11 Court St.
Exeter, NH 03833
(603) 778-1020
Fax: (603) 778-7265
email@allvertical.com
www.allfishermen.com
AllFishermen.com offers information to fishermen via
the Internet, including news, free e-mail, talk, and
links to sport license sites as well as fishing
businesses and stores.
✔ Online shop.
- **Products:** • Online information

AllFlyFishermen.com

P.O. Box 990
11 Court St.
Exeter, NH 03833
(603) 778-1020
Fax: (603) 778-7276
email@allvertical.com
www.allflyfishermen.com
AllFlyFishermen.com is a sister Web site to
AllFishermen.com and provides fly fishing
information, including news, free e-mail, talk, and
links to fishing businesses and stores.
✔ Online shop.
- **Products:** • Fly fishing information

American Rod & Gun

2500 E. Kearney St.
Springfield, MO 65898
(417) 873-5085
(800) 332-5377
Fax: (417) 864-6558
tivie@basspro.com
www.basspro.com
American Rod & Gun is a wholesale distributor of
major name brands of fishing, hunting, camping,
marine, and sporting goods. It is the exclusive
wholesale source for Bass Pro Shops, Offshore
Angler, Salt Water, White River Fly Shops.
- **Products:** • Fishing equipment

American Sportfishing Association

225 Reinekers Lane, Suite 420
Alexandria, VA 22314
(703) 519-9691
Fax: (703) 519-1872
info@asafishing.org
www.asafishing.org
The American Sportfishing Association is a fishing
industry group that works for conservation through its
FishAmerica Foundation and Government Affairs
Program. It also promotes fishing through its Water
Works Wonders program. It runs the annual ICAST
show.
- **Brand Name(s):** ICAST.
- **Products:** • Conservation • Fishing promotion •
Trade show

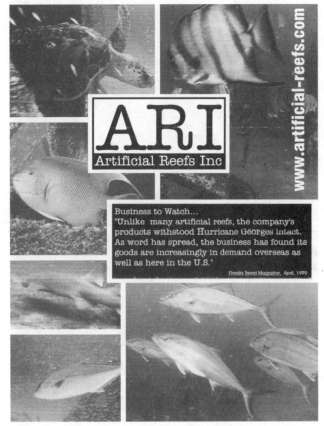

Artificial Reefs makes four types and sizes of Fish Haven and Lobster Haven ocean reef habitats.

Artificial Reefs Inc.

6536 East Bay Blvd.
Gulf Breeze, FL 32563
Near Pensacola
(850) 934-7201
(866) 805-6833
Fax: (850) 934-9189
debatkinson@hotmail.com
www.artificialreefs.com
Concrete structures, ranging from 600 to 3,000 pounds, are placed on the ocean floor to act as shelters for fish, shrimp and lobsters.
- **Brand Name(s):** Artificial Reefs
- ✔ Brochure.
- **Products:** Fish habitats, including Fish Haven Tower, Fish Haven and Lobster Haven.

B.A.S.S./ESPN Outdoors

5845 Carmichael Road
Montgomery, AL 36117
(334) 272-9530
Fax: (334) 279-7148
adv@bassmaster.com
www.bassmaster.com
B.A.S.S. runs fishing tournaments, has publications including Bassmaster, B.A.S.S. Times and Fishing Tackle Retailer, and has TV shows on ESPN and ESPN Outdoors. It also has fishing news and articles on its Web site and a membership program.
- **Brand Name(s):** B.A.S.S., Bassmaster, ESPN.
- **Products:** • TV shows • Publications • Tournaments

Big Rock Sports

173 Hankinson Drive
Newport, NC 28570
(252) 726-6186
Fax: (252) 726-8352
www.bigrocksports.com
Big Rock Sports is comprised of five of the fishing tackle and shooting sports industry's top distributors. They provide merchandise for more than 14,000 retailers.
- **Products:** • Fishing equipment

Black's Fly Fishing

P.O. Box 2029
Red Banks, NJ 07701
(732) 224-8700
(800) 224-9464
Fax: (732) 741-2827
Black's Fly Fishing is a national directory that covers more than 1,600 companies and individuals offering fly fishing products and services, fly fishing schools, and more than 3,000 fly tackle retailers.
- **Products:** • Fly fishing directory

Carson Optical

175A E. 2nd St.
Huntington Station, NY 11746
(631) 547-5000
8009-OPTICS
Fax: (631) 427-6749
info@carson-optical.com
www.carson-optical.com
Carson Optical makes a variety of binoculars and night vision instruments.
- **Brand Name(s):** Carson Optical.
- ✔ Brochure.
- **Products:** • Binoculars • Night vision scopes

D&E Enterprises

201 State Highway 108
P.O. Box 212
Dent, MN 56528
(218) 758-2448
(800) 554-4916
Fax: (800) 554-4916
deent@eot.com
www.dandenteprises.com
D&E Enterprises manufactures Trophy Fishouses and
   distributes H & H Trailers.
■ **Brand Name(s):** Trophy Fishouses, H & H Trailers.
■ **Products:** • Ice fishing houses

Discover the Outdoors.com Inc.

P.O. Box 7008
Shawnee Mission, KS 66207
(913) 498-3100
Fax: (913) 498-3104
www.dto.com
Discover the Outdoors provides online fishing
   information, including news, tips, tide tables, and
   outdoors forums. It also hosts and produces the
   Heartland Adventures Outdoor Show.
■ **Products:** • Fishing information

Federation of Fly Fishers

P.O. Box 1595
Bozeman, MT 59771
(406) 585-7592
Fax: (406) 585-7596
conserve@fedflyfishers.org
www.fedflyfishers.org
The Federation of Fly Fishers is an organization
   dedicated to conserving, restoring and educating
   through fly fishing. The Federation includes more
   than 300 local fly fishing clubs as well as individual
   members. It publishes a national magazine.
■ **Products:** • Fly fishing information

Fishing Hot Spots Inc.

P.O. Box 1167
Rhinelander, WI 54501
(715) 375-5555
(800) 338-5957
Fax: (715) 365-5525
www.fishinghotspots.com
Fishing Hot Spots is the nation's largest publisher of
   fishing maps, books, and inland freshwater fishing
   data. It has added saltwater directions charts.
   Accessories include vinyl waterproof rulers, map
   cases, GPS logbooks, and clothing.
■ **Brand Name(s):** Fishing Hot Spots.

✔ Online shop.
■ **Products:** • Maps • Fishing information • Books

Great Lakes Fishery Commission

2100 Commonwealth Blvd. Suite 100
Ann Arbor, MI 48105
(734) 662-3209
Fax: (734) 741-2010
info@glfc.com
www.glfc.com
The Great Lakes Fishery Commission develops
   programs of research on the Great Lakes and
   recommends measures to permit the maximum
   sustained productivity of stocks of fish. It also works
   to eradicate or minimize sea lamprey populations in
   the Great Lakes.
■ **Products:** • Fishing information

Half Hitch Tackle

2206 Thomas Drive
Panama City, FL 32408
(850) 234-2621
(888) 668-9810
Fax: (850) 235-1700
pc@halfhitch.com
www.halfhitch.com
Half Hitch Tackle has stores in Panama City and
   Destin, Fla., and issues a catalog of products
   available. Its Web site has fishing information,
   weather reports, regulations and licensing
   information, and tournament schedules.
✔ Brochure. ✔ Retail shop.
■ **Products:** • Fishing gear • Fishing information

Hooked On The Outdoors

11 Dunwoody Park, Suite 140
Atlanta, GA 30338
(770) 396-4320
www.ruhooked.com
Hooked On The Outdoors produces a magazine about
   outdoors activities including fishing, biking, camping,
   climbing and water sports. It also features fishing
   feature stories, discussion boards, and contests on its
   Web site.
■ **Products:** • Fishing information

In-Fisherman

2 In-Fisherman Drive
Brainerd, MN 56425
(218) 829-1648
Fax: (218) 829-3091
info@in-fisherman.com
www.in-fisherman.com
- **Brand Name(s):** In-Fisherman and Walleye In-Sider magazines; Walleye, Bass, Catfish In-Sider and Ice Fishing Guides; In-Fisherman television; In-Fisherman radio; Professional Walleye Trail (PWT).
- ✔ Online shop.
- **Products:** • Fishing magazines • TV and radio show • Books • Videos • Internet

Interactive Outdoors Inc.

183 Pancake Hollow Road
Highland, NY 12528
(845) 483-7191
info@interactiveoutdoors.tv
www.interactiveoutdoors.tv
Interactive Outdoors produces a fishing publication delivered on CD monthly.

International Game Fish Association

300 Gulf Stream Way
Dania Beach, FL 33004
(954) 922-4212
Fax: (954) 924-4220
www.igfa.org
International Game Fish Association keeps world fish size records, provides conservation information and education, and maintains databases on the subject of fishing. It also has a museum in Florida.
- **Products:** • Fishing records

International Women Fly Fishers

107 N. Main St.
Farmville, VA 23901
(888) 811-4933
IWFF@intlwomenflyfishers.org
www.intlwomenflyfishers.org
The International Women Fly Fishers club was formed in 1996 and the non-profit group has more than 300 members. Its goal is to help the environment through children's education. It publishes a quarterly newsletter.
- **Products:** • Fly fishing education

Izaak Walton League of America

707 Conservation Lane
Gaithersburg, MD 20878
(301) 548-0150
Fax: (301) 548-0149
www.ilwa.org
The Izaak Walton League of America, founded in 1922, is a national organization that works through volunteer, community-based action and education programs to ensure sustainable use of America's natural resources.
- **Products:** • Conservation

Jersey Coast Anglers Association

1201 Route 37 East, Suite 9
Toms River, NJ 08753
(732) 506-6565
Fax: (732) 506-6975
www.jcaa.org
The Jersey Coast Anglers Association works for marine recreation anglers on conservation and environmental concerns.
- **Products:** • Conservation

King Sailfish Mounts Inc.

P.O. Box 2962
Pompano Beach, FL 33702
(954) 784-8377
(800) 809-0009
Fax: (954) 784-8453
kingsails@aol.com
www.kingsailfish.com
King Sailfish Mounts makes highly detailed Fiberglass fish reproductions for display, including sailfish, grouper, snapper, snook, tarpon, shark, tuna, and bass. Orders are taken online or by phone or catalog.
- ✔ Brochure. ✔ Online shop.
- **Products:** • Fish reproductions

A wide variety of fish, from bass to sharks, are available for display from King Sailfish Mounts.

Lake Fork Taxidermy

P.O. Box 880
Emory, TX 75440
(903) 765-9999
jason@lakeforktaxidermy.com
www.lakeforktaxidermy.com
Lake Fork Taxidermy specializes in trophy fish reproductions in fiberglass. Samples and prices are available on the Web site.
✔ Online shop.
■ **Products:** • Fish reproductions

National Teen Anglers

1177 Bayshore Drive, #207
Ft. Pierce, FL 34949
(772) 468-0824
www.teenanglers.org
Reservations: (772) 519-0482
Teen Anglers is a free boating and fishing education program for teen-agers from 13 through 18. Capt. Al Bernetti is president and Capt. Tony Strickland is vice president.
■ **Products:** • Education

Outdoor Intelligence LLC

4410 Arapahoe Ave., Suite 135
Boulder, CO 80303
(303) 441-2412
info@outdoorintelligence.com
www.outdoorintelligence.com
Outdoor Intelligence uses Fishing Hot Spots data to provide information about 350 inland bodies of water, including maps, fishing areas, access, boat ramps, marinas, campgrounds, tackle shops, and contact information.
■ **Brand Name(s):** Outdoor Intelligence, Fishing Hot Spots.
✔ Online shop.
■ **Products:** • Maps • Fishing information

Ritz Interactive Inc.

2010 Main St., Suite 400
Irvine, CA 92614
(949) 442-0202
Fax: (949) 442-0210
info@ritzinteractive.com
www.ritzinteractive.com
Ritz Interactive operates a number of Web sites, including FishingOnly.com, BoatersWorld.com, and BoatingOnly.com. The sites offer online shopping, fishing or boating tips and links, weather reports, fishing reports, discussion boards, and articles.
■ **Brand Name(s):** FishingOnly.com, BoatingOnly.com, BoatersWorld.com.
✔ Online shop.
■ **Products:** • Fishing information • Boating information • Online shopping

Russell's For Men

1920 N. 26th St.
Lowell, AR 76745
(479) 631-0130
(800) 255-9034
Fax: (479) 631-8493
ag@agrussell.com
www.russellsformen.com
Russell's is a mail order catalog of fine gifts for men, including fillet knives and sporting knives, fishing tools, compasses, emergency gear, and fishing and boating displays. Online shopping is available.
■ **Brand Name(s):** Several leading brands.
✔ Brochure. ✔ Online shop.
■ **Products:** • Knives • Tools • Display items

Salamander Graphix

10 Hangar Way
Watsonville, CA 95076
(831) 763-1067
Fax: (831) 722-0586
www.salamandergraphix.com
Salamander Graphix makes novelty fishing items, including fish hot mitts, a cooler bag shaped like a fish, boxer shorts, sox and slippers with fish designs, and fish-shaped pillows.
■ **Products:** • Novelty fish items

Saltwater Directions

731 S. Highway 101, Suite 1K
Solana Beach, CA 92075
(858) 793-9295
Fax: (858) 793-9818
www.saltwaterdirections.com
Saltwater Directions specializes in creative highly detailed fishing charts for saltwater fishing. They include where to catch fish, detailed GPS fishing and waypoints, latitude and longitude grids, compass headings for offshore charts, and marina.
■ **Brand Name(s):** Saltwater Directions.
✔ Online shop.
■ **Products:** • Saltwater fishing maps

Solunar Sales Co.

P.O. Box 207
Montoursville, PA 17754
(570) 368-8042
Fax: (570) 368-8179
solunar@uplink.net
www.solunartables.com
Solunar Sales publishes the Solunar Tables of sun and moon cycles that many anglers use to determine the best times of day to catch fish. Products include a solunar booklet, Sportsman's Almanac, LeadeRule, and the book Moon Up Moon Down.
✔ Brochure. ✔ Online shop.
■ **Products:** • Solunar Tables

Surfcaster.com

12 Market Square, Suites 6-9
Amesbury, MA 01950
(978) 388-4703
Fax: (978) 477-6397
info@Zdezigns.com
www.surfcaster.com
Surfcaster.com, owned by Z deZigns Inc., is a Web site covering fishing information about New England. Included are tide charts, articles, recipes, photos, a resource guide, a Fish Forum, classified ads, and an event calendar.
■ **Products:** • Fishing information

Swift Instruments Inc.

952 Dorchester Ave.
Boston, MA 02125
(800) 446-1116
www.swift-optics.com
Swift Instruments makes a variety of binoculars, including a line of marine binoculars.
■ **Brand Name(s):** Swift Optics.
✔ Brochure.
■ **Products:** • Binoculars

Van Patten Industries

P.O. Box 6694
Rockford, IL 61125
(815) 332-4812
Fax: (815) 332-7455
www.theinhibitor.com
Van Patten Industries makes the Inhibitor rust-prevention system. The environmentally safe technology prevents rust and corrosion of fishing tackle and other outdoors equipment.
■ **Brand Name(s):** Inhibitor.
✔ Brochure. ✔ Online shop.
■ **Products:** • Rust prevention

Virtual Flyshop

3665 JFK Parkway, Building 1, Suite 310
Fort Collins, CO 80525
(970) 484-8650
Fax: (970) 484-8256
info@flyshop.com
www.flyshop.com
The Virtual Flyshop is the Web site of Fly Fisherman magazine and features a wide variety of information about fly fishing, including a bulletin board, chat room, classified ads and auctions, fishing tips, articles, and fishing reports.
✔ Online shop.
■ **Products:** • Fly fishing information

West Virginia Division of Tourism

90 MacCorkle Ave. SW
South Charleston, WV 25303
800CALLWVA
www.callwva.com
Division of Tourism promotes parks and tourism in West Virginia and offers a variety of facilities, activities, parks, lodging.
✔ Brochure.

Fishing Guides

Many anglers prefer to experiment on their local lake or river until they find a fishin' hole where they can frequently hook a lunker. But there's not always time for that lengthy process while traveling or planning to fish unfamiliar waters.

Enter the guide or charter. A professional, equipped with the proper equipment, boat, and know-how, can find fish and provide a fun day on the water for anglers, no matter what their level of expertise.

The authoritative source fishing guides and charters is the Fishing Guides Home Page (on the Web at www.1fghp.com). Jim Dicken, owner and Webmaster of that site, provided the following list of American and Canadian guides to Fishing Digest.

The Fishing Guides Home Page includes guides and charter services in all 50 states, plus Canada, Mexico, and other international destinations. It also provides links to other fishing information, including weather, tides, licenses, fishing regulations, and clubs.

ALABAMA

Carl's Guide Service, Carl Boaz, Rogersville, AL 35652, Phone: (256) 247-0752, e-mail: carlboaz@mindspring.com

Tennessee River Guide Service, 1114 N Main St., Tuscumbia AL 35674, Phone: (256) 383-7481 e-mail:Bassnut306@aol.com

South States Fish'in, Dano Bratton, P.O.Box 492, Wedowee, AL 36278, Phone: (256) 357-4195, e-mail: megabass2@juno.com

Central Alabama Guide Service, Roger Perkins, 2300 Co Rd 495, Verbena, AL 36091, Phone: (888) 300-9837

Tee's Guide Service, 5008 Lumary Drive, Huntsville, AL 35810, Phone: (256) 859-1465, e-mail: molly.kitchens@gte.net

Lake Weiss Guide Service, Phone: (256) 927-6617, e-mail: CLP-POPE@tds.net Reeds Guide Service, Reed Montgomery, 1805 28 St., Birmingham, AL 35218, Phone: (205) 787-5133, e-mail: ALABASSGYD@aol.com

S&S Guide Service, Captain Steve Kinard, P.O. Box 851, Gardendale, AL 35071, Phone: 205-223-5098, e-mail: slkinard@bellsouth.net

TJ's Fishing and Guide Service, Tommy J. Smith, Gadsden, AL, Phone: (256) 442-8969

Envision Guide Service, Roger Perkins, 2300 Co Rd 495, Verbena, AL 36091, Phone: (888) 300-9837, e-mail:ENVISIONLURES@cs.com

Dauphin Charters, Captain David Dunnam, Dauphin Island, AL, Phone : (334) 580-9490 e-mail: dauphincharters@cs.com

Fish-Finder, Captain Mike Foto, Phone: (228) 594-0801

Ed Blank's Adventures on the Fly, P.O. Box 180446, Boston, AL, Phone: (617) 974-8764

Shirley R. Charters, *(formerly Small Boat Charters)*, Capt. Dan Ratliff, 31883 River Road, Orange Beach, AL 36561, Phone: (877) 980-FISH (3474), e-mail: info@shirleyr.com

Nellie G, Captain Earl Griffiths, Orange Beach, AL, Phone: (334) 981-9044

Flaid Back, Captain Mike Garrett, Phone: (334) 660-8561

ALASKA

Alaskan Adventure Charters, Phone: (907) 262-7773, Fax: (907) 262-7765, e-mail: rufishn@alaska.net

Classic Alaska Charters, Captain Rob Scherer, Box 6117, Ketchikan, AK 99901, Phone: (907) 225-0608, e-mail: captrob@classicalaskacharters.com

Dave's Alaskan River & Sea Charters, Dave Essert, P.O. Box 1172, Sterling, AK 99672, Phone: (877) 512-3824, e-mail: Akfishguide@ak.net

Jake's Alaska Wilderness Outfitters, Jake Gaudet, P.O. Box 104179, Anchorage, AK 99510, Phone: (907) 522-1133, e-mail: jakesawo@alaska.net

Glacier's Edge Sportfishing Charters, Inc., Cliff Young, P.O. Box 772442, Eagle River, AK 99577-2442, Phone: (907) 227-3151, young@ptialaska.net

Mystic Waters "Fly-fishing," Fred Telleen, P.O. Box 791, Cooper Landing, AK 99572, Phone: (907) 227-0549, e-mail: telleen@gvii.net

Fringe Benefit Charters, David Flower, P.O.Box 1949, Homer, AK 99603, Phone: (888) 420-7038, e-mail: flower@xyz.net

Martin's Fishing Guide Service, P.O.Box 1343, Soldotna, AK 99669, Phone: (877) 248-9547

Grizzly Charters Homer, Alaska, John Earls, P.O. Box 1664, Homer, AK 99603, Phone: (888) 948-4388

Sea Bear Charters, Inc., John Phillips, 32915 Williams St., Anchor Point, AK 99556, Phone: (888) 825-1828

Trophy Catch Charters, James D. Booth, P.O. Box 245, Palmer, AK 99645, Phone: (907) 745-4101

Ron's Alaska Charters, Ron Phillips, P.O. Box 1438, Wrangell, AK 99801, Phone: (907) 874-3624

Kenny Bingaman King Size Adventures, P.O. Box 2163, Soldotna AK 99669, Phone: (907) 262-8386

Eruk's Wilderness Floats, Eruk Williamson, 12720 Lupine Rd., Anchorage, AK 99516, Phone: (888) 212-2203

Greg Nicol Guide Service, P.O. Box 155, Smith River, CA 95567, Phone: (707) 464-7320

Wilson's Guided Sportfishing, Jim Wilson, P.O. Box 4386, Soldotna, AK 99669, Phone: (907) 260-4838

Drifter's Landing Lodge, Ken Smith, 909 Ames Road, Kenai, AK 99611, Phone: (907) 283-9328

Affordable Alaska Fishing & Lodging, George Stek, Soldotna, AK, Phone: (800) 770- 3701, e-mail: akfishing@gci.net or funmoose@alaska.net

Alaska Rainbow Adventures, Paul Hansen, P.O. Box 456, Anchor Point, AK 99556, Phone: (877) 235-2647

Alaska's Bentalit Fishing Lodge, Bill Brion, Mile 50 Yentna River, P.O. Box 52, Skwentna, AK 99667, Phone: (907) 733-2716, e-mail: bentalit@ptialaska.net

Silver Fox Charters, P.O. Box 402, Homer, AK 99603, Phone: (800) 478-8792, e-mail: silvfox@xyz.net

George Siavelis Guide Service, George Siavelis, P.O. Box 74, Aniak, AK 99557, Phone: (907) 675-4510, e-mail: explore@arctic.net

Alaska Top Dog Charters, Lauren Burch, P.O. Box 20424, Juneau, AK 99802, Phone: (907) 586-4656, e-mail: topdogch@alaska.net

Weeping Trout Sports Resort, Greg Brask, P.O. Box 129, Haines, AK 99827, Phone: (877) 94-TROUT, e-mail: trout@weepingtrout.com

The Farm Lodge, Inc., Glen R. Alsworth, Box 1, Port Alsworth, AK 99653, Phone: (800) 662-7661

Clearwater Angling Adventures, Scott Limbourne, P.O. Box 57022, North Pole, AK 99702, Phone: (907) 372-3139

Chilkoot Charters, Larry Pierce, P. O. Box 1336, Skagway, AK 99840, Phone: (907) 983-3400, Fax: (877) 983-3400

Midnight Sun Trophy Pike Adventures, Dean Nelsen, P.O. Box 62, Aniak, AK 99557, Phone: (800) 440-PIKE

Parker Guide Service, Steven J. Priddle, P.O. Box 6290, Sitka, AK 99835, Phone: (907) 747-6026, Fax: (907) 747-8596

The Sports Den Fishing Team, Jim Golden, 44176 Sterling Highway, Soldotna, AK 9669, Phone: (907) 262-7491, Fax: (907) 260-9190

Silver Bullet Kenai River Guide Service and B&B, John Joseph Resident Guide, Phone: (907) 262-0887

Alaska Good Time Charters, David Pinquoch, P.O. Box 876257, Wasilla, AK 99687, Phone: (907) 373-7447

Alagnak Lodge, Alaska, P.O. Box 351, King Salmon, AK 99613, Phone: (800) 877-9903

Seldovia Fishing Adventures, David and Peggy Cloninger, P.O. Box 121, Seldovia, AK 99663, Phone: (907) 234-7417

Freebird Guide Service, Peter H. Mueller, P.O. Box 887, Sterling, AK, Phone: (877) 600-5001

Aurora Sportfishing, Mark Millspaugh, P.O. Box 2824, Homer, AK 99642, Phone: (800) 848-3495, e-mail: akfishing@gci.net

ARIZONA

Big Bass Alley, Bill Warman, P.O. Box 2982, Mesa, AZ 85214-2982, Phone: (480) 380-2901, e-mail: bass@vsps.com

Arizona Fishing Shack Guides & Charter Services, 9222 No.14th Ave., Phoenix, AZ 85021, Phone: 602-944-6577

Bill Schultz, HC-67 Box 2, Marble Canyon, AZ. 86036, Phone: 1-800-962-9755

Ambassador Guide Services, Inc., Bill McBurney, P.O. Box 6229, Marble Canyon, AZ 86036, Phone: (800) 256-7596, e-mail: judyf@ambassadorguides.com

Angling Arizona Guide Service, Inc., Tim Galloway, 4499 E. Acrete Lane, Flagstaff, AZ 86004-7569, Phone: (928) 714-9541, e-mail: TiGalloway@aol.com

Hooked Up Fishing, Mike Stone, 1976 Ironwood Drive, Mohave Valley, AZ 86440, Phone: (520) 768-1940, e-mail: mstone@citlink.net

C & C Guide Service, P.O. Box 738, Roosevelt, AZ 85545, Phone: (520) 467-2770

Exclusive Outdoor Adventures, 1219 SE 14th Ave., Canby, OR 97013, Phone: (503) 266-4753

Fish On Guide Service, Phone: (602) 618-8072

ARKANSAS

Millwood Lake Guide Service, Mike Siefert, Texarkana, AR, Phone: (870) 772-6840, e-mail: MillwoodLakeGSvc@aol.com

Dave's Striper Service, David R. Luttrell, 1516 Berry Lane, Mountain Home, AR 72653, Phone: (877) STRYPER (787-9737)

All For Fishing, John Miskelley, Phone: (800) 558-BAIT

Charlies Rainbow Trout Resort, 270 River Acres Drive, Salesville, AR 72653-9795, Phone: (870) 499-7214

Sportfishing Striper Guide Service, Ron Schneider, Schneider's Rod Shop, 2796 Highway 5 North, Mountain Home, AR 72653, Phone: (888) 946-2427

Ozark Mountains Fish & Game Guide Service, Dennis Whiteside, 4389 SR164W Dover, AR 72837, Phone: (501) 331-2712

Ozark Waters, Everett Middleton, 61 Woodside Lane, Flippin, AR 72634, Phone: (870) 453-8441

Breckenridge Guide Service, Russell and Russ Breckenridge, 131 Crestline Drive, Mountain Home, AR 72653, Phone: (870) 492-5552 or (870) 488-5555

Grand Prairie Outdoors & Guide Service, Inc., Jerry Lochridge, Darrell Lockridge and Bill Lockridge, Hwy 33S & Broadway St., Roe, AR 72134, Phone: (870) 241-9047, e-mail: info@gpoutdoors.com

Blanton's Fishing Guide Service, Frank G. Blanton, P.O. Box 664, Flippin, AR 72634, Phone: (870) 449-6362

Ron Crawford's Fishing Service, 20432 Four Seas, Rogers, AR 72756, Phone: (501) 925-4266

Chucks Fishing Service, Chuck McCarney, P.O. Box 289, Gassville AR 72635, Phone: (870) 435-6958

Clyde's Guide Service, Clyde E. Packer, 1812 Pinetree Lane, Mountain Home, AR 72653, Phone: (870) 424-2316

Dave's Guide Service, Dave Selvey, P.O. Box 416, Dumas, AR 71639, Phone: (870) 382-2353

Big 1's Striper Guide, Johnny Glantz, 1301 S. 11th St., Rogers, AR 72756, Phone: (501) 633-0662

Lindsey's Guide Service, Lindsey Lewis, Conway, AR, Phone: (501) 328-0485

Just Fishin' Guides, Ken Richards, 2309 Southeast 16th, Bentonville, AR 72712, Phone: (501) 273-0276

CALIFORNIA

Doctor's Orders Sportfishing, Captain Skip Driggers, 33012 Calle Perfecto, San Juan Capistrano, CA 92675, Phone: (949) 489 FISH (3474); e-mail: doctorsorders@worldnet.att.net

River Pirate Guide Service, Ken Hoffman, 17622 China Gulch Drive, Anderson, CA 96007, Phone: (530) 365-5833, e-mail: webmaster@riverpirate.com

Sierra Drifters Guide Service, Tom Loe, HCR 79 Box 165-A, Mammoth Lakes, CA 93546, Phone: 760-935-4250, driftfish@qnet.com

Byrd's Guide Service, Doug Byrd, 12068 Hwy. 99E, Red Bluff, CA 96080, Phone: (800) 527-3332, dougbyrd@cwnet.com

Three Rivers Guide Service, Alan Blankenship, Phone: (530) 926-1743, Mitchell Barret, Phone: (539) 964-2044, McCloud General Store (HQ), Phone: (530) 964-2934

Free Willy's Professional Fishing Guide Service, Willy Hauptmann, 600 Whispering Pines, Angwin, CA 94508, Phone: (707) 965-3261

Riptide Sportfishing & Whale Watching, Captain Smitty, 549 Grafton Ave., San Francisco, CA 94112, Phone: (888) RIPTIDE (888-747-8433)

Mike Bogue's Guide Service, 5887 Live Oak Lane, Redding, CA 96001, Phone: (530) 246-8457

Phil's Smiling Salmon Guide Service, P.O. Box 841, Smith River, CA 95567,

Phone: (707) 487-0260

Big Bear Charter Fishing, Aaron Armstrong, Phone: (760) 961-8779

Chartle Charters, Capt. Joe Stoops, P.O. Box 4202, Santa Cruz, CA 95063-4202, Phone: (831) 336-2244

Butchie B Sportfishing, Captain Phil Bentivegna, San Francisco Fishermen's Wharf, Phone: (415) 457-8388

Byrd's Guide Service, Doug Byrd, 12068 Hwy. 99E, Red Bluff, CA 96080, Phone: (800) 527-3332

Salvador's Sportfishing Charters, Salvador Nunez Ocampo, contact Jim Dillon, P.O. Box 9069, San Diego, CA 92169-0069, Phone: (858) 483-3771, e-mail : elbudster@aol.com

Stillwater Guide Service (Flyfishing), Chris Wharton, 5410 Simons Drive, Reno, NV 89523, Phone: (775) 747-0312, e-mail: Chris@out4trout.com

Bear Ridge Fishing Charters, P. O. Box 9156, Santa Rosa, CA 95405, Phone: (707) 539-9534, e-mail: john@salmonandsteelhead.com

Big George's Guide Service, P.O. Box 855, Kelseyville, CA 95451, Phone: (707) 279-9269, e-mail: info@biggeorgesguide.com

Fish'n Dan's Guide Service, Danny Layne, 22701 Confidence Rd., Twain Harte, CA 95383, Phone: (209) 586-2383, e-mail: fishndans@caltechnet.net

S&C Guide Service, Steven Adams, 630 Mockingbird Lane, Oakley, CA 94561, Phone: (925) 625-8718, e-mail: Steveshogheaven@AOL.COM

Greg Nicol Guide Service, Greg Nicol, P.O. Box 155, Smith River, CA 95567, Phone: (707) 464-7320

Jerry's Guide Service, Guide: Jerry Bertagna, Phone: (530) 533-4572

Dan Carter's Guide Service, Dan Carter, 5470 North Bank Rd., Crescent City, CA 95531, Phone: (707) 458-3527

Tim Bermingham's Drift Boat Guide Service, Tim Bermingham, 8400 Old Melones Dam Rd. #70, Jamestown, CA 95327, Phone: (209) 984-4007, e-mail: tim@driftfish.com

Tahoe Fly Fishing Outfitters, 3433 Lake Tahoe Blvd., So. Lake Tahoe, CA 96150, Phone: (530) 541-8208

Seiad Valley Guide Service, P.O.Box 676, Seiad Valley, CA 96086-0676, Phone: (530) 496-3291

Southern California Charter Fishing, Aaron Armstrong, Pleasure Point Marina, Big Bear Lake, CA 92315, Phone: (760) 961-8779

Primetime Sportfishing, Captain Nate Foster, Fishermans Wharf, San Francisco, CA, Phone: (888) 405-9333 or (415) 706-4947

22nd Street Landing, San Pedro, CA, Phone: (310) 832-8304

Adventure at Sea, Newport Beach, CA, Phone: (800) 229-2412

American Yacht Charters, Newport Beach, CA, Phone: (714) 673-4453

Anchor Charter Boats, Inc., Fort Bragg, CA,
Phone: (707) 964-3854
Aqua Adventures Kayak School, San Diego, CA,
Phone: (619) 523-9577
Avanti Sportfishing, La Mesa, CA,
Phone: (619) 464-6264
Balboa Pavillion, Balboa, CA, Phone: (714) 673-5245
Basshole, Lakehead, CA, Phone: (916) 238-2170
Belmont Pier Sportfishing, Long Beach, CA,
Phone: (301) 434-6781
Bongos Sportfishing, Newport Beach, CA,
Phone: (714) 673-2810
Capt. Bill Poole, San Diego, CA,
Phone: (619) 223-7493
Capt. Ferreira, Chula Vista, CA,
Phone: (619) 585-7190
Capt. Ward's My Fair Lady Charters, San Diego,
CA, Phone: (619) 523-0520
Catala Charters & Lodge, Port Hardy, CA,
Phone: (250) 949-7560
Club Nautico Rental, San Diego, CA,
Phone: (800) 628-8426
Coronado Boat Rental, Coronado, CA,
Phone: (619) 437-1514
Cortez Club, La Paz, Mexico, Phone: +5211216120/1
Dana Wharf Sportfishing, Dana Point, CA,
Phone: (714) 496-5794
Dream Chaser Charters, Dana Point, CA,
Phone: (800) 590-9994
Gail Force Charters, San Pedro, CA,
Phone: (310) 833-8400
Grander Sportfishing, Fallbrook, CA,
Phone: (760) 728-6809
Huck Finn Sportfishing, El Granada, CA,
Phone: (800) 572-2934
Impulse Sportfishing, San Diego, CA,
Phone: (619) 689-4731
Jerry's Guide Service, Oroville, CA,
Phone: (530) 533-4572
Ken Cunningham Guide Service, Kelseyville, CA,
Phone: (707) 928-4762
L A Harbor Sportfishing, Inc., San Pedro, CA,
Phone: (310) 547-9916
Liquid Web, San Pedro, CA, Phone: (714) 585-7599
Loch Lomond Live Bait & Tackle, San Rafael, CA,
Phone: (415) 456-0321
Lucky Strike Sportfishing, Costa Mesa, CA,
Phone: (949) 645-5745
Martini's Bait & Tackle, Stockton, CA,
Phone: (209) 951-1692
Matson Maritime Services, San Diego, CA,
Phone: (619) 223-2278
Newport Landing Sportfishing, Balboa, CA,
Phone: (714) 675-0550
Party Boat Patty-C, Fort Bragg, CA,
Phone: (707) 964-0669
PIZAZ III, San Diego, CA, Phone: (760) 431-0385

Rancho Buena Vista, Santa Maria, CA,
Phone: (800) 258-8200
Seaside Yacht Charters, Newport Beach, CA,
Phone: (949) 675-1853
Shadow Cliffs Park Co., Pleasanton, CA,
Phone: (510) 846-9263
Silver King Lodge, Modesto, CA,
Phone: (800) 847-3474
Skip'n Out Charters, South Laguna, CA,
Phone: (714) 240-7226
Sportfishing Concepts, Anaheim, CA,
Phone: (714) 304-0130
Suntan Charters, Santa Cruz, CA,
Phone: (831) 423-2211
The Fisherman's Friend, Lodi, CA,
Phone: (209) 369-0204
Tony Reyes Fishing Tours, Orange, CA,
Phone: (714) 538-9300

COLORADO

Bar-H Outfitters, Randy Horne, 2036 CR 43, Meeker,
CO 81641, Phone: (800) 230-HUNT (4868)
Troll-In Thunder Freshwater Charters, Charley
Stull, P.O. Box 270015, Littleton, CO 80127-0001,
Phone: (888) 922-9783
Mountain Angler Guide Service, Doug Hardwick,
P.O. Box 467, Main Street Mall, 311 South Main
Street, Breckenridge, CO 80424,
Phone: (970) 453-HOOK (4665) or (800) 453-4669
Thomas B. Rossi, 6762 N. Bighorn Trail, Littleton, CO
80125, Phone: (303) 932-2241
Thomas M. Murphy, 299 CR 307, Durango, CO
81301, Phone: (970) 259-5469
Van E. Johnson, 20980 Hwy 666, Yellow Jacket, CO
81335, Phone: (970) 562-4593
Alpine Outfitters, Chris Cassidy, 520 N. Cherry St.,
Colorado Nation, CO 81521, Phone: (970) 858-7393
Backcountry Outfitters, Inc., David L. Guilliams Sr.,
Box 4190, Pagosa Springs, CO 81157,
Phone: (970) 731-4630
Chuck Davies Guide Services, Inc., P.O. Box 8, Loma,
CO 81524, Phone: (970) 858-7079 or
(970) 858-0370.
Green River Drifters, Gregg "Bomar" Tipton, 1327
Saratoga Ave., Steamboat Springs, CO 80487, Phone:
(970) 879-0370
Hill's Summer Camp, Route 1, Box 189, Collbran,
CO 81624, Phone: (970) 487-3433
Jerry L. Smith, 7175 CR 501, Bayfield, CO 81122,
Phone: (970) 884-2074
John D. Orourke, 4210 E 100th Ave. #612, Thornton,
CO 80229, Phone: (303) 450-4131
Michael S. Ray, Box 1286, Pagosa Springs, CO 81147,
Phone: (970) 264-2812
Richard H. Ray, 4821 A Hwy 84, Pagosa Springs, CO

81147, Phone: (970) 264-5546

CONNECTICUT

Jims LLC., jadams01@snet.net

Marla Blair's Flyfishing Guide Service & Instruction, Marla Blair, Phone: (413) 583-5141

Talon Guide Service & Outfitters, 120 North Road, Shelburne NH 03581, Phone: (603) 466-3403

North East Saltwater Flyfishing, Capt. Jeff Northrop, Westport Outfitters, 570 Riverside Ave., Westport, CT 06880, Phone: (203) 226-1915, e-mail: Godzilla41@AOL.com

Benmar Custom Charters, Captain John Groff, Mystic, CT, Phone: (860) 521-3168, e-mail: SEACAPJG@AOL.COM

Daystar, Capt Bob Bociek, 295 Gilman St., Bridgeport, CT 06605, Phone: (203) 615-0070

Early Bird Charters, Capt. Tony Barone, Clinton, CT, Phone: (860) 664-4540

Bill Fish Charters, Capt. Bill Herold, Greenwich, CT, Phone: (914) 967-8246

Blue Waters Charters, Capt. Don Caddick, Groton, CT, Phone: (860) 445-5190

Lady Margaret, Capt. Claude Adams, New London, CT, Phone: (860) 739-3687

North Coast Charters, Capt. Bob Turley, 40 San Pedro Ave., Stratford CT 06614, Phone (203) 378-1160, e-mail: Flats2020@aol.com

My Bonnie Charters, Capt. Sal Tardella, Norwalk, CT, Phone: (203) 866-6313

Eden Charters, Capt. Paul Retano, Old Saybrook, CT, Phone: (860) 388-5897

The Reel Thing, Capt. James Ring, Stratford, CT, Phone: (203) 377-1682

Catch'Em, Capt. Dick Siedzik, Westbrook, CT, Phone: (860) 399-5853

DELAWARE

Pisces Charters, Capt. Jim Neyhart, Slaughter Beach, DE, Phone: (302) 697-0647

Fishhawk Charters, Capt. Thom Brejwa, Route 2 Box 168-K, Frankford, DE 19945, Phone: (302) 539-8523

Keely Ann, Capt. Neil McLaughlin, 108 West Bay Park, Lewes, DE 19958, Phone: (302) 945-0451

Brandywine Outfitters 2000, Pennsylvania Avenue, Wilmington, DE, Phone: (302) 656- 6008

FLORIDA

Hawkeye Charters, Inc., Capt. George Halper, P.O. Box 91, Matlacha FL 33993, Phone: (941) 282-1263, e-mail: fishwithhawkeye@aol.com

AJ's Freelancer Bass Guide Service, Captain A. James Jackson, Phone: (407) 348-8764 or (800) 738-8144, e-mail: capjackson@aol.com

Renegade Guide Service, Capt. Harry Simmons, 148 Chobee St., Okeechobee, FL 34974, Phone: (800) 685-7309, e-mail: captdexter@prodigy.net

Fresh/Saltwater Fishing Charters, Captain Charlie Clyne, Jupiter, FL, Phone: 561-762-7146, e-mail: captain@flinet.com

Central Florida Guide Service, John Leech, 2442 Spring Lake Rd., Fruitland Park, FL, Phone: (800) 507-0058, e-mail: JLeech1014@aol.com

Hillbilly Charters, Capt. Chester Rowe, 1201 S.E. Eighth Ave., Okeechobee, FL 34974, Phone: (800) 472-2036, e-mail: captskid@strato.net

Bud Andrews Big Bass Fishing Guide Service, Bud Andrews, 10811 N. Coveview Terrace, Crystal River, FL 34428, Phone: (352) 795-6336, e-mail: info@lakerousseaufishingresort.com

Hawghunter Guide & Taxidermy Service, Capt. Todd Kersey, 1000 NW 48 St., Ft. Lauderdale, FL 33309, Phone: (800) 235-1349, e-mail: hawghunter@bellsouth.net

Easy Days Guide Service, Capt. Terry Lamielle, 385 Hammonton St. S.W., Palm Bay FL 32908, Phone: (321) 725-7255, e-mail: Zaracrazy@aol.com

Bud Keefer Guide Service, Capt. Bud Keefer, 2730 SE 25th Drive, Okeechobee, FL 34974, Phone: (800) 465-8805

Oh Son Lures and Guide Service, 4561 Iola Drive, Sarasota, FL 34231, Phone: (941) 922-0706

A-Action Professional Bass Guide Services, Captain Chuck Matthews, P.O. Box 701625, St. Cloud, FL 34770, Phone (800) 936-7398

Fargo's Guide Service, 1550 Sassy Road, Clewiston, FL 33440, Phone: (800) 793-5741, fargo@gate.net

MFCTOO, 4500 Joe Overstreet Road, Kenansville, FL 34739, Phone: (800) 347-4007, e-mail: MFCTOO@aol.com

A Bass Guide, Hugh Crumpler III, 2808 Dorsey Place, Melbourne, FL 32901-7016, Phone: (321) 722-3134, e-mail: bsncoach@gate.net

Champion Pro Guide Services Central Florida, Capt. Tony Weatherman, Kissimmee/ Orlando, FL, Phone: (888) 715-7661, e-mail: captain@championbass.com

Chuck's Guide Service, Capt. Chuck Pippin Jr., Clewiston, FL at Roland Martin's Marina, Phone: (941) 564-4273, e-mail: cpippin@onearrow.net

Memory Makin' Guides, Captain Reno Alley, Phone: (800) 749-2278, e-mail: mmguides@gte.net

Playing Hooky Guide Service, Steve McNeely, 2445 Empire Ave., Melbourne, FL 32934, Phone: (321) 751-4042, Playhooky@aol.com

Balon's Pro Guide Service, Capt. Mike Balon, based at Roland Martin's Marina, Clewiston, FL, Phone: (863) 983-3461, e-mail: balon@gate.net

Tom and Jerry's Pro Guide Service, 1780 King Charles Drive, Kissimmee, FL, Phone: (800) 328-5686

Imagination Bassin Guide Services, 738 Jensen Beach Blvd., Jensen Beach, FL 34957, Phone: (877) 890-6809

Stickmarsh Bait, Tackle & Guide Service, Shane Allen, 9 S. Mulberry St., Fellsmere, FL, Phone: (561) 571-9855

Capt. Mike's Charters, Capt. Mike Fay, Florida Everglades, Phone: (954) 474-3242, e-mail: captmf13@aol.com

Lamar Middleton's Guide Service, Lamar Middleton, 144 Chaucer Lane, Winter Haven, FL 33884, Phone: (863) 324-0433 or (877) 912-5161

The Art of Fishing Guide Service, Art Ferguson, Lake Okeechobee, FL, Phone: (941) 983-2812

Capt. Bob's Lunker Bass Guide Service, Capt. Bob Bloom, 4050 Oberry Road, Kissimmee, FL 34746, Phone: (888) 847-6424 or (407) 931-3118

Elite Anglers Fishing Charters, Captain Daniel Goode, 228 Hibiscus St., Tavernier FL 33070, Phone: (305) 853-0346, Fax: (305) 852-8951, e-mail: phishman91@aol.com

Flats Fishing Key West.com, Capt. Paul Down Ollariu, Phone: (800) 581-3659 or (305) 304-1805, e-mail: Captpaulinkw@aol.com

Sea Level Fishing Charters, Captain David L. Ribeca, 4609 S.W. 22nd Ave., Cape Coral, FL 33914, Phone: (941) 549-8594, e-mail: sealevelcharters@mindspring.com

Bass Challenger Guide Service, Eddie Bussard, 195 Heather Lane Drive, Deltona, FL 32738, Phone: (800) 241-5314 or (407) 273-8045, e-mail: bassineddie@cs.com

GEORGIA

Southern Fishing Schools Inc., Ken Sturdivant, 106 Hickory Ridge, Cumming, Ga. 30040, Phone: (770) 889-2654, e-mail: kensturdivant@southernfishing.com

Harold Nash Professional Fishing Guide Service, 5931 Nacoochee Trail, Flowery Branch, GA 30542, Phone: (770) 967-6582, e-mail: nashfish@bellsouth.net

Bill Vanderford, P.O. Box 1222, Lawrenceville GA 30046, Phone: (770) 962-1241, e-mail: info@fishinglanier.com

Glenn Morrison's Lake Lanier Guide Service, 2066 Pine Tree Drive, Buford, GA 30518, Phone: (770) 962-8738, e-mail: HGMFish@aol.com

Billy Darby's Fishing Guide Service, Rt. 1, Fort Gaines, GA 31751, Phone: (229) 768-3919

Mountain Lake Outfitters, Dave Kaetzel, Blairsville, GA/Murphy, NC, Phone: (828) 837-8045

Georgia Mountain Guide Service, Jeffery Hughes,

988 Fairview Road, Ball Ground, GA 30107, Phone: (770) 735-2625, e-mail: jeff.guide@tds.net

Striper-Hybrid Guide Service, Fred Duncan, 3235 Brandywine Place, Marietta, GA 30064, Phone: (770) 422-6539, fred@biglanierstripers.com

Lake Lanier Outfitters, Inc., Tom Branch Jr., 4603 Fox Forrest Drive, Flowery Branch, Ga 30542, Phone: (770) 764-0191

Lanier Fishing Adventures, Rick Ramey, Lawrenceville, GA, Phone: (770) 806-8253

HAWAII

Lahela Ocean Adventures, Captain Scott Akana, Kauai, HI, Phone: (808) 635-4020, e-mail: lahela-adventures@aloha.net

Catchem Sportfishing, Capt. Chuck Haupert, 77-6456 Pualani St., Kailua-Kona, HI 96740, Phone: (808) 938-1400, e-mail: fishkona@gte.net

Kona Hawaii fishing with K-IX Charters, Capt. Jeff Rogers, 73-1295 Kaiminani Drive, Kona, HI 96740, Phone: (808) 895-1852

No Mercy Sportfishing, Mike Berg, P.O. Box 5451, Kailua-Kona, HI 96745, Phone: (808) 331-2217

Live Bait Sport Fishing, Captain Shannon Frazier, P.O. Box 4100, Waianae, HI 96792, Phone: (808) 696-1604

Inter Island Sportfishing, Phone: (877) 806-FISH or (808) 591-8888

Stand Up Fishing Charters, Poipu Kauai Inc., Captain Danny Waugh, P.O. Box 3650, Lihue, Kauai, HI 96766, Phone: (808) 635-TUNA or (877) 887-0412, e-mail: fishingkauai@fishingkauai.com

Hana Pa'a Sport Fishing Charters Kauai, 6370 Kalama Rd., Kapaa HI 96746, Phone: (866) PRO-FISH, e-mail: julietim@aloha.net

Sportfish Hawaii, 197 Opihikao Way, Honolulu, HI 96825, Phone: (877) 388-1376

Intrepid Sportfishing, Captain Cintas, Honokohau Harbor, HI, Phone: (808) 987-9889

IDAHO

Idaho Angling Services, LLC, P.O. Box 703, Picabo, Idaho 83348, Phone: (208) 788-9709, e-mail: david@anglingservices.com

Sevy Guide Service and River Expeditions, Bob Sevy, P.O. Box 24, Stanley, ID 83278, Phone: (208) 774-2200

Bighorn Outfitters, Rt. 10, Box 30-MU, Carmen, ID 83462, Phone: (208) 756-3992 or (800) 259-3992

Clearwater River Trips, Jim Cook, Route 1, Box 108 F, Lenore, ID 83541, Phone: (208) 276-3199

Solitude River Trips, Al & Jeana Bukowsky, P.O. Box 907-MU, Merlin, OR 97532, Phone: (800) 396-1776;

Summer: P.O. Box 702-MU, Salmon, ID 83467

ILLINOIS

Big Goomba Musky Hunter Guide Service, Rich Gallagher, 1253 Cobblers Crossing, Elgin, IL, Phone: (847) 741-9771, bigoomba@aol.com

Lone Eagle Lake Michigan Sport Fishing Charters, Captain Norm Sanford, Slip AA7, North Point Marina, Winthrop Harbor, IL 60097, Phone (800) 566-3245

Hawg Hunter Charters, Capt. Dave Bentham, 1008 Catalpa Lane, Naperville, IL 60540, Phone: (630) 355-6353

Muskie "62" Guide Service, Phillip Gutmann, 4200 Greenfield Lane, Lake in the Hills, IL 60156, Phone: (847) 669-8286

Fatman's Fly Fishing Guide Service, Rich "The Fatman" Brown, 209 Kendall St., Burlington, WI 53105, Phone: (847) 781-2526, e-mail: fishinfatman@fishinfatman.com

X-stream Bassin,' Chicago, IL, Phone: (708) 672-1966

Geno Altiery's Guide Service, Kankakee River, Phone: (815) 476-4056
Cajun Illinois River Guide Service, Illinois River, Phone: (815) 667-4222

Kristy Lynn II Sportfishing Charter, Terry & Bonnie Nied, 280 Cypress Lane, Libertyville, IL 60048, Phone: (800) 487-0199, e-mail: TNied680@aol.com

Into The Outdoors, Todd Berg, 25705 Arrowhead Drive, Mundelein IL 60060, Phone: (847) 922-1271, e-mail: sales@intotheoutdoors.net

Spendthrift Sportfishing Charters, Captain Jerry Nied, 1091 West Dearborn Lane, Vernon Hills IL 60061, Phone: (800) 726- 7309, e-mail: fishjerry@aol.com

Urbahn's Guide Service, Gary Urbahn, 190 Park Ct., Hinckley IL 60520, Phone: (815) 286-9500, e-mail: fastbass@hinckleyaccess.com

Jay Angel: Shabbona Lake Guide, Shabonna Lake, Phone: (815) 756-8914, e-mail: dekalbfish@aol.com

Professional Guide Service, 1521 College Ave., Dixon, IL, Phone: (815) 288-6855

Illinois Valley Guide Service, Phone: (815) 664-4159

Limit Guide Service, Phone: (815) 667-4862

Spendthrift Sportfishing Charters, Captain Jerry Nied, 1091 West Dearborn Lane, Vernon Hills, IL 60061, Phone: (800) 726-7309, e-mail: fishjerry@aol.com

Chip Porter's Salmon Master Charters, Capt. Chip Porter, 740 Summit Road, Lake Zurich, IL 60047, Phone: (847) 726-8877, e-mail: chip@chipporter.com

INDIANA

Fatal Attraction Guide Service, Captain Chip Mertens, 1928 Utica Pike, Jeffersonville, IN, Phone: (812) 284-4352, e-mail: fishinCmertens53@aol.com

Brother Nature Fishing Adventures, Mike Schoonveld, 6312W 100N, Enos, IN 47963, Phone: (219) 285-2123

Tim's Patoka Lake Guide Service, Tim Gibson, Patoka Lake, IN, Phone: (812) 723-4195, e-mail: fishin@bluemarble.net

Ranger Nick's Guide Service, Nick Teeters, Bloomington, IN 47401, Phone: (812) 335-6636, e-mail: fishinteetersn@city.bloomington.in.us

IOWA

Jim McDonnell Guide Service, P.O. Box 148, Royal, IA, Phone: (712) 933-5532

Talaview Resorts, Jacob Hunget, 924 143rd Ave., Indianola, IA 50125, Phone: 515-961-5554

F&S Guide Service, F. Sharkey, 222 Dream St., Des Moines, IA 33561, Phone: (312) 222-6161

Jimmy O's Bait & Tackle, Jim Oberfoell, 11917 Sherrill Rd., Dubuque, IA 52002, Phone: (319) 552-1424

KANSAS

Madd Jack Striper Guide, Jack Hoskinson, 1821 W. 13th, Hutchinson, KS 67501, Phone: (316) 669-8120 or (316) 664-2794, e-mail: orval@mindspring.com

Mike Cook, Four Lake Guides, Phone: (316) 522-1720, e-mail: fourlake@kscable.com

Timber Creek Wildlife Adventures, Mark Womacks, 4858 231st Road, Atlanta, KS 67008, Phone: (620) 394-2393, mmmmw@sktc.net

Ozark and Prairie Outfitter, 2632 N. Payne, Wichita, KS, Phone: (316) 838-1619

Clyde Holscher Guide Lines Guide Service, 3608 Hackberry Drive, Topeka, KS 66605, Phone: (785) 267-0065, e-mail: fshguide@swbell.net

H&R Outfitters, Inc., Cody Heitschmidt, 11502 W69th, Nickerson, KS 67561, Phone: (316) 422-3273, e-mail: cody@huntingkansas.com

R&T Guide Service, Chuck Tidball, 314 N. Main, Wakeeney KS, Phone: (785) 743-2418

KENTUCKY

Colonel Duncan's Barren River Lake Guide Service, Barren River Lake, KY, Phone:(270) 622-4328, e-mail: finweb01@aol.com

Double D Outfitters, Dave DeBold, 270 Harrison Circle, Mt. Washington, KY 40047, Phone: (502) 538-8919, e-mail: Ddflyfisher@cs.com
Fish Tales Guide Service, Randall Gibson, Phone: (502) 426-1839

Rainbow Guide Service, John Rush, Burkesville, KY, Phone: (270) 864-2248

Crash's Landing Inc., Crash Mullins, Cave Run Lake, KY, Phone: (606) 780-4260, e-mail: crashky@mis.net

Cave Run Muskie Guide Service, P.O. Box 112, Denniston, KY 40316, Phone: (800) 452-1600, e-mail: dcsquare@mrtc.com

Buckhorn Guide Service, Chris Haley, 421 Memorial Drive, Hazard, KY 41701, Phone: (606) 436-6501

AJ's Guide Service, A.J. Reid, 1085 Shadow Road, Russell Springs, KY 42642, Phone: (270) 866-6207

Micah's Guide Service, Magic Micah Brown, 1071 E. Lexington Ave., Danville, KY 40422, Phone: (859) 236-3796

Bates Guide Service, Gerald Bates, 219 M. Tucker Road, Russell Springs, KY 42642, Phone: (270) 866-8703, e-mail: frizzell@duo-county.com

Phil Glass Striper Guide Service, 1854 Hwy. 790, Bronston, KY 42518, Phone: (606) 561-5324

Striper Time Guide Service, Mark Wasiloski, P.O. Box 538, Monticello, KY 42633, Phone: (606) 348-9927
Dave Stewart Bass Buster Guide Service, Kentucky Lake, KY, Phone: (270) 354-5039, e-mail: ky-barkleyguide@home.com

Crappie Action Guide Service, Ken Riddick, Kentucky Lake, 95 Elmwood Drive, Paris, TN, Phone: (731) 285-3551, e-mail: crappieaction@yahoo.com

Mr. Clean's Professional Guide Service, Jerry Schwartz, 696 Cedar Point Rd., Benton, KY 42025, Phone: (270) 354-8673

Mike Shelton Guide Service, Barkley Lake, Phone: (270) 522-1539

Wicks's Guide Service, Lyndon Wicker, 859 Keniana Drive, New Concord, KY 42076, Phone: (270) 436-6025, e-mail: wicksguideservice@apex.net

Malcolm Lane Hook Line & Sinker Guide Service, 1408 Lake Barkley Drive, Kuttawa, KY 42055, Phone: (270) 388-0525, e-mail: mlane@ziggycom.net

Weakley's Guide Service, Brad Weakley, 527 E. Unity Church Rd., Hardin, KY 42048, Phone: 1-877-547-FISH, bweakley@apex.net

Fatal Attraction Guide Service, Captain Chip Mertens, 1928 Utica Pike, Jeffersonville, IN, Phone: (812) 284-4352

Bob Coan's Dale Hollow Lake Guide Service, Phone: (931) 243-3827

Dale Hollow Smallmouth Guide Service, Ralph Sandfer, 8836 Poplar Grove Road, Celina, TN 38551, Phone: (931) 243-4795

Eck's Guide Service, Tony Eckler, Dale Hollow Lake,
Phone: (931) 243-6349

Trophy Guides Service, Fred McClintock, Dale Hollow Lake, Phone: (931) 243-2142

LOUISIANA

Bayou Bass, Jerry Lochridge, Darrell Lockridge & Bill Lockridge, Hwy 33S & Broadway Street, Roe, AR 72134, Phone: (870) 241-9047, e-mail: info@gpoutdoors.com

Adventure South Guide Service, Capt. Shane Mayfield, P.O. Box 341, Buras, LA 70041, Phone: (504) 392-1700, e-mail: shanemay@bellsouth.net

Toledo Bend Guide Service, Toledo Bend Cottage, Route 1 Box 1347, Shelbyville, Texas 75973, Phone: (409) 368-7151

Toledo Bend Guides Association, Guides on the Bend, Mark Stewart (318) 645-7274; Paul Eason (409) 698-9491; Maurice Jackson (318) 645-6863; Ray Pellerin (318) 645-5215; Robert Anderson (318) 925-2880; Mike Wheatley (318) 697-2136; Gary Hartley (318) 352-2744; Shawn Stinson (318) 645-7243; Glen Freeman (318) 872-6110; Glen Teer (318) 256-2758; Mike Echols (318) 687-9037; Willard Moore (318) 894-8770; Bubba Rivers (318) 645-4862.

Caddo Lake Guide Service, Paul Keith, 6774 Spring Valley Drive, Shreveport, LA 71107, Phone: (318) 309-3474, e-mail: caddoguide1@att.net

Louisiana Fishing Expeditions, Capt. Ben H. Leto, 23288 Hwy. 1084, Covington, LA 70435, Phone: (877) 271-2059
Bassmasters Guide Service, 225 Carolyn Ave., Denham Springs, LA 70726, Phone: (504) 665-0899

Griffin Fishing Charters, Raymond Griffin, Hc 99 Bx 604, Lafitte, LA 70067, Phone: (800) 741-1340, e-mail: CAJINN1@aol.com

Capt. Phil Robichaux's Saltwater Guide Service, 4775 Jean Lafitte Blvd., Lafitte, LA 70067, Phone: (504) 689-2006, e-mail: phil@accesscom.net

Big Easy Adventures Inc., P.O. Box 73299, Metarie, LA 70033, Phone: (504) 456-2820 or (877) 523-0757, e-mail: bill@noaa1.com

Bayou Charters L.L.C. Professional Guide Services, Capt. Charlie Thomas, 3415 Delille St., Chalmette, LA 70043, Phone: (504) 278-FISH

Osprey Charters, Capt. James Peters, Venice, LA, Phone: (504) 834-7097

Gotcha Charters, Captain Bobby Terrebonne, P.O. Box 518, Grand Isle, LA 70358, Phone: (504) 787-2481

Escape Charters, Capt. Tim Ursin, 210 Blackfin Cove, Slidell, LA 70458, Phone: (888) 932-2824 or (985) 643-5905

New Orleans Saltwater Charters, Capt. John Pounders, P.O. Box 178, Lafitte, LA 70767, Phone: (504) 689-3148, e-mail: dehinton1@home.com

Capt. John L.'s Charters, Capt. John L. Taylor, 190 Louis Morel Lane, Buras, LA 70041, Phone: (504) 657-9739 or (318) 688-9900, e-mail: captjohnl@captjohnl.com

Big Bayou Blue Marina, Capt. T-Man Charamie, 1352 Bourg-Larose Hwy., P.O. Box 1453, LaRose LA 70373, Phone: (504) 693-6828

Reel Time Charters, Captain Roland Felarise, 106 Ouski Bayou Drive, Houma, LA 70360, Phone: (504) 876-1185

Super Strike II Charters, Capt. Damon McKnight, 14 Oil Well Road, Venice, LA 70461, Phone: (800) 318-1720

Paradise Outfitters, Capt. Scott Avanzino, P.O. Box 611, Venice, LA 70091, Phone: (504) 451-7579, e-mail: avanzino@yahoo.com

MAINE

Fat Bass Tours, Eric Eklund, 25 Lantern Lane, Windham, ME 04062, Phone (207) 892-3095, e-mail: fbtours@aol.com

Hillbilly Charters, Capt. Chester Rowe, (June-August in Maine), 1201 S.E. Eighth Ave., Okeechobee, FL 34974, Phone: (800) 472-2036, e-mail: captskid@strato.net

Katahdin Lake Wilderness Camps, Alfred J. Cooper III, P.O.Box 398, Millinocket, ME 04462, Phone: (207) 723-4050, e-mail: t3r8lake@ime.net

Katahdin Region Wilderness Guide Service, Thomas Chase, P.O. Box 731, Patten, ME 04765, Phone: (207) 528-2967

Gary C's Guiding, Gary Corson, P.O. Box 22, New Sharon, ME 04955, Phone: (207) 778-0529

Raio's Guide Service Bass Fishing Adventures, Phone: (207) 727-3215

White Birch Guide Service, Capt. Paul Bois, RR 1 Box 300, West Lovell Rd., Lovell, ME 04051, Phone: (207) 925-1740

Portland Guide Service, Capt. John Ford, P.O. Box 10318, Portland, ME 04104, Phone: (207) 471-5858, e-mail: captjohn@loa.com

Loon Lodge in the Allagash, Michael Yencha, P.O. Box 404, Millinocket, ME 04462 Phone: (207) 745-8168 or (570)287-6915, e-mail: relax@loonlodgemaine.com

Gateway Recreation and Lodging, Victor Smith, P.O. Box 291, Bingham, ME 04920, Phone: (207) 672-9395 or (800) 440-0053, e-mail: gateway@gwi.net

Caratunk Wilderness Lodging and Guide Service, Scott Underhill, P.O. Box 38, Caratunk, ME 04925, Phone: (877) 254-8021

Northern Horizons Guide Service, Allan Albert, P.O. Box 52 St. Francis, ME, Phone (207) 398-3292

Northeast Anglers Inc., 551 Atlantic Highway, Northport, ME 04849, Phone: (800) 558-7658

MARYLAND

Potomac Guide Service, Bill Kramer, 1 Apache Ct., Gaithersburg, MD 20878, e-mail: billkramer@potomacguides.com

Life Outdoors Unlimited, 4708 Sellman Road, Beltsville, MD 20705, Phone: (301) 937-0010

National Bass Guide Service, Steve Chaconas, 8619 Camden St., Alexandria, VA 22308, Phone: (703) 360-3472, e-mail: NationalBass@aol.com

Mark Kovach Fishing Services, six guides: Mark Kovach, Dave Motes, John Hayes, Richard Larkin, Butch Murphy, Mark Frondorf, 406 Pershing Drive, Silver Spring, MD 20910-4253, Phone: (301) 588-8742

"Master" Sportfishing Charters, Capt. Ben Franklin, Fisherman's Marina, Ocean City, MD, Phone: (800) 240-5025 or (410) 208-1067, e-mail: masterfishing@patmos-international.com

Bounty Hunter Charters, Captain Glenn James, 8076 Windward Key Drive, Chesapeake Beach, MD 20732, Phone: (800) 322-4032, gjamescapt@aol.com

Chesapeake Charter Fishing on The Darlene II, Captain Kerry Muse, Happy Harbor, Deale, MD, Phone: (800) 381-2727, e-mail: CaptKerry@aol.com

Waterdog Sportfishing Charters, Capt. Tom Henry, P.O. Box 1138, Saint Michaels, MD 21663, Phone: (800) 787-3474

"Muff Diver" Sportfishing Charters, Sunset Marina, Chesapeake Bay, Phone: (877) 514-3474

"Magic" Sportfishing Charters, Old Town Marina, Dorchester St. at the Inlet, Phone: (410) 208-1555

"Always Late" (not) Sportfishing Charters, Ocean City Fishing Center, Phone: (410) 749-9764

"My Sanity" Sportfishing Charters, Bahia Marina, Phone: (410) 289-6491

"Box Lunch" Sportfishing Charters, Bahia Marina, Phone: (800) 210-0023

"Gales Warning" Sportfishing Charters, Fisherman's Marina, Phone: (800) 825-5948

"Fish Hunter" Sportfishing Charters, Ocean City Fishing Center, Phone: (410) 213-2972

Dockside Charters, Jeff Pfister, P.O. Box 108, Queenstown, MD 21658, Phone: (410) 827-4313, e-mail: jeffro@friend.ly.net

Tuna the Tide Charter Service, 404 Greenwood Creek Lane, Grasonville, MD 21638, Phone: (410) 827-6188, fax: (410) 827-9331, e-mail: capmarco@friend.ly.net

Babu Sport Fishing Charters, Capt. John Wilkinson, 626 Dunberry Drive, Arnold, MD 21012, Phone: (410) 757-1466, e-mail: wilk@erols.com

Capt. Clyde's Charters, Capt. Clyde McGowan, Capt. Eddie McGowan, Capt. Dave Badwak, 1058 Deep Creek Ave., Arnold, MD 21012, Phone: (410) 974-4314, e-mail:Clyde@Captclyde.com

Marica, Capt. Gary Sacks, 48862 Curley's Road, Ridge, MD 20680, Phone: (301) 872-5506 or (301) 904-3670

Sea Dux Outfitters, Captain Randy Townsend, Duck Neck Point, Chestertown, MD 21620, Phone: (410) 778-4362

"Huntress" Sportfishing Charters, Bahia Marina, Phone: (410) 289-7438

"Infinity" Sportfishing Charters, Sunset Marina, Phone: (877) 514-3474

"Second to None" Sportfishing Charters, Fisherman's Marina, Phone: (302) 645-5912

"Islander" Sportfishing Charters, Fisherman's Marina, Phone: (410) 641-4604

"Good Vibrations" Sportfishing Charters, Ocean City Fishing Center, Phone: (302) 227-0728

Upper Bay (Chesapeake Bay) Charter Captains Association:

Capt. Russell Green, Phone: (410) 574-7067, "Carol G" (Middle River)

Capt. Bob Spore, Phone: (410) 437-2715, "Catherine M" (Magothy)

Capt. Clyde McGowan, Phone: (410) 974-4314, "Christina" (Magothy River)

Capt. Bernie Michael, Phone: (410) 974-0238, "Dottie M II" (Magothy)

Capt. George W. Bentz, Phone: (410) 360-2376, "Drizzle Bar" (Bodkin Creek)

Capt. Bob Hunter, Phone: (410) 682-6077, "Gloria Jean" (Back River)

Capt. Charles T. Reichert, Jr., Phone: (410) 465-6880, "Interlude" (Bodkin)

Capt. Skip Slomski, Phone: (410) 255-9597, "Jenny Beck" (Patapsco)

Capt. Bud Thomas, Phone: (410) 866-4994, "Lar Joy II" (Seneca)

Capt. Jerry Schultz, Phone: (410) 574-3853, "Little M" (Middle River)

Capt. Joseph Anderson, Phone: (410) 284-3709, "Loaded Deck" (Back River)

Capt. John Collison, Phone: (410) 761-8846, "Mary Emma" (Magothy River)

Capt. Jim Moore III, Phone: (410) 574-9066, "Misty Dawn" (Back River)

Capt. Bob Dukehart, Phone: (410) 465-6857, "My Girl" (Magothy)

Capt. Woody Ensor, Phone: (410) 429-3948, "Pandora" (Middle River)

Capt. James T. Coppinger, Phone: (410) 663-8983, "Princess" (Middle River)

Capt Salvaotre D. Marani Jr., Phone: (410) 342-2004, "Slapshot" (Baltimore Harbour)

Capt. Leonard Poole, Phone: (410) 760-7854, (Bodkin)

MASSACHUSETTS

Marla Blair's Flyfishing Guide Service & Instruction, Marla Blair, Phone: (413) 583-5141

Northeast FlyFishing Guide Service, Walt Geryk, 38 Elm St., Hatfield, MA 01038, Phone: (413) 575-5421, Fax: (413) 247-9971

B-Fast Charters, Capt. Mike Bartlett, P.O. Box 122, N. Pembroke, MA 02358, Phone: (781) 293-6402, e-mail: bfastcharters@yahoo.com

Reel to Reel Sportfishing Charters, Captain Scott Lundberg, 35 Windsor Ridge Drive, Whitinsville MA 01588, Phone (508) 234-5944

Alloverit Fishing Guide Service Nantucket, Mike Cody, 165 Orange St., Nantucket, MA, Phone: (508) 325-6043, e-mail: mcody@alloveritfishing.com

Tuna Hunter Charters, Captain Gary Cannell, 4 Heritage Drive, Rockport, MA 01966, Phone: (978) 546-7992 or (978) 407-1351

Coastline Sport Fishing Inc., Capt. R.J. Silvester, Chatham Yacht Basin, West Chatham, MA, Phone: (508) 945-4971

MICHIGAN

CoHooker Charter Service, Capt. Ron and Kevin Westrate, 6545 128th Ave., Holland, MI 49423, Phone: (616) 335-2076 or (888) 253-8372, e-mail: captron@chartermichigan.com

Gnat's Charters, Captain Mike Gnatkowski, 6934 W. Illinois St., Ludington, MI 49431, Phone: (231) 845-8400, e-mail: 1012gnat@inet.westshore.cc.mi.us

Trophy Specialists Fishing Charters, Capt. Michael Veine, 15555 Cassidy Rd., Chelsea, MI 48118, Phone: (734) 475-9146, e-mail: veinemr@aol.com

Reel Teaser Sportfishing Charters, Captain Mitch Modrzynski, 11175 LaSalle Road, Manistee, MI 49660, Phone: (231) 398-0619, e-mail: reel-teaser@juno.com

Moose Crossing Outfitters, Steve Taylor, One Old Homestead Rd., Glen Arbor, MI 49636, Phone: (231) 334-7550, e-mail: info@moosecrossingoutfitters.com

The Art of Fishing Guide Service, Art Ferguson (Michigan, May-November), Florida, December-April, Phone: (810) 997-7702

F.B.I. Charters, Wallace Hodges, 5876 Country View, Allendale, MI 49401, Phone: (616) 895-4813 or (231) 845-8042

FirstLight Charters, Ben Gillette, 2395 Terrace Ave., Holland, MI 49424, Phone: (616) 836-3660

Bialik Charters, Captain Jason Bialik, Big Manistee River, MI, Phone: (231) 723-0591

Walleye Express Fishing Charters, Captain Dan Manyen, 1686 SE Boutell Rd., Essexville MI 48732-1562, Phone: (517) 892-1920

Captain Bill's Charters, 3333 Ravenswood Lot 51, Marysville, MI 48040-1168, Phone: (810) 364-3494

Sundowner Charters, Capt. Gary Gamble, 7068 Evans Rd., Eau Claire, MI 49111, Phone: (616) 461-3099

First Class Fishing Charters, Captain Steve Hamilton, 6219 Miller Rd., Manistee, MI 49660, Phone: (800) 392-3129, Ext. 98, e-mail: firstclass@micharterboats.com

Rivers North Sport Fishing Guide Service, Brad Petzke, P.O. Box 371, Marquette, MI 49855, Phone: (906) 226-8125, e-mail: Riversnorth@yahoo.com

Stormy Chinook Charters, Captain Dan Cruchon, 4140 S. Lakeshore Road, Lexington, MI 48450, Phone: (810) 359-5192 or (810) 212-4030, fishing@greatlakes.net

30 Pounder III Charters, John Schwartz, 6128 Deckerville Rd., Deford, MI 48729, Phone: (517) 872-4182

A1 Ludington Charters, Captain Ed Stell, 6501 Woodbrook SE, Grand Rapids, MI 49546 Phone: (877) 272-0688

Ruddy Duck Sport Fishing, Barry Aspenleiter, 3175 Country Club Rd., Petoskey MI 49770, Phone: (231) 347-3232

Reel Adventure, Mark Veurink, 19041 West Spring Lake Road, Spring Lake, MI 49456, Phone: (800) 846-1018 or (616) 846-6637

Betts Flyfishing Guide Service, Chad Betts, P.O. Box 608, Newaygo, MI 49337, Phone: (231) 652-3189

Summer Remedy, Eric Gatza, P.O. Box 585, Bay City, MI 48707, Phone: (517) 684-2368

MINNESOTA

Agape Bass Guides, Wayne Ek, 2032 Eaglewood Circle, Alexandria, MN 55379, Phone: (612) 445-4028, e-mail: week@rea-alp.com

Jonny Jaws All Species, Metro Guide Service, Jonny (Hase) Jaws, 4338 Leander Lane, Columbia Heights, MN 55421, Phone: (763) 788-4072, e-mail: jonnyjaws@qwest.net

International Angling Adventures, Northern Minnesota/Ontario, Canada, Phone: (877) 246-7762, e-mail: smallies@rainylakefishing.com

Pike Dreams Guide Service, Gregg Melstrom, 4600 Lynwood Terrace, Minnetonka MN 55345, Phone: (952) 474-9380, e-mail: gregg@pikedreams.com

KDK Charter Service, 4894 Drake Rd., Duluth MN 55803-1253, Phone: (888) 724-1264

Lake Superior Fishing, Captain Steve Johnson, 1006 N. 8th Ave. East, Duluth MN 55905, Phone: (800) 531-3474 or (218) 724-4214

Upper Mississippi River Professional Guide Service, Dale Radcliffe, 550 Rublee St., Apt. #10, La Crosse, WI 54603, Phone: (608) 779-5934

La Tourell's Guide Service, P.O. Box 239, Ely, MN 55731, Phone: (800) 365-4531

Musky 101 Guide Service, Brian Kaiser, 7367 360 Ave., Minneapolis, MN, Phone: (507) 835-8922

Gonzo's Guide Service, Tom Stay, 112 5th Ave. SE, Baudette, MN 56623, Phone: (218) 634-2781

Honey Hole Guides Service, 101 3rd St., Holdingford, MN, Phone: (320) 746-2958, e-mail: mjsinner@uswest.net

Musky Tom's Guide Service, Tom Wehler, (Winter) 325 Maryland Ave. W, St. Paul, MN 55117; (Summer) Mallard Island, Lake Vermilion, Tower, MN, Phone: (651) 470-9774 or (651) 578-2569, e-mail: muskitom@aol.com

Jeff Sundin's Early Bird Fishing, Jeff Sundin, P.O. Box 627, Deer River, MN 56636, Phone: (218) 246-2375, e-mail: jsundin@paulbunyan.net

Tom Wilson's Leech Lake Guide Service, Leech Lake, MN, Phone: (218) 224-2815, e-mail: fish@walleyetrips.com

Muskie Breath Guide Service, Jason Hamernick & Jason Summers, 62 102nd Lane, Blaine, MN 55434, Phone: (763) 717-7241

Ed's Guide Service, Tim Edinger, 5984 Royal Oaks Road, Royalton, MN 56373, Phone: (320) 584-8019

Bret's Guide Service, Bret Setterholm, P.O. Box 684, Battle Lake, MN 56515, Phone: (218) 367-3503 or (218) 864-3149

Ultimate Outdoors, Travis Peterson, 9329 Oman Rd. NE, Bemidji, MN 56601, Phone: (218) 586-3743

The Fly Guys Guide Service, Brian J. Swartling & Todd Olson, 507 Wall St., Winona, MN 55987, Phone: (507) 454-0158

Jakes Teaching Guide Service, Randy "Jake" Jacobs, e-mail: jakej@prairie.lakes.com

MISSISSIPPI

Captain Ron's Charters, Captain Ron Harmon, 14107 Old Hwy. 67, Biloxi, MS 39532-8846, e-mail: CaptRono1@aol.com

BreakAway Fishing Charters, Mike Brackin, 12309 Windward Drive, Gulfport, MS 39503, Phone: (228) 832-6131, e-mail: BBEAN052@aol.com

Affordable Fishing Adventures, Mike Moore, Phone: (228) 392-3396, e-mail: strictlytoo@telesouth1.com

Fish-On Charters, Captain Kenny Bellais, 13054 Three Oaks Rd., Biloxi, MS 39532-7715, Phone: (228) 392-7485 or (228) 617-HOOK

FishTales Charters, Capt. Jim Bradley, P.O. Box 21, Pass Christian, MS 39571-0021, Phone: (228) 452-0420 or (228) 332-0061, e-mail: msfishtales@hsiweb.com

Fish-Finder Charters, Captain Mike Foto, 985 Campbell Drive, Biloxi, MS, Phone:

(877) 351-0734 or (228) 860-0314, e-mail: CaptainMike@Fish-Finder.net

Capt. Brent Roy's Venice Charters Unlimited, 41113 Lee Drive, Gonzales, LA 70737, Phone: (225) 907-8420

Saltwater Charter Listings by Mississippi Ports ConspiraSEA, Captain Patrick Peterson, Biloxi 374-5449 or 380-6980

Baja 31, Captains Joseph E. Fountain and Joe Scott Byrd, Biloxi (slip 34) 392-1520

Fish-On, Captain Kenny Bellais, Point Cadet Marina (slip D-3) 392-7485

Beachwater, Capt. Dean Gladney, Biloxi (slip 82) 875-7804 or 938-1838

Blue Bayou, Capt. Andy Burns, Biloxi (slip 63) 392-4731

Happy Hooker, Capt. James McClellon, Biloxi (slip 102) 872-3007

The Michael J., Capt. Albert Lechner, Biloxi (slip 61) 392-1238

Quick Silver, Capt. Gary Geno, Biloxi (behind McElroy's Rest.) 435-2245

Sebastes, Capt. A.J. Taconi, Biloxi (slip 66) 435-5336

Southern Belle, Capt. Richard Desporte, Sr. Biloxi (slip 85) 436-6570

Three Sons, Capt. Bobby Williams, Biloxi (slip 103) 392-8243 or 392-1553

Becuna, Capt. Danny Stanley, Broadwater (slip 138) 374-6295

Big Fish, Capt. Mark Sepe, Broadwater (slip 40) 872-3412

Double Trouble, Capt. Brandon Trochesset, Broadwater (slip 36) 388-2209 or 388-2211

Happy Snapper Headboat, Capt. Stanley Fournier, Broadwater (slip 26) 432-9856 or 388-2211

Bad Company, Capt. Bryan Richard, Biloxi 392-0458

Amberjack, Captains Skeeter Raymond and Greg Hebert Biloxi, (slip 60) 392-1745 or 374-3176

Mr. Champ, Capt. Steve West, Broadwater (slip 41) 432-0172 or 388-2211

Mystic Angel, Capt. Derek Groves, Broadwater (slip 38) 872-4874 or 388-2211

Speck Tacular, Capt. John Lewis, Bay St. Louis 467-4852

Silver Dollar, Capt. Jay Trochesset, Broadwater (slip 138) 388-2209 or 388-2211

Barbara Teresa, Capt. Jim Mowrey, D'Iberville 392-0600

D-N-D, Capt. Alan Wade, Mary Walker Marina, Gautier 934-0836

Mistral II, Capt. Mike Hill, Mary Walker Marina, Gautier 872-2935

Offshore Express, Capt. Don Gautier, Gautier 497-6152

Speckled Trout Express, Capt. Don Gautier, Gautier 497-6152

Cavu, Capt. Robert Hatch, Gulfport 896-7969

Fishy Business, Capt. Lenny Desroche, Gulfport (Pier 1, slip 1) 865-9801

P.J., Capt. Alan Jones, Gulfport (Pier A, slip 3) 863-2362 or (800) 377-3630

Sugar Bear, Capt. Sammy Carver, Gulfport (Pier 4, slip 10) 863-4471

Top Gun Charters, Capt. Frank Dendis, Gulfport (Pier A, slip 10) 452-7384

Tuff-E-Nuff, Capt. Jerry Holland, Gulfport (Pier A, slip 13) 832-7215

Gulf Dancer, Capt. Toni King, Ocean Springs 875-9491

The Fisha-Tracter, Capt. Les Osborne, Pascagoula (slip 7) 769-8984

The Big Bite, Capt. Toni King, Point Cadet (slip 1-10) 875-9491

Bonnie Amie, Capt. Roland Skinner, Point Cadet (Pier A, slip 37) 392-3346 or (800) 484-2076

Breakaway, Capt. Mike Brackin, Point Cadet (Pier D) 832-6191

Due South Charters, Captains Robbie and Greg Thornton, Point Cadet 436-4232

Capt. Mike McRaney, Point Cadet (Pier A, slip 3) 875-9462 or 872-3443

Happy Landing, Capt. Mark Compton, Point Cadet 875-3825 or 861-9485

Hide-A-Way, Capt. Mike McRaney, Point Cadet (Pier A, slip 11) 875-9462 or 872-3443

Joka's Wild, Capt. George Pelaez Jr., Point Cadet 392-0989

Kingfish, Capt. Gerald Skinner, Point Cadet (Pier E, slip 10) 392-3448

Omeco III, Capt. Joe Kuljis, Point Cadet (Pier E, slip 33) 432-2054

Outrageous, Capt. Mike McRaney, Point Cadet (Pier A, slip 1) 875-9462 or 872-3443

Play Pretty, Capt. Tom Parker, Point Cadet (slip 76) 872-3102

Prime Time, Capt. Timmy Holley, Point Cadet (Pier B, slip 3) 392-6137

The Silver King III, Capt. Mark Compton, Point Cadet (Pier E, slip 35) 875-3825 or 861-9485

Strictly Business, Capt. Mike Moore, Point Cadet (Pier G, slip 9) 436-3128 or 392-4047

TunaSea, Captains Jimmy Taylor and Ralph Case, Point Cadet (slip A-36) 388-1120 or 863-1653

Unit 1, Capt. Mark Compton, Point Cadet 875-3825 or 861-9485

Pa$$ion Charters, Capt. Robert Henley, Bay St. Louis 467-1941 or (800) 239-0908

Anytime, Capt. Jason Jakimczuk, Point Cadet (Pier E) 1-800-FISH-132

SYL Charters, Capt. Clarence Seymour, Point Cadet (slip D-1) 1-877-SYL-BOAT

MISSOURI

Pete's Professional Guide Service, Pete Wenners, 2025 Pioneer Point Road, Galena, MO 65656, Phone: (417) 538-2159, e-mail: coryw@inter-linc.net

Show Me Mo Outdoors, Dale Williams, 7055 Portage Rd., Portage Des Sioux, MO 63373, Phone: (636) 899-0007, e-mail: bowhuntr@gateway. net

Coaches Guide Service, Jim Wilson, Rt. 2 Box 2106, Hermitage, MO, Phone: (417) 745-2163, e-mail: spinnerbait@mailcity.com

Rick's Chauferred Guide Service, 3322 S. Kimbrough, Springfield, MO 65807, Phone: (800) 869-2210 or (417) 861-3899

Lenny's Guide Service, 2632 N. Payne, Wichita, KS, Phone: (316) 838-1619

Buster Loving, P.O. Box 132, Rockaway Beach, MO 65740, Phone: (417) 561-2256

Lake of the Ozarks Guide Service, Cory Knoke, 8 KK Ranch Rd., Osage Beach, MO 65065, Phone: (573) 348-5104

White River Basin Guide Service, Inc., Jeff Martin, 3074 Longbend Rd., Galena, MO 65656, Phone: (888) 221-6141, e-mail: jeff@whiteriverbasin.com

Hook's Guide Service, Jim Van Hook, 129 McIntosh Lane, Reeds Spring, MO 65737, Phone: (417) 338-2277, e-mail: HOOKSBASS@aol.com

Cedar Creek Cove, Ron Misek, HC 3, Box 3770, Theodosia, MO 65761, Phone: (417) 273-4927

Randy's Guide Service, Randy Turnbough, P.O. Box 129, Steelville, MO 65565, Phone: (888) 486-FISH (3474)

Chaonia Landing, Dave Bowman, Rt. 2, Williamsville, MO 63967, Phone: (314) 297-3206

River of Life Farm, Rt. 1, Box 4560, Dora, MO 65637, Phone: (417) 261-7777

MONTANA

Pat Straub's Montana Anglers, Pat and Terri Straub, 1426 Knight St., Helena, MT 59601, Phone: (406) 439-6008, e-mail: info@montanaanglers.com

Marvin and Connie Loomis, Box 312, Jordan, MT 59337, Phone: (406) 557-2787 or (406) 557-2224

Two Leggins Outfitters Provides, Box 2120 Star Route, Hardin, MT 59034, Phone: (406) 665-2825 Wild Trout Outfitters, P.O. Box 160003, Big Sky, MT 59716, Phone: (800) 4AFISH2

Crain Outfitting & Guide Service, Clark Fork Reservoir, Phone: (406) 649-7220

A-1 Fishing, Craig Renfro, P.O. Box 784, Lakeside, MT 59922, Phone: (406) 844-3602

Paul Tunkis Flyfishing Guide Service, Paul Tunkis, 128 South F St., Livingston, MT 59047, Phone: (406) 222-8480, mtflyfish@imt.net

Potosi Hot Springs Resort, Nick Kern, P.O. Box 269, Pony, MT 59747, Phone: (406) 685-3330 or (888) 685-1695, e-mail: potosi@potosiresort.com

Wolf Creek Guide Service, Stephen Butt Outfitter, 420 Broadway, Helena, MT 59601, Phone: (406) 442-5148

Campbell's Guided Fishing Trips, Rodney Campbell, 511 East Olive St., Bozeman, MT 59715, Phone: (406) 587-0822

Montana Trout Stalkers, Joe Dilschneider, P.O. Box 1406, Ennis, MT 59729, Phone: (406) 682-5356

Grossenbacher Guides, P.O. Box 6704, Bozeman, MT 59771, Phone: (406) 582-1760

Big Hole River Guide, Bob Folkedahl, 315 S. Jackson, Butte, MT 59701, Phone: (406) 782-0567

NEBRASKA

Greg's Guide Service, Greg Adams, 17831 Quantum Place, Pierre, SD 57501, Phone: (605) 264-5426, e-mail: Greg@oahewalleye.com

Merritt Trading Post, Joe Dodd, Merritt Reservoir, Phone: (402) 376-3437

Shore Line Charters, 5107 Ventura Drive, Fremont, NE 68025, Phone: (402) 721-0182 Missouri River Guide Service, Capt. James A. Mason II, 408 Water P.O. Box 162, Brownville, NE 68321, Phone: (402) 825-6151, e-mail: JAM24U@webtv.net

Great Plains Guide Service, Kerry Keane, 220719 Sandberg Rd., Gering NE 69341, Phone: (866) LAKE MAC

Steve Lytle, 1304 W. 2nd St., McCook, NE 69001, Phone: (308) 345-1472

NEVADA

Stillwater Guide Service, Chris Wharton, 5410 Simons Drive, Reno, NV 89523, Phone: (775) 747-0312, e-mail: Chris@out4trout.com

Striper Guide Service, Captain Joe F. Wegener, Las Vegas, NV, Phone: (702) 263-7375 or (800) 556-0929 #43

Anglers Edge Guide Service, Capt. John R. Wood, 915 Highland Trails Ave., Henderson, NV 89015, Phone: (702) 285-2814

NEW HAMPSHIRE

New Hampshire Lakes Area Bass Guide, Jim Flanders, P.O. Box 457, Merrimack, NH 03054, Phone: (603) 424-4946, e-mail: jimfnh@aol.com

Tight Lines Fishing Services, P.O. Box 236, Elkins Business Loop, Elkins, NH, Phone: (603) 526-9299 or

(800) 526-6550

Fin Fighters Guide Service, Richie Bernard, 11 King Edward Drive, Londonderry, NH 03053, Phone: (603) 434-2193

Strictly Trout Guides Service, David L. Deen, 5607 Westminister West Rd., Putney, VT 05346, Phone: (802) 869-3116

Henry H. Achilles, 3 Kingsbury St., Derby, NH 03038, Phone: (603) 432-8214

Marshall Adams, 400 Monadnock St., Troy, NH 03465, Phone: (603) 242-3750

Akela Fishing Tours, Douglas K. Plasencia, P.O. Box 282, 113 Lehner St., Wolfeboro, NH 03894, Phone: (603) 569-6035

Charles R. Allard, 111 Govenor Wentworth Hwy., Mirror Lake, NH 03853, Phone: (603) 569-4902

Michael P. Allard, 97 Summerside Ave., Manchester, NH 03102, Phone: (603) 668-8928

Peter Basta, P.O. Box 540, Dorset, VT 05251, Phone: (802) 867-4103

Mark Beauchesne, 37 High St., Penacook, NH 03303, Phone: (603) 753-8380

William Bernhardt III, P.O. Box 1401, No. Conway, NH 03860, Phone: (603) 356-8366

Angus Boezeman, 39 Shaker Rd., Concord, NH 03301, Phone: (603) 224-1766

John Brancato, P.O. Box 28, Dundee Rd., Intervale, NH 03845, Phone: (603) 356-5358

James I. Brown, 4586 Brown Ave., Manchester, NH 03103, Phone: (603) 627-9041

W. Scott Canelas, 9 Island Pond Rd., Pehham, NH 03076, Phone: (603) 635-1717

Thomas Carens, 14 Depot St., Sunapee, NH 03782, Phone: (603) 863-9087

Joe Catalano, 230 Lawrence Rd., Salem, NH, Phone: (603) 890-0526

Kevin M. Cote, 11 Cheryl Drive, Concord, NH 03303, Phone: (603) 229-1669

Raymond Cotnoir, RR1, Box 1412, Randolph, NH 03570, Phone: (603) 466-5179

Thomas A. Crompton, 27 Golden Drive, Bedford, NH 03110, Phone: (603) 471-0861 Wayne A. Derby, P.O. Box 670, Bethlehem, NH 03574, Phone: (603) 869-2634

Kim Dubuque, P.O. Box 653, Moultonboro, NH 03254, Phone: (603) 476-8291

Peter M. Eldridge, #6 N. Division, Silver Lake, NH 03875, Phone: (603) 367-8772

Richard A. Estes Jr., P.O. Box 506, Ossipee, NH 03864, Phone: (603) 539-7354

Mark Clayton Ewing III, P.O. Box 280, Hanover, NH 03755, Phone: (603) 643-6745

Daniel L. Fitzgerald, P.O. Box 443, One Westwood Lane, Henniker, NH 03242, Phone: (603) 428-3133

Richard K. Forge, RFD 1 Box 500C, Centre Harbor, NH 03226, Phone: (603) 253-6119

Douglas H. Gagnon, 9 Old Bye Rd., Raymond, NH

03077, Phone: (603) 895-0654

Curtis W. Golder, 79 Middleton Rd., Wolfeboro, NH 03894, Phone: (603) 569-6426

Peter A. Grasso, 95 Roller Coaster Rd., Laconia, NH 03246, Phone: (603) 366-4115

Larry Guile, RR #2 Box 129, Lancaster, NH 03581, Phone: (603) 636-2946

Kenneth B. Hastings, P.O. Box 121, Colebrook, NH 03576-0121, Phone: (603) 922-3800

Andrew E. Hemmerling, Rt. 4A Box 55, Enfield Center, NH 03749, Phone: (603) 632-7794

Jonathan K. Howe, P.O. Box 1646, North Conway, NH 03860, Phone: (603) 356-0071

Erik Hufnagle, P.O. Box 962, Intervale, NH 03845, Phone: (603) 356-8072

Alan E. Jones, P.O. Box 443, Hampton, NH 03843-0443, Phone: (603) 926-2541

Kenneth J. Keating, 1030 Roxbury Rd., Keene, NH 03431, Phone: (603) 357-3291

Charles W. Kenney, P.O. Box 1071, Meredith, NH 03253, Phone: (603) 279-5407

Talon Guide Service & Outfitters, Richard Lariviere, 120 North Road, Shelburne, NH 03581, Phone: (603) 466-3403

Keith A. Leclair, 27 Post Rd., North Hampton, NH 03862, Phone:(603) 964-9242
Rick Lillegard, 21 Hemlock Heights Road, Atkinson, NH 03811, Phone: (603) 329-6438

Jonathan E. Lockwood, P.O. Box 592, New London, NH 03257, Phone: (603) 526-9383

Stephen Lucarelli, P.O. Box 464, Meredith, NH 03253, Phone: (603) 279-2248

Gordon Marceau, 340 Prospect St., Franklin, NH 03235, Phone: (603) 934-4846

Daniel R. Marchi, 291 Mammoth Rd., Pelham, NH 03076, Phone: (603) 635-7035

John G. Marshall, P.O. Box 65, Hartland Corners, VT 05049, Phone: (802) 457-4021

Shawn Marzerka, P.O. Box 402, Wolfeboro Falls, NH 03896, Phone: (603) 569-3881

Stuart D. May, 453 Center Rd., Lyndeborough, NH 03082, Phone: (603) 672-1315 William J. Murphy, RD 2 Box 42, South Royalton VT 05068, Phone: 802-763-8887

Joseph Nassar, P.O. Box 185, Holderness, NH 03245, Phone: (603) 968-7577

Gregory M. Nault, P.O. Box 300, New Boston, NH 03070, Phone: (603)487-3388

Kathleen Noonan, P.O. Box 7, Intervale, NH 03845, Phone: (603) 356-6240

Daniel Parent, 16 Twighlight Path, Derry, NH 03038, Phone: (603) 425-6523

David M. Pellerin, P.O. Box 660, Windham, NH 03087, Phone: (603) 893-8673

Douglas Plasencia, P.O. Box 282, Wolfeboro, NH 03894, Phone: (603) 569-6035

Thomas R. Remick, Box 57B Rte.3, Pittsburg, NH

03592, Phone: (603) 538-7123

James St. Laurent, East Hill Farm, Troy, NH 03465, Phone: (603) 242-3242

Drew Santa Barbara, 84 Leslie Drive, Portsmouth, NH 03801, Phone: (603) 436-9302

Lisa and Timothy R. Savard, RR1 Box 49, Pittsburg, NH 03592, Phone: (603) 538-9955 Sarah E. Sanders, 68 Stoney Hill Rd., Hampden, MA 01036, Phone: (413) 566-3465

Thomas R. Schwendler, P.O. Box 519, Bradford, NH 03221, Phone: (603) 938-5611

John M. Starkey, 234 Shackford Corner Rd., Ctr. Barnstead, NH 03225, Phone: (603) 269-7451

Cindy Sullivan, 231 Beach St., Pittsburg, NH 03592, Phone: (603) 538-6651

Jeffrey Thomas, 1251 US Rte. 10, Lempster, NH 03605, Phone: (603) 863-0865

Janet and William Thompson, RFD 1 Box 2788, Freedom, NH 03836, Phone: (603) 539-6680

Mark D. Whitman, RR 1 Box 516 Bean Rd., Center Harbor, NH 0322, Phone: (603) 253-6752

NEW JERSEY

Norma K III Deep Sea Fishing Party Boat, Captains Ken Keller & John Hawryluk, 1104 Dell D'or Drive, Point Pleasant, NJ, Phone: (732) 899-5656, e-mail: NormaK123@aol.com

Babu Sport Fishing Charters, Capt. John Wilkinson, 219 2nd St. North, Brigantine, NJ 08203, Phone: (410) 757-1466, e-mail: wilk@erols.com

Bounty Hunter Sportfishing, Capt. Paul Regula, Clarks Landing Marina, Pt. Pleasant, NJ, Phone (732) 323-8700

Calypso Sportfishing, Capt. James Rivelli, Marina on the Bay, Highlands, NJ and Clarks Landing Marina, Point Pleasant, NJ, Phone: (732) 899-2313

Blue Water Adventures, Edward Collet, New Jersey Avenue and the Bay, Atlantic City, NJ, Phone: (609) 926-5353

Tampa VII Charters, Captain Gene Becker, P.O. Box 1001, Point Pleasant, NJ 08742, Phone: (888) 31-TAMPA, e-mail: CaptainGene@tampaVII.com

Off Duty Charters, Capt. Joe Safaryn, 618 2nd Ave., West Cape May, NJ 08204, Phone: (609) 425-8859, e-mail: offduty@pro-usa.net

"Just One More" Sportfishing, Capt. Rich Newallis Jr., 736 Johnston Drive, Watchung, NJ 07069, Phone: (908) 412-9147

The Angler, 645 Main St., Cedarville, NJ 08311, Phone: (856) 447-0036

K-KAT Sportfishing, Captain Ken Dubman, Bahr's Landing, 2 Bay Ave., Highlands, NJ, Phone: (732) 935-1708

Muskie Daze Guide Service, John Brylinski, P.O. Box 160, Layton, NJ 07851, Phone: (973) 948-4724, e-mail: Muskiedaze@aol.com

Trout & Shad Chasers, P.O. Box 242, High Bridge, NJ 08829 and P.O. Box 116 Starlight, PA 18461, Phone: (908) 735-5787

NEW MEXICO

JR's Desert Bass Fishing Guide Service, P.O. Box 1486, Elephant Butte, NM 87935, Phone: (505) 744-5314, e-mail: jr@jrdesertbass.com

Yong Special Flies and Guide Service, Andy Kim, P.O. Box 6482, Navajo Dam NM 87419, Phone: (505) 334-0909 or (818) 909-9707

High Mountain Angler Rods & Guide Service, Manuel Sandoval, 5404 NDCBU, Taos, NM 87571, Phone: (505) 751-4358 or (505) 770-0211

NEW YORK

"The Bass Coach," Roger Lee Brown, Route1, Box 65, Pearl Street, Crown Point, NY 12928, Phone: (518) 597-4240, e-mail: rlbrown@capital.net

Niagara River Guide Service, Capt. John V. DeLorenzo, 2493 Michigan Ave., Niagara Falls, NY 14305, Phone: (716) 297-9424, e-mail: ljnrgs@AOL.com

Greene Connection Charters, Capt. Arden Greene, 13738 Greene St., Adams Center, NY 13606, Phone: (888) 330-9083, e-mail: agreene@imcnet.net

Papasmurf Fishing Charters, Capt. Roger Young, 39a River St., Hoosickfalls, NY 12090 Phone: (800) 548-0067

Northeast FlyFishing Guide Service, Walt Geryk, 38 Elm St., Hatfield, MA 01038, Phone: (413) 575-5421, e-mail: walt@neffguide.com

Raindance Charters, Capt. John C. Allen, Fair Haven, NY, Phone: (888) 699-0929, e-mail: jcallen@bluewtr.com

My Dream Charters, Capt. Martin J. Ruk, 40 Starner Rd., Danville, PA 17821, Phone: (570) 437-2756, e-mail: VRUK1@HOTMAIL

First Class Bass Charters, Captain Terry Jones, 70 Huetter Ave., Tonawanda, NY 14207, Phone: (716) 875-4946

D.C. Outdoor Adventures, Capt.Dennis Caracciolo, P.O. Box 26, Selden, NY 11784, Phone: (631) 451-1941

The Backwoods Angler Guide Service, Blaine Mengel, Jr., Delware River, Phone: (610) 867-5985

Brushwolfs Adirondack Fishing, Larry DeLoria, Chestertown, NY, 12817, Phone: (518) 494-7878

Jerry Hadden's Guide Service, Capt. Jerry Hadden, 33 East River St., Susquehanna, PA 18847, Phone: (570) 853-4048, e-mail: fly@jerryhadden.com

Lake George Fishing with Mike's Charter Fishing,

Captain Mike Mollica, 710 Route 28, Warrensburg, NY 12885, Phone: (877) 234-7446, e-mail: mcmcharter@aol.com

Jon-Boy Fishing Charters, Captain John Delorme, P.O. Box 176, Henderson Harbor, NY 13651, Phone: (315) 938-5718 or (800) 824-3474, e-mail: jonboy738@cs.com

HWC Guide Service, 25 Roosevelt Ave., Stamford, NY 12167, Phone: (607) 652-8049, e-mail: cioccari58@aol.com

Northern Waters Guide Service, Terry Mostyn Jr., 357 T Chase Lake Rd., Glenfield, NY 13343, Phone: (315) 376-7228, e-mail: twmostjr@northnet.org

Bayguide, Larry Kernehan, 54 Anthony St., Alexandria, NY 13607, Phone: (315) 482-9368 or (877) 229-4843, e-mail: bayguide@email.msn.com

Landing Zone Charters on Lake Ontario, Capt. Dick Dennie, 4839 County Line Rd., Macedon, NY 14502, Phone: (800) 872-3691

Trout & Shad Chasers, P.O. Box 242, High Bridge, NJ 08829, Phone: (908) 735-5787

Moby Dick Charters, Captain Bob Dick, 13684 Harborview Rd., P.O. Box 455, Henderson Harbor, NY 13651, Phone: (315) 938-5871 or (888) 232-2827

Justy-Joe Sportfishing Charters, Capt. Joe Greco & Capt. Jim "Jasper" McCormick, 30 Iris Ave., South Glens Falls, NY 12803, Phone: (877) 530-8183

Great White Charters, Captain Jack Prutzman, 301 White Springs Rd., Geneva, NY, 14456, Phone: (315) 781-1038

Lake Ontario/Black River Bay Charter Guides Association:

Gone Fishin Charter, Sandra Bliven, Phone: (315) 649-5352

Moby Dick Charter, Bob Dick, Phone: (888) 232-2827

Ewing Charter, Tom Ewing, Phone: (315) 376-6921

The Bear Charter, Carl Golas, Phone: (315) 376-7695

Green Connection Charter, Arden Green, Phone: (888) 330-9083

Fish Taxi Charter, Charles Rawson, Phone: (315) 639-3632

Two Forty Charter, Bill Toumbacaris, Phone: (315) 821-7837

Ron Ditch & Sons Charter, Ron Ditch, Phone: (315) 938-5234

Reba Charter, Rudy Ford, Phone: (315) 393-5384

Trophy Angler Charter, Bob Gregory, Phone: (315) 649-5856

Sharon Lee Charter, Scott Hanson, Phone: (315) 232-2758

C.R. Charter, Ron Stein, Phone: (315) 568-5017

Kingfisher Charter, Paul Jernigan, Phone: (315) 656-3070

C Gypsy Charter, Dick Smith, Phone: (315) 788-0178

Reel Time Charter, Bob Savage, Phone: (315) 639-6574

Ginny Pauline Charter, Gene Musselman, Phone: (800) 419-5181

Mickey Finn Charter, Steve Lemieux, Phone: (207) 379-2035

Flyfishing Long Island, Capt.Ken Rafferty, 1 Olive St., East Hampton, NY, Phone: (631) 324-8746

Dragon Fly Charters, Capt. Scott Holder, P.O. Box 12451, Hauppauge, NY 11788, Phone: (516) 840-6522

Captain Gillen Fishing, Captain Patrick Gillen, Captree Boat Basin, NY, Phone: (631) 586-5511

On the Bite Charters, Capt. Joe Mattioli, 408 Chelsea St., Staten Island NY 10308, Phone: (718) 967-9095 or (908) 337-2984

NORTH CAROLINA

Jordan Lake Outdoors, Jeffrey Thomas, Broadway, NC, Phone: (919) 258-3757, e-mail: flipper@wave-net.net

Bigfoot Guide Service, Joe Whisnant, Rt. 5 Box 324A, Horse Shoe NC 28742, Phone: (828) 891-2784, e-mail: bigfoot15e@hotmail.com

Outdoor Adventures, Thomas L. Andrews, 2131 Hwy. 21 North, Sparta, NC 28675, Phone: (336) 372-8188

Asheville Drifters, LLC, Andrew Tashie, Asheville, NC 28801, Phone: (828) 215-7379

Cape Fear Sportsman Guide Service, Tom Morketter, 2770 Breezewood Ave., Fayetteville NC 28303, Phone: (910) 484-2532, e-mail: cfflyfish@aol.com

Angler's Choice Adventures, Capt. Rodney Duke, 1024 Indian Creek Trail, Garner, NC 27529, Phone: (919) 782-6873, e-mail: cptduke@hotmail.com

Mountain Lake Outfitters, Dave Kaetzel, Blairsville, GA/Murphy, NC, Phone: (828) 837-8045

Captain Darryl's Guide Service, Captain Darryl Smith, 3145 Long Meadow Road, Rock Hill, SC 29732, Phone: (803) 324-7912 or (803) 372-1398

Flyfish North Carolina, Capt. Gordon Churchill, Hwy. 24, Newport, NC, Phone: (252) 726-5667

Waterdog Sportfishing Charters, Capt. Tom Henry, P.O. Box 1138, Saint Michaels, MD 21663, Phone: (800) 787-3474

Gecko Sportfishing, Capt. Ernie Doshier, P.O. Box 624, Ocracoke NC 27960, Phone: (252) 928-5561 or 921-0095

Dudley's Guiding Services, Nagshead, NC, Phone: 252-475-1555, e-mail: captdudley@nagsheadfishing.com

Spec Fever Guide Service, Capt. Gary Dubiel, P.O. Box 1029, Oriental, NC 28571, Phone: (252) 249-1520

Flounder Fishing Guide Service, Capt. Eddie O'Briant, 1412 N. Old Wire Rd., Shannon, NC 28386, Phone: (910) 843-5516

Outdoor Expeditions Guide Service, Joel Munday/Clay Ausley, 8206 Falls of Neuse Rd., **Raleigh**, NC 27615, Phone: (919) 345-2767, e-mail: info@haulingbass.com

NORTH DAKOTA

Angler's Adventures & Outfitters, Guide/Outfitter Brian Ringeisen, P.O. Box 991, Devils Lake, ND 58301, Phone: (701) 662-8683 or (701) 351-2621, e-mail: itbeme@stellarnet.com

1st Choice Guides, Keith Pierson, P.O. Box 343, Minnewaukan, ND 58351, Phone: (701) 438-2325, e-mail: 1stchoice@1stchoiceguides.com

Mitchell's Guide Service, 1012 Woodland Drive, Devils Lake, ND 58301, Phone: (701) 351-1890

Perch Patrol Guide Service, Devils Lake, ND, Phone: (701)DL1-FISH or (701)351-3474

Shad Rap Guide Service, Devils Lake, ND, Phone: (701) 662-5996

OHIO

Coe Vanna Charters & Lodging, Captains Dave Whitt, Bob McCoy, Jeff Krieling, Lake Erie, Phone: (419) 355-4732 or (419) 355-4732, e-mail: coevannacharters@aol.com

Double J Charters, Captain Joe Mehalic Jr., 611 Regina Pkwy., Toledo, OH 43612, Phone: (800) 950-4887 or (419) 476-9983, e-mail: doublej@greatlakescharters.cc

Hawg Alert Charters, Capt. Doug Krabacher, 212 E. Maplewood Ave. #3, Dayton, OH 45405, Phone: (888) 304-8767, e-mail: hawgalert@voyager.net

Sea Breeze Charters, Captain Bob Witt, 8680 Genzman Road, Oak Harbor, OH 43449, Phone: (419) 898-4003 or (419) 898-1655

Lake Erie Walleye Adventures, Capt. Tony Denslow, 130 Villanova Circle, Elyria, OH 44035, Phone: (888) 930-9932, e-mail: captlad@yahoo.com

Trophy Charters, 7041 Lake Road South, Andover, OH 44003, Phone: (440) 293-7249 or (216) 387-2656

Parker Guide Service, Captain Jeff Parker, 3108-131st St., Toledo, OH 43611, Phone: (800) 700-ERIE or (419) 726-3557, e-mail: Wizardfishing@aol.com

Pooh Bear Sport Fishing Charters, Captain Keith Unkefer, P.O. Box 237, Grand River, OH 44045-0237, Phone: (888) 698-2381 or (330) 697-2381, e-mail: Walleyecharter@aol.com

Captain Park's Charters, Capt. Park Schafer, 526 Mariner Village, Huron, OH 44839, Phone: (888) 306-7835 or (419) 656-5029, e-mail: Capt1Park@aol.com

LeisurLee Charters, Captain Lee Brown, 3131 W. Washington St., Bradford, PA 16701, Phone: (814)

362-4008 or (440) 964-7864, e-mail: elee@penn.com

Sunshine Charters, Captain Jim Bonner, 5650 E. Harbor Road #204, Lakeside, OH 43440, Phone: (419) 732-2488 or (412) 824-1912, e-mail: sunshineii1@prodigy.net

La - Grele Fishing Charters, Captain Wayne Hickman, 2166 Buckeye Drive, Sharpsville, PA 16150, Phone: (724) 962-2838 or (800) 214-0690

Trophy Hunter Charter Services, Capt. Gary Hopp, 1600 North Buck Road, Marblehead, OH 43440, Phone: (888) 601-5800 or (419) 734-3799, e-mail: charter@trophyhuntercharters.com

OKLAHOMA

The Cheaper Angler, Rick Williams, P.O. Box 7, Commerce, OK 74339, Phone: (918) 675-4106, e-mail: wilric@datalinkok.com

Talbots Guide Service, Jimmy Talbot, 321 S. Delawar, Okmulgee, OK, 74447, Phone: (918) 756 4208

Lenny's Guide Service, 2632 N. Payne, Wichita, KS, Phone: (316) 838-1619

Cartel Guide Service, Bing Korb, HC 72, Box 435A, Kingston, OK 73439, Phone: (800) 564-4316

J.C.'s Trophy Tracking Guide Service, JC McCullough, 610 W. 7th St., Hendrix, OK 74741, Phone: (580) 838-2225

(For more Lake Texoma guides, see Texas listings)

OREGON

Martin's Big Fish Adventures, Larry Martin, 1140 N.W. Warrenton Drive #306, Warrenton, OR 97146, Phone: (503) 680-9787, e-mail: larry@martinsbigfishadventures.com

David Anderson's Guide Service, David Anderson, southern Oregon Coast, Phone: (541) 247-0420, e-mail: dsand@harborside.com

Charles Ireland Guide Service, 3389 N. Myrtle Rd., Myrtle Creek, OR 97457, Phone: (541) 863-6082, e-mail: cirelandguide@yahoo.com

Fishpatrick's Guide Service, Patrick Roelle, Oregon waters, e-mail: fishpatric@aol.com

Bob Houghton's Guide Service, Bob Houghton, 4186 Normandy Way, Eugene, OR 97405, Phone: (541) 344-9024

Dave Skeeter's Guide Service, Dave Skeeters, 136 Onyx St., Eagle Point, OR 97524, Phone: (541) 830-8294

"The Local Fisherman News" Guides & Charter Services Directory, Portland, OR, Phone: (503) 255-5958, e-mail: fishnews@qwest.net

Don Nelson Guide Service, Don Nelson, P.O. Box 2, Riddle, OR 97469, Phone: (541) 874-2065, e-mail: nelson@mcsi.net

Oregon Outdoors, Dennis Dobson, 11880 Hwy. 101 S, Tillamook, OR 97141, Phone: (503) 815-2766, e-mail: oreoutdd@pacifier.com

Greg Nicol Guide Service, Greg Nicol, P.O. Box 155, Smith River,
CA 95567, Phone: (707) 464-7320

Page's NW Guide Service, Larry Page, 14321 SE Bush, Portland OR 97236, Phone: (866) 760-3370

Mah-Hah Outfitters, Steve Fleming, P.O. Box 428, Fossil, OR 97830, Phone: (888) 624-9424, e-mail: bassinbuddy@centurytel.net

Fishboss Guide Service, Ron Buntrock, P.O. Box 1124, Gold Beach, OR 97444, Phone: (800) 263-4351, e-mail: fishboss@harborside.com

PENNSYLVANIA

Jerry Hadden's Guide Service, 33 East River St., Susquehanna, PA 18847, Phone: (570) 853-4048, e-mail: fly@jerryhadden.com

Tom's Fly-Fishing Service, Tom Brtalik, 75 Pleasant View Terrace, New Cumberland, PA 17070, Phone: (717) 770-0796, e-mail: flyfishing@tomsflyfishing.com

Expert Guide Service, Bill Boysha, 11 Lee St., Bloomsburg, PA 17815, Phone: (570) 784-0765, e-mail: smalliefever777@aol.com

Trout & Shad Chasers, P.O. Box 116, Starlight, PA 18461, Phone: (908) 735-5787

Cross Current Guide Service, Joe Demalderis, 100 Laurel Acres Rd., Milford, PA 18337,
Phone: (570) 296-6919

Steelheadguides, Michael Hilf, Erie, PA, Phone: (724) 934-4983

Lunker Guide Service, Fred Davoli, RR#1 Box 96 River Road, Alexandria, PA
Phone: (814) 669-8887

Bill's Guide Service, Bill Albright, 190 W. Shore Drive, P.O. Box 256, Lake Ariel, PA 18436, Phone: (570) 347-4484 or (570) 698-6035

Ray "PeeWee " Serfass Guide Service, Ray Serfass, P.O. Box 194, Heath Lane, Pocono Summit, PA, Phone: (570) 839-7736, e-mail: rayserfass@mail.noln.com

The Backwoods Angler Guide Service, Blaine Mengel Jr., 1428 Monocacy St., Bethlehem, PA 18018, Phone: (610) 867-5985, e-mail: fishinontheriver@aol.com

Fish Tale Charters, Capt. Mike Stilin, 32 S.13th St., Lewisburg, PA, Phone: (717) 523-0753 or 850-7624

Mountain Top Outfitters, Harold Grimm, P.O. Box 201, Emporium, PA 15834, Phone: (814) 486-0363 Trophy Guide Service, Sparky Price, RD3, Box 50, Huntingdon, PA 16652, Phone: (814) 627-5231

Susquehanna River Guides, Brian Shumaker, 209 Oak Knoll Road, New Cumberland, PA 17070, Phone: 717-774-2307

Jet Set River Guides, Gene 'Duber' Winters and Andy Null, 332 Rohrer Rd., Mountville, PA 17554 and 1277 Loop Rd., Columbia, PA 17512, Phone: (717) 285-2092 or (717) 653-7329

RHODE ISLAND

L'il Toot Charters Inc., Capt. John Rainone, 431 Mourning Dove Drive, Saunderstown, RI 02874, Phone: (401) 294-1132, e-mail: liltoot@juno.com

White Ghost Guide Service, Capt. Jim White, 43 York Drive, Coventry, RI 02816, Phone: (401) 828-9465

C-Devil II Sportfishing, Capt. Kelly Smith, 331 Burdickville Rd., Charlestown, RI 02813, Phone: (401) 364-9774, e-mail: cdevilii@aol.com

Gail Frances, Lady Frances and Miss Frances, Captain Frank Blount, Phone: 783-4988
Seven B's V, Captain Russel Bean, Phone: 789-9250

Fly Swatter, Ed Hughes (Pt. Judith/Jerusalem), Phone: 364-8502

The Saltwater Edge, Greg Weatherby (Newport) Phone: 842-0062

Bonito Bandido, Chris Lembo, Phone: 423-1402

SOUTH CAROLINA

Fish Call Charters, Capt. J.R. Waits, Seven Shem Drive, Mt. Pleasant, SC 29464, Phone: (843) 509-REDS (7337), e-mail: jrwaits@internetx.net

Charleston Fishing Guide, Captain Adam Ridgeway, 4131 Flynn Drive, North Charleston, SC 29405, Phone: (843) 860-FISH(3474)

Risky Business Charters, 445 Cheves Drive, Charleston, SC 29412, Phone: (843) 559-6029 or (843) 209-8921

Charleston Fishing Charters, Captain Marsha, 1215 Pembrooke Drive, Charleston, SC 29407, Phone: (843) 556-6555 or (843) 442-6555, e-mail: marshgrass1@home.com

Second Chance Charters, Captain Richard Boone, 301 Dazmy Way, Nakina, NC 28455, Phone:(888) 640-3981, e-mail: cptwaccamaw@ncez.net

Delta Guide Service, Gene Dickson, 2417 ? Highmarket St., Georgetown, SC 29440, Phone: (843) 546-3645

Complete Fishing Guide, Capt. Tom Gregory, 145 Sinkler Ave., Eutawville, SC 29048, Phone: (803) 492-7274, e-mail: bestfishman@tri-countyelectric.net

Fishfinder Guide Service, Jim Glenn, P.O. Box 106, Bonneau, SC 29431, Phone: (843) 825-4239, e-mail: fishfindersc@icqmail.com

Captain Darryl's Guide Service, Captain Darryl

Smith, 3145 Long Meadow Road, Rock Hill, SC 29732, Phone: (803) 324-7912 or (803) 372-1398

Carolina Cajun Guide Service, Steve Sylvester, 5813 East Lakeside Drive, Hanahan, SC 29406, Phone: (843) 566-9059, e-mail: carolinacajn@home.com

Inky Davis Bass Fishing, Capt. Inky Davis, Santee Cooper, Phone: (803) 473-3783

Captain Brad's Guide Service, Captain Brad Browder, P.O. Box 66, Cross, SC 29436, Phone: (888) 854-9635

Tomkats Professional Fishing Guide Service, Tom Cravens, 116 Veteran Lane, Pineville, SC 29468, Phone: (843) 351-4579

SOUTH DAKOTA

Gary's Guide Service, Gary Humpal, 37949 286th St., Geddes, SD 57342, Phone: (605) 337-2887
Mac's Outdoor Adventures, Gerrick McComsey, Box 580, Ft. Pierre, SD 57532, Phone: (605) 945-1260

Lon's Guide Service, Lon Tschumper, 302 Scotty Phillips, Ft. Pierre, SD 57532, Phone: (605) 223-2615

TENNESSEE

Wetland Outfitters, John Marshall, 119 Yukon Ct., Murfreesboro, TN 37129, Phone: (615) 904-2556, e-mail: john@wetlandoutfitters.com

Fishing Tennessee Inc., T.K. Walker, Old Hickory Lake, e-mail: StriperTKW@aol.com

Jim Story, Rt. 1 Box 729, Tennessee Ridge, TN 37178, Phone: (931) 721-3548

Reelfoot Lake, Steve Coleman (901) 253-7148; Leonard Douglas (901) 538-3741; Elmer Parker (901) 538-2200; Golden Mathis (901) 536-5002, Boyette's Resort, TN

Trophy Guides Service, Fred McClintock, Phone: (931) 243-2142, e-mail: Rockfishman@webtv.net

Seein' Stripes, Shawn McNew, 9011 Fox Lake Drive, Knoxville, TN 37923, Phone: (865) 531-3888, e-mail: SeeinStripes@aol.com

Crappie Action Guide Service, Ken Riddick, 95 Elmwood Drive, Paris, TN, Phone: (731) 285-3551, crappieaction@yahoo.com

Percy Priest Guide Service, Jack Kuhn, 1708 Wright Meadow Court, Mount Juliet, TN, Phone: (615) 758-8594

"Cap'n Jack's James and New River Experience," Captain Jack West, 209 Boyd St., Johnson City, TN 37604, Phone: (423) 926-8539

Crappie Action Guide Service, Ken Riddick, Kentucky Lake, 95 Elmwood Drive, Paris, TN, Phone: (731) 285-3551, e-mail: crappieaction@yahoo.com

TEXAS

Lake Texoma Guides:

Tinker's Striper Guide Service, Jean Tinker Toney, 605 Lee Blvd., Pottsboro, TX 75076, Phone: (888) TINKERS, e-mail: tinker@tinker.net

Bill Bannister's Striper Guide Service, 1620 Mill Creek Rd., Pottsboro, TX 75076, Phone: 903-786-8400, e-mail: bannist9@aol.com

Gone Fishing Striper Guide, Bob Faulkner, P.O. Box 699, Gordonville, TX 76245, Phone: (866) 760-FISH [3474], e-mail: gonefishingrvpark@yahoo.com

J.C.'s Trophy Tracking Guide Service, J.C. McCullough, 610 W. 7th St., Hendrix, OK 74741, Phone: (580) 838-2225

A Trophy Guide Service, Phone: (800) 920-1450
Billy's Striper Guide Service, Phone: (903) 965-9316
Captain Ron's Guide Service, P.O. Box 755, Kingston, OK 73439, Phone: (800) 317-2260

Chuck Pilant Striped Bass Guide Service, 1505 Idlewood Drive, Sherman, TX 75090, Phone: (903) 892-6875

Cross Creek Guide Service, Jerry D. Dorsey, Phone: (580) 564-2871

Fireball's Striper Guide Service, Phone: (903) 364-2311
FishHawk Guide Service, Mike Anderson, Phone: (972) 680-Fish (3474)

Fish-On Striper Guide Service, Jack Hamlin, Phone: (903) 786-8386

Forman's Striper Guide Service, Jeff Forman, Phone: (903) 786-3050 or (903) 464-1393

Lake Texoma Guide Services, HC 68, Box 96, Kingston, OK 73439

Stan Constant, Liberty Guide Service, Allen Schnoor, Phone: (580) 564-2217

J&G Striper Guide Service, Gary Gear, Phone: (580) 564-3258

James' Striper Guide Service, Phone: (903) 786-8381

Slice's Striper Guide Service, Phone: (903) 463-2565

Speedy's Guide Service, Cliff Moss, Kingston, OK, Phone: (580) 564-3964 or (580) 513-2760

Southern Oklahoma Guide Service, Steve Walker, Phone: (580) 564-2208

Texoma Outfitters, Tim Hall, Phone: (903) 786-2748

Texoma Striper, Bob Faulkner, Phone: (903) 523-4879

Tim Littell Striper Guide Service, HC 73 Box 814, Kingston, OK 73439, Phone: (800) 325-9716 or (580) 564-1031

TNT Guide Service, Terry Johnson, Phone: (580) 564-2235 or (405) 623-0855

Turners Guide Service, HC 73 Box 895, Kingston, OK, Phone: (580) 564-2675

Armstrong Outfitters Professional Guide Service, Kirk R. Armstrong, 2808 Terry Court, Denton, TX 76201, Phone: (817) 821-5407, e-mail: txbassman2@aol.com

Fishing With the Melman, Lake Meredith, e-mail: Fishman@netjava.com

The Reel Guide Service, Jeff Donahue, 1890 N. Meadow Circle, McKinney, TX 75069, Phone: (972) 658-5069, e-mail: jdonahue@reelguide.net

Carter Tours Guide Service, Bryan Carter, 105 Barry Hand, Waco, TX 76705, Phone: (254) 744-6600

H&S Fishing, Steven Hill & Billy Swaim, Phone: Central trips (512) 341-0671, South trips (210) 945-2781

Centex Bass Guide Service, Tom Richardson, 4511 Slick Rock, Austin, TX 78747, Phone: (512) 291-9084 or (210) 865-1400

J&J Guide Service, J.W. Peterson & Jim Purdy, Rt. 2 Box 349, Yantis, TX 75497, Phone: (903) 383-3282

Messin With the Fish Guide Service, Keith Parks, Phone: (972) 545-1010

WWW Guide Service, Wes W. Winget, 12825 Friendship Rd., Pilot Point,TX 76258, Phone: (940) 365-9549, e-mail: wwwguideservice@prodigy.net

Hogge's Guide Service, central Texas, Phone: (254) 698-4744

Mike's Guide Service, Lake Travis, Phone: (512) 733-5689

Professional Guide Service.Com, Dennis States, 390 RCR 3317, Emory, TX 75440, Phone: (903) 473-2039

Kris Chitty's Guide Service, 123 Gateway Drive, Wills Point, TX 75169, Phone: (903) 873-8543

Fishin' With Jeff, Jeff Kirkwood, 4010 Seventh St., Sachse, TX 75048, Phone: (972) 414-5189 or (800) 965-0350, e-mail: FISHWJEFF@MSN.COM

West Side Adventures, Kent Clifton, 9499 W. FM 515 Suite 1, Alba, TX 75410, Phone: (800) 840-8781, e-mail: kent@westsideadventures.com

John Tanners, Lake Fork Guide Service, 682 vz cr 1815, Grand Saline TX , 75140, Phone: (800) 865-2282

Toledo Bend Guide Service, Greg Crafts, Rt. 1 Bx. 1347, Shelbyville, TX 75973, Phone: (409) 368-7151, e-mail: gcrafts@bigfoot.com

Fish & Fowl Guide Service, Shane Allman, P.O. Box 5116, Sam Rayburn, TX 75951 Phone: (409) 698-2227

East Texas Pro Guide Service, Chris Wilkerson, P.O. Box 1663, Livingston, TX 77351, Phone: (936) 327-8001 or (936) 329-2750

Caddo Lake Guide Service, Paul Keith, 6774 Spring Valley Drive, Shreveport, LA 71107, Phone: (318) 309-3474

Fish-Tales Guide Service, Ron Jones, 385 Perkins Loop, Diana TX 75640, Phone: (903) 777-BASS

Tex-Mex Bassin', Mike Perez, Rt. 25 Box 721-V, Mission, TX 78572, Phone: (956) 584-9887

Shawn's Guide Service, Shawn Reese, 441 Settlers View, Adkins, TX 78101, Phone: (210) 649-2760

Southwest Fishing Charters & Guide Service, Jeffrey Snyder, 11398 New Sulphur Springs Rd., San Antonio, TX 78263, Phone: (210) 649-2435

Lone Star Coastal Outfitters, Capt. Everett Johnson, 1497 South Oaks Drive, College Station, Texas 77845, Phone: (361) 785-3420 or (979) 690-0034, e-mail: ejohnson@tca.net

Capt. Terry's Rip Tide Charters, Terry Haun, 1139 B. Haun Rd. Box 41, Meyersville, TX 77974, Phone: (888) 990-6460, e-mail: haun@captainterry.com

Capt Bill Jarrard`s Bay Charters, Capt Bill Jarrard, Box 3350, 206 W. Redsnapper #105,

South Padre Island, Texas 79597, Phone: (800) 683-3390 or (956) 761-2067, e-mail: captbilljarrard@aol.com

Tarpon Adventures of Galveston, Capt. Jim Leavelle, 5447 Beechnut, Houston, TX 77096, Phone: (713) 667-8034 or (888) TX-TARPON, e-mail: jim@tarponadventures.com

Red's Coastal Charters, Captain J.M. "Red" Childers, P.O. Box 11, Port O'Connor, TX 77982, Phone: (361) 983-2937, e-mail: reds@tisd.net

Affordable Fisherman Charters, 95 West Shady Oak Lane, Rockport, TX 78382, Phone: (361) 790-5944, e-mail: bigfish@shelley.dbstech.com

S & S Guide Service, Capt. Marsh Steussy, P.O. Box 262, Port Mansfield, TX, Phone: (956) 944-2816

Claude`s Guides Service, Claude "Cowboy" Ward, P.O. Box 1423, Aransas Pass, TX 78335, Phone: (361) 758-6171 or (888) 321-4711 (7550)

Bob's Bay Fishing, Robert Sirvello, P.O. Box 571, Port Isabel, TX, Phone: (956) 943-1010

Bayrat Guide Service, Gary Gray, P.O. Box 626, Seadrift, TX 77983, Phone: (361) 785-6708

Topwater Guide Service, Capt. Mike Singleterry, 13969 Seafarer, Corpus Christi, TX 78418, Phone (361) 949 9455

Xtreme Sportfishing, J.T. Bottoms, Galveston, TX, Phone: (918) 246-0033 or (918) 269-3804

Ramirez Guide Service, Capt.Tommy Ramirez, 102 South Crescent, Victoria, TX 77901, Phone: (361) 576-9857, e-mail: captram@tisd.net

Bay Flats Waterfowl and Fishing Guide Services, Capt. Chris Martin, P.O. Box 534, Seadrift, TX 77983, Phone: (888) 677-4868, e-mail: Martin391@aol.com

Capt. Jay's Saltwater Guide Service, Capt. Jay Huitt, 3120A Ave F., Bay City, TX 77414, Phone: (979) 240-3597 or (979) 245-1190, e-mail: thecaptjay@yahoo.com

Texas Saltwater Adventures, Capt. Leaf Potter, 258 Plum Circle, Lake Jackson, TX 77566, Phone: (832) 428-3340, e-mail: Leaf@TexasSaltwaterFishingGuide.com

The Original Sabine Lake Guide Service, Capt. Jerry Norris, 3262 Bell St., Port Arthur, TX, Phone: (409) 736-3023, e-mail: sabinecapt@aol.com

Skipper's Guide Service, Skipper Osborne, 3404 Briar Lane, Bay City, TX 77414, Phone: (979) 245-6670, e-mail: skipper@skippersguideservice.com

Back Bay Guide Service, Capt. Lynn Smith, P.O. Box 522, Port O'Connor, TX 77982, Phone: (361) 983-4434, e-mail: Lynn@tisd.net

"Reel" McCoy Guide Service, Kevin M. McCoy, P.O. Box 1712, Aransas Pass, TX 78335, Phone: (888) 94TROUT or (888) 948-7688, e-mail: reelmccoy@intcomm.net

Sabine Lake Guide Service, Capt. Skip James, 4452 Memorial Drive, Orange, TX 77632, Phone: (409) 886-5341

RB Charters, Rodney Blackman, P.O. Box 825, Port O'Connor, TX 77982, Phone: (361) 983-2291

UTAH

Red Elk Outfitters, Gary H. Richins, 230 East 700 North, American Fork, UT 84003, Phone: (801) 763-9036 or (877) 880-3644, e-mail: outfitters@redelk.com

River Excursions, multiple guides, 585 N. 100 W. #7, Provo, UT 84601, Phone: (801) 792-1852

Uinta Fishing Co., Chris Barkey, 14361 Lapis Drive, **Draper**, UT 84020, Phone: (801) 523-6159

Fishing Adventures, Kevin Anderson, P.O. Box 1092, Bountiful, UT 84011-1092, Phone: (801) 292-8460

Park City Outfitters, Brandon Bertagnole, 1295 E. Whileaway Rd., Park City, UT 84098, Phone: (435) 647-0677

Green River Drifters, Gregg "Bomar" Tipton, 1327 Saratoga Ave., Steamboat Springs, CO 80487, Phone: (970) 879-0370

VERMONT

Trout on the Fly, P.O. Box 236, East Randolph, VT 05041, Phone: (802) 728-6599

Talon Guide Service & Outfitters, 120 North Road, Shelburne, NH 03581, Phone: (603) 466-3403

Nomad Fishing Charters, Capt. Art Martin, 2355 Mountain View Rd., Williston, VT 05495, Phone: (802) 878-2080

Blue Ridge Outfitters, Greg Newton, 20 Chittenden Road, South Chittenden, VT 05701, Phone: (802) 747-4878

VIRGINIA

Finstalkers Guide Service, Denny Seabright, 278 Akern Lane, Cross Junction, VA 22625, Phone: (540) 888-4064, e-mail: DENNISSEABRIIGHT@email.msn.com

The Fishin' Musician, P.O. Box 50102, Richmond, VA, e-mail: FISHINMUSICIANS@hotmail.

Trout & About, Phil Gay, 3488 N. Emerson St., Arlington, VA 22207, Phone: (703) 536-7494, e-mail: trotabot@mindspring.com

Razorback Guide Service, Brian J. Bodine, P.O. Box 449, Scottsville, VA 24590, Phone: (804) 923-9305, e-mail: JRVRBASS@aol.com

Mark Kovach Fishing Services, guides: Mark Kovach, Dave Motes, John Hayes, Richard Larkin, Butch Murphy, Mark Frondorf, 406 Pershing Drive, Silver Spring, MD 20910-4253, Phone: (301) 588-8742

James River Angler, Darren Raynor, RR 1 Box 9B, Arvonia, VA 23004, Phone: (804) 581-1817

James River Bronzeback, Steve Garrett, Travis Garrett, 2193 Mountain Brook Drive, Charlottesville, VA 22902, Phone: (434) 293-2008, e-mail: JRBRONZEBACK@msn.com

Tangent Outfitters, 4747 State Park Road, Dublin, VA 24084, Phone: (540) 674-5202, e-mail: TangentOutfitters@yahoo.com

Dudley's Guide Service, Capt. Dave Dudley, Capt. James Dudley, 543 Dawnridge Drive, Lynchburg, VA 24502, Phone: (804) 239-2533, e-mail: DUDSFISHN@AOL.COM

National Bass Guide Service, Steve Chaconas, 8619 Camden St., Alexandria, VA 22308, Phone: (703) 360-3472, e-mail: NationalBass@aol.com

Hatchmatcher Flies Guide Service, L.E. Rhodes, Scottsville,VA, Phone: (804) 286-3366

"Cap'n Jack's James and New River Experience," Captain Jack West, 209 Boyd St., Johnson City, TN 37604, Phone: (423) 926-8539

Captain Hogg's Charter Service, Captain J. Chandler Hogg, 800 S. Armistead Ave., Hampton, VA 23669, Phone: (757) 723-3200 or (757) 876-1590, e-mail: info@captainhoggscharters.com

Reel Reel Gone Charters, Captain Len Gerylo, 802 Deer Path Trail, Newport News, VA 23608, Phone: (757) 877-6015, e-mail: lgerylo@aol.com

Spec Fever Guide Service, Capt. Gary Dubiel, P.O. Box 1029, Oriental, NC 28571, Phone: (252) 249-1520, e-mail: captgary@specfever.com

Greasy Creek Outfitters, Mike Smith, P.O. Box 211, Willis, VA 24380, Phone: (540) 789-7811, e-mail: msmith@swva.net

WASHINGTON

Bent Rods Fishing Guide Service, Jordan Smith, 1900 NW 92 St., Vancouver, WA 98665, Phone: (360) 910-2104, e-mail: public.enterprise@juno.com

Olsen's Guide Service, Kris Olsen, 5821 11th Ave W., Everett, WA 98203, Phone: (425) 407-1013, e-mail: fisherman@seanet.com

Drifting Fly Guide Service, Scott G. Fierst, P.O. Box 643, Woodinville, WA 98072, Phone: (888) 204-5327, e-mail: info@driftingfly.com

Ship's Guide Service, Stephen Shipley, 1518 228th St.

SW, Bothell, WA 98021, Phone: (425) 483-8388, e-mail: shipfishing@aol.com

The Evening Hatch Guide Service, P.O. Box 1295, Ellensburg, WA 98926, Phone: (509) 962-5959, e-mail: jack@theeveninghatch.com

Bob's Piscatorial Pursuits, May-August: P.O. Box 1207 Soldotna, Alaska 99669, September-April, P.O. Box 919 Forks, WA 98331, Phone: (907) 260-5362 or (907) 398-4917

Mansfield Outfitter Service, Jim Mansfield, 963 Fifth Ave., Forks, WA 98331, Phone: (360) 374-9018

Kulshan River Excursions, Rob Endsley, P.O. Box 1313, Bellingham, WA 98227, Phone: (360) 676-1321, e-mail: rendsley@earthlink.net

Graybill's Guide Service, Rick Graybill, P.O. Box 2621, Chelan, WA 98816, Phone: (509) 682-4294, e-mail: rick@rgraybill.com

Special Moments Guide Service, 14204 140 Ave. S.E., Renton , WA 98059, Phone (425) 226-6327 or (206) 300-8209, e-mail: CLWELCH000@aol.com

Snake River Guide Service, 2227 5th Ave., Clarkston, WA 99403, Phone: (509)751-0410

Yakima River Angler Guide Service, Bruce Skotland, P.O. Box 905, Selah, WA 98942, Phone: (509) 697-6327

Adventurous Charters, P.O. Box 1718, Sequim,WA 98382, Phone: (360) 683-6677 or (360) 683-9604

Olsen's Guide Service, 5821 11th Ave W., Everett, WA 98203, Phone: (425) 407-1013

John's Guide Service, P.O. Box 727, Concrete, WA 98237, Phone: (360) 853-9801

Puget Sound Salmon Charters, Capt. John Keizer, 6909 35th St. West, Tacoma, WA 98466, Phone: (253) 565-6598, e-mail: Salcht@cs.com

Quillayute River Guide Service, P.O. Box 71, LaPush WA 98350, Phone: (360) 374-2660

Izzy's Guide Service, 108 N. 39th Place, Mount Vernon, WA 98273, Phone: (360) 424-5786

Onco Sportfishing & Guide Services, Inc., Brad Shride, P.O. Box 2043, Vashon, WA 98070, Phone: (877) 483-0047 or (206) 463-9230, e-mail: onco@seanet.com

Puget Sound Salmon Charters, Capt. John Keizer, 6909 35th St. West, Tacoma WA 98466, Phone: (253) 565-6598, e-mail: Salcht@cs.com

Sunrise Guide Service, Jerry Schroeder, 305 Collins Road, Toledo, WA 98591, Phone: (360) 864-6960, e-mail: JSFlyfishing@aol.com

WEST VIRGINIA

New River Outfitters & Guide Service, P.O. Box 968, Craborchard, WV 25827, Phone: (877) 982-3474 or (304) 255- 4769, e-mail: chief@newwave

Valley Fork Fly Fishing, Dave Breitmeier, HC86 Box 20, Monterville,WV 26282, Phone: (304) 339-8232

Mark Kovach Fishing Services, guides: Mark Kovach, Dave Motes, John Hayes, Richard Larkin, Butch Murphy, Mark Frondorf, 406 Pershing Drive, Silver Spring, MD 20910-4253, Phone: (301) 588-8742

Tracy Samples, 1220 Jordan Road, Marlinton, WV 24954, Phone: (304) 799-4733

River Riders, Inc., Frank Baker, RR 5 Box 1260, Harpers Ferry, WV, Phone: (304) 535-2663 or (800) 326-7238

WISCONSIN

Sorry Charlie Sport Fishing, Capt. Randy Even, 4226 S. 13th St., Sheboygan, WI 52081, Phone: (920) 452-9964, e-mail: uchart@excel.net

Renegade Sportfishing Charters, Capt. Tim Mueller, P.O. Box 436, Port Washington, WI 53074, Phone: (800) 343-0089, e-mail: Rengad@aol.com

Salmon Depot Charters, Captain Bill Silbernagel and Captain Jeff Haleen, P.O. Box 484, Baileys Harbor, WI 54202, Phone: (920) 839-2272, e-mail: silber@itol.com

"Adventure Fishing Company," Guide Steve Slutsky, W5923 Mariner Hills Court, Elkhorn, WI, Phone (262) 742-3090, e-mail: stejan@elknet.net

Fatman's Fly Fishing Guide Service, Rich "The Fatman" Brown, 209 Kendall St., Burlington, WI 53105, Phone: (847) 781-2526, e-mail: fishinfatman@fishinfatman.com

Angling Adventures, Herb Leuthe Jr., RR 1 Box 86B, Drummond, WI 54832, Phone: (715) 798-4665

Strike Master Guide Service, Larry Smith, N585 32nd Ave., Berlin, WI 54923, Phone: (920) 361-4996

Upper Mississippi River Professional Guide Service, Dale Radcliffe, 550 Rublee St. Apt #10, La Crosse, WI 54603, Phone: (608) 779-5934

P&P Guide Service, Paul Olson and Ryan (Pie) Krings, 540 Meadow Lane, Winneconne, WI 54986, Phone: (920) 582-0518

Sennett's Guide Service, Ty Sennett, 8712 N Co. Highway CC, Hayward, WI 54843, Phone: (715) 462-9403

Muskie "62" Guide Service, Phillip Gutmann, 4200 Greenfield Lane, Lake in the Hills, IL 60156, Phone: (847) 669-8286

Double "B" Guide Service, Bill Baldauf, 4894 West Fairview Rd., Larsen,WI 54947, Phone: (920) 582-0263 or (920) 836-2377

Sea Dog Sport Fishing Charters of Sheboygan, Capt. James Schlegel, P.O. Box 912, Sheboygan, WI 53082, Phone: (800) 582-9694, e-mail: schled@nconnect.net

Dumper Dan's Lake Michigan Sportfishing Charters, Captain Dan Welsch, 4022 N. 51st St., Sheboygan, WI 53083, Phone: (920) 457-2940, e-mail: dmprdan@bytehead.com

Into The Outdoors, Todd Berg, 25705 Arrowhead Drive, Mundelein, IL 60060, Phone: (847) 922-1271, e-mail: sales@intotheoutdoors.net

Hutch's Tackle & Guide Services, Tim Hutchison, P.O. Box 442, Prairie du Chien, WI 53821, Phone: (608) 326-6764, e-mail: jigman@mhtc.net

Hodag Guide Service, Scott Biscobing, 5621 Squirrel Drive, Rhinelander, WI 54501, e-mail: biscob@newnorth.net

Jim Stroede Fishing Guide Service, W7004 County Hwy. E, Spooner, WI 54801, Phone: (715) 635-7927, e-mail: jim@fishhayward.com

Solidarity Guide Service, Captain Mike Ekholm, 24-16th St., Cloquet, MN 55720, Phone: (218) 879-7214 or (218) 390-221

W-3 Guide Service, Rick Gennrich, W1002 Augies Drive, Gleason, WI, Phone: (715) 536-3198

Top Tackle Guide Service, Joel Tinker, P.O. Box 1423, Superior, WI 54880 Phone: (715) 399-0440

Reel Hooked Guide Service, Brian J. Keller, P.O. Box 48, Butte des Morts, WI 54927, Phone: (920) 420-3351

Walleyesplus Guide Service, Steve Hafemeister, 8028 Island Ave., Omro, WI 54963, Phone: (920) 685-5435

Genson Fish Hunts, LLC, Eric Genson, 122 W. Vine, River Falls, WI, Phone (715) 425-7550

Wisconsin River Guide Service, Richard Unbehaun, 392 N. Park St., Richland Center, WI 53581, Phone: (608) 647-4035

CSA Guide Service, Dan Horwich, P.O. Box 212, Lodi, WI 53555, Phone: (608) 592-5076

G & S Guide Service, Steve Huber, 2882 N. Pelican Lake Road, Rhinelander, WI 54501, Phone: (715) 362-3857

Ocooch Mountain Fishing Guides, Lawrence Ecklor and Brian Ecklor, 100 Viking St., Coon Valley, WI. 54623, Phone: (608) 452-3700, e-mail: ecklor@hotmail.com

WYOMING

Great Rocky Mountain Outfitters, Robert Smith, Box 1677, Saratoga, WY 82331, Phone: (307) 326-8750 or (800) 326-5390, e-mail: grmo@union-tel.com

North Platte Anglers, Paul Kiser, Glenn Pease, Dave Mandrella, Box 31, Alcova, WY 82620, Phone: (307) 472-9190, e-mail: flyfishpdk@earthlink.net

Angler's West Boating Adventures, Gary Meredith, Buffalo, WY, Phone: (877) WYO-BOAT

John Henry Lee Outfitters, Inc., John Henry Lee, P.O. Box 8368, Jackson, WY 83002, Phone: (800) 352-2576, e-mail: infojhl@johnhenrylee.com

High Country Anglers, John Douville, P.O. Box 9552, Jackson, WY 83002, Phone: (877) 589-7191

Wyoming Fly Fishing Guide Service, Mark Boname and Greg Mueller, 7400 Alcova Hwy 220, Casper, WY 82604, Phone: (307) 237-5997, e-mail: platterat@aol.com

Wyoming Adventures, John Schwalbe, 484 Wakeley Rd., Thermopolis, WY 82443, Phone: (307) 864-2407, e-mail: anglingadv@yahoo.comGuides

Canada Fishing Guides

ALBERTA

Southern Alberta Fly Fishing Outfitters, Mark MacDonald, Box 546 Turner Valley, Alberta Canada T0L 2A0, Phone: (403) 931-2211, e-mail: bowriver@albertaflyfish.com

Alberta Bound Fishing Adventures, Chris Gerritse, 123 McKenna Way S.E., Calgary, Alberta, T2Z 1W9, Phone (403) 257-1994, e-mail: albertaboundfishing@shaw.ca

The Water Boatman, Mike Guinn, 612 Queensland Drive, S.E., Calgary, AB. T2J 4G7, Phone: (403) 271-0799

West Winds Fly Shop Ltd., Gord Kennedy, #109--9919 Fairmount Drive S.E., Calgary, Alberta, Canada, T2J 0S3, Phone: (403) 278-6331, e-mail: flyshop@telusplanet.net

Banff Fishing Unlimited, Jeff Perodeau, P.O.Box 8281, Canmore, Ab. Canada T1W 2V1, Phone: (403) 762-4936, e-mail: banffish@expertcanmore.net

Kimball River Sports, Kip Barnes, Tim Ruggles Guides, Cardston, Alberta, Canada, Phone: (403) 382-0997

Trout Chasers River Company Ltd., Dee Chatani, 3741 Douglas Ridge Way, S. E. Calgary, Alberta T2Z 3C3, Phone: (403) 236-4409

Alberta Drift Company, Bow River, Phone: (403) 256-9172

Angling Adventures, Phone: (403) 274-7221

Bow Valley Guides Ltd., Calgary Bow River, Phone: (403) 276-5013

Eagle Eye Drifters, Bow River, (403) 605-4631

Great Waters Alberta, Calgary Bow River, Phone: (403) 256-3090

Rainbow & Brown Flyfishing float trips, Dewinton Bow River, Phone: (403) 256-9622

North Raven Lodge, Caroline Stauffer Creek, Phone: (877) 68-TROUT

Tailwater Drifter, s 71 Hammond Cresc., Red Deer, Ab. T4N 6J5, Phone: (403) 314-5444

Before the Hatch Anglers, Phone: (403) 845-4435

Currie's Guiding & Tackle Ltd., Jasper Maligne, Amethyst, Medicine Lakes; Phone: (780) 852-5650

Maligne Lake Guided Fly Fishing, Phone: (780) 852-3370

On-Line Sport & Tackle, Jasper, Alpine lakes, Phone: (780) 852-3630

Streamside Adventures, Phone: (780) 475-9297

High Country Outdoor Adventures, 123 Ranchero Place, NW. Calgary, Ab. T3G 1C6,
Phone: (403) 241-8666

Crowsnest Angler, P.O. Box 400, Bellevue Ab. T0K 0C0, Phone: (403) 564-4333

Bow River Company, Phone: (403) 640-2464

Hanson's Fishing Tours, Calgary Bow River, Phone: (800) 784-3312

Rocky River Outfitters, Calgary Bow River, Phone: (403) 251 5286

Silvertip Outfitters, Calgary Bow River, Phone: (403) 256-5018

South Bow Anglers, Calgary Bow River, Phone: (403) 271-7756

Get Hooked Fishing Tours, Keith Rae, Box 10 Site 201 RR2, Stony Plain AB T7Z 1X2, Phone: (780) 963-4279, e-mail: gethooked@trinustech.com

BRITISH COLUMBIA

Nechako Lodge & Aviation, Joe Doerig, Box 2413, Vanderhoof, BC Canada, V0J 3A0m, Phone: (250) 690-7740 or (800) 567-7022, e-mail: nelo@hwy16.com

Ospray Charters and Guide Service, Shawn Hillier, Box 608, Tofino, BC V0R 2Z0, Phone: (888) 286-3466, e-mail: shawn@ospray.com

Destiny Sportfishing, David Manson, 2753 Vargo Rd., Campbell River, B.C.; V9W 4W9, Phone: (250) 286-9610, e-mail: destiny@oberon.ark.com

Quigley Sport Fishing, Larry Quigley, 7048 West Coast Rd., Sooke BC V0S 1N0, Phone: (250) 642-2321, e-mail: larry@quigleysportfishing.com

Fraser Valley Outdoor Adventures Ltd., Steve and Nancy Arcand, 8944 Hammond St., Mission, BC, Canada, V2V 6X8, Phone: (888) 826-3862, e-mail: fvoa@mindlink.bc.ca

ReelFishingBC.com Fly Fishing Charters, Rick Baerg, Chilliwack B.C. Canada, Phone: (604) 302-4590, e-mail: info@reelfishingbc.com

Ex-Stream Steelhead Guide Service, Scott Blewett, 1040 Jenkins Ave., Victoria, BC V9B 2N7, Phone: (877) 474-3619 or (250) 474-3619

Northwest Fishing Guides & Lodge, P.O. Box 434, Terrace, BC V8G 4B1 Canada, Phone: (250) 635-5295

Bites-on Charter Group, Vancouver, BC, Phone: (877) 688-2483 or (604) 688-2483

Double Down Fishing Adventures, Brian Kangas, Vancouver, BC, Phone: (250) 478-2135

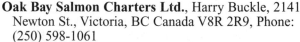

Oak Bay Salmon Charters Ltd., Harry Buckle, 2141
   Newton St., Victoria, BC Canada V8R 2R9, Phone:
   (250) 598-1061
Catala Charters, Jim Witton, 6170 Hardy Bay Rd.
   Box 526, Port Hardy BC Canada V0N2P0, Phone:
   (250) 949-7560 or (800) 515-5511, e-mail:
   info@catalacharters.net
STS Guiding Service, 32374 Ptarmigan Drive,
   Mission, British Columbia V2V 5R5, Phone (604)
   671-FISH (3474), e-mail: sts@guidebc.com
Naden Lodge, Brian Hillier, P.O. Box #648 1496
   Delkatla St., Masset B.C. V0T 1M0, Phone: (800)
   771-TYEE (8933), e-mail: info@nadenlodge.bc.ca
Coho Sports Salmon Fishing British Columbia, Fred
   Kuzyk, 4152 Penticton St., Vancouver, British
   Columbia, V5R1Y1, Phone: (604) 435-7333, e-mail:
   fishing@cohosports.ca
South Cariboo Fishing Adventures, Matt Harper &
   Sean Paterson, P.O. Box 494, 108 Mile Ranch, B.C.,
   Canada, V0K 2Z0, Phone: (250) 791-7313
Jay's Clayoquout Ventures, Tofino, B.C.(Vancouver
   Island), Box 652 Tofino, B.C. vor 2zo, Phone: (888)
   5FISHBC or (250) 725-2700, e-mail:
   jay@steelheadsalmonhalibut.com
Kelly's Sportfishing, Brad Kelly, 9674 5 St., Sidney
   BC V8L2W8, e-mail: kelly@kellysportfishing.com
Cascade Fishing Charters, Marc Laynes or Alexis
   Heaton, P.O. Box 682, AgassizB.C. V0M 1A0,
   Phone: (87-S)TURGEON
Polar Bear Outfitters, Billy Konopelky, Box 2436,
   Cichrane Ontario P0L 1C0, Phone: (705) 272-5680
Wilderness River Adventure Tours, Joen Nelson, 943
   Denewood Place, Shirley Sooke, BC V0S 1N0
   Canada, Phone: (250) 646-2820
Northwest Fishing Guides & Lodge, P.O. Box 434,
   Terrace BC V8G 4B1 Canada, Phone: (250) 635-5295

MANITOBA

True North Adventures, Tim Matheson, Box 8,
   Sherridon, Mb. Canada R0B 1L0,
   Phone: (888) 590-5544
Rene's Guiding Service, Rene Dubé, Box 45,
   Powerview, Manitoba, Canada R0E 1P0,
   Phone: (204) 367-8064,
   e-mail: bdube@mb.sympatico.ca
Cat-Eye Outfitter, Dan Kiazyk, Box 629, Minnedosa,
   Manitoba Canada, Phone: (204) 867-3550

NEW BRUNSWICK

Byron Coughlan, Country Haven Lodge, 601rt118
   Gray Rapids, NB Canada E9B1G9 1877,
   Phone: (877) flyhook, e-mail: flyhook@nbnet.nb.ca
Beech Nut Outfitters, Nelson C. Grant, 350 Upper

Skiff Lake Road, Dead Creek, NB e9c 1T8,
   Phone: (506) 279-2984
Long Meadow Cabins, Darren Johnson, 2104 Route 3,
   Harvey, NB E6K 1M6, Phone: (506) 366-2043
Craswell Guide Service, Karl Craswell, 28
   Restigouche Drive, Tide Head, New Brunswick,
   Canada, e3n 4h4, Phone: (506) 759-9890
North View Hunting & Fishing Lodge, Wayne
   DeLeavey, P.O. Box 1132, Plaster Rock, NB, Canada
   E7G 4G9, Phone: (506) 356-7212
Lake Retreat Outfitters & Charters, Rob Wilson,
   P.O. Box 902, Saint John, NB E2L 4C3,
   Phone: (506) 757-8062
Adairs Wilderness Lodge, Larry Adair, 900 Creek
   Road, Shepody, NB E4E 5R9, Phone: (506) 432-6687

NEWFOUNDLAND

Gander River Tours, Peter Stacey, Site 5, Box 18,
   Appleton, NF Canada, A0G-2K0,
   Phone: (709) 679-2271, e-mail: grt@nf.sympatico.ca
Flyfishing the Island, Dwayne Miller, 161 Westridge
   Crescent Apt. #7, Charlottetown, PEI C1A 8P1,
   Phone: (902) 628-6175
Eagle Lake Sport Fishing, Rick Dawes, P.O. Box 358
   Station "C" Happy Valley - Goose Bay, Labrador A0P
   1C0, Phone: (709) 896-3363 or (877) 677-3633,
   e-mail: info@fishinglabrador.com
Gander River Outfitters Inc., P.O. Box 21017, St.
   John's, Newfoundland Canada A1A 5B2, Phone:
   (888) SALMON3 (725-6663) or (709) 753-9163

NORTHWEST TERRITORIES

Barbara Ann Charters, 9-705 Williams Ave.,
   Yellowknife Northwest Territories X1A 3W,
   Phone: (867) 873-9913

NOVA SCOTIA

Dave's Guide Service, 331 Lacewood Drive, Suite 208
   B3S 1K6 Nova Scotia, Canada,
   Phone: (902) 489-1938

ONTARIO

Lecuyer's Tru-Tail Lodge, Dan Lecuyer, P.O. Box 55,
   Nestor Falls, Ontario Canada, Pox 1KO,
   Phone: (807) 484-2448 or (800) 201-2100,
   e-mail: lecuyer@earthlink.net
Canada Outfitters, P.O. Box 572, Kenora, Ont.
   Canada, Phone: (807) 548-7654,
   e-mail: fishing@norcomcable.ca

On The Water Fishing Adventures, Ken Puddicombe, 202 Melbourne Drive, Bradford Ontario L3Z 2Y8, Phone: (905) 775-0819, e-mail: ken.puddicombe@sympatico.ca

Chasen Fish Charters, James Dexter, 184 Ferguson Drive, Brockville, Ontario, Canada, K6V 4R6, Phone: (613) 342-3102

Ewing Charters, Captain Tom Ewing, RD 1, Box 280, Lowville, NY 13367, Phone: (315) 376-6921

Voyageur Ventures, 8356 50th Ave N, New Hope, MN 55428, Phone: (877) 240-9112

TrophyMuskiecharters.com, Richard Collin, R.R.#1 Hammond, Ontario K0A 2A0, Phone: (613) 487-3934

All Canadian Fly-In Lodge & Outposts at Kesagami, Northern Ontario, Canada, e-mail: fishkesagami@aol.com

Bear Lake Wilderness Camp, Bill Drane, P.O. Box 5262, Espanola, Ontario P5E 1S3, Phone: (705) 866-7100, blwc@aol.com

Canadian Carpin Holidays, Paul Hunt, RR#3, Ingleside, Ontario K0C 1M0, Phone: (613) 534-3883, e-mail: canadian.carpin@sympatico.ca

1000 Islands Guide Service, Doug Amos, 1000 Islands Bridge, Rt. 81, Rockport, Ontario, Phone: (613) 923 5257

Alan Meline Fishing Guides, Nestor Falls, Ontario, Canada, Phone: (800) 561-3166 or (807) 484-2483

International Angling Adventures, Northern Minnesota/Ontario, Canada, Phone: (877) 246-7762

Nickel's Charters, Stan Nickel, 30 Southpark Drive, Ottawa Ontario, Canada K1B 3A5, Phone: (877) 763-9326

QUEBEC

Safari Nordik, Rich Sopko, 408 South Freedom St., Ravenna, Ohio 44266, Phone: (330) 296-5463, Fax: (330) 297-1373

SASKATCHEWAN

Mclaren Outfitting/Guiding, Quentin Fauth, Box 182, Richmound, Saskatchewan, Son 2eo, Phone: (306) 669-2161, e-mail: qfauth@sk.sympatico.ca

Fishing Books

Where to fish? What to fish? How to fish?

They're all good questions. Each has a thousand answers, and at least that many books written on the subject. Whether you're a "complete idiot," a "dummy," an experienced angler, or a professional, there's always something more to learn about fishing.

We've selected a bookshelf, maybe even a good-sized library, chock full of volumes that will keep anglers turning pages for weeks. Besides the specialty books on fly fishing, specific species, regional fishing spots, techniques, and fishing collectibles, there are some classics, such as *Hemingway on Fishing* and *A River Runs Through It*.

We sorted through the shelves for books that are current, in print, and commercially available. Prices listed are suggested retail and are subject to change. There are many other books on fishing. Check your local library or book store for even more selections.

FLY FISHING

Bob Zeller's No Nonsense Business Travelers Guide to Fly Fishing in the Western States, by Bob Zeller, David Marketing Communications, paperbound, 100 pages, 1999 . . . .$18.95

Cast from the Edge: Tales of an Uncommon Fly Fisher, by Scott Sadil, Greycliff Publishing, hardcover, 192 pages, 1999 . . . .$24.95

Castwork: Reflections of Fly Fishing Guides and the American West, by Kirk D. Deeter and Andrew W. Steketee, Willow Creek Press, hardcover, 208 pages, 2002 . . . .$40

The Complete Idiot's Guide to Fly Fishing, by Michael D. Shook and Mel Krieger, Alpha Books, paperbound, 400 pages, 1999 . . . .$16.95

Death, Taxes, and Leaky Waders: A John Gierach Fly-Fishing Treasury, by John Gierach and Glenn Wolff, Fireside, paperbound, 414 pages, 2001 . . . .$14

The Everything Fly-Fishing Book, by Jeff Zhorne, Adams Media Corp., paperbound, 304 pages, 1999 . . . .$12.95

Flyfisher's Guide to Colorado, by Marty Bartholomew and Barry Reynolds, Wilderness Adventures, paperbound, 520 pages, 1998 . . . .$26.95

Fly Fisher's Guide to Idaho, by Ken Retallic and Rocky Barker, Wilderness Adventures, paperbound, 367 pages, 1996 . . . .$26.95

Flyfisher's Guide to Montana, by Greg Thomas,

Handcrafting a Graphite Fly Rod by L.A. Garcia

Wilderness Adventures, paperbound, 374 pages, 1997 . . . .$26.95

Flyfisher's Guide to Northern New England: Vermont, New Hampshire, and Maine, by Steve Hickoff and Rhey Plumley, Wilderness Adventures, paperbound, 500 pages, 1999 . . . .$26.95

Flyfisher's Guide To Pennsylvania, by Dave Wolf, Wilderness Adventures, paperbound, 544 pages, 2000 . . . .$26.95

Flyfisher's Guide To Texas, by Phil H. Shook, Wilderness Adventures, paperbound, 443 pages, 2001 . . . .$26.95

Fly-Fishing Alaska's Wild Rivers, by Dan Heiner, Stackpole Books, paperbound, 176 pages, 1998 . . . .$19.95

Fly Fishing: A Trailside Guide, by John Merwin, W.W. Norton & Co., paperbound, 1996 . . . .$19.95

Fly Fishing in North Carolina, by Buck Paysour and Bob Timberlake, Down Home Press, paperbound, 288 pages, 1995 . . . .$14.95

Fly Fishing Pacific Northwest Waters: Trout & Beyond II, by John Shewey, Frank Amato Publications, paperbound, 80 pages, 1997 . . . .$19.95

Fly Fishing the Madison, by Craig Mathews and Gary

LaFontaine, The Lyons Press, paperbound, 148 pages, 2002 . . . .$18.95

Fly Pattern Encyclopedia, Federation of Fly Fishers, by Al Beatty and Gretchen Beatty, Frank Amato Publishcations, spiral-bound, 150 pages, 2000 . . . .$49.95

Fly Patterns for Stillwaters: A Study of Trout, Entomology and Tying, by Phillip Rowley, Frank Amato Publications, paperbound, 2000 . . . . . .$29.95

The Fly Tier's Benchside Reference, by Ted Leeson and Jim Schollmeyer, Frank Amato Publications, hardcover, 464 pages, 1998 . . . .$100

Fly Tying Made Clear and Simple, by Skip Morris, Frank Amato Publications, spiral bound, 80 pages, 1992 . . . .$19.95

Fly-Tying Techniques & Patterns (The Complete Fly Fisherman), by John Van Vliet, Creative Publishing International, hardcover, 144 pages, 1996 . . . .$18.95

Fly Tying With Poly Yarn, by Lee Clark, Joe Warren and John Shewey, Frank Amato Publications, paperbound, 56 pages, 2000 . . . .$19.95

Hatch Guide for New England Streams, by Thomas Ames Jr., Frank Amato Publications, 271 pages, 2000 . . . .$19.95

The Orvis Fly-Fishing Guide, by Tom Rosenbauer, The Lyons Press, paperbound, 272 pages, 1988 . . .$17.95

Pardon My Backcast, by Alan Pratt, Frank Amato Publications, paperbound, 80 pages, 1996 . . . . .$6.95

Rocky Mountain Fly Fishing, by Steve Cook, Utah Outdoors, paperbound, 416 pages, 2000 . . . . .$24.95

Top Rated Fly Fishing, Maurizio Valerio editor, Derrydale, paperbound, 250 pages, 2000 . . . . .$18.95

Trout Flies: The Tier's Reference, by Dave Hughes, Stackpole Books, hardcover, 480 pages, 1999 . . .$75

Tying Dry Flies (Third Edition), by Randall Kaufmann, Western Fisherman's Press, paperbound, 144 pages, 2001 . . . .$32.95

Tying Glass Bead Flies, by Joe J. Warren, Frank Amato Publications, spiral bound, 64 pages, 1997 . . .$19.95

Tying Trout Flies, by C. Boyd Pfeiffer, Krause Publications, spiral bound, 160 pages, 2002 . .$24.95

Upstream: Fly-Fishing in the American West, by Charles Lindsay and Thomas McGuane, Aperture, hardcover, 96 pages, 2000 . . . .$40

Which Fly Do I Use? by Darren Banasch, Frank Amato Publications, paperbound, 48 pages, 2000 . . . .$8.95

SALTWATER FISHING

American Big Game Fishing, Eugene V. Connet III editor, Derrydale, paperbound, 278 pages, 1999 . . . .$27.95

Coastal Fishing in the Carolinas: From Surf, Pier, and Jetty (3rd ed.), by Robert J. Goldstein, John F. Blair Publishers, paperbound, 208 pages, 2000 . . . .$15.95

Saltwater Gamefishing: Offshore and Onshore by Peter Goadby

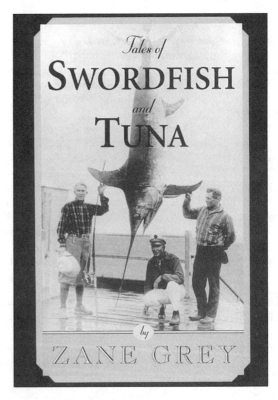

Tales of Swordfish and Tuna by Zane Grey

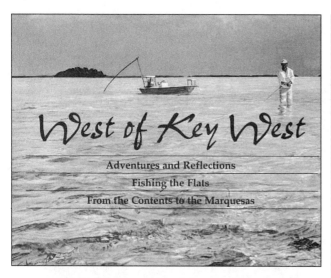

West of Key West: Adventures and Reflections, Fishing the Flats From the Contents of the Marquesas

L.L. Bean: Fly Fishing for Bass Handbook by Dave Whitlock

The Complete Book of Saltwater Fishing, by Milt Rosko, Krause Publications, paperbound, 288 pages, 2001 . . . .$29.95

Engulfed: A Photographic Celebration of People, Places and Fish Around the Gulf Coast, by David J. Sams and Doug Pike, Tapestry Press, hardcover, 112 pages, 2001 . . . .$39.95

Fish Florida: Saltwater/Better Than Luck-The Fool

Proof Guide to Florida Saltwater Fishing, by Boris Arnov, Gulf Publishing, paperbound, 232 pages, 2002 . . . .$13.95

Fishing the Big Four: A Guide for Saltwater Anglers, by Milt Rosko, Burford Books, paperbound, 256 pages, 2001 . . . .$16.95

Flats Fishing II: A Shoalwater Handbook, by Jan S. Maizler, Writer's Club Ltd., paperbound, 188 pages, 2001 . . . .$14.95

Fly Fishing for Bonefish, by Dick Brown, The Lyons Press, paperbound, 372 pages, 1993 . . . .$35

Giant Bluefin, by Douglas Whynott, North Point Press, paperbound, 1996 . . . .$12

Good Luck and Tight Lines! : A Sure-Fire Guide to Florida's Inshore Fishing, by R.G. Schmidt, Gulf Publishing, paperbound, 1996 . . . .$12.95

Offshore Salt Water Fishing, by Barry Gibson and Saltwater Sportsman magazine staff, Creative Publishing International, hardcover, 128 pages, 2002 . . . .$21.95

Pacific Shore Fishing, by Michael R. Sakamoto, University of Hawaii Press, paperbound, 272 pages, 1985 . . . .$14.95

Saltwater Angler's Guide to the Southeast : Flyfishing and Light Tackle in the Carolinas and Georgia (Saltwater Angler's Guide Series), by Bob Newman, Wilderness Adventures, paperbound, 375 pages, 1999 . . . .$26.95

Saltwater Gamefishing: Offshore and Onshore, by Peter Goadby, McGraw-Hill, hardcover, 352 pages, 1992 . . . .$44.95

Sight-Fishing for Striped Bass: Fly-Fishing Strategies for Inshore, Offshore and the Surf, by Alan Caolo, Frank Amato Publications, hardcover, 100 pages, 2001 . . . .$39.95

Striper Hot Spots, 2nd Ed., by Frank Daignault, Globe Pequot, paperbound, 256 pages, 1996 . . . .$14.95

Top Rated Saltwater Fishing, by Maurizio Valerio, Derrydale, paperbound, 300 pages, 2000 . . . . .$18.95

Tuna, by Bill Smith, Burford Books, hardcover, 256 pages, 2001 . . . .$30

Veiled Horizons: Stories of Big Game Fish of the Sea, by Ralph Bandini, Buckingham Mint, paperbound, 222 pages, 2001 . . . .$24.95

West of Key West, John N. Cole and Hawk Pollard editors, Stackpole Books, hardcover, 224 pages, 1996 . . . .$50

BASS FISHING

The Bass Angler's Almanac: More Than 650 Tips and Tactics, by John Weiss, The Lyons Press, hardcover, 296 pages, 2001 . . . .$29.95

The Bass Fisherman's Bible (3rd Ed.), by Erwin A. Bauer and Mark Hicks, Main Street Books,

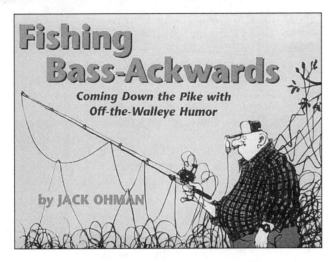

Fishing Bass-Ackwards: Coming Down the Pike with Off-the-Walleye Humor by Jack Ohman

paperbound, 213 pages, 1989 . . . .$12.95

Bassing With the Best: Techniques of America's Top Pros, by Gary White, William Morrow & Co., paperbound, 192 pages, 1997 . . . .$12.95

Bassin' With the Pros, by Mark Romanack, Krause Publications, paperbound, 232 pages, 2001 . . .$19.95

Bass Pro Shops Hunting and Fishing Directory: Outfitters, Guides and Lodges, by Marv Fremerman, Derrydale, paperbound, 167 pages, 2001 . . . .$18.95

Bass Wisdom, by Homer Circle, The Lyons Press, paperbound, 240 pages, 2000 . . . .$16.95

The Complete Book of Striped Bass Fishing (3rd ed.), by Nick Karas, The Lyons Press, paperbound, 368 pages, 2000 . . . .$24.95

Hooked! America's Passion for Bass Fishing, Tehabi Books, Simon & Schuster, hardcover, 192 pages, 2001 . . . .$30

L. L. Bean Fly Fishing for Bass Handbook, by Dave Whitlock, The Lyons Press, paperbound, 176 pages, 2000 . . . .$18.95

The Moon Pulled Up an Acre of Bass: A Flyrodder's Odyssey at Montauk Point, by Peter Kaminsky, Hyperion, hardcover, 244 pages, 2001 . . . . . .$23.95

Peacock Bass Explosions! Where, When & How to Catch America's Greatest Gamefish!, by Larry Larsen, Larsens Outdoor Publishing, 192 pages, 1993 . . . .$12.95

Roland Martin's 101 Bass-Catching Secrets (2nd Ed.), by Roland Martin, New Win Publishing, 1988 . . . .$19.95

Smallmouth Bass, by Dick Sternberg, Creative Publishing International, paperbound, 160 pages, 1986 . . . .$7.25

The Trophy Striper, by Frank Daignault, Burford Books, paperbound, 182 pages, 1999 . . . .$16.95

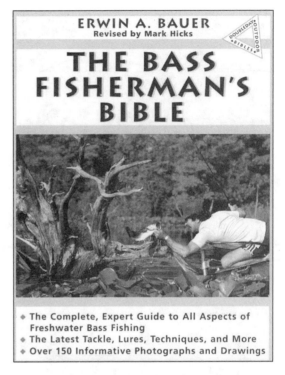

The Bass Fisherman's Bible by Erwin A. Bauer

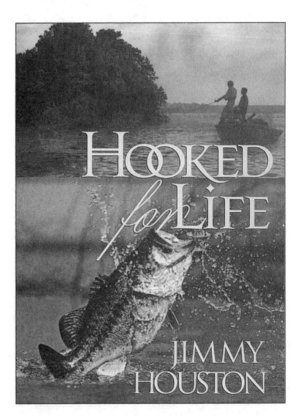

Hooked for Life by Jimmy Houston

Hooked on Ice Fishing II: Panfish by Tom Gruenwald

Trout Streams of Pennsylvania: An Angler's Guide by Dwight Landis

ICE FISHING

Hooked on Ice Fishing, by Tom Gruenwald, Krause Publications, paperbound, 256 pages, 2000 . . . .$14.95
Hooked on Ice Fishing II: Panfish, by Tom Gruenwald, Krause Publications, paperbound, 256 pages $16.95
Ice Fishing Secrets, by Al Lindner, Dave Genz and Doug Stange, In-Fisherman, paperbound, 1998 . . . .$9.95

REGIONAL FISHING

Alaska Blues: A Season of Fishing the Inside Passage, by Joe Upton, Sasquatch Books, paperbound, 256 pages, 1998 . . . .$15.95
The Barefoot Fisherman's Guide to the Emerald Coast: From Gulf Shore, Alabama, to Apalachicola, Florida, by Gregory Dew, Crane Hill Publishers, paperbound, 180 pages, 1999 . . . .$10.95
Boats of Alaska: An Artist's Guide to Commercial Fishing Boats, by Pedro Denton and Clem Tilliom, Publication Consultants, paperbound, 80 pages, 1998 . . . .$24.95
A Boundary Waters Fishing Guide, by Michael Furtman, Birch Portage Press, paperbound, 2001 . . . . $12.95
Cleveland Fishing Guide, by John Barbo, Gray & Co., 240 pages, 1998 . . . .$13.95
The Colorado Angling Guide (3rd Edition), by Bob Sterling and Chuck Fothergill, Stream Stalker, paperbound, 2000 . . . .$29.95
The Complete Angling Guide to the Roaring Fork Valley (Colorado), by Michael Shook, paperbound, 66 pages, 1997 . . . .$10.95
The Complete Guide to Freshwater Fishing (The Freshwater Angler), Creative Publishing International, hardcover, 288 pages, 2002 . . . .$29.95
Fishing Arkansas: A Year-Round Guide to Angling Adventures in the Natural State, by Keith B. Sutton, University of Arkansas Press, 304 pages, 2000 $24.95
Fishing California Freshwater : A Travel Guide to Proven Spots & Proven Methods, by David Colby, Sabertooth Publications, 184 pages, 1994 . . . .$14.95
Days on the Water: The Angling Tradition in Pennsylvania, by Mike Sajna, University of Pittsburgh Press, hardcover, 174 pages, 1999 . . . .$22.95
Fishing for Dummies, by Peter Kaminsky, Hungry Minds Inc., paperbound, 348 pages, 1997 . . . .$21.99
Fishing in Oregon's Deschutes River, by Scott Richmond, Flying Pencil Publications, paperbound, 173 pages, 1993 . . . .$14.95
Fishing Maine, by Tom Seymour, Falcon Publishing Co., paperbound, 194 pages, 1997 . . . .$12.95

Fish Michigan: One Hundred Northern Lower Michigan Lakes, 2nd ed., by Tom Huggler and Thomas E. Huggler, Friede Publications, paperbound, 104 pages, 2000 . . . .$17.95

Fishing New England: A Rhode Island Shore Guide, by Gene Bourque, On the Water LLC, paperbound, 162 pages, 2001 . . . .$14.95

Foghorn Outdoors: California Fishing 6th Ed: The Complete Guide to More Than 1,000 Fishing Spots in the Golden State, by Tom Stienstra, Avalon Travel Publishing, paperbound, 650 pages, 2001 . . . .$19.95

Foghorn Outdoors: Washington Fishing (3rd ed.), by Terry Rudnick, Avalon Travel Publishing, paperbound, 537 pages, 2000 . . . .$19.95

Fishing Alaska (2nd ed.), by Evan Swensen and Margaret Swensen, Falcon Publishing Co., paperbound, 208 pages, 1997 . . . .$16.95

Fishing Florida, by Kris W. Thoemke, Falcon Publishing Co., paperbound, 374 pages, 1996 . . . .$18.95

Fishing Georgia, by Kevin Dallmier, Falcon Publishing Co., paperbound, 350 pages, 2000 . . . .$19.95

Fishing in New Mexico, by R. Titus Piper, University of New Mexico Press, paperbound, 285 pages, 1989 . . . .$15.95

Fishing the Beartooths, by Pat Marcuson, Falcon Publishing Co., paperbound, 186 pages, 1997 . . . .$14.95

Fishing Wyoming, by Ken Graham, Falcon Publishing Co., paperbound, 300 pages, 1998 . . . .$16.95

Gene Kilgore's Ranch Vacations 6th Ed: The Complete Guide to Guest and Resort, Fly-Fishing, and Cross-Country Skiing Ranches in the United States and Canada, by Gene Kilgore, Jeff Cahill, George Gaines and Barnaby Conrad, Avalon Travel Publishing, paperbound, 550 pages, 2001 . . . .$22.95

Gone Fishin' in N.J. Saltwater, Rivers & Bays, by Manny Luftglass, Gone Fishin' Enterprises, paperbound, 110 pages, 1997 . . . .$14.95

Housatonic River : Fly Fishing Guide, by Jeff Passante, Frank Amato Publications, paperbound, 56 pages, 1998 . . . .$14.95

Idaho Fishing Guide: Hook, Line & Sinker, by Pete Zimowsky, Frank Amato Publications, 1995 . . .$7.47

The James River Guide, by Bruce Ingram, Ecopress, paperbound, 136 pages, 2000 . . . .$11.95

Joe Bucher's Crankbait Secrets, by Joe Bucher, Krause Publications, paperbound, 256 pages, 2001 . . .$19.95

Maine Fishing Maps : Rivers and Streams, by Harry Vanderweide, DeLorme Publishing, paperbound, 88 pages, 1991 . . . .$10.95

North American Fishing: The Premier Guide to Angling in Freshwater and Saltwater, by Ken Schultz, Carlton, hardcover, 256 pages, 2001 . . . .$40

North America's Greatest Fishing Lodges: More Than 250 Prime Destinations in the U.S., Canada & Central America, by John Ross and Katie Anders,

Trout Streams of Michigan: A Fly-Angler's Guide by Bob Linsenman and Steve Nevala

Willow Creek Press, paperbound, 352 pages, 2000 . . . .$19.95

Ozark Hideaways : Twenty-Seven Day Trips for Hiking and Fishing, 2nd ed., by Louis C. White, University of Missouri Press, paperbound, 256 pages, 1998 . . . .$19.95

Reeling in Russia, by Fen Montaigne, St. Martin's Press, hardcover, 320 pages, 1998 . . . .$24.95

Snake River Secrets, by Lanny Harward, Frank Amato Publications, paperbound, 96 pages, 1996 . . . . .$8.95

Wisconsin's Top Muskie Lakes, by Chuck Petrie, Bob Knops, Mark C. Martin and Brian Vaughn, Fishing Hot Spots, paperbound, 256 pages, 1993 . . . .$19.95

SALMON FISHING

Atlantic Salmon Fishing, by Charles Phair, Derrydale, paperbound, 218 pages, 1999 . . . .$27.95

Field Guide to the Pacific Salmon (Adopt-A-Stream Foundation), by Robert Steelquist, Sasquatch Books, paperbound, 64 pages, 1992 . . . .$7.95

King Salmon: A Guide To Salmon Fishing in California, by Greg Goddard, Paradise Cay Publications, paperbound, 132 pages, 2000 . . . .$14.95

Leaper: The Wonderful World of Atlantic Salmon Fishing, Charles Gaines and Monte Burke editors, The Lyons Press, hardcover, 224 pages, 2001 . . . .$50

Trout Flies: The Tier's Reference by Dave Hughes

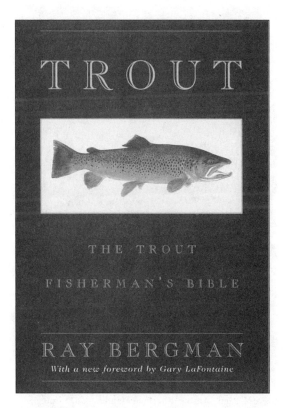

Trout: The Trout Fisherman's Bible by Ray Bergman

Maximum Salmon: Fishing in the West Coast from Alaska to California, by Dennis Colin Reid, Gorman & Gorman, paperbound, 2002 . . . .$24.95

River Salmon Fishing, by Bill Stinson, Frank Amato Publications, paperbound, 148 pages, 1995 . . .$14.95

Saltwater Salmon Angling, by Bob Mottram, Frank Amato Publications, paperbound, 140 pages, 1990 . . . .$9.95

Shrimp & Spey Flies for Salmon & Steelhead, by Chris Mann and Robert Gillespie, Stackpole Books, hardcover, 222 pages, 2001 . . . .$32.95

STEELHEAD FISHING

Color Guide to Steelhead Drift Fishing, by Bill Herzog, Frank Amato Publications, paperbound, 80 pages, 1984 . . . .$16.95

Float Fishing for Steelhead: Techniques & Tackle, by Dave Vedder, Frank Amato Publications, paperbound, 64 pages, 1995 . . . .$15.95

Fly Fishing for Great Lakes Steelhead - An Advanced Look at an Emerging Fishery, by Rick Kustich and Jerry Kustich, West River Publishing Co., hardcover, 280 pages, 1999 . . . .$39.95

Steelhead Dreams: The Theory, Method, Science and Madness of Great Lakes Steelhead Fly Fishing, by Matt Supinski, Frank Amato Publications, hardcover, 2001 . . . .$39.95

Steelhead: Fly Fishing, by Trey Combs, The Lyons Press, paperbound, 494 pages, 1999 . . . .$29.95

Steelhead Guide: Fly Fishing Techniques and Strategies for Lake Erie Steelhead (second edition), by John Nagy, Great Lakes Publishing, paperbound, 192 pages, 2000 . . . .$24.95

Steelhead Jig Fishing Techniques & Tackle: Techniques & Tackle, by Dave Vedder and Drew Harthorn, Frank Amato Publications, paperbound, 48 pages, 1996$8.95

The Teeny Technique for Steelhead and Salmon, by Jim Teeny, The Lyons Press, paperbound, 160 pages, 2001 . . . .$17.95

TROUT FISHING

Arizona Trout Streams and Their Hatches: Fly-Fishing in the High Deserts of Arizona and Western New Mexico, by Charles R. Meck and John Rohmer, Countryman Press, paperbound, 204 pages, 1998 . . . .$17.95

Mid-Atlantic Trout Streams and Their Hatches: Overlooked Angling in Pennsylvania, New York, and New Jersey, by Charles R. Meck, Countryman Press, paperbound, 206 pages, 1997 . . . .$13.60

The New North American Trout Fishing, by John

Merwin, hardcover, 240 pages, 2001 . . . .$9.99

Reading the Water: A Fly Fisher's Handbook for Finding Trout in All Types of Water, by Dave Hughes, Stackpole Books, paperbound, 224 pages, 1988 . . . .$16.95

Small Fly Adventures in the West: A Guide to Angling for Larger Trout, by Neale Streeks, Pruett Publishing Co., paperbound, 1996 . . . .$12.50

Specks: Louisiana's Top 10 Trout Destinations, and Exactly How to Fish Them Year-Round, by Todd Masson, Louisiana Publishing, paperbound, 192 pages, 2001 . . . .$19.95

Trout, by Ray Bergman, Derrydale, paperbound, 512 pages, 2000 . . . .$29.95

Trout Dreams: A Gallery of Fly-Fishing Profiles, by J.I. Merritt, Derrydale, hardcover, 2000 . . . .$24.95

Trout Streams of Michigan: A Fly-Angler's Guide (Second Edition), by Bob Linsenman, Steve Nevala and Ernest Schwiebert, Countryman Press, paperbound, 336 pages, 2001 . . . .$21.95

Trout Streams of Northern New England: A Guide to the Best Fly-Fishing in Vermont, New Hampshire, and Maine, First Edition, by David Klausmeyer, Countryman Press, paperbound, 224 pages, 2001 . . . .$18.95

Trout Streams of Pennsylvania: An Angler's Guide (third edition), by Dwight Landis, Hempstead-Lyndell, paperbound, 256 pages, 2000 . . . .$20.95

Trout Streams of Southern Appalachia: Fly-Casting in Georgia, Kentucky, North Carolina, South Carolina, and Tennessee, Second Edition, by Jimmy Jacobs, Countryman Press, paperbound, 352 pages, 2001 . . . .$19.95

Trout Streams of Southern New England: An Angler's Guide to the Watersheds of Massachusetts, Connecticut, and Rhode Island, by Tom Fuller and Patricia Fuller, Countryman Press, paperbound, 240 pages, 1999 . . . .$18.95

Trout Unlimited's Guide to America's 100 Best Trout Streams, by John Ross, Falcon Publishing Co., paperbound, 353 pages, 1999 . . . .$18.95

Trout Unlimited's Guide to Pennsylvania Limestone Streams (2nd ed.), by A. Joseph Armstrong, Stackpole Books, paperbound, 256 pages, 2000 . . . .$14.95

Virginia Trout Streams: A Guide to Fishing the Blue Ridge Watershed, by Harry Slone, Backcountry Publications, paperbound, 1994 . . . .$32.55

Wisconsin Blue-Ribbon Trout Streams, by R. Chris Halla, Frank Amato Publications, paperbound, 2001 . . . .$24.95

WALLEYE FISHING

Catch More Walleyes, by Mark Romanack, Krause Publications, paperbound, 256 pages $19.95

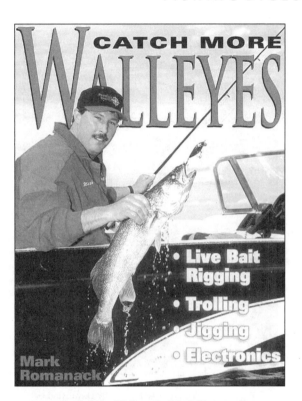

Catch More Walleyes by Mark Romanack

Walleye Wisdom: An In-Fisherman Handbook of Strategies by Al Linder, Dave Csanda, Tony Dean, Ron Linder, Bob Ripley and Doug Stange

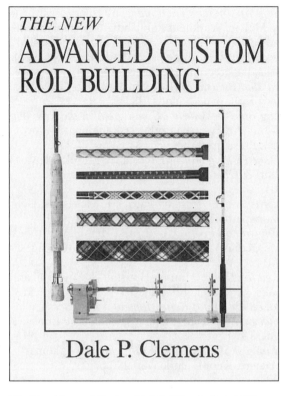

The New Advanced Custom Rod Building by Dale P. Clemens

Fishing for Dummies by Peter Kaminsky

Successful Walleye Fishing, by Freshwater Angler, Creative Publishing International, paperbound, 160 pages, 1999 . . . .$21.95
Walleye Fishing Simplified, by Ed Inman, Lenox Dick andGordon Steinmetz, Frank Amato Publications, paperbound, 106 pages, 1999 . . . .$9.95
Walleye Wisdom : An In-Fisherman Handbook of Strategies, by Al Lindner, paperbound, 1994 . . . .$11.95

FISHING COLLECTIBLES

19th Century Fishing Lures: A Collector's Guide to U.S. Lures Manufactured Prior to 1901, by Alan Carter, Collector Books, hardcover, 304 pages, 2000 . . . .$29.95
The Angler's Life: Collecting and Traditions, by Larry Sheehan, Clarkson Potter, hardcover, 240 pages, 2000 . . . .$50
Antique & Collectible Fishing Reels: Identification, Evaluation, and Maintenance, by Harold Jellison and Daniel B. Homel, Forest Park Publishing, paperbound, 144 pages, 1998 . . . .$23.95
Classic Fishing Lures: And Angling Collectibles, by Daniel B. Homel, Forrest Park Publishing, paperbound, 144 pages, 1997 . . . .$19.95
Collecting Fishing: Instant Expert, by Carl Caiati, Alliance Publishing, paperbound, 130 pages, 1997 . . . .$14
Collector's Guide to Antique Fishing Tackle, by Silvio Taccalabi and Sylvio Calabi, Wellfleet, hardcover, 224 pages, 1996 . . . .$19
Collector's Guide to Creek Chub: Lures & Collectibles, by Harold E. Smith, Collector Books, 176 pages, 1997 . . . .$24.95
Fishing Lure Collectibles : An Identification and Value Guide to the Most Collectible Antique Fishing Lures (Fishing Lure Collectibles, 2nd Ed), by Dudley Murphy and Rick Edmisten, Collector Books, hardcover, 368 pages, 2000 . . . .$29.95
Old Fishing Lures & Tackle, 6th Edition, by Carl F. Luckey and Clyde "The Bassman" Harbin Sr., Krause Publications, paperbound, 768 pages, 2002 . . .$34.95

FISHING EQUIPMENT

Advanced Custom Rod Building, by Dale P. Clemens, New Win Publishing, 348 pages, 1998 . . . . . .$29.95
The Book of the Fly Rod, Hugh Sheringham and John C. Moore editors, Derrydale, paperbound, 192 pages, 1999 . . . .$19.95
The Complete Book of Fishing Knots : Fundamental

Knots/Loop Knots/Joining Knots/Hook, Lure, Swivel and Sinker Knots, Other Useful Knots, by Geoffrey Budworth, The Lyons Press, paperbound, 160 pages, 1999 . . . .$18.95

The Complete Book of Tackle Making, by C. Boyd Pfeiffer, The Lyons Press, paperbound, 544 pages, 1999 . . . .$19.95

Fishing Bamboo, by John Gierach, The Lyons Press, hardcover, 128 pages, 1997 . . . .$19.95

Handcrafting Bamboo Fly Rods, Wayne Cattanach, The Lyons Press, hardcover, 288 pages, 2000 . . . .$50

Handcrafting a Graphite Fly Rod, by Tony Oswald and L.A. Garcia, Frank Amato Publishing, paperbound, 48 pages, 1994 . . . .$15.95

Hook, Line, and Sinker: The Complete Angler's Guide to Terminal Tackle, by Gary Soucie, Henry Holt, paperbound, 477 pages, 1994 . . . .$17

Ingenious Angler: Hundreds of Do-It-Yourself Projects and Tips to Improve Your Fishing Boat and Tackle, by Keith Walters, McGraw-Hill, paperbound, 176 pages, 2001 . . . .$16.95

Luremaking: The Art and Science of Spinnerbaits, Buzzbaits, Jigs, and Other Leadheads, by A.D. Livingston, McGraw-Hill, paperbound, 161 pages, 1993 . . . .$16.95

A Master's Guide to Building a Bamboo Fly Rod, by Everett Garrison and Hoagy B. Carmichael, Meadow Run Press, hardcover, 1994 . . . .$75

The Field & Stream Tackle Care and Repair Handbook, by C. Boyd Pfeiffer, The Lyons Press, paperbound, 128 pages, 1999 . . . .$9.95

Vic Dunaway's Complete Book of Baits, Rigs and Tackle, by Vic Dunaway, Wickstrom Publishing, paperbound, 1998 . . . .$11.95

FISHING LITERATURE

The Best of Hook & Bullet: Fishing Falsities and Hunting Hoaxes from a Magazine That Never Existed, by W. Hardbark McLoughlin, Pubs Overstock, paperbound, 128 pages, 1996 . . . .$14.95

Dogs That Point, Fish That Bite: Outdoor Essays, by Jim Dean, University of North Carolina Press, paperbound, 168 pages, 2000 . . . .$10.95

Down in Bristol Bay: High Tides, Hangovers, and Harrowing Experiences on Alaska's Last Frontier, by Bob Durr, Dunne Books, hardcover, 240 pages, 1999 . . . .$23.95

The Earth Is Enough: Growing Up in a World of Fly Fishing, Trout, & Old Men, by Harry Middleton and Russell Chatham, Pruett Publishing Co., paperbound, 208 pages, 1996 . . . .$18

Fishing: An Angler's Dictionary, by Henry Beard and Roy McKie, Workman Publishing Co., paperbound, 96 pages, 1983 . . . .$7.95

Fishing With the Presidents, by Bill Mares, Stackpole Books, paperbound, 272 pages, 1999 . . . .$14.95

A Fine and Pleasant Misery, by Patrick F. McManus, Henry Holt, paperbound, 1987 . . . .$12

Fishing Bass-Ackwards : Coming Down the Pike With Off-The-Walleye Humor, by Jack Ohman, Willow Creek Press, paperbound, 144 pages, 1995 . . . .$9.95

Go Fish: Fishing Journal, by James Prosek, Stewart Tabori & Chang, hardcover, 144 pages, 2001 . . . .$17.95

The Grasshopper Trap, by Patrick F. McManus, Henry Holt, paperbound, 1986 . . . .$12

Hemingway on Fishing, by Ernest Hemingway (Nick Lyons, editor), Lyons Press, hardcover, 308 pages, 2000 . . . .$29.95

Hooked for Life, by Jimmy Houston, J. Countryman Books, hardcover, 129 pages, 1999 . . . .$13.99

A Jerk on One End: Reflections of a Mediocre Fisherman, by Robert Hughes, Ballantine Books, 128 pages, 1999 . . . .$18.95

The Longest Silence: A Life in Fishing, by Thomas McGuane, Knopf, hardcover, 280 pages, 1999 . . . .$25

Outdoor Life: If Nature Calls...Hang Up!, Outdoor Life magazine, Creative Publishing International, paperbound, 224 pages, 1999 . . . .$14.95

Richard Brautigan's Trout Fishing in America, the Pill versus the Springhill Mine Disaster, and In Watermelon Sugar, by Richard Brautigan, Mariner Books, 138 pages, 1989 . . . .$15

The River Home: An Angler's Explorations, by Jerry Dennis, Dunne Books, hardcover, 1998 . . . .$8.95

A River Runs Through It, by Norman Maclean, University of Chicago Press, 161 pages, 1989 . . . .$27.50

The Secret Lives of Fishermen: More Outdoor Essays, by Jim Dean, University of North Carolina Press, paperbound 176 pages, 2000 . . . .$24.95

Tales of Swordfish and Tuna, by Zane Grey, Derrydale, paperbound, 320 pages, 2000 . . . .$24.95

Tales of the Angler's Eldorado, by Zane Grey, Derrydale, paperbound, 384 pages, 2000 . . . . .$24.95

This Book Is Full of Carp, by Peter Bradley and Jeff Tolbert, Ruminator Books, paperbound, 1997 . . . .$7.95

A Treasury of Hunting & Fishing Humor, James E. Myers editor, Lincoln Herndon, paperbound, 1990 . . . .$10.95

Uncommon Waters: Women Write About Fishing (2nd ed.), Holly Morris editor, Seal Press Feminist Publications, paperbound, 320 pages, 1998 . . .$16.95

Fishing Magazines

Whether an angler likes freshwater, saltwater, fly, trout, bass, or salmon fishing, there's a magazine that can provide articles and tips. Here's a sampling of periodicals available on fishing topics:

American Angler *(fly fishing)*, 160 Benmont Ave., Bennington, VT 05201; Phone: (802) 447-1518; fax (802) 447-2471.

The Angling Report *(travel newsletter)*; 9300 S Dadeland Blvd. #605, Miami, FL 33156; Phone: (305) 670-1361.

BACKCASTS *(A Journal for the Northeastern Council of the Federation of Fly Fishers)*, 600 Warren Road, Bldg.1, Apt. 3-A, Ithaca, NY 14850.

Bassin', NatCom Inc., 15115 S. 76 E. Ave., Bixby, OK 74008; Phone: (918) 491-6100.

Bassmaster , B.A.S.S. Inc., 5845 Carmichael Rd., Montgomery, AL 36117; Phone: (205) 272-9530.

British Columbia Sport Fishing Magazine *(Canadian fishing)*, 909 Jackson Crescent, New Westminster, B.C., Canada, V3L 4S1; Phone: (604) 606-4644.

Crappie *(fishing for crappies)*, Natcom Inc., 15115 S. 76th E. Ave., Bixby, OK 74008; Phone: (918) 491-6100 or (800) 554-1999.

The Fisherman *(New York fishing)*, 14 Ramsey Road, Shirley, NY 11967; Phone: (516) 345-5200.

Fishing Facts Magazine *(freshwater fishing)*, 312 E. Buffalo, Milwaukee, WI 53202; Phone: (414) 273-0021.

Fishing World *(salt and freshwater fishing)*, KC Publishing, Inc., 700 W. 47th St., Suite 310, Kansas City, MO 64112.

Fly Fisherman, Cowles Magazines, 6405 Flank Drive, P.O. Box 8200, Harrisburg, PA 17105-8200; Phone: (717) 657-9555.

Fly Rod and Reel Magazine *(fly fishing)*, Down East Enterprises, Inc., Rt. 1, Roxmont, Rockport, ME 04856; Phone: (207) 594-9544.

Fly Tyer, 160 Benmont Ave., Bennington, VT 05201; Phone: (802) 447-1518, fax (802) 447-2471.

Flyfishing, Frank Amato Publications, P.O. Box 82112, Portland, OR 97282; Phone: (503) 653-8151.

In-Fisherman *(freshwater fishing)*, In-Fisherman Inc., Two In Fisherman Drive, Brainerd, MN 56401; Phone: (218) 829-1648.

Marlin (billfishing), World Publications, Inc., 330 W. Canton Ave., Winter Park, FL 32789; Phone: (407) 628-4802.

Nor'east Saltwater, 732 Smithtown By-Pass, Suite 301, Smithtown, NY 11787; Phone: (631) 863-0170; Fax: (631) 543-1492.

North American Fisherman, North American Outdoor Group, Inc., 12301 Whitewater Drive, Suite 260, Minnetonka, MN 55343; Phone (612) 936-0555.

The PanAngler, 5348 W. Vermont St. Suite 300A, Indianapolis, IN 46224; Phone: (800) 533-4353; fax (317) 227-6803

Pike & Muskie Magazine, BroadScape, Inc., P.O. Box 387, Ashland, MA 01721.

Salmon Trout Steelheader, P.O. Box 82112, Portland, OR 97282; Phone: (503) 653-8108.

Saltwater Fly Fishing, 160 Benmont Ave., Bennington, VT 05201; Phone: (802) 447-1518; fax (802) 447-2471.

Salt Water Sportsman, 263 Summer St., Boston, MA 02210; Phone: (617) 303-3660 Fax: (617) 303-3661; e-mail: editor@saltwatersportsman.com.

Sport Fishing *(saltwater fishing)*, World Publications, Inc., 330 W. Canton Ave., Winter Park, FL 32789; Phone: (407) 628-4802

TROUT *(The official magazine of Trout Unlimited)*, c/o Trout Unlimited, 1500 Wilson Blvd., Suite 310, Arlington, VA 22209-2404; Phone: (703) 284-9412; fax (703) 284-9400.

Tournament Angler News, P.O. Box 1989, Lindale, TX 75771; Phone: (903) 882-8877; fax (903) 882-3110.

Walleye In-Sider, In-Fisherman Inc., Two In Fisherman Drive, Brainerd, MN 56401; Phone: (218) 829-1648.

Walleye Magazine, P.O. Box 40210, Cleveland, OH 44140; Phone: (216) 333-9494.

Warmwater Fly Fishing, 160 Benmont Ave., Bennington, VT 05201; Phone: (802) 447-1518; fax (802) 447-2471

Chapter Four: The Digest

International Game Fish Association World Record Fish

The International Game Fish Association Fishing Hall of Fame & Museum, located in Sportsman's Park, Fla., is the world headquarters for the IGFA and home to a world-class museum featuring both traditional and interactive exhibits that capture the thrill, beauty, and universal appeal of recreational fishing.

IGFA maintains and publishes world records for saltwater, freshwater, fly fishing catches, U.S. state freshwater records, and junior angler records, awarding certificates of recognition to each record holder. Recognized as the official keeper of world saltwater fishing records since 1939, IGFA entered the field of freshwater record keeping when Field & Stream transferred its 68 years of records to the association in 1978. The equipment and fishing regulations adopted worldwide are formulated, updated, and published by IGFA to promote sporting angling practices, to establish uniform rules for world record catches, and to provide angling guidelines for use in tournaments and other group fishing activities. Rules and regulations for registering world record fish can be found on the Web site www.igfa.org.

The 60,000 square foot, three-story museum building, designed to appeal to the entire family, contains five galleries, a theater, the Fishing Hall of Fame, an outdoor marina, a 3.5-acre wetlands, meeting room facilities, and a one-of-a-kind research library. Visitors begin their museum experience in the Orientation Theater with its larger-than-life sights and sounds. Then, children can discover the fun of fishing in the Discovery Room, while adults experience the thrill of trying to catch a thousand-pound marlin (and four other species) on interactive fishing simulators in The Catch Gallery. The journey continues to the Marina, where an assortment of fishing boats are on display; the Legacy Gallery, which traces the history of recreational angling; and the intriguing Fish Gallery, where visitors experience first-hand what it is like to be a fish.

Junior Angler Program

The IGFA Junior Angler World Record Program kicked off in January 1997. Since that time, more than 700 junior world records have been approved in 31 countries. The program instills ethical and conservation-oriented fishing practices in today's youth by encouraging them to release their catches. Junior anglers are allowed to weigh their catch on a certified portable scale, and release their catch alive after taking the proper measurements and photos. The program also awards monthly prizes for the heaviest saltwater and heaviest freshwater fish caught in each junior world record division. Winners are listed in the International Junior Angler newsletter, in the World Record Game Fishes book, and on the IGFA Web site. The junior section of www.igfa.org is an interactive educational tool for all young people; it is loaded with fun facts, games, printable versions of record application forms, photos and letters, record updates, kids' quotes, fishing tips, and much more.

Greats hall: Dozens of huge mounted fish hang from the ceiling of the IGFA Museum.

All-Tackle Records
(as of September, 2002)

Species	Weight	Place of Catch	Date	Angler
Albacore	40.00 kg (88 lb 2 oz)	Gran Canaria, Canary Islands, Spain	Nov. 19, 1977	Siegfried Dickemann
Amberjack, greater	70.59 kg (155 lb 10 oz)	Challenger Bank, Bermuda	June 24, 1981	Joseph Dawson
Amberjack, greater	70.64 kg (155 lb 12 oz)	Bermuda	Aug. 16, 1992	Larry Trott
Angelfish, gray	1.83 kg (4 lb 0 oz)	South Beach Jetty, Miami, Florida, USA	July 12, 1999	Rene G. de Dios
Angler	57.50 kg (126 lb 12 oz)	Sagnefiorden, Hoyanger, Norway	July 4, 1996	Gunnar Thorsteinsen
Ara	2.00 kg (4 lb 6 oz)	Kshima, Ibaraki-ken, Japan	Jan. 30, 2000	Masato Ishizuka
Arawana	4.60 kg (10 lb 2 oz)	Puraquequara Lake, Amazon, Brazil	Feb. 3, 1990	Gilberto Fernandes
Argentine, greater	0.70 kg (1 lb 8 oz)	Hardangerfjord, Norway	Aug. 6, 2001	Sandra Marquard
Asp	5.66 kg (12 lb 7 oz)	Lake Vanern, Sweden	Sept. 25, 1993	Jan-Erik Skoglund
Ayamekasago	2.50 kg (5 lb 8 oz)	Irozaki, Shizuoka, Japan	Aug. 13, 1998	Mikio Suzuki
Barb, giant	47.00 kg (103 lb 9 oz)	Bung Sam Lan Lake, Thailand	Nov. 19, 2001	Arnout Terlouw
Barb, golden belly	1.40 kg (3 lb 1 oz)	Srinakarin Dam, Thailand	Apr. 28, 2002	Tsang Sau Yin
Barb, golden belly	1.40 kg (3 lb 1 oz)	Srinakarin Dam, Thailand	Apr. 28, 2002	Jean-Francois Helias
Barb, hampala	5.40 kg (11 lb 14 oz)	Temengor Lake, State of Perak, Malaysia	Mar. 3, 2002	Lye Chuan Hong
Barb, Smith's	0.80 kg (1 lb 12 oz)	Srinakarin Dam, Thailand	May 2, 2002	Jean-Francois Helias
Barbel	2.55 kg (5 lb 10 oz)	Rhine River, Germany	Sept. 12, 1990	Marc David Hartmann
Barenose, bigeye	5.89 kg (13 lb 0 oz)	Otec Beach, Kailua, Kona, Hawaii, USA	July 12, 1992	Rex C. Bigg
Barracuda, blackfin	7.14 kg (15 lb 12 oz)	Puerto Quetzal, Guatemala	June 10, 1995	Estuardo Vila S.
Barracuda, great	38.55 kg (85 lb 0 oz)	Christmas Island, Republic of Kiribati	Apr. 11, 1992	John W. Helfrich
Barracuda, great	38.50 kg (84 lb 14 oz)	Scarborough Shoals, Philippines	Mar. 1, 1991	Jessie D. Cordova
Barracuda, Guinean	30.30 kg (66 lb 12 oz)	Mondia Branca, Luanda, Angola	Feb. 24, 1998	Nisa Ekberg
Barracuda, Mexican	9.52 kg (21 lb 0 oz)	Phantom Isle, Costa Rica	Mar. 27, 1987	E. Greg Kent
Barracuda, Pacific	12.02 kg (26 lb 8 oz)	Playa Matapalo, Costa Rica	Jan. 3, 1999	Doug Hettinger
Barracuda, pickhandle	11.50 kg (25 lb 5 oz)	Scottburgh, Natal, Republic of South Africa	July 3, 1996	Demetrios Stamatis
Barracuda, yellowmouth	8.20 kg (18 lb 1 oz)	Isla Graciosa, Canary Islands, Spain	Aug. 26, 1994	Guiseppe Parini
Barracuda, yellowmouth	8.35 kg (18 lb 6 oz)	Isla Graciosa, Canary Islands, Spain	Oct. 4, 2001	Elide Legnani
Barramundi	37.85 kg (83 lb 7 oz)	Lake Tinaroo, N. Queensland, Australia	Sept. 23, 1999	David Powell
Bass, barred sand	5.98 kg (13 lb 3 oz)	Huntington Beach, California, USA	Aug. 29, 1988	Robert Halal
Bass, black sea	4.65 kg (10 lb 4 oz)	Virginia Beach, Virginia, USA	Jan. 1, 2000	Allan P. Paschall
Bass, European	9.48 kg (20 lb 14 oz)	Cap d'Agde, France	Sept. 8, 1999	Robert Mari
Bass, giant sea	255.60 kg (563 lb 8 oz)	Anacapa Island, California, USA	Aug. 20, 1968	James D. McAdam, Jr.
Bass, goldspotted sand	2.72 kg (6 lb 0 oz)	San Francisco, Baja California, Mexico	June 13, 1993	Charles F. Ulrich
Bass, goldspotted sand	2.72 kg (6 lb 0 oz)	Vista del Oro, Mexico	Nov. 13, 1999	William E. Favor
Bass, Guadalupe	1.67 kg (3 lb 11 oz)	Lake Travis, Austin, Texas, USA	Sept. 25, 1983	Allen Christenson, Jr.

This Guinean Barracuda was caught in Mondia Branca by Nisa Ekberg on Mar. 1, 1991. It measured in at 4.7 ft. 66.6 lbs.

This Albacore was caught at Gran Canaria, Canary Islands by Siegfried Dickemann on Nov. 19, 1977. It measured in at 88 lb 2 oz.

Photo courtesy of IGFA

263

THE DIGEST

All-Tackle Records, *continued*

Species	Weight	Place of Catch	Date	Angler
Bass, Guadalupe x smallmouth	1.90 kg (4 lb 3 oz)	Blanco River, Texas, USA	June 18, 1995	John Ryan Weaver
Bass, kelp (calico)	6.54 kg (14 lb 7 oz)	Newport Beach, California, USA	Oct. 2, 1993	Thomas Murphy
Bass, largemouth	10.09 kg (22 lb 4 oz)	Montgomery Lake, Georgia, USA	June 2, 1932	George W. Perry
Bass, leather	12.47 kg (27 lb 8 oz)	Isla Clarion, Revillagigedo Islands, Mexico	Jan. 26, 1988	Allan J. Ristori
Bass, Ozark	0.45 kg (1 lb 0 oz)	Bull Shoals Lake, Arkansas, USA	May 13, 1997	Gary Nelson
Bass, Roanoke	0.62 kg (1 lb 5 oz)	Nottoway River, Virginia, USA	Nov. 11, 1991	Thomas F. Elkins
Bass, rock	1.36 kg (3 lb 0 oz)	Lake Erie, Pennsylvania, USA	June 18, 1998	Herbert G. Ratner, Jr.
Bass, rock	1.36 kg (3 lb 0 oz)	York River, Ontario, Canada	Aug. 1, 1974	Peter Gulgin
Bass, shadow	0.82 kg (1 lb 13 oz)	Spring River, Arkansas, USA	July 5, 1999	James E. Baker
Bass, shoal	3.99 kg (8 lb 12 oz)	Apalachicola River, Florida, USA	Jan. 28, 1995	Carl W. Davis
Bass, smallmouth	4.93 kg (10 lb 14 oz)	Dale Hollow, Tennessee, USA	Apr. 24, 1969	John T. Gorman
Bass, splittail	0.68 kg (1 lb 8 oz)	Playa Zancudo, Costa Rica	June 10, 1995	Craig Whitehead, MD
Bass, spotted	4.65 kg (10 lb 4 oz)	Pine Flat Lake, California, USA	Apr. 21, 2001	Bryan Shishido
Bass, spotted sand	0.90 kg (2 lb 0 oz)	Playa Hermosa, Mexico	Mar. 30, 1997	William E. Favor
Bass, striped	35.60 kg (78 lb 8 oz)	Atlantic City, New Jersey, USA	Sept. 21, 1982	Albert R. McReynolds
Bass, striped (landlocked)	30.61 kg (67 lb 8 oz)	O'Neill Forebay, Los Banos, California, USA	May 7, 1992	Hank Ferguson
Bass, Suwannee	1.75 kg (3 lb 14 oz)	Suwannee River, Florida, USA	Mar. 2, 1985	Ronnie Everett
Bass, white	3.09 kg (6 lb 13 oz)	Lake Orange, Orange, Virginia, USA	July 31, 1989	Ronald L. Sprouse
Bass, whiterock	12.38 kg (27 lb 5 oz)	Greers Ferry Lake, Arkansas, USA	Apr. 24, 1997	Jerald C. Shaum
Bass, yellow	1.16 kg (2 lb 9 oz)	Duck River, Waverly, Tennessee, USA	Feb. 27, 1998	John T. Chappell
Bass, yellow (hybrid)	1.51 kg (3 lb 5 oz)	Big Cypress Bayou, Marion County, Texas, USA	Mar. 27, 1991	Patrick Collin Myers
Biara	2.10 kg (4 lb 10 oz)	Xingu River, Brazil	Apr. 21, 2000	Marcio Mattos Borges de Oliveira
Bicuda	4.76 kg (10 lb 8 oz)	Xingu River, Brazil	Apr. 16, 2000	Marcio Martins Loureiro
Bigeye	2.85 kg (6 lb 4 oz)	Baja da Guanabara, Rio de Janeiro, Brazil	Aug. 30, 1997	Jayme Garcia
Binga	0.51 kg (1 lb 2 oz)	Maleri Island, Lake Malawi	Nov. 30, 1996	Garry Seymer Whitcher
Blackfish, smallscale	3.40 kg (7 lb 7 oz)	Hachijokojima, Hachijo Island, Japan	Jan. 8, 1998	Papa Otsuru
Bludger	9.70 kg (21 lb 6 oz)	Bartholmeu Dias, Mozambique	June 17, 1997	Joh Haasbroek
Blue, big	1.05 kg (2 lb 5 oz)	Lake Malawi, Malawi	Nov. 4, 2000	Deon R. Haigh
Bluefish	14.40 kg (31 lb 12 oz)	Hatteras, North Carolina, USA	Jan. 30, 1972	James M. Hussey
Bluegill	2.15 kg (4 lb 12 oz)	Ketona Lake, Alabama, USA	Apr. 9, 1950	T. S. Hudson

This Bluefish was caught in Hatteras, North Carolina by James M. Hussey on Jan. 30, 1972. It measured in at 31 lb 12 ozs.

CHAPTER FOUR

All-Tackle Records, *continued*

Species	Weight	Place of Catch	Date	Angler
Bocaccio	10.09 kg (22 lb 4 oz)	Elfin Cove, Alaska, USA	Aug. 25, 2001	Gaylord A. Saetre
Bonefish	8.61 kg (19 lb 0 oz)	Zululand, Republic of South Africa	May 26, 1962	Brian W. Batchelor
Bonito, Atlantic	8.30 kg (18 lb 4 oz)	Faial Island, Azores	July 8, 1953	D. Gama Higgs
Bonito, Australian	9.40 kg (20 lb 11 oz)	Montague Island, N.S.W., Australia	Apr. 1, 1978	Bruce Conley
Bonito, leaping	0.96 kg (2 lb 2 oz)	Macleay River, Australia	May 7, 1995	Wayne Colling
Bonito, Pacific	9.62 kg (21 lb 3 oz)	Malibu, California, USA	July 30, 1978	Gino M. Picciolo
Bonito, striped	10.65 kg (23 lb 8 oz)	Victoria, Mahe, Seychelles	Feb. 19, 1975	Anne Cochain
Bowfin	9.75 kg (21 lb 8 oz)	Forest Lake, Florence, South Carolina, USA	Jan. 29, 1980	Robert L. Harmon
Bream	6.01 kg (13 lb 3 oz)	Hagbyan Creek, Sweden	May 11, 1984	Luis Kilian Rasmussen
Bream, African red	5.55 kg (12 lb 3 oz)	Nouadhibou, Mauritania	Mar. 13, 1986	Bernard Defago
Bream, black	6.17 kg (13 lb 9 oz)	Lake Tinaroo, Queensland, Australia	Jan. 16, 1997	Brian G. Seawright
Bream, blue-lined large-eye	5.50 kg (12 lb 2 oz)	Amami-oshima, Kagoshima, Japan	May 28, 2000	Hitoshi Suzuki
Bream, collared large-eye	2.72 kg (6 lb 0 oz)	Great Barrier Reef, Cairns, Australia	Oct. 30, 2001	Dennis Triana
Bream, gilthead	7.36 kg (16 lb 3 oz)	Florn Estuary, Brest, France	Oct. 13, 2000	Jean Philippe Serra
Bream, twoband	1.30 kg (2 lb 13 oz)	Europa Point, Gibraltar	Sept. 3, 1995	Ernest Borrell
Bream, white	0.58 kg (1 lb 4 oz)	Nok, Germany	May 19, 1998	Holger Damerius
Brotula, bearded	8.52 kg (18 lb 12 oz)	Destin, Florida, USA	Apr. 10, 1999	Joe M. Dollar
Buffalo, bigmouth	31.89 kg (70 lb 5 oz)	Bastrop, Louisiana, USA	Apr. 21, 1980	Delbert Sisk
Buffalo, black	28.74 kg (63 lb 6 oz)	Mississippi River, Iowa, USA	Aug. 14, 1999	Jim Winters
Buffalo, smallmouth	37.29 kg (82 lb 3 oz)	Athens Lake, Alabama, USA	June 6, 1993	Randy Collins
Bulleye	2.95 kg (6 lb 8 oz)	Rio de Janeiro, Brazil	May 18, 2002	Eduardo Baumeier
Bullhead, black	3.37 kg (7 lb 7 oz)	Mill Pond, Wantagh, Long Island, NY, USA	Aug. 25, 1993	Kevin Kelly
Bullhead, brown	2.74 kg (6 lb 1 oz)	Waterford, New York, USA	Apr. 26, 1998	Bobby Triplett
Bullhead, yellow	1.92 kg (4 lb 4 oz)	Mormon Lake, Arizona, USA	May 11, 1984	Emily Williams
Bullseye, longfinned	2.08 kg (4 lb 9 oz)	Rio de Janeiro, Brazil	Apr. 4, 1996	Eduardo Baumeier
Burbot	8.50 kg (18 lb 11 oz)	Angenmanalren, Sweden	Oct. 22, 1996	Margit Agren
Buri (Japanese amberjack)	17.10 kg (37 lb 11 oz)	Setozaki, Shirahama, Wakayama, Japan	Jan. 4, 1999	Hideyuki Kitamura
Burrfish, striped	0.63 kg (1 lb 6 oz)	Delaware Bay, New Jersey, USA	Aug. 13, 1989	Donna L. Ludlam
Cabezon	10.43 kg (23 lb 0 oz)	Juan De Fuca Strait, Washington, USA	Aug. 4, 1990	Wesley S. Hunter
Captainfish	12.00 kg (26 lb 7 oz)	Archipelago dos Bijagos, Guinea Bissau	May 17, 1998	Eric Legris
Carp, bighead	28.09 kg (61 lb 15 oz)	Old Hickory Lake, Tennessee, USA	Mar. 27, 2002	Rick Richard
Carp, black	18.50 kg (40 lb 12 oz)	Edo River, Chiba, Japan	Apr. 1, 2000	Kenichi Hosoi
Carp, common	34.35 kg (75 lb 11 oz)	Lac de St. Cassien, France	May 21, 1987	Leo van der Gugten
Carp, crucian	2.30 kg (5 lb 1 oz)	Lago Caldaro, Kalterersee, Italy	July 16, 1997	Jorge Marquard
Carp, grass	31.18 kg (68 lb 12 oz)	Somerland's Pond, North Carolina, USA	June 8, 1998	David Stowell
Carp, silver	16.00 kg (35 lb 4 oz)	Danube River, Austria	Nov. 10, 1983	Josef Windholz
Carpsucker, river	3.48 kg (7 lb 11 oz)	Canadian Co., Oklahoma, USA	Apr. 18, 1990	W.C. (Bill) Kenyon
Catfish, amur	2.30 kg (5 lb 1 oz)	Raikougawa, Shizuoka, Japan	May 21, 2001	Hiromitsu Fukasawa
Catfish, blue	52.95 kg (116 lb 12 oz)	Mississippi River, Arkansas, USA	Aug. 3, 2001	Charles Ashley, Jr.
Catfish, channel	26.30 kg (58 lb 0 oz)	Santee-Cooper Reservoir, South Carolina, USA	July 7, 1964	W. B. Whaley
Catfish, chao phraya giant	9.00 kg (19 lb 13 oz)	Bung Sam Lan Lake, Thailand	Mar. 25, 2002	Jean-Francois Helias
Catfish, duckbill	1.30 kg (2 lb 13 oz)	Xingu River, Brazil	Apr. 20, 2000	Capt. Kdu Magalhaes
Catfish, Eurasian	17.20 kg (37 lb 14 oz)	Imazuhama, Lake Biwa, Shiga, Japan	July 4, 1997	Shoji Matsuura

All-Tackle Records, *continued*

Species	Weight	Place of Catch	Date	Angler
Catfish, flathead	55.79 kg (123 lb 0 oz)	Elk City Reservoir, Independence, Kansas, USA	May 14, 1998	Ken Paulie
Catfish, flatwhiskered	7.68 kg (16 lb 15 oz)	Xingu River, Brazil	Aug. 7, 2001	Ian-Arthur de Sulocki
Catfish, forked tail	2.30 kg (5 lb 1 oz)	Temmengor Dam, Malaysia	June 14, 2001	Jean-Francois Helias
Catfish, gafftopsail	4.36 kg (9 lb 10 oz)	Heron Bay, Mississippi, USA	Aug. 26, 2000	Shane A. Ardis
Catfish, giant (Mekong)	40.10 kg (88 lb 6 oz)	Benjamin Lake, Sukhapibal, Thailand	May 18, 2001	Gerard Parruite
Catfish, gilded	38.80 kg (85 lb 8 oz)	Amazon River, Amazon, Brazil	Nov. 15, 1986	Gilberto Fernandes
Catfish, granulated	6.50 kg (14 lb 5 oz)	Xingu River, Mato Grosso, Brazil	Oct. 16, 1999	Kdu Magalhaes
Catfish, grey eel	8.50 kg (18 lb 11 oz)	Nakorn Nayok River, Thailand	Apr. 4, 2002	Anongnart Sungwichien
Catfish, hardhead	1.50 kg (3 lb 5 oz)	Mays Marina, Sebastian, Florida, USA	Apr. 18, 1993	Amanda Steed
Catfish, redtail (pirarara)	44.20 kg (97 lb 7 oz)	Amazon River, Amazon, Brazil	July 16, 1988	Gilberto Fernandes
Catfish, ripsaw	11.00 kg (24 lb 4 oz)	Xingu River, Mato Grosso, Brazil	Oct. 19, 1999	Kdu Magalhaes
Catfish, sharptoothed	36.00 kg (79 lb 5 oz)	Orange River, Upington, Republic of South Africa	Dec. 5, 1992	Hennie Moller
Catfish, smoothmouth sea	10.00 kg (22 lb 0 oz)	Archipelago des Bijagos, Guinea Bissau	Apr. 3, 2002	Jacques Sibieude
Catfish, striped (swai)	15.50 kg (34 lb 2 oz)	Bung Sam Lan Lake, Thailand	Mar. 22, 2002	Daniel R. Walter
Catfish, walking	1.19 kg (2 lb 10 oz)	Delray Beach, Florida, USA	July 15, 2001	Patrick Keough
Catfish, white	9.75 kg (21 lb 8 oz)	Gorton Pond, East Lyme, Connecticut, USA	Apr. 22, 2001	Thomas Urquhart
Catshark, smallspotted	1.32 kg (2 lb 14 oz)	Mausundvar, Norway	Dec. 18, 1998	Alan Steinsvoll
Char, Arctic	14.77 kg (32 lb 9 oz)	Tree River, Canada	July 30, 1981	Jeffery L. Ward
Char, whitespotted	7.37 kg (16 lb 4 oz)	Samarga River, Russia	Aug. 20, 1994	Pete Moring
Chilipepper	1.54 kg (3 lb 6 oz)	San Clemente Island, California, USA	Mar. 11, 2000	George Bogen
Chilipepper	1.54 kg (3 lb 6 oz)	San Clemente Island, California, USA	Mar. 11, 2000	Stephen D. Grossberg
Chinamanfish	13.20 kg (29 lb 1 oz)	Dampier, Australia	Mar. 8, 1996	Mark Cottrell
Chub, Bermuda	6.01 kg (13 lb 4 oz)	Ft. Pierce Inlet, Florida, USA	Mar. 5, 1997	Sam Baum
Chub, European	2.62 kg (5 lb 12 oz)	Helige, Gemla, Sweden	July 26, 1987	Luis Kilian Rasmussen
Chub, gray sea	1.85 kg (4 lb 1 oz)	Midway Islands, Pacific Ocean	July 26, 1998	George Handgis
Chub, yellow	3.85 kg (8 lb 8 oz)	Sabine Pass, Texas, USA	May 29, 1994	Stephen L. McDonald
Cichlid, Mayan	1.13 kg (2 lb 8 oz)	Holiday Park, Florida, USA	Feb. 20, 1999	Jay Wright, Jr.

This Flathead Catfish was caught in Elk City Reservoir, Independence, Kansas by Ken Paulie on May 14, 1998. It measured in at 123 lb 0 oz.

All-Tackle Records, *continued*

Species	Weight	Place of Catch	Date	Angler
Cichlid, parrot	0.73 kg (1 lb 9 oz)	Rio Negro, Brazil	Nov. 7, 1999	James B. Wise, M.D.
Cisco	3.35 kg (7 lb 6 oz)	North Cross Bay, Cedar Lake, Manitoba, Canada	Apr. 11, 1986	Randy K. Huff
Cobia	61.50 kg (135 lb 9 oz)	Shark Bay, W.A., Australia	July 9, 1985	Peter William Goulding
Cod, Atlantic	44.79 kg (98 lb 12 oz)	Isle of Shoals, New Hampshire, USA	June 8, 1969	Alphonse J. Bielevich
Cod, cow	11.79 kg (26 lb 0 oz)	San Clemente Island, California, USA	Jan. 9, 1999	Stephen D. Grossberg
Cod, Pacific	15.87 kg (35 lb 0 oz)	Unalaska Bay, Alaska, USA	June 16, 1999	Jim Johnson
Conger	60.44 kg (133 lb 4 oz)	Berry Head, South Devon, England	June 5, 1995	Vic Evans
Coralgrouper, blacksaddled	24.20 kg (53 lb 5 oz)	Hahajima, Ogasawara Island, Tokyo, Japan	Sept. 27, 1997	Hideo Morishita
Coralgrouper, highfin	1.20 kg (2 lb 10 oz)	Buso Point, Huon Gulf, Papua New Guinea	May 1, 1994	Justin Mallett
Coralgrouper, leopard	7.00 kg (15 lb 6 oz)	Bourake, New Caledonia, France	Jan. 26, 2002	Patrick Sebile
Corb (shi drum)	3.10 kg (6 lb 13 oz)	Corse, France	June 7, 2001	Patrick Sebile
Corbina, California	2.95 kg (6 lb 8 oz)	Dana Harbor, California, USA	May 23, 1997	Scott Matthews
Coris, yellowstripe	4.62 kg (10 lb 3 oz)	Keahole Point, Kailua Kona, Hawaii, USA	Jan. 1, 1996	Rex C. Bigg
Cornetfish, bluespotted	1.00 kg (2 lb 3 oz)	Dania Beach, Florida, USA	Oct. 11, 2001	Jean Paul Lafage
Corvina, hybrid	4.76 kg (10 lb 8 oz)	Calaveras Lake, San Antonio, Texas, USA	Jan. 27, 1987	Norma E. Cleary
Corvina, orangemouth	24.60 kg (54 lb 3 oz)	Sabana Grande, Guayaquil, Ecuador	July 29, 1992	Felipe Estrada E.
Corvina, shortfin	3.15 kg (6 lb 15 oz)	Playa Hermosa, Mexico	Apr. 26, 1998	William E. Favor
Crappie, black	2.05 kg (4 lb 8 oz)	Kerr Lake, Virginia, USA	Mar. 1, 1981	L. Carl Herring, Jr.
Crappie, white	2.35 kg (5 lb 3 oz)	Enid Dam, Mississippi, USA	July 31, 1957	Fred L. Bright
Croaker, Atlantic	2.49 kg (5 lb 8 oz)	Dauphin Island, Alabama, USA	Aug. 26, 2000	Carl N. Billings
Croaker, Boeseman	7.00 kg (15 lb 6 oz)	Chaopraya River, Pakkred, Thailand	Nov. 18, 1998	Jean-Francois Helias
Croaker, longneck	15.02 kg (33 lb 2 oz)	Banjul, Gambia	Mar. 25, 1998	Alberto Madaria Hernandez
Croaker, S. A. silver	4.50 kg (9 lb 14 oz)	Xingu River, Brazil	Sept. 7, 2000	Capt. Kdu Magalhaes
Croaker, spotfin	1.72 kg (3 lb 12 oz)	Black's Beach, La Jolla, California, USA	Apr. 18, 2001	Ervin S. Wheeler
Croaker, yellowfin	2.49 kg (5 lb 8 oz)	East Cape, Mexico	May 22, 2001	Capt. Jay Wright, Jr.
Cui-ui	2.72 kg (6 lb 0 oz)	Pyramid Lake, Arizona, USA	June 30, 1997	Mike Berg
Cunner	0.99 kg (2 lb 3 oz)	Two Lights State Park, Maine, USA	July 7, 1999	Joseph Henry Pinault
Cusk	16.30 kg (35 lb 14 oz)	Langesund, Norway	Apr. 26, 1998	Fredrik Amdal
Cutlassfish, Atlantic	3.68 kg (8 lb 1 oz)	Rio de Janeiro, Brazil	Sept. 6, 1997	Felipe Ricciulli Soares
Dab (Kliesche)	0.57 kg (1 lb 4 oz)	East Sea, Kappeln, Germany	Sept. 20, 1998	Holger Damerius
Dentex	14.25 kg (31 lb 6 oz)	Los Cristianos Tenerife, Canary Islands	Jan. 29, 1999	Torsten Wetzel
Dentex, pink	13.80 kg (30 lb 6 oz)	Gibraltar	Apr. 5, 1996	P.A. Dunham
Doctorfish	0.57 kg (1 lb 4 oz)	Stetson Rock, Texas, USA	Apr. 14, 1997	Jerry Dee McCullin
Dogfish, small-spotted	4.33 kg (9 lb 8 oz)	La Baule, France	Oct. 13, 2001	Lionel Minier
Dogfish, smooth	12.15 kg (26 lb 12 oz)	Galveston, Texas, USA	Mar. 2, 1998	George A. Flores
Dogfish, spiny	7.14 kg (15 lb 12 oz)	Kenmare Bay, Co. Kerry, Ireland	May 26, 1989	Horst Willi Muller
Dolly Varden	9.46 kg (20 lb 14 oz)	Wulik River, Alaska, USA	July 7, 2001	Raz Reid
Dolphinfish	39.91 kg (88 lb 0 oz)	Highbourne Cay, Exuma, Bahamas	May 5, 1998	Richard D. Evans
Dorado	23.30 kg (51 lb 5 oz)	Toledo (Corrientes), Argentina	Sept. 27, 1984	Armando Giudice
Drum, black	51.28 kg (113 lb 1 oz)	Lewes, Delaware, USA	Sept. 15, 1975	Gerald M. Townsend
Drum, freshwater	24.72 kg (54 lb 8 oz)	Nickajack Lake, Tennessee, USA	Apr. 20, 1972	Benny E. Hull
Drum, red	42.69 kg (94 lb 2 oz)	Avon, North Carolina, USA	Nov. 7, 1984	David G. Deuel
Durgon, black	0.68 kg (1 lb 8 oz)	Port Lucaya, Bahamas	Feb. 3, 2002	Dennis Triana
Eagleray, plain	13.93 kg (30 lb 11 oz)	Himeji Port, Hyogo, Japan	Aug. 19, 2000	Masahiro Oomori
Eel, American	4.21 kg (9 lb 4 oz)	Cape May, New Jersey, USA	Nov. 9, 1995	Jeff Pennick
Eel, European	3.59 kg (7 lb 14 oz)	River Lyckeby, Sweden	Aug. 8, 1988	Luis Kilian Rasmussen
Eel, European	3.60 kg (7 lb 14 oz)	River Aare, Buren, Switzerland	July 10, 1992	Christoph Lave
Eel, Japanese	0.76 kg (1 lb 10 oz)	Kandase River, Tokushima, Japan	Aug. 12, 2000	Hiroyoshi Yamada
Eel, king snake	23.58 kg (52 lb 0 oz)	Gulf of Mexico, Texas, USA	Feb. 11, 1997	Patrick L. Lemire
Eel, marbled	16.36 kg (36 lb 1 oz)	Hazelmere Dam, Durban, South Africa	June 10, 1984	Ferdie Van Nooten
Eel, shortfin	7.48 kg (16 lb 8 oz)	Lake Bolac, Victoria, Australia	Nov. 17, 1998	Bernard Murphy
Emperor, longface	4.85 kg (10 lb 11 oz)	Christmas Island, Republic of Kiribati	Oct. 16, 1988	Jeff Konn

All-Tackle Records, *continued*

Species	Weight	Place of Catch	Date	Angler
Emperor, spangled	8.40 kg (18 lb 8 oz)	Anijima, Ogasawara Island, Japan	Dec. 16, 1996	Osamu Toji
Emperor, yellowlip	5.44 kg (12 lb 0 oz)	Lifuka Island, Kingdom of Tonga	Nov. 25, 1991	Peter Dunn-Rankin
Escolar	28.50 kg (62 lb 13 oz)	El Hiero, Spain	Sept. 8, 1996	Joep Stolwyk
Fallfish	1.61 kg (3 lb 8 oz)	Lake Winnipesaukee, New Hampshire, USA	July 12, 1991	John Conti
Featherback, clown	4.95 kg (10 lb 14 oz)	Srinakarine Lake, Thailand	July 7, 2001	Gerard Chen Shang
Filefish, scrawled	2.15 kg (4 lb 11 oz)	Pompano Beach, Florida, USA	Jan. 20, 1998	Jonathan Mark Angel
Filefish, unicorn	2.71 kg (5 lb 15 oz)	Orange Beach, Alabama, USA	Mar. 10, 1993	Yvonne Hanek
Flathead, bar-tailed	3.50 kg (7 lb 11 oz)	Amami-oshima, Kagoshima, Japan	July 2, 2001	Yasunori Haraguchi
Flathead, dusky	6.33 kg (13 lb 15 oz)	Wallis Lake, Forster, N.S.W., Australia	June 7, 1997	Glen Edwards
Flier	0.56 kg (1 lb 4 oz)	Little River, Spring Lake, North Carolina, USA	Aug. 24, 1988	Dr. R. D. Snipes
Flier	0.56 kg (1 lb 4 oz)	Lowndes Co., Georgia, USA	Feb. 26, 1996	Curt Anthony Brooks
Flounder, European	1.20 kg (2 lb 10 oz)	Bua Harbor, Halland County, Sweden	Sept. 3, 1993	Henning Madsen
Flounder, gulf	2.83 kg (6 lb 4 oz)	Dauphin Island, Alabama, USA	Nov. 2, 1996	Don Davis
Flounder, marbled	1.15 kg (2 lb 8 oz)	Koshiba, Kanagawa, Japan	Mar. 9, 2002	Junzo Okada
Flounder, olive	9.10 kg (20 lb 0 oz)	Esashi, Hokkaido, Japan	Aug. 19, 1999	Yoshiaki Yamamoto
Flounder, slime (babagarei)	1.76 kg (3 lb 14 oz)	Sendai Bay, Miyagi, Japan	Dec. 28, 1998	Tomoyasu Ishikawa
Flounder, southern	9.33 kg (20 lb 9 oz)	Nassau Sound, Florida, USA	Dec. 23, 1983	Larenza W. Mungin
Flounder, starry	1.70 kg (3 lb 12 oz)	Gastineau Channel, Alaska, USA	July 16, 2000	Mike Gallion
Flounder, summer	10.17 kg (22 lb 7 oz)	Montauk, New York, USA	Sept. 15, 1975	Charles Nappi
Flounder, winter	3.17 kg (7 lb 0 oz)	Fire Island, New York, USA	May 8, 1986	Einar F. Grell
Forkbeard	3.91 kg (8 lb 10 oz)	Mahon-Menorca Island, Spain	Dec. 12, 2000	Ciceron Mercadel Pascual
Forkbeard, greater	3.54 kg (7 lb 12 oz)	Straits of Gibraltar, Gibraltar	July 12, 1997	Susan Anne Holgado
Gar, alligator	126.55 kg (279 lb 0 oz)	Rio Grande, Texas, USA	Dec. 2, 1951	Bill Valverde
Gar, Florida	4.53 kg (10 lb 0 oz)	Florida Everglades, Florida, USA	Jan. 28, 2002	Herbert G. Ratner, Jr.
Gar, longnose	22.82 kg (50 lb 5 oz)	Trinity River, Texas, USA	July 30, 1954	Townsend Miller
Gar, shortnose	2.60 kg (5 lb 12 oz)	Rend Lake, Illinois, USA	July 16, 1995	Donna K. Willmert
Gar, spotted	4.44 kg (9 lb 12 oz)	Lake Mexia, Mexia, Texas, USA	Apr. 7, 1994	Rick Rivard
Gar, tropical	2.89 kg (6 lb 6 oz)	Rio Frio, Los Chiles, Costa Rica	Nov. 22, 1994	John A. Corry
Garpike	1.18 kg (2 lb 9 oz)	La Teste, France	May 14, 2002	David Mesure
Geelbek	14.91 kg (32 lb 14 oz)	Algoa Bay, Port Elizabeth, South Africa	June 16, 1994	Carel Sanders
Gengoro-buna	1.50 kg (3 lb 4 oz)	Chigusagawa, Hyogo, Japan	May 28, 2002	Masahiro Oomori

This Escolar was caught in El Hiero, Spain by Joep Stolwyk on Sept. 8, 1996. It measured in at 62 lb 13 oz.

All-Tackle Records, *continued*

Species	Weight	Place of Catch	Date	Angler
Globefish	4.30 kg (9 lb 7 oz)	Nouadhibou, Mauritania	Mar. 10, 1986	Raphael Levy
Gnomefish (mutsu)	16.10 kg (35 lb 7 oz)	Nanbu, Wakayama, Japan	May 5, 2000	Takayuki Nishioka
Goldeye	1.72 kg (3 lb 13 oz)	Pierre, South Dakota, USA	Aug. 9, 1987	Gary Wayne Heuer
Goldfish	3.00 kg (6 lb 10 oz)	Lake Hodges, California, USA	Apr. 17, 1996	Florentino M. Abena
Goldfish, Asian	1.14 kg (2 lb 8 oz)	Kako River, Hyogo, Japan	Oct. 29, 1994	Masahiro Oomori
Goldfish/Carp hybrid	1.58 kg (3 lb 8 oz)	Cermak Quarry, Lyons, Illinois, USA	Aug. 22, 1990	Donald A. Czyzewski
Goosefish	22.56 kg (49 lb 12 oz)	Perkins Cove, Ogunquit, Maine, USA	July 9, 1991	Nancy Lee Regimbald
Grayling	1.69 kg (3 lb 11 oz)	Dessau, Bavaria, Germany	Sept. 12, 1991	Jean-Paul Pequegnot
Grayling, Arctic	2.69 kg (5 lb 15 oz)	Katseyedie River, N.W.T., Canada	Aug. 16, 1967	Jeanne P. Branson
Graysby	1.13 kg (2 lb 8 oz)	Stetson Rock, Texas, USA	Mar. 2, 1998	George A. Flores
Greenling, fat (ainame)	2.41 kg (5 lb 5 oz)	Todogasaki,, Iwate, Japan	Dec. 29, 1997	Akira Tazawa
Greenling, kelp	1.42 kg (3 lb 2 oz)	Rivers Inlet, British Columbia, Canada	June 23, 1990	Dave Vedder
Greenling, rock	0.83 kg (1 lb 13 oz)	Adak, Alaska, USA	Aug. 15, 1988	George D. Cornish
Grenadier, roundnose	1.69 kg (3 lb 11 oz)	Trondheimsfjorden, Norway	Nov. 26, 1993	Knut Nilsen
Grouper, black	51.71 kg (114 lb 0 oz)	Galveston, Texas, USA	Jan. 2, 1997	Stanely W. Sweet
Grouper, blue & yellow	3.60 kg (7 lb 14 oz)	Sardunia Bay, Port Elizabeth, South Africa	Mar. 22, 1995	Mario Enzio Bruno
Grouper, broomtail	45.35 kg (100 lb 0 oz)	El Muerto Island, Ecuador	Dec. 29, 1998	Ernesto Jouvin
Grouper, brown-marbled	7.65 kg (16 lb 13 oz)	Amami-oshima, Kagoshima, Japan	Sept. 10, 2000	Takumi Matsuda
Grouper, comet	6.70 kg (14 lb 12 oz)	Chichijima, Ogasawara, Tokyo, Japan	Nov. 10, 1998	Jin Tsukada
Grouper, convict (mahata)	62.80 kg (138 lb 7 oz)	Amami-oshima, Kagoshima, Japan	Sept. 24, 1997	Shinichi Tsurumi
Grouper, dusky	21.25 kg (46 lb 13 oz)	Porto Cervo, Sardinia, Italy	Nov. 15, 1990	Luca Bonfanti
Grouper, gag	36.46 kg (80 lb 6 oz)	Destin, Florida, USA	Oct. 14, 1993	Bill Smith
Grouper, giant	119.50 kg (263 lb 7 oz)	Anguruki Creek, Groote Eylandt, Australia	Sept. 9, 1988	Peter C. Norris
Grouper, goldblotch	1.35 kg (2 lb 15 oz)	Detached Mole, Gibraltar	Apr. 9, 1995	Joseph Anthony Triay
Grouper, goliath	308.44 kg (680 lb 0 oz)	Fernandina Beach, Florida, USA	May 20, 1961	Lynn Joyner
Grouper, gulf	51.25 kg (113 lb 0 oz)	Loreto, Baja California Sur, Mexico	Apr. 25, 2000	William Klaser
Grouper, Hawaiian	14.42 kg (31 lb 12 oz)	Midway Islands, Pacific Ocean	July 3, 2001	Gary Giglio
Grouper, Hong Kong	2.47 kg (5 lb 7 oz)	Kanmon, Shimonoseki, Yamaguchi, Japan	Dec. 30, 2000	Tetsuya Kataoka
Grouper, leopard	9.64 kg (21 lb 4 oz)	Cabo San Lucas, Baja California, Mexico	July 11, 1995	Jeff Klassen

This Goosefish was caught in Perkins Cove, Ogunquit, Maine by Nancy Lee Regimbald on July 9, 1991. It measured in at 49 lb 12 oz.

All-Tackle Records, *continued*

Species	Weight	Place of Catch	Date	Angler
Grouper, longtooth	33.00 kg (72 lb 12 oz)	Hachijo Island, Tokyo, Japan	July 16, 1998	Yasuhiko Nagasaka
Grouper, Malabar	38.00 kg (83 lb 12 oz)	Bourake, New Caledonia, France	Jan. 27, 2002	Patrick Sebile
Grouper, marbled	10.20 kg (22 lb 8 oz)	Ship Shoal, Louisiana, USA	July 8, 2001	Daniel W. Landry
Grouper, mottled	49.70 kg (109 lb 9 oz)	East Side, Gibraltar	Aug. 13, 1996	Albert Peralta
Grouper, moustache	55.00 kg (121 lb 4 oz)	Desroches Island, Seychelles	Jan. 1, 1998	Charles-Antoine Roucayrol
Grouper, Nassau	17.46 kg (38 lb 8 oz)	Bimini, Bahamas	Feb. 14, 1994	Lewis Goodman
Grouper, olive	22.31 kg (49 lb 3 oz)	Clarion Island, Baja California, Mexico	Apr. 18, 1994	Norman Y. Taniguchi
Grouper, red	19.16 kg (42 lb 4 oz)	St. Augustine, Florida, USA	Mar. 9, 1997	Del Wiseman, Jr.
Grouper, sawtail	14.06 kg (31 lb 0 oz)	Palmas Secas, Mexico	Apr. 1, 2001	William E. Favor
Grouper, snowy	12.43 kg (27 lb 6 oz)	St. Augustine, Florida, USA	June 2, 2000	Burt Hood
Grouper, speckled blue	17.30 kg (38 lb 2 oz)	Magojima, Ogasawara, Tokyo, Japan	July 7, 2001	Kenichi Uchikomi
Grouper, spotted (cabrilla)	22.31 kg (49 lb 3 oz)	Cedros/Natividad Islands, Baja California, Mexico	Nov. 18, 1990	Barry T. Morita
Grouper, tiger	6.57 kg (14 lb 8 oz)	Bimini, Bahamas	May 30, 1993	Michael John Meeker
Grouper, Warsaw	198.10 kg (436 lb 12 oz)	Gulf of Mexico, Destin, Florida, USA	Dec. 22, 1985	Steve Haeusler
Grouper, white	6.85 kg (15 lb 1 oz)	Dakar, Senegal	Jan. 24, 1984	Michel Calendini
Grouper, yellowedge	18.64 kg (41 lb 1 oz)	Gulf of Mexico, Destin, Florida, USA	May 24, 1998	Christopher D. Allen
Grouper, yellowfin	18.48 kg (40 lb 12 oz)	Gulf of Mexico, Texas, USA	Nov. 15, 1995	Karl O. Loessin
Grouper, yellowmouth	10.20 kg (22 lb 8 oz)	Murrell's Inlet, South Carolina, USA	Sept. 2, 2001	Brian J. Ford
Grunt, burrito	3.57 kg (7 lb 14 oz)	Morro Santo Domingo, Baja Norte, Mexico	July 5, 1996	Bryan M. Cupp
Grunt, burro	1.85 kg (4 lb 1 oz)	Los Chiles, Rio Fio, Costa Rica	Dec. 4, 1995	John A. Corry
Grunt, Pacific roncador	1.58 kg (3 lb 8 oz)	Rio Grande de Terraba, Costa Rica	Jan. 28, 1990	Craig Whitehead, MD
Grunt, rubberlip	7.92 kg (17 lb 7 oz)	Europa Point, Gibraltar	Sept. 10, 1996	Michael Berllaque
Grunt, white	2.94 kg (6 lb 8 oz)	North Brunswick, Georgia, USA	May 6, 1989	J.D. Barnes, Jr.
Grunt, white (Pacific)	0.59 kg (1 lb 5 oz)	Mazatlan, Mexico	June 20, 1999	David S. Boswell, III
Grunter, saddle	3.20 kg (7 lb 0 oz)	St. Lucia, Republic of South Africa	Dec. 11, 1991	J.J. van Rensburg
Guapote	6.80 kg (15 lb 0 oz)	Lago Apanas, Jinotega, Nicaragua	Feb. 14, 1999	Hubert J. Gordillo
Guapote, jaguar	1.58 kg (3 lb 8 oz)	Ludlum Rd. canal, Florida, USA	Aug. 15, 1999	Jay Wright, Jr.
Guitarfish, blackchin	49.90 kg (110 lb 0 oz)	Batanga, Gabon	June 11, 1998	Philippe Le Danff
Guitarfish, giant	54.00 kg (119 lb 0 oz)	Bird Island, Seychelles	Oct. 9, 1995	Peter Lee
Guitarfish, shovelnose	9.75 kg (21 lb 8 oz)	Manhattan Beach, California, USA	Sept. 22, 1996	Robert B. Young
Gurnard, flying	1.81 kg (4 lb 0 oz)	Gulf of Mexico, Panama City, Florida, USA	June 7, 1986	Vernon Carl Allen
Gurnard, grey	0.62 kg (1 lb 5 oz)	La Middleground, Kattegatt, Sweden	Apr. 20, 1998	Lars Kraemer
Gurnard, red (hobo)	0.95 kg (2 lb 1 oz)	Togawa, Chiba, Japan	Nov. 6, 1999	Mikio Kambara
Haddock	6.80 kg (14 lb 15 oz)	Saltraumen, Germany	Aug. 15, 1997	Heike Neblinger
Hake, European	7.08 kg (15 lb 9 oz)	Longva, Norway	Sept. 1, 2000	Knut Steen
Hake, gulf	2.54 kg (5 lb 9 oz)	Gulf of Mexico, Texas, USA	Apr. 16, 1996	Patrick Lemire
Hake, Pacific	0.98 kg (2 lb 2 oz)	Tatoosh Island, Washington, USA	June 26, 1988	Steven D. Garnett
Hake, red	3.60 kg (7 lb 15 oz)	Mud Hole, New Jersey, USA	Mar. 23, 1994	Stephen Schauermann
Hake, silver	2.04 kg (4 lb 8 oz)	Perkins Cove, Ogunquit, Maine, USA	Aug. 8, 1995	Erik M. Callahan
Hake, white	20.97 kg (46 lb 4 oz)	Perkins Cove, Ogunquit, Maine, USA	Oct. 26, 1986	John Audet
Halibut, Atlantic	161.20 kg (355 lb 6 oz)	Valevag, Norway	Oct. 20, 1997	Odd Arve Gunderstad
Halibut, California	26.58 kg (58 lb 9 oz)	Santa Rosa Island, California, USA	June 26, 1999	Roger W. Borrell
Halibut, Greenland	2.31 kg (5 lb 1 oz)	Andenes, Norway	July 6, 1998	Torunn Handeland
Halibut, Pacific	208.20 kg (459 lb 0 oz)	Dutch Harbor, Alaska, USA	June 11, 1996	Jack Tragis
Happy, pink	2.45 kg (5 lb 6 oz)	Upper Zambezi, Zambia, Africa	Aug. 14, 1998	Graham J. Glasspool
Hawkfish, giant	4.16 kg (9 lb 3 oz)	Salinas, Ecuador	Aug. 21, 1993	Hugo Tobar
Herring, Atlantic	0.69 kg (1 lb 8 oz)	South Amboy Beach, New Jersey, USA	Nov. 28, 2001	Alex Gerus
Herring, skipjack	1.70 kg (3 lb 12 oz)	Watts Bar Lake, Kingston, Tennessee, USA	Feb. 14, 1982	Paul D. Goddard
Hind, red	2.74 kg (6 lb 1 oz)	Dry Tortugas, Florida, USA	Jan. 23, 1993	Mark Johnson
Hind, rock	4.08 kg (9 lb 0 oz)	Ascension Island, South Atlantic	Apr. 25, 1994	William F. Kleinfelder
Hind, speckled	23.81 kg (52 lb 8 oz)	Destin, Florida, USA	Oct. 21, 1994	Russell George Perry
Hogfish	8.84 kg (19 lb 8 oz)	Daytona Beach, Florida, USA	Apr. 28, 1962	Robert E. Batson

All-Tackle Records, *continued*

Species	Weight	Place of Catch	Date	Angler
Hottentot	1.70 kg (3 lb 12 oz)	Cape Point, Republic of South Africa	May 28, 1989	Byron Ashington
Houndfish	3.40 kg (7 lb 8 oz)	N. Hollywood, Florida, USA	Jan. 12, 1999	Roger F. Ploneis
Houndfish, Mexican	9.86 kg (21 lb 12 oz)	Cabo San Lucas, Baja California Sur, Mexico	Aug. 10, 1993	John J. Kovacevich
Huchen	34.80 kg (76 lb 11 oz)	Gemeinde Spittal/Drau, Austria	Feb. 19, 1985	Hans Offermanns
Huchen, Japanese	7.10 kg (15 lb 10 oz)	Sarufutsu River, Hokkaido, Japan	Nov. 12, 2001	Nozomi Sato
Ide	3.36 kg (7 lb 6 oz)	Grangshammaran, Borlange, Sweden	June 24, 2001	Sonny Pettersson
Inconnu	24.04 kg (53 lb 0 oz)	Pah River, Alaska, USA	Aug. 20, 1986	Lawrence E. Hudnall
Isaki	1.05 kg (2 lb 5 oz)	Futo, Ito-shi, Sizuoka, Japan	June 15, 2000	Yasufumi Tahara
Iwatoko-namazu	1.50 kg (3 lb 4 oz)	Kozuhama, Lake Biwa, Shiga, Japan	June 26, 2001	Yoshitaka Sakurai
Izukasago	1.50 kg (3 lb 4 oz)	Numazu, Shizuoka, Japan	Oct. 28, 2000	Kouji Kimura
Jack, almaco (Atlantic)	35.38 kg (78 lb 0 oz)	Argus Bank, Bermuda	July 11, 1990	Joey Dawson
Jack, almaco (Pacific)	59.87 kg (132 lb 0 oz)	La Paz, Baja California, Mexico	July 21, 1964	Howard H. Hahn
Jack, bar	3.51 kg (7 lb 12 oz)	Miami, Florida, USA	Dec. 18, 1999	Martini Arostegui
Jack, black	17.94 kg (39 lb 9 oz)	Isla Roca Partida, Revillagigedo Islands, Mexico	Apr. 13, 1995	Calvin R. Sheets
Jack, cornish	11.25 kg (24 lb 12 oz)	Zambezi River, Zambia	Aug. 24, 1996	Pieter Willem Jacobsz
Jack, cottonmouth	2.04 kg (4 lb 8 oz)	Cat Island, Bahama	May 17, 1991	Linda R. Cook
Jack, crevalle	26.50 kg (58 lb 6 oz)	Barra do Kwanza, Angola	Dec. 10, 2000	Nuno Abohbot P. da Silva
Jack, green	2.81 kg (6 lb 3 oz)	Cabo San Lucas, Mexico	May 28, 2000	Jamey Damon
Jack, horse-eye	13.38 kg (29 lb 8 oz)	Ascension Island, South Atlantic	May 28, 1993	Mike Hanson
Jack, island	6.61 kg (14 lb 9 oz)	Oahu, Hawaii, USA	Jan. 2, 1995	Alex Ancheta
Jack, mangrove	8.70 kg (19 lb 2 oz)	Fish Rock, N.S.W., Australia	Apr. 22, 1994	Ken Lyons
Jack, Pacific crevalle	17.69 kg (39 lb 0 oz)	Playa Zancudo, Costa Rica	Mar. 3, 1997	Ingrid Callaghan
Jack, yellow	10.65 kg (23 lb 8 oz)	Key Largo, Florida, USA	Mar. 14, 1999	Richard Rodriguez
Jacunda	0.68 kg (1 lb 8 oz)	Matapuri River, Brazil	Oct. 13, 1999	Jack W. Wadkins
Janamecem	1.38 kg (3 lb 1 oz)	Cuibara River, Mato Grosso, Brasil	Aug. 12, 1996	Sandy Blum
Jandia	4.02 kg (8 lb 14 oz)	St. Benedicto River, Brazil	Aug. 17, 1996	Rogerio E. Cabral de Menezes
Jau	25.00 kg (55 lb 1 oz)	Mato Grosso, Piguiri River, Brazil	Apr. 16, 1998	Romulo Coutinho
Jawfish, finespotted	1.13 kg (2 lb 8 oz)	Turner Island, Sonora, Mexico	June 11, 1988	Lorna R. Garrod
Jobfish, green	15.40 kg (33 lb 15 oz)	Cape Vidal, Republic of South Africa	July 9, 2000	Nicholas G. Dubber
Jobfish, lavender	8.40 kg (18 lb 8 oz)	Chichijima, Ogasawara, Tokyo, Japan	Apr. 5, 1998	Yusuke Nakamura
Jobfish, rusty	6.60 kg (14 lb 8 oz)	Tokara, Kagoshima, Japan	May 19, 2002	Yuuko Hirashima
Jurupoca	1.47 kg (3 lb 4 oz)	Caceres, Paraguai River, Brazil	Sept. 9, 1996	Alacyr Beghini de Moraes
Kahawai (Australian salmon)	8.74 kg (19 lb 4 oz)	Currarong, Australia	Apr. 9, 1994	Stephen Muller
Kasago	2.80 kg (6 lb 2 oz)	Niijima, Tokyo, Japan	June 23, 1996	Osamu Hida
Kawahagi	0.50 kg (1 lb 1 oz)	Hayama, Kanagawa, Japan	Nov. 11, 2001	Eijin Suzuki
Kawakawa	13.15 kg (29 lb 0 oz)	Isla Clarion, Revillagigedo Islands, Mexico	Dec. 17, 1986	Ronald Nakamura
Kingfish, gulf	1.38 kg (3 lb 0 oz)	Salvo, North Carolina, USA	Oct. 9, 1999	Betty Duke
Kingfish, northern	1.11 kg (2 lb 7 oz)	Salvo, North Carolina, USA	July 12, 2000	William Graham
Kingfish, southern	1.07 kg (2 lb 5 oz)	Rodanthe, North Carolina, USA	July 29, 1999	Michael Graham
Kitsune-mebaru	1.54 kg (3 lb 6 oz)	Oshika-cho, Miyagi, Japan	Feb. 11, 2002	Yousuke Goto
Kob	66.75 kg (147 lb 2 oz)	Sunday's River, Port Elizabeth, South Africa	Nov. 22, 1998	Ronnie Thomas Botha
Kobudai	14.66 kg (32 lb 5 oz)	Shiroura, Mie, Japan	July 4, 1999	Shunzo Takada
Kokanee	4.27 kg (9 lb 6 oz)	Okanagan Lake, British Columbia, Canada	June 18, 1988	Norm Kuhn
Kurosoi	3.45 kg (7 lb 9 oz)	Tomari, Aomori, Japan	Mar. 31, 2002	Yasuyuki Umetsu
Ladyfish	2.73 kg (6 lb 0 oz)	Sepetiba Bay, Rio de Janeiro, Brazil	Jan. 24, 1999	Ian Arthur de Sulocki
Ladyfish	2.72 kg (6 lb 0 oz)	Loxahatchee River, Jupiter, Florida, USA	Dec. 20, 1997	Michael Baz
Ladyfish, Hawaiian	6.60 kg (14 lb 8 oz)	Southwest Reef, Dampier, W.A., Australia	Dec. 16, 2001	Anthony La Tosa
Ladyfish, Senegalese	5.90 kg (13 lb 0 oz)	Guinea Bissau, Bijagos Isles	Apr. 12, 1994	Gerard Cittadini
Ladyfish, springer	10.80 kg (23 lb 12 oz)	Ilha do Bazaruio, Mozambique	Oct. 28, 1993	Zaqueu Paulo
Largemouth, humpback	3.85 kg (8 lb 7 oz)	Upper Zambezi River, Zambia	Aug. 15, 1998	Richie Peters
Largemouth, purple-faced	0.58 kg (1 lb 4 oz)	Kariba, Zimbabwe	Oct. 4, 1999	Graham Mitchell
Largemouth, thinface	1.66 kg (3 lb 10 oz)	Upper Zambezi River, Zambia	Sept. 13, 1999	Howard Voss

All-Tackle Records, *continued*

Species	Weight	Place of Catch	Date	Angler
Lates, forktail	8.30 kg (18 lb 4 oz)	Lake Tanganyika, Zambia	Dec. 1, 1987	Steve Robinson
Lates, Japanese (akame)	33.00 kg (72 lb 12 oz)	Shimanto River, Kochi, Japan	May 31, 1996	Yoshio Murasaki
Lau-lau (piraiba)	116.40 kg (256 lb 9 oz)	Solimoes River, Amazon, Brazil	Apr. 3, 1981	Gilberto Fernandes
Leaffish, Malayan	0.50 kg (1 lb 1 oz)	Srinakarin Dam, Thailand	May 3, 2002	Johnny Jensen
Leatherjack, longjaw	1.58 kg (3 lb 8 oz)	Rio Coto, Puntarenas, Costa Rica	Feb. 6, 1990	Craig Whitehead, MD
Leatherjack, longjaw	1.58 kg (3 lb 8 oz)	Playa Zancudo, Costa Rica	May 27, 1995	Craig Whitehead, MD
Leerfish (Garrick)	27.80 kg (61 lb 4 oz)	L'Ampolla, Spain	Apr. 30, 2000	Oriol Ribalta
Lenok	4.08 kg (9 lb 0 oz)	Anui River, Russia	June 2, 2000	Thomas Cappiello
Ling, blue	16.05 kg (35 lb 6 oz)	Trondheimsfjorden, Norway	Nov. 23, 1993	Oyvind Braa
Ling, European	40.10 kg (88 lb 6 oz)	Shetland Islands, United Kingdom	Apr. 5, 2002	Gareth Angus Laurenson
Lingcod	34.74 kg (76 lb 9 oz)	Gulf of Alaska, Alaska, USA	Aug. 11, 2001	Antwan D. Tinsley
Lizardfish, inshore	0.90 kg (2 lb 0 oz)	Boca Grande, Florida, USA	Oct. 25, 1994	Robert L. Hill, Jr.
Lizardfish, inshore	0.90 kg (2 lb 0 oz)	Bellair Shores, Florida, USA	Nov. 17, 1990	Todd Staley
Lookdown	2.10 kg (4 lb 10 oz)	Angra Dor Reis Bay, Rio de Janeiro, Brazil	Nov. 11, 1993	Adolpho A. Mayer Neto
Lord, Red Irish	1.11 kg (2 lb 7 oz)	Depoe Bay, Oregon, USA	Apr. 26, 1992	Ronald L. Chatham
Lyretail, yellow-edged	5.00 kg (11 lb 0 oz)	Chichijima, Ogasawara Island, Tokyo, Japan	June 25, 1999	Hiromasa Kobayashi
Machaca	4.32 kg (9 lb 8 oz)	Barra del Colorado, Costa Rica	Nov. 24, 1991	Barbara Ann Fields
Mackerel, Atlantic	1.20 kg (2 lb 10 oz)	Kraakvaag Fjord, Norway	June 29, 1992	Jorge Marquard
Mackerel, blue	1.36 kg (2 lb 15 oz)	Ashizuri-misaki, Kochi, Japan	May 6, 2000	Kenji Tamura
Mackerel, broadbarred	9.30 kg (20 lb 8 oz)	The Patch, Dampier, Australia	June 12, 1997	Tammy Denise Yates
Mackerel, bullet	1.60 kg (3 lb 8 oz)	St. Laurent du Var, France	July 12, 2001	Patrick Sebile
Mackerel, cero	7.76 kg (17 lb 2 oz)	Islamorada, Florida, USA	Apr. 5, 1986	G. Michael Mills
Mackerel, chub	2.17 kg (4 lb 12 oz)	Guadalupe Island, Mexico	June 5, 1986	Roy R. Ludt
Mackerel, frigate	1.72 kg (3 lb 12 oz)	Hat Head, N.S.W., Australia	Apr. 17, 1998	Glen Beers
Mackerel, Japanese jack	0.66 kg (1 lb 7 oz)	Kenzaki, Kanagawa, Japan	Apr. 30, 2000	Junzo Okada
Mackerel, Japanese jack	0.70 kg (1 lb 8 oz)	Kannonzaki, Kanagawa, Japan	Dec. 22, 2001	Junzo Okada
Mackerel, Japanese Spanish	7.10 kg (15 lb 10 oz)	Nakanose, Tokyo Bay, Japan	Oct. 8, 2000	Kazushige Ozawa
Mackerel, king	42.18 kg (93 lb 0 oz)	San Juan, Puerto Rico	Apr. 18, 1999	Steve Perez Graulau
Mackerel, narrowbarred	44.90 kg (99 lb 0 oz)	Scottburgh, Natal, Republic of South Africa	Mar. 14, 1982	Michael John Wilkinson
Mackerel, Pacific sierra	8.16 kg (18 lb 0 oz)	Salinas, Ecuador	Sept. 15, 1990	Luis Alberto Flores A.
Mackerel, Pacific sierra	8.16 kg (18 lb 0 oz)	Isla de la Plata, Ecuador	Mar. 24, 1990	Jorge Begue W.
Mackerel, shark	12.30 kg (27 lb 1 oz)	Bribie Island, Brisbane, Queensland, Australia	Mar. 24, 1989	Kathy Maguire
Mackerel, Spanish	5.89 kg (13 lb 0 oz)	Ocracoke Inlet, North Carolina, USA	Nov. 4, 1987	Robert Cranton
Mackerel, West African Spanish	6.00 kg (13 lb 3 oz)	Grand Bereby, Ivory Coast	Dec. 27, 1998	Dorchies Jacques
Madai	9.72 kg (21 lb 6 oz)	Kouzu Island, Tokyo, Japan	Aug. 18, 1998	Yoshiaki Nakajima
Mahseer	43.09 kg (95 lb 0 oz)	Cauvery River, India	Mar. 26, 1984	Robert Howitt
Mahseer, Thai	12.00 kg (26 lb 7 oz)	Jeram Besu, Benta, Pahang, Malaysia	July 24, 2001	Mohamed Zainudin bin Ibrahim
Manduba	2.50 kg (5 lb 8 oz)	Xingu River, Brazil	Apr. 26, 2000	Capt. Kdu Magalhaes
Margate, black	5.78 kg (12 lb 12 oz)	Ft. Pierce Inlet, Florida, USA	May 28, 1994	Carol Napierala
Margate, white	7.14 kg (15 lb 12 oz)	Reef Point, San Pedro, Ambergris Cay, Belize	Feb. 14, 1996	Carol Barrows
Marlin, black	707.61 kg (1560 lb 0 oz)	Cabo Blanco, Peru	Aug. 4, 1953	Alfred C. Glassell, Jr.
Marlin, blue (Atlantic)	636.00 kg (1402 lb 2 oz)	Vitoria, Brazil	Feb. 29, 1992	Paulo Roberto A. Amorim
Marlin, blue (Pacific)	624.14 kg (1376 lb 0 oz)	Kaaiwi Point, Kona, Hawaii, USA	May 31, 1982	Jay Wm. de Beaubien
Marlin, striped	224.10 kg (494 lb 0 oz)	Tutukaka, New Zealand	Jan. 16, 1986	Bill Boniface
Marlin, white	82.50 kg (181 lb 14 oz)	Vitoria, Brazil	Dec. 8, 1979	Evandro Luiz Coser
Matrincha	3.36 kg (7 lb 6 oz)	Rio Arinos, Brazil	Sept. 3, 1997	Marcio Mattos Borges de Oliveira
Matrincha	3.31 kg (7 lb 5 oz)	Sao Benedicto River, Para, Brazil	Apr. 26, 1997	Luiz Carlos Nolasco
Mcheni (lake tiger)	0.65 kg (1 lb 6 oz)	Maleri Islands, Lake Malawi, Malawi	May 31, 1997	Brendon Garry Whitcher
Meagre	48.00 kg (105 lb 13 oz)	Nouadhibou, Mauritania	Mar. 30, 1986	Laurent Morat
Mebaru	0.80 kg (1 lb 12 oz)	Ito-shi, Shizuoka, Japan	Dec. 9, 1999	Keiji Kurihara

All-Tackle Records, *continued*

Species	Weight	Place of Catch	Date	Angler
Medai (Japanese Butterfish)	10.20 kg (22 lb 7 oz)	Tokara, Kagoshima, Japan	July 24, 2001	Hiroki Yano
Megrim	0.95 kg (2 lb 1 oz)	Hardangerfjord, Norway	Aug. 5, 2001	Sandra Marquard
Menada	3.40 kg (7 lb 8 oz)	Hanami River, Chiba City, Chiba, Japan	Aug. 20, 1995	Kazuyoshi Nagasawa
Mihara-hanadai	1.00 kg (2 lb 3 oz)	Irozaki, Shizuoka, Japan	Aug. 13, 1998	Mikio Suzuki
Milkfish	11.11 kg (24 lb 8 oz)	Hilo Bay, Hilo, Hawaii, USA	Aug. 25, 1991	Rory Tokeshi
Mojarra, striped	1.02 kg (2 lb 4 oz)	West Palm Beach, Florida, USA	Aug. 21, 1987	James B. Black, Jr.
Mojarra, yellowfin	0.53 kg (1 lb 3 oz)	Marathon, Florida, USA	Jan. 13, 1999	George D. Cornish
Monkfish, European	25.96 kg (57 lb 4 oz)	Fenit, Tralee Bay, County Kerry, Ireland	May 20, 1989	Jim Dooley
Mooneye	0.70 kg (1 lb 8 oz)	Lake of the Woods, Minnesota, USA	June 13, 2001	Dan McGuire
Moray, blackedge	1.40 kg (3 lb 1 oz)	Gulf of Mexico, Texas, USA	May 30, 1999	Ronnie Vaughn
Moray, blacktail	1.09 kg (2 lb 6 oz)	Gulf of Mexico, Texas, USA	Mar. 24, 1998	George A. Flores
Moray, green	15.19 kg (33 lb 8 oz)	Marathon Key, Florida, USA	Mar. 15, 1997	Rene de Dios
Moray, purplemouth	0.75 kg (1 lb 10 oz)	Port Everglades Reef, Florida, USA	June 19, 1998	Rene G. de Dios
Moray, slender giant	5.35 kg (11 lb 12 oz)	St. Lucia, Republic of South Africa	Aug. 29, 1987	Graham Vollmer
Moray, spotted	2.51 kg (5 lb 8 oz)	Marathon Key, Florida, USA	Apr. 1, 2000	Rene G. de Dios
Moray, viper	1.32 kg (2 lb 14 oz)	Fowey Light, Florida, USA	May 25, 1998	Rene G. de Dios
Mullet, hog	3.25 kg (7 lb 2 oz)	Rio Sarapiqui, Costa Rica	Aug. 9, 1995	Carlos M. Barrantes R.
Mullet, liza	1.45 kg (3 lb 3 oz)	Rio de Janeiro, Brazil	Sept. 20, 1999	Erich Baumeier Filho
Mullet, striped	3.14 kg (6 lb 15 oz)	Hanami River, Chiba City, Chiba, Japan	Sept. 4, 1995	Makoto Hanaki
Mullet, thicklip	3.52 kg (7 lb 12 oz)	Ymuiden, Zuid Pier, Holland	Aug. 20, 1996	Frits Kromhout vander Meer
Mullet, thicklip	3.48 kg (7 lb 11 oz)	Barseback, Sweden	Mar. 16, 1991	Bengt Olsson
Mullet, thinlip	2.38 kg (5 lb 4 oz)	River Taw, Barnstaple, England	June 14, 1984	Raymond John White
Mullet, white	0.68 kg (1 lb 7 oz)	Rio de Janeiro, Brazil	Apr. 13, 2001	Erich Baumeier Filho
Murasoi	1.56 kg (3 lb 7 oz)	Oarai, Ibaraki, Japan	May 30, 2001	Noboru Gunji
Muskellunge	30.61 kg (67 lb 8 oz)	Lake Court Oreilles, Hayward, Wisconsin, USA	July 24, 1949	Cal Johnson
Muskellunge, tiger	23.21 kg (51 lb 3 oz)	Lac Vieux-Desert, Michigan, USA	July 16, 1919	John A. Knobla
Musselcracker, black	32.20 kg (70 lb 15 oz)	Richards Bay, South Africa	Aug. 25, 1996	John Rex Harvey
Myleus, redhook	1.50 kg (3 lb 4 oz)	Xingu River, Mato Grosso, Brazil	Oct. 18, 1999	Kdu Magalhaes
Naga-buna	0.69 kg (1 lb 8 oz)	Mino River, Miki-shi, Hyogo, Japan	Jan. 14, 2002	Masahiro Oomori
Needlefish, Agujon	4.08 kg (9 lb 0 oz)	Garza, Costa Rica	Aug. 16, 2001	David M. Dickman
Needlefish, Atlantic	1.47 kg (3 lb 4 oz)	Brigantine, New Jersey, USA	July 18, 1990	Charlie Trost
Needlefish, flat	4.80 kg (10 lb 9 oz)	Zavora, Mozambique	Dec. 25, 1997	Leon Paul deBeer
Nembwe	3.50 kg (7 lb 11 oz)	Tiger Camp, Zambezi River, Zambia	Sept. 27, 1998	W. F. Reitsma
Nkupe	5.50 kg (12 lb 2 oz)	Chete Gorge, Lake Kariba, Zimbabwe	Dec. 12, 2000	Malcolm Pheasant
Oilfish	63.50 kg (139 lb 15 oz)	White Island, New Zealand	Apr. 12, 1986	Tim Wallace
Okuchi-ishinagi	84.80 kg (186 lb 15 oz)	Gentatsuse, Fukui, Japan	June 21, 2000	Takehiro Isaka
Oniokoze	0.48 kg (1 lb 0 oz)	Ikitsukijima, Nagasaki, Japan	Nov. 8, 1999	Masaki Takano
Opah	73.93 kg (163 lb 0 oz)	Port San Luis Obispo, California, USA	Oct. 8, 1998	Thomas R. Foran
Oscar	1.58 kg (3 lb 8 oz)	Pasadena Lakes, Florida, USA	July 30, 1999	Jay Wright, Jr.
Otolithe (Law croaker)	12.50 kg (27 lb 8 oz)	Archipelago dos Bijagos, Guinea Bissau	Mar. 14, 2001	Jean-Louis Savall
Oxeye	2.99 kg (6 lb 9 oz)	Tide Island, Queensland, Australia	May 14, 2000	Neil Schultz
Pacu	9.58 kg (21 lb 2 oz)	Parana River, Paso de la Patria, Argentina	Jan. 3, 1993	Ken Bohling
Pacu, black (pirapatinga)	19.95 kg (44 lb 0 oz)	Ft. Lauderdale, Florida, USA	Mar. 19, 2000	Todd A. Ewing
Palometa	0.55 kg (1 lb 3 oz)	Bimini, Bahamas	Feb. 3, 1991	Dan Kipnis
Palometa	0.56 kg (1 lb 4 oz)	Key Largo, Florida, USA	Nov. 28, 2000	Dennis Triana
Palometa	0.56 kg (1 lb 4 oz)	Key Largo, Florida, USA	Sept. 22, 2001	David Pesi
Pandora	3.24 kg (7 lb 2 oz)	Monte Gordo, Portugal	May 16, 1996	Geoff Flores
Pangasius, shortbarbel	22.00 kg (48 lb 8 oz)	Seletar Reservoir, Singapore	Sept. 27, 2001	Khoo Wee Lee
Parrotfish, rainbow	2.94 kg (6 lb 8 oz)	Key Largo, Florida, USA	Nov. 20, 2001	Dennis Triana
Parrotperch, Japanese	6.40 kg (14 lb 1 oz)	Hatusima, Sizuoka, Japan	Sept. 11, 1993	Yoshikatu Higuchi
Parrotperch, spotted	12.08 kg (26 lb 10 oz)	Hachijo Island, Tokyo, Japan	May 5, 1978	Tsunehisa Kanayama
Payara	17.80 kg (39 lb 4 oz)	Uraima Falls, Venezuela	Feb. 10, 1996	Bill Keeley

All-Tackle Records, *continued*

Species	Weight	Place of Catch	Date	Angler
Peacock, blackstriped	3.00 kg (6 lb 9 oz)	Caurama Lodge, Caura River, Venezuela	Mar. 22, 1999	Carlos Aristeguieta L.
Peacock, blue	2.73 kg (6 lb 0 oz)	Lago do Pade, Valparaiso-Goias, Brazil	Nov. 21, 1999	Andre Luiz Penna Ranna
Peacock, butterfly	5.71 kg (12 lb 9 oz)	Chiguao River, Bolivar State, Venezuela	Jan. 6, 2000	Antonio Campa G.
Peacock, speckled	12.24 kg (27 lb 0 oz)	Rio Negro, Brazil	Dec. 4, 1994	Gerald "Doc" Lawson
Pellona, Amazon	7.10 kg (15 lb 10 oz)	Caurama Lodge, Caura River, Venezuela	Jan. 15, 1999	Stephen E. Ray
Perch, creole	0.89 kg (1 lb 15 oz)	Maullin River, Chile	Mar. 21, 2002	Kdu Magalhaes
Perch, European	1.50 kg (3 lb 4 oz)	Eidsvoll, Norway	June 13, 1998	Johnny Hogli
Perch, Nile	104.32 kg (230 lb 0 oz)	Lake Nasser, Egypt	Dec. 20, 2000	William Toth
Perch, Sacramento	1.44 kg (3 lb 3 oz)	Crowley Lake, California, USA	Sept. 22, 1995	Richard J. Fischer
Perch, white	1.38 kg (3 lb 1 oz)	Forest Hill Park, New Jersey, USA	May 6, 1989	Edward Tango
Perch, yellow	1.91 kg (4 lb 3 oz)	Bordentown, New Jersey, USA	May, 1865	Dr. C. C. Abbot
Permit	25.45 kg (56 lb 2 oz)	Ft. Lauderdale, Florida, USA	June 30, 1997	Thomas Sebestyen
Piau	2.00 kg (4 lb 6 oz)	Cel. Vanick River, Brazil	Sept. 13, 2000	Capt. Kdu Magalhaes
Pickerel, chain	4.25 kg (9 lb 6 oz)	Homerville, Georgia, USA	Feb. 17, 1961	Baxley McQuaig, Jr.
Pickerel, grass	0.45 kg (1 lb 0 oz)	Dewart Lake, Indiana, USA	June 9, 1990	Mike Berg
Pickerel, redfin	1.02 kg (2 lb 4 oz)	Gall Berry Swamp, North Carolina, USA	June 27, 1997	Edward C. Davis
Pike, northern	25.00 kg (55 lb 1 oz)	Lake of Grefeern, West Germany	Oct. 16, 1986	Lothar Louis
Pike-conger, common	7.10 kg (15 lb 10 oz)	Markham River, Lae, Huon Gulf, Papua New Guinea	Mar. 7, 1993	Barry Mallett
Pikeminnow, Sacramento	2.92 kg (6 lb 7 oz)	Shasta Lake, California, USA	June 13, 2001	James W. Schmidt
Pinfish	1.51 kg (3 lb 5 oz)	Horn Island, Mississippi, USA	Sept. 4, 1992	William Davis Fountain
Pinook	7.25 kg (16 lb 0 oz)	Sault Ste. Marie, Ontario, Canada	Sept. 20, 1999	David P. Conlin
Piranha, black	3.17 kg (6 lb 15 oz)	Rio Autana, Venezuela	Feb. 27, 1995	Alejandro Mata
Piranha, black spot	0.56 kg (1 lb 4 oz)	Hato Cedral, Apure, Venezuela	Jan. 18, 1991	William T. Miller
Piranha, Manueli's	2.50 kg (5 lb 8 oz)	Xingu River, Brazil	Sept. 9, 2000	Capt. Kdu Magalhaes
Piranha, red	3.85 kg (8 lb 8 oz)	Xingu River, Para, Brazil	July 9, 1997	Jedediah Smith Colston
Piraputanga	0.62 kg (1 lb 6 oz)	Mato Grosso, Piguiri River, Brazil	Apr. 16, 1998	Helder Coutinho
Pirarucu	67.13 kg (148 lb 0 oz)	Rupununi River, Karanambu, Guyana	Apr. 1, 1953	Ed Migdalski
Pollack, European	12.41 kg (27 lb 6 oz)	Salcombe, Devon, England	Jan. 16, 1986	Robert Samuel Milkins
Pollock	22.70 kg (50 lb 0 oz)	Salstraumen, Norway	Nov. 30, 1995	Thor-Magnus Lekang
Pomfret	3.80 kg (8 lb 6 oz)	Orange Beach, Alabama, USA	Mar. 23, 2002	Dan Foster
Pomfret, big scale	3.06 kg (6 lb 12 oz)	Bimini, Bahamas	Nov. 16, 1998	Horst Martin Schneider
Pomfret, Pacific	1.56 kg (3 lb 7 oz)	San Diego, California, USA	Oct. 8, 2001	William "Baja Billy" Theroux
Pompano, African	22.90 kg (50 lb 8 oz)	Daytona Beach, Florida, USA	Apr. 21, 1990	Tom Sargent
Pompano, Florida	3.76 kg (8 lb 4 oz)	Port St. Joe Bay, Florida, USA	Oct. 16, 1999	Barry Huston
Pompano, gafftopsail	1.30 kg (2 lb 14 oz)	Cabo San Lucas, Mexico	Apr. 16, 1997	Bruce Coale
Pompano, Irish	0.68 kg (1 lb 8 oz)	St. Lucie River, Florida, USA	Dec. 17, 2000	Richard J. Morgan, Sr.

This Northern Pike was caught in Lake of Grefeern by Lothar Louis on Oct. 16, 1986. It measured in at 55 lb 1 oz.

All-Tackle Records, *continued*

Species	Weight	Place of Catch	Date	Angler
Pompano, snubnose	3.40 kg (7 lb 7 oz)	Port Hedland, W.A., Australia	Apr. 29, 2001	Anthony Boekhorst
Porcupinefish	2.80 kg (6 lb 3 oz)	Oakhill, Florida, USA	May 22, 1997	Bill Whipple
Porgy, black	3.20 kg (7 lb 0 oz)	West Port, Niigata, Japan	Mar. 30, 1992	Yoichi Suzuki
Porgy, black	3.20 kg (7 lb 0 oz)	Daisan-kaiho, Tokyo Bay, Japan	Mar. 30, 1995	Shigenobu Takahashi
Porgy, bluepointed	9.40 kg (20 lb 11 oz)	Europa Point, Gibraltar	Mar. 17, 1996	Derek Apap
Porgy, Canary	8.06 kg (17 lb 12 oz)	Monte Gordo, Portugal	July 14, 1997	Joseph Anthony Triay
Porgy, jolthead	10.54 kg (23 lb 4 oz)	Madeira Beach, Florida, USA	Mar. 14, 1990	Harm M. Wilder
Porgy, knobbed	2.63 kg (5 lb 12 oz)	Gulf of Mexico, Texas, USA	Feb. 21, 2000	Stanley W. Sweet
Porgy, red	7.72 kg (17 lb 0 oz)	Gibraltar	July 12, 1997	Richard Gomila
Porgy, saucereye	0.68 kg (1 lb 8 oz)	Snake Cay, Abaco, Bahamas	Feb. 23, 2001	Donald Carson, Jr.
Porkfish	0.93 kg (2 lb 1 oz)	St. Lucie Inlet, Florida, USA	Aug. 29, 2001	Leonard R. Lopes
Powan	5.39 kg (11 lb 14 oz)	Skrabean, Nymolla, Sweden	Dec. 15, 1994	Allan Englund
Puffer, oceanic	3.17 kg (7 lb 0 oz)	Sandy Hook, New Jersey, USA	Aug. 28, 1991	Jane Lee Jagen
Puffer, smooth	5.21 kg (11 lb 7 oz)	Cape May Inlet, New Jersey, USA	Aug. 24, 2001	Shawn F. Clark
Puffer, whitespotted	2.01 kg (4 lb 7 oz)	Iroquois Point, Hawaii, USA	Oct. 31, 1992	George D. Cornish
Pumpkinseed	0.63 kg (1 lb 6 oz)	Mexico, New York, USA	Apr. 27, 1985	Heather Ann Finch
Queenfish, doublespotted	2.26 kg (5 lb 0 oz)	Midway Islands, Pacific Ocean	Nov. 14, 1999	Michael J. Botha
Queenfish, needlescaled	0.51 kg (1 lb 2 oz)	Hope Reef, Cairns, N. Queensland, Australia	Nov. 24, 1998	Renee E. Andrews
Queenfish, talang	16.00 kg (35 lb 4 oz)	Waterpark Creek, Yeppoon, Australia	Feb. 3, 2001	Ron Fordham
Quillback	2.94 kg (6 lb 8 oz)	Lake Michigan, Indiana, USA	Jan. 15, 1993	Mike Berg
Raven, sea	1.47 kg (3 lb 4 oz)	Manasquan Inlet, New Jersey, USA	Jan. 17, 1996	Allan Ristori
Ray, backwater butterfly	82.60 kg (182 lb 1 oz)	Knysna Lagoon, Republic of South Africa	July 11, 1992	Hilton Gervais
Ray, bat	82.10 kg (181 lb 0 oz)	Huntington Beach Pier, California, USA	June 30, 1978	Bradley A. Dew
Ray, black	37.50 kg (82 lb 10 oz)	Weston Point Bay, Newhaven, Australia	Jan. 20, 1993	Peter Ronald Blondell
Ray, blonde	14.28 kg (31 lb 8 oz)	Jersey Channel Islands, United Kingdom	Apr. 3, 1989	John Thompson
Ray, bull	46.60 kg (102 lb 11 oz)	Cape Skirring, Senegal	Feb. 18, 1999	Daniel Bidel
Ray, bull (Australian)	56.50 kg (124 lb 8 oz)	Neptune Island, Port Lincoln, S.A., Australia	Apr. 13, 1991	Rolf Czabayski
Ray, discus	53.00 kg (116 lb 13 oz)	Rio Negro and Blanco, Brazil	Dec. 20, 2000	Keith B. Sutton
Ray, painted	4.50 kg (9 lb 15 oz)	Jersey, Channel Islands, England	Aug. 2, 1988	Andrew R. J. Mitchell
Ray, pale	11.15 kg (24 lb 9 oz)	Langesund, Stavern, Norway	June 13, 1999	Bjorn Persson
Ray, southern eagle	41.50 kg (91 lb 7 oz)	American River, Kangaroo Island, Australia	Mar. 16, 1999	Xenia Dodt
Ray, southern fiddler	6.70 kg (14 lb 12 oz)	Marion Bay, S.A., Australia	Aug. 11, 1990	Marcel Vandergoot
Ray, spiny butterfly	60.00 kg (132 lb 4 oz)	Nouadhibou, Mauritania	May 5, 1984	Robin Michel
Ray, thornback	7.59 kg (16 lb 12 oz)	Jersey, Channel Islands, United Kingdom	July 11, 1988	John Thompson
Rebeca	2.23 kg (4 lb 15 oz)	Xingu River, Estado Mato Grosso, Brazil	June 6, 1996	Sergio Roberto Rothier
Redfish (ocean perch)	7.50 kg (16 lb 8 oz)	Andenes, Norway	June 7, 1998	Das Kjelsaas
Redhorse, black	1.02 kg (2 lb 4 oz)	French Creek, Franklin, Pennsylvania, USA	Feb. 22, 1998	Richard E. Faler, Jr.
Redhorse, golden	4.08 kg (9 lb 0 oz)	Muskegon River, Michigan, USA	June 9, 2001	Andy Tulgetske
Redhorse, greater	4.16 kg (9 lb 3 oz)	Salmon River, Pulaski, New York, USA	May 11, 1985	Jason A. Wilson
Redhorse, river	3.96 kg (8 lb 11 oz)	Trent River, Ontario, Canada	Aug. 6, 1997	Geoff J. Bernado
Redhorse, shorthead	3.99 kg (8 lb 12 oz)	North River, Ontario, Canada	May 23, 1988	Bruce E. Johnstone
Redhorse, silver	5.18 kg (11 lb 7 oz)	Plum Creek, Wisconsin, USA	May 29, 1985	Neal D.G. Long
Remora, common	1.07 kg (2 lb 6 oz)	Pensacola, Florida, USA	Sept. 30, 2000	Matthew Finelli
Roach	1.84 kg (4 lb 1 oz)	Colwick, Nottingham, England	June 16, 1975	R. G. Jones
Rockfish, bank	1.98 kg (4 lb 6 oz)	San Clemente Island, California, USA	Feb. 14, 1998	Stephen D. Grossberg
Rockfish, black	4.56 kg (10 lb 0 oz)	Puget Sound, Washington, USA	July 20, 1986	William J. Harris, DDS
Rockfish, blackgill	3.53 kg (7 lb 12 oz)	San Clemente Island, California, USA	Dec. 27, 2000	Stephen D. Grossberg
Rockfish, blue	3.79 kg (8 lb 6 oz)	Whaler's Cove, Alaska, USA	July 27, 1994	Dr. John F. Whitaker
Rockfish, bronzespotted	4.96 kg (10 lb 15 oz)	San Clemente Island, California, USA	Mar. 25, 2000	George Bogen
Rockfish, canary	4.53 kg (10 lb 0 oz)	Westport, Washington, USA	May 17, 1986	Terry Rudnick
Rockfish, chameleon	1.22 kg (2 lb 11 oz)	San Clemente Island, California, USA	Mar. 14, 2001	Stephen D. Grossberg
Rockfish, China	1.67 kg (3 lb 11 oz)	Tatoosh Island, Neah Bay, Washington, USA	Aug. 24, 1992	Edward Schultz

All-Tackle Records, *continued*

Species	Weight	Place of Catch	Date	Angler
Rockfish, copper	2.74 kg (6 lb 1 oz)	Mink Bay, Alaska, USA	June 17, 1995	Jack. H. Simon
Rockfish, dusky	2.26 kg (5 lb 0 oz)	Marmot Bay, Kodiak, Alaska, USA	Aug. 2, 2001	Paul Leader
Rockfish, flag	1.45 kg (3 lb 3 oz)	San Clemente Island, California, USA	Feb. 14, 1999	Stephen D. Grossberg
Rockfish, greenspotted	1.01 kg (2 lb 3 oz)	San Clemente Island, California, USA	Nov. 4, 2000	Stephen D. Grossberg
Rockfish, greenstriped	0.63 kg (1 lb 6 oz)	San Clemente Island, California, USA	Mar. 18, 2000	Stephen D. Grossberg
Rockfish, honeycomb	0.57 kg (1 lb 4 oz)	San Martin Island, Baja California Sur, Mexico	Oct. 27, 2000	Stephen D. Grossberg
Rockfish, Mexican	2.72 kg (6 lb 0 oz)	San Clemente Island, California, USA	Dec. 9, 2000	Stephen D. Grossberg
Rockfish, olive	1.63 kg (3 lb 9 oz)	Los Coranados Islands, Mexico	Mar. 23, 2001	Stephen D. Grossberg
Rockfish, pink	2.44 kg (5 lb 6 oz)	San Clemente Island, California, USA	Mar. 25, 2000	George Bogen
Rockfish, quillback	3.28 kg (7 lb 4 oz)	Depoe Bay, Oregon, USA	Mar. 18, 1990	Kelly H. Canaday
Rockfish, redbanded	4.44 kg (9 lb 12 oz)	Whaler's Cove, Alaska, USA	July 11, 1999	Thomas D. Stroud
Rockfish, rougheye	0.90 kg (2 lb 0 oz)	Hoggatt Bay, Alaska, USA	Aug. 11, 2000	Martin Arostegui
Rockfish, shortraker	16.24 kg (35 lb 13 oz)	Ketchikan, Alaska, USA	June 28, 1994	Jeffrey A. Hendrickson
Rockfish, silvergray	4.71 kg (10 lb 6 oz)	Seward, Alaska, USA	June 12, 2001	Corey Green
Rockfish, speckled	0.95 kg (2 lb 1 oz)	Santa Barbara Island, California, USA	Dec. 4, 1999	Bill Grossberg
Rockfish, splitnose	0.81 kg (1 lb 12 oz)	San Clemente Island, California, USA	Mar. 17, 2001	Stephen D. Grossberg
Rockfish, starry	1.04 kg (2 lb 4 oz)	San Clemente Island, California, USA	Jan. 9, 1999	Stephen D. Grossberg
Rockfish, tiger	2.22 kg (4 lb 14 oz)	Depoe Bay, Oregon, USA	Sept. 4, 1993	Ronald L. Chatham
Rockfish, vermillion	5.45 kg (12 lb 0 oz)	Depoe Bay, Oregon, USA	June 2, 1990	Joseph William Lowe
Rockfish, yelloweye	17.82 kg (39 lb 4 oz)	Whalers Cove, Alaska, USA	July 18, 2000	David Mundhenke
Rockfish, yellowtail	2.51 kg (5 lb 8 oz)	Cape Flattery, Washington, USA	Aug. 28, 1988	Steven D. Garnett
Roosterfish	51.71 kg (114 lb 0 oz)	La Paz, Baja California, Mexico	June 1, 1960	Abe Sackheim
Rosefish, blackbelly	1.55 kg (3 lb 6 oz)	Langesund, Norway	Sept. 4, 1998	Per Magne Grefstad
Rudd	1.58 kg (3 lb 7 oz)	Ljungan River, Sweden	July 31, 1988	Luis Kilian Rasmussen
Runner, blue	5.05 kg (11 lb 2 oz)	Dauphin Island, Alabama, USA	June 28, 1997	Stacey Michele Moiren
Runner, rainbow	17.05 kg (37 lb 9 oz)	Isla Clarion, Revillagigedo Islands, Mexico	Nov. 21, 1991	Tom Pfleger
Sabaleta	0.47 kg (1 lb 0 oz)	Rio Churimo, Colombia	June 23, 1999	Alejandro Linares
Sabalo	4.35 kg (9 lb 9 oz)	Rio Tambopata, Peru	Oct. 10, 1992	James B. Wise, MD
Sailfish, Atlantic	64.00 kg (141 lb 1 oz)	Luanda, Angola	Feb. 19, 1994	Alfredo de Sousa Neves
Sailfish, Pacific	100.24 kg (221 lb 0 oz)	Santa Cruz Island, Ecuador	Feb. 12, 1947	Carl W. Stewart
Salmon, Atlantic	35.89 kg (79 lb 2 oz)	Tana River, Norway	1928	Henrik Henriksen
Salmon, Atlantic (landlocked)	10.76 kg (23 lb 11 oz)	Lake Vaernern, Djuroe, Sweden	Mar. 17, 2002	Thomas Johansson
Salmon, chinook	44.11 kg (97 lb 4 oz)	Kenai River, Alaska, USA	May 17, 1985	Les Anderson
Salmon, chinook/coho	16.10 kg (35 lb 8 oz)	Salmon River, Pulaski, New York, USA	Oct. 21, 2001	Brooks Gerli
Salmon, chum	15.87 kg (35 lb 0 oz)	Edye Pass, British Columbia, Canada	July 11, 1995	Todd A. Johansson
Salmon, coho	15.08 kg (33 lb 4 oz)	Salmon River, Pulaski, New York, USA	Sept. 27, 1989	Jerry Lifton
Salmon, pink	6.74 kg (14 lb 13 oz)	Monroe, Washington, USA	Sept. 30, 2001	Alexander Minerich
Salmon, sockeye	6.88 kg (15 lb 3 oz)	Kenai River, Alaska, USA	Aug. 9, 1987	Stan Roach
Samsonfish	36.50 kg (80 lb 7 oz)	Cape Naturaliste, W.A., Australia	Jan. 31, 1993	Terry Coote
Sandperch, namorado	20.20 kg (44 lb 8 oz)	Rio de Janeiro, Brazil	Mar. 7, 1998	Eduardo Baumeier
Sauger	3.96 kg (8 lb 12 oz)	Lake Sakakawea, North Dakota, USA	Oct. 6, 1971	Mike Fischer
Saugeye	5.81 kg (12 lb 13 oz)	Clendening Reservoir, Ohio, USA	Nov. 19, 2001	Fred Sulek
Sawfish	403.92 kg (890 lb 8 oz)	Fort Amador, Canal Zone, Panama	May 26, 1960	Jack D. Wagner
Scabbardfish, channel	3.89 kg (8 lb 9 oz)	Rio de Janeiro, Brazil	Apr. 6, 2002	Eduardo Baumeier
Scabbardfish, silver	6.40 kg (14 lb 1 oz)	Europa Point, Gibraltar	July 16, 1995	Ernest Borrell
Scamp	13.44 kg (29 lb 10 oz)	Dauphin Island, Alabama, USA	July 22, 2000	Robert Andrew Conklin
Scombrops, Atlantic	9.88 kg (21 lb 12 oz)	Bimini, Bahamas	July 15, 1997	Doug Olander
Scorpionfish, black	0.87 kg (1 lb 14 oz)	Detached Mole, Gibraltar	Feb. 3, 1997	Julius Gafan
Scorpionfish, red	2.96 kg (6 lb 8 oz)	Gibraltar	May 30, 1996	Stuart Brown-Giraldi
Scorpionfish, spotted	1.55 kg (3 lb 7 oz)	Angra Dor Reis Bay, Rio de Janeiro, Brazil	May 25, 1997	Pedro L.D. Cabral de Menezes
Sculpin, great	3.40 kg (7 lb 8 oz)	Ugak Bay, Kodiak, Alaska, USA	Aug. 30, 2000	Brian R. Phelps
Scup	2.06 kg (4 lb 9 oz)	Nantucket Sound, Massachusetts, USA	June 3, 1992	Sonny Richards

All-Tackle Records, *continued*

Species	Weight	Place of Catch	Date	Angler
Seabass, blackfin	9.10 kg (20 lb 0 oz)	Muroto, Kochi, Japan	July 13, 1997	Yuji Shimasaki
Seabass, Japanese (suzuki)	8.70 kg (19 lb 2 oz)	Kano River, Numazu-shi, Shizuoka, Japan	Nov. 26, 1988	Yasuaki Ohshio
Seabass, white	37.98 kg (83 lb 12 oz)	San Felipe, Mexico	Mar. 31, 1953	Lyal C. Baumgardner
Seabream, axillary	0.60 kg (1 lb 5 oz)	Anglet, France	June 8, 2001	Jean Pierre Baibarac
Seabream, black	1.22 kg (2 lb 11 oz)	Detached Mole, Gibraltar	Jan. 14, 1996	Albert Ward
Seabream, bluespotted	11.62 kg (25 lb 9 oz)	Detached Mole, Gibraltar	June 4, 2000	Charles Bear
Seabream, daggerhead	7.30 kg (16 lb 1 oz)	Algoa Bay, Port Elizabeth, South Africa	Oct. 10, 1993	Eddie De Reuck
Seabream, Okinawa	2.80 kg (6 lb 2 oz)	Otana, Amami-oshima, Kagoshima, Japan	Sept. 24, 2001	Yasunori Haraguchi
Seabream, redbanded (murudai)	3.00 kg (6 lb 9 oz)	Nouadhibou, Mauritania	Mar. 9, 1986	Serge Bensa
Seabream, Scotsman	7.80 kg (17 lb 3 oz)	St. Lucia Estuary, South Africa	Nov. 25, 1994	G.J. Van Der Westhuizen
Seabream, sharpsnout	1.68 kg (3 lb 11 oz)	La Sela, Gibraltar Bay, Gibraltar	Nov. 23, 1996	Brian Anthony Soiza
Seabream, white	1.87 kg (4 lb 1 oz)	Gibraltar Bay, Gibraltar	Apr. 28, 1996	Anthony William Loddo
Seabream, yellowfin	1.68 kg (3 lb 11 oz)	Kobe port, Hyogo, Japan	Dec. 2, 2001	Ryo Kinoshita
Seabream, zebra	2.74 kg (6 lb 0 oz)	Detached Mole, Gibraltar	Mar. 19, 2000	Albert Gonzalez
Seaperch, spotted scale	10.50 kg (23 lb 2 oz)	Cairns, Queensland, Australia	Mar. 2, 1986	Mac Mankowski
Searobin, striped	1.55 kg (3 lb 6 oz)	Mt. Sinai, Long Island, New York, USA	June 22, 1988	Michael B. Greene, Jr.
Seatrout, sand	2.78 kg (6 lb 2 oz)	Dauphin Island, Alabama, USA	May 24, 1997	Steve V. Scoggin
Seatrout, spotted	7.92 kg (17 lb 7 oz)	Ft. Pierce, Florida, USA	May 11, 1995	Craig F. Carson
Seerfish, Australian	9.25 kg (20 lb 6 oz)	South West Rocks, N.S.W., Australia	July 5, 1987	Greg Laarkamp
Seerfish, Chinese	59.67 kg (131 lb 9 oz)	Lema Islands, Hong Kong	May 31, 1998	Peter Sprung
Seerfish, kanadi	12.50 kg (27 lb 8 oz)	Mapelane, Zululand, Natal, South Africa	July 11, 1997	Daniel J. Van Tonder
Sennet, southern	1.14 kg (2 lb 8 oz)	Indian River, Florida, USA	Jan. 29, 1999	Chris Kirkhart
Seventy-four	16.00 kg (35 lb 4 oz)	Mapuzi, Transkei, Republic of South Africa	Aug. 17, 1985	Nolan Sparg
Shad, allis	1.19 kg (2 lb 9 oz)	Dordogne River, Lalinde, France	June 28, 2001	Stephane Giraudeau
Shad, American	5.10 kg (11 lb 4 oz)	Connecticut River, Massachusetts, USA	May 19, 1986	Bob Thibodo
Shad, gizzard	1.98 kg (4 lb 6 oz)	Lake Michigan, Indiana, USA	Mar. 2, 1996	Mike Berg
Shad, hickory	0.85 kg (1 lb 14 oz)	James River, Virginia, USA	Apr. 4, 2002	W. Scott Johnston
Shad, Mediterranean	0.76 kg (1 lb 10 oz)	Ombrone River, Grosseto, Italy	Apr. 16, 1994	Marco Sammicheli
Shad, skipjack	1.16 kg (2 lb 9 oz)	Pickwick Dam, Tennessee, USA	Mar. 26, 2000	Tim Shea, Jr.
Shad, twaite	0.70 kg (1 lb 8 oz)	North Sea, Netherlands	Aug. 21, 1998	P.C. Ouwendijk
Shark, Atlantic sharpnose	7.25 kg (16 lb 0 oz)	Port Mansfield, Texas, USA	Oct. 12, 1994	R. Bruce Shields
Shark, bigeye thresher	363.80 kg (802 lb 0 oz)	Tutukaka, New Zealand	Feb. 8, 1981	Dianne North
Shark, bignose	167.80 kg (369 lb 14 oz)	Markham River, LAE, Papua New Guinea	Oct. 23, 1993	Lester J. Rohrlach
Shark, blackmouth cat	1.37 kg (3 lb 0 oz)	Mausundvar, Trondheim, Norway	Sept. 17, 1994	Per Arne Hagen
Shark, blacknose	18.86 kg (41 lb 9 oz)	Little River, South Carolina, USA	July 30, 1992	Jon-Paul Hoffman
Shark, blacktail	33.70 kg (74 lb 4 oz)	Kosi Bay, Zululand, Republic of South Africa	May 25, 1987	Trevor Ashington
Shark, blacktip	122.75 kg (270 lb 9 oz)	Malindi Bay, Kenya	Sept. 21, 1984	Jurgen Oeder
Shark, blacktip reef	13.55 kg (29 lb 13 oz)	Coco Island, Indian Ocean	Oct. 22, 1995	Dr. Joachim Kleidon
Shark, blue	239.49 kg (528 lb 0 oz)	Montauk Point, New York, USA	Aug. 9, 2001	Joe Seidel
Shark, bonnethead	10.76 kg (23 lb 11 oz)	Cumberland Sound, Georgia, USA	Aug. 5, 1994	Chad Wood
Shark, bull	316.50 kg (697 lb 12 oz)	Malindi, Kenya	Mar. 24, 2001	Ronald de Jager
Shark, Caribbean reef	69.85 kg (154 lb 0 oz)	Molasses Reef, Florida, USA	Dec. 29, 1996	Rene G. de Dios
Shark, dusky	346.54 kg (764 lb 0 oz)	Longboat Key, Florida, USA	May 28, 1982	Warren Girle
Shark, Galapagos	85.45 kg (188 lb 6 oz)	Midway Islands, Pacific Ocean	Aug. 15, 2000	David B. Holmer
Shark, great hammerhead	449.51 kg (991 lb 0 oz)	Sarasota, Florida, USA	May 30, 1982	Allen Ogle
Shark, Greenland	775.00 kg (1708 lb 9 oz)	Trondheimsfjord, Norway	Oct. 18, 1987	Terje Nordtvedt
Shark, gulper	7.34 kg (16 lb 3 oz)	Bimini, Bahamas	July 15, 1997	Doug Olander
Shark, gummy	30.80 kg (67 lb 14 oz)	Mcloughins Beach, Victoria, Australia	Nov. 15, 1992	Neale Blunden
Shark, lemon	183.70 kg (405 lb 0 oz)	Buxton, North Carolina, USA	Nov. 23, 1988	Colleen D. Harlow
Shark, leopard	18.42 kg (40 lb 10 oz)	Oceanside, California, USA	May 13, 1994	Fred Oakley
Shark, milk	5.00 kg (11 lb 0 oz)	Archipelago dos Bijagos, Guinea Bissau	Apr. 1, 2001	Adrien Bernard
Shark, narrowtooth	242.00 kg (533 lb 8 oz)	Cape Karikari, New Zealand	Jan. 9, 1993	Gaye Harrison-Armstrong

All-Tackle Records, *continued*

Species	Weight	Place of Catch	Date	Angler
Shark, night	76.65 kg (169 lb 0 oz)	Bimini, Bahamas	July 13, 1997	Ron Schatman
Shark, nurse	109.58 kg (241 lb 9 oz)	South Beach, Ft. Pierce, Florida, USA	Apr. 14, 2001	Jeffery L. Chism
Shark, oceanic whitetip	167.37 kg (369 lb 0 oz)	San Salvador, Bahamas	Jan. 24, 1998	Reid Hodges
Shark, porbeagle	230.00 kg (507 lb 0 oz)	Pentland Firth, Caithness, Scotland	Mar. 9, 1993	Christopher Bennett
Shark, salmon	104.32 kg (230 lb 0 oz)	Port Gravina, Alaska, USA	June 13, 2002	Ken Higginbotham
Shark, sand tiger	158.81 kg (350 lb 2 oz)	Charleston Jetty, South Carolina, USA	Apr. 29, 1993	Mark Thawley
Shark, sandbar	117.93 kg (260 lb 0 oz)	Gambia Coast, Gambia	Jan. 2, 1989	Paul Delsignore
Shark, scalloped hammerhead	152.40 kg (335 lb 15 oz)	Latham Island, Tanzania	Dec. 3, 1995	Jack Reece, Q.P.M.
Shark, sevengill	32.80 kg (72 lb 4 oz)	Weymouth Channel, Manukou Harbour, New Zealand	Oct. 23, 1995	Shane Sowerby
Shark, shortfin mako	553.84 kg (1221 lb 0 oz)	Chatham, Massachusetts, USA	July 21, 2001	Luke Sweeney
Shark, sicklefin lemon	10.60 kg (23 lb 5 oz)	Darwin Harbour, Australia	Dec. 7, 1998	Craig Johnston
Shark, silky	346.00 kg (762 lb 12 oz)	Port Stephen's, N.S.W., Australia	Feb. 26, 1994	Bryce Robert Henderson
Shark, silvertip	180.60 kg (398 lb 2 oz)	Malindi, Kenya	Sept. 16, 2001	Billy Furnish
Shark, sixgilled	485.00 kg (1069 lb 3 oz)	Faial, Azores	Oct. 18, 1990	Jack Reece
Shark, smallfin gulper	2.40 kg (5 lb 4 oz)	Lae, Huon Gulf, Papua New Guinea	Feb. 13, 1993	Justin Mallett
Shark, smooth hammerhead	164.65 kg (363 lb 0 oz)	Horta, Faial, Azores	July 31, 1999	Georg Geyer
Shark, spinner	89.70 kg (197 lb 12 oz)	Malindi, Kenya, East Africa	Sept. 21, 1999	Emiel Van De Werf
Shark, thresher	348.00 kg (767 lb 3 oz)	Bay of Islands, New Zealand	Feb. 26, 1983	D.L. Hannah
Shark, tiger	807.40 kg (1780 lb 0 oz)	Cherry Grove, South Carolina, USA	June 14, 1964	Walter Maxwell
Shark, tope	33.00 kg (72 lb 12 oz)	Parengarenga Harbor, New Zealand	Dec. 19, 1986	Melanie B. Feldman
Shark, velvet belly lantern	0.85 kg (1 lb 13 oz)	Langesundbukta, Norway	Oct. 7, 2000	Arild Borresen
Shark, white	1208.38 kg (2664 lb 0 oz)	Ceduna, South Australia	Apr. 21, 1959	Alfred Dean
Shark, whitetip reef	18.25 kg (40 lb 4 oz)	Isla Coiba, Panama	Aug. 8, 1979	Jack Kamerman
Sharksucker	5.38 kg (11 lb 14 oz)	Molasses Reef, Florida, USA	Aug. 9, 2001	Yolanda Morejon
Sheephead, California	12.88 kg (28 lb 6 oz)	Isla Roca Partida, Revillagigedo Islands, Mexico	Nov. 4, 1999	Marshall Madruga
Sheepshead	9.63 kg (21 lb 4 oz)	Bayou St. John, New Orleans, Louisiana, USA	Apr. 16, 1982	Wayne Desselle
Sierra, Atlantic	6.71 kg (14 lb 13 oz)	Mangaratiba, Brazil	June 20, 1999	Paula Breves Boghossian
Skate	97.07 kg (214 lb 0 oz)	Scapa Flow, Orkney, Great Britain	July 16, 1968	Jan A. E. Olsson
Skate, big	41.27 kg (91 lb 0 oz)	Humbolt Bay, Eureka, California, USA	Mar. 6, 1993	Scotty A. Krick
Skate, starry	4.25 kg (9 lb 5 oz)	Hvasser, Norway	Oct. 10, 1982	Knut Hedlund
Skipjack, black	11.79 kg (26 lb 0 oz)	Thetis Bank, Baja California, Mexico	Oct. 23, 1991	Clifford K. Hamaishi
Sleeper, bigmouth	2.03 kg (4 lb 7 oz)	Rio Sarapiqui, Costa Rica	Mar. 17, 2001	Alexander Arias A.
Smoothhound, Florida	13.78 kg (30 lb 6 oz)	Gulf of Mexico, Destin, Florida, USA	Apr. 1, 1992	Stephen L. Wilson
Smoothhound, star-spotted	5.72 kg (12 lb 9 oz)	Lae, Huon Gulf, Papua New Guinea	Feb. 13, 1993	Justin Mallett
Smoothhound, starry	4.76 kg (10 lb 8 oz)	Nab Rocks, Isle of Wight, England	July 18, 1984	Sylvia M. Steed
Snakehead	6.35 kg (13 lb 15 oz)	Meimaike, Kagawa, Japan	Dec. 2, 2001	Hiroyoshi Yamada
Snakehead	1.97 kg (4 lb 5 oz)	Kako River, Hyogo, Japan	Apr. 19, 2002	Masahiro Oomori
Snakehead, chevron	3.00 kg (6 lb 9 oz)	Peekree River, Sangklaburi, Thailand	Feb. 15, 2001	Jean-Francois Helias
Snakehead, giant	7.50 kg (16 lb 8 oz)	Khao Laem Dam, Sangklaburi, Thailand	Apr. 23, 2000	Jean-Francois Helias
Snakehead, great	2.55 kg (5 lb 10 oz)	Srinakarine Lake, Thailand	July 6, 2001	Gerard Cittadini
Snapper (squirefish)	17.20 kg (37 lb 14 oz)	Mottiti Island, New Zealand	Nov. 2, 1992	Mark Hemingway
Snapper, black	3.17 kg (7 lb 0 oz)	Little San Salvador, Bahamas	Apr. 24, 1992	Donald E. May
Snapper, blackfin	3.28 kg (7 lb 3 oz)	Bimini, Bahamas	Aug. 25, 1993	Ron Mallet
Snapper, colorado	9.29 kg (20 lb 8 oz)	Playa Zancudo, Costa Rica	Mar. 19, 1993	Craig Whitehead, MD
Snapper, cubera	55.11 kg (121 lb 8 oz)	Cameron, Louisiana, USA	July 5, 1982	Mike Hebert
Snapper, dog (Atlantic)	10.90 kg (24 lb 0 oz)	Hole in the Wall, Abaco, Bahamas	May 28, 1994	Wayne Barder
Snapper, emperor	17.90 kg (39 lb 7 oz)	Chichijima, Ogasawara, Tokyo, Japan	Nov. 9, 1999	Tadashi Kawabata
Snapper, gorean	5.50 kg (12 lb 2 oz)	Archipelago dos Bijagos, Guinea Bissau	Mar. 23, 2001	Patrick Sebile
Snapper, gray	7.71 kg (17 lb 0 oz)	Port Canaveral, Florida, USA	June 14, 1992	Steve Maddox
Snapper, greenbar	9.58 kg (21 lb 2 oz)	Solmar Beach, Baja California, Mexico	June 15, 1994	Walt Geiger
Snapper, Guinean (Afr. cubera)	60.00 kg (132 lb 4 oz)	Keur Saloum, Senegal	Feb. 18, 2001	Stephane Talavet
Snapper, lane	3.72 kg (8 lb 3 oz)	Horseshoe Rigs, Mississippi, USA	Aug. 25, 2001	Stephen Edward Wilson

All-Tackle Records, *continued*

Species	Weight	Place of Catch	Date	Angler
Snapper, Malabar	7.91 kg (17 lb 7 oz)	Cairns, Queensland, Australia	Aug. 3, 1989	Gregory Ronald Albert
Snapper, mullet	14.96 kg (33 lb 0 oz)	Cano Island, Costa Rica	Sept. 23, 1997	Jose Francisco Reyes Astorga
Snapper, mutton	13.72 kg (30 lb 4 oz)	Dry Tortugas, Florida, USA	Nov. 29, 1998	Richard Casey
Snapper, Pacific cubera	35.72 kg (78 lb 12 oz)	Bahia Pez Vela, Costa Rica	Mar. 23, 1988	Steven C. Paull
Snapper, Pacific red	7.90 kg (17 lb 7 oz)	Uncle Sam Banks, Mexico	Oct. 20, 2001	Lon Mikkelsen
Snapper, Papuan black	19.20 kg (42 lb 5 oz)	Fly River, Papua New Guinea	Sept. 22, 1992	Len Bradica
Snapper, queen	5.30 kg (11 lb 11 oz)	Bimini, Bahamas	July 15, 1997	Jeff Dry
Snapper, red	22.79 kg (50 lb 4 oz)	Gulf of Mexico, Louisiana, USA	June 23, 1996	Doc Kennedy
Snapper, schoolmaster	6.02 kg (13 lb 4 oz)	North Key Largo, Florida, USA	Sept. 3, 1999	Gustavo Pla
Snapper, silk	8.32 kg (18 lb 5 oz)	Gulf of Mexico, Venice, Florida, USA	July 12, 1986	James M. Taylor
Snapper, spotted rose	1.31 kg (2 lb 14 oz)	Playa Hermosa, Mexico	July 4, 1999	William Favor
Snapper, twospot red	12.50 kg (27 lb 8 oz)	Ogasawara Islands, Hahajima, Tokyo, Japan	Aug. 9, 1990	Fujiko Shimazaki
Snapper, vermillion	3.26 kg (7 lb 3 oz)	Gulf of Mexico, Mobile, Alabama, USA	May 31, 1987	John W. Doss
Snapper, yellow (amarillo)	5.44 kg (12 lb 0 oz)	Golfito, Costa Rica	Aug. 11, 1998	John Gunnar Olson
Snapper, yellowtail	4.62 kg (10 lb 3 oz)	Eugene Island, Louisiana, USA	Aug. 27, 2001	Michael Ledet
Snook, common	24.32 kg (53 lb 10 oz)	Parismina Ranch, Costa Rica	Oct. 18, 1978	Gilbert Ponzi
Snook, fat	4.23 kg (9 lb 5 oz)	Barra Una, Sao Paulo, Brazil	Mar. 14, 1999	Vander Afonso
Snook, Pacific black	26.19 kg (57 lb 12 oz)	Rio Naranjo, Quepos, Costa Rica	Aug. 23, 1991	George Beck
Snook, Pacific blackfin	3.14 kg (6 lb 14 oz)	Rio Parrita, Costa Rica	Dec. 7, 1997	Victor Miranda Golfin
Snook, Pacific white	21.54 kg (47 lb 8 oz)	Cabo San Lucas, Mexico	July 4, 2001	Vito M. Allessandro
Snook, swordspine	0.60 kg (1 lb 5 oz)	Stuart, Florida, USA	Apr. 6, 1997	Robert R. Pelosi, Sr.
Snook, tarpon	1.42 kg (3 lb 2 oz)	Dona Bay, Nokomis, Florida, USA	Sept. 19, 1996	David B. Coudal
Sole	0.80 kg (1 lb 12 oz)	North Sea, Netherlands	July 12, 1997	P.C. Ouwendijk
Sole, fantail	3.99 kg (8 lb 12 oz)	San Clemente Island, California, USA	June 3, 2001	Allan Sheridan
Sole, lemon	1.03 kg (2 lb 4 oz)	Fedje, Norway	May 20, 1999	Nicklas Kolbeck
Sorubim, barred	13.50 kg (29 lb 12 oz)	Kuluene River, Brazil	Sept. 17, 2000	Capt. Kdu Magalhaes
Sorubim, spotted	53.50 kg (117 lb 15 oz)	Rio Parana, Corrientes, Argentina	Feb. 16, 2000	Joao Batista Marches Neto
Sorubim, tiger	16.55 kg (36 lb 8 oz)	Rupinuni River, Karanambo, Guyana	Dec. 4, 1981	William T. Miller
Spadefish, Atlantic	6.35 kg (14 lb 0 oz)	Chesapeake Bay, Virginia, USA	May 23, 1986	Geo. F. Brace
Spearfish, longbill	58.00 kg (127 lb 13 oz)	Puerto Rico, Gran Canaria, Spain	May 20, 1999	Paul Cashmore
Spearfish, Mediterranean	41.20 kg (90 lb 13 oz)	Madeira Island, Portugal	June 2, 1980	Joseph Larkin

This Red Snapper was caught in Gulf of Mexico, Louisiana by Doc Kennedy on June 23, 1996. It measured in at 50 lb 4 oz.

All-Tackle Records, *continued*

Species	Weight	Place of Catch	Date	Angler
Spearfish, shortbill	33.80 kg (74 lb 8 oz)	Bay of Islands, New Zealand	Mar. 16, 1999	Leonie Kai Patterson
Splake	9.39 kg (20 lb 11 oz)	Georgian Bay, Ontario, Canada	May 17, 1987	Paul S. Thompson
Spot	0.45 kg (1 lb 0 oz)	Nags Head, North Carolina, USA	July 16, 2000	Sean William McKinney
Squirrelfish, sabre	2.55 kg (5 lb 10 oz)	Keahole Point, Kailua Kona, Hawaii, USA	Mar. 26, 1995	Rex C. Bigg
Stargazer	0.94 kg (2 lb 1 oz)	Gibraltar, United Kingdom	Dec. 4, 1994	Albert Ward
Stargazer, northern	4.87 kg (10 lb 12 oz)	Cape May, New Jersey, USA	June 20, 1998	John E. Jacobsen
Steed, barbel (nigoi)	2.15 kg (4 lb 11 oz)	Ibo-River, Hyogo, Japan	Feb. 18, 1996	Masahiro Oomori
Steed, barbel (nigoi)	2.16 kg (4 lb 12 oz)	Ukawa, Niigata, Japan	Jan. 29, 2000	Shinichi Akiyama
Steed, barbel (nigoi)	2.18 kg (4 lb 12 oz)	Ibo River, Hyogo, Japan	Apr. 27, 2002	Masahiro Oomori
Steenbras, red	56.60 kg (124 lb 12 oz)	Aston Bay, Eastern Cape, South Africa	May 8, 1994	Terry Colin Goldstone
Stingray, Atlantic	4.87 kg (10 lb 12 oz)	Galveston Bay, Texas, USA	July 3, 1994	David Lee Anderson
Stingray, black	57.50 kg (126 lb 12 oz)	Laurieton, N.S.W., Australia	July 3, 1994	David Shearing
Stingray, common	201.39 kg (444 lb 0 oz)	Faial, Horta, Azores	Sept. 1, 1999	Bob de Boeck
Stingray, diamond	46.26 kg (102 lb 0 oz)	Mission Bay, San Diego, California, USA	Aug. 7, 1993	Roger Ehlers
Stingray, Haller's round	1.36 kg (3 lb 0 oz)	Santa Clara River, Ventura, California, USA	Sept. 3, 1989	Paul David Bodtke
Stingray, red (akaei)	19.30 kg (42 lb 8 oz)	Kashiwazaki, Niigata, Japan	Apr. 24, 2002	Youji Yamaguchi
Stingray, roughtail	183.70 kg (405 lb 0 oz)	Islamorada, Florida, USA	Feb. 1979	Geoff Flores
Stingray, round	84.00 kg (185 lb 2 oz)	Archipelago dos Bijagos, Guinea Bissau	Mar. 14, 2001	Pierre Verot
Stingray, S.A. freshwater	12.59 kg (27 lb 12 oz)	Rio Agua Boa, Roraima, Brazil	Jan. 9, 2000	Ben P. Wise
Stingray, southern	111.58 kg (246 lb 0 oz)	Galveston Bay, Texas, USA	June 30, 1998	Carissa Egger
Stumpnose, red	5.80 kg (12 lb 12 oz)	St. Croix Island, Port Elizabeth, South Africa	Dec. 20, 1993	Craig Saunders
Sturgeon, beluga	102.00 kg (224 lb 13 oz)	Guryev, Kazakhstan	May 3, 1993	Merete Lehne
Sturgeon, lake	76.20 kg (168 lb 0 oz)	Georgian Bay, Ontario, Canada	May 29, 1982	Edward Paszkowski
Sturgeon, shortnose	5.04 kg (11 lb 2 oz)	Kennebacis River, New Brunswick, Canada	July 31, 1988	Lawrence Guimond
Sturgeon, shovelnose	4.88 kg (10 lb 12 oz)	Missouri River, Loma, Montana, USA	June 14, 1985	Arthur James Seal
Sturgeon, white	212.28 kg (468 lb 0 oz)	Benicia, California, USA	July 9, 1983	Joey Pallotta, III
Sucker, flannelmouth	1.09 kg (2 lb 6 oz)	Colorado River, Colorado, USA	July 7, 1990	Karen A. DeVine
Sucker, longnose	2.97 kg (6 lb 9 oz)	St. Joseph River, Michigan, USA	Dec. 2, 1989	Ben Knoll
Sucker, northern hog	0.48 kg (1 lb 1 oz)	Clarion River, Pennsylvania, USA	Oct. 8, 1994	Richard E. Faler, Jr.
Sucker, spotted	1.23 kg (2 lb 11 oz)	Hall's Lake, Rome, Georgia, USA	Mar. 6, 1985	J. Paul Diprima, Jr.

This Splake was caught in the Georgian Bay by Paul S. Thompson on May 17, 1987. It measured in at 20 lb 11 oz.

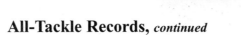

All-Tackle Records, *continued*

Species	Weight	Place of Catch	Date	Angler
Sucker, white	2.94 kg (6 lb 8 oz)	Rainy River, Loman, Minnesota, USA	Apr. 20, 1984	Joel M. Anderson
Sunfish, green	0.96 kg (2 lb 2 oz)	Stockton Lake, Missouri, USA	June 18, 1971	Paul M. Dilley
Sunfish, green (hybrid)	0.97 kg (2 lb 2 oz)	Patagonia Lake State Park, Arizona, USA	June 5, 1998	Mikey A. Porter
Sunfish, hybrid	0.48 kg (1 lb 1 oz)	Shakey Slough, Indiana, USA	May 2, 1998	Steven M. Berg
Sunfish, hybrid	0.48 kg (1 lb 1 oz)	Shakey Slough, Indiana, USA	May 2, 1998	Mike Berg
Sunfish, longear	0.79 kg (1 lb 12 oz)	Elephant Butte Lake, New Mexico, USA	May 9, 1985	Patricia Stout
Sunfish, redbreast	0.79 kg (1 lb 12 oz)	Suwannee River, Florida, USA	May 29, 1984	Alvin Buchanan
Sunfish, redear	2.48 kg (5 lb 7 oz)	Diversion Canal, South Carolina, USA	Nov. 6, 1998	Amos M. Gay
Surfperch, barred	1.87 kg (4 lb 2 oz)	Oxnard, California, USA	Mar. 30, 1996	Fred Oakley
Sweetlip, painted	6.90 kg (15 lb 3 oz)	Moreton Island, Queensland, Australia	July 24, 1993	Kathy McGuire
Swordfish	536.15 kg (1182 lb 0 oz)	Iquique, Chile	May 7, 1953	Louis B. Marron
Taimen	41.95 kg (92 lb 8 oz)	Keta River, Siberia, Russia	Aug. 11, 1993	Yuri Orlov
Takenokomebaru	1.60 kg (3 lb 8 oz)	Oshika, Miyagi, Japan	Feb. 22, 2002	Norihiko Shiotsu
Tambaqui	28.50 kg (62 lb 13 oz)	Guapore, Estado de Rondonia, Brazil	Sept. 7, 1998	Laerte Batista de Oliveira Alves
Tarpon	128.36 kg (283 lb 0 oz)	Lake Maracaibo, Venezuela	Mar. 19, 1956	Mario Salazar
Tarpon	128.50 kg (283 lb 4 oz)	Sherbro Island, Sierra Leone	Apr. 16, 1991	Yvon Victor Sebag
Tautog	11.33 kg (25 lb 0 oz)	Ocean City, New Jersey, USA	Jan. 20, 1998	Anthony R. Monica
Tench	4.64 kg (10 lb 3 oz)	Ljungbyan, Sweden	July 2, 1985	Dan Dellerfjord
Thornyhead, shortspine	2.31 kg (5 lb 1 oz)	Los Coranados Islands, Baja California Sur, Mexico	Feb. 3, 2001	Stephen D. Grossberg
Threadfin, African	3.17 kg (7 lb 0 oz)	Guinea-Bissau	May 21, 1996	Yvon Mabileau
Threadfin, giant African	49.60 kg (109 lb 5 oz)	Barra do Kwanza, Angola	Jan. 17, 1999	Marco Roberto da Silva Couto
Threadfin, king	12.50 kg (27 lb 8 oz)	Dampier Creek, Broome, Australia	Apr. 24, 1996	Brian William Albert
Threadfin, moi	3.17 kg (7 lb 0 oz)	Hanalei, Hawaii, USA	Sept. 3, 1988	Harry H. Paik
Threadfin, smallscale	0.62 kg (1 lb 6 oz)	Jensen Beach, Florida, USA	Oct. 9, 1998	Ralph E. Bailey, III
Threadfin, striped	1.65 kg (3 lb 10 oz)	Ukenmura, Amami-oshima, Kagoshima, Japan	Oct. 24, 1999	Masaaki Sudo
Tigerfish	16.10 kg (35 lb 7 oz)	Kariba, Zimbabwe	Sept. 12, 2001	Jennifer Lynne Daynes
Tigerfish, giant	44.00 kg (97 lb 0 oz)	Zaire River, Kinshasa, Zaire	July 9, 1988	Raymond Houtmans
Tilapia, blue	2.01 kg (4 lb 7 oz)	Santiago Pond, Orlando, Florida, USA	Oct. 14, 1998	Charles D. Scheerschmidt
Tilapia, Mozambique	1.13 kg (2 lb 8 oz)	Delray Beach, Florida, USA	Nov. 10, 1997	Nick Cardella
Tilapia, Nile	4.32 kg (9 lb 8 oz)	Antelope Island, Kariba, Zimbabwe	Apr. 22, 2001	David Barnard
Tilapia, redbreast	1.62 kg (3 lb 9 oz)	Zambezi River, Namibia	Nov. 14, 1994	Bill Staveley
Tilapia, spotted	1.36 kg (3 lb 0 oz)	Pembroke Pines, Florida, USA	Mar. 20, 1999	Jay Wright, Jr.
Tilapia, threespot	4.71 kg (10 lb 6 oz)	Upper Zambezi, Zambia	Nov. 3, 1998	Ben Van Wyk
Tilefish, Bahama	1.31 kg (2 lb 14 oz)	Grand Bahama Island, Bahamas	Aug. 22, 2000	Capt. Jay Cohen
Tilefish, blueline	4.79 kg (10 lb 9 oz)	Sea Girt, New Jersey, USA	Dec. 5, 2001	Jim Zigarelli
Tilefish, golden-eyed	0.68 kg (1 lb 8 oz)	Playa Zancudo, Costa Rica	Mar. 10, 1993	Craig Whitehead, MD
Tilefish, great northern	9.18 kg (20 lb 4 oz)	Murrell's Inlet, South Carolina, USA	Apr. 30, 2000	Jeffrey Pifer

This Giant Tigerfish was caught on the Zaire River by Raymond Houtmans on July 9, 1988. It measured in at 35 lb 7 oz.

All-Tackle Records, *continued*

Species	Weight	Place of Catch	Date	Angler
Tilefish, red	1.25 kg (2 lb 12 oz)	Manazuru, Kanagawa, Japan	Nov. 19, 2000	Yuji Mita
Tilefish, sand	1.02 kg (2 lb 4 oz)	Key Largo, Florida, USA	June 23, 1991	Rachel S. Olander
Tilefish, southern	3.75 kg (8 lb 12 oz)	Rio de Janeiro, Brazil	May 18, 2002	Eduardo Baumeier
Toadfish, oyster	2.23 kg (4 lb 15 oz)	Ocracoke, North Carolina, USA	June 4, 1994	David R. Tinsley
Torpedo, Atlantic	16.01 kg (35 lb 4 oz)	Perkins Cove, Ogunquit, Maine, USA	Aug. 24, 1995	Don Carignan
Trahira	1.41 kg (3 lb 2 oz)	Rio Piqueri, Mato Grosso, Brazil	Aug. 11, 1996	Sandy Blum
Trahira, giant	13.15 kg (29 lb 0 oz)	Uraima Falls, Venezuela	Mar. 2, 2001	Jace Spencer
Trevally, bigeye	14.30 kg (31 lb 8 oz)	Poivre Island, Seychelles	Apr. 23,1997	Les Sampson
Trevally, blue	2.26 kg (5 lb 0 oz)	Midway Islands, Pacific Ocean	May 30, 2001	Matthew Stewart
Trevally, bluefin	11.99 kg (26 lb 7 oz)	Clipperton Island, E. Pacific Ocean	Mar. 24, 1997	Tom Taylor
Trevally, brassy	4.40 kg (9 lb 11 oz)	Isigaki Island, Okinawa, Japan	Apr. 12, 1991	Fumio Suzuki
Trevally, giant	65.99 kg (145 lb 8 oz)	Makena, Maui, Hawaii, USA	Mar. 28, 1991	Russell Mori
Trevally, golden	14.15 kg (31 lb 3 oz)	Port Hedland, Australia	Aug. 16, 1997	Tammy Yates
Trevally, white	15.25 kg (33 lb 9 oz)	Hahajima, Ogasawara, Tokyo, Japan	July 6, 1998	Kazuhiko Adachi
Trevally, yellowspotted	11.20 kg (24 lb 11 oz)	Inhaca Island, Maputo	Apr. 3, 1998	Peter Kidd
Triggerfish, gray	6.15 kg (13 lb 9 oz)	Murrells Inlet, South Carolina, USA	May 3, 1989	Jim Hilton
Triggerfish, ocean	6.12 kg (13 lb 8 oz)	Pompano Beach, Florida, USA	Mar. 7, 1995	Frederick J. Lauriello
Triggerfish, queen	2.87 kg (6 lb 5 oz)	Murrell's Inlet, South Carolina, USA	July 12, 2000	Alicea Ann Novak
Tripletail	19.20 kg (42 lb 5 oz)	Zululand, Republic of South Africa	June 7, 1989	Steve Hand
Trout, Apache	2.36 kg (5 lb 3 oz)	White Mtn. Apache, Reservoir, Arizona, USA	May 29, 1991	John (TRES) Baldwin
Trout, aurora	2.21 kg (4 lb 14 oz)	Carol Lake, Ontario, Canada	Oct. 8, 1996	Robert J. Bernardo
Trout, biwamasu	1.25 kg (2 lb 12 oz)	Lake Biwa, Shiga, Japan	May 21, 1993	Shoji Matsuura
Trout, brook	6.57 kg (14 lb 8 oz)	Nipigon River, Ontario, Canada	July, 1916	W. J. Cook
Trout, brown	18.25 kg (40 lb 4 oz)	Little Red River, Heber Springs, Arkansas, USA	May 9, 1992	Howard L. (Rip) Collins
Trout, bull	14.51 kg (32 lb 0 oz)	Lake Pend Oreille, Idaho, USA	Oct. 27, 1949	N. L. Higgins
Trout, cutbow	5.10 kg (11 lb 4 oz)	Delta Co., Colorado, USA	Apr. 15, 1999	Brent Curtice
Trout, cutthroat	18.59 kg (41 lb 0 oz)	Pyramid Lake, Nevada, USA	Dec. 1925	John Skimmerhorn
Trout, golden	4.98 kg (11 lb 0 oz)	Cooks Lake, Wyoming, USA	Aug. 5, 1948	Chas. S. Reed
Trout, lake	32.65 kg (72 lb 0 oz)	Great Bear Lake, N.W.T., Canada	Aug. 19, 1995	Lloyd E. Bull
Trout, masu	5.25 kg (11 lb 9 oz)	Kuzuryu River, Fukui, Japan	May 6, 1995	Takeshi Matsuura
Trout, ohrid	6.46 kg (14 lb 4 oz)	Platte River, Wyoming, USA	Jan. 26, 1986	Kim Darwin Durfee
Trout, ohrid	6.49 kg (14 lb 4 oz)	Watauga Lake, Tennessee, USA	Mar. 28, 1986	Richard L. Carter
Trout, rainbow	19.10 kg (42 lb 2 oz)	Bell Island, Alaska, USA	June 22, 1970	David Robert White
Trout, red-spotted masu	1.54 kg (3 lb 6 oz)	Yoshino River, Tokushima, Japan	May 17, 1998	Akihiko Masutani
Trout, tiger	9.44 kg (20 lb 13 oz)	Lake Michigan, Wisconsin, USA	Aug. 12, 1978	Pete M. Friedland
Trunkfish	3.31 kg (7 lb 4 oz)	Palm Beach, Florida, USA	Apr. 1, 2000	Charlie Colon
Tuna, bigeye (Atlantic)	178.00 kg (392 lb 6 oz)	Puerto Rico, Gran Canaria, Spain	July 25, 1996	Dieter Vogel
Tuna, bigeye (Pacific)	197.31 kg (435 lb 0 oz)	Cabo Blanco, Peru	Apr. 17, 1957	Dr. Russel V. A. Lee
Tuna, blackfin	20.63 kg (45 lb 8 oz)	Key West, Florida, USA	May 4, 1996	Sam J. Burnett
Tuna, bluefin	678.58 kg (1496 lb 0 oz)	Aulds Cove, Nova Scotia, Canada	Oct. 26, 1979	Ken Fraser
Tuna, dogtooth	131.00 kg (288 lb 12 oz)	Kwan-Tall Island, Cheju-Do, Korea	Oct. 6, 1982	Boo-Il Oh
Tuna, longtail	35.90 kg (79 lb 2 oz)	Montague Island, N.S.W., Australia	Apr. 12, 1982	Tim Simpson
Tuna, northern bluefin	198.00 kg (436 lb 8 oz)	Kiapra Trench, New Zealand	Sept. 17, 2000	Peter Jackson
Tuna, skipjack	20.54 kg (45 lb 4 oz)	Flathead Bank, Baja California, Mexico	Nov. 16, 1996	Brian Evans
Tuna, slender	11.85 kg (26 lb 1 oz)	Taiaroa Heads, Otago, New Zealand	May 1, 2001	Gary Wilson
Tuna, southern bluefin	158.00 kg (348 lb 5 oz)	Whakatane, New Zealand	Jan. 16, 1981	Rex Wood
Tuna, yellowfin	176.35 kg (388 lb 12 oz)	Isla San Benedicto, Revillagigedo Islands, Mexico	Apr. 1, 1977	Curt Wiesenhutter
Tunny, little	15.95 kg (35 lb 2 oz)	Cap de Garde, Algeria	Dec. 14, 1988	Jean Yves Chatard
Tuskfish, blackspot	9.50 kg (20 lb 15 oz)	Bribie Island, Queensland, Australia	June 19, 1988	Olga Mack
Ugui	0.80 kg (1 lb 12 oz)	Ibi River, Gifu, Japan	June 23, 1995	Kaoru Hosoe
Ugui	0.81 kg (1 lb 12 oz)	Shimoda Port, Shizuoka, Japan	July 20, 1995	Motoshi Aihara
Ugui	0.85 kg (1 lb 13 oz)	Kuzuryu River, Fukui, Japan	May 13, 1996	Kaoru Hosoe

Vimba (Zahrte)	1.14 kg (2 lb 8 oz)	Olandsan, Sweden	May 1, 1990	Sonny Pettersson
Vimba (Zahrte)	1.11 kg (2 lb 7 oz)	Hossmoan, Kalmar, Sweden	June 9, 1987	Luis Kilian Rasmussen
Vundu	32.50 kg (71 lb 10 oz)	Lake Kariba, Zimbabwe, Africa	Dec. 26, 2000	Rob Konschel
Wahoo	71.89 kg (158 lb 8 oz)	Loreto, Baja California, Mexico	June 10, 1996	Keith Winter
Walleye	11.34 kg (25 lb 0 oz)	Old Hickory Lake, Tennessee, USA	Aug. 2, 1960	Mabry Harper
Warmouth	1.10 kg (2 lb 7 oz)	Guess Lake, Yellow River, Holt, Florida, USA	Oct. 19, 1985	Tony David Dempsey
Weakfish	8.67 kg (19 lb 2 oz)	Delaware Bay, Delaware, USA	May 20, 1989	William E. Thomas
Weakfish	8.67 kg (19 lb 2 oz)	Jones Beach Inlet, Long Island, New York, USA	Oct. 11, 1984	Dennis Roger Rooney
Weakfish, acoupa	17.00 kg (37 lb 7 oz)	Canal do Boqueirao, Ilha do Governador, Brazil	Aug. 23, 1997	Gilberto Ferreira
Weakfish, green	13.60 kg (29 lb 15 oz)	Ilha de Comandatuba, Hotel Transamerica, Brazil	Nov. 3, 1998	Martin Holzmann
Weakfish, gulf (corvina)	2.43 kg (5 lb 5 oz)	Vista del Oro, Mexico	Sept. 16, 2000	William E. Favor
Weakfish, Stolzmann's	9.52 kg (21 lb 0 oz)	Mazatlan, Sinaloa, Mexico	Dec. 20, 2000	Sergio Escutia
Weakfish, striped (corvina)	1.13 kg (2 lb 8 oz)	Mazatlan, Sinaloa, Mexico	Feb. 22, 2001	Sergio Escutia
Weever, greater	1.67 kg (3 lb 11 oz)	Gran Canaria, Canary Islands, Spain	Mar. 31, 1984	Arild J. Danielsen
Wels	91.62 kg (202 lb 0 oz)	River Ile Delta, Kazakhstan	Aug. 16, 1999	Kevin Maddocks
Wenchman	1.99 kg (4 lb 6 oz)	Bimini, Bahamas	July 13, 1997	Dan Upton
Whipray, pink	18.50 kg (40 lb 12 oz)	Bali Beach, Bali	July 20, 1995	Bo T. Johansson
Whitefish, broad	4.08 kg (9 lb 0 oz)	Tozitna River, Alaska, USA	July 17, 1989	Al Mathews
Whitefish, lake	6.52 kg (14 lb 6 oz)	Meaford, Ontario, Canada	May 21, 1984	Dennis M. Laycock
Whitefish, mountain	2.51 kg (5 lb 8 oz)	Elbow River, Calgary, Alberta, Canada	Aug. 1, 1995	Randy G. Woo
Whitefish, ocean	5.76 kg (12 lb 11 oz)	San Martin Island, Mexico	Aug. 21, 2000	Nicholas K. Sullivan
Whitefish, round	2.72 kg (6 lb 0 oz)	Putahow River, Manitoba, Canada	June 14, 1984	Allan J. Ristori
Whiting, blue	0.83 kg (1 lb 13 oz)	Drobak, Norway	Sept. 19, 1998	Trond Raade
Whiting, European	3.11 kg (6 lb 13 oz)	Dypdalen, Norway	June 10, 1997	John Kofoed
Wolffish, Atlantic	23.58 kg (52 lb 0 oz)	Georges Bank, Massachusetts, USA	June 11, 1986	Frederick Gardiner
Wolffish, northern	17.00 kg (37 lb 7 oz)	Holsteinsborg, Greenland	Aug. 19, 1982	Jens Ploug Hansen
Wolffish, spotted	27.90 kg (61 lb 8 oz)	Vannoy, Trohs Fylke, Norway	May 29, 2000	Kolbjorn Melien
Wrasse, ballan	4.35 kg (9 lb 9 oz)	Clogher Head, Co. Kerry, Ireland	Aug. 20, 1983	Bertrand Kron

This Spotted Wolffish was caught in Vannoy, Trohs Fylke, Norway by Kolbjorn Melien on May 29, 2000. It measured in at 61 lb 8 oz

This Wels was caught in River Ile Delta by Kevin Maddocks on Aug. 16, 1999. It measured in at 202 lb 0 oz.

Chapter Four: The Digest
National Fresh Water Fishing Hall of Fame Freshwater Record Fish

Straight through the musky's mouth. That's how thousands of anglers and tourists in northern Wisconsin view the grounds of the National Fresh Water Fishing Hall of Fame and Museum each week.

The highlight of the museum is a gigantic fish, measuring five stories tall and a half-city block long and loaded with fishing exhibits. The musky's mouth is an observation deck to view the museum's grounds. It's part of the seven acres and four buildings that comprise the museum, which is open seven days a week from April 15 to Nov. 1 from 10 a.m. to 5 p.m. The winter office is open Monday through Friday from 9 a.m. to 5 p.m.

The museum is the official qualifier and recorder of world record freshwater fish, from bass and bluegills to muskies and walleyes. A non-profit educational organization, the museum has about 30,000 members, whose membership includes free admission.

Founded in 1960, the museum also collects and displays fishing artifacts, including:

- 400 fish mounts of 200 species.
- 300 classic and antique outboard motors.
- 5,000 classic fishing lures.
- 200 historical fishing rods
- Hundreds of dated fishing reels
- Hundreds of fishing accessories.

A national committee of fishing industry volunteers elects persons and organizations to the Hall of Fame for their accomplishments.
About 100,000 visitors tour the museum annually. Hayward is located in northwest Wisconsin, 70 miles south of Duluth, Minn, 140 miles northeast of Minneapolis, and 400 miles northwest of Chicago. For more information about the museum, call (800) 724-2992.

Photos courtesy of The National Fresh Water Fishing Hall of Fame

Besides the outboard motors collection, the National Fresh Water Fishing Hall of Fame has 400 fish mounts decorating its walls.

FRESHWATER FISH RECORDS

The National Fresh Water Fishing Hall of Fame, located in Hayward, Wis., keeps a list of record fish for all freshwater species, by overall size as well as by line class. Here is the list for all tackle, courtesy of the Hall of Fame.

Size	Angler	Where caught	Date
AMUR, white (grass carp) 69 lb. 8 oz.	Daniel A. McDougall	Lake Petersburg, Ill.	7-13-00
BASS, Guadalupe (hybrid) 4 lb. 10 oz.	Brian R. Baeke	Blanco River, Texas	7-5-97
BASS, Largemouth 22 lb. 4 oz.	George W. Perry	Montgomery Lake, Ga.	6-2-32
BASS, Ozark 1 lb. 0 oz.	Gary Nelson	Bull Shoals Lake, Ark.	5-3-97
BASS, Peacock 9 lb. 1 oz.	Jerry Gomez	Kendale Lake, Fla.	3-11-93
BASS, Redeye 3 lb. 2 oz.	William T. Johnson	Choccolocco Creek, Ala.	3-28-00
BASS, Roanoke 2 lb. 7 oz.	James S. Ricks	Tar River, N.C.	4-15-90
BASS, Rock 3 lb. 0 oz.	Peter Gulgin	York River, Ontario, Canada	8-1-74
BASS, Shoal 8 lb. 3 oz.	David A. Hubbard	Flint River, Ga.	10-23-77
BASS, Smallmouth 11 lb. 15 oz.	David L. Hayes	Dale Hollow Lake, Tenn.	7-9-55
BASS, Spotted or Kentucky 8 lb. 15 oz.	Philip C. Terry Jr.	Lewis Smith Lake, Ala.	3-18-78

A collection of 270 antique and classic outboard motors greets visitors to the National Fresh Water Fishing Hall of Fame.

A giant musky forms a walk-through museum at the National Fresh Water Fishing Hall of Fame in Hayward, Wis. The museum "musky" is a half-city block long and stands five stories tall on the seven-acre museum grounds.

FRESHWATER FISH RECORDS
(continued)

Size	Angler	Where caught	Date
BASS, Striped (inland) 67 lb. 1 oz.	Jeff Smith	Colorado River, Ariz.	8-15-97
BASS, Suwannee 3 lb. 9 oz.	Laverne Norton	Ochlockonee River, Ga.	10-6-84
BASS, White 6 lb. 7 oz.	David S. Kraushaar	Saginaw Bay, Mich.	9-19-89
BASS, Whiterock or Rockfish hybrid 27 lb. 5 oz.	Jerald C. Shaum	Greers Ferry Lake, Ark.	4-24-97
BASS, Yellow 2 lb. 8 oz.	Dennis Michael	Tennessee River, Ala.	4-12-00
BASS, Yellow/hybrid 2 lb. 11 oz.	Dennis Hammersmith	Sabine River, Texas	3-10-97
BLUEGILL (brim or bream) 4 lb. 12 oz.	T.S. Hudson	Ketona Lake, Ala.	4-9-5
BLUEGILL, Hybrid 1 lb. 7 oz.	Daniel J. Manville	Arbulus Lake, Mich.	5-28-88
BOWFIN or dogfish 21 lb. 8 oz.	Robert L. Harmon	Forest Lake, S.C.	1-29-80
BUFFALO, Bigmouth 70 lb. 5 oz.	Delbert Sisk	Bussey Brake, La.	4-21-80
BUFFALO, Black 63 lb. 6 oz.	Jim Winters	Mississippi River, Iowa	8-14-90
BUFFALO, Smallmouth 88 lb. 0 oz.	Tony Crawford	Lake Wylie, N.C.	11-14-93
BULLHEAD, Black 8 lb. 15 oz.	Charles M. Taylor	Sturgis Pond, Mich.	8-19-97
BULLHEAD, Brown 6 lb. 2 oz.	Bobby L. Gibson Jr.	Pearl River, Miss.	1-19-91
BULLHEAD, Yellow 4 lb. 8 oz.	Patricia Simmon	Mormon Lake, Ariz.	7-15-89
BURBOT (Eelpout/lawyer) 22 lb. 8 oz.	Vaughn J. Kshywiecki	Little Athapapuskow Lake, Manitoba, Canada	4-2-94
CARP, Big Head 90 lb. 0 oz.	Timothy B. Conner	Kirby Lake, Texas	7-22-00
CARP, Common 57 lb. 13 oz.	David Nikolow	Tidal Basin, Washington, D.C.	6-19-83
CARP, Hybrid 3 lb. 8 oz.	Donald A. Czyzewski	Cermack Quarry, Ill.	8-22-90
CARP, Mirror 47 lb. 0 oz.	Gary A. Johnson	Farm Pond, W.Va.	7-2-98

FRESHWATER FISH RECORDS
(continued)

Size	Angler	Where caught	Date
CARPSUCKER (Quillback) 6 lb. 14 oz.	Craig F. Merchant	Kalamazoo River, Mich.	4-30-88
CARPSUCKER, River 7 lb. 15 oz.	Paulette HisGun	Lake Sharpe, S.D.	5-15-99
CATFISH, Blue 111 lb. 0 oz.	William P. McKinley	Wheeler Reservoir, Ala.	7-5-96
CATFISH, Channel 58 lb. 0 oz.	W.B. Whaley	Santee Cooper Reservoir, S.C.	7-7-64
CATFISH, Channel (Albino) 10 lb. 14 oz.	Henry "Buddy" Durden	Lake Laura, Ga.	6-12-98
CATFISH, Channel (Hybrid) 7 lb. 1 oz.	Chris E. Carothers	Holcombe Flowage, Wis.	5-4-93
CATFISH, Flathead (Mud-Cat) 123 lb. 0 oz.	Ken Paulie	Elk City Reservoir, Kans.	5-14-98
CATFISH, Walking 1 lb. 0 oz.	Stephen H. Helvin	Dade County, Fla.	3-9-97
CATFISH, White 22 lb. 0 oz.	James Robinson	William Land Pk. Pond, Calif.	3-21-94
CHAR, Arctic 32 lb. 9 oz.	Jeffery Lee Ward	Tree River, N.W.T., Canada	7-29-81
CHUB, Round Tailed 2 lb. 5 oz.	Daron W. Coombs	Verde River, Ariz.	12-10-83
CISCO or Lake Herring *(Tullibee)* 7 lb. 4 oz.	Randy Huff	Cedar Lake, Manitoba, Canada	4-11-86
CRAPPIE, Black (Specks) 6 lb. 0 oz.	Lettie Robertson	Westwego Canal, La.	11-28-69
CRAPPIE, Hybrid 2 lb. 1 oz.	Scott S. Szafran	Lake Elizabeth, Wis.	5-26-88
CRAPPIE, White (Specks) 5 lb. 3 oz.	Fred L. Bright	Enid Dam, Miss.	7-31-57
CUI-UI 6 lb. 0 oz.	Mike Berg	Pyramid Lake, Nev.	6-30-97
DRUM, Freshwater (Sheepshead) 54 lb. 8 oz.	Benny E. Hull	Nickajack Lake, Tenn.	4-20-72
DRUM, Red (freshwater) 26 lb. 0 oz.	Jeff Heimer	Tradinghouse Creek Lake, Texas	5-7-97
EEL, American 8 lb. 8 oz.	Gerald G. LaPierre Sr.	Cliff Pond, Mass.	5-17-92
FALLFISH 3 lb. 12 oz.	Wayne S. Morey Sr.	Sibley Pond, Maine	9-12-86

FRESHWATER FISH RECORDS
(continued)

Size	Angler	Where caught	Date
FLIER 1 lb. 2 oz.	Edward B. Smith	Pope's Pond, Ga.	6-19-95
GAR, Alligator 279 lb. 0 oz.	Bill Valverde	Rio Grande River, Texas	12-2-51
GAR, Florida 20 lb. 4 oz.	Randolph G. Copeland	St. John's River, Fla.	6-27-87
GAR, Longnose 50 lb. 5 oz.	Townsend Miller	Trinity River, Texas	7-30-54
GAR, Shortnose 5 lb. 13 oz.	Robert Mills	Enid Lake Spillway, Miss.	8-22-99
GAR, Spotted 28 lb. 8 oz.	John W. Shouppe	Lake Seminole, Fla.	3-4-87
GOLDEYE 3 lb. 13 oz.	Gary Heuer	Oahe Tailwater, S.D.	8-9-87
GOLDFISH 2 lb. 13 oz.	Thomas Berg	Lake Michigan, Ind.	2-27-93
GRAYLING, Arctic or American 5 lb. 15 oz.	Jeanne P. Branson	Katseyedie River, N.W.T., Canada	8-16-67
HERRING, River or Skipjack 3 lb. 12 oz.	Paul D. Goddard	Watts Bar Lake, Tenn.	2-14-82
INCONNU (Arctic Sheefish) 53 lb. 0 oz.	Lawrence E. Hudnall	Pah River, Alaska	8-20-86
KOI 5 lb. 0 oz.	Christina Berg	Hawkins Pond, Ind.	8-31-97
MOONEYE 1 lb. 12 oz.	Gary Schwersenka	Lake Poygan, Wis.	4-22-00
MUSKELLUNGE, Natural 69 lb. 11 oz.	Louis Spray	Chippewa Flowage, Wis.	10-20-49
MUSKELLUNGE, Hybrid or Tiger Musky 51 lb. 3 oz.	John A. Knobla	Lake Vieux Desert, Wis./Mich.	7-16-19
PACU 11 lb. 11 oz. 9-21-98	Joseph W. McPherson	DeKalb Lake, Ala.	
PADDLEFISH (Spoonbill) 50 lb. 8 oz.	Dr. Monte A. Wheeler	Beaver Lake, Ark.	1-31-98
PERCH, Rio Grande (Cichlid) 1 lb. 5 oz.	Paul E. Mueller	Concho River, Texas	9-20-96
PERCH, White 4 lb. 12 oz.	Mrs. Earl Small	Messalonskee Lake, Maine	6-4-49
PERCH, Yellow 4 lb. 3 oz.	Dr. C.C. Abbot	Bordentown, N.J.	5-1865

FRESHWATER FISH RECORDS
(continued)

Size	Angler	Where caught	Date
PICKEREL, Chain 9 lb. 6 oz.	Baxley McQuaig Jr.	Homerville, Ga.	2-17-61
PICKEREL, Grass 1 lb. 0 oz.	Mike Berg	Dewart Lake, Ind.	6-9-90
PICKEREL, Red Fin 2 lb. 10 oz.	Gene D. Brantley	Lewis' Lake, Ga.	7-7-82
PIKE, Amur 24 lb. 3 oz.	Fred Daley	Glendale Lake, Pa.	8-30-77
PIKE, Blue-Silver 18 lb. 0 oz.	Chuck Hinchman	La LeGardeur, Quebec, Canada	9-20-84
PIKE, Hybrid 14 lb. 0 oz.	Joseph C. Seidl	Lake Wapogasset, Wis.	5-30-83
PIKE, Northern 46 lb. 2 oz.	Peter Dubuc	Sacandaga Reservoir, N.Y.	9-15-40
PIRANHA 4 lb. 0 oz.	Richard E. Koeppen	Secaucus Duck Pond, N.J.	8-20-93
REDHORSE, Black 1 lb. 14 oz.	Richard E. Faler Jr.	French Creek, Pa.	3-27-97
REDHORSE, Golden 3 lb. 12 oz.	Richard E. Faler Jr.	Conneaut Marsh Outlet, Pa.	3-28-97
REDHORSE, Greater 11 lb. 13 oz.	Mitch Kunde	S. Long Lake, Minn.	5-18-95
REDHORSE, River 8 lb. 11 oz.	Geoff Bernardo	Trend River, Ontario, Canada	8-6-97
REDHORSE, Shorthead/Northern 11 lb. 5 oz.	Bill Barnaby	Brunet River, Wis.	5-21-83
REDHORSE, Silver 14 lb. 14 oz.	Chris A. Stephenson	Pickwick Lake, Ala.	4-2-95
SACRAMENTO PERCH 4 lb. 9 oz.	John Battcher	Pyramid Lake, Nev.	7-18-71
SALMON, Atlantic (inland) 22 lb. 11 oz.	Frank J. McGrath	Lobstick Lake, Newfoundland, Canada	8-24-82
SALMON, Atlantic (Sea-run) 30 lb. 0 oz.	Joseph A. Montgomery	St. Jean River, Quebec, Canada	6-24-79
SALMON, Chinook (King, inland) 44 lb. 14 oz.	Josh Bostedt	Lake Michigan, Wis.	1-15-95
SALMON, Chinook (King, sea-run) 97 lb. 4 oz.	Lester S. Anderson	Kenai River, Alaska	5-17-85
SALMON, Chum 25 lb. 15 oz.	Johnnie R. Wilson	Satsop River, Wash.	10-19-97

FRESHWATER FISH RECORDS
(continued)

Size	Angler	Where caught	Date
SALMON, Coho (Silver, inland)			
33 lb. 4 oz.	Jerry Lifton	Salmon River, N.Y.	9-27-89
SALMON, Coho (Silver, sea-run)			
31 lb. 0 oz.	Mrs. Lee Hallberg	Cowichan Bay, B.C. Canada	10-11-47
SALMON, Kokanee			
9 lb. 6 oz.	Norm Kuhn	Okanagan Lake, B.C. Canada	6-18-88
SALMON, Pink (inland)			
3 lb. 14 oz.	Steven L. Ratte	Poplar River, Minn.	9-13-83
SALMON, Pink (sca-run)			
12 lb. 9 oz.	Steven Alan Lee	Moose & Kenai Rivers, Alaska	8-17-74
SALMON, Pink (hybrid)			
19 lb. 8 oz.	Tino Del Signore	Garden River, Ontario, Canada	9-28-97
SALMON, Sockeye (Red)			
13 lb. 9 oz.	Eugene N. Marre	Kenai River, Alaska	7-26-92
SAUGER			
8 lb. 12 oz.	Mike Fischer	Lake Sakakawea, N.D.	10-6-71
SAUGEYE, Hybrid			
15 lb. 10 oz.	Myron Kibler	Fort Peck Reservoir, Mont.	1-11-95
SHAD, American			
11 lb. 4 oz.	Bob Thibodo	Connecticut River, Mass.	5-19-86
SHAD, Gizzard			
4 lb. 6 oz.	Richard "Slim" Rutschke	Missouri River, S.D.	10-8-92
SHAD, Hickory			
3 lb. 8 oz.	Ralph Dan Johnson	Tar River, N.C.	2-20-92
SPLAKE (Hybrid/trout)			
20 lb. 11 oz.	Paul S. Thompson	Georgian Bay, Ontario, Canada	5-17-87
SQUAWFISH/Northern			
2 lb. 4 oz.	Jeff L. Frederick	Snake River, Wash.	6-1-91
STURGEON, Lake			
168 lb. 0 oz.	Edward Paszkowski	Nottawasaga River, Ontario, Canada	5-29-82
STURGEON, Pallid			
49 lb. 8 oz.	Robert C. Carlson	Missouri River, N.D.	5-19-84
STURGEON, Shovelnose			
7 lb. 5 oz.	Kathleen J. Morrison	Mississippi River, Wis.	9-8-98
STURGEON, White (sea-run)			
468 lb. 0 oz.	Joey Pallotta	Carquinez Straits, Calif.	7-9-83
SUCKER, Blue			
14 lb. 3 oz.	Bruce A. Edwards	Mississippi River, Minn.	2-28-87
SUCKER, Bluehead			
2 lb. 9 oz.	Ray Johnson	Strawberry River, Utah	6-6-92

FRESHWATER FISH RECORDS
(continued)

Size	Angler	Where caught	Date
SUCKER, Desert 2 lb. 10 oz.	Edith E. Toney	Verde River, Ariz.	9-20-92
SUCKER, Flannelmouth 4 lb. 5 oz.	Ray Johnson	Flaming Gorge, Utah	4-11-92
SUCKER, Humpback or Razorback 6 lb. 4 oz.	A.J. DiLucino	Colorado River, Idaho	10-14-77
SUCKER, Largescale 6 lb. 3 oz.	Jesse Brown	Cascade Reservoir, Idaho	6-25-99
SUCKER, Longnose 6 lb. 14 oz.	David W. Rose	St. Joseph River, Mich.	3-22-86
SUCKER, Utah 7 lb. 11 oz.	Craig Curtiss	Portneuf River, Idaho	6-99
SUCKER, White 7 lb. 4 oz.	Bob Kramer	Big Round Lake, Wis.	5-4-78
SUNFISH, Green 2 lb. 2 oz.	Paul Dilley	Stockton Lake, Mo.	6-18-71
SUNFISH, Green/hybrid 2 lb. 10 oz.	Ron Fountain	Farm Pond, Kans.	5-17-99
SUNFISH, Longear 1 lb. 12 oz.	Patricia Stout	Elephant Butte Lake, N.M.	5-9-85
SUNFISH, Pumpkinseed 2 lb. 4 oz.	Scott Hart	North Saluda River, S.C.	5-26-97
SUNFISH, Redbreast 2 lb. 1 oz.	Jerrel R. De Wees Jr.	Suwannee River, Fla.	4-29-88
SUNFISH, Redear/hybrid 1 lb. 1 oz.	Mike Berg	Shakey Slough, Ind.	5-2-98
SUNFISH, Redear (Shell cracker) 5 lb. 7.5 oz.	Amos M. Gay	Diversion Canal, S.C.	11-6-98
TENCH 3 lb. 13 oz.	Louie Adams	Freeman Lake, Idaho	9-11-94
TILAPIA 6 lb. 4 oz.	Matthew P. Gross	Gibbons Creek Reservoir, Texas	12-19-95
TROUT, Apache 5 lb. 15 oz.	Jeffrey Banegas	Hurricane Lake, Ariz.	6-6-93
TROUT, Aurora 6 lb. 10 oz.	Luc M. Pilon	Carol Lake, Ontario, Canada	8-1-99
TROUT, Brook (Speckled) 14 lb. 8 oz.	Dr. W.J. Cook	Nipigon River, Ontario, Canada	7-1916
TROUT, Brown 40 lb. 4 oz.	Howard "Rip" Collins	Little Red River, Ark.	5-9-92

FRESHWATER FISH RECORDS
(continued)

Size	Angler	Where caught	Date
TROUT, Bull 32 lb. 0 oz.	N.L. Higgins	Lake Pend Crelle, Idaho	10-27-49
TROUT, Cutbow (hybrid) 30 lb. 4 oz.	Pat Kelly	Ashley Lake, Mont.	5-16-82
TROUT, Cutthroat 41 lb. 0 oz.	John Skimmerhorn	Pyramid Lake, Nev.	12-19-25
TROUT, Dolly Varden 17 lb. 8 oz.	James M. Hasenack	Unnamed river, Alaska	7-23-99
TROUT, Golden 11 lb. 4 oz.	Charles S. Reed	Cook Lake, Wyo.	8-5-48
TROUT, Lake (Mackinaw) 72 lb. 4 oz.	Lloyd E. Bull	Great Bear Lake, N.W.T., Canada	8-19-95
TROUT, Ohrid 14 lb. 5 oz.	Richard L. Carter	Watauga Lake, Tenn.	3-28-86
TROUT, Palomino (Golden Rainbow) 2 lb. 9 oz.	Christina Berg	Beaver Springs, Wis.	7-29-99
TROUT, Rainbow or Steelhead or Kamloops (inland) 37 lb. 0 oz.	Wes Hamlet	Lake Pend Oreille, Idaho	11-25-47
TROUT, Rainbow or Steelhead (sea-run) 42 lb. 2 oz.	David Robert White	Bell Island, Alaska	6-22-70
TROUT, Sunapee 11 lb. 8 oz.	Ernest Theoharis	Lake Sunapee, N.H.	8-1-54
TROUT, Tiger (hybrid) 20 lb. 13 oz.	Pete M. Friedland	Lake Michigan, Wis.	8-12-78
WALLEYE 22 lb. 11 oz.	Al Nelson	Greer's Ferry Lake, Ark.	3-14-82
WARMOUTH 2 lb. 7 oz.	Tony D. Dempsey	Yellow River, Fla.	10-19-85
WHITEFISH, Lake 15 lb. 6 oz.	Chris T.D. Webster	Clear Lake, Ontario, Canada	5-21-83
WHITEFISH, Mountain 5 lb. 14 oz.	Robert K. Hall	Indland Park Reservoir, Idaho	8-26-97
WHITEFISH, Mule (hybrid) 8 lb. 10 oz.	Theodore R. Chaney	Lake Superior, Wis.	3-16-91
WHITEFISH, Round or Menominee 4 lb. 0 oz.	Kenneth E. Bilski	Lake Michigan, Mich.	11-19-92

CATCH AND RELEASE RECORDS

Length	Name	Where caught	Date
AMUR, White (Grass Carp) 44"	Mark Banczak	Alabama River, Ala.	11-23-00
BASS, Largemouth 30"	Larry Spears	Sam Rayburn Lake, Texas	7-12-95
BASS, Rock 12"	Mike Berg	Lake Michigan, Ind.	2-8-96
BASS, Shoal 19"	Jimmy Jacobs	Flint River, Ga.	7-9-98
BASS, Smallmouth 24"	Zelma Wilson	Fall Lake, Minn.	9-6-94
BASS, Spotted or Kentucky 22"	Brandon Blankenship	Lake Neely Henry, Ala.	6-12-99
BASS, Striped (inland) 40"	Tim Feeser	Susquehanna River, Md.	7-25-94
BASS, White 21"	Jed Martin	Pickwick Lake, Ala.	4-8-99
BASS, Whiterock or Rockfish Hybrid 33"	Mark Alexander Foster	Ohio River, Ohio	10-5-99
BLUEGILL, (Brim, Bream) 12" (tie) 12"	William F. Byrd Jr. Alex Benson	Chicadee Pond, Ga. Jeter Lake, S.C.	11-22-96 10-17-98
BLUEGILL, Hybrid 11"	Jim Sprengelmeyer	Lake Eileen, Ill.	9-24-00
BULLHEAD, Black 14"	Jim Sprengelmeyer	Lake Eileen, Ill.	9-9-00
CARP, Common 42"	Scott Osmond	Hudson River, N.Y.	9-20-98
CATFISH, Blue 57"	James C. Edmiston	Missouri River, Kans.	7-14-00
CATFISH, Channel 40"	Dave Tigges	Irvine Lake, Calif.	6-29-97
CATFISH, Flathead (Mud-Cat) 59"	Eddie R. Robinson	Ohio River, Ind.	9-24-96
CHAR, Arctic 37"	Dave Youngquist	West Lake, N.W.T., Canada	8-7-93
CRAPPIE, Black (Specks) 16"	Ed Raymond	Derby Pond, Del.	3-31-00
CRAPPIE, White (Specks) 16"	Gabriel Brown	Kentucky Lake, Tenn.	4-10-00

CATCH AND RELEASE RECORDS

Length	Name	Where caught	Date
DRUM, Freshwater (Sheepshead)			
32"	Robert Barnhard	Lake Erie, Ohio	6-8-99
GAR, Longnose			
48"	Mark Alexander Foster	Ohio River, Ohio	8-21-00
GAR, Spotted			
50"	Al Cox	Lay Lake, Ala.	3-21-99
GRAYLING, Arctic			
25"	Daryl H. Koch	Fond du Lac River, Saskatchewan, Canada	6-25-93
MUSKELLUNGE, Natural			
62"	William Howard Craig	Ottawa River, Quebec, Canada	7-12-97
MUSKELLUNGE, Hybrid or Tiger Musky			
53"	Ray Johnson	Pineview Reseroir, Utah	11-28-98
PERCH, Yellow			
14"	Mike Berg	Red Cedar Lake, Wis.	6-15-98
PICKEREL, Chain			
28"	Jillian Texera	Farrar Pond, Mass.	5-25-96
PIKE, Blue-Silver			
48"	Jon D. Freeman	Favourable Lake, Ontario, Canada	5-22-00
PIKE, Northern			
54"	Rick Jensen	Anoko River, Alaska	7-28-94
SALMON, Atlantic (inland)			
26"	Brian Bockhahn	Niagara River, N.Y.	10-27-96
SALMON, Chinook (King, inland)			
45"	Ken Westfahl	Silver River, Wis.	10-11-99
SALMON, Chinook (King, sea-run)			
52"	David S. Wagoner	Indian Creek, Alaska	7-9-99
SALMON, Chum			
33"	Michael McKelvey	Skykomish River, Wash.	11-12-98
SALMON, Coho (Silver, inland)			
38"	Ken Westfahl	Kewaunee River, Wis.	10-15-99
SALMON, Coho (Silver, sea-run)			
34"	Leonard J. Kouba	Kiklukh River, Alaska	9-14-98
SALMON, Kokanee			
23"	Ray Johnson	Flaming Gorge Reservoir, Wyo.	8-29-96
SALMON, Pink (inland)			
22"	Daniel Du Russel	Garden River, Ontario, Canada	8-27-00
SALMON, Pink (sea-run)			
26"	David S. Wagoner	Resurrection Creek, Alaska	8-2-98
SALMON, Pinook (hybrid)			
33"	Joyce Smith	Manistee River, Mich.	10-1-99

CATCH AND RELEASE RECORDS

Length	Name	Where caught	Date
SALMON, Sockeye (Red)			
31" (tie)	Keith A. Thoreson	Crescent River, Alaska	8-27-96
31"	David S. Wagoner	Quartz Creek, Alaska	8-31-98
SAUGER			
27"	Dan Majeske	Fort Peck Lake, Mont.	8-27-94
SAUGEYE, Hybrid			
27"	Gary L. DuBois	Mississippi River, Minn.	7-26-96
STURGEON, Lake			
75"	Bruce Stanley	Nottawasaga River, Ontario, Canada	6-15-95
STURGEON, White			
114"	Tony Riley	Snake River, Idaho	5-12-93
SUNFISH, Pumpkinseed			
10" (tie)	Nicole Berg	Red Cedar Lake, Wis.	8-8-00
10"	John Regan	Lake Lorraine, Mass.	11-1-00
SUNFISH, Redbreast			
11"	William F. Byrd Jr.	Whipporwill Lake, Ga.	4-20-97
SUNFISH, Redear (Shell cracker)			
12"	William F. Byrd Jr.	Bluebird Lake, Ga.	11-22-97
TILAPIA			
20"	David S. Wagoner	Sun-N-Shade Pond, Fla.	3-29-00
TROUT, Brook			
25"	Eric Taylor	Menominee River, Wis.	4-1-95
TROUT, Brown			
37"	Mark Seeley	Root River, Wis.	12-16-97
TROUT, Bull			
25"	Dr. W. Richard Dukelow	Flathead River, Mont.	7-23-93
TROUT, Cutthroat			
30"	Fred Turner	Pyramid Lake, Nev.	4-26-99
TROUT, Dolly Varden			
33"	Donna Lea Nicholson	Unnamed river, Alaska	7-22-99
TROUT, Lake (Mackinaw)			
52"	Don Robbins	Great Bear Lake, N.W.T. Canada	7-14-94
TROUT, Rainbow (Steelhead, inland)			
41"	George Warburton	Little Bitterroot River, Mont.	5-3-95
TROUT, Rainbow (Steelhead, sea-run)			
44"	Spud Renzelman	Babine River, B.C. Canada	10-5-95
WALLEYE			
35" (tie)	Suezanne Tyler	Columbia River, Ore.	9-17-95
35"	Dean M. Van	Columbia River, Ore.	7-5-96
WARMOUTH			
9"	Steven M. Berg	Great Bear Lake, Mich.	5-16-98

Fishing Licenses and Fees

Fishing license fees and rules vary widely from state to state. Generally, anglers who are state residents must obtain licenses, with no licenses required for youths (ages vary). Senior citizens have special rates in many states, and some states don't require licensing for anglers over 62 or 65. Non-resident fees are usually higher, but many states offer special, short-term licenses for tourists.

The following license fees and rules were in effect in 2002, subject to change. Check with the state fishing bureau for further information, including locations where licenses can be purchased.

ALABAMA

Alabama Department of Conservation and Natural Resources
License Section
Suite 457, 64 North Union St.
Montgomery, AL 36130
(888) 848-6887
www.dcnr.state.al.us/
Resident: Annual freshwater fishing, $9.50; seven-day freshwater $6; annual combination freshwater and saltwater, $24.50; annual combination freshwater fishing and hunting, $24.50; sportsman's license, $59.50. License required age 16 up to 65. Lifetime resident licenses: Freshwater, $150; freshwater and saltwater, $400; hunting and freshwater, $450; hunting, freshwater and saltwater, $700.
Non-resident: Annual freshwater fishing, $31 (except Louisiana residents $61); seven-day freshwater, $11 (except Louisiana and Tennessee residents $16); annual combination freshwater and saltwater, $61 **(except Louisiana residents $90)**.

ALASKA

Alaska Department of Fish and Game
P.O. Box 25526
Juneau, Alaska 99802-5526
(907) 465-4100
www.state.ak.us/local/akpages/FISH.GAME/
E-mail: ADFG-Commissioner's Office
Resident: Sport fishing, $15; sport fishing for blind, $0.25; hunting and sport fishing, $39; annual king salmon stamp, $10.
Non-resident: Annual sport fishing, $100; one-day, $10; three-day, $20; seven-day, $30; 14-day, $50; annual hunting and sport fishing, $185; seven-day hunting and sport fishing, $115, annual king salmon stamp, $100; one-day stamp, $10; three-day stamp, $20; seven-day stamp, $30; 14-day stamp, $50.

ARIZONA

Arizona Game & Fish Department
2221 W. Greenway Road
Phoenix, AZ 85023
(602) 942-3000 or (866) 462-0433
www.azgfd.com
Resident: General fishing, $18; general fishing purchased in November and December, $9; one-day fishing, $12.50; combination hunting and fishing, $44; youth combination, $25.50; youth group two-day, $25; family fishing, $28.50 for first parent, $22.80 for second parent, $2 each dependent ages 14-17; urban fishing, $16; trout stamp, $10.50; two-pole stamp, $4; disabled veteran, free; age 70 or resident for 25 years, free.
Non-resident: General fishing, $51.50; general fishing purchased in November and December, $25.75; one-day fishing, $12.50; five-day, $26; four-month, $37.50; Colorado River only, $42.50; combination hunting and fishing, $177.50; youth combination, $25.50; urban fishing, $16; trout stamp, $49.50; 2-pole stamp, $4.
Colorado River special use stamps: Arizona stamp (for California, Nevada licenses), $3; Arizona Lake Powell stamp (Utah licenses), $3; California stamp (for Arizona licenses), $3; Nevada stamp (for Arizona licenses), $3; Utah Lake Powell stamp (Arizona licenses), $8.

ARKANSAS

Arkansas Game & Fish Commission
2 Natural Resources Drive
Little Rock, AR 72205
(501) 223-6300 or (800) 364-3263
www.agfc.state.ar.us/
e-mail: webmaster@agfc.state.ar.us
Resident: Fishing (16 or older), $10.50; three-day fishing, $7.50; combination sportsman's license, $35.50; trout permit, $5; White River Border Lakes Permit (Missouri), $10; 65-plus lifetime fishing, $10.50; 65-plus lifetime combination, $35.50; non-expiring lifetime sportsman's permit, $1,000.

Non-resident: Fishing annual, $32; three-day license, $11; seven-day license, $17; 14-day license, $22; trout permit, $9. (State has reciprocal agreements with Mississippi, Missouri, Tennessee.)

CALIFORNIA

California Department of Fish and Game
License and Revenue Branch
3211 S Street, Sacramento, CA 95816
(916) 227-2245
www.dfg.ca.gov/
   Resident: Fishing annual (16 or older), $30.45; Pacific Ocean only, $17.85; 2-day, $11.05; one-day Pacific Ocean only, $6.55; one-day Pacific Ocean only with ocean enhancement, $7.10; duplicate, $6.30. Non-resident: Fishing annual, $81.65; 10-day license, $30.45; 2-day, $11.05; one-day Pacific Ocean only, $6.55; one-day Pacific Ocean only with ocean enhancement, $7.10.
   Stamps and cards: Second rod stamp, $9.70; resident fishing upgrade, $12.60; Ocean enhancement annual, $2.65; Colorado River, $3; Abalone report card, $12.60; salmon punch card, $1.05; steelhead report card, $3.40.

COLORADO

Colorado Division of Wildlife
6060 Broadway
Denver, CO 80216
(303) 297-1192
wildlife.state.co.us
   Resident: Fishing annual, $20.25; senior annual, $10.25; five-day, $18.25; one-day, $5.25; 2nd rod stamp, $4; small game and fishing, $30.25; youth small game, furbearers and fishing (under 16), $1.
   Non-resident: Fishing annual, $40.25; five-day, $18.25; one-day, $5.25; 2nd rod stamp, $4; youth small game, furbearers and fishing (under 16), $1.

CONNECTICUT

Department of Environmental Protection
79 Elm St.
Hartford, CT 06106-5127
www.dep.state.ct.us
e-mail: dep.webmaster@po.state.ct.us
   Resident: Fishing annual (16 or older), $15; fishing and small game hunting, $21; senior citizen (65 or older), free; mentally retarded, blind or disabled, free.
   Non-resident: Fishing annual, $25; three-day license, $8; fishing and small game hunting, $55; armed forces fishing, $15; armed forces fishing and small game hunting, $21.

DELAWARE

Delaware Division of Fish & Wildlife
Department of Natural Resources & Environmental Control
89 Kings Hwy
Dover, DE 19901
(302) 739-4403
www.dnrec.state.de.us/fw
   Resident: Fishing annual (16 to 65), $8.50; youth trout stamp (12-15), $2.10; adult trout stamp, $4.20. No license needed for hook and line fishing in tidal waters. Non-resident: Fishing annual (16 and older), $15; seven-day license, $5.20; trout stamp, $6.20.

DISTRICT OF COLUMBIA

D.C. Environmental Health Administration
Fisheries and Wildlife Division
51 N Street, NE
Washington, DC 20002
(202) 535-2260
www.dchealth.com/dcfishandwildlife/
   Resident: Fishing annual (16 to 65), $7.
   Non-resident: Fishing annual, $10; 14-day license, $5.

FLORIDA

Florida Fish and Wildlife Conservation Commission
620 South Meridian St.
Tallahassee, FL 32399-1600
Phone: (850) 488-0520; Fax: (850) 413-0381
www.floridafisheries.com
   Resident: Freshwater annual license (ages 16-64), $13.50; hunting and fishing 64 or older, $13.50; sportsman's license, $64.50; saltwater annual, $13.50; snook or crawfish permit, $2 each; tarpon tag, $51.50; freshwater and saltwater combination, $25.50. Lifetime and five-year licenses also available.
   Non-resident: Freshwater annual, $31.50; 7-day, $16.50; saltwater annual, $31.50; saltwater three-day, $6.50; saltwater seven-day, $16.50; snook or crawfish permit, $2 each; tarpon tag, $51.50.

GEORGIA

Georgia Department of Natural Resources
License and Boat Registration Unit
2189 Northlake Parkway, Building 10, Suite 108
Tucker, GA 30084
(770) 414-3333 or (888) 748-6887
www.georgianet.org/dnr/wild/
   Resident: Fishing annual, $9; one-day, $3.50; trout, $5; combination fishing and hunting, $17; sportsman's license, $60; senior lifetime license (65 and older), $10. Lifetime licenses available.
   Non-resident: Fishing annual, $24; one-day, $3.50; seven-day, $7; trout, $13.

HAWAII

Department of Land and Natural Resources
Division of Aquatic Resources
1151 Punchbowl St., Room 330
Honolulu, HI 96813
(808) 587-0100
Fax: 808-587-0115
www.hawaii.gov/dlnr
e-mail: dlnr_aquatics@exec.state.hi.us
   Resident: Freshwater fishing annual (ages 15-65), $5; minor (ages 9-15), $3; senior (65 or older), free; armed forces personnel, $5; commercial marine license, $25.
   Non-resident: Freshwater annual, $25; seven-day tourist license, $10; 30-day tourist license, $20; commercial marine license, $50.

IDAHO

Idaho Fish and Game
600 S. Walnut, P.O. Box 25
Boise, ID 83707
(208) 334-3700 or (800) 554-8685
Fax: (208) 334-2114 or (208) 334-2148
www2.state.id.us/fishgame/
   Resident: Fishing annual, $23.50; junior (14-17), $12.50; disabled, $4.50; military furlough fishing, $16; commercial fishing, $101.50; combination hunting and fishing, $30.50; Sportsman package, $107; senior combination (65 and older), $4.50; junior combination, $16; two-pole permit, $12.50; salmon or steelhead permit, $11.50.
   Non-resident: Fishing annual, $74.50; daily fishing, $10.50; three-day salmon/steelhead, $28.50; junior fishing, $38; commercial fishing, $201.50; combination hunting and fishing, $181.50; two-pole permit, $12.50; salmon or steelhead permit, $11.50.

ILLINOIS

Illinois Department of Natural Resources
Lincoln Tower Plaza
524 S. Second St., Room 500
Springfield, IL 62701-1787
(217) 782-7454
dnr.state.il.us/
   Resident: Fishing annual (16 and older), $13; senior (65 and over), $6.75; sportsman's combined hunting and fishing, $19.25; senior sportsman's, $10; Lake Michigan salmon stamp, $6.50; inland trout stamp, $6.50; lifetime fishing, $375; lifetime sportsman's, $555. Blind or disabled do not need a license.
   Non-resident: Fishing annual, $24.50; 10-day, $13; 24-hour, $5.50; Lake Michigan salmon stamp, $6.50; inland trout stamp, $6.50.

INDIANA

Division of Fish and Wildlife
Indiana Department of Natural Resources
402 W. Washington St., W273
Indianapolis, IN 46204
(317) 232-4080
www.in.gov/dnr/fishwild/
   Resident: Fishing annual (17 and older), $14.25; one-day, $7; hunting and fishing, $20.75; trout/salmon stamp, $9.25; lifetime fishing, $285; lifetime comprehensive fishing, $427.50; senior (65 and older), no license needed.
   Non-resident: Fishing annual, $24.75; one-day, $7; seven-day, $12.75; trout/salmon stamp, $9.25.

IOWA

Iowa Department of Natural Resources
900 E. Grand
Wallace State Office Building
Des Moines, IA 50319-0034
(515) 281-4515
www.state.ia.us/dnr
   Resident: Fishing annual (16 and older), $11; lifetime fishing (65 or older), $51; lifetime combined (disabled veteran or POW), $31; seven-day, $9; boundary water sport trotline, $11; trout fee, $11; fish habitat fee, $3.50.
   Non-resident: Fishing annual, $36; seven-day, $27; trout fee, $13; fish habitat fee, $3.50; boundary water sport trotline, $21.

KANSAS

Kansas Department of Wildlife and Parks

900 Jackson St., Suite 502
Topeka, KS 66612
(785) 296-2281
ww.kdwp.state.ks.us/
e-mail: feedback@wp.state.ks.us
    Resident: Fishing annual, $18.50; combination fishing and hunting, $36.50, 24-hour, $5.50; lifetime fishing, $300.50; trout permit, $10; guide license, $50.50.
    Non-resident: Fishing annual, $40.50; five-day, $20.50; 24-hour, $5.50, trout permit, $10.

KENTUCKY

Kentucky Department of Fish and Wildlife Resources

#1 Game Farm Road
Frankfort, KY 40601
(800) 858-1549
www.kdfwr.state.ky.us/
e-mail: info.center@mail.state.ky.us
    Resident: Fishing annual, $15; one-day, $6; two-day, $12; joint husband/wife, $27; combination hunting and fishing, $22.50; sportsman, $80; trout permit, $10.
    Non-resident: Fishing annual, $35; one-day, $7; two-day, $14; three-day, $21; 15-day, $25; trout permit, $10.

LOUISIANA

Louisiana Department of Wildlife and Fisheries

2000 Quail Drive
Baton Rouge, La. 70808
(225) 765-2887 or (888) 765-2602
www.wlf.state.la.us
    Resident: Freshwater, $9.50; saltwater, $5.50; hook and line, $2.50. Lifetime licenses available.
    Non-resident: Freshwater, $60; saltwater, $30; freshwater four-day, $15; saltwater four-day, $45; freshwater one-day, $5; one-day saltwater, $15; charter passenger, $5.

MAINE

Maine Department of Inland Fisheries and Wildlife

284 State St.
41 State House Station
Augusta, ME 04333-0041
(207) 287-8000 or (207) 287-8003

www.state.me.us/ifw
    Resident: Fishing annual (16 or older), $21; supersport and fishing, $36; combination hunting and fishing, $38; supersport combination hunting and fishing, $53; archery and fishing, $38. (Supersport money goes to Landowner Relation Program.)
    Non-resident: Fishing annual, $51; junior fishing (12-15), $8; one-day, $10; three-day, $22; seven-day, $35; 15-day, $39; combination hunting and fishing, $124. Alien season fishing, $71; combination hunting and fishing, $177.

MARYLAND

Maryland Department of Natural Resources

580 Taylor Ave.
Annapolis, MD 21401
(877) 620-8DNR (8367)
Out of state (410) 260-8100
www.dnr.state.md.us/
    Resident: Sport fishing (16 or older), $9; consolidated senior sportfishing, $5; bay sport pleasure boat (Chesapeake Bay), $40, five-day bay sport, $6; freshwater, $10; trout stamp, $5. Complimentary licenses to disabled veterans, POWs, blind persons.
    Non-resident: Sport fishing, $14; bay sport pleasure boat (Chesapeake Bay), $40, five-day bay sport, $6; freshwater, varies by state; trout stamp, $5.

MASSACHUSETTS

Mass Wildlife (freshwater fishing) Department of Fisheries, Wildlife and Environmental Law Enforcement

251 Causeway St., First Floor
Boston, MA 02114
(617) 626-1590
www.state.ma.us/dfwele
    Resident: Annual, $27.50; minor (15-17), $11.50; age (65-69), $16.25; age (70 or over or paraplegic, blind, mentally retarded), free; sporting (fishing and hunting combined), $45; age sporting (65-69), $25.
    Non-resident: Annual, $37.50; three-day, $23.50; youth (15-17), $11.50.

Division of Marine Fisheries (saltwater fishing)

251 Causeway St., Suite 400
Boston, MA 02114
(617) 626-1520
www.state.ma.us/dfwele/dmf
    Saltwater permits are not required for recreational fishing, but commercial licenses are needed if fish are to be sold.

MICHIGAN

Michigan Department of Natural Resources
Mason Building, Eighth Floor
P.O. Box 30446
Lansing, MI 48909
(517) 373-1280 or (800) 275-3474
Fax: (517) 373-0381
www.dnr.state.mi.us/
    Resident: Fishing restricted (does not include trout and salmon), season, $14; senior, $5.60; fishing upgrade to all species, season, $13; senior, $5.20; fishing all-species, $27; fishing all-species senior, $10.80; fishing all-species young angler, $2; 24-hour, $7; senior 24-hour, $3; military, $1.
    Non-resident: Fishing restricted (does not include trout and salmon), season, $30; fishing upgrade to all species, season, $11; fishing all-species, $41; 24-hour, $7.

MINNESOTA

Minnesota Department of Natural Resources
500 Lafayette Road
St. Paul, MN 55155-4040
(651) 296-6157 or (888) MINNDNR
www.dnr.state.mn.us/
e-mail: info@dnr.state.mn.us
    Resident: Fishing annual (16-64), $18; senior, $6.50; 24-hour, $9.50; combination (husband and wife), $26; fish house or dark house, $12.50; fish house or dark house rental, $27; dark house spearing, $18; whitefish netting, $11; trout and salmon stamp, $8.50; sports, $28; sports combination (husband and wife), $37.
    Non-resident: Fishing annual, 35; 24-hour, $9.50; 72-hour, $21; seven-day, $25; combination (husband and wife) 14-day, $36; angling family (husband, wife and children under 16), $47; fish house (portable only), $34; fish house (portable only) seven-day, $20; trout and salmon stamp, $8.50.

MISSISSIPPI

Mississippi Wildlife, Fisheries & Parks
1505 Eastover Drive
Jackson, MS 39211-6374
(601) 432-2400
    Resident: Freshwater fishing (16-64), $8; three-day freshwater, $3; saltwater fishing, $4; sportsman's (does not include saltwater fishing), $32; all-game hunting/freshwater fishing, $17. Anglers over 65 do not need a license. Lifetime licenses: sportsman (age 13 and over), $1,000; sportsman (birth to 12), $500.
    Non-resident: Freshwater fishing, $30; saltwater fishing, $30; three-day freshwater fishing, $15; three-day saltwater fishing, $15. Lifetime license: $1,500.

MISSOURI

Missouri Department of Conservation
P.O. Box 180
2901 W. Truman Blvd.
Jefferson City, MO 65109
(573) 751-4115
Fax: (573) 751-4467
www.conservation.state.mo.us
    Resident: Fishing annual, $11; hunting and fishing, $19; White River border lakes (Missouri and Arkansas residents only), $10; daily fishing, $5; trout, $7. Lifetime permits: 15 and under, $275; 16-29, $400; 30-39, $350; 40-59, $300; 60-64, $35.
    Non-resident: Fishing annual, $35.

MONTANA

Montana Fish, Wildlife & Parks
1420 East Sixth Ave.
Helena, MT 59620
(406) 444-6759
    Resident: Fishing ages 12-14, conservation license only, $4; ages 15-61, conservation license, $4, plus fishing license, $13; 62 and older, conservation license only, $4; warm water game fish stamp, $5; paddlefish, $2.50; disability, $4.
    Non-resident: Fishing ages 12-14, $13; ages 15 and older, conservation license, $5, and fishing license, $10 for two consecutive days or $45 for season; warm water game fish stamp, $5; paddlefish, $7.50.

NEBRASKA

Nebraska Game and Parks Commission
2200 North 33rd St.
Lincoln, NE 68503
(402) 471-0641
www.ngpc.state.ne.us/fish/
    Resident: Fishing annual (16 and older), $12.75; combination fishing and hunting, $21.75; three-day, $8.25; special fishing permit, $5; aquatic habitat stamp, $5; veterans 65 and older, and all residents 70 and older can get fee-exempt permits. Lifetime permits: fishing, $257.50; combination hunting and fishing, $448.
    Non-resident: Fishing annual, $35; three-day, $8.25.

NEVADA

Nevada Division of Wildlife
1100 Valley Road
Reno, NV 89512
(775) 688-1500
www.nevadadivisionofwildlife.org/
 Resident: Fishing annual (16 and older), $21;
junior (12-15), $5; senior (65 and older), $5;
serviceman, $6; disabled, $5; one-day, $7 plus $2 per
day; Indian fishing and hunting, free; combination
hunting and fishing, $39; junior combination (12-15),
$8; senior combination, $8; disabled combination, $8.
 Non-resident: Fishing annual (16 and older), $51;
junior (12-15), $9; Colorado River license, $21; one-
day, $12 plus $4 per consecutive day.
 Stamps: Trout, $5; Arizona Colorado River special
use, $3; Nevada Colorado River special use, $3.

NEW HAMPSHIRE

New Hampshire Fish and Game Department
2 Hazen Drive
Concord, NH 03301
(603) 271-3211
www.wildlife.state.nh.us/
e-mail: info@wildlife.state.nh.us
 Resident: Fishing annual, $31; combination, $41;
salmon permit, $10; clam, $27; oyster, $27. Lifetime
licenses available with cost determined by age.
 Non-resident: Fishing annual, $47; combination,
$127; salmon permit, $10; clam, $27; oyster, $27; one-
day fishing, $15; three-day, $25; seven-day, $32.

NEW JERSEY

**New Jersey Division of Fish and Wildlife
(freshwater fishing)
Bureau of Marine Fisheries (saltwater
fishing)**
P.O. Box 400, 501 E. State St.
Trenton, NJ 08625-0400
(609) 292-2965
www.state.nj.us/dep/fgw/
e-mail: njwildlife@nac.net
 Resident: Fishing annual (16 and older), $22.50;
senior (65-69), $12.50; over 70, no license required;
trout stamp, $10.50; all-around sportsman, $72.25.
 Non-resident: Fishing annual, $34; trout stamp,
$20; two-day, $9; seven-day, $19.50.

NEW MEXICO

New Mexico Game and Fish
1 Wildlife Way, P.O. Box 25112
Santa Fe, NM 87507
(505) 476-8000 or (800) 862-9310
www.gmfsh.state.nm.us/
 Resident: Fishing annual (12 and older), $17.50;
junior, senior or handicapped, $5; one-day, $8;
additional days, $8; five-day, $16; over 70, free.
 Non-resident: Fishing annual, $39; junior, $18.50;
one-day, $8; five-day, $16.

NEW YORK

**New York Department of
Environmental Conservation**
625 Broadway
Albany, NY 12233-4790
(518) 402-8920; fax (518) 402-9027
www.dec.state.ny.us/website/dfwmr
 Resident: Fishing annual (16 and older), $14;
three-day, $6; senior, $5. Lifetime licenses available.
 Non-resident: Fishing annual, $35; five-day, $20;
one-day, $11; combination fishing and hunting, $225.

NORTH CAROLINA

**North Carolina Wildlife Resources
Commission :Division of Inland Fisheries**
1721 Mail Service Center
Raleigh, NC 27699-1721
(919) 733-3633
 www.ncwildlife.org
 Resident: Fishing basic, $15; combination hunting
and fishing, $20; county fishing, $10; comprehensive
fishing, $20; one-day, $5; sportsman, $40. Lifetime
licenses available.
 Non-residents: Fishing basic, $30; one-day, $10;
three-day, $15.
 Note: North Carolina currently does not require a
license for recreational saltwater fishing with rod and
reel - from the beach, piers, and boats in most coastal
waters. A license is required for freshwater fishing.

NORTH DAKOTA

North Dakota Game and Fish Department
100 N. Bismarck Expressway
Bismarck, ND 58501-5095
(701) 328-6300 or (701) 328-6335
Fax: (701) 328-6352
www.state.nd.us/gnf/
e-mail: ndgf@state.nd.us
Resident: Fishing annual (16 and older), $10; husband and wife, $14; 65 and older, $3; disabled, $3; fishing, hunting & furbearer certificate, $1; sportsmen's license, $27; paddlefish tag, $3.
    Non-resident: Fishing, $25; husband and wife, $35; seven-day, $15; three-day, $10; fishing, hunting & furbearer certificate, $2; paddlefish tag, $7.50.

OHIO

Ohio Department of Natural Resources : Division of Wildlife
1840 Belcher Drive, Building G
Columbus OH 43224-1329
(614) 265-6300 or (800) WILDLIFE
www.dnr.state.oh.us/wildlife
    Resident: Fishing annual (ages 16-65), $15; one-day, $7.
    Non-resident: Fishing, $24; three-day, $15.

OKLAHOMA

Oklahoma Department of Wildlife Conservation
P.O. Box 53465
Oklahoma City, Oklahoma 73152
(405) 521-3851
www.wildlifedepartment.com/
    Resident: Fishing annual (16 and older), $12.50; combination fishing and hunting, $21; lifetime fishing, $150; lifetime fishing and hunting, $525; trout license, $7.75; Lake Texoma license, $7.75; senior citizen (64 or older), $6 for lifetime; senior citizen fishing and hunting, $10 for lifetime; disability, $10 for five years.
    Non-resident: Fishing, $28.50; five-day, $10; 14-day, $20; lifetime fishing, $250; lifetime hunting and fishing, $650; trout license, $7.75; Lake Texoma license, $7.75.

OREGON

Oregon Department of Fish & Wildlife
2501 SW First Ave., P.O. Box 59
Portland, OR 97207
(503) 872-5275
www.dfw.state.or.us
e-mail: Odfw.info@state.or.us
    Resident: Fishing annual, $19.75; combination hunting/angling, $33.75; junior angling (ages 14-17), $6.75; senior citizen combination hunting/angling, $16.50; senior citizen angling, $9.50; sports pac license, $105; Pioneer hunting and angling permanent license (65 and older, with 50 years as resident), free.
    Non-resident: Fishing, $48.50; one-day, $8; two-day, $14.50; three-day, $21; four-day, $27.50; seven-day, $34.75.
    Tags (resident and non-resident): Adult combined harvest tag (salmon, sturgeon, steelhead, halibut), $16.50; juvenile combined harvest tag (under 18), $6.50; hatchery harvest tag (hatchery salmon or steelhead), $12.

PENNSYLVANIA

Pennsylvania Fish and Boat Commission
1601 Elmerton Ave.
Harrisburg, PA 17110
717-705-7800
www.fish.state.pa.us/
    Resident: Fishing annual (ages 16-64), $17; senior (65 and older), $4; senior lifetime, $16; trout and salmon permit, $5.50.
    Non-resident: Fishing, $35; seven-day, $30; three-day, $15; trout and salmon permit, $5.50.

RHODE ISLAND

Department of Environmental Management Fish and Wildlife
235 Promenade St.
Providence, RI 02908-5767
(401) 222-6800
Fax: (401) 783-4460
www.state.ri.us/dem
    Resident: Freshwater fishing annual, $9.50; combination hunting and fishing, $15, trout conservation stamp, $5.50; 65 or older or disabled, free. No license is needed for non-commercial saltwater fishing.
    Non-resident: Fishing, $31; three-day, $16; trout conservation stamp, $5.50.

SOUTH CAROLINA

**South Carolina Department
of Natural Resources**
PO Box 11710
Columbia, SC 29202
www.dnr.state.sc.us/
    Resident: Annual freshwater fishing (16 and older), $10; 14-day, $5; annual saltwater fishing $10, 14-day saltwater fishing $5. Lakes and reservoirs permit for use of cane pole and natural bait in any public waters, $3.
    Non-resident: Annual freshwater fishing, $35; 7-day $11; annual saltwater $35, 14-day saltwater $11.

SOUTH DAKOTA

South Dakota Division of Wildlife
412 West Missouri
Pierre, SD 57501
(605) 773-3485
www.state.sd.us/gfp
    Resident: Fishing annual, $21; one-day, $7; small game hunting and fishing, $44; senior, $5; Lake Oahe only, $7.
    Non-resident: Fishing, $59; one-day, $12; three-day, $30; family annual, $59; Lake Oahe, $20.

TENNESSEE

Tennessee Wildlife Resources Agency
P.O. Box 40747
Nashville, TN 37204
(615) 781-6500
www.state.tn.us/twra
    Resident: Annual fishing and hunting, $21; junior fish, hunt and trap (13-15), $8; one-day, $2.50; annual trout, $12; sportsman's, $101; county of residence fishing, $6. Lifetime licenses available with fees depending on age.
    Non-resident: Fishing, no trout, $26; junior hunting and fishing, no trout, $6; three-day, no trout, $10.50; 10-day, no trout, $15.50; all fish annual, $51; three-day, all fish, $20.50; 10-day, all fish, $30.50.
    Permits: Special permits required, in addition to licenses, for Gatlinburg, Reelfoot, Agency Lake.

TEXAS

Texas Parks & Wildlife
4200 Smith School Road
Austin, TX 78744
(800) TX LIC 4 Y or (512) 389-4800
www.tpwd.state.tx.us
    Resident: Fishing annual (17 and older), $19; three-day, $10; 14-day, $12; special (65 or older or blind), $6.
    Non-resident: Fishing, $30; five-day, $20.
    Stamps and tags: Freshwater trout, $7; sport oyster boat, $10 for resident and $40 for non-resident; saltwater fishing stamp, $10; tarpon tag, $100; saltwater trotline tag, $3; bait-shrimp trawl tag, $23; red drum tag, free for one fish per year.

UTAH

Utah Wildlife Resources
1594 W. North Temple
Box 146301
Salt Lake City UT 84114
(801) 538-4700
Fax: (801) 538-4745
    Resident: Fishing annual (ages 14-64), $24; age 65 and older, $14; one-day, $7; seven-day, $15; small game and fishing, $32.
    Non-resident: Fishing, $46; one-day, $8; seven-day, $21.

VERMONT

Vermont Fish and Wildlife Department
103 South Main St.
Waterbury, VT 05671-0501
(802) 241-3700
Fax: (802) 241-3295
www.anr.state.vt.us/fw
    Resident: Fishing annual (18 and older), $20; youth (15-17), $8; three-day, $10; fishing and hunting combination, $29.
    Non-resident: Fishing, $41; youth, $15; one-day, $15; three-day, $20; seven-day, $30; combination hunting and fishing, $110.

VIRGINIA

**Virginia Department of
Game & Inland Fisheries**
4010 West Broad St.
Richmond, VA 23230
(804) 367-1000
www.dgif.state.va.us
 Resident: Fishing annual (16 and older), $12;
fishing in county or city of residence, $5; five-day, $5;
stocked trout waters, $12 in addition to license; 65 and
older, $1; lifetime 65 and older, $10; disabled, $5.
 Non-resident: Fishing, $30; five-day, $6; stocked
trout waters, $30 in addition to license; lifetime, $500.

WASHINGTON

Washington Department of Fish and Wildlife
1111 Washington St. SE
Olympia, WA 98501
(360) 902-2200 or (360) 902-2945
Fax: (360) 902-2230
www.wa.gov/wdfw
 Resident: Freshwater fishing (ages 16-69), $21.90;
saltwater, $19.71; senior (70 and older), $5.48 for each;
shellfish/seaweed, $7.67; two-day fish/shellfish, $6.57;
combination fish/shellfish, $39.42; youth (age 15),
$5.48; disabled, $5.48.
 Non-resident: Freshwater fishing, $43.80;
saltwater, $39.42; shellfish/seaweed, $21.90; two-
fish/shellfish, $6.57; combination fish/shellfish,
$78.84.

WEST VIRGINIA

West Virginia Division of Natural Resources
State Capitol Complex, Building 3
1900 Kanawha Blvd.
Charleston, WV 25305-0060
(304) 558-3399
www.dnr.state.wv.us
 Resident: Fishing annual (ages 16-65), $11; trout
stamp, $7.50; conservation stamp, $3; sportsman, $25;
junior sportsman (15-17), $15; national forest
hunting/trapping/fishing, $2.
 Non-resident: Fishing, $30; trout stamp, $10;
conservation stamp, $10; three-day, $5; national
forest hunting/trapping/fishing, $2.

WISCONSIN

Wisconsin Department of Natural Resources
101 S. Webster St.
Madison, WI 53703
(608) 266-2621
Fax: (608) 261-4380
www.dnr.state.wi.us
 Resident: Fishing annual, $14; junior (16-17), $7;
senior citizen, $7; husband and wife, $24; inland trout
stamp, $7.25; Great Lakes salmon and trout stamp,
$7.25; two-day Great Lakes fishing, $10; disabled, $7;
disabled veteran, $3; combination sports, $43;
conservation patron, $110.
 Non-resident: Fishing, $34; family (includes ages
16-17), $52; four-day, $15; 15-day, $20; 15-day family,
$30; inland trout stamp, $7.25; Great Lakes salmon and
trout stamp, $7.25; two-day Great Lakes fishing, $10;
combination sports, $240; conservation patron, $575.

WYOMING

Wyoming Game and Fish Department
5400 Bishop Blvd.
Cheyenne, WY 82006
(307) 777-4600
Fax: (307) 777-4699
www.gf.state.wy.us
 Resident: Fishing annual, $15; daily, $3; youth
(ages 14-18), $3; lifetime fishing, $250; lifetime
bird/small game/fishing, $400.
 Non-resident: Fishing, $65; daily, $10; youth (ages
14-18), $15.

State Tourism Offices

Alabama

Alabama Bureau of Tourism and Travel
401 Adams Ave.
P.O. Box 4927
Montgomery, AL 36103-4927
800-ALABAMA
www.touralabama.org

Alaska

Alaska Travel Industry Association
2600 Cordova Street, Ste. 201
Anchorage, AK 99503
www.travelalaska.com
info@alaskatia.org

Arkansas

Arkansas Department of Parks & Tourism
One Capitol Mall
Little Rock, AR 72201
800-NATURAL
www.arkansas.com
info@arkansas.com

Arizona

Arizona Office of Tourism
2702 North 3rd Street, Suite 4015
Phoenix, AZ 85004
Phone: 602-230-7733, Fax: 602-540-5432
Toll-Free visitor information: 888-520-3434
www.arizonavacationvalues.com

California

caltour@commerce.ca.gov
800-GOCALIF

Colorado

Colorado Tourism Office
1625 Broadway, Ste. 1700
Denver, CO 80202
800-COLORADO
www.colorado.com

Connecticut

Connecticut Office of Tourism
Department of Economic and
Community Development
505 Hudson Street
Hartford, CT 06106
(860) 270-8080 Fax (860) 270-8077
www.tourism.state.ct.us

Delaware

Delaware Tourism Office
99 Kings Highway
Dover, DE 19901
(302) 739-4271
(866) 2-VISITDE
Fax (302) 739-5749
www.visitdelaware.net

Florida

VISIT FLORIDA
661 East Jefferson Street, Suite 300
Tallahassee, FL 32301
(850) 488-5607 Fax (850) 224-2938
www.flausa.com

Georgia

Georgia Tourism
285 Peachtree Center Ave., Suite 1000
Atlanta, GA 30303
800-VISITGA (1-800-847-4842)
www.georgia.org/tourism

Hawaii

Hawaii Visitors and Convention Bureau
2270 Kalakaua Ave., 8th Floor
Honolulu, HI 96815
(808) 923-1811 Fax: (808) 924-0290
www.gohawaii.com

Idaho

Idaho Department of Commerce
700 W. State St.
P.O. Box 83720
Boise, ID 83720-0093
(208) 334-2470
(800) 842-5858
Fax: (208) 334-2631
www.visitid.org
tourism@idoc.state.id.us

Illinois

Illinois Bureau of Tourism
James R. Thompson Center
100 W. Randolph St., Suite 3-400
Chicago, IL 60601
800-2CONNECT
www.enjoyillinois.com
Tourism@commerce.state.il.us

Indiana

Indiana Tourism Division
Indiana Department of Commerce
One North Capitol, Suite 700
Indianapolis, IN 46204-2288
888-ENJOY-IN fax: 317-233-6887
www.enjoyindiana.com
webmaster@enjoyindiana.com

Iowa

Iowa Department of Economic Development
Iowa Tourism Office
200 East Grand Ave.
Des Moines, IA 50309
(515) 242-4705
(888) 472-6035
Fax: 515-242-4718
www.traveliowa.com

Kansas

Kansas Department of Commerce & Housing
Travel & Tourism Development Division
1000 S.W. Jackson St., Suite 100
Topeka, Kansas 66612-1354
(785) 296-8478, Fax: (785) 296-6988
www.kansas-travel.com
travtour@kdoch.state.ks.us

Kentucky

Kentucky Department of Travel
PO Box 2011, Dept WWW,
Frankfort, KY 40602
(800) 225-8747
www.kytourism.com

Louisiana

Louisiana Office of Tourism
P.O. Box 94291
Baton Rouge, LA 70804-9291
(225) 342-8100
Fax: (225) 342-8390
www.louisianatravel.com
free.info@crt.state.la.us

Maine

Maine Office of Tourism
59 State House Station
Augusta, ME 04330
(207) 287-5711
www.visitmaine.com

Maryland

Maryland Office of Tourism Development
217 East Redwood St., 9th Floor
Baltimore, MD 21202
800-MDISFUN
www.mdisfun.org

Massachusetts

Massachusetts Office of Travel & Tourism
10 Park Plaza, Suite 4510
Boston, MA 02116
Phone: (617) 973-8500
Toll-free: (800) 227-MASS
Fax: (617) 973-8525
www.massvacation.com

Michigan

Travel Michigan
Michigan Economic Development Corporation
 P.O. Box 30226
Lansing, MI 48909-7726
(800) 676-1743
travel.michigan.org

Minnesota

Minnesota Office of Tourism
100 Metro Square
121 7th Place East
St. Paul, MN 55101-2146
(800) 657-3700
(651) 296-5029
exploreminnesota.com
explore@state.mn.us

Mississippi

Mississippi Development Authority
Division of Tourism Development
P. O. Box 849
Jackson, MS 39205
(601) 359-3297
Fax (601) 359-5757
(800) 927-6378
 www.visitmississippi.org
 lturnage@mississippi.org

Missouri

Missouri Division of Tourism
P.O. Box 1055
Jefferson City, MO 65102
(573) 751-4133
Fax: (573) 751-5160
 (800) 877-1234
www.missouritourism.org
tourism@mail.state.mo.us

Montana

Travel Montana
PO Box 7549
Missoula MT 59807-7549
1-800-VISITMT
(1-800-847-4868)
www.visitmt.com

Nebraska

Nebraska Department of Economic Development
P.O. Box 94666
301 Centennial Mall South
Lincoln, NE 68509-4666
(800) 228-4307 or (877) 632-7275
FAX: (402) 471-3778
www.visitnebraska.org

Nevada

Nevada Commission on Tourism
401 North Carson St.
Carson City, NV 89701
Telephone: 800-NEVADA-8, (775) 687-4322
Fax (775) 687-6779
www.travelnevada.com
 ncot@travelnevada.com

New Hampshire

New Hampshire Division of Travel
and Tourism Development
172 Pembroke Road
P.O. Box 1856
Concord, NH 03302-1856
1-800-FUN-IN-NH (1-800-386-4664) - FAX: 603-271-6870
www.visitnh.gov

New Jersey

New Jersey Commerce & Economic
Growth Commission
P.O. Box 820
20 W. State St.
Trenton, NJ 08625
 (800) VISIT NJ
 (609) 777-0885
/www.visitnj.org

New Mexico

New Mexico Tourism Department
491 Old Santa Fe Trail
The Lamy Building
Santa Fe, 87503
(800) 733-6396 ext 0643
www.newmexico.org

New York

New York State Division of Tourism
Empire State Development
30 S. Pearl St., 2nd Floor
Albany, NY 12245
800 CALL-NYS
(518) 474-4116
www.iloveny.com

North Carolina

North Carolina Division of Tourism, Film, and Sports Development
301 N. Wilmington St.
Raleigh, NC 27601
800 VISITNC
www.visitnc.com

North Dakota

North Dakota Tourism
Liberty Memorial Building
604 East Blvd.
Bismarck, N.D. 58505-0825
800-HELLO ND
www.ndtourism.com

Ohio

Ohio Department of Development-Travel&Tourism
77 S. High St.
P.O. BX 1001
Columbus, Ohio 43216-1001
800-BUCKEYE
www.ohiotourism.com
AskOhioTourism@CallTech.com

Oklahoma

Oklahoma Tourism and Recreation Department
Travel & Tourism Division
P.O. Box 60789
Oklahoma City, OK 73146-0789
(800) 652-6552
information@travelok.com

Oregon

Oregon Tourism Commission
775 Summer St. NE
Salem, OR 97301-1282
(800) 547-7842
www.traveloregon.com

Pennsylvania

Tourism, Film and Economic
Development Marketing Office
4th Floor, Commonwealth Keystone Building
400 North St.
Harrisburg, PA 17120-0225
(800) 237-4363
(717) 787-5453
Fax: 717-787-0687
www.experiencepa.com

Rhode Island

Rhode Island Tourism Division
One W. Exchange St.
Providence, RI 02903
(401) 222-2601
(800) 556-2484
Fax: (401) 273-8270
www.visitrhodeisland.com

South Carolina

South Carolina Department of Parks,
Recreation & Tourism
1205 Pendleton St.
Columbia, SC 29201
888-SCSMILE
www.discoversouthcarolina.com

South Dakota

Department of Tourism
Capitol Lake Plaza
711 East Wells Ave.
c/o 500 East Capitol Ave.
Pierre, SD 57501-5070
(605) 773-3301
1-800-S-DAKOTA (1-800-732-5682)
www.travelsd.com
SDINFO@state.sd.us

Tennessee

Tennessee Department of Tourist Development
320 Sixth Avenue N., 5th Floor Rachel Jackson Bldg.
Nashville, TN 37243
(615) 741-2159
www.tourism.state.tn.us

Texas

Texas Department of Transportation Travel Division
125 E. 11th Street
Austin, TX 78701
(512) 486-5900
800-8888-TEX
Fax: (512) 486-5909
www.traveltex.com

Utah

Utah Travel Council
 P.O. Box 147420
Salt Lake City, UT 84114-7420
(801) 538-1030
www.utah.com
travel@utah.com

Vermont

Vermont Department of Tourism & Marketing
Vermont Dept. of Tourism and Marketing
6 Baldwin St., Drawer 33
Montpelier, VT 05633-1301
800-VERMONT
www.travel-vermont.com
vttravel@dca.state.vt.us

Virginia

Virginia Tourism Corp.
901 E. Byrd St.
Richmond, VA 23219
(800) 321-3244
www.virginia.org
VAinfo@virginia.org

Washington

Washington State Office of Trade and Economic Development
210-11th Ave SW, Room 101
PO Box 42500
Olympia, WA 98504-2500
(360) 725-5052.
tourism@cted.wa.gov

West Virginia

West Virginia Division of Tourism
90 MacCorkle Ave., SW
South Charleston, WV 25303
(304)558-2200
800-CALL WVA (800-225-5982)
www.callwva.com

Wisconsin

Wisconsin Department of Tourism
P.O. Box 7976
Madison, WI 53707-7976
(800) 432-TRIP
www.travelwisconsin.com

Wyoming

Wyoming Business Council Travel & Tourism
I-25 at College Drive
Cheyenne, WY 82002
(307) 777-7777
Fax: (307) 777-2877
www.wyomingtourism.org

Photo courtesy of the Wisconsin Department of Tourism

Fishing Associations and Groups

There are dozens of fishing clubs, groups, and associations across the United States. Here is a selection:

American Bass Association, 2810 Trotters Trl., Wetumpka, AL 36092; Phone: (205) 567-6035; FAX (205) 567-8632.

American Casting Association, 1773 Lance End Ln, Fenton, MO 63026; Phone (314) 225-9443.

American League of Anglers and Boaters, 1010 Massachusetts Ave. NW, Suite 320, Washington, DC 20001; Phone: (202) 898-0770; FAX (202) 371-2085.

Association of Northwest Steelheaders, P.O. Box 22065, Milwaukie, OR 97222; Phone: (503) 653-4176.

Bass Anglers Sportsman Society (B.A.S.S.), P.O. Box 17900,Montgomery, AL 36141; Phone: (205) 272-9530; FAX 205-279-7148.

Brown Trout Club, 134 Skillings St., South Portland, ME 04106; Phone: (207) 773-8561.

Colorado Fishing Federation, P.O. Box 17852, Colorado Springs, CO. 80935; Phone: (719) 473-6060.

Federation of Fly Fishers, P.O. Box 1595, Bozeman, MT 59771; Phone: (406) 585-7592; FAX 406-585-7596.

Future Fisherman Foundation, 1250 Grove Ave., Suite 300, Barrington, IL 60010; Phone: (708) 381-4061.

Gulf Coast Angler's Association, Sebastian Ct. #719, Nassau Bay, TX 77058.

International Casting Federation, 3960 Patterson Ave., Oakland, CA 94619; Phone: (510) 531-1336.

International Game Fish Association, 1301 E. Atlantic Blvd., Pompano Beach, FL 33060-6744; Phone: (305) 941-3474; FAX (305) 941-5868.

International Light Tackle Tournament Association, 2044 Federal Ave., Costa Mesa, CA 92627; Phone: (714) 548-4273; FAX (714) 631-7642.

International Women's Fishing Association, P.O. Box 3125, Palm Beach, FL 33480.

Marina Del Rey Anglers, 4230 Del Rey Ave., Box 530, Marina Del Rey, CA 90292.

North American Fishing Club, 12301 Whitewater Dr., Suite 260, Minnetonka, MN 55343; Phone: (612) 936-0555; (800) 843-6232; FAX (612) 936-9755.

Ocean City Maryland Marlin Club, 12902 Kelly Bridge Road, Ocean City, MD 21842;Phone: (410) 213-1613, FAX: (410) 213-1833.

Pensacola Big Game Fishing Club, P.O. Box 401 Pensacola, FL 32592-0401; Phone: (850) 453-4638.

Salmon Unlimited, 4548 N. Milwaukee Ave., Chicago, IL 60630; Phone: (312) 736-5757.

Sport Fishing Institute, 1010 Massachusetts Ave. NW, Suite 320, Washington, DC 20001; Phone: (202) 898-0770; FAX (202) 371-2085.

United Fly Tyers, P.O. Box 220, Maynard, MA 01754; Phone: (603) 329-5211.

Western Washington Walleye Club, P.O. Box 4204, Kent, WA 98032; Phone: (253) 833-7184.

Fishing Licenses

State	Sales
Alabama	511,055
Alaska	421,975
Arizona	436,544
Arkansas	710,655
California	2,206,382
Colorado	752,060
Connecticut	171,100
Delaware	22,859
Florida	1,102,562
Georgia	666,389
Hawaii	6,005
Idaho	419,189
Illinois	749,091
Indiana	619,383
Iowa	405,599
Kansas	311,744
Kentucky	615,606
Louisiana	613,843
Maine	262,003
Maryland	386,430
Massachusetts	163,019
Michigan	251,146
Minnesota	1,565,708
Mississippi	412,189
Missouri	888,376
Montana	375,032
Nebraska	222,141
Nevada	161,495
New Hampshire	158,920
New Jersey	181,053
New Mexico	227,319

State	Sales
New York	1,056,841
North Carolina	690,038
North Dakota	174,399
Ohio	938,602
Oklahoma	637,154
Oregon	689,669
Pennsylvania	1,082,850
Rhode Island	36,851
South Carolina	505,573
South Dakota	218,384
Tennessee	959,366
Texas	1,479,070
Utah	455,725
Vermont	122,992
Virginia	647,775
Washington	765,061
West Virginia	284,822
Wisconsin	1,430,714
Wyoming	279,621
Total	**29,452,379**

Source: American Sportfishing Association. Figures are for 2001, the most recent statistics available.

Photos courtesy of The Alaska State Travel Guide

Website Directory

3rd Grip Products - www.3rdgrip.com
A Bass Guide - www.hughcrumpler.com
AA Worms - www.aaworms.com
Abu Garcia - www.abu-garcia.com
ACDelco - www.acdelco.com
Acme Tackle Co. - www.acmetackle.com
Action Craft Inc. - www.actioncraft.com
Action Optics - www.actionoptics.com
Action Performance Co.
    www.action-performance.com
Action Products Inc. - www.actionp.com
Aerated Bait Container Co. Inc. -
    www.ecenet.com/abccoinc
Airguide - www.airguideinstruments.com
Alaska Top Dog Charters
    www.alaskaboatcharter.com
Alaska Travel Industry Association
    www.sportfishinginalaska.com
Albackore - www.albackore
All Star Graphite Rods Inc. - www.allstarrods.com
AllFishermen.com - www.allfishermen.com
AllFlyFishermen.com - www.allflyfishermen.com
Altrec.com - www.altrec.com
American Angler - www.quikut.com
American Fishing Tackle Co. (AFTCO Mfg.)
    www.aftco.com
American Fishing Wire
    www.americanfishingwire.com
American Fly Fishing Co. - www.americanfly.com
American Rod & Gun - www.basspro.com
American Sportfishing Association -
    www.asafishing.org
American Suzuki Motor Corp. -
    www.suzukimarine.com
Angler Sports - www.anglersports.com
Angler's Aluminum Products - www.rodrack.com
Angler's Warehouse - www.anglerswarehouse.com
Anglers Adventures & Outfitters - www.anglers-
    adventures.com
Anglers Attic - www.anglersattic.com
Anglers Mart - www.anglersmart.com
Apex Outfitters Inc. - www.thetangletamer.com
Aqua Gem - www.aquagemtackle.com
Aquasport - www.aquasport.com
Aries Boats/Fiberglass Works Inc
    www.ariesboats.com
Artificial Reefs Inc. - www.artificialreefs.com
Atlantic & Gulf Fishing Supply Corp. -
    www.atagulf.com
Attwood Corp. - www.attwoodmarine.com
Avet Reels - www.avetreels.com
Axial Technologies Inc. - www.axialtech.com
B.A.S.S./ESPN Outdoors - www.bassmaster.com

B3 Sports Manufacturing Inc. - www.b3sports.com
Backbone Fishing Products -
    www.backbonefishing.com
Backlash Tackle LLC - www.backlashtackle.com
Bag-em Products LLC - www.bag-em-com
Bagley International - www.baghome.com
Bandit Lures - www.banditlures.com
Bass Assassin Lures Inc. - www.bassassassin.com
Bass Baby - www.connectadock.com
Bass Cat - www.basscat.com
Bass Hunter - www.basshunter.com
Bass Pro Shops - www.basspro-shops.com
Bassmaster Boats - www.bassmasterboats.com
Basstackle.com - www.basstackle.com
Bay de Noc Lure Co. - www.baydenoclure.com
Bayliner - www.baylinerboats.com
Bear Paw Tackle Co. - www.bearpawtackle.com
Bentalit Lodge - www.bentalitlodge.com
Berkley - www.berkley-fishing.com
Bert's Custom Tackle - www.teclausa.com
Big Rock Sports - www.bigrocksports.com
Big Ten Tackle - www.bigtentackle.com
Bigfishtackle.com Inc. - www.bigfishtackle.com
Bill Lewis Lures - www.rat-l-trap.com
Bill's Sport Shop - www.billssportshop.com
Biscayne Rod Manufacturing Inc. -
    www.biscaynerod.com
Blakemore Lure Co. - www.blakemore-lure.com
Blazer Boats Inc. - www.blazerboats.com
BnM Pole Co. - www.bnmpoles.com
Boat Master Trailers - www.boat-trailers.com
BobWards.com - www.bobwards.com
Boston Whaler - www.whaler.com
Bottomline Electronics/Cannon -
    www.bottomlinefishfinders.com
Bowker's - www.bowkersbait.com
Boyette's Resort - www.boyettesresort.com
Bradley Technologies - www.bradleysmoker.com
Braid Products Inc. - www.braidproducts.com
Brunswick Corp. - www.brunswick.com
Buck Knives - www.buckknives.com
Bug-Out Outdoorwear Inc. - www.bug-out-
    outdoorwear.com
Bullet Boats Inc. - www.bulletboats.com
Bullet Weights Inc. - www.bulletweights.com
Bumble Bee Boats - www.bumblebeeboats.com
Bushnell Performance Optics - www.bushnell.com
Byrd's Guide Service - www.wecatchum.com
C&H Lures - www.candhlure.com
C-Devil II Sportfishing and Lil' Devil Guide Servi -
    www.cdevilsportfishing.com
C.C. Filson Co. - www.filson.com
Cabela's - www.cabelas.com

Caddis Manufacturing Inc. - www.caddis.com
Cajun Line Co. - www.cajunline.com
Calcutta Baits - www.calcuttabaits.com
Cape Fear Rod Co. - www.capefearrodcompany.com
Capt. Harry's Fishing Supply - www.captharry.com
Carlisle Paddles Inc. - www.carlislepaddles.com
Carlson Tackle Co. Inc. - www.carlsontackle.com
Carson Optical - www.carson-optical.com
CastAway Graphite Rods - www.castawayrods.com
Cat Tracker Bait Co. - www.cattracker.com
Catalina Technologies Inc. - www.technocat.com
Challenge Plastic Products Inc. -
  www.fishingbuckets.com
Champion Boats - www.championboats.com
Champion Trailer Parts Supply -
  www.championtrailers.com
Charger Boats Inc. - www.chargerboats.com
Charles Ireland Guide Service -
  www.cirelandguide.com
Charlie Brewer's Slider Co. -
  www.fishingworld.com/slider/
Chota Outdoor Gear - www.chotaoutdoorgear.com
Church Tackle Co. - www.churchtackle.com
Classic Alaska Charters -
  www.classicalaskacharters.com
CMC - www.cook-mfg.com
Co-Star VII - www.co-starvii.com
Coleman Company Inc. - www.coleman.com
Columbia River Knife & Tool - www.crkt.com
Competitive Edge - www.cefishing.com
Component Systems Inc. - www.csipaint.com
Cordura/DuPont - www.dupont.com/cordura
Costa Del Mar - www.costadelmar.com
Covema Filaments Ltd. - www.covema.com
Coverlay Manufacturing Inc. - www.coverlaymfg.com
Crafty's TackleWorks - www.ScentHead.com
Crave Fishing Research - www.cravebait.com
Creme Lure Co. - www.cremelure.com
Crestliner - www.crestliner.com
D&E Enterprises - www.dandeenteprises.com
D.O.A. Lures - www.doalures.com
Dabbie Products - www.dabbie.net
Daiichi - www.daiichihooks.com
Daiwa Corp. - www.daiwa.com
Dan Bailey's Fly Shop - www.dan-bailey.com
Danner Inc. - www.danner.com
Davis Boats - www.davisboats.com
DeLorme Mapping Co. - www.delorme.com
Discover the Outdoors.com Inc. - www.dto.com
Do-It Corp. - www.do-itmolds.com
Don Iovino Products - www.iovino.com
Dorado Marine Inc. - www.doradoboats.com
Duckworth Boat Works Inc. -
  www.duckworthboats.com
Duluth Pack - www.duluthpack.com
Dumper Dan's Lake Michigan Sportfishing
Charters - www.fishdumperdancharters.com

Eagle Claw Fishing Tackle - www.eagleclaw.com
Eagle Electronics - www.eaglesonar.com
Eagle Lake Lodge - www.eaglelakelodge.com
eAngler Inc. - www.eangler.com
Ed Cumings Inc. - www.cumingsnets.com
eders.com - www.eders.com
Erie Dearie Lures Inc. - www.eriedearie.com
Evercel - www.evercel.com
Evergreen Fly Fishing Co. -
  www.evergreenflyfishing.com
Exide Technologies - www.exideworld.com
EZ Loader Boat Trailers - www.ezloader.com
Falcon Graphite Rods - www.falconrods.com
Falcon Lures - www.falconlures.com
Fatman's Flyfishing Guides - www.fishinfatman.com
Federation of Fly Fishers - www.fedflyfishers.org
Fentress Marine - www.fentressmarine.com
Fenwick Fishing - www.fenwickfishing.com
Fish Hawk Electronics Corp. -
  www.fishhawkelectronics.com
Fish-N-More Inc. - www.fishnmore.com
Fishboy - www.fishboy.com
Fisherman Eyewear - www.fishermaneyewear.com
Fisherman's Landing - www.fishermanslanding.com
Fisherman's Line - www.fishermansline.com
Fishin' Musician - www.thefishinmusician.com
Fishing Buddy System - www.fishingbs.netmegs.com
Fishing Hot Spots Inc. - www.fishinghotspots.com
Fishypete's Fly Co. - www.fishypete.net
Fitovers Eyewear USA - www.fitovers.com
Flambeau Products Corp. - www.flambeau.com
Flow-Rite - www.flow-rite.com
Fly Logic Inc. - www.flylogic.com
Fly Shop International -
  www.flyshopinternational.com
Flying Fisherman - www.flyingfisherman.com
Force Fin - www.forcefin.com
Form Plus Industries - www.formplusindustries.com
Frabill - www.frabill.com
Frogg toggs - www.froggtoggs.com
Fulton/Wesbar Corp. - www.wesbar.com
Furuno USA Inc. - www.furunousa.com
G. Loomis Inc. - www.gloomis.com
G. Pucci and Sons - www.p-line.com
G3 Boats - www.g3boats.com
Gamakatsu USA Inc. - www.gamakatsu.com
Garmin International Inc. - www.garmin.com
Gator Grip - www.gatorgrip.com
Gearout Outdoor GearStore - www.gearout.com
Gene Larew Tackle - www.genelarew.com
Gibbs/Nortac Industries Ltd. -
  www.gibbsfishing.com
Glacier's Edge Sportfishing Charters Inc. -
  www.glaciersedge.net
Glastron - www.glastron.com
Godfrey Marine - www.godfreymarine.com
Gonefishinshop.com - www.gonefishinshop.com

Gorge Fly Shop - www.gorgeflyshop.com
Grady-White Boat Co. - www.gradywhite.com
Great Lakes Fishery Commission - www.glfc.com
Great Rocky Mountain Outfitters - www.grmo.com
Greg Tatman Wooden Boats Inc. -
   www.gregboats.com
Griffin Enterprises - www.griffinenterprisesinc.com
Gudebrod - www.gudebrod.com
Hagen's - www.hagensfish.com
Half Hitch Tackle - www.halfhitch.com
Hanggee-Koehler Corp. - www.reelegood.com
Hawaii Lure - www.hawaiilure.com
Hawk Boats - www.hawkboats.com
Headlights - www.headlightlures.com
Hi-Liner Fishing Gear & Tackle Inc. -
   www.hiliner.com
High Country Flies - www.highcountryflies.com
HighRoller Fishing Lure Co. LLC - www.hroller.com
Hildebrandt Co. LLC - www.hildebrandt.net
HillBilly Charters - www.CaptsKid.com
Hillman Marine - www.hillmanmarine.com
Hobie Cat Co. - www.hobiekayaks.com
HoldZit Products Inc. - www.holdzit.com
Honda Marine Group - www.honda-marine.com
Hooked On The Outdoors - www.ruhooked.com
Hookhider Fishing Rods - www.hookhider.com
Hopkins Fishing Lures - www.hopkinslures.com
Hot Spot Fishing Lures Ltd. - www.hotspotlures.com
Housatonic River Outfitters - www.dryflies.com
Hover-Lure - www.hover-lure.com
Hydra-Sports - www.hydrasports.com
Hydra-Sports Boats - www.hydrasports.com
Idaho Angling Services LLC -
   www.anglingservices.com
Illusion Lures Inc. - www.illusionlures.com
In-Fisherman - www.in-fisherman.com
Inside Sportfishing - www.insidesportfishing.com
Interactive Outdoors Inc. -
   www.interactiveoutdoors.tv
International Concepts Inc. - www.motowasher.com
International Game Fish Association - www.igfa.org
International Women Fly Fishers
   www.intlwomenflyfishers.org
Interphase Technologies Inc. -
   www.interphase-tech.com
Interstate Batteries - www.interstatebatteries.com
Intruder Inc. - www.intruderinc.com
Izaak Walton League of America - www.ilwa.org
Jack's Juice - www.jacksjuice.com
James Acord's Leather - www.turtlemoon.com/acord/
Javelin Boats - www.javelinboats.com
Jersey Coast Anglers Association - www.jcaa.org
Johnson - www.fishjohnson.com
Johnson Outdoors Inc. - www.johnsonoutdoors.com
Katahdin Lake Wilderness Camps -
   www.katahdinlakecamps.com
KeepAlive Inc. - www.keepalive.net

King Sailfish Mounts Inc. - www.kingsailfish.com
KL Industries Inc. - www.klindustries.com
Korkers - www.korkers.com
L&S Bait Co. - www.mirrolure.com
L.L. Bean - www.llbean.com
La Reserve Beauchene - www.beauchene.com
LaCrosse Footwear Inc. - www.lacrosse-outdoors.com
Lake Fork Taxidermy - www.lakeforktaxidermy.com
Lake Hawk Inc. - www.lakehawk.com
Lake Products Co. - www.knottying.com
Lake Texoma Striper Guide Service - www.texoma-
   fishing.com
Lamiglas Inc. - www.lamiglas.com
Land O' Lakes Tackle Co. -
   www.landolakestackle.com
Lansky Sharpeners - www.lansky.com
Larson Boats - www.larsonboats.com
Lee Fisher International Inc. -
   www.cherrybombmarkerbuoy.com
Lee's Tackle - www.leetackle.com
Legend Boats - www.legendboats.com
Leisure Life Limited - www.llboats.com
Lew's - www.lews.com
Lil' Hustler Tackle Co. - www.lilhustler.com
Lindy Legendary Fishing Tackle -
   www.lindylittlejoe.com
Loon Haunt Outposts - www.loonhaunt.com
Loon Outdoors - www.loonoutdoors.com
Lowe - www.lowe.com
Lowrance Electronics Inc. - www.lowrance.com
Luck E Strike - www.luckestrike.com
Lucky Craft - www.luckycraft.com
Lucky Strike Bait Works Ltd. -
   www.luckystrikebaitworks.com
Luhr Jensen & Sons - www.luhr-jensen.com
Lund - www.lundboats.com
Lunker Lure - www.lunkerlure.com
Lure-Eyes - www.lureeyes.com
M and N Distributing - www.mandndistributing.com
Mad Man Lures - www.madmanlures.com
Magellan - www.magellangps.com
Magic Products Inc. - www.magicproducts.com
Magic Tilt Trailers - www.magictilt.com
Magnum Trailers - www.magnumtrailers.com
Mann's Bait Co. - www.mannsbait.com
Maptech Inc. - www.maptech.com
Marado Rods & Reels - www.marado.com
Marine Metal Products Inc. - www.marinemetal.com
Marine Products Group LLC - www.mplures.com
Mark Kovach Fishing Services - www.mkfs.com
Martin Classic Fly Tackle - www.martinfishing.com
Matzuo America Inc. - www.matzuo.com
Maverick Boat Co. Inc. - www.maverickboats.com
Maxima America - www.maxima-lines.com
McNett Corp. - www.mcnett.com
Meier's Fish Bait - www.predatorfishbait.com
Melton International Tackle - www.meltontackle.com

Mengo Industries Inc. - www.mengo-ind.com
Mercury Marine - www.mercurymarine.com
Meyerco USA - www.meyercousa.com
Midwest Industries Inc. - www.shorelandr.com
Mil-Comm Products - www.reelsaver.com
Millennium Lures Inc. - www.millennium-lures.com
Minn Kota - www.minnkotamotors.com
Mitchell - www.fishmitchell.com
Mizmo Bait Co. - www.mizmo.com
Montana Flywater Fishing Co. -
    www.montanaflywater.com
Morning Dew Anglers - www.morningdewanglers.com
Mountain Angler - www.mountainangler.com
Mud Hole Custom Tackle Inc. - www.mudhole.com
Musky Tom Wehler's Guide Service -
    www.muskytomsguideservice.com
N.A.S. Bait & Tackle - www.bestbait.com
National Bass Guide Service - www.nationalbass.com
National Marine Manufacturers Association -
    www.nmma.org
National Teen Anglers - www.teenanglers.org
Nature Vision Inc. - www.naturevisioninc.com
Navarro Weather Gear - www.navarro.ca
New Hampshire Lakes Area Bass Guide -
http://members.aol.com/jimfnh/ newhampshirebassguid
NGC Sports - www.ngcsports.com
Nikon USA - www.nikonusa.com
Nikwax - www.nikwax-usa.com
Nils Master USA Inc. - www.nilsmaster.com
Nissan Marine & Power Products -
    www.nissanmarine.com
Normark Corp./Rapala - www.normark.com
Norris Craft Boat Co. Inc. -
    www.norriscraftboats.com
North Platte Anglers - www.northplatteanglers.com
Northern Sport Fishing Products Ltd. -
    www.flyline.net
Northwest Angler - www.nwangler.com
O. Mustad & Sons (USA) Inc. - www.mustad.no
Ocean Anglers Unlimited LLC - www.theanglers.net
Ocean Waves Sunglasses Inc. - www.oceanwaves.com
Old Bayside Tackle Co. - www.oldbayside.com
Old Whiskers Catfish Bait -
    www.oldwhiskersbait.com
Ole Florida Fly Shop - www.oleflorida.com
OmniGlow - www.omniglow.com
Optronics Inc. - www.optronicsinc.com
Orion Safety Products - www.orionsignals.com
Osprey Products - www.ospreyproducts.com
Outcast Sporting Goods - www.outcastboats.com
Outdoor Intelligence LLC -
    www.outdoorintelligence.com
Overton's - www.overtons.com
Owner American Corp. - www.ownerhooks.com
Pace Products Inc. - www.pacemarine.com
Panther Marine Products -
    www.panthermarineproducts.com

Panther Martin/Harrison Hoge Industries -
    www.panther-martin.com
Para-Tech Engineering Co. - www.seaanchor.com
Paragon Plastics Inc. - www.lunkerlure.com
Patagonia Inc. - www.patagonia.com
Pelican International Inc. - www.pelican-intl.com
Penn Fishing Tackle Mfg. Co. - www.pennreels.com
Penn Yan Boat Co. - www.pennyanboats.com
Persuader American Angling -
    www.persuaderamerican.com
Pflueger - www.pfluegerfishing.com
Plano Molding Co. - www.planomolding.com
Playbuoy Pontoon Manufacturing Inc. -
    www.playbuoy.com
Pokee Fishing Tackle Co. Ltd. -
    www.pokeefishing.com
PolarEyes - www.polaroptics.com
Porta-Bote International - www.porta-bote.com
PowerPro - www.powerpro.com
Pradco Outdoor Brands - www.lurenet.com
Preston Lures - www.prestonlures.com
Princecraft - www.princecraft.com
Pro Image Distribution Co. - www.ezfishing.com
Pro-Troll Products - www.protroll.com
Pure Fishing - www.purefishing.com
Quantum - www.quantumfishing.com
Quarrow - www.quarrow.com
Rain Shield Inc. - www.rainshield.com
Rainbow Plastics - www.rainbowplastics.com
Ranger Boats - www.rangerboats.com
Rapala-Normark Group - www.rapala.com
Raymarine Inc. - www.raymarine.com
Realures LLC - www.realures.com
Recreational Equipment Inc. (REI) - www.rei.com
Red Lodge Resort - www.manitoulin.com/redlodge
Red Wing Shoe Co. - www.irishsetterboots.com
Redfish-Bluefish Tackle Co. -
    www.redfishbluefishtackle.com
Reliance Products - www.relianceproducts.com
Relic Lures - www.reliclures.com
Renegade Guide Service -
    www.fishfla.com/renegade.html
Renegade Sportfishing Charters LLC -
    www.renegadecharterfishing.com
Renzetti Inc. - www.renzetti.com
Rio Products International Inc. -
    www.rioproducts.com
Ritz Interactive Inc. - www.ritzinteractive.com
River Ridge Custom Canoes -
    www.riverridgecustomcanoes.com
River's Edge Products Inc. -
    www.riversedgeproducts.com
Roaring Stony Lodge - www.fishingresorts.com
RodMounts - www.rodmounts.com
Rods by Sirrus - www.sirrusrods.com
rose plastic USA LP - www.rose-plastic.com
Russell's For Men - www.russellsformen.com

S&C Brinkman Corp. - www.slidingweight.com
Salamander Graphix - www.salamandergraphix.com
Salmon Depot Charter Fishing
  www.salmondepot.com
Saltwater Directions - www.saltwaterdirections.com
Sampo Inc. - www.sampoinc.com
San Augustine Fiberglass Products Inc.
  www.raycraftboats.com
Schott International Inc. - www.schottint.com
Scotty Fishing and Outdoor Products
  www.scotty.com
Sea Dog Sportfishing Charters
  www.fishsheboygan.com
Sea Ray International - www.searay.com
Seaswirl Boats - www.seaswirl.com
Shakespeare Fishing Tackle - www.shakespeare-fishing.com
Shark River Mail Order - www.srmo.com
Shikari Inc. - www.shikariblanks.com
Shimano American Corp. - www.fish.shimano.com
SI-TEX Marine Electronics Inc. - www.si-tex.com
Sierra Drifters Guide Service
  www.sierradrifters.com
Sierra Stream - www.tie-fast.com
Silstar/Pinnacle Corp. of America Inc.
  www.silstar.com
Silver Buddy Lures - www.silverbuddy.com
SKB Corp. - www.skbcases.com
Sliding Weight Hooks & Baits
  www.slidingweighthooksandbaits.com
Smirk Tackle Co. - www.smirktackle.com
Snag Proof Mfg. Inc./Sea Bay Lures
  www.snagproof.com
Solunar Sales Co. - www.solunartables.com
South Bend Sporting Goods - www.south-bend.com
Southern Fishing Schools Inc.
  www.southernfishing.com
Speedtech Instruments - www.speedtech.com
Spidercast - www.fishspidercast.com
Spiderline - www.fishspiderwire.com
Splash Marine Inc. - www.busterboats.com
Sportif USA - www.sportif.com
SPRO Corp. - www.spro.com
St. Croix Rods - www.stcroixrods.com
Stearns Inc. - www.stearnsinc.com
Stillwater Fishing - www.stillwaterfishing.com
Storm Boats - www.stormboats.com
Stratos Boats - www.stratosboats.com
Stren Fishing Lines - www.stren.com
Strike King Lure Co. - www.strikeking.com
Strike On Lures - www.strikeon.com
StrikeMaster Ice Augers - www.strikemaster.com
Stroker Boats - www.strokerboats.com
Sufix USA - www.sufixfishing.com
Surfcaster.com - www.surfcaster.com
Swift Instruments Inc. - www.swift-optics.com
T&L Products - www.tandlproducts.com

Tackle Factory - www.tackle-factory.com
TackleDirect - www.tackledirect.com
Tarponwear International - www.tarponwear.com
Taylor Creek Fly Shop - www.taylorcreek.com
Taylor Cutlery - www.taylorcutlery.com
Team Nu-Mark - www.teamnumark.com
Techsonic Industries Inc. - www.humminbird.com
Tempress Products/Fish-On! - www.fish-on.com
Teton Fly Reels Inc. - www.tetonflyreels.com
The Complete Sportsman
  www.rareandunusual.com/tcs
The Fisherman's Store - www.thefishermansstore.com
The Fly Factory - www.troutbums.com
The Fly Rod Shop - www.flyfishvt.com
The Hook-Up! - www.thehookupcapecod.com
The Worth Co. - www.worthco.com
Thomas & Thomas Rodmakers Inc.
  www.thomasandthomas.com
Thompson-Pallister Bait Co. Inc.
  www.lenthompson.com
Thornwood Lures Inc. - www.thornwoodlures.com
TICA USA Inc. - www.ticaglobal.com
Tight Lines Fishing Services - www.nhfishguide.com
Timberline Fisheries - www.timberlinefisheries.com
Titan Rods - www.titanrods.com
Tite Line Fishing - www.titeline.com
Tite-Lok - www.titelok.com
Tomahawk Resort - www.tomahawkresort.com
Tooltron Industries - www.tooltron.com
Top Brass Tackle - www.topbrasstackle.com
Top Line Manufacturing Co. - www.toplineus.com
Tracker Marine - www.trackermarine.com
Triton Boats - www.tritonboats.com
Triumph Boats - www.triumphboats.com
Trojan Battery Co. - www.trojanbattery.com
Trondak Inc. - www.aquaseal.com
Trophy Specialists Fishing Charters
  www.trophyspecialists.com
Trophy Sportfishing Boats - www.trophyfishing.com
Trout & About - www.troutandabout.com
Tru-Turn Hook More Fish - www.truturnhooks.com
TyGer Leader - www.tygerleader.com
Uchi Lake Lodge - www.uchilake.com
Ultimate Angler Inc. - www.ultimateangler.com
Ultimate NiTi Technologies - www.ultimateniti.com
Ultracom International - www.okumafishing.com
Uncle Josh Bait Co. - www.unclejosh.com
Van Patten Industries - www.theinhibitor.com
Van Staal - www.vanstaal.com
Vexilar Inc. - www.vexilar.com
Viper Boats Inc. - www.viperboatsinc.com
Virtual Flyshop - www.flyshop.com
Vivian Industries - www.vipboats.com
VMC Inc. - www.vmchooks.com
W.L. Gore & Associates - www.gore.com
W.R. Case & Sons Cutlery Co. - casesales.com
Warrior Boats - www.warrior-boats.com

Water Gremlin Co. - www.watergremlin.com
Wellcraft Marine - www.wellcraft.com
West Coast Nets Inc. - www.westcoastnets.com
West Marine - www.westmarine.com
West Virginia Division of Tourism
   www.callwva.com
Westport Outfitters - www.saltwater-flyfishing.com
Wetland Outfitters - www.wetlandoutfitters.com
Whistle Creek - www.whistlecreek.com
White's Outdoor - www.whitesoutdoor.com
Wickers America - www.wickers.com
WiggleFin Inc. - www.wigglefin.com

Wiggy's Inc. - www.wiggys.com
Wigston's Lures - www.wigstonslures.com.au
Wolf Wire Forms Inc. - www.wolfwire.com
Wonder Winder Inc. - www.linewinder.com
WristSaver Rods Inc. - www.wristsaverrods.com
Xplores Inc. - www.xplores.com
XPoint - www.xpointhooks.com
Xpress Boats - www.xpressboats.com
Yakima Bait Co. - www.yakimabait.com
Yamaha Motor Corp. USA - www.yamaha-motor.com
Zebco - www.zebco.com
Zephyr Boats - www.zephyrboats.com

Reel in the Big Ones
With Some Help From the Pros

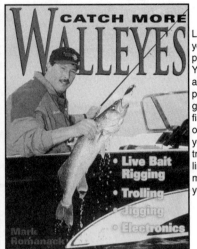

Catch More Walleyes
by Mark Romanack
Learn the skills that will help you catch more walleyes from pro angler Mark Romanack. You'll understand the tactics and equipment needed for popular fishing styles like jigging, rigging and slip sinker fishing. He also shows you tips on boat control and teaches you how to best use your electronics to find fish. Enjoy your limited time on the water even more by bringing more fish to your boat.
Softcover • 8½x11
256 pages
250 b&w photos
Item# WALL • $19.95

Bassin' With the Pros
by Mark Romanack
If you want big bass, let the pros tell you how they can be caught. Author Mark Romanack has brought together 20 of the nation's top bass anglers to teach you every facet of catching big bass. This book reveals the secrets of the biggest names in bass fishing and provides valuable tips to help you succeed where other may fail.
Softcover • 8½x11
232 pages
250 b&w photos
Item# BWTP • $19.95

The Complete Book of Saltwater Fishing
by Milt Rosko
"Fun for the whole family" describes this ultimate saltwater fishing guide. Learn the methods, tackle, techniques, and fish species of saltwater fishing on the U.S. Atlantic, Pacific, and Gulf coasts. Extensive illustrations and photographs demonstrate the joys of saltwater fishing. From fishing to cleaning to cooking, every member of your family can get involved in this contemplative sport.
Softcover • 8¼x10⅞
288 pages
200 color photos
Item# SAWF • $29.95

Tying Trout Flies
by C. Boyd Pfeiffer
Match the hatch with flies you've tied. You'll learn to tie effective and popular trout flies with step-by-step instruction from an expert angler. Close-up photos make tying perfect flies as easy as 1, 2, 3. Includes patterns for 100 flies such as dry flies, wet flies, nymphs, and streamers.
Softcover W/Concealed Spiral
8¼x10⅞ • 160 pages
150 color photos
Item# TYTF • $24.95

Joe Bucher's Crankbait Secrets
by Joe Bucher
Learn the secrets of casting, trolling and working your crankbaits to keep them in front of the fish you want to catch. This is the first book of it's kind covering all types and crankbaits and all fishing conditions. Grab a copy today and learn the secrets of a pro fisherman.
Softcover • 8½x11
256 pages
100 b&w photos
Item# JBCS • $19.95

Tying Warmwater Flies
by C. Boyd Pfeiffer
There's no greater satisfaction than landing a fish on a fly you've tied. Using easy step-by-step instructions, noted fly fishing expert, C. Boyd Pfeiffer, shows you how to tie 100 flies designed to trick North America's most popular fish. You'll learn how to tie flies that will take bass, northern pike, and panfish. Each fly listing includes a full-color photo of the finished fly, materials needed, and the tying sequence.
Softcover W/Concealed Spiral
8¼x10⅞ • 160 pages
250 color photos
Item# TYWF • $24.99

To order call **800-258-0929** Offer OTB3

 Krause Publications, Offer OTB3
P.O. Box 5009, Iola WI 54945-5009
www.krausebooks.com

Please add $4.00 for the first book and $2.25 each additional for shipping & handling to U.S. addresses. Non-U.S. addresses please add $20.95 for the first book and $5.95 each additional.

Residents of CA, IA, IL, KS, NJ, PA, SD, TN, WI please add appropriate sales tax.

order your subscription online at www.outdoorworldmag.com
FREE T-SHIRT
WITH YOUR PAID SUBSCRIPTION TO OUTDOOR WORLD MAGAZINE
• Extra large and extra comfortable
• Made exclusively for subscribers of Outdoor World Magazine
• 100% pre-shrunk cotton for a perfect fit every time
Outdoor World Magazine
Bass Pro Shops
12 issues for just $16.95 and a FREE Outdoor World Magazine t-shirt!
FREE BASS PRO SHOPS T-SHIRT! DETAILS INSIDE!
NEW SOUNDS! Hot 2003 Turkey Calls
MAY 2003
Outdoor World
Spring's Bounty
YOUR GUIDE TO TURKEY SUCCESS
• A Pro's Woodsmanship Secrets
• Trouble-Shooting Tough Gobblers
• Fundamentals That Kill Longbeards
HIGH TIMES BEATING BASS FISHING'S SPRING-FLOOD BLUES
COLD TRUTHS ICE-FISHING REVEALS SUMMER PANFISH SECRETS
Bass Pro Shops
Outdoor World
MAGAZINE
call toll-free 800-627-9218 offer ABBC1P
Mon. - Fri. 7am - 8pm; Sat. 8am - 2pm, CST